Moviegoing in America

In memory of my father, Irving T. Waller

★ ★ ★ ★ ★ ★ ★ ★ ★ ★ ★ ★ ★ ★ ★

MOVIEGOING IN AMERICA

A Sourcebook in the
History of Film Exhibition

★ ★ ★ ★ ★ ★ ★ ★ ★ ★ ★ ★ ★ ★

Edited by Gregory A. Waller

BLACKWELL
Publishers

Copyright © Blackwell Publishers Ltd 2002
Editorial organization and introduction copyright © Gregory A. Waller 2002

First published 2002

2 4 6 8 10 9 7 5 3 1

Blackwell Publishers Inc.
350 Main Street
Malden, Massachusetts 02148
USA

Blackwell Publishers Ltd
108 Cowley Road
Oxford OX4 1JF
UK

Library of Congress Cataloging-in-Publication Data has been applied for.

Moviegoing in America : a sourcebook in the history of film exhibition/edited by Gregory A. Waller.
    p. cm.
  Includes bibliographical references and index.
  ISBN 0–631–22591–9 (alk. paper)—ISBN 0–631–22592–7 (pbk : alk. paper)
   1. Motion pictures—United States—History. 2. Motion picture theaters—United States—History. I. Waller, Gregory A. (Gregory Albert), 1950–

  PN1993.5.U6 M669 2001
  791.43'0973—dc21

                                     2001035004

British Library Cataloguing in Publication Data
A CIP catalogue record for this book is available from the British Library.

Typeset in 9.5pt/11.5pt MPhotina
by Kolam Information Services Pvt Ltd, Pondicherry, India.
Printed in Great Britain by MPG Books Ltd, Bodmin, Cornwall.
This book is printed on acid-free paper.

Contents

List of Illustrations   ix

Acknowledgments   x

Introduction: A Century at the Movies   1
Gregory A. Waller

Part I   Capturing an Audience, Creating a Business: 1896–1916   **9**

Introduction   11

1   Introducing Cinema to the American Public: The Vitascope in the United States, 1896–7   13
    Charles Musser

2   From Rum Shop to Rialto: Workers and Movies   27
    Roy Rosenzweig

3   Cheap Amusements (1908)   46
    John Collier

4   Some Picture Show Audiences (1911)   50
    Mary Heaton Vorse

5   Motion-Picture Work (1911)   54
    David Hulfish

6   Hints to Exhibitors (1908)   64
    W. Stephen Bush

7   Handling the Visitor (1909)   66
    Moving Picture World

8   Posteritis (1910)   68
    F.H. Richardson

9   Swelling the Box Office Receipts (1911)   70
    George Rockhill Craw

Contents

10 The Murder of *Othello* (1911)   73
   H.F. Hoffman

11 Projection (1912)   75
   F.H. Richardson

12 The Regulation of Motion Picture Theaters (1912)   77
   Boyd Fisher

13 Architectural Treatment of the Moving Picture Theatre (1914)   81
   Aymar Embury II

Part II   Palatial Palaces and Everyday Practices: 1916–1930   83

Introduction   85

14 "You Can Have the Strand in Your Own Town": The Struggle
   between Urban and Small-Town Exhibition in the Picture Palace Era   88
   Kathryn H. Fuller

15 What the Public Wants in the Picture Theater (1925)   100
   Samuel L. Rothafel ("Roxy")

16 Theater Entrances and Lobbies (1925)   104
   E.C.A. Bullock

17 A Description of the Capitol Theater, Chicago (1925)   106
   John Eberson

18 Building Theatre Patronage (1927)   110
   John F. Barry and Epes W. Sargent

19 Motion Picture Theater Management (1928)   116
   Harold B. Franklin

20 Fashioning an Exhibition Empire: Promotion, Publicity,
   and the Rise of Publix Theaters   124
   Douglas Gomery

21 Where "Movie Playing" Needs Reform (1920)   138
   K. Sherwood Boblitz

22 Musical Presentation of Motion Pictures (1921)   140
   George W. Beynon

23 Music (1927)   144
   John F. Barry and Epes W. Sargent

24 Future Developments (1927)   147
   Harry M. Warner

25 Motion Pictures as a Phase of Commercialized Amusement in Toledo,
   Ohio (1919)   151
   J.J. Phelan

Contents

26 The Motion Picture and the Upbuilding of Community Life (1920)   153
Orrin G. Cocks

27 Our Movie Made Children (1934)   155
Henry James Foreman

28 Ethnography and Exhibition: The Child Audience, the Hays Office,
and Saturday Matinees   159
Richard deCordova

**Part III   Picture Shows and New Theaters: The 1930s and
1940s**   **171**

Introduction   173

29 Hillbilly Music and Will Rogers: Small-Town Picture Shows in the 1930s   175
Gregory A. Waller

30 Bank Night (1936)   189
H.O. Kusell

31 The Management of Motion Picture Theatres (1938)   192
Frank H. Ricketson, Jr.

32 Show Lady (1939)   197
Carlie Beach Roney

33 What's Playing at the Grove? (1948)   203
Fortune

34 Give the Movie Exhibitor a Chance! (1935)   211
P.S. Harrison

35 Economic Control of the Motion Picture Industry (1944)   214
Mae D. Huettig

36 New Theaters for the Cinema (1932)   219
Ben Schlanger

37 Motion Picture Theaters (1937)   221
Ben Schlanger

38 A New Architecture for the Movie Theater (1948)   225
Architectural Record

39 Psychology of the Theater (1948)   228
Walter A. Cutter

Part IV   Drive-In, Art House, Multiplex: The 1950s and Beyond   **233**

Introduction   235

40 Spectator and Screen   238
John Belton

Contents

41 Big Boom in Outdoor Movies (1956)   247
    Frank J. Taylor

42 Free Lances (1929)   252
    Alexander Bakshy

43 Sure-Seaters Discover an Audience (1952)   255
    Stanley Frank

44 Some Considerations on the Rise of the Art-Film Theater (1956)   259
    John E. Twomey

45 Domestic Theatrical and Semi-Theatrical Distribution and Exhibition
    of American Independent Feature Films: A Survey in 1983   265
    Betsy McLane

46 The Harlem Theater: Black Film Exhibition in Austin, Texas: 1920–1973   268
    Dan Streible

47 The Exhibitors (1972)   279
    Stanley H. Durwood

48 The K-Mart Audience at the Mall Movies   282
    William Paul

49 Modern Times (1993)   296
    Barbara Stones

50 From Exhibition to Reception: Reflections on the Audience in Film
    History   300
    Robert C. Allen

Part V   Research and Resources   309

A Guide to Research and Resources   311
Research Projects in the History of Moviegoing and Film Exhibition   322
Bibliography   324

Index   346

Illustrations

Youngsters with *White Zombie* display in theater lobby (1932)   xii

Movie audience illustration from Mary Heaton Vorse, "Some Picture
Show Audiences" (1911)   49

Annotated photos of theater displays from James F. Hodges, *Owning and
Operating a Motion Picture Theatre* (1912)   63

Alfred Jackson, "Hiram and Cynthia" (1916)   80

Ahern, "The Crazy Quilt" (1912) and "Our Boarding House"   87

Cover of *Capitol Theatre Weekly* (August 14, 1921)   99

Strand weekly program (May 12, 1918)   103

Promotional giveaway, Chicago Theatre   109

Illustrations from Harold Franklin, *Motion Picture Theater Management* (1928)   119

Promotion of *American Tragedy* at a Publix theater (1931)   137

American Federation of Musicians' advertisement (1931); Fontaine
Fox cartoon (1929)   150

Theater front with youngsters and man on stilts (1933)   158

Handout flyer (later 1920s) and newspaper advertisement (1935)
for the Alhambra Theatre   177

Parade float for the projectionists' union (ca. 1932)   196

Illustration from *National Parent–Teacher* (March 1938)   213

Ben Schlanger, "Design for a Theater for Motion Pictures," *Architectural
Record* (June 1944)   224

Illustrations from Freeman Lincoln, "The Comeback of the Movies,"
Fortune 51 (February 1955)   237

Cover for Surrealist and Fantastic Film Festival at 5th Avenue Playhouse (1941)   254

Table of film schedules for New York City repertory cinemas, June 24–June 30, 1981   263

Canned food drive and *Tom Sawyer* promotion (ca. 1932)   321

Acknowledgments

Thanks once more to Richard Angelo, David Durant, Walter C. Foreman, Armando Prats, and other good friends and colleagues at the University of Kentucky; to the graduate students who have assisted in different ways with this project, Joe DeSpain, Jason McEntee, and Katherine Ledford; to Lucy Combs, who helped me complete this project while I negotiated my way through my first two years as chair of the Department of English; to Dean Howard Grotch and Associate Dean Richard Greissman of the College of Arts and Sciences and to the office of Research and Graduate Studies at UK for providing time and resources that helped to make this book possible; to copyeditor Brigitte Lee; and to Jayne Fargnoli, Annie Lenth, and their colleagues at Blackwell for their enthusiasm for this project, their advice along the way, and their willingness to let *Moviegoing in America* take the shape it has.

Kudos on top of kudos to the knowledgeable, patient, and efficient reference, special collections, architecture, fine arts, and interlibrary loan librarians at the University of Kentucky, without whom a project like this would have been impossible. For information, images, and instruction, my ongoing gratitude to Claire McCann and Lisa Carter (of Special Collections), Barbara Hale (of ILL), and Linda Cantara (of the Collaboratory for Research in Computing for Humanities). I am still making use of material provided by former UK audio-visual archivist, Tom House, who is now at the University of New Hampshire.

Let my thanks to Fred Mills for his commitment to keeping Lexington's Kentucky Theater (1922) alive and well stand here as a sign of grateful appreciation for all who labor for historic theater preservation and for independent film exhibition. It is likely that without the repertory screenings and midnight movies at the Kentucky Theater – and therefore without Fred, who has managed this venue for more than a quarter century – I would not have become fascinated by the sites, occasions, and practices that make up the history of film exhibition.

If *Moviegoing in America* encourages new research in film history, it will pay back a portion of my debt to and gratitude for the groundbreaking scholarship, good spirits, and high standards of Richard Abel, Robert Allen, Lucy Fischer, Jane Gaines, Douglas Gomery, Tom Gunning, Richard Maltby, Charles Musser, Dan Streible, and all those who have in different ways influenced and encouraged my own work and made it so rewarding to belong to this particular academic community.

As always, my sisters, Andrea Miera and Beth Kamhi, and my dad, Irving Waller, have provided love and support that stretches across the miles between us. As my sons, Moby and Graham, move through the worlds of high finance and haute cuisine, I hope that they find the satisfaction in their work that I have found in mine.

Most of all, daily thanks to my best reader (in every sense of the word), Brenda Weber, for, in Lucinda's words, "all of this"– and much, much more.

Acknowledgments

The authors and publishers gratefully acknowledge the following for permission to reproduce copyright illustrations:

Architectural Record, for Ben Schlanger, "Design for a Theater for Motion Pictures," *Architectural Record* (June 1944). Reprinted with permission from *Architectural Record*, a publication of The McGraw-Hill Cos., Inc.

The Special Collections Library at the University of Kentucky for the illustrations on pages xii, 99, 103, 137, 158, 196, 254, 321.

The publishers apologize for any errors or omissions in the above list and would be grateful to be notified of any corrections that should be incorporated in the next edition or reprint of this book.

Youngsters with *White Zombie* display in theater lobby (1932)

Introduction: A Century at the Movies

Gregory A. Waller

How can we get at the influential, continuing role that the movies have played in the lives of so many people in the United States during the twentieth century? How can we best acknowledge and understand the important function of movie theaters as public spaces locally situated but providing nationally available cultural products? By paying due heed, I would argue, both to the stories and stars that filled the screen and also to where, when, and how the movies were made available to and consumed by American audiences. This grand ambition involves, first of all, realizing that the sites where motion pictures have been publicly screened and the sorts of entertainment programs offered at those sites have varied considerably over the past century. So, too, has moviegoing itself changed, in terms of the particular activities and pleasures it entailed and in terms of the social and cultural connotations it carried.

In 1937, Gilbert Seldes, a long-time commentator on the movies, concluded that while people sometimes do choose to attend motion picture theaters because they want to see a film starring Charlie Chaplin or Shirley Temple, "the fundamental passion is a desire to go to the movies, which means to go to any movie rather than not go at all." And this passion, Seldes claimed, "is the prime phenomenon of our time" (Seldes 1937, 13–14). Few of us today would make so sweeping a claim for moviegoing, by which we would likely mean a trip to a multiplex to see a first-run feature film. Two decades into the age of home video, there are still some screening sites beyond the multiplex: the occasional drive-in, the struggling repertory theater, the thriving second-run house, the refurbished picture palace become civic showplace, the metropolitan art cinema. But, judging from box-office revenues and sheer visibility, the primary or privileged destination for moviegoers is a freestanding, state-of-the-art multiplex located some distance from anything resembling an older downtown area. Attending this type of theater means selecting among the first-run options at a computerized ticket counter, passing through a high-gloss, efficiently organized central concession area sporting displays for next season's would-be blockbusters, and then settling into climate-controlled, deep-cushioned comfort. A good size screen fills the front wall, biding the time with trivia contests, commercials, and trailers. There is no stage or proscenium, no sense whatsoever that this site was ever intended to be anything but a movie theater. This screening space is pared down but not artsily austere; above all, it's proud of its own technology and ready to rumble. All is effectively designed to showcase the scheduled first-run film, which is presented so as to command the spectator's undivided attention. This sort of multiplex movie experience is readily accessible for a sizable number of Americans. For example, in Lexington, Kentucky (population 243,000), where I live, Cinemark operates three freestanding multiplexes with 26 total screens, and Regal

Cinemas has a 16-screen facility. On an ordinary summer day, these 42 screens together offer some 17 different films.

However, Lexington – to continue with my example – has other options for moviegoers. Two renovated Main Street theaters built in the 1920s now screen new foreign films, American independents, the occasional midnight movie, and, of necessity, some first-run bookings. There is also a boxy duplex in an older mall, a couple of drive-ins within 20 miles offering double features, and a thriving ten-screen multiplex devoted solely to mainstream movies returning for a second-run at discount prices. In recent years there also have occasionally been special screenings at libraries and universities in Lexington, even a city-sponsored Friday night family film series in the summertime at a local park.

Enumerating this array of screening sites – hardly unique to Lexington – reminds us that the chain-operated first-run multiplex is not the only game in town, though it is by far the dominant player. The range of possibilities expands almost immeasurably when we set our contemporary experiences of the movies against the variety of film exhibition venues, occasions, and practices in the United States throughout the last century. Again, consider the situation in Lexington, this time in 1908, when it had a population of around 35,000. Moving pictures were then screened in several quite distinct venues: summer parks, fairs, churches, vaudeville theaters, the opera house, and at least five storefront nickelodeons downtown, each offering daily changing programs comprised of several one-reel films and some sort of live entertainment, usually a pianist and a singer who performed songs illustrated by colorful slides. By 1925 (with the city's population approaching 45,000), Lexington's Main Street was home to three self-styled picture palaces, each seating well over 1,000 and offering "balanced" programs that included a newsreel, several shorts, a feature film, and a substantial helping of live entertainment by in-house orchestras, organists, touring marimba bands, "vodvil" acts, Charleston dancers, and so on.

Down the block there were two more theaters: a former vaudeville house now given over to the movies, a resident musical comedy troupe, and local amateur performers, and a much smaller relic from the nickelodeon era that screened little more than westerns and serial episodes. By 1980, only one of the big downtown theaters was still standing, its ceiling-wide skylight removed years before to accommodate an improved sound system that was installed, the story goes, to guarantee a first-run booking of *The Sound of Music*. This 1,100-seat picture palace was then in its third or fourth incarnation, this time as a flourishing repertory cinema, bolstered by popular weekend midnight shows. Each of the three malls and the three bigger strip malls around the city (then home to 200,000 people) had its own chain-operated "twin" cinema for first-run movies and the occasional midnight cult classic. Five drive-ins perched in the darkness on the edge of town (actually, right on the other side of the county line), showing mostly low-budget horror and soft-core sexploitation to carloads of teenagers.

Even these snapshot views of one locality, which don't begin to document a century's worth of film exhibition, underscore a simple yet significant point: commercial screening sites have not always been designed, equipped, managed, and socially situated as they are in a suburban, chain-operated multiplex. Not only have theaters varied in countless ways, from the configuration of the box office and the price of admission to the shape of the auditorium and the size of the screen; so, too, have programming policies and practices differed across time and place, as the material included in this anthology so vividly demonstrates. What this material also proves is that within the vast and diverse array of sites, occasions, and practices there are identifiable trends, industry standards, competing models, and widely adopted strategies. There is, in other words, a history of film exhibition, which merits our attention because it offers more than the very real and abiding pleasures of nostalgia and antiquarian curiosity that are so often associated with nickel dumps, opulent cathedrals for the movies, and 1950s passion pits. Gaining a deeper sense of the changes during the past century in movie theaters, film booking practices, and entertainment packaging contributes to our understanding of the history of Hollywood cinema and, perhaps more important, to how we think about the larger cultural history of film in America.

In one respect there is no "film" apart from exhibition; we seek out, pay for, take pleasure or displeasure in the *experience* of a film – even if the film is shown in a "home theater" rather than a public venue. That we can now own the object itself, amass an archive, shelve our own copy of *Mary Poppins* or *Mystery Train*, has made movie watching potentially more private, fragmented, and repetitive, but it hasn't done away with public exhibition. And there is no "Hollywood" apart from all those sites that have screened Hollywood product. "Despite the glamour of Hollywood," the author of a Rockefeller Foundation-funded study wrote in 1944, "the crux of the motion picture industry is the theatre" (Huettig 1944, 54). From the opening night of the first vitascope screening in April, 1896, exhibitors have shaped the history of this industry as much as have highly visible stars, moguls, and innovative auteurs. This is, in part, a matter of marketplace economics, the result of theater owners exerting influence on producers and distributors by electing to offer one movie or genre or form of film as opposed to another or by putting pressure on Hollywood to "give the public what it wants."

But there are other ways to gauge the influence of exhibition on production. For instance, William Paul convincingly argues that "both the architectural screen and the technological screen [in the movie theater] have changed in their 100 years, and changed in ways that directly affect our perception of the movie image." "The screen itself," Paul proposes, "might have influenced the development of film style" (Paul 1996, 245–6). We can extend this argument further to take into account other instances where aspects of film style correspond to or somehow suit the technological and architectural characteristics of particular screening sites. The specific uses and the overall foregrounding of the soundtrack in contemporary Hollywood blockbusters, for example, seem to me directly related to the fact that high-end sound systems have become standard equipment in first-run multiplexes.

The interrelations between production and exhibition are probably most evident when it comes to programming – the way motion pictures (features, shorts, trailers, advertisements) are combined to create what is billed as a single program, which in the past often included live performance. Programming strategies vary greatly over the course of film history, allowing more or less opportunity for the exhibitor to shape the entertainment experience he or she sells. To cite one striking example, Charles Musser's research on early cinema explores the creative role of exhibitors who packaged and combined short motion pictures into saleable shows at venues like New York City's Eden Musee (Musser 1991b, 103–56). Furthermore, the illustrated-song-and-moving-picture show of the nickelodeon era, the balanced program of shorts, live entertainment, and a feature film in the later silent era, the double features of the 1930s, the pared-down, single-film program favored by the multiplex – each of these formats requires the producer to deliver films that differ in any number of ways, including running time. Current multiplexes, for example, look to be much more flexible in their ability to regularly accommodate movies that run more than 120 minutes than were previous first-run theaters. In addition, well before the advent of multi-channel cable TV, certain studios and independent producers targeted niche markets that were often associated with specific kinds of theaters: drive-ins or art cinemas or, before that, segregated "colored" theaters and the approximately 500 "ethnic" or foreign-language theaters that operated in metropolitan areas of the United States in the 1930s

3

(see Gomery 1992, 175–80). There is no question but that the existence of these venues and the audiences they served helped promote production outside the Hollywood mainstream.

A reasonably full picture of American cinema, then, should take into account the ownership and operation of theaters as well as of studios; that is, it should consider film exhibition practices along with what David Bordwell, Janet Staiger, and Kristin Thompson call the "style and mode of production" of classical Hollywood cinema.[1] Charles Musser's *The Emergence of Cinema*, Eileen Bowser's *The Transformation of Cinema*, and Richard Koszarski's *An Evening's Entertainment*, the first three volumes in Scribner's *History of American Cinema* series, are exemplary in this regard. And, further, any broad sense of the social and cultural history of film in America should necessarily take into account exhibition policies, theater design, and moviegoing practices. We can know precious little about how audiences – across racial, regional, gender, and class lines – made sense of and responded to, for example, *The Birth of a Nation* (much less to a run-of-the-mill, now lost movie from 1915). The history of film exhibition does, however, afford us some feel for the particular conditions of reception at a given place in a given time. (Robert C. Allen's essay in this collection explores the relations between exhibition and reception.) Such information, it seems to me, is especially important when we undertake historically grounded interpretations of specific texts, i.e., how a certain movie or genre functions culturally or ideologically in terms of, for instance, the representation of working women or social-class-crossing romance.[2]

Historicizing film exhibition and moviegoing is more than a bit ironic given that there has been a long-standing tendency to design, promote, celebrate, or condemn the movie theater as a place apart, insulating the spectator, warding off distractions from the outside world. "The initial requisite" for the ideal movie theater is "darkness: complete, solid, unbroken," declared a writer in the *National Board of Review Magazine* in 1927 (Stern 1927, 9).[3] As I've noted, this ambition toward enclosure and separation is also evident in the way that the contemporary multiplex is designed to be a cinematic inner sanctum.[4] Yet as P. Morton Shand somewhat hyperbolically put it in *Modern Picture-Houses and Theaters* (1930), "the cinema is...at once the most public and the most secluded of places" (Shand 1930, 9). Much of the research on theaters and audiences that has been published over the past 20 years by social historians and cinema scholars, by specialists in American studies, architecture, gender, working-class history, critical theory, and the mass entertainment business, quite convincingly manages to draw us away from the screen and, figuratively, out of the theater and into the street – that is, into the complexities of twentieth-century America. This impressive body of work proves just how much is at issue in the ways we fill, monitor, and participate in leisure time and public space. Recent scholarship on the history of film exhibition and moviegoing provides an important perspective on the growth and transformation of the commercial entertainment industry at large and – more specifically – on the relations between film and theater, radio, and television. It foregrounds the role of promotion and advertising in a consumer society and charts both the emergence of a metropolitan-based national culture and the enduring appeal of locality, neighborhood, and community. It highlights revealing examples of the business practices associated with the entrepreneur, the chain store, and the vertically integrated corporation. And last, but surely not least, studying the design, operation, and patronage of movie theaters – as well as the broad and often passionate discourse concerning moviegoing in America – reveals much that illuminates the day-by-day negotiation of class, race, age, and gender identities and relations across a century of life in the United States.

This anthology, as its subtitle suggests, is intended to serve as a sourcebook in the history of film exhibition and moviegoing in America, from the first commercial screenings of motion pictures to the generation of new and improved multiplexes that opened at the end of the twentieth century. It does not take up that branch of film theory concerned with spectatorship in the abstract, nor does it address local censorship initiatives, film advertising and exploitation at large, or mass communication research on film viewers and audience demographics.[5] For reasons of space, I have restricted my field to the United States, though there is a substantial body of scholarship on movie theaters in Europe and the United Kingdom and on exhibition practices in different national contexts, including, for example, the tradition of *benshi* (live lecturers) in Japan. Furthermore, while a survey of screen exhibition could surely be understood to include important precursors of projected moving pictures, such as magic lantern shows and single-viewer "peepshow" machines like the kinetoscope, I have elected to focus on the history of public, commercial film exhibition. And, again primarily for reasons of space, I have not included material concerned with the history of movie presentation on commercial television nor with certain key home exhibition formats and practices that have emerged in the past 20 years, notably VHS tape, cable TV, laserdisc, and DVD.

I approach the history of film exhibition and moviegoing in the United States in terms of four basic components that elicit the following questions:

1 **The theater or screening site**: How is it designed, decorated, and equipped? What are its architectural characteristics? How large is its work staff? How is it managed? Where is it located? How is it marketed? What is its status and identity in the community?

2 **Booking and promoting films**: How are films acquired and promoted by the exhibitor? Who oversees these activities? What are the relations between the exhibitor and the distributor?

3 **The program**: What's on the bill? What is the length of the program? How frequently is it offered? What is the role of music and live performance? How much control does the exhibitor wield in designing, modifying, "localizing" the program? Is it a specialized programming format, like the Saturday matinee or the midnight movie?

4 **Moviegoing**: Who is in the audience? How often and how regularly do they attend? Is seating segregated by race, gender, or age? What activities and behaviors occur inside and around the theater?

It is possible to consider each of these areas separately – to look, for example, at lighting as a specialized problem in theater design or to focus solely on the moviegoing opportunities open to, say, Hispanic audiences in the Southwest during the 1940s. There is no question, however, but that these four topics connect and overlap. Precisely how they do so is one of the most basic issues in film history: what are the relations between screening sites, for example, and programming, between programming and the economics of exhibition, between exhibition policies and moviegoing practice?

To frame and explore such issues, *Moviegoing in America* juxtaposes two quite different types of material. First, it includes a sampling of recent academic research by scholars who think across traditional disciplinary lines in work that often bridges film studies, social history, and cultural analysis. These essays, quite distinct in focus, method, and explanatory ambitions, demonstrate the vitality and diversity of contemporary work in film history. They include case studies of specific localities (Worcester, Massachusetts; Austin, Texas; rural Kentucky) or the moviegoing practices and experiences of specific audiences (African Americans, working-class immigrants); they examine particular historical moments (the first public motion picture screenings), specific business practices (the model of chain store management), influential technological changes (the spread of widescreen processes), and various exhibition sites (the small town picture show, the urban picture palace, the suburban multiplex).

Intercut with this academic scholarship is a collection of what I would loosely call "primary" documents drawn from diverse sources across the twentieth century. These are not individual accounts of personal moviegoing experiences, such as might appear in diaries or letters or be represented in novels or poems. They are, instead, public documents, including advertisements, photographs, souvenirs, theater programs and flyers, newspaper comics, feature articles from mass-market magazines, specialized studies of architecture, business practices, and legal issues, advice from motion picture trade journals and handbooks for theater managers, editorials, interviews, and exposés. From different perspectives within and around the industry, these documents speak of what film exhibition was, and they seek to influence what it might become. In so doing, they open up, enliven, and complicate the cultural history of the movies.

Although this book does survey the entire span of American cinema, space permits that certain important topics be covered, at best, only in passing: pre-nickelodeon screenings at fairs, circuses, vaudeville theaters, and chautauquas; traveling motion picture exhibitors large and small who worked the provinces town by town; specialized newsreel theaters and venues featuring foreign-language films; particular screening occasions like the midnight movie and the Hollywood premiere; booking policies like the double feature and the roadshow attraction; porn houses and exhibitors specializing in exploitation movies; high- and low-visibility film festivals; and non-theatrical exhibition in churches, schools, museums, community centers, and homes. I will give some indication of where to look for information about these and other such topics, including scholarship on the history of exhibition practices outside the United States, in my guide to sources and resources.

In conducting research for this project, I have been continually pleased to discover that there is a treasure trove of additional material that could have been included in *Moviegoing in America*. The past decade has seen an increasing number of scholarly articles, monographs, and dissertations in this particular area of film studies. The primary documents reprinted here only hint at the amount of material waiting to be reclaimed from the vast published discourse concerning the movies in twentieth-century America. And then there is all that has gone unpublished and remains to be gathered by researchers from public archives, personal scrapbooks, memorabilia collections, and oral history interviews. (In Part V I suggest some possible research projects along these lines.) Heavily illustrated books like Q. David Bowers' *Nickelodeon Theatres and Their Music* and Barbara Stones' *America Goes to the Movies* attest to the extraordinary visual record – the countless snapshots, postcards, and publicity photographs documenting the American movie theater in all its many manifestations. Perhaps in some later multimedia project on moviegoing and exhibition, the full range of these images can be adequately sampled, along with excerpts from relevant documentaries, recordings of germane popular songs, and a selection of clips illustrating the motion picture industry's own take on what happens in movie theaters, from celebratory newsreel coverage of grand premieres to irreverent animated parody, from *Uncle Josh at the Moving Picture Show* (1902) and *Sherlock Jr.* (1924) through *Sullivan's Travels* (1941), *The Last Picture Show* (1971), *Desperately Seeking Susan* (1985), *The Purple Rose of Cairo* (1985), *Matinee* (1992), and *Get Shorty* (1995). There might even be room for a scene or two from *Drive-In Massacre* (1974).

Notes

1 Lewis Jacobs' *The Rise of the American Film* (1939) and most subsequent one-volume histories give at best passing attention to a few exhibition highpoints: the nickelodeon boom, the practice of block-booking, the emergence of

the picture palace, the methods used to draw audiences during the Depression. Jacobs devotes fewer pages to 40 years of film exhibition practices than he does to D.W. Griffith's *Intolerance*. Exhibition typically is given extensive treatment only in those studies that focus on the "economics" of the industry, like Seabury and Huettig.

2   For examples and a sense of the issue involved with studying the historical reception of specific films and genres, see Staiger (1986, 1992); Uricchio and Pearson (1993); Smoodin (1995); and Klinger (1997).

3   An alternate model is what Dudley Andrew, in discussing the drive-in, calls the "social ethic of distracted viewing" as opposed to the "promise of 'engulfment'" (Andrew 1988, 15).

4   Certain critical writing on the history of theaters shares this approach by, for example, becoming lost in the magnificent picture palaces and cascading organ overtures of the 1920s.

5   See collections edited by Williams, Pribram, and Penley for key essays in the debate over spectatorship and gender. Important work on studio advertising film exploitation includes Eckert (1978); Gaines (1990); Haralovich (1984, 1985); and Staiger (1990). Austin (1983) provides a useful bibliography of the communications research on audiences. The trade press during the early silent era paid considerable attention to local censorship efforts, along with all other laws pertaining to the operation of theaters (see *Moving Picture World*'s listing of relevant state laws, which appeared from November 21, 1914 through July 24, 1915). For studies of local censorship efforts, see, for example, Jowett (1976, 113–19); McCarthy (1976); Bernstein (1995); Waller (1995, 136–47); and O'Leary (1996).

★ ★ ★ ★ ★ ★ ★ ★ ★ ★ ★ ★ ★ ★

PART I

**Capturing an Audience,
Creating a Business:
1896–1916**

★ ★ ★ ★ ★ ★ ★ ★ ★ ★ ★ ★ ★

Introduction

The selections in Part I cover approximately the first 20 years of film exhibition in the United States. They begin with the initial commercial vitascope screenings in 1896–7 and move through the nickelodeon boom to the early 'teens, when multi-reel feature films had come to play a much more prominent role in theater programming and when new venues began to be designed and built specifically as movie theaters. Charles Musser's "Introducing Cinema to the American Public: The Vitascope in the United States, 1896–7" surveys the first year of film screenings, when moving pictures were an exploitable novelty attraction, ready-made for entrepreneurial exhibitors across the country. Relying on business records and newspaper accounts, Musser considers both the larger national situation and the particular circumstances of different cities and towns across the United States. In so doing, he foregrounds an essential point: moving pictures were, from the start, a nationally available product that was programmed, marketed, exhibited, and consumed locally. As we will see, throughout the cultural history of film in America, this relation between the national and the local will be reconfigured in a variety of ways.

Looking at the nickelodeon era and beyond, Roy Rosenzweig's richly detailed study of the role of movies and movie theaters in the ethnic working-class communities of Worcester, Massachusetts, also explores locality and nationality, but takes up a different set of questions: Who owned and operated moving picture shows? What audiences did they attract and how did these customers behave inside the theater? What did it mean to be part of the growing movie audience? Did theater operation, programming policies, and audience behavior change so as to attract middle-class patrons to the movies? Such questions, as Rosenzweig proves, point to larger issues about the role of mass entertainment in early twentieth-century America – above all, to the losses and gains accrued when moviegoing immigrants with strong working-class and ethnic ties "moved," in Rosenzweig's phrase, "gradually to the mainstream of American life."

The period documents in Part I supplement and complicate the issues raised by Musser and Rosenzweig. Typical of contemporary reform discourse, John Collier's 1908 article reports on an "investigation" of nickelodeons and other cheap amusement sites in Manhattan, with an eye toward uplift by progressive legislation. Unlike Collier's account, Mary Heaton Vorse's 1911 description of Jewish and Italian immigrant picture show audiences, published in the general-interest weekly, *Outlook*, is framed much more as a piece of journalistic ethnography, complete with rendered dialect and vividly etched character types. These two early articles raise significant questions: Is the site itself or the particularized audience the most important aspect of film exhibition? On what grounds should we be suspicious of Vorse's sympathetic reportage or Collier's social-scientific investigation? Compare both of these accounts of the nickelodeon with the matter-of-fact catalogue of different types of motion picture theaters by David Hulfish, in the selection taken from his manual on theater operation, first published in 1911. Audiences for Hulfish are customers or potential customers; he is principally concerned with explaining the range of venues in operation, from the small vaudeville theater using films to the "large exclusive picture house" and the airdome. The emergence of distinct types of screening sites has potentially major implications for our understanding of the historical reception of the movies. Is, say, Griffith's *The Girl and Her Trust* (1912) the same film when shown in each of the quite distinct venues Hulfish enumerates? Furthermore, Hulfish's advice on how to boost profits suggests that the independent theater operator had a good deal of discretion in arranging and promoting programs with a particular audience in mind. At what point, we can ask, do certain of these screening sites and programming configurations disappear or become especially predominant?

The material included from *Moving Picture World* (1908–11) samples how this important trade magazine perceived the business of film exhibition, specifically, how it sought to "swell the box office receipts" by improving a range of practices – projection, programming, staffing, design, advertising, and "handling" the patron. In the anxieties expressed and ideals promoted by *Moving Picture World*, we can glimpse what was at stake in attempts to legitimize the movies and standardize and uplift exhibition. Boyd Fisher's survey in *American City* (1912), a journal devoted to municipal government and urban problems, captures a more general apprehension concerning the movie theater as a ubiquitous, unsafe physical and moral presence in the city that civic authority must regulate. Writing in a 1914 special moving picture theater issue of the architectural journal, the *Brickbuilder*, Aymar Embury is less concerned about cultural uplift, moral danger, or day-to-day business practices than about the moving picture theater's emergence as a vital form of indigenous American "street architecture." Thus these readings on the theater bring us back to certain of Rosenzweig's concerns about moviegoing and Americanization, and, more broadly, to thinking about the movie theater as a constructed place, as an economic opportunity, as a site of Americanization, and as a zone requiring regulation.

1

Introducing Cinema to the American Public: The Vitascope in the United States, 1896–7

Charles Musser

Although motion pictures were occasionally projected onto a screen in the United States during 1895, by the Lathams' eidoloscope and C. Francis Jenkins' and Thomas Armat's phantoscope, these efforts never reached a level of sufficient achievement either technically or commercially. It was the vitascope – often known as "Edison's Vitascope" – that effectively launched projected motion pictures as a screen novelty in the United States. In late April 1896, the vitascope was showing films in only one American theater – at Koster & Bial's Music Hall in New York City. The subsequent pace of diffusion was remarkable, for both the vitascope and the cinema. By spring 1897, as the year-long novelty period came to a close, exhibitors were using several hundred projectors to present films across the country. Honolulu had its first picture show in early February 1897, while Phoenix, in Arizona Territory, followed that May 1897.[1] In the Northeast and Midwest, towns of a few thousand inhabitants had been visited by showmen with motion pictures not once but two or three times. The vast majority of Americans had had the opportunity to see motion pictures on a screen, and many took it. Their responses were not unlike those that greeted the magic lantern in the 1650s or the stereopticon in the 1860s – astonishment at the lifelike quality of the images. Likewise, during this brief 13- or 14-month period, a new industry was established and staffed.[2] It was a period of ferment and rapid change. By its close, a framework existed within which subsequent motion picture practices developed.

The vitascope was launched by Norman Raff and Frank Gammon, who already controlled the North American sales rights for the kinetoscope. The kinetoscope, invented by Thomas A. Edison and his staff (notably W.K.L. Dickson and William Heise), was a peep-hole machine used for the individual viewing of short films (initially 40–50 feet in length, later as much as 150 feet). It was a key component of the first commercially successful motion picture system in the world. The adaptation of kinetoscope films to projection (to the magic lantern) was an obvious step in the improvement of this system – one which occurred to many customers and was realized in different forms within a very short time frame in both the United States and Europe. The Lathams' eidoloscope was the first effort at adaptation in the United States,

The following essay reworks elements of chapter 4, "The Vitascope," from *The Emergence of Cinema: The American Screen to 1907*, in combination with more recent research, some of which appeared in Musser, "Nationalism and the Beginnings of Cinema: The Lumière Cinématographe in the United States, 1896–1897." *Historical Journal of Film, Radio and Television* 19, no.2 (June 1999), 149–76.

but the machine lacked an intermittent mechanism that stopped the film frame in front of the light source. This resulted in a small and unsteady image. The phantoscope did have an intermittent, and was technically successful, but had a disastrous debut at the Cotton States Exhibition in Atlanta, Georgia, in October 1895. At this point co-inventors Jenkins and Armat had a falling out, with Armat reaching an agreement to exploit the machine with Raff & Gammon (leaving Jenkins out of the picture entirely).

Raff & Gammon faced an array of challenges in marketing Armat's phantoscope, which they quickly renamed the vitascope, but one of the most serious soon proved to be the certain invasion of competing "screen machines" from Europe, particularly England and France. The kinetoscope had been an international novelty, selling equally in Europe and the United States even as it featured performers from around the world. When it came to the vitascope, international markets were seriously compromised while the domestic market was likewise threatened from without (as well as, obviously, from domestic competitors). Quick and aggressive action was required if they were to have any reasonable chance of success.

The New York Debut

Working closely with Thomas Edison in the first months of 1896, Raff & Gammon choreographed an abbreviated but effective promotional campaign to launch the new "screen machine." From the outset, they had decided to have the premiere in New York City, the nation's entertainment and media capital. "Judging from our experience with the Kinetoscope, we are pretty well satisfied that we can do much better and make more money for both parties by exhibiting the machine at the start exclusively in New York City. The reports through the news-papers go throughout the country, and we shall do a lot of advertising in the shape of news-paper articles which will excite the curiosity of

parties interested in such things," they explained to Armat.[3]

The name and involvement of Thomas Edison, by this time a semi-mythic figure in American life, guaranteed extensive media attention and a favorable outlook from the American public. The degree of his cooperation, however, remained uncertain until the popular hero had actually attended a private screening on March 27, 1896. Not only did the machine receive his complete approval, but the "Wizard of Menlo Park" stood ready to play the role of inventor, which the press desired and Raff & Gammon had assigned to him. Participating in a press screening at his laboratory on April 3, the Wizard stole the show, and if Thomas Armat was present, he stayed discreetly in the background. As the *New York Journal* reported on the following day,

> For the first time since Edison has been working on his new invention, the vitascope, persons other than his trusted employees and assistants were allowed last night to see the workings of the wonderful machine. For two hours dancing girls and groups of figures, all of life size, seemed to exist as realities on the big white screen which had been built at one end of the experimenting rooms.[4]

Representatives of the *New York World* and other dailies also attended, and their reports soon appeared in newspapers nationwide.

On March 23, Raff & Gammon approached Albert Bial and asked him to book the vitascope at his Koster & Bial's Music Hall on 34th Street and Broadway for a fee of $800 a week. These negotiations were concluded in early April.[5] After the novelty premiered on Thursday, April 23, the *New York Dramatic Mirror* declared the entertainment "was a success in every way and the large audience testified its approval of the novelty by the heartiest kind of applause."[6] The debut helped to sell additional territory; soon only exhibition rights for the South were available for purchase.[7]

Although Koster & Bial's program promised as many as 12 views,[8] only six scenes were shown on opening night according to New York newspapers:

The first view showed two dancers holding between and in front of them an umbrella and dancing the while. The position of the umbrella was constantly changed, and every change was smooth and even, and the steps of the dancing could be perfectly followed.

Then came the waves, showing a scene at Dover pier after a stiff blow. This was by far the best view shown, and had to be repeated many times. As in the umbrella dance, there was absolutely no hitch. One could look far out to sea and pick out a particular wave swelling and undulating and growing bigger and bigger until it struck the end of the pier. Its edge then would be fringed with foam, and finally, in a cloud of spray, the wave would dash upon the beach. One could imagine the people running away.[9]

This was followed by a burlesque boxing bout, in which the contestants were a very tall, thin man and a very short, stout one. The little fellow was knocked down several times, and the movements of the boxers were well represented. A scene from "A Milk White Flag" was next shown, in which soldiers and a military band perform some complex evolutions. A group representing Uncle Sam, John Bull, Venezuela and the Monroe doctrine got a good welcome from the patriotic. The last picture was a serpentine dancer. The color effects were used in this, and it was one of the most effective of the series.[10]

The Music Hall band accompanied the images with appropriate music. Two of the films were in color, using a hand-tinting process similar to that for stereopticon slides. This was almost certainly done by the wife of Edmund Kuhn in Orange, New Jersey.[11]

Reviewers considered the "projection of [Edison's peep-hole] kinetoscope figures in stereopticon fashion" to be a screen novelty.[12] The *New York Mail and Express* explained to its readers, "In the vitascope the figures of the kinetoscope are projected, enlarged to life-size, upon a screen in much the same manner as ordinary, everyday stereopticon images."[13] The exhibition methods that typified later vitascope screenings were already in use at the premiere. As with the kinetoscope, each film was spliced end-to-end to form a continuous band so that a brief 20-second scene could be shown over and over again. Jump cuts regularly appeared at the splice. With dances and the wave rolling onto the beach, this jump was not disruptive. With most other subjects, however, the splice created "a few hitches in the changes."[14] Although one exhibitor reported showing each endless band of film only three times before turning off his machine, a subject was usually repeated at least half a dozen times. As was to be the case at some other important showings, two vitascopes were used at Koster & Bial's, "housed in a little turret-like structure built above two of the middle boxes."[15] While one film was being shown on one vitascope, the subject on the other machine could be taken off and replaced by a new one – a process that took approximately two minutes.

By projecting one-shot films in an endless band, the vitascope emphasized movement and life-like images at the expense of narrative. As Raff & Gammon claimed in their prospectus, "When the machine is started by the operator, the bare canvas before the audience instantly becomes a stage, upon which living beings move about, and through their respective acts, movements, gestures and changing expressions, surrounded by appropriate settings and accessories – the very counterpart of the stage, the field, the city, the country – yes, more, for these reproductions are in some respects more satisfactory, pleasing and interesting than the originals."[16] The spectators were thus assumed to make a conscious comparison between the projected image and the everyday world as they knew and experienced it directly. It was the unprecedented congruence between the two that was being celebrated. Projected images were conceived as a novelty for which life-like movement in conjunction with a life-size photographic image provided a sense of heightened realism.

This new level of realism at least temporarily expanded the screen's importance as a source of commercial amusement.

The opening night program of the vitascope, however, was something more than a casually assembled collection of entertaining views. The sequence of films was built around *The Monroe Doctrine*, the only film on the program which we know for certainty was made by the Edison Manufacturing Company for this new era of projected motion pictures. *The Monroe Doctrine* responded to a "crisis" in foreign affairs, involving a long-standing border dispute between British Guiana and Venezuela, which had heated up after gold miners rushed into the disputed area. When Great Britain threatened to use force to assert its claims, the United States intervened by evoking the Monroe Doctrine, "the favorite dogma of the American people."[17] The Monroe Doctrine hardly had the stature of international law, and its new and expanded application in this context could be seen to signal the true beginning of "the American century." The Edison film, which was doubtlessly inspired by a political cartoon on this subject, "shows John Bull bombarding a South American shore, supposedly to represent Venezuela. John is seemingly getting the better of the argument when the tall lanky figure of Uncle Sam emerges from the back of the picture. He grasps John Bull by the neck, forces him to his knees and makes him take off his hat to Venezuela."[18] A burlesque, this editorial cartoon on film showed "Uncle Sam teaching John Bull a lesson."[19] England was only the specific object of a doctrine that the United States sought to apply to all European powers. A synecdochal or allegorical tale seems to be at play: one in which the forbidden interference of Europeans in American affairs could be expanded to include the expected invasion of European motion picture machines into the American market.

Of the six films shown on opening night, three or four others were old kinetoscope films, made in 1894–5: the Leigh sisters in *Umbrella Dance*, *Band Drill* with an excerpt of "The Milk White Flag," and *Walton & Slavin*

showing a burlesque boxing match from *Little Christopher Columbus*. New subjects within the familiar genre of dance films may have included a skirt dance by an unidentified performer (this may well have been an old film). In all these instances, the performers were American (and white). The most novel film was Robert Paul's *Sea Waves at Dover* – duly credited as an English subject but without acknowledging its true author. The film provides a fascinating complement to *The Monroe Doctrine*: *Sea Waves at Dover* suggested not only the geographic mobility of the American machine, but its ability to keep the heart of the British Empire within its vision. And as the waves crashed on the cinematic shore and failed to sweep away its vaudeville spectators, did not this film hint that British power in the Americas was only an illusion? Or that British waves (and John Bull) should stay on British shores? The vitascope's opening night program strongly indicates that Raff & Gammon had consciously chosen to fight the expected influx of international machines (English as well as French) by appealing to American patriotism – even as they (like Maguire & Baucus) had marketed the kinetoscope on the basis of a cosmopolitan internationalism.[20]

The order of the films was (1) *Umbrella Dance*, (2) *Sea Waves at Dover*, (3) *Walton & Slavin*, (4) *Band Drill*, (5) *The Monroe Doctrine*, and (6) Serpentine or Skirt Dance.[21] The program thus started off by showing two young female dancers, asserting a continuation between stage and screen. (According to one critic, "It seemed as though they were actually on the stage, so natural was the dance, with its many and graceful motions.")[22] The proscenium arch established by this first film was then broken in *Sea Waves at Dover*. The British waves metaphorically wash away the stage and the Leigh Sisters even as they assault American patrons, causing initial consternation and excitement. This is followed by a familiar subject that reasserted the proscenium. The burlesque bout was between "the long and the short of it," featuring lanky Charles Walton and the stout

John Slavin. According to some sources, *The Monroe Doctrine* also featured Walton as Uncle Sam as well as Slavin's replacement, John Mayon, as John Bull. In any case, Walton and Slavin visually evoked, at least subliminally and retrospectively, Uncle Sam and John Bull engaging in a fistic encounter. The fourth film showed a marching band in uniform: suggesting a mobilization of the American military, it "elicited loud cries of 'Bravo!'"[23] *Band Drill* thus prepared the way for *The Monroe Doctrine*, which "twinned" *Sea Waves at Dover*. The British bombard the shoreline of another American nation – with guns instead of cinematic waves. Uncle Sam forces John Bull to stop. According to one report, "This delighted the audience, and applause and cheers rang through the house, while someone cried, 'Hurrah for Edison.'"[24] With this victory there was a return to the status quo as patrons again viewed a dance film, one similar in style and subject matter to the opening selection. The program began and ended with films of women that indulge male voyeuristic pleasures. A masculinist-nationalist (English–American) confrontation thus forces these pleasures aside until an American triumph is achieved (on the screen), and audiences are returned to their sensual pleasures. More than a miscellaneous collection of self-contained films organized on variety principles and "supplying pleasure through an exciting spectacle – a unique event, whether fictional or documentary, that is of interest in itself,"[25] this opening night program displays a highly organized, if oblique, narrative structure. It demonstrates one of the ways in which exhibitors of the 1890s played a creative force. They were responsible for giving more than a "good show." In organizing and presenting sequences of short films they not only shaped meaning but created it. By sequencing the short films in their repertoire (the equivalent of shots or short scenes), showmen effectively had editorial control over their programs. Programming and editing were, in this respect, not yet distinct phenomena. Throughout the 1890s, the exhibitor thus had creative control over a variety of elements that we would now call post-production.

Local Debuts of the Vitascope

While the vitascope's New York debut created intense demand for "the latest Edison invention" (and the imminent arrival of competing machines from abroad necessitated rapid deployment of machines), the ability to satisfy this desire was hampered by delays in the manufacturing of vitascope projectors. This was particularly frustrating for "state rights" owners because the most lucrative commercial arrangements occurred during the regular theatrical season, which drew to a close in most parts of the country sometime during May. These investors had to watch enticing contracts disappear for lack of a machine. Allen Rieser, who had been promised a machine in mid-March, was impatient and "D — mad" by the second week in May. "The [Summer] Parks that want to engage the Vitascope that I know of wire us if we cannot show them what we have and conclude our engagement they will drop us," he told Raff & Gammon. "Just now I got a telegram from Cleveland Ohio asking whether I could be there on the 16th with the machine. This is the biggest Park in that section of the country. I have to reject them which may be a matter of a couple of thousand dollars."[26] W.R. Miller could have extended his phonograph tour and made another $500 instead of vainly waiting in Tennessee for a promise to be kept.[27] It was not until mid-May that the Edison Manufacturing Company completed the first group of projectors.

The vitascope opened in a dozen major cities and resorts between mid-May and mid-June, with many others to follow in subsequent weeks:

Boston – May 18
Camden, New Jersey(?) – May 21
Hartford, Ct. – May 21
Atlantic City – May 23
Philadelphia – May 25

New Haven, Ct. – May 28
Providence – June 4
Buffalo – June 8
San Francisco – June 8
Meriden, Ct. – June 8
Nashville – June 13
Baltimore – June 15
Bridgeport, Ct. – June 15
New London, Ct. – June 15
St. Louis – June 15
Rochester, NY – by July 20
Portland, Maine – June 22
Bergen Beach (Coney Island) – ca. June 22
Scranton, Pa. – June 22
New Orleans – June 28
Wilkes-Barre, Pa. – June 29
Cleveland – July 1
Asbury Park, NJ – July 1
Detroit – July 1
Los Angeles – July 5
Chicago – July 5
Milwaukee – July 26
Kansas City, Mo. – July 26

Vitascope exhibitions occurred throughout the continental United States in any locality large enough to boast an electrical system. Although the rapid pace of these debuts strained Raff & Gammon's resources beyond the breaking point (Norman Raff even suffered a nervous breakdown), they were generally well received; and the resulting popularity, publicity, and broad diffusion established "Edison's Vitascope" as the first motion picture projector in the minds of the American public.

The vitascope was presented in various types of entertainment venues, thus extending the eclectic nature of sites that had been used for motion picture exhibitions by the Lathams with their eidoloscope. Vaudeville introduced amusement-goers to projected motion pictures in many major cities:

- The vitascope ran at B.F. Keith's Boston theater for 12 weeks and his Philadelphia theater for nine. In each locale, it remained the principal feature on the bill throughout the run.

- The California states rights owners made arrangements with Gustave Walker to play his Orpheum houses in San Francisco (three weeks) and Los Angeles (two weeks).

- The vitascope had its Chicago premiere at Hopkins' South Side Theater where it ran on the vaudeville bill for 20 consecutive weeks. "It is not only an interesting and instructive novelty for the regular patrons of the house," manager J.D. Hopkins declared, "but is drawing scores and hundreds of people who never before attended this popular form of entertainment." He went on to claim that the previous Sunday's business "was the heaviest ever known in the 'ten–twenty–thirty' style of entertainment in this country."[28]

- In Louisville, the vitascope was introduced on September 20 at a newly opened vaudeville house and helped to make it a success.[29]

- In Cleveland, where no vaudeville was presented during the summer, A.F. Rieser engaged a hall and presented the vitascope along with his own small vaudeville company.[30]

Theaters offering other entertainment forms also featured the vitascope. Films were shown in conjunction with plays, musicals, and even operas.

- In St. Louis, vitascope moving pictures were exhibited immediately after the opera, *The Bohemian Girl*.[31] Spectators could either see the films from an outdoor garden or remain inside the theater.

- In Milwaukee, the manager of the Academy of Music arranged for Hixson and Wollam to show the vitascope exclusively at his theater. Each week his stock company put on a new play and a few specialities were performed between acts. Receiving $400 per week, the vitascope entrepreneurs played two weeks in late July and early August, returned for another two weeks in mid-September, and a single week in early November.

- In Albany, New York, on August 17, the vitascope debuted between acts of a play presented by the Corse Payton Company.[32]
- At an opening in Atlanta, Georgia, on November 16, the Florence Hamilton Company put on a different play each night, with moving pictures concluding each performance. Although Jenkins and Armat had failed to draw audiences of any size at the city's Cotton States Exposition, their invention now became "the reigning fad."[33]

In a few instances, the vitascope was linked to occult figures whose mysterious performances equaled Edison's most remarkable achievements.

- In Connecticut, "Wizard Edison's most marvelous Invention" joined with the touring hypnotist Santanelli.[34] Starting in Hartford and moving next to New Haven's Grand Opera House, Santanelli regularly hypnotized subjects in his entourage and made them perform outlandish feats. These performances were ultimately condemned by the conservative *New Haven Register*, which declared, "ENOUGH OF SANTANELLI. Public Should Be Glad When He Leaves With His Men."[35] His performance was not considered educational and "his freak-like, weak-willed sleeping boys" seemed to be throwing their lives away. The work of this mysterious wizard often received more attention than the vitascope.
- At Melodeon Hall in Lexington, Kentucky, the vitascope co-starred with Miss Winnie Anderson, who conducted a "séance of Spiritualism and Theosophy."[36]

Storefronts were a frequently used outlet for vitascope entrepreneurs. Such premises had already been occupied by phonograph exhibitors and other showmen anxious to avoid the expense and brief runs associated with a regular theater. Once an appropriate space was rented, they could give exhibitions

for weeks at a time and pocket all the income above expenses.

- Residents of Providence, Rhode Island – including the Mayor and the city's leading citizens – flocked to a storefront show at 305 Westminister Street during the first part of June. There they could see ten films for 25¢. Screenings went on 12 hours a day (11:00 a.m. to 11:00 p.m.) over four weeks. The "Standing Room Only" sign was often on display both in the afternoons and evenings.[37]
- After playing for a month at a nearby summer park, Walter Wainwright and William Rock operated a storefront moving picture show at 623 Canal Street in New Orleans. With a 10¢ admission fee, this profitable effort (one of the few) ran from July 26 through September.
- After earlier turns in nearby summer parks, the New York Vitascope Company opened storefronts in Rochester on September 4 and in Buffalo later in the month.[38] Although the Rochester venue at 64 South Street was "a very fine store in the best location in the city," McLoughlin grossed only $100 during the first seven days – much less than expenses.[39] Nonetheless, he remained there at least a month. In late December, he opened another storefront in Utica and stayed for five weeks. Fifteen films were presented at each showing with an admission fee of 10¢ to 15¢.[40]

Many of these storefronts were variations on phonograph and kinetoscope parlors.

- In Nashville, Tennessee, the main room featured the vitascope but nickel-in-the-slot phonographs were in the foyer.[41] There, W.R. Miller tried various methods of ballyhooing his films. "I started giving a half hour show for 25¢ but it didn't work, so I put the price [at] 10¢ and run one film and change every fifteen minutes in the evening. In that way many people spend

50¢ or more where they would not spend a quarter."[42]

- The California vitascope exhibitors began to show their machine in the rear of Tally's kinetoscope and phonograph storefront in late July.
- In Asbury Park, Edison's Electrical Casino had the vitascope in its small theater while kinetoscopes and phonographs were in the annex.[43]

Summer parks and resorts provided popular locations for vitascope exhibitions during the warm weather. In most cases these venues were either small theaters that functioned like the urban storefronts or summer theaters adapted for vaudeville.

- The vitascope was presented at three summer parks near Philadelphia. One, Willow Grove Park, opened a new theater on August 5 with the vitascope, an X-ray machine ("through the medium of which can be seen the bones in the hand and other portions of the body"), kinetoscopes, and phonographs.[44]
- At the Casino, a summer vaudeville theater at Baltimore's Arlington Electric Park (run by Charles E. Ford, who owned and managed Ford's Theater), there was only one projector in operation, and a film was shown between each vaudeville act. By the second week of the vitascope run, 3,500 people attended on a single day, with each paying 25¢. Most were drawn by the screen novelty; and, according to the *Baltimore Sun*, the show became "a favorite point for cyclers out on an evening ride."[45]
- In Atlantic City, which relied heavily on Philadelphia vacationers, Peter Kiefaber exhibited the vitascope at the Scenic Theater, at "the very centre of the 'Boardwalk' and the only room fitted up in theatrical style, finely lit up by electricity and with drop seats."[46] Arthur Hotaling, who saw his first motion pictures there, felt that Kiefaber's lack of showmanship was responsible for his poor box-office receipts.

Hotaling, who had previously run a "living picture show" in which performers formed tableaux in imitation of well-known paintings, offered his expertise to the inexperienced showman and was soon managing the theater. Later he recalled,

As a showman one of my best assets was an ability to handle a brush, and the first thing I did was to plaster the front with banners. The two star films were Cissy Fitzgerald in her dance and the John C. Rice-May Irwin kiss, and I decorated the front with these in vivid color. Then I fixed up the entrance so that the curtain could be drawn back to display the screen. If we saw anyone in the crowd getting interested we would drop the curtain and he would have to pay his dime to see the rest. Generally, though, we would show part of the Fitzgerald picture and I would make a "spiel" about the kiss picture, which was from "The Widow Jones," then a recent Broadway hit. Business picked up.[47]

In August Kiefaber was running another vitascope in a second Atlantic City location, probably a storefront.[48]

- At Bergen Beach, a resort near Coney Island that was run by Percy Williams, the vitascope played in its own small theater and each day delighted "hundreds by its almost perfect simulation of moving scenes in real life."[49]

These different venues suggest some of the different ways that early films were marketed and understood. This new form of screen entertainment – an up-to-date magic lantern – could serve as a vaudeville novelty, as a vehicle to re-present theatrical performances, or as a new form of technology for mechanical reproduction like the X-ray or phonograph (one of several "new media" making their appearance at this time). Above all, impresarios eagerly associated the new screen novelty with a wide range of entertainment forms, cutting across genres and in some cases even high–low cultural distinctions. In its methods of production and exhibition, as well as in its subject matter, the vitascope continued the profound transformation of American life and performance culture that the kinetoscope had already begun.

Problems with the Vitascope

A wide range of problems plagued the vitascope entrepreneurs. At first, only a handful of people (Thomas Armat and his brothers, Edward Murphy, James White, and one or two others) knew how to set up and operate the machines; these experts raced from city to city trying to salvage dire situations. Eurio Hopkins' terse telegram from Providence was typical: "Rush Murphy quick. In trouble. Also competent man permanent. Turned five hundred away. Unable to give performance."[50] There were no instructions to send out with the machines. In the best of circumstances, mechanically minded men such as Tennesee rights owner W.R. Miller figured out how to assemble the parts and run the machine on their own.[51] Adjustments were often imperfect and sometimes resulted in unnecessary technical difficulties.

The electricity needed to power the vitascopes was one of the entrepreneurs' biggest headaches. The machines were designed to run on the direct current favored by Edison, but many locations were wired for alternating current instead. As Robert C. Allen has pointed out, the nation's patchwork of conflicting currents and voltages meant that the projectors frequently had to be adapted to different conditions when moved to a new locale.[52] In some instances, electricity had to be pulled off streetcar lines. When J. Hunter Armat confronted this situation in Baltimore, he declined to take charge of the show, and it was several days before his more experienced brother Christopher arrived and tied in. With streetcars using 500 volts, the vitascope was overloaded and frequently subjected the motion picture operator to painful shocks.[53] The electrical problem was so severe that theater manager Charles Ford decided not to renew his contract after a four-week run but rather waited for a more amenable machine to come along.[54] Meanwhile, from Halifax, Nova Scotia, Andrew Holland wrote Raff & Gammon, "If I have to get a special motor for every town I go into I may as well drop this country altogether, except in towns large enough to support an electric railway system. In Ottawa the alternating system is 52 volts 1600 frequency; here it is 104 volts. I do not know the frequency, but I thought you had overcome the difficulty of differences in frequency by the adoption of cone pulleys."[55] The Halifax showing was a failure due to electrical problems and Holland lost $200 out of pocket.

Solutions were diverse, often ingenious, but rarely satisfactory. In Los Angeles, R.S. Paine, Charles H. Balsley, and Edwin S. Porter relied on batteries to power their machine. After working imperfectly on opening night, the vitascope was soon performing up to standard. Such a solution was not generally practical, however, since the quantity of batteries needed to project the films would have been prohibitive for someone moving from town to town.[56] Many locales simply did not have electricity. In North Dakota, for example, only four towns could supply electrical power of any kind. In Canada, Holland tried bicycle power in the hope that "I can make myself entirely independent of electric light and power, and consequently will be able to work the small towns through this country to advantage."[57] The results were somewhat disappointing. "The motive power run by hand proves to be a complete success so far as speed is concerned, but it does not give the same even, steady power as an electric motor," he explained. "I have more difficulty with the lamp of the new machine. Do my best I cannot get a good clean light from it the same as we have with the first machine."[58]

Films were another major expense, costing as much as $12.50 for a new 50-foot (actual length 42-foot) subject. To make matters worse, the Edison Manufacturing Company often failed to turn out film prints of acceptable quality. The first exhibitions relied on the semitranslucent strips intended for kinetoscopes. When the Blair Camera Company finally produced a clear-base celluloid film stock, it quickly proved unsatisfactory as the emulsion peeled off the base.[59] Exhibitors despaired at the poor quality of films; A.F. Rieser was reduced to sending back only those that would wear out in less than a week. Some prints only lasted a couple of nights.[60] Edmund McLoughlin complained that his films were very gray and discussed the problem with experts at the Eastman Company in Rochester, New York, already the country's leading supplier of photographic supplies. They suggested that Edison was not using the proper emulsion. McLoughlin also informed them, "The Eastman Co. are shipping very heavily to France. They make a positive and negative emulsion and claim better results than you get."[61] Finally, in mid-September the Edison Manufacturing Company shifted its purchases of raw stock to Eastman. From that time on, the photographic manufacturer has been the principal American supplier of motion picture raw stock.

Individual vitascope entrepreneurs faced still other problems. In more rural areas, the screen novelty was greeted with little enthusiasm or patronage. "After the thing becomes ancient history these Yankees may become interested. But it is a harder task to interest the Maine natives in something new, than it is to preach free silver coinage to Wall Street bankers," declared C.O. Richardson in a letter to the Vitascope Company.[62] W.R. Miller apparently had the same problem with Southerners as his gross income with the vitascope generally fluctuated between $5 and $34 a day. Far from major urban centers, people were often suspicious of urban popular amusements. In Skowhegan, Maine, Richardson reported that *Watermelon Contest* was considered "nasty and vulgar because of the spitting and slobbering,"[63] and he thus had to ask Raff & Gammon for a replacement. City, county, and state licenses often reflected this hostility. As the owner of the Tennessee rights

complained, "the only city where a good business can be done is Memphis where the City license is $22.50 per day. State and county are extra so you see that is prohibitive."[64] Eventually many of the problems evoked by "state rights" owners were ameliorated if not completely eliminated; Eastman's satisfactory film stock was adopted; and although vitascope exhibitors complained about the shortage of film subjects, their choice of titles continued to grow.

Despite these improvements, "state rights" owners rarely recouped their investment. Most did little more than meet expenses. Wainwright and Rock were the only ones ever to claim a profit. In early September a Holland brother wrote to Raff:

I am completely disheartened about the Vitascope business in consequence of the wretched films we have been receiving of late. If there is no improvement, it is simply out of the question altogether doing business under present conditions, and I do not wonder at the statements I hear from exhibitors in the United States that they are not making money to warrant paying large bonuses for territory.[65]

A month later, C.O. Richardson reported:

The Vitascope business in Maine has been no picnic by any means. Without counting a dollar for services of myself, wife and daughter, who have done all the work, we have since June, profited enough above running expenses to just pay costs of film and rental. After four months work with state two thirds covered I am still out my original $1000 for state.[66]

The expense and difficulty of introducing a new technology became their burden, allowing others to prosper.

Raff & Gammon, Thomas Armat, and Thomas Edison were the chief people to profit from the vitascope. Although the vitascope's New York run at Koster & Bial's ended in mid-August 1896, Raff & Gammon reopened at Proctor's two New York vaudeville houses in

Table 1 Premieres of "Edison's Vitascope," the Lumière Cinématographe, and the American biograph in selected US cities

Cities	Vitascope	Cinématographe	Biograph
New York	April 23	June 29	Oct 5/12
Boston	May 18	Aug 10	Jan 11 (1897)
Hartford, Ct.	May 21	Dec 3	Feb 4 (1897)
Philadelphia	May 25	July 27	Dec 28
New Haven, Ct.	May 28	Sept 14	Nov 30
Providence	June 4	Sept 7	Dec 21
San Francisco	June 8	Aug 30 (1897)	Oct 25 (1897)
Baltimore	June 15	by Jan 15 (1897)	Nov 2
Brooklyn[a]	June 22	Aug 17	Sept 28
New Orleans[b]	June 28	June 21 (1897)	Sept 11 (1898)
Wilkes-Barre, Pa.[c]	June 29	–	Dec 9 (1899)[d]
Detroit[e]	July 1	Jan 17 (1897)	Dec 6
Cleveland	July 1	March 29 (1897)	May 3 (1897)
Chicago	July 5	Sept 14	Nov 16[f]
Los Angeles	July 5	Aug 9 (1897)	Dec 6 (1897)
Rochester, NY[g]	by July 20	Nov 2	Nov 30
Milwaukee	July 26	Dec 10	April 4 (1897)
Kansas City, Mo.	July 26	Dec 20	Nov 30[f]
Denver[h]	Aug 16	Jan 23 (1898)	Jan 11 (1897)
Pittsburgh	Sept 7	Sept 7	Sept 14
Cincinnati	Sept 13	Dec 20	March 14 (1897)
Louisville, Ky.	Sept 20	Nov 9	Jan 4 (1897)
Washington, DC[i]	Sept 21	Jan 1 (1897)	Feb 2 (1897)
Lexington, Ky.[j]	Dec 23	–	Jan 25 (1900)[d]
Utica, NY	Dec 29	–	April 12 (1897)

Dates are for 1896 unless the year is provided in parentheses. Information is derived from searches of local newspapers with supplemental sources as noted.

[a] The local Brooklyn premiere of the vitascope was at Coney Island.

[b] Sylvester Quinn Breard, "A History of Motion Pictures in New Orleans, 1896–1908" (M.A. thesis; Louisiana State University, May 1951), published on microfiche in *Historical Journal of Film, Radio and Television* 15, no. 4 (1995).

[c] Charles Musser with Carol Nelson, *High-Class Moving Pictures: Lyman H. Howe and the Forgotten Era of Traveling Exhibition, 1880–1920* (Princeton, New Jersey: Princeton University Press, 1991).

[d] Biograph did not screen its regular films in this city, but showed *The Jeffries-Sharkey Fight* on this date.

[e] Detroit was one of the few cities where the vitascope did not introduce local amusement-goers to projected motion pictures. Manager Whitney of the Detroit Opera House had bought the Michigan rights to the improved eidoloscope (i.e., with an intermittent) and exhibited them in his Opera House to somewhat disappointing results beginning May 28, 1896. According to one report, "thus far it has had very light attendance. The Bull Fight is the only novelty it offers – the other scenes have been seen here before at the Wonderland. The machine is still far from perfection" (*New York Clipper*, June 12, 1896, 231). See also "Eidoloscope at Fresco," *Detroit Free Press*, July 2, 1896, 10.

[f] As part of show with Palmer Cox's Brownies *Chicago Inter-Ocean*, November 15, 1896, 4D. It then moved to St. Louis (*St. Louis Republican*, November 22, 1896, 5) and Kansas City (*Kansas City Star*, November 29, 1896, 6).

[g] The vitascope premiered in Rochester, New York, at Ontario Beach (E.M. McLoughlin to Vitascope Co., July 21, 1896, Raff & Gammon Collection, Baker Library, Harvard University). See also George C. Pratt, "No Magic, No Mystery, No Sleight of Hand: The First Ten Years of Motion Pictures in Rochester," *Image* 8, no. 4 (December

1959). In Marshall Deutelbaum (ed.), *"Image": On the Art and Evolution of the Film* (New York: Dover, 1979), 20–2.

[h] Roger William Warren, "History of Motion Picture Exhibition in Denver, 1896–1911" (M.A. thesis; University of Denver, 1960), published on microfiche in *Historical Journal of Film, Radio, and Television* 15, no. 4 (1995). The phantoscope/phantascope opened on the same day as the vitascope (August 16).

[i] Washington, DC, was one of the few cities where the vitascope was preceded by an international rival, in this instance R.W. Paul's animatographe, which opened September 7, 1896 (*Washington Star*, September 8, 1896, 12).

[j] Gregory A. Waller, *Main Street Amusements: Movies and Commercial Entertainment in a Southern City, 1896–1930* (Washington, DC: Smithsonian Institution Press, 1995).

mid-September and remained for almost two months. By the time this run was concluded, Raff & Gammon had made over $10,000 from their exhibition contracts in that city alone.[67] Sale of territory and business dealings with the "state rights" owners must have roughly tripled that amount. Armat probably accrued more than $10,000. The Edison Manufacturing Company's film-related profits for the 1896 business year were almost $25,000, while the famed inventor received additional compensation from Raff & Gammon in an informal royalty arrangement. Their success was thus in stark contrast to the fate of most "state rights" owners, who never regained the money from their purchase of territory. These local entrepreneurs faced many impediments to success but only one that could not be overcome or ameliorated: the problem created by competing motion picture enterprises.

Although "Edison's Vitascope" was the first successful screen machine in the American amusement field, competing projectors and enterprises began to appear within a month of its Koster & Bial's debut. In fact, even before its premiere, F.F. Proctor promised the imminent presentation of a mysterious "Kinematographe" – a promise he did not keep but one that told amusement-goers that the vitascope was not unique. During the spring and summer of 1896, several other companies quickly established themselves as leading enterprises in the field: the Eidoloscope Company (by adding an intermittent to its eidoloscope projector), the Lumière Agency with its cinématographe, and the American Mutoscope Company with its biograph service. While organized somewhat differently, they shared underlying similarities with the Vitascope Company. Each company developed a complete motion picture system, built its own equipment (cameras as well as projectors) and acted as a self-sufficient entity. All four sought to control the exhibition as well as the production of their films. This was the characteristic structure of film companies in the initial stages of the novelty period.

Some histories have suggested that the vitascope was quickly vanquished by the Lumière cinématographe.[68] Although this did happen at specific venues, notably some top-line vaudeville houses where the European views offered by the cinématographe provided a welcome change of pace from the American views featured on the vitascope. The arrival of the cinématographe was hardly decisive in the vitascope's demise. Indeed, as table 1 shows, the Lumière cinématographe was quickly challenged (and just as often replaced) by the American Mutoscope Company's biograph exhibition service, which also featured American views and made its initial appeal on the basis of patriotic nationalism. Despite their apparent rivalry, the Edison and Lumière companies were in some way complementary. The biograph service challenged the vitascope group more directly because it offered the same type of subject matter, though of substantially higher technical quality. Indeed, it was Biograph's expensive, large-format system that made it the premier service in the field, potentially leaving room for the vitascope in more moderately priced venues.[69]

In the end, the Vitascope Company and its "state rights" owners could have withstood the challenges coming from rival full-service motion picture companies. It was the activities of independent exhibitors, usually working with the 35 mm, four-perforation format established by Edison, but not yet protected by his patents (despite years of litigation, such protection proved elusive). Rather than building a self-contained company that created its own technological system, these showmen bought their projectors and films from various manufacturers, either in Europe (primarily England) or domestically. Unencumbered by the restrictions and royalty payments that Raff & Gammon imposed on the vitascope exhibitors, these showmen occupied the low and moderate end of the market where they could compete very effectively and to which the vitascope "state rights" owners had been relegated. Inevitably, the vitascope alliance of Edison, Raff & Gammon, Thomas Armat and "state rights" owners fell apart. Nonetheless, the vitascope provided a key role in the introduction of projected motion pictures to the American public and did much to establish a framework within which subsequent exhibition practices were developed.

Notes

1 *Honolulu Evening Bulletin*, February 4, 1897, 5 and February 6, 1897, 1 in Robert C. Schmitt, "Movies in Hawaii, 1897–1932." *Hawaiian Journal of History*, 1 (1967); *Phoenix Gazette*, May 17 and 18, 1897, courtesy George C. Hall.

2 Most owners of film production companies associated with the Motion Picture Patents Company (formed at the end of 1908) entered the field during this year.

3 Raff & Gammon to Daniel and Armat, n.d. [ca. December 26, 1895], 3:179, Harvard Business School, Baker Library (hereafter MH-BA).

4 *New York Journal*, April 4, 1896, clipping, Raff & Gammon Collection, MH-BA.

5 Raff & Gammon to Albert Bial, March 23, 1896, 3:402; and Raff & Gammon to Albert Bial, April 7, 1896, 2:108, MH-BA; this figure

is extremely difficult to decipher and may have been $300 per week.

6 *New York Dramatic Mirror*, May 2, 1896, 19.

7 For a discussion of "state rights" owners for the vitascope see Charles Musser, *The Emergence of Cinema: The American Screen to 1907* (New York: Scribner's, 1990), 112–15ff.

8 A portion of the Koster & Bial program is reproduced in Terry Ramsaye, *A Million and One Nights* (New York: Simon and Schuster, 1926), opposite p. 249.

9 "Figures on the Screen" *New York Mail and Express*, April 24, 1896, 12.

10 "Amusements." *New York Daily News*, April 24, 1896, clipping, MH-BA.

11 E. Kuhn to Frank Gammon, July 28, 1896, incoming letters, July 1896, MH-BA.

12 "Edison's Vitascope Cheered." *New York Times*, April 24, 1896, 5.

13 *New York Mail and Express*, April 24, 1896, 12.

14 Ibid.

15 *New York Daily News*, April 24, 1896, clipping, MH-BA.

16 Raff & Gammon, *The Vitascope*, 2.

17 Dexter Perkins, *The Monroe Doctrine, 1867–1907* (Baltimore: Johns Hopkins University Press, 1937), 136.

18 *Boston Herald*, May 17, 1896, 32.

19 F.Z. Maguire & Co., *Catalogue* [March 1898], 31.

20 Reports of the Lumière cinématographe reached Raff & Gammon from England. These London screenings destroyed their hope for a lucrative sale of European rights. British "screen machines" were also showing films by the vitascope's Koster & Bial's debut. In this respect Great Britain was an appropriate if somewhat misplaced object of Raff & Gammon's barbs.

21 I misidentified *Band Drill* as *Finale of 1st Act of Hoyt's "Milk White Flag,"* in Musser, *Before the Nickelodeon: Edwin S. Porter and the Edison Manufacturing Company* (Berkeley: University of California Press, 1991), 62.

22 "Wonderful is the Vitascope." *New York Herald*, April 24, 1896, 11. In Charles Musser, *Edison Motion Pictures, 1890–1900: An Annotated Filmography* (Washington, DC: Smithsonian Institution Press, 1997), 200–1.

23 Ibid.

24 Ibid.

25 Tom Gunning, "The Cinema of Attractions: Early Film, Its Spectator and the Avant-

Garde." In Thomas Elsaesser with Adam Barker (eds.), *Early Cinema: Space–Frame–Narrative* (London: British Film Institute, 1990), 58.

26 A.F. Rieser to Raff & Gammon, May 8, 1896, MH-BA.

27 W.R. Miller to Raff & Gammon, May 19, 1896, MH-BA.

28 *Chicago Tribune*, July 26, 1896, 34. "Ten–twenty–thirty" refers to theaters with an admission price ranging from 10¢ in the gallery to 30¢ in the orchestra.

29 *Louisville Courier-Journal*, September 20, 1896, 6B.

30 *Cleveland Plain-Dealer*, July 12, 1896, 15.

31 *St. Louis Republic*, June 16, 1896, 11.

32 *Albany Times-Union*, August 18, 1896, 1.

33 *Atlanta Constitution*, November 21, 1896, 7.

34 *New Haven Journal-Courier*, May 29, 1896, 7.

35 *New Haven Register*, June 5, 1896, 2.

36 Gregory A. Waller, *Main Street Amusements: Movies and Commercial Entertainment in a Southern City, 1896–1930* (Washington, DC: Smithsonian Institution Press, 1995), 30.

37 *Providence Journal*, June 7, 1896, 8.

38 Edmund McLoughlin to Raff & Gammon, September 12, 1896, MH-BA.

39 Edmund McLoughlin to Raff & Gammon, September 3, 1896, MH-BA.

40 *Utica Observer*, December 29, 1896, 1.

41 Miller to Vitascope Co., June 21, 1896, MH-BA.

42 Miller to Vitascope Co., June 14, 1896, MH-BA.

43 *Asbury Park Daily Press*, July 17, 1896, 4.

44 *Philadelphia Record*, August 9, 1896, 11.

45 *Baltimore Sun*, June 23, 1896, 10. This method of exhibition celebrated each film as a self-contained attraction and differed markedly from the methods of presentation used at Koster & Bial's Music Hall on opening night.

46 P.W. Kiefaber to Raff & Gammon, March 31, 1896, MH-BA.

47 "Arthur Hotaling Recalls the 'Good Old Days.'" *Moving Picture World*, July 15, 1916, 380. Kiefaber eventually became a prominent producer-director for Sigmund Lubin.

48 *Atlantic City Daily Union*, August 19, 1896, 1.

49 *Brooklyn Eagle*, June 21, 1896, 23.

50 E. Hopkins, Jr. to Raff & Gammon, June 2, 1896, MH-BA.

51 W.R. Miller to Raff & Gammon, May 24, 1896, MH-BA.

52 Robert C. Allen, *Vaudeville and Film 1895–1915*, 97–8.

53 J. Hunter Armat to P.W. Kiefaber, June 17, 1896, MH-BA.

54 P.W. Kiefaber to Vitascope Co., June 11, 1896, MH-BA.

55 Andrew Holland to Raff, September 8, 1896, MH-BA.

56 See Musser, *Before the Nickelodeon*, 81–91.

57 Holland to Gammon, September 26, 1896, MH-BA.

58 Holland to Raff & Gammon, October 1, 1896, MH-BA.

59 H.R. Kiefaber to Raff & Gammon, July 29, 1896; Purdy and Kiefaber to Vitascope Co., August 17, 1896, MH-BA.

60 A.F. Rieser to Raff & Gammon, September 25, 1896, MH-BA.

61 Edmund McLoughlin to Raff & Gammon, August 4, 1896, MH-BA.

62 C.O. Richardson to Vitascope Co., October 4, 1896, MH-BA.

63 C.O. Richardson to Vitascope Co., November 13, 1896, MH-BA. Richardson called the picture *Eating Watermelon for a Wager*.

64 W.R. Miller to Raff & Gammon, August 14, 1896, MH-BA.

65 Holland to Norman Raff, September 3, 1896, MH-BA.

66 C.O. Richardson to Vitascope Co., October 4, 1896, MH-BA.

67 Holland to Raff, December 28, 1896, MH-BA.

68 In *A Million and One Nights* Ramsaye states, "Within two months of the introductory showing of the Vitascope at Koster & Bial's Music Hall in New York, the precedents to govern the next ten years of presentation of the motion picture were laid down. It is whimsically true that these precedents came not with the exploitation of the American-made Vitascope but rather with its French rival, the Lumière Cinématographe" (p. 262). See also Robert C. Allen, "Vitascope/Cinématographe: Initial Patterns of American Film Industrial Practice." In John Fell (ed.), *Film Before Griffith* (Berkeley: University of California Press, 1983), 144–52.

69 Biograph continued to thrive into the twentieth century (though as part of an international group of sister companies), while the vitascope and Lumière cinématographe had ceased to be a significant presence in the American exhibition field by 1897–8.

2

From Rum Shop to Rialto: Workers and Movies

Roy Rosenzweig

G. Stanley Hall was not alone in pointing out the close connection between the decline of the saloon and the rise of the motion pictures. "Often when a moving picture house is set up," Vachel Lindsay wrote in 1915 in his study of *The Art of the Moving Picture*, "the saloon on the right hand or the left declares bankruptcy." Movies, according to Lindsay, had emerged as "the first enemy of King Alcohol with real power where that king has deepest hold." Saloonkeepers ruefully conceded Lindsay's point. Almost from the opening of the very first movie theaters in 1905, they had "protested excitedly against the nickelodeon as a menace to their trade," according to one national magazine. What saloonkeepers bemoaned, temperance leaders celebrated. "I believe the movies now occupy the attention of a great many persons who would otherwise be in a saloon," exulted a prominent Worcester no-licence crusader and building contractor.[1] While the Worcester saloon had already begun a process of internal transformation, the development of a new form of working-class leisure – the movies – proved to be a much more potent force in the displacement of the saloon from the center of ethnic working-class life.

Of course, the nickelodeon's triumph over the saloon was never as complete as temperance and movie promoters liked to

believe. Analyzing the results of a detailed 1910 study of the leisure-time pursuits of 1,000 New York workingmen, a temperance reformer cautioned that the five-cent show "hasn't quite put the saloon out of business." But the balance had shifted: Of the men in the study, 60 percent patronized the movies, whereas only 30 percent frequented the saloon. And certainly by the dry decade of the 1920s the movies had triumphed as the most popular form of public working-class recreation. But by that time the movies were no longer merely the private preserve of the urban, immigrant working class. They had become a truly mass entertainment, attracting a weekly attendance of well over 50 million – equivalent to half the total US population.[2] This dramatic emergence of the movie theater as a center of interclass, nationally distributed mass entertainment and its impact on the late nineteenth-century working-class world of the saloon and the holiday picnic forms the subject of this chapter.

The Movies Come to Worcester

As in most cities, moving pictures first appeared in Worcester in the late 1890s as

Excerpted from Roy Rosenzweig, "From Rum Shop to Rialto." In *Eight Hours for What We Will: Workers and Leisure in an Industrial City, 1870–1920* (New York: Cambridge University Press, 1983), 191–212, 280–6. Reprinted with permission from Cambridge University Press.

a sporadic novelty. By 1904, however, they had found a regular spot on the program of two of the city's vaudeville theaters. The next year movies acquired their first full-time outlet when Nathan and Isaac Gordon converted a Main Street furniture store into a "penny arcade," which they filled with Edison peep-show machines. In the fall of 1906 the Gordon brothers joined with local theater managers P.F. Shea and Alf T. Wilton in opening the city's first full-fledged movie theater. With the Gordons' machines in the lobby, Shea and Wilton transformed the Palace Museum, a 1,000-seat showcase for low-priced vaudeville and Friday-night wrestling, into the Nickel Theatre, which premiered on September 24, 1906, with a program of motion pictures and illustrated songs. Other Worcester theaters continued to exhibit films as part of vaudeville programs or as special presentations, but only the Nickel offered the continuous shows and the "democratic" seating and pricing that characterized the nickelodeons, which were rapidly proliferating throughout the nation's cities.[3]

The prices and programs proved a local success; the Nickel claimed 10,000 customers in its first week of business. Although it faced both criticism and censorship early in 1907 for showing *The Unwritten Law*, a film about the sensational Thaw–White murder case, the Nickel soon found itself surrounded by imitators. Within a few months in the spring of 1907, three other Worcester theaters, which had previously presented melodrama or vaudeville, switched to so-called pictorial vaudeville. Of course, the separation between these two entertainments was not always absolute – some theaters mixed live vaudeville and motion pictures. But the movies were now leading the way. "The unusual demand for moving picture shows has caught the people of Worcester as it has those in every other city and town in the country," the *Worcester Gazette* reported.[4]

Although the "nickel madness" that gripped the country equally infected Worcester, the precise pattern of growth differed from that of the largest cities. Entrepreneurs in metropolitan centers like New York and Chicago, spurred by licensing regulations, had established small storefront theaters usually seating fewer than 300 people. Only later did they open larger and more centrally located theaters. But in Worcester the movies came first to the full-sized downtown theaters and only spread to three smaller cinemas over the next two and a half years. Even more than the city's first movie houses, these smaller theaters had an ethnic or working-class management, an immigrant, working-class clientele, and the lowest prices in the city.[5]

In 1909 John W. Raymond, a former machinist, opened the 350-seat Majestic Theatre in what had been a downtown variety store. Later Aduino Feretti and Carmine Zamarro, who ran an employment and steamship ticket agency, took it over. Also in 1909, a Jewish shoe operator, Max Graf, launched the 300-seat, five-cent Pastime Theatre. Subsequently, "Gaspard and Charlie," two French Canadians who performed between film reels, reportedly took charge. Finally, in early 1910, the larger Bijou opened its doors on the site of what ten years earlier had been Michael McGaddy's saloon. For the first time in Worcester a theater had located itself well outside the city's central business district. Significantly, the Bijou chose Millbury Street, the heart of the city's multiethnic, working-class East Side. "At Last – A High Class Amusement Temple for the East Side" its advertisements proclaimed.[6]

Thus, by 1910 Worcester had about 4,250 seats devoted exclusively to moving pictures. Furthermore, in the first ten years of the twentieth century the total number of seats in Worcester available for all forms of commercial entertainment – theater, burlesque, vaudeville, and movies – had almost tripled from 3,438 to 9,338. In the process, the number of Worcester residents for each theater seat dropped sharply from thirty-four to fewer than sixteen.[7] The most important explanation for the rapid expansion in theatrical seats lies with the opening of the new, cheap movie houses and the development of a working-class movie audience.

Workers Go to the Movies

In 1912 Clark professor and social reformer Prentice Hoyt scrutinized Worcester's three cheap movie theaters, the Bijou, the Family (formerly the Nickel), and the Majestic. "All the world of a certain class meets together for an hour or two a day" at these theaters, Hoyt concluded. The poorest immigrants dominated at the Bijou, while "the slightly better class of workmen and their wives and children" filled the Family. The Majestic, located only a few steps from the Family, drew a similar crowd. Hoyt's analysis of Worcester's movie audiences confirmed the patterns found in other cities. In 1910, for example, a Russell Sage Foundation study found that in New York City blue-collar workers made up only 2 percent of the audiences at theaters showing live dramatic productions but almost three-quarters of moving picture audiences. Around the same time, a Columbia University sociology graduate student, writing his doctoral thesis on the leisure activities of New York workingmen, discovered that only reading newspapers or socializing with family or friends occurred more frequently or occupied more spare time than movie-going for most workers. "Motion pictures," John Collier explained to a middle class suddenly noticing this new amusement, "are the favorite entertainment today of the wage earning classes of the world." And journalists and other commentators penned such phrases as "the academy of the workingman," the "drama of the multitude," "the workingman's college," and the "true theater of the people" to dramatize the new development.[8]

While reformers, sociologists, and journalists rushed to report on this new working-class movie audience, few paused to ask where it had come from. In part, the crowds that flocked to the early nickelodeons had simply transferred their allegiances from the existing varieties of cheap commercial entertainment. As early as the 1870s, the Worcester Theatre, while primarily offering dramatic productions aimed at the city's "well-to-do," occasionally presented minstrel shows and plays appealing to Irish and German audiences. But the high tariff charged at the Worcester Theatre kept away many blue-collar workers. By 1883 Bristol's Dime Museum gave them Bohemian glass blowers, comedy sketches, ventriloquists, acrobats, and human-faced chickens at a much more affordable price. In the following decade those with only ten cents to spend could sit in the gallery of Lothrop's Opera House and watch melodramas and minstrel shows or visit the nearby Front Street Musee for burlesque or vaudeville. And such outlets for cheap amusement multiplied further in the first decade of the twentieth century.[9]

The lower prices, the "democratic" seating, the novelty, and the excitement of the five-cent movie houses appealed strongly to the patrons of these cheap theaters. With the coming of the movies, actors in local melodramas – what a historian of Worcester theaters referred condescendingly to as "dramatic pablum of the masses for two generations" – reported "the loss of gallery patronage." Thousands of theatergoers voted with their nickels and dimes for the new entertainment sensation. Movies benefited not only from the patronage of those who had always attended the city's lower-priced theatrical amusements but even more from the general expansion of the leisure market in early twentieth-century Worcester. The amusement parks discussed in the preceding chapter are one example of that boom. And the four "dime museums" featuring a combination of melodrama, farces, vaudeville, and wrestling, which opened on Front Street between 1900 and 1905, are another. Thus, even before the nickel madness of 1907 swept through Worcester, the number of theatrical seats in the city had more than doubled.[10] In effect, a good portion of the new movie audience had found its way to older, live entertainments in the years immediately preceding the birth of the nickelodeon.

Why was commercial entertainment enjoying such prosperity around the turn of the century in both Worcester and the rest of the country? As previously noted, the rise in real incomes and the decline in work hours crucially fueled the expansion of the leisure market. Yet, significantly, movies, with their low admission price and their short programs, were also regularly accessible to workers who still had low wages and long hours. Thus, in 1912 when a Worcester labor lawyer worked out a relatively generous budget for a working-class family, he could only find room in it for a weekly expenditure of about twenty cents for amusements. In this context, the five-cent movie house had a decisive edge over not only the twenty-five-cent gallery seats at the Worcester Theatre but also the ten-cent melodrama in competing for the working-class entertainment dollar (or quarter).[11] Similarly, nickelodeons, because their shows were continuous and short, proved compatible with long work hours. Although the US Steel Corporation, a major employer in both Worcester and Pittsburgh, maintained the twelve-hour day for some workers until 1923, investigators for the 1908 Pittsburgh Survey still encountered long lines of overworked steel-mill hands at that city's nickelodeons.[12]

Part of the success of the movies thus rested on their ability to attract the underpaid and overworked as well as those who were gaining a bit more disposable income and a few more free hours in the early twentieth century. By accommodating both kinds of schedules and pocketbooks, the movie theater managed to become – like the saloon, the church, and the fraternal lodge – a central working-class institution that involved workers on a sustained and regular basis.

Yet there was an even more obvious source for the growth in movie audiences: more people. America's cities were booming and Worcester was no exception. Its population grew by 72 percent between 1890 and 1910.

Immigrants, of course, played a disproportionately large part in that population growth. In those twenty years, the city's foreign-born increased by 82 percent, adding almost 22,000 immigrants to Worcester's already substantial foreign population. These new immigrants – almost entirely non-English speaking and often from southern and eastern Europe – proved particularly important to the growth of Worcester's movie theaters. "It doesn't matter whether a man is from Kamchatka or Stamboul, whether he can speak English or not. He can understand pictures and he doesn't need to have anyone explain that to him," commented a Worcester movie theater manager in accounting for the burgeoning of the movies. The silence of the movies beckoned immigrants unable to comprehend so many other facets of American life. "Its very voicelessness," one student of popular amusements wrote of the new medium in 1909, "makes it eloquent for Letts, Finns, Italians, Syrians, Greeks, and pigtailed Celestials. It has pulled down the Tower of Babel, abolished the hyphenated dictionary, and fulfilled the Esperantist's dearest dream."[13]

For many Worcester immigrants – circumscribed by their language to the social institutions of their own ethnic communities – movies offered their first nonwork contact with the larger American society. "I never saw a movie in Italy," recalls Fred Fedeli, who arrived in Worcester in 1907 at age thirteen. "I was on the farm; when I came here I got interested in going to the movies." In his limited spare time from his sixty-hour per week factory job, Fedeli would spend part of the sixty cents he had left each week after paying room and board to attend the newly opened Nickel Theatre. In 1912, realizing the appeal of the new medium for his fellow immigrants, Fedeli, along with his older brother and a cousin, leased the Bijou Theatre on Millbury Street in the heart of Worcester's immigrant, working-class district. "The [Bijou] audiences," commented Professor Hoyt, "are of every nationality under the sun, every type which has its home in the region around Vernon Square." As a moviegoer and an immigrant himself, Fedeli understood this audience well. Explaining the popularity of silent films, he recalls: "My people, the Polish people and the Lithuanian and Jewish people... didn't talk any more English than I did."[14]

Of course, some observers probably exaggerated the ease with which the most recent immigrants adapted to the new entertainment medium. A Worcester woman wrote that it was only through evening English-language classes that she had learned to "red a newspaper and to red de moving pekses."[15] Reading movie captions was much less likely to be a problem for the children of immigrants, and this second generation took to the movies with even more enthusiasm than their parents. Virtually all observers of early movie theater audiences noted the presence of large numbers of children and young people. "The nickelodeon," wrote one in 1908, "is almost the creation of the child, and it has discovered a new and healthy cheap-amusement public." "Children are the best patrons of the nickelodeon," added a trade press correspondent that same year. So great was the hold of the movies on immigrant children, according to reformer Jane Addams, that a group of young girls, "accustomed to the life of a five-cent theater, reluctantly refused an invitation to go to the country for a day's outing because the return of a late train would compel them to miss one evening's performance. They found it impossible to tear themselves away not only from the excitements of the theater but from the gaiety of the crowd of young men and girls invariably gathered outside discussing the sensational posters." Children, a range of different studies agreed, composed about one-quarter to one-half of the new movie audience.[16]

As Edward Chandler told the First Conference on Child Welfare in Worcester in 1909, the "simplest reason" why so many children and young people found their way to the movies was "the low price. A nickel or a dime is far easier to get than a quarter." But for the children of immigrants, movie houses may have had a particular attraction: freedom from the surveillance mandated by a constricted and conservative family life. One woman, a New York Italian garment worker brought up by strict parents, recalls that "the one place I was allowed to go by myself was the movies. My parents wouldn't let me go out anywhere else, even when I was 24." Another woman of the same background recalls meeting her future husband on the sly at the local movie house.[17]

While some immigrant teen-agers relished the freedom provided by the movie house, much moviegoing was actually done in family groups. Reformer Frederic Howe noted with satisfaction that "men now take their wives and families for an evening at the movies where formerly they went alone to the nearby saloon." Mary Heaton Vorse visited a movie house on Bleecker Street in the heart of New York's Italian section and reported: "Every woman has a baby in her arms and at least two children clinging to her skirts." Whereas Worcester's Deputy Sheriff James Early complained that a mother "should be at home, attending her household duties," not patronizing "this popular form of amusement," the *Labor News* leapt to the defense of "these overworked women" who take advantage of the few hours' time during which "the older children are at school or at the playgrounds" to attend the movie theater, "very often carrying a babe in arms."[18]

Worcester movie theater managers assiduously courted this female patronage. Press releases from the newly opened Nickel Theatre announced the management's intention "to cater especially to the patronage of women and children," and its advertisements labeled it "The Ladies and Children's Resort." After its first week of operation, it claimed that women and children made up 60 percent of the audience.[19] The young working-woman joined working-class mothers in this new female audience. In the early twentieth century, increasing numbers of women took jobs outside the home. In Worcester, which mirrored national trends, women's labor force participation rates went from 19.5 to 23.7 percent between 1890 and 1910. As Elizabeth Butler documented in the Pittsburgh Survey, these women – especially those living alone in cheap rooming houses – had few outlets for their hard-earned leisure time and money. Often "the only relief for nervous weariness and the desire for stimulation" was the picture show.[20]

The working-class movie audience thus drew on a variety of sources. The movie house attracted former patrons of other cheap amusements as well as tapped what one contemporary reporter called "an entirely new stratum of people." It appeared at a moment when workers had more time and money for leisure, but its low price and convenient time schedule made it available to workers who still remained poorly paid and overworked. Finally, it had particular appeals for the non-English-speaking immigrant who was effectively shut out of other entertainment forms; the child with only a nickel to spend; the immigrant teen-ager seeking freedom from restrictive family life; and the wife and mother, who had traditionally shunned, or been barred from, many other working-class social centers. "As a business, and as a social phenomenon," writes historian Robert Sklar, "the motion pictures came to life in the United States when they made contact with working-class needs and desires." "The art of the photo-play," the *Nation* concluded in a similar contemporary comment, was "created for the masses and largely by them."[21]

Moviegoing as Working-Class Culture

Working-class audiences were decisive in the early success of the movies. But did the new medium actually reflect the values and traditions of its new patrons? Analyzing the relationship between audience and movies before 1920 is fraught with more than the usual difficulties of popular cultural analysis. Prewar films, unlike those popular in the 1920s, seem to have "dealt mostly with the working man and his world," according to one prominent film historian. Yet even this general characterization of movie content remains open to debate, given the paucity of films surviving from this period. Additionally, even if we could see all the films produced in these years, how would we know which ones particularly appealed to working-class viewers or how they responded to the picture on the screen? D.W. Griffith's *The Fatal Hour*, which was shown at Worcester's Nickel Theatre in September 1908, may have offered a moralistic attack on the white slave trade, but working-class viewers may have simply seen it as an action-packed melodrama.[22]

With these difficulties in mind, it may be more fruitful to focus on the moviegoing experience, rather than movie content. Whatever the degree of control of the middle and upper classes over movie content, the working class was likely to determine the nature of behavior and interaction within the movie theater. Although theater managers mediated the audience's self-determination, they were, like saloonkeepers, usually cut from the same cloth as their customers. They shared similar backgrounds, values, and perspectives, and even, as with Fred Fedeli, a similar language disadvantage. Together, the immigrant working-class movie manager and the immigrant working-class audience developed a style of moviegoing that accorded with, and drew upon, earlier modes of public working-class recreation.

Working-class movie theater conduct built on a long tradition of crowd behavior that could be found at a variety of earlier popular amusements from melodramas to saloons to July Fourth picnics to working-class parks. Indeed, such patterns of public sociability and boisterousness can also be discerned in eighteenth-century French and English middle- and upper-class theater audiences. But by the mid-nineteenth century, historian Richard Sennett notes, "restraint of emotion in the theater became a way for middle-class audiences to mark the line between themselves and the working class." The "silence" that descended over bourgeois public behavior in the nineteenth century did not also blanket working-class public life.[23] Modes of conviviality, active sociability, and liveliness remained the norms for the working class. And workers brought these behavior styles with them when they entered the world of commercial amusement.

Working-class audiences at the melodramas, minstrel shows, and burlesque acts of the late nineteenth and early twentieth centuries gave repeated evidence of interactive, lively, and often rowdy public behavior. Even when the upper-class men and women of the theater boxes maintained a restrained decorum, the lower-class inhabitants of the gallery could be counted on for vocal and high-spirited spontaneity. "In all theaters," writes a historian of early nineteenth-century melodrama, "the gallery was the place most suitable for rowdyism, the best point from which to bombard disliked actors, members of the orchestra who failed to play popular tunes, or even the helpless 'middling classes' ensconced in the pit." Similarly, despite a placard proclaiming "no guying, whistling, or cat-calls," the gallery of the early twentieth-century urban burlesque house would rage with "whistling, stamping, and hand-clapping."[24]

Naturally, in theaters that drew exclusively working-class patronage such lively behavior was not confined to the gallery. In the late 1890s drama critic John Corbin described the friendly and expressive audiences that filled the Teatro Italiano on New York's East Side: "They would speak to you on the slightest pretext, or none, and would relate all that was happening on the stage... At the tragic climaxes they shouted with delight, and at the end of each act yelled at the top of their lungs." Making the reverse comparison, a letter writer to a Yiddish newspaper pointed out that "the English Theater" is "not like our Jewish theater.... I found it so quiet there... There are no cries of 'Sha!' 'Shut up!' or 'Order!' and no babies cried – as if it were no theater at all!"[25]

Although ethnic theater companies made only occasional stops in a medium-sized industrial city like Worcester, audiences at its other low-priced commercial entertainments revealed these same patterns of theatrical behavior. At melodrama productions in the 1880s, most of the action took place "down stage," a local historian comments laconically. The "dime museums," which sprang up on Front Street in the early twentieth century, attracted particularly lively working-class crowds. At the always popular Amateur Night, singers met shouts of "If you can't sing get off the stage" and persistent howls and hisses from an audience filled with friends of their competitors. Only the presence of "several policemen in full uniform in the building put a quietus on what may have easily terminated in a miniature riot," the *Worcester Sunday Telegram* reported after one Amateur Night. Professional companies at Worcester's ten-cent music halls faced equally demanding and vocal audiences. Charles Baker, the man charged with writing, directing, performing in, and even selling tickets for productions at the Palace Museum, noted that stale jokes would never wash since "the dime audience knows more about a good joke than half of the two dollar theatre patrons." "If it isn't a go," the opening-night audience would quickly let him know, and a new production would have "to be written before the next afternoon for two o'clock."[26]

The Nickel movie theater inherited not only the actual building of the Palace Museum but also the lively and demanding crowds that had filled it and such other centers of working-class sociability as the saloon, the fraternal lodge, and the cheap theater. Indeed, the particular structure of the movie-going experience – especially prices, seating arrangements, time schedules, and internal conditions – reinforced and heightened pre-existing behavior patterns. The lack of seating differentiation by price at the early movie house exemplified its egalitarian social style. Whereas the Worcester Theatre carefully stratified patrons according to their ability to pay, the Nickel Theatre placed all customers on an equal plane. Even many other cheap forms of commercial entertainment such as the melodrama or vaudeville had often resisted this radical "leveling."

This "democratic" pricing fostered what one critic called an "atmosphere of independence" and "a kind of proprietorship in the playhouse" and along with that an air of informality and relaxed socializing at early movie houses. The lack of a structured time schedule further encouraged these tendencies. Workers could casually stop at the movie theater on their way home from work or shopping and catch all or part of the twenty- to sixty-minute show. Since no single item on the program lasted very long, there was little pressure to arrive at a specific time. Workers, already burdened with exacting time demands on the job, undoubtedly appreciated this lack of structure. The slogan "Stay as Long as You Like," from an early Nickel Theatre advertisement, captured the casual spirit of the enterprise.[27]

This informality sanctioned a wide variety of behaviors that were disdained at most higher-priced theaters. Commenting on the timelessness of movie shows, a reporter for the *Moving Picture World* noted that some patrons watched the same performances all day and into the night, eating their lunch in the theater along the way. In Worcester, the use of the movie house as a lunchroom brought complaints from the middle-class press: "One can go into any theatre in town prior to the noon hour and find at least one-half of the women patrons nibbling lunch biscuits, cakes, or sweet meals of some kind," one reporter grumbled. Even less acceptable to middle-class observers was drinking alcohol or exhibiting drunken behavior. Part of the job of the ticket taker at the Nickel Theatre was keeping out intoxicated patrons. Despite his efforts, "a choice collection of drunks" could be found in the back rows, perhaps sleeping off a binge. Still others undertook more animated, if still less acceptable, pursuits. "The very darkness" of the movie house, observed Jane Addams, "is an

added attraction to many young people, for whom the place is filled with the glamour of love making." Newspapers labeled the last row of Worcester movie theaters "lovers' lane" and youths filled these seats well before those that provided better views.[28]

Such unacceptable public behavior – eating, drinking, sleeping, necking – was actually incidental to the larger function of the movie house as a vehicle for informal socializing. The Bijou, for example, apparently served as a social center for Worcester's immigrant working-class East Side – "the gathering place of the women of the neighborhood with their babies and little children, a crude sort of tea-room gossiping place," according to Professor Hoyt. Similarly, in 1915, the theater correspondent of the *Worcester Sunday Telegram* complained of some Irish women at the Family Theatre who "substitute seats in the orchestra for seats at the tea table." In New York in 1909 a movie house visitor similarly observed "regulars" who "stroll up and down the aisles between reels and visit friends." "The five-cent theater," Jane Addams reported from Chicago that same year, "is also fast becoming the general social center and club house in many crowded neighborhoods... The room which contains the... stage is small and cozy, and less formal than the regular theater, and there is much more gossip and social life as if the foyer and pit were mingled."[29]

Overall, then, moviegoing was far from the passive experience that some critics accused it of being. The working-class audience interacted volubly not only with each other but also with the entertainment presented. The large number of children at the movie houses reinforced this boisterous atmosphere. "When the hero triumphs during a children's performance, shouting, whistling, and stomping combine in a demonstration which at times is most remarkable," noted the *Worcester Telegram*. Various nonmovie features also encouraged audience participation. The illustrated song used as a "filler" between movie reels promoted group singing with its injunction: "All Join in the Chorus."

Amateur Night, of course, stimulated audience participation, with friends and neighbors shouting for their favorites and the crowd usually selecting the winner. Other forms of working-class recreation from bike racing to wrestling complemented movie shows and stimulated audience cheering.[30]

Not only did movie theater conduct grow out of traditions of working-class public recreational behavior based on sociability, conviviality, communality, and informality, but movie theater conditions also accorded with the realities of working-class life. The movie house might offer some relief from crowded urban tenements or three-deckers, but it did not offer a radically different environment. Unlike the ornate movie palaces of later years, recalls an old-time Worcester manager, the early and cheaper movie theaters were just "four walls." Another early manager remembers the closely packed wooden seats. But a former patron paints an even less flattering picture. He recollects the old Gem Theatre as nothing more than a "shack" and remembers rats from the city's sewers scurrying under his seat while he was watching movies at the Bijou.[31]

Spartan, and even unsanitary, conditions made little impression on working-class moviegoers; such surroundings were part of their daily lives. But middle-class commentators reacted with horror. "A room that is stuffy and congested is not a proper place for a growing child to be, and it doesn't look at first glance as if it were the place for the mother either," Worcester Deputy Sheriff James Early asserted. Only the word "filth" could adequately describe these theaters according to Professor Hoyt: "The floors are dirty and the air is stagnant and charged with the vileness and disease that is poured into it."[32]

But part of the shocked reaction of middle-class observers was not to the actual physical conditions of theaters themselves but simply to the presence of large numbers of working-class people, who acted, looked, and smelled differently from themselves. The *Worcester Sunday Telegram* drama correspondent, for example, was obsessed by the odors of theaters: "Unclean persons should be influenced to respect the rights of others. The best ventilating system made will not rid playhouses of odors which have become component parts of individuals." Despite this pessimism, he offered such remedies as distributing soap to patrons or burning incense. On one occasion he recommended that patrons who "eat garlic and spread their breath promiscuously should be given seats on the roof or in the alley." In the early twentieth century odors had important class and cultural implications. Indeed, Rollin Lynde Hartt, the author of a 1909 study of *The People at Play*, whimsically suggested that "some modern sage might devote study to the graded aromas of our entertainments." Whereas Hartt characterized the opera as "the breath of roses," he labeled burlesque "an unwashed odor, mitigated with vile tabacco [*sic.*]" and the dime museum "the same and more of it, though unfortunately without the tobacco." "With the nose we knows," Hartt concluded.[33] And so observers like the *Telegram's* drama correspondent could not only see and hear working-class movie audiences, they could also smell them.

Conflict over the Working-Class Movie Theater

As the "odor issue" indicates, the development of a new entertainment medium with a distinctive working-class presence and style occasioned a variety of social and cultural conflicts. On the one hand, the forces of middle-class reform, morality, and order perceived the movie house as a barrier to their efforts not only to control and redirect working-class leisure but also to shape changing middle-class leisure patterns. On the other hand, the movie theater also challenged the prevailing working-class culture and its twin institutional pillars, the saloon and the church. Accordingly, over the next twenty years advocates of the status quo within both the middle and working classes struggled to control, restrict, regulate, and redirect the new medium. In effect, both the middle and working classes split over their willingness to accept the emerging mass culture. Nevertheless, the efforts of both groups had only limited impact. More influential in transforming the movie house were those actually assembled there: the theater owner, the working-class audience, and the new, developing middle-class audience.

In January 1910 the *Worcester Telegram* began a series of sensationalized front-page stories about the city's juvenile gangs, which stressed that many of the gangs' allegedly immoral activities centered around the city's movie theaters. According to the *Telegram*, female gang members with their "short, close fitting dresses" and "paint on their faces" could usually be found at "the opening matinees" of the downtown theaters, and male gang members also "hung about the cheap moving picture places on Front Street." The police responded swiftly to this ostensible problem of immorality and movies. Noting that girls involved in the alleged "orgies" had "confessed that their early tendencies toward evil came from seeing moving pictures... and from certain houses where conditions were permitted that made temptations easy," Police Chief David Matthews appointed Police Lieutenant George Hill, who had been serving as head of the police liquor squad (a job made less necessary by the impending end of no-license), as movie censor.[34]

Just as he had fought to control working-class drinking habits, Police Censor Hill zealously battled to bring Worcester movies in line with his own narrow conceptions of propriety. Within his first two weeks as police censor in 1910, he scissored out the duel and hell scenes from *Faust*, the murder of Julius Caesar from the Shakespeare play, and a scene from a labor film in which strikers murdered a scab. The police went beyond the picture on the screen to regulate conduct within the theater. In late January, for example, Chief Matthews banned standing in theaters. And in March, Censor Hill stopped

the Nickel Theatre's popular and lively Amateur Night because it "attracted lots of young girls and boys, ... [and] it was thought best to ... keep the girls and boys at home."[35]

Such censorial zeal did not meet with uniform approval. The Worcester *Labor News* commented that "Hill might make an excellent rum sleuth, but that as a censor of picture films, he is an out-and-out failure," and suggested "that someone with more brains might have been selected for the position." But opposition was not confined to the labor press. The *Worcester Evening Gazette* ran a satirical poem, which commented that "the picture shows don't have a thrill/since censored by Lieutenant Hill. / There'll be no kissing scenes, you bet / no Romeo and Juliet!/...No bar-room scenes – ten nights or one – / are all cut out – are simply done." The poem concluded with the suggestion that his excesses might drive movie patrons back to the saloons, which were soon to reopen with the end of no-license.[36]

While some voices of native-American middle-class public opinion, like the *Gazette*, opposed zealous censorship, some representatives of ethnic constituencies, like the *Catholic Messenger*, gave it wholehearted support. As early as 1907 it had denounced moving pictures as "The Devil's Lieutenants." When the city closed *The Unwritten Law*, the paper congratulated the police, urging them to carry on an "axe raid" on the moving picture shows, particularly the Gordon Brothers' penny arcade machines. Can the mayor and City Council, they asked, "permit on Main and Front Streets a public nuisance which is being driven from the Tenderloin and the Bowery of New York?" Again, in the 1910 controversy the *Catholic Messenger* called for even more drastic action than the city had taken: "Since these shows are the breeding places of a moral plague far worse than any physical ills, why hesitate to close them?"[37]

The *Catholic Messenger* of these years spoke more for the emerging middle-class and second-generation Irish American than it did for the laborer or the recent immigrant. Nevertheless, even such a well-known champion of the Worcester worker as the now aging James H. Mellen apparently shared the *Messenger's* distrust of the new medium. In 1910 he urged a state investigation into the moving picture business, maintaining that "the corruption these places breed is great." "Motion pictures rightly conducted," Mellen declared, "could be made a great educational and instructive institution but the business has degraded [fallen] into the hands of men without any moral conception and the main idea is to make money at the sacrifice of the community." Mellen's moralistic strictures about popular entertainment were not simply a product of his old age. Twenty-five years earlier, as editor of the *Worcester Daily Times*, he had bitterly denounced the Worcester Theatre for posting "show bills about the city ... bedaubed with disgusting pictures of shameless women ... exhibiting their limbs in a series of indecent gyrations."[38]

The Swedish evangelical churches with their large immigrant working-class congregations shared Mellen's long-standing and morally based suspicion of uncontrolled commercial amusements. But they were even more absolute in their condemnation of the latest entertainment sensation. Swedish ministers considered attendance at movies, like card playing and dancing, a serious sin. So strong were the denunciations that one Swedish woman recalls that "some youngsters developed a morbid fear just walking by a movie theater." The daughter of a Swedish foundry worker who grew up in Quinsigamond Village at the beginning of the century similarly recounts how her father gave her five cents every Saturday to prove that he was not cheap but forbade her to use the money to go to the movies.[39]

As with temperance, the motives of working-class critics of moviegoing often differed from those of their middle-class counterparts. For workers, the threat was from within rather than from without; it was an issue of maintaining ethnic and religious traditions, not controlling a disorderly mob. One Slovak commentator explained that with "a public school education" children are "lost comple-

tely to the Slovaks. Their idea of life is a breezy and snappy novel, a blood curdling *movie* and lots of money."[40] The movies, like the amusement park, challenged traditional cultural authorities both inside and outside the ethnic working-class community.

Despite this lingering distrust, controversy over the content of movies shown in Worcester soon faded. Compulsory local censorship boards, such as that set up in Chicago in 1907, as well as the voluntary National Board of Review established in New York in 1909, began to bring movies under outside surveillance, if not total control.[41] At the same time, the red pencil of the accountant often had more impact on film content than the blue pencil of the censor. "It is an expensive business, the making of films only to have them thrown away," noted one 1910 commentator. Indeed, as early as the 1907 controversy over *The Unwritten Law*, the nascent trade press urged the withdrawal of the film "*for the sake of the future prosperity of the five cent theaters*, all of whom are now menaced by public opinion."[42] For businessmen interested in building a national market, self-censorship appeared to be the most prudent – and profitable – course.

Such commercial considerations also operated powerfully on the local level. "Those interested in the moving picture business realize that it is to their advantage to have pictures of the highest type," the manager of the Majestic Theatre commented in 1910. Not only did managers begin to cooperate with Police Censor Hill, but they also carefully watched other sources of public disapproval. Bijou proprietor Fred Fedeli, for example, recalls that "we were amongst six [Catholic] churches in them days, and if you played a movie, that wasn't fit to be seen, they could crucify you by saying 'don't go and see it.'" So when Fedeli feared possible clerical criticism, he immediately canceled the offending film and repeated an old one. He recounts that "you would put a slide on the screen: 'By Popular Demand This Picture Brought Back.' And we were the one that was demanding it, because we were afraid; after all, you had to be careful."[43]

Thus, by 1912 movie content rarely caused trouble in Worcester. Professor Hoyt noted that while a 1909 report on Worcester movies had revealed "a coarseness and . . . a suggestiveness of crime and sin that was frankly appalling . . . now, thanks to the most careful censorship of films we get little note of criticism." But the elimination of what he called "the story of clever vice and of trickery triumphant" did not eliminate conflict over moviegoing. "As we turn to the consideration of the conditions existing in the theatres themselves," Hoyt warned, "there is another story to tell." The reform-oriented Worcester Public Education Association agreed: "The chief weakness of the moving picture lies in the conditions of presentation rather than in the picture itself. The halls and buildings are very dirty and poorly ventilated, and the audiences [are] under no *supervision* or *surveillance* as to age or character." Other middle-class commentators also complained about poor ventilation, odor, dirt, eye-strain, and darkness at movie houses.[44] As the now-censored films became palatable to middle-class critics, they increasingly focused their disapproval on the conditions of the theaters and the behavior of their patrons. Just as anti-saloon agitators concentrated their attacks on the saloon, not alcohol, movie reformers increasingly concerned themselves with the cheap movie theaters, not the movies. It was autonomous working-class institutions and behavior that troubled the middle class.

The Middle Class Goes to the Movies

Middle-class complaints about theatrical conditions and behavior reflect, in part, fears about a hidden and unknown working-class culture and a desire to control that culture and limit its autonomy. But behind all the talk about filth and body odor lay the entrance, in large numbers and for the first time, of middle-class people into movie houses and their forced encounters with a resident working-class audience, which smelled and acted in ways that jarred middle-class standards of decorum. It was the emergence of this new middle-class audience – and the theater managers' fervent efforts to cultivate it – that led to an alteration of some of the basic characteristics of the early movie-going experience.

As late as 1914 the Worcester working class still seems to have dominated the city's movie houses. The controversy that burst forth early in that year over Sunday moving pictures confirms this alignment. Whereas the city's Protestant establishment – virtually all the Protestant ministers, the Women's Christian Temperance Union, as well as most city officials – vehemently denounced this desecration of the sabbath, "those favoring Sunday shows," according to the *Worcester Telegram*, "were composed mostly of the working class of people and persons directly or indirectly connected with the Worcester playhouses and moving picture places." To those who fought over Sunday movies, the reason for this division was obvious: "The movies always was and always will be the poor man's amusement," declared one Worcester theater manager.[45]

Yet this very controversy also suggested that the association of the working class with the movie house was neither timeless nor total. Some of the more moderate ministers insisted that they opposed a commercialized Sunday, not moviegoing *per se*. "We believe in moving pictures . . . it is not moving pictures that we oppose," the Reverend Francis Poole told his Union Church congregants. Furthermore, the city's manufacturers – aligned with the Protestant clergy on issues like drinking – do not seem to have joined in the attack on Sunday movies. Donald Tulloch, secretary of the Worcester Metal Trades Association, endorsed the idea of "well-regulated, suitable movies Sunday afternoon, leaving the forenoon and evenings entirely to the Church services and home life."[46]

These new, more approving attitudes toward movies by middle-class Worcesterites reflected not only the success of earlier censorship efforts but also the growing appeal of movies for middle-class audiences, a trend increasingly evident in pre-World War I Worcester. In December 1913 the *Worcester Sunday Telegram's* drama correspondent noted that Worcester theaters had suffered a bad season, and he blamed the competition of moving pictures. He pointed out that the movie version of *Quo Vadis* had attracted more Worcesterites in three days than had its live version in an entire week. "Whether the play be popular priced or of a higher scale," he concluded, "the moving pictures are drawing bigger." Vaudeville suffered less directly from the competition of movies, since many movie houses offered vaudeville acts in addition to their film programs, and most vaudeville bills included some moving pictures. Still, the balance seemed to be shifting in favor of movies. In February 1914 Sylvester Poli, Worcester's leading vaudeville promoter, recognizing "the prominent part that moving pictures have come to play in the amusement world," added feature films to the program at his flagship theater. By the following year, the *Worcester Sunday Telegram*, distressed by the dismal quality of vaudeville shows, wondered whether "the silent drama" had given vaudeville "the count."[47]

By the end of World War I movies had not only captured many theater and vaudeville patrons but also expanded the market for commercial entertainment in general. Between 1910 and 1918 the number of theatrical seats in Worcester nearly doubled, going from about 9,300 to about 17,600. The rate of increase greatly exceeded even Worcester's rapidly growing population; the number of people for each theatrical seat declined sharply from sixteen to ten. Even more significantly, the percentage of seats devoted primarily to moving pictures almost doubled. In 1910 moving picture houses contained only 44 percent of Worcester's theatrical seats, whereas eight years later they included 82 percent. Since moving picture houses usually had continuous or multiple performances and legitimate theater, stock,

and vaudeville offered only two shows per day, these figures actually understate the ascendance of moving pictures. By 1919, according to conservative estimates, more than 128,000 Worcesterites attended the movies each week.[48]

The burgeoning of the Worcester movie audience indicates the expansion of moviegoing into the city's middle class and the creation of the first medium of regular interclass entertainment, a development that local observers increasingly noticed around World War I. In 1917, for example, the *Worcester Telegram* observed that the new Strand movie theater was "catering to the best class of theatrical patronage in Worcester." Pointing to the "long line of touring cars and limousines" parked in front of the theater every night, it concluded that "society folks have acquired the movie habit."[49]

How had middle- and upper-class Worcesterites found their way into the previously disdained movie theater? In part, the theater managers and movie producers brought them there.[50] The search for larger markets, which had motivated the movie industry to accept censorship from without and promote self-censorship within, also encouraged the quest for a middle-class audience. In pursuit of these new customers, exhibitors modernized their theaters, and producers experimented with different kinds of films. The cries of reformers to improve movie theater conditions and conduct had gone largely unheeded, but the quest for a larger and more respectable audience accomplished the same purpose: the transformation of the shabby nickelodeon into the opulent movie palace.

After 1913 Worcester movie theaters became increasingly lavish. At first the changes were rather modest. The Pleasant Theatre, reopened in November 1913 after a fire, simply advertised itself as "safe" and "clean." But a further remodeling three years later involved more extensive alterations, such as "new carpets of the finest Wilton velvet," a "colorful electric fountain," and a large rooftop electric sign. The *Worcester*

Telegram theater correspondent enthusiastically celebrated this "real high-class house of feature photoplays" with its "elegance," "refinement," and "dignity." The building of the Strand Theatre in 1917 culminated the trend toward lavish theaters – until the still more impressive structures of the 1920s. Lauded as a "modern photoplay house," it included "red plush seats," no obstructed views, frosted ceiling globes, a "rich chandelier," drinking fountains, a gold fiber screen, "luxurious carpets," loges for private parties, "rich velour curtains," marble pillars, an advanced ventilating system, a $15,000 Austin organ, and, most important, "finely appointed toilet rooms."[51]

The more elaborate accouterments of the newer Worcester theaters were often complemented by more professional theatrical management, which brought greater internal order to the theaters. Early Worcester movie managers were often local men from immigrant backgrounds who went directly from working-class jobs or small businesses to movie management. Increasingly after 1915, however, Worcester movie theaters came under the control of theatrical chains and the direction of professional theater managers, men with long experience in theaters in different cities, who had worked their way up to the position of manager.[52]

These more professional managers – often college graduates – hired large and well-disciplined staffs to impose order on their theaters. By way of contrast, the East Side Bijou had a staff of only four, mostly relatives. Discipline within the theater was far from tight. Fred Fedeli, who served as usher in the theater's early days, complained that "you would call people in the aisle where there were the seats and they would go the other way." But the newer and more elegant movie houses employed large corps of ushers, who strictly enforced standards of decorum. At the Plaza Theatre ushers donned summer uniforms of "military coats, white trousers and white oxfords." The military attire was perhaps deliberate, an effort to assure middle-class patrons that this was a well-run and well-ordered establishment. Indeed, by 1928 theaters like Worcester's new Plymouth were hiring army officers to drill their ushers in "bearing and discipline as well as in courteous handling of the public." The thrust of all these efforts to improve theater conditions and control theater behavior was, as historian Lary May has observed, to remove any "unease" the middle class might have over entering the previously "disreputable movie house."[53]

While the movie exhibitor pursued middle-class patrons with carpeting and well-disciplined ushers, the movie producer enticed them with feature films, which approximated the form and length of theatrical production. By 1914 feature films had met with such success that the Paramount Pictures Corporation, the first national distributor of feature films, could guarantee exhibitors two features each week. Worcester's Pleasant Theatre, for example, immediately signed up with Paramount, believing that the combination of longer films and well-known stars would win "a patronage that will be quality and quantity combined." The exhibition of *The Birth of a Nation* sealed the marriage of middle-class audiences and movies. "It is the greatest thing I have ever seen in the way of a moving picture," Worcester's Mayor Wright declared.[54]

Wright's enthusiasm for *The Birth of a Nation* represented a radical departure from the disapproving stance he took in the 1910 controversies. In this shift he followed the path trod by many other middle-class Worcesterites in these years. Initially perceiving movies and movie houses as a threat to the social fabric, by 1916 he joined in the hometown frenzy over the local filming of *A Romance in Worcester*. Wright even agreed to play the role of the father of the heroine, but when the Republican National Convention took him out of town, the president of the Board of Aldermen replaced him.[55]

Mayor Wright's newfound passion for the movies reminds us of the relatively recent recognition by the middle class of its own need for non-instrumental recreation, for "fun." In going to the movies, as in playing more active sports, the middle class at least partially adapted some of the leisure patterns that characterized working-class life. As Lary May has argued, the movie theater, with its mixing of sexes and classes, its lack of formality, and its intimacy, represented a radically new experience for the native middle class.[56] Thus, in many ways the development of moviegoing habits was a sharper break in middle-class culture than it had been in working-class culture. Moreover, it was a shift toward working-class norms.

But the process was hardly one way. The entrance of the middle class into the movie houses had altered moviegoing conduct and conditions. The new and more lavish movie theaters represented a more distinct change from the everyday conditions of working-class life than had the old storefront, five-cent theaters. More important, the new environment prescribed a more formal and structured moviegoing experience. Ushers instructed by handbooks of theater management carefully controlled conduct within the new theaters and politely guided customers to a specific seat. The longer programs made necessary by the feature films meant specific show times and even sometimes reserved seats. In effect, the new moviegoing experience was both more public and informal than that normally expected by the native middle class but also more privatistic and formal than that traditionally followed by the immigrant working class.[57]

Notes

1 Vachel Lindsay, *The Art of the Moving Picture*, rev. ed. (1922; rpt. New York, 1970), 235, 242; Lucy France Pierce, "The Nickelodeon," *World Today* 15 (Oct. 1908):1052; *Worcester Telegram (WT)*, Oct. 26, 1915. For other discussions of the relation of the saloon and the movie theater, see Kathleen D. McCarthy, "Nickel Vice and Virtue: Movie Censorship in Chicago, 1907–1915," *Journal of Popular Film* 5, no. 1 (1976):37–55; William T. Foster, *Vaudeville and Motion Picture Shows: A Study of Theaters in Portland, Oregon* (Portland, Ore., 1914), 28–9; Charles Stelzle, "Movies Instead of Saloons," *Independent* 85 (Feb. 28, 1916): 311; John Collier, "Cheap Amusements," *Charities and the Commons* 20 (Apr. 11, 1908):73–6; John J. Phelan, *Motion Pictures as a Phase of Commercialized Amusements in Toledo, Ohio* (Toledo, 1919), 22, 108–9; Barton W. Currie, "The Nickel Madness," *Harper's Weekly* 51 (Aug. 24, 1907):1245–6; Simon Patten, *Product and Climax* (New York, 1909), 45; Adele F. Woodward, "The Motion Picture as Saloon Substitute," in Raymond Calkins, ed., *Substitutes for the Saloon*, rev. ed. (Boston, 1919), 358–67.

2 Charles Stelzle, "How One Thousand Working-men Spend Their Spare Time," *Outlook* 106 (Apr. 4, 1914):762; Garth Jowett, *Film: The Democratic Art* (Boston, 1976), 192.

3 *Worcester Sunday Telegram (WST)*, July 7, 1947; *Worcester Directory, 1907* (Worcester, 1907); *Labor News (LN)*, Sept. 22, 1906; *Worcester Evening Gazette (WEG)*, Sept. 22, 1906. On the early development of movies in Worcester, see *WT*, Aug. 30, 31, 1897, Nov. 14, 1898; *WEG*, Aug.–Sept. 1898; Nov. 11, 1898; *Park Theatre Program*, Theater Pamphlet Collection, *Worcester Historical Museum (WHM)*. Showings of movies in these years can be traced in the advertisements in the local newspapers and in the records of the Worcester License Board, Worcester City Hall; hereafter cited as Lic. Bd.

4 *Worcester Evening Post (WEP)*, Sept. 29, 1906; *WEG*, Apr. 4, 5, 1907; *WT*, Apr. 5, 1907; *WEP*, May 21, 1907; *WEG*, Apr. 8, May 11, 25, 18, 1907. For an excellent discussion of the relationship between early movies and vaudeville, see Robert C. Allen, "Vaudeville and Film, 1895–1915: A Study of Media Interaction" (Ph.D. thesis, Univ. of Iowa, 1977). On vaudeville in general, see John DiMeglio, *Vaudeville U.S.A.* (Bowling Green, Ohio, 1973); Albert McLean, *American Vaudeville as Ritual* (Lexington, Ky., 1965); Douglas Gilbert, *American Vaudeville: Its Life and Times* (New York, 1940); Gunther Barth, *City People: The Rise of Modern City Culture in Nineteenth-Century America* (New York, 1980), 192–228.

5 The Pastime charged five cents; the Bijou's pricing varied between a mix of five- and ten-cent charges (lower price during the day) and a

flat five-cent charge; *WT*, Dec. 9, 1909; *WST*, Jan. 16, 1910; *LN*, Sept. 27, 1915. Since the cheap theaters did not regularly advertise, it is difficult to follow their prices with precision. On the development of the nickelodeon, see Robert Sklar, *Movie-Made America: A Social History of American Movies* (New York, 1975), 14–19; Russell Merritt, "Nickelodeon Theaters, 1905–1914: Building an Audience for the Movies," in Tino Balio, ed., *The American Film Industry* (Madison, Wis., 1976), 59–79; Jowett, *Film*, 29–46; George Pratt, ed., *Spellbound in Darkness: A History of the Silent Film*, rev. ed. (Greenwich, Conn., 1973), 39–54; Daniel Joseph Czitrom, "Media and the American Mind: The Intellectual and Cultural Reception of Modern Communication" (Ph.D. thesis, Univ. of Wisconsin, 1980), 60–127; Robert C. Allen, "Motion Picture Exhibition in Manhattan 1906–1912: Beyond the Nickelodeon," *Cinema Journal* 17 (Spring 1979):2–15; Jeffrey Kmet, "Milwaukee's Nickelodeon Era: 1906–1915," and Douglas Gomery, "Movie Exhibition in Milwaukee, 1906–1947: A Short History," both in special issue of *Milwaukee History* 2 (Spring 1979):2–17. Gomery notes that Milwaukee's first nickelodeons, like Worcester's first movie houses, were located downtown.

6 *LN*, May 22, 1909; *WST*, Jan. 16, 1910. Information on proprietors is from *Worcester Directory, 1900–20.* The Pastime may have been originally known as the Star; *LN*, Mar. 13, 1909. Information on Graf is from *Worcester Directory* and on "Gaspard and Charlie" from James L. Gilrein, interview, Worcester, Mar. 1, 1978, and Lic. Bd., May 27, 1909.

7 Most of the data on numbers of seats was obtained from the *Worcester Directory*, but this listing is incomplete. The rest of the material is derived from newspaper reports and personal interviews. Thus, the figures here are only estimates, but they are probably quite close to the actual numbers.

8 Prentice G. Hoyt, "Conditions of Three of the Cheaper Theaters of Worcester," *Worcester Bulletin* 1 (Nov. 16, 1912):5; Michael Davis, *The Exploitation of Pleasure* (New York, 1911), 30–1; George Esdras Bevans, *How Workingmen Spend Their Spare Time* (New York, 1913); John Collier, "Moving Pictures: Their Function and Regulation," *Playground* 4 (Oct.

1910):232; Pierce, "The Nickelodeon," 1052; George E. Walsh, "Moving Picture Drama for the Multitude," *Independent* 64 (Feb. 6, 1908):306–20; Jane E. Snow, "The Workingman's College," *Moving Picture World* 7 (Aug. 27, 1910):458; Collier, "Cheap Amusements," 75. Bevans did not even attempt to construct a random or representative sample of New York City workers; he took whatever questionnaires he could get filled out. However, there are probably not any egregious biases in the data, and it is the only information from this period giving such detailed data on the spare time of *any* workingmen.

9 Philip H. Cook, "History of the Drama in Worcester" (paper, 1947, copy available at American Antiquarian Society), 12; Charles A. Nutt, *History of Worcester and Its People*, 4 vols. (New York, 1919), 2:795; Elizabeth A. Johnson, *Worcester Illustrated, 1875–1885* (Worcester, 1978), 14–15. On Bristol's Dime Museum and other cheap amusements, see, for example, *Worcester Daily Times (WDT)*, Dec. 13, 1883, Dec. 1, 17, 1884, Jan. 1, Feb. 21, June 17, 1885, Jan. 15, Apr. 29, June 25, 1886, June 24, 1889; *WST*, Dec. 21, 1884, Jan. 4, 1885, May 8, 1904; *Worcester Weekly Amusement Bulletin*, Jan.–May, Sept.–Oct. 1892 (copy available at WHM); Lic. Bd., 1902–10.

10 Cook, "History of the Drama in Worcester," 54. In the absence of regular advertisements and press coverage, these theaters are difficult to trace with precision, but see Lic. Bd., 1902–6, and *WST*, May 1, 8, 1904. Another factor in the shift from live entertainment to movies may have been an effort by theater managers to avoid problems with actors' unions and theatrical "trusts"; see *WT*, Dec. 13, 1904, Aug. 4, 6, 1906; *WEG*, Oct. 13, 1905.

11 *WST*, Aug. 8, 1912. According to a pamphlet published in 1927 by the *Worcester Telegram and Gazette* (*The Story of the Worcester Telegram and Gazette*), which was likely to exaggerate local prosperity, the average wage in Worcester was $650 in 1915, $1,080 in 1918, and $1,360 in 1927. The 1912 budget was for a family earning $896.15, an above average wage. The average recreational spending in a study of New York workers was about sixteen cents per

week. For a family earning between $1,000 and $1,100 per year (the range of a skilled construction worker), the average recreational spending was about twenty-eight cents per week. On this basis, a family of five could go to a five-cent movie once each week. (The lowest priced seats at the Worcester Theatre, which presented live drama, were usually twenty-five cents.) See Robert Coit Chapin, *The Standard of Living Among Workingmen's Families in New York City* (New York, 1909), 210–13. See also National Industrial Conference Board, *The Cost of Living Among Wage Earners, Worcester, Mass., June, 1920* (New York, 1920), 8.

12 David Brody, *Steelworkers in America: The Nonunion Era* (1960; rpt. New York, 1969), 34–40, 279; Elizabeth Beardsley Butler, *Women and the Trades, Pittsburgh, 1907–1908* (1909; rpt. New York, 1969), 333. See also Margaret F. Byington, *Homestead: The Households of a Mill Town* (1910; rpt. Pittsburgh, 1974), 111, and discussion of hours in chapter 7, this volume. Gunnar Forslund recalls workers stopping at downtown movie theaters on their way home from work, but this was probably in the years around World War I and after; interview, Worcester, Mar. 29, 1978.

13 US Bureau of the Census, *Thirteenth Census, 1910*, 11 vols. (Washington, DC, 1913), 1:858–9; *WST*, Feb. 7, 1915; Rollin L. Hartt, *The People at Play* (1909; rpt. New York, 1975), 133. See also Frederick J. Haskin, "The Popular Nickelodeon," *Moving Picture World* 2 (Jan. 18, 1908):37.

14 Interview with Fred Fedeli, Shrewsbury, Mass., Feb. 23, 1978; Hoyt, "Conditions of Three of the Cheaper Theaters," 5.

15 Thomas F. Power, comp., *Messages From Recent Pilgrims* (Worcester, 1921), 12.

16 Collier, "Cheap Amusements," 75; Haskin, "Popular Nickelodeon," 37; Jane Addams, *The Spirit of Youth and the City Streets* (New York, 1909), 91; John Collier, "The Motion Picture," in *Proceedings of the Child Conference for Research and Welfare*, 2 vols. (New York, 1910), 2:109; Davis, *Exploitation of Pleasure*, 29–35; Charles V. Tevis, "Censoring the Five-Cent Drama," *World Today*, 19 (Oct. 1910): 1137.

17 Edward Chandler, "How Much Children Attend the Theater: The Quality of the Enter-

tainment They Choose and Its Effect Upon Them," *Proceedings of the Child Conference*, 1:57; women quoted in Elizabeth Ewen, "City Lights: Immigrant Women and the Rise of the Movies," *Signs* 5, no. 3 (1980):58. On parent–child conflicts over movies, see also Herbert Blumer, *Movies and Conduct* (New York, 1933), 157–61.

18 Frederic C. Howe, "What to Do With the Motion-Picture Show: Shall It Be Censored?" *Outlook* 107 (June 20, 1914):413; Mary Heaton Vorse, "Some Picture Show Audiences," *Outlook* 98 (June 24, 1911):445; *WST*, Apr. 10, 1910; *LN*, Aug. 27, 1910.

19 *WEP*, Sept. 22, 25, 29, 1906. Russell Merritt finds that Boston movie houses also solicited female patronage; he sees this effort as part of a larger strategy to develop respectable, middle-class audiences; "Nickelodeon Theaters," 73–4.

20 US Bureau of the Census, *Eleventh Census, 1890* (Washington, DC, 1897), 2:742-3; *Thirteenth Census, 1910* (Washington, DC, 1914), 4:194-207; Butler, *Women and the Trades*, 333. See also *LN*, July 18, 1908.

21 Joseph M. Patterson, "The Nickelodeon," *Moving Picture World* 2 (Jan. 4, 1908):21; this article originally appeared in *Saturday Evening Post* (Nov. 23, 1907):10–11, 38; Sklar, *Movie-Made America*, 16; "A Democratic Art," *Nation* 97 (Aug. 28, 1913):193. See similarly Allen, "Vaudeville and Film," 324.

22 Lewis Jacobs, *The Rise of the American Film: A Critical History* (1939; rpt. New York, 1968), 156. For an interesting discussion of the favorable depiction of immigrants in early films, see Thomas Cripps, "The Movie Jew as an Image of Assimilationism, 1903–1927," *Journal of Popular Film* 4, no. 3 (1975):193. For the debate over the influence of progressive reform on these early films, see Robert Sklar's review of Lary May's *Screening Out the Past: The Birth of Mass Culture and the Motion Picture Industry* (New York, 1980) in *American Historical Review* 86 (Oct. 1981):945, and May's response in the June 1982 issue of the same journal (pp. 913–14). The paper prints deposited at the Library of Congress and restored to film by Kemp Niver are a valuable resource for the pre-1912 years, but even these 3,000 films are not a full or

representative sample of the films of those years; Kemp R. Niver, *Motion Pictures from the Library of Congress Paper Print Collection, 1894–1912* (Berkeley and Los Angeles, 1967). I viewed *The Fatal Hour* at the Library of Congress.

23 Richard Sennett, *The Fall of Public Man* (New York, 1977), 206–7, 73–81.

24 David Grimsted, *Melodrama Unveiled: American Theater and Culture, 1800–1860* (Chicago, 1968), 53; Hartt, *People at Play*, 7–8. See similarly Robert C. Toll, *Blacking Up: The Minstrel Show in Nineteenth-Century America* (New York, 1974), 12.

25 John Corbin, "How the Other Half Laughs," *Harper's New Monthly Magazine* (Dec. 1898), reprinted in Neil Harris, ed., *The Land of Contrasts, 1880–1901* (New York, 1970), 160–1, 162, 164; Irving Howe and Kenneth Libo, eds., *How We Lived: A Documentary History of Immigrant Jews in America, 1880–1930* (New York, 1979), 246. See also A. Richard Sogliuzzo, "Notes for a History of the Italian-American Theatre of New York," *Theatre Survey*, 14 (Nov. 1973):59–75; Irving Howe, *World of Our Fathers* (New York, 1976), 484.

26 Cook, "History of the Drama in Worcester," 19; *WST*, Apr. 4, May 1, 1904. For appearances of Yiddish companies in Worcester, see *LN*, Nov. 17, 1906, Apr. 6, 1912.

27 Walter Prichard Eaton, "Class Consciousness and the 'Movies,'" *Atlantic Monthly* 115 (Jan. 1915):51; *WEP*, Oct. 6, 1906.

28 "The Nickelodeon," *Moving Picture World* 1 (Apr. 27, 1908):140; *WST*, June 20, 1915; *LN*, Dec. 28, 1907; Hoyt, "Conditions of Three of the Cheaper Theaters," 5; Addams, *Spirit of Youth*, 86; *WST*, Jan. 8, Nov. 8, 1914, Apr. 4, 1915. Drinking was not limited to the movie audience, apparently. In 1910 the projectionist at the Pastime Theatre was arrested in the theater for drunkenness; *WT*, Feb. 25, 1910. For national concern about sex and movie theaters, see the Vice Commission of Chicago, *The Social Evil in Chicago* (Chicago, 1911), 217–18.

29 Hoyt, "Conditions of Three of the Cheaper Theaters," 5; *WST*, Nov. 21, 1915; Ewen, "City Lights," 52; Addams, *Spirit of Youth*, 85–6.

30 *WT*, Feb. 28, 1916; John W. Ripley, "All Join in the Chorus," *American Heritage* 10 (June 1959):50–9; *WEP*, Jan. 9, 1908; interview with Frank Nagle, Worcester, Mar. 1, 1978; interview with Fedeli; *WEP*, May 7, 14, 1910; *LN*, Aug. 6, 1910, Jan. 28, 1911. Exactly how bike races fit on a small theater stage is not clear.

31 Interview with Leo LaJoie, Worcester, Feb. 28, 1978; interview with Fedeli; interview with Robert Werme, Worcester, Mar. 1, 1978.

32 *WST*, Apr. 10, 1910; Hoyt, "Conditions of Three of the Cheaper Theaters," 5. See also *Catholic Messenger*, Jan. 17, 1908.

33 *WST*, Sept. 6, 13, Apr. 26, 1914, Feb. 13, 1916; Hartt, *People at Play*, 90–1. See also *WST*, May 16, 1915. There is some evidence that Worcester movie theater managers took this criticism to heart. The poet Stanley Kunitz, who grew up in Worcester's Jewish community in the early twentieth century, writes in a poem entitled "The Magic Curtain" that between shows at the Front Street movie houses: "ushers with atomizers ranged the aisles, emitting lilac spray"; *The Testing Tree* (Boston, 1971), 33.

34 *WT*, Jan. 24, 25, 27, Feb. 1, 5, 7, 14, 1910. See also Thomas C. Carrigan, "Juvenile Delinquency in Worcester" (M.A. thesis, Clark Univ., 1910), 227–31; *Catholic Messenger*, Feb. 11, 18, 25, 1910; on Hill, see *WT*, Aug. 7, 1912.

35 *WT*, Jan. 25, Feb. 28, Mar. 7, 14, 21, 1910. See also the controversy over the showing of the film of the Johnson–Jeffries heavyweight fight in *WT*, July 4, 7, 1910; *LN*, July 9, 1910.

36 *LN*, Mar. 26, 1910; *WEG*, Mar. 30, July 6, 1910.

37 *Catholic Messenger*, May 10, 17, 24, 31, 1907, May 20, 1910. See also Feb. 11, 18, 25, Mar. 4, 1910. (References courtesy of Timothy J. Meagher.)

38 *WT*, Jan. 20, 1910; *WDT*, Dec. 15, 1884.

39 Interview with Ms. Forslund, Mar. 29, 1978; interview with Chester Olson, Mar. 1, 1978; interview with Ted Bergsten, Feb. 23, 1978, all in Worcester. Further insight on Swedes and moviegoing in Worcester came from interviews with Mr. and Mrs. Algot Eckstrom, Mar. 1, 1978, and Ethel Nelson Bigelow, Aug. 5, 1980, both in Worcester.

40 Quote in John Bodnar, "Materialism and Morality: Slavic-American Immigrants and Education, 1890–1940," *Journal of Ethnic*

Studies 3 (Winter 1976):9 (emphasis added). For movies and the challenge to middle-class culture, see Sklar, *Movie-Made America*, 88–90; May, *Screening Out the Past*, xi–xv.

41 There is a vast literature on movie censorhip. Two good starting places on this subject are Jowett, *Film*, 108–82, and Arthur McClure, "Censor the Movies! Early Attempts to Regulate the Content of Motion Pictures in America, 1907–1936," in Arthur McClure, ed., *The Movies: An American Idiom* (Rutherford, NJ, 1971), 117–52. Also see McCarthy, "Nickel Vice and Virtue"; Robert Fisher, "Film Censorship and Progressive Reform: The National Board of Censorship of Motion Pictures, 1909–1922," *Journal of Popular Film* 4, no. 2 (1975): 143–56; Richard Corliss, "The Legion of Decency," *Film Comment* 4 (Summer 1968): 24–61; Paul W. Facey, *The Legion of Decency: A Sociological Analysis of the Emergence and Development of a Social Pressure Group* (1945; rpt. New York, 1974). Some interesting contemporary comment can be found in Tevis, "Censoring the Five-Cent Drama"; William Inglis, "Morals and Moving Pictures," *Harper's Weekly* 54 (July 30, 1910): 12–13; Howe, "What To Do With the Motion-Picture Show"; John Collier, "Censorship and the National Board," *Survey* 35 (Oct. 2, 1915): 9–14; Orrin G. Cocks, "Applying Standards to Motion Picture Films," *Survey* 32 (June 27, 1914): 337–8; Boyd Fisher, "The Regulation of Motion Picture Theaters," *American City* 7 (Sept. 1912): 520–2; John Collier, "Should the Government Censor Motion Pictures?" *Playground* 6 (July 1912): 129–32.

42 Tevis, "Censoring the Five-Cent Drama," 1138; "The Film Manufacturer and the Public," *Moving Picture World* 1 (May 25, 1907): 179.

43 *WT*, Mar. 21, 1910; *WST*, Apr. 17, 1910; interview with Fedeli. Kmet, "Milwaukee's Nickelodeon Era," 5, discusses self-regulation by exhibitors.

44 Hoyt, "Conditions of Three of the Cheaper Theatres," 3; Public Education Association of Worcester, Mass., *Seventh Annual Report, May, 1912* (Worcester, 1912), 15 (emphasis added). For similar complaints elsewhere, see Vice Commission, *Social Evil in Chicago*, 247; Phelan, *Motion Pictures*, 23.

45 *WT*, Feb. 5, 1914. For further discussion of the sabbath movie question, see *WT*, Jan. 26, 30, 31, Feb. 1–3, 4, 7–10, 12, 14–17, 22, Mar. 6, 8, June 4, 1914; "Report of Sunday Recreation Commission," *Worcester Magazine* 17 (July 1914): 201; *LN*, Feb. 7, 1914.

46 *WT*, Feb. 9, 3, 1914.

47 *WST*, Dec. 21, 1913, Feb. 1, 1914, Apr. 18, 1915. See also Cook, "History of the Drama in Worcester," 54. Allen, "Vaudeville and Film" provides an extensive discussion of the relationships between the two forms.

48 *WEG*, Jan. 18, 1919. Data on seats from *Worcester Directory*, newspaper reports, and interviews. Merritt, "Nickelodeon Theaters," 75, estimates that movie attendance probably doubled between 1908 and 1914.

49 *WT*, Nov. 19, 1917.

50 My argument here follows that of Russell Merritt, "Nickelodeon Theaters," 65, 67.

51 *WT*, Mar. 9, 1913, Sept. 11, 18, 25, Dec. 29, 1916, Feb. 19, 1917. For other examples of the upgrading of conditions in Worcester movie theatres, see *WST*, Jan. 17, Feb. 14, 21, Apr. 18, Sept. 26, Nov. 14, 1915; "New England Column," *Moving Picture World* 23 (Feb. 20, Mar. 6, 1915): 1168, 1483; 24 (Apr. 17, 1915): 429; 25 (July 24, 1915): 693; *WT*, Aug. 21, 1916.

52 See, for example, *WST*, Feb. 7, Sept. 5, 19, Nov. 7, 1915, Jan. 2, 23, 1916; *WT*, Aug. 21, 1916, June 25, Aug. 1, 13, 1917.

53 Samuel Katz, "Theatrical Management," in Joseph P. Kennedy, ed., *The Story of Films* (Chicago, 1927), 266–7; interview with Fedeli; *WST*, July 8, 1915, Nov. 18, 1928; May, *Screening Out the Past*, 148. See also Harold B. Franklin, *Motion Picture Management* (New York, 1927).

54 Sklar, *Movie-Made America*, 42; Tino Balio, "Struggles for Control: 1908–1930," in Balio, *American Film Industry*, 109–10; *WST*, Mar. 21, 1915; *WT*, Sept. 29, 1915.

55 *WT*, May 15, 16, 22, 29, June 7, 8, 14, 15, 19, 1916.

56 May, *Screening Out the Past*, 147–66.

57 Katz, "Theatrical Management," 269; A.J. Balaban (as told to Carrie Balaban), *Continuous Performance* (New York, 1942): 69–71; May, *Screening Out the Past*, 166.

3

Cheap Amusements (1908)

John Collier

For four months a joint-committee of the Woman's Municipal League and the People's Institute has been engaged in an investigation of the cheap amusements of Manhattan Island. The committee has been composed as follows: Michael M. Davis. Jr., secretary of the People's Institute, chairman; Mrs. Josephine Redding, secretary of the Woman's Municipal League, secretary; Mrs. R.H. McKelvey, Miss Henrietta B. Rodman, Miss Alice Lewisohn, Mrs. F.R. Swift, Michael H. Cardoza, Charles H. Ayres, Jr., John Collier, and W. Frank Persons. The investigation has been made financially possible through the Spuyten Duyvil branch of the Woman's Municipal League. The writer has acted as field investigator.

Attempt has been made to cover all phases of the cheap amusement problem, excluding from the detailed investigation dance-halls and skating-rinks on the one hand and high-priced theaters on the other. Legal and business aspects have been studied as well as educational and sanitary. The subject-matter has been fourfold: melodrama, vaudeville and burlesque; nickelodeons, or moving picture variety shows; penny arcades; and miscellany. The miscellany are anatomical museums, fake beauty-shows, etc., which are confined to a limited area of the city [...]

Five years ago the nickelodeon was neither better nor worse than many other cheap amusements are at present. It was often a carnival of vulgarity, suggestiveness and vio- lence, the fit subject for police regulation. It gained a deservedly bad name, and although no longer deserved, that name still clings to it. During the present investigation a visit to more than two hundred nickelodeons has not detected one immoral or indecent picture, or one indecent feature of any sort, much as there has been in other respects to call for improvement. But more than this: in the nickelodeon one sees history, travel, the reproduction of industries. He sees farce- comedy which at worst is relaxing, innocu- ous, rather monotonously confined to horse- play, and at its best is distinctly humanizing, laughing with and not at the subject. Some real drama: delightful curtain-raisers, in per- fect pantomime, from France, and in the judgment of most people rather an excess of mere melodrama, and in rare cases even of sheer murderous violence. At one show or another a growing number of classic legends, like Jack and the Beanstalk or Ali Baba and the Forty Thieves, can be seen any night. The moving picture repertoire amounts to tens of thousands, and is amazingly varied. One firm alone in the city has two million feet of "film" stored away until it can be used again as fresh material, after the public has forgotten it. In addition to the moving-picture, the nickel- odeon as a rule has singing, and almost invariably the audience joins in the chorus with a good will. Thus has the moving- picture-show elevated itself. But the penny

Excerpted from John Collier. "Cheap Amusements." *Charities and the Commons* 20 (April 1908), 73–6.

arcade has not elevated itself, and the cheap vaudeville, if anything, has grown worse.

The nickelodeon is a family theater, and is almost the creation of the child, and it has discovered a new and healthy cheap-amusement public. The penny arcade is a selfish and costly form of amusement, a penny buying only a half-minute's excitement for one person. Its shooting-gallery and similar features are likewise costly. In the short-lived pictures there is no time for the development of human interest, but the gist of a murder or of a salacious situation can be conveyed. So the penny arcade has resembled the saloon, from which the family has stayed away; and everything artificial has been mustered in to draw the floating crowd. As for the cheap theater, it has had a false tradition behind it, and managers have taken for granted that a low-priced performance could be given only by an inferior cast. So when the cheap theater has departed from the crudest melodrama it has gone over into inferior vaudeville and has depended on illegitimate methods for its success. This is the rule, although there are exceptions, and vaudeville at best has only a limited interest for the great, basic, public of the working and immigrant classes in New York.

But the nickelodeon started with a free field and a marvelous labor-saving device in the moving-picture, and it began above all as a neighborhood institution, offering an evening of the most varied interest to the entire family for a quarter. Thus the nickelodeon grew as solidly as it grew swiftly, and developed a new amusement seeking public, the public that has made the nickelodeon what it is. Right here is found the most significant aspect of the present amusement situation. All the settlements and churches combined do not reach daily a tithe of the simple and impressionable folk that the nickelodeons reach and vitally impress every day. Here is a new social force, perhaps the beginning of a true theater of the people, and an instrument whose power can only be realized when social workers begin to use it.

The investigation led almost immediately to constructive opportunities. On the legal side, an anomalous situation was found. In no existing law, state or municipal, was penny arcade or moving picture mentioned. These theaters were grouped by construction as common shows, along with ferris wheels and bicycle carrousels, and were put under the authority of the license bureau. But where the standard theater is regulated in the minutest detail as regards its building requirements, by written law, there is no law and no printed specification for the moving picture show, which plays with fire. The theaters are controlled by the police, in whom responsibility is centered, and who co-operate with the proper departments. But the nickelodeon is controlled by the license bureau, a clerical department, and up to ten months ago it went to all intents and purposes unsupervised. Then popular agitation and the initiative of a hard working official in the fire department, set the city's machinery at work, and a good deal has been done. The moving picture show is reasonably safe from fire now; it is not yet safe from contagious disease, and the air is often very bad.

As a first step toward adjusting the legal situation, the investigation committee framed a bill, which has been introduced by Assemblyman Samuel A. Gluck at Albany, and which has passed the Assembly by a large majority. Barring unforeseen obstacles it will pass the Senate at the present session. This bill provides for the raising of license fees on nickelodeons from $25 to $150 a year, for the placing of this license under the direct control of the police, along with the license for standard theaters, and for the exclusion of school children from nickelodeons during school hours and after eight o'clock at night, except when accompanied by guardians. This bill went to Albany with the endorsement of various civic organizations, the Board of Education, and the Moving Picture Association itself which has shown every desire to co-operate in the improvement of moving picture standards.

On the side of co-operation with the moving-picture business looking toward more elevated performances, and even the improvement of the artistic and educational quality and of sanitary conditions through direct competition on a commercial basis, the opportunity is immediate and large. In this field it is probable that the drama machinery of the People's Institute will be turned to use in some co-operative plan, giving endorsement to the best of the shows and receiving in return the right to regulate their programs. Settlements on their own initiative could do valuable work in this way. The investigation committee, which is to be perpetuated as a sub-committee of the drama committee of the People's Institute, will in all probability start one or more model nickelodeons, with the object of forcing up the standard through direct competition, of proving that an unprecedentedly high class of performance can be made to pay, and perhaps, in the event of success, of founding a people's theater of the future.

THEY WERE PERMITTED TO DRINK DEEP OF OBLIVION OF ALL THE TROUBLE IN THE WORLD

Movie audience illustration from Mary Heaton Vorse, "Some Picture Show Audiences" (1911)

4

Some Picture Show Audiences (1911)

Mary Heaton Vorse

One rainy night in a little Tuscan hill town I went to a moving-picture show. It was market-day; the little hall was full of men in their great Italian cloaks. They had come in from small isolated hamlets, from tiny fortified towns perched on the tops of distant hills to which no road led, but only a *salita*. I remember that there was in the evening's entertainment a balloon race, and a pilgrimage to the Holy Land, and a mad comic piece that included a rush with a baby-carriage through the boulevards of Paris; and there was a drama, "The Vendetta," which had for its background the beautiful olive terraces of Italy.

I had gone, as they had, to see pictures, but in the end I saw only them, because it seemed to me that what had happened was a latter-day miracle. By an ingenious invention all the wonderful things that happened in the diverse world outside their simple lives could come to them. They had no pictures or papers; few of them could read; and yet they sat there at home and watched the inflating of great balloons and saw them rise and soar and go away into the blue, and watched again the strange Oriental crowd walking through the holy streets of Jerusalem. It is hard to understand what a sudden widening of their horizon that meant for them. It is the door of escape, for a few cents, from the realities of life.

It is drama, and it is travel, and it is even beauty, all in one. A wonderful thing it is, and to know just how wonderful I suppose you must be poor and have in your life no books and no pictures and no means of travel or seeing beautiful places, and almost no amusements of any kind; perhaps your only door of escape or only means of forgetfulness more drink than is good for you. Then you will know what a moving-picture show really means, although you will probably not be able to put it into words.

We talk a good deal about the censorship of picture shows, and pass city ordinances to keep the young from being corrupted by them; and this is all very well, because a great amusement of the people ought to be kept clean and sweet; but at the same time this discussion has left a sort of feeling in the minds of people who do not need to go to the picture show that it is a doubtful sort of a place, where young girls and men scrape undesirable acquaintances, and where the prowler lies in wait for the unwary, and where suggestive films of crime and passion are invariably displayed. But I think that this is an unjust idea, and that any one who will take the trouble to amuse himself with the picture show audiences for an afternoon or two will see why it is that the making of films has become a great industry, why it is that the picture show has driven out the vaudeville and the melodrama.

You cannot go to any one of the picture shows in New York without having a series of

Excerpted from Mary Heaton Vorse, "Some Picture Show Audiences." *Outlook* 98 (June 24, 1911), 441–7.

touching little adventures with the people who sit near you, without overhearing chance words of a *naïveté* and appreciation that make you bless the living picture book that has brought so much into the lives of the people who work.

Houston Street, on the East Side, of an afternoon is always more crowded than Broadway. Push-carts line the street. The faces that you see are almost all Jewish – Jews of many different types; swarthy little men, most of them, looking undersized according to the Anglo-Saxon standard. Here and there a deep-chested mother of Israel sails along, majestic in *shietel* and shawl. These are the toilers – garment-makers, a great many of them – people who work "by pants," as they say. A long and terrible workday they have to keep body and soul together. Their distractions are the streets, and the bargaining off the push-carts, and the show. For a continual trickle of people detaches itself from the crowded streets and goes into the good-sized hall; and around the entrance, too, wait little boys – eager-eyed little boys – with their tickets in their hands, trying to decoy those who enter into taking them in with them as guardians, because the city ordinances do not allow a child under sixteen to go in unaccompanied by an older person.

In the half-light the faces of the audience detach themselves into little pallid ovals, and, as you will always find in the city, it is an audience largely of men.

Behind us sat a woman with her escort. So rapt and entranced was she with what was happening on the stage that her voice accompanied all that happened – a little unconscious and lilting *obbligato*. It was the voice of a person unconscious that she spoke – speaking from the depths of emotion; a low voice, but perfectly clear, and the unconsciously spoken words dropped with the sweetness of running water. She spoke in German. One would judge her to be from some part of Austria. She herself was lovely in person and young, level-browed and clear-eyed, deep-chested; a beneficent and lovely

woman one guessed her to be. And she had never seen Indians before; perhaps never heard of them.

The drama being enacted was the rescue from the bear pit of Yellow Wing, the lovely Indian maiden, by Dick the Trapper; his capture by the tribe, his escape with the connivance of Yellow Wing, who goes to warn him in his log house, their siege by the Indians, and final rescue by a splendid charge of the United States cavalry; these one saw riding with splendid abandon over hill and dale, and the marriage then and there of Yellow Wing and Dick by the gallant chaplain. A guileless and sentimental dime novel, most ingeniously performed; a work of art; beautiful, too, because one had glimpses of stately forests, sunlight shifting through leaves, wild, dancing forms of Indians, the beautiful swift rushing of horses. One must have had a heart of stone not to follow the adventures of Yellow Wing and Dick the Trapper with passionate interest.

But to the woman behind it was reality at its highest. She was there in a fabled country full of painted savages. The rapidly unfolding drama was to her no make-believe arrangement ingeniously fitted together by actors and picture-makers. It had happened; it was happening for her now.

"Oh!" she murmured. "That wild and terrible people! Oh, boy, take care, take care! Those wild and awful people will get you!" "*Das wildes und grausames Volk*," she called them. "Now – now – she comes to save her beloved!" This as Yellow Wing hears the chief plotting an attack on Dick the Trapper, and then flies fleet-foot through the forest. "Surely, surely, she will save her beloved!" It was almost a prayer; in the woman's simple mind there was no foregone conclusion of a happy ending. She saw no step ahead, since she lived the present moment so intensely.

When Yellow Wing and Dick were besieged within and Dick's hand was wounded –

"The poor child! how can she bear it? To see the *geliebte* wounded before one's very eyes!"

And when the cavalry thundered through the forest –

"God give that they arrive swiftly – to be in time they must arrive swiftly!" she exclaimed to herself.

Outside the iron city roared; before the door of the show the push-cart venders bargained and trafficked with customers. Who in that audience remembered it? They had found the door of escape. For the moment they were in the depths of the forest following the loves of Yellow Wing and Dick. The woman's voice, so like the voice of a spirit talking to itself, unconscious of time and place, was their voice. There they were, a strange company of aliens – Jews, almost all; haggard and battered and bearded men, young girls with their beaus, spruce and dapper youngsters beginning to make their way. In that humble playhouse one ran the gamut of the East Side. The American-born sat next to the emigrant who arrived but a week before. A strange and romantic people cast into the welter of the terrible city of New York, each of them with the overwhelming problem of battling with strange conditions and an alien civilization. And for the moment they were permitted to drink deep of oblivion of all the trouble in the world. Life holds some compensation, after all. The keener your intellectual capacity, the higher your artistic sensibilities are developed, just so much more difficult it is to find this total forgetfulness – a thing that for the spirit is as life-giving as sleep.

And all through the afternoon and evening this company of tired workers, overburdened men and women, fills the little halls scattered throughout the city and throughout the land.

There are motion-picture shows in New York that are as intensely local to the audience as to the audience of a Tuscan hill town. Down on Bleecker Street is the Church of Our Lady of Pompeii. Here women, on their way to work or to their brief marketing, drop in to say their prayers before their favorite saints in exactly the same fashion as though it were a little church in their own parish. Towards evening women with their brood of children go in; the children frolic and play subdued tag in the aisles, for church with them is an every-day affair, not a starched-up matter of Sunday only. Then, prayers finished, you may see a mother sorting out her own babies and moving on serenely to the picture show down the road – prayers first and amusement afterwards, after the good old Latin fashion.

It is on Saturday nights down here that the picture show reaches its high moment. The whole neighborhood seems to be waiting for a chance to go in. Every woman has a baby in her arms and at least two children clinging to her skirts. Indeed, so universal is this custom that a woman who goes there unaccompanied by a baby feels out of place, as if she were not properly dressed. A baby seems as much a matter-of-course adjunct to one's toilet on Bleecker Street as a picture hat would be on Broadway.

Every one seems to know everyone else. As a new woman joins the throng other women cry out to her, gayly:

"Ah, good-evening, Concetta. How is Giuseppi's tooth?"

"Through at last," she answers. "And where are your twins?"

The first woman makes a gesture indicating that they are somewhere swallowed up in the crowd. [. . .]

In the Bowery you get a different kind of audience. None of your neighborhood spirit here. Even in what is called the "dago show" – that is, the show where the occasional vaudeville numbers are Italian singers – the people seem chance-met; the audience is almost entirely composed of men, only an occasional woman.

It was here that I met the moving-picture show expert, the connoisseur, for he told me that he went to a moving-picture show every night. It was the best way that he knew of spending your evenings in New York, and one gathered that he had tried many different ways. He was in his early twenties, with a tough and honest countenance, and he spoke the dialect of the city of New York with greater richness than I have ever heard it spoken. He was ashamed of being caught by a compatriot in a "dago show."

"Say," he said, "dis is a bum joint. I don't know how I come to toin in here. You don't un'erstan' what that skoit's singin', do you? You betcher I don't!"

Not for worlds would he have understood a word of the inferior Italian tongue.

"I don't never come to dago moving-picter shows," he hastened to assure me. "Say, if youse wanter see a real show, beat it down to Grand Street. Dat's de real t'ing. Dese dago shows ain't got no good films. You hardly ever see a travel film; w'en I goes to a show, I likes to see the woild. I'd like travelin' if I could afford it, but I can't; that's why I like a good travel film. A good comic's all right, but a good travel film or an a'rioplane race or a battle-ship review – dat's de real t'ing! You don't get none here. I don't know what made me come here," he repeated. He was sincerely displeased with himself at being caught with the goods by his compatriots in a place that had no class, and the only way he could defend himself was by showing his fine scorn of the inferior race.

You see what it means to them; it means Opportunity – a chance to glimpse the beautiful and strange things in the world that you haven't in your life; the gratification of the higher side of your nature; opportunity which, except for the big moving picture book, would be forever closed to you. You understand still more how much it means opportunity if you happen to live in a little country place where the whole town goes to every change of films and where the new films are gravely discussed. Down here it is that you find the people who agree with my friend of the Bowery – that "travel films is de real t'ing." For those people who would like to travel they make films of pilgrims going to Mecca; films of the great religious processions in the holy city of Jerusalem; of walrus fights in the far North. It has even gone so far that in Melilla there was an order for the troops to start out; they sprang to their places, trumpets blew, and the men fell into line and marched off – all for the moving-picture show. They were angry – the troops – but the people in Spain saw how their armies acted.

In all the countries of the earth – in Sicily, and out in the desert of Arizona, and in the deep woods of America, and on the olive terraces of Italy – they are making more films, inventing new dramas with new and beautiful backgrounds, for the poor man's theater. In his own little town, in some far-off fishing village, he can sit and see the coronation, and the burial of a king, or the great pageant of the Roman Church.

It is no wonder that it is a great business with a capitalization of millions of dollars, since it gives to the people who need it most laughter and drama and beauty and a chance for once to look at the strange places of the earth.

5

Motion-Picture Work (1911)

David Hulfish

A Store-Front City Theater Building

A vacant business house having been selected both for location and for size, the process of converting it into a motion-picture theater is to remove the glass front and framing for the door and window, to replace it with a closed front a few feet back from the sidewalk line into which are built the ticket seller's booth and the entrance and exit doors and on the inside of which is built the projection operator's booth. At the inner end of the room a muslin screen about 3 by 4 yards is stretched. The room is filled with rows of chairs, either kitchen chairs or opera chairs, as the expense justified by the location will permit, and a piano is placed near the picture screen. [...]

The complete change in the store room, ready for chairs, piano, wiring and projecting machine, should not exceed $150; 200 chairs of the kitchen variety at $100; electric lamps and wiring at $100; a projecting machine at $165; and a rented piano – the total expense amounting to about $500. With a small additional amount for supplies and initial advertising expense, the manager will be able to open his doors to the public at a total cash expense of not more than $600, and no debts. [...]

The cost of operating this theater, evenings only – for it would be either in a small town or in a residence territory of a city – for a program of two reels of film and a song, would be, by the week, about as follows:

Rent and heat	$ 10.00
Electricity	5.00
Film	20.00
Song Slides	2.00
Supplies	13.00
Operator	15.00
Cashier	3.00
Doorkeeper	5.00
Pianist	5.00
Singer	5.00
Weekly Expense	$ 83.00

In a non-competitive small city, not only will the rent be lower, but the wage rate will be lower throughout.

Elaborate Store-Front

The floor plan will be the same in this case [...] the difference being found in the quality and appearance of the elements going to make up the theater.

A decorative front [...] will cost $500 to $2,000 for the front partition complete with operating room and cashier's booth, including all the decoration in front of the partition. Another $500 or more will be needed to raise

Excerpted from David Hulfish, *Motion-Picture Work: A General Treatise on Picture Taking, Picture Making, Photo-Plays, and Theater Management and Operation* (Chicago: American Technical Society, 1915), 12–45.

the floor and to install 200 opera chairs at $1.20 to $1.60 each. The inside decorations and the picture screen of modern type will raise the expense $200 to $300 at least. The total expense need not exceed $6,000; with any pretensions toward beauty and luxury, it cannot be kept below $2,000.

For designing and building the front, a firm in the special work should be employed [...]

In selecting or approving a plan by a professional designer, the manager should see that the cashier's booth is large enough for comfort all the year round and that the projection operator's booth is large enough for two operators and two projecting machines. Not only may competition enforce the employment of two operators, but it will be found positive economy to give the operator an assistant during the rush hours of Saturday night.

In a house of this class, a manager's control panel and signal system should be installed at the door where the ticket-taker stands, that he may signal the operator to begin projection, and may ring for the singer, etc., controlling the conduct of the program particularly during the rush hours when the passing of numbers of people in or out may delay the beginning of the next picture.

The program selected – by this term "program" is included the quality as well as quantity of pictures, song, music, and vaudeville – must follow the custom of the city in which the theater is located, if the certainty of a proper division of patronage is desired. A departure from the custom of the city may result in a larger success, or may result in failure. [...]

A specimen expense sheet of a high-class store-front picture theater is here given.

WEEKLY EXPENSE SHEET

Rent, of complete theater, week	$ 40.00
Film rent, three reels daily change	50.00
Carbons	1.00
Pianist	15.00
Violinist	10.00
Drummer	12.00
Usher	2.50
Electricity	18.00
Song Slides	2.00
Cashier	5.00
Singer	18.00
License	4.00
Projection operator	18.00
Porter	4.00
Ticket taker	5.00
General Expense	10.00
Total weekly expense, not including manager	$214.50

Receipts, average, six nights $240, Sunday $100; total weekly receipts, average, $340.

Specimen Expense Sheet of a High-Class Store-Front Picture Theater. The figures given above are the actual expense sheet of a house of this class in a residence district of Chicago. [...] The cost of opening this house for business was in the neighborhood of $3,000.

This particular theater charges a five-cent admission seven days in the week. The seating capacity is 300. A one-hour program is given at 7, 8, 9, and 10 p.m. on week days and at 2, 3, 4, 5, 6, 7, 8, 9, 10 p.m. on Sundays – thirty-three shows per week, three reels and a song in each program. The film is one reel third-run, one reel not more than ten days old, and one reel not more than three months old, daily change, for which $50 per week is paid. Two different songs are given, alternating in every other program, with one singer. Music is furnished by an orchestra of three. The item of "Sundry Expense" includes tickets, coal, condensers, poster service, machine repairs, lamp renewals, piano tuning, etc.

In this theater, the manager takes profits rather than a salary. He has no capital invested, but in the $40 per week rent he is paying a return to the capitalist for the investment. [...]

Small Vaudeville Theater

The class of theater occupying a specially constructed building, in the residence districts of Chicago, is well represented by the particular theater from which the following facts are taken:

The lot, 50 by 125 feet, upon which the building is erected, was estimated in value at $10,000; and the erection of the building and its equipment ready for the public, cost $15,000, making a total expense in the building itself of $25,000. For this investment the owner takes a rental of $5,200 per year from the receipts of the theater. This item is considered an item of rent in the theater expense sheet, and is paid weekly at the rate of $100 per week, as rent.

The program consists of four acts of vaudeville, two reels of film, and a song. There is an orchestra of four pieces. The program lasts about an hour and a half to an hour and three-quarters. The program is given twice each night, once on Wednesday afternoon, once on Saturday afternoon, and twice on Sunday afternoon; eighteen performances per week, of which four are on Sunday. In case of a long vaudeville program, the song is omitted.

The house contains 800 seats, of which 600 are on the main floor and 200 on the balcony. Of these, 350 seats are sold at twenty cents and 450 at ten cents; the total value of a full house is $115. An average evening in fair weather is a house and a half for the two performances. Of the twenty-cent seats, fifty are the front rows of the balcony; this raises the tone of the balcony as a seat location and helps to sell the house out when nearly full.

The film service is one reel ten days old and one reel not more than three months old, change twice a week; for this service, the price paid is $20 per week. The entire program, vaudeville and film and song, is changed twice each week.

The illustrated song slides, when used, and the singer as well, are furnished free by the music publishers for the advertising value.

WEEKLY EXPENSE OF A SMALL VAUDEVILLE THEATER

Rent, per week	$100.00
Film service, per week............	20.00
Carbons...............................	1.00
Orchestra of four pieces, per week	91.00
Two ushers	5.00
One fire guard	7.00
One stage manager.................	20.00
One stage helper	7.00
Electricity, per week...............	30.00
Cashier...............................	7.00
License...............................	4.00
Poster title service	5.00
Projection operator.................	18.00
Vaudeville, average weekly	500.00
Porter and watchman.............	12.00
Ticket taker.........................	8.00
Sundry small expenses, average per week	25.00
Weekly expense sheet	$860.00

Average receipts for six days, fourteen performances, $900.00; for Sunday, four performances, $315. Average weekly receipts, $1,215.

Large Exclusive Picture House

Only in the shopping district of a city can a sufficient number of patrons be found to fill a large house repeatedly for short programs. The data given here for such a theater is taken from a theater on the busiest retail business street of one of the largest cities of the United States, a theater representative of the highest class of motion-picture theater.

The house is open fourteen hours per day, seven days each week, from 9 a.m. until 11 p.m. The program is three reels of film (or three pictures, not necessarily each a full reel) and two illustrated songs. The film is all first run, changing the three reels three times each week, without holdovers, but a good film picture frequently will be repeated a few weeks later, with the advertising sign, "Repeated by request." The songs are changed weekly. Two singers are employed for the two songs of each program, one male voice and one female voice.

Three projection operators, working at the same time in the operating room, put on the program. Two of these operators have motion-picture projecting machines, while the third operator projects nothing but stereopticon slides, both announcement slides and song slides, attending also to the illumination of the auditorium during the intermission.

The order of the program is as follows: The show starts with a few announcement slides; then the first motion-picture operator puts on the first film picture. As the end of the film picture approaches the stereopticon operator stands ready and projects the song title upon the tailpiece of the film, the pianist opens the introduction to the song as the title appears and the song follows without a second of lost time. At the close of the song, the second motion-picture operator stands ready and begins projection at a signal from the stereopticon operator, the last slide of the song dissolving into the title of the next film picture. In the same manner the screen continues without interruption of projection into the second song and then into the third film picture by the first projection operator. At the close of the third film picture the lights are turned on, the crowd is allowed a few minutes for passing out and in, the candy man makes a trip, and the program is repeated. The house is "dark" about fifty minutes for the program of three pictures and two songs, and is "light" for about five minutes for the intermission.

For the ordinary day, fifteen performances are given in the fourteen hours. On Saturday, the busy day, an extra performance is given, making sixteen in all.

The house, equipped fully for the operation of the theater, represents an invested capital of $160,000. The building was completely remodeled for the theater, under lease to the theater managers. It is not owned by the theater managers, and a rental of $48,000 per year is paid. This includes heating. Figured upon a weekly basis for the weekly expense sheet, this rental is $923 per week.

The theater seats seven hundred people. The admission price is ten cents, anywhere in the house, giving a value for a "full house" of $70.

The attendance averages about six-tenths of the total capacity – six-tenths of seven hundred seats, filled fifteen times on an average for six days, 6,300 tickets per day for six days and 400 more on Saturday for the extra performance, about 44,500 tickets per week, or $4,450 weekly receipts at the ticket window. On many Saturdays – the busy day with sixteen performances – the ticket sale reaches nearly 10,000, or $1,000.

The theater is operated by two sets of employes, called the day force and the night force, each working seven hours continuously. The day force works from 9 a.m. until 4 p.m., the night force then coming on and working until 11 p.m. Thirty-five employes are on the pay roll of the theater itself, aside from the manager and his clerical help.

The orchestra comprises pianist and drummer, and a "sound effect" man for adding something of realism to the pictures by supplying some of the sounds attendant in nature upon the scene represented. [...]

WEEKLY EXPENSE SHEET

Rent and heat, per week	$923.00
Electricity, per week	200.00
Film rental	126.00
Song slides	2.00
Sundry expenses, per week	130.00
License	8.00
6 Projection operators	112.00
2 Cashiers	30.00
2 Uniformed police at door	36.00
2 Fire guards	28.00
2 Ticket takers	30.00
6 Orchestra and sound effects	210.00
4 Singers	100.00
3 Porters	36.00
8 Ushers	80.00
Manager, per week	40.00
Assistant manager, per week	25.00
Stenographer and bookkeeper	15.00
Messenger boy	6.00
Telephone	2.00
Office supplies and sundry	6.00
Average weekly expenses	$2,145.00

Average weekly receipts, $4,450.

Country Theater (1)

The theater from which this expense sheet was taken was unsuccessful. The expense seems about a minimum for a theater in which the manager must employ help for all of his service, yet the gross receipts of the theater did not justify even this expense.

WEEKLY EXPENSE SHEET

Rent	$3.50
Film service, 7 reels weekly	18.00
Express charges	1.00
Electricity	3.00
Operator..............................	10.00
Ticket seller..........................	1.50
Pianist	3.00
Coal (winter expense)..............	2.00
Tickets, carbons and sundry.....	1.00
Total weekly expense...............	$43.00

Average weekly receipts, $40.
This town had a census population of 1,100 people, giving a probable weekly ticket window income of $27.50 to $55.

Country Theater (2)

In the same town, under a different manager. The experience of the first theater had shown about what gross income could be expected. The expense account was planned to fall below the anticipated income by enough to leave a profit for the manager.

WEEKLY EXPENSE SHEET

Rent	$3.50
Film, eight reels, express paid ...	12.00
Electricity	3.00
Operator..............................	
Ticket seller..........................	1.00
Pianist	2.50
Coal (winter expense)..............	2.00
Tickets, carbons and sundry.....	1.00
Newspaper advertisements.......	.50
Total weekly expense...............	$25.50

Average weekly receipts, $45.

The commerical run of film satisfied his audience for quality, and age of subject was immaterial, as all were new to his patrons. The eight reels were run as follows: Two on Monday night, one new and one hold-over on Tuesday night; one new and one holdover Wednesday night; one new and one holdover Thursday night; one new and one holdover Friday night; two new reels and one holdover Saturday afternoon and Saturday evening. This gave a three-reel show on Saturday and prices of ten cents for adults and five cents for children were charged.

The manager ran the projecting machine himself, thus avoiding an expenditure for an operator's salary.

The ticket seller sold tickets and noted that the patrons dropped them into a ticket box at the door, which box could be seen by the manager from time to time as he chanced to look.

The pianist seems the only luxury on the bill of expense. The small advertisement in the local newspaper seems good business judgment.

Country Theater (3)

In the same town, during the summer. During this season the patronage of the country folk is largely withdrawn except on Saturdays. The operation of the picture theater was changed to suit the changed conditions for the summer months.

The theater building or room was held over the summer at the uniform rental rate for the following winter's business. The film service was reduced to three reels for the Saturday show, and shows were given only on Saturday afternoon and evening. Admission was five and ten cents, as on Saturdays during the winter.

WEEKLY EXPENSE SHEET

Rent	$3.50
Film, three reels express paid	5.00
Electricity	1.00

Ticket seller............................	.25
Pianist	.75
Sundry expense......................	.50
Newspaper advertisements.......	1.00
Total weekly expense..............	$12.00

Receipts averaged between $15 and $20 weekly. In addition to the profit of the one day at the theater, the manager had other employment during the week. [...]

Airdome

This name has been adopted to define a motion-picture theater in the open air. A fenced enclosure is chosen, or a canvas 8 to 10 feet high is erected upon stakes to form an enclosed yard. At one end a projection house or even a projection platform is built; at the other end, a picture screen of usual theater size is erected. Chairs are arranged before the screen as in any motion-picture theater, and the entire conduct of the airdome is quite the same. A platform may be built before the screen for vaudeville.

The airdome is for fair weather only. The novel idea seems to please the general public, whether the airdome is operated in a country town or upon a vacant lot in a large city.

Operation

Studying audiences

The manager will learn much about his show by watching his patrons as they come out. It is not necessary to inquire what they think of the show. Comments will pass among them which may be overheard by the manager and by the cashier as they pass the ticket window, commenting favorably and unfavorably upon the film pictures which they have seen a few minutes before. In this manner the manager may learn when any particular picture has favorable comment, and may endeavor to have his film exchange supply more of the same class; likewise, when any

picture has a flood of unfavorable comment among the theatergoers themselves, the manager may try to influence his film exchange to avoid sending him that class of subject.

The words, "try to influence his film exchange," are chosen carefully to express the true position of the exhibitor, or theater manager, in the matter of obtaining film pictures acceptable to his patrons. The film exchanges as a rule take all the film pictures produced by the particular manufacturers from whom they buy. All of these film reels look alike to the film exchange man, and he would like to send them indiscriminately to his customers, to the exhibitors, or to theater managers. The service the theater manager will get, therefore, will be "hit or miss" of the film exchange stock of reels unless some influence is used by the manager to govern the classes of pictures furnished him. Film exchanges are notoriously lax in the matter of selecting pictures for particular theaters. If the film service is to be what the manager desires, the deliveries of the film exchange must be watched constantly and carefully.

The manager who has learned the tastes of his audience should consider their tastes as a requirement upon him to obtain the preferred classes of pictures from his film exchange. The responsiveness of the audience in the theater is one barometer of public approval; the attitude and conduct of patrons leaving the theater is another. The ticket sales will be another, but this last is not so quick in its indications of response.

When a picture pleases the audience, it may be the specific picture, or it may be the general class to which the picture belongs; in one neighborhood, dramatic and scenic may please more than comic or historical; in another nothing but comics can draw the crowds and send them away smiling.

The program

Whether vaudeville is advisable and profitable, and whether the song is a drawing card or whether the audience would rather have solid pictures, all may be learned from watching the house during the performance and watching the faces and comments of the patrons as they pass out after seeing the performance.

Choice of a program is a great factor where the theater is in a competitive position. There is but little difference in expense between a three-reel program and two reels and a song. [...]

Special programs

An entire program made up of films of some specific nature may be called a special program, and advertised accordingly. "Biograph Night" on which nothing but biograph reels are used, might strike the popular fancy of some neighborhood, while "Travel Night" on which the majority of films are scenic, might "make a hit" with another neighborhood.

School children. A special program of films particularly pleasing to children, and to some extent educational or travel, may be given in the afternoon after the close of school, and the result of the experiment noted. Special arrangements with the film exchange will be necessary, and a talk will be needed with the educational or travel films, otherwise they are usually too unfamiliar to the child mind and, therefore, dry and uninteresting.

Amateur night. As a part of one show of the evening, amateurs are invited to entertain the audience, with a time limit of five minutes each; after all have done their acts, each walks upon the stage; each patron in the audience has been requested to decide upon the prize-winning act, and when the selected amateur enters the patrons favoring him applaud. The amateur getting the greatest applause is awarded the advertised prize of the evening. "Amateur Night" is usually made a weekly event in theaters where it is introduced.

Contests. This is merely a specialized "amateur night" in which all acts are limited to the same nature, thereby placing the several acts in direct contest with each other.

Double price. A five-cent theater may run on Saturday night at a ten-cent admission fee. This not only increases the gross receipts for Saturday evening but acts as an advertising feature for the theater. A better show should be given, to justify the double price, in order that the patrons may not think the double price is being charged merely because the manager can get it on Saturday. The program, however, should not require double time, or there will be no gain by the double price. It may be slightly longer in time, and may have advertisable differences in quality if desired.

The live manager will find some excuse to make a special noise once in a while to get a few new patrons to come to his theater because of the special feature advertised. [...]

Side lines for profit

The patron has a sentiment against any form of advertising *in the theater*. For the theater in a competitive position, it is a good plan to avoid all semblance of advertising inside the theater – upon the walls or upon the picture screen, either drop curtain or lantern slides. The tone of the theater is improved by leaving the show clean and free from advertising of any kind, particularly if the competing theaters offer objectionable advertising matter. At the same time, the big vaudeville houses of the cities use their advertising drop curtain before the performance and put advertising matter in their street scenes. Also, the legitimate theaters sell candy in the auditorium between the acts and before the performance begins. The manager must judge his people on these points and handle his advertising accordingly.

Following are a few plans available for increasing the revenue of a theater beyond ticket-window receipts:

Wall posters. This plan is borrowed from the street-car practice of assigning a wall space for advertising matter. The street-car practice is not objectionable, because the space is well chosen and advertising matter is confined strictly to the selected space. As to its application in any specific theater, the sentiment of the patrons must be judged. Many things will pass in a small country town which would not be endured by patrons in a city.

Advertising drop curtain. The picture screen is an unsightly object in the theater when there is no projected picture upon it. The appearance of the room is improved greatly during the intermission by lowering an ornamental drop curtain over the picture screen. This drop curtain may contain advertising matter. It should be well put on – at the expense of the advertising client – and a liberal price charged.

Advertising slides. Advertising slides bear advertising matter for the advertising patron, and such slides are thrown upon the screen along with the set of announcement slides with which the program begins, before the motion pictures start. A single advertising slide is hardly objectionable anywhere, but too many will ruin the show. [...]

Program advertising. This is a practice set by the large theaters. No theater program is complete without advertising matter upon it, and this can be obtained from local merchants at prices which will assist in paying the expense of printing the theater's program, or even yield a profit. [...]

Handbills. The weekly handbill is worth its cost in any city show. The cost may be reduced by carrying the advertisement of a local merchant, or two or three in different lines of business, for a price in excess of the added cost of the bills at the printer's. [...]

Candy kid. The practice of selling candy in theaters before and between acts is well established. Remember in this connection that the patrons come to the theater to be amused. The candy vendor can help much in their entertainment if his "act" is studied. One successful candy vendor waits only until the old crowd is out and then as soon as the new patrons start in he walks before the picture screen and says something like this: "I know, ladies and gentlemen, that you have come here tonight for a little fun, sport and amusement, and I am going to add to your fun just as much as I possibly can; I have tonight a package of —— candy which I am selling for five cents; as I pass up the aisle please have your change ready." He passes up the aisle with his basket as soon as the aisle is clear, selling candy and making remarks to entertain the crowd: "Don't be afraid to buy it; it's worth the money;" "The young man takes two packages because the young lady knows it's good;" "Every package guaranteed to send you home fat and happy;" "After you eat it, if you don't like it, give it back and I'll refund the nickel;" when the show starts before he has finished his trip, he says, "Keep your eyes on the pictures and hand me your money." Your people have come to your theater to be entertained; your candy vendor is making the intermission seem shorter and is positively adding to their entertainment. [...]

Slot machines. The lobby, or entrance of the theater in front of the partition, offers space for a few compact automatic vending machines, if, in the manager's best judgement, such a plan is advisable. If the police regulations of the town will permit, an automatic vending machine may stand on the sidewalk at each side of the theater, just in the foot square of sidewalk space at the end of the theater's side walls.

Sheet music sales. It is a favor to many patrons to advise them where sheet music of the song may be obtained. An announcement slide, "The song on our program is always for sale at our ticket window," has no objection and does not seem advertising matter because it pertains to the theater.

Refreshment annex. In the airdome, the refreshment business is so much associated with the motion-picture business, and they are so mutually helpful to each other that they usually are run in conjunction, each to boost the other. In the motion-picture winter theater, the relation cannot be so boldly emphasized or the departure from custom will be noted and adversely commented upon, but a candy store and soda fountain located near a motion-picture theater will do a larger business than if the theater were not there.

Types of Smaller Theatres With Overcrowded Lobby
Display.

Annotated photos of theater displays from James F. Hodges, *Owning and Operating a Motion
Picture Theatre* (1912)

6

Hints to Exhibitors (1908)

W. Stephen Bush

It is one of the cheerful facts in the moving picture business that within recent times the exhibitors are abler, better educated, more intelligent and experienced men than ever before. The great boom which followed in the wake of the novelty of the moving picture has passed away, the business rests on more solid foundations and the exhibitors, like water, have found their level. How much money has been sunk in electric theaters by the ill-judged enterprise of the incompetent it is hard to calculate, but I fear the aggregate amount runs into the hundreds of thousands. Even at this day the percentage of failures is large. In this business no man has success thrust upon him, he must achieve it by hard, steady work. The man who wants to make money out of amusing the public with moving pictures must, among other qualifications, possess tact, knowledge of the business, judgment, and he must understand the public in general and his own little public in particular. His personality must count for something with the patrons. He cannot leave the conduct of his business to others and expect to thrive. He is the head of affairs and for him there are few idle moments. Once he succeeds in convincing his employees that his supervising eye never sleeps, he has made a good start on the journey, whose goal is success. It will not be long before the patrons will have the same conviction, and with that conviction comes confidence in the place. [...]

It is not the noisy element that pays and makes the solid foundation of an electric theater's patronage. Take no picture that was made for this element alone. The rough and the vulgar are in the minority everywhere; and the moment you begin to cater to them you place yourself on the sliding board. The MOVING PICTURE WORLD will keep you posted in this respect and will do its very best to kill off vulgarity, cheapness and garbage generally. Next to vulgarity avoid anything that is at all suggestive, and if you are in doubt resolve the doubt adversely to the picture in question. The Pathes were at one time open to objection on that score, but they certainly have reformed and taken a new tack. Everything they have turned out recently has been absolutely clean.

I state with pleasure that all exhibitors realize the importance of catering to women and children, without whom, indeed, the electric theater could not long exist. Special matinees for women and children, which really do show special features, are as a rule paying arrangements. The fairy tales of Pathe's, the children's stories of Edison and Essanay, are rich in materials for such a programme.

The Effect of Music

No picture was ever made that could not be improved by music and effects. This fact is

Excerpted from W. Stephen Bush, "Hints to Exhibitors." *Moving Picture World* 3 (October 24, 1908), 316–17.

being more generally recognized than ever before. I have been in theaters where the piano player helped the success of the pictures almost as much as the operator. There are many places where an occasional operatic will come in very prettily and effectively. A good piano player is essential to the success of the progressive and successful electric theater. Do not idolize the illustrated song as if it were a fetish. It easily grows tiresome because of its monotony. Instead of allowing some cheap singer to inflict himself upon the audience night after night, do without any song for a week or two and then hire a really competent singer, one who possesses tried merit, art and talent, and give him a week. The illustrated song, I am sorry to say, has developed a breed of "singers" in the cheaper theaters that in many cases calls for suppression by either the police or the board of health, or both. The "illustrated singers" need never fear the coming of the wolf to their doors. All they have to do is to sing one verse and the wolf will make hasty tracks back to the forest.

Value of the Lecture and Effects

There are films, some of the very best, that should not be put on without a lecture. If for any reason you cannot secure a trained lecturer, take an encyclopedia, look the subject up, write out a short story of the thing, get a man who can read English, and whose voice can plainly be heard, and then before you start the picture give the people an inkling of what it is about. No matter how poor the effort, it is better than no effort at all, and your patrons will appreciate the explanation.

In the matter of effects too great care cannot be taken. A good effect will go well with any audience; a bad one is likely to create a demand for the "hook." The imitation behind the screen of the murmur of a mob growing by degrees into a roar is a splendid effect, but it is a very difficult undertaking, and in the process of rehearsal a good stage manager would be too frequently tempted to do bodily violence to the "supers" composing the mob. I have seen productions of Julius Caesar, where the mob around the rostrum was as interesting as anything Mark Antony said or did. A touch of that great art would help such and similar scenes very much. Attempt no effects that have not been thoroughly rehearsed. In the famous dagger scene in "Macbeth" (I am speaking of the Vitagraph film) a grand effect can be introduced at the end by having someone strike upon the bell three times – the signal by Lady Macbeth to her husband to go and murder Duncan. I lectured on the picture one night in a theater not a thousand miles from Philadelphia. The young man who had charge of effects was enthusiastic and determined, but a fine perception of dramatic possibilities was not among his strong points. I gave him the cue. "Remember," I said, "three strokes upon the bell." The fatal moment came. The audience was spellbound and listened intently for the "stern alarum." The bell rang – it rang loud and hard and long – it might have called Macbeth to his supper, but never to midnight murder. All effects that work well and are skilfully prepared will delight, all others will disgust.

7

Handling the Visitor (1909)

Moving Picture World

The first impressions are the most durable. When we enter a moving picture house the impression formed on our minds at the threshold of the theater is the one that lasts. If we meet a polite and courteous usher, who shows us to our seats, we are disposed *ab initio* to take a favorable view of the entertainment. If there is not too much light in the auditorium but just light enough to enable us to distinguish surrounding objects and persons, then we are disposed to compliment the management upon its adroitness in striking the happy mean between darkness and light. For the proper lighting of a moving picture house is a problem of adjustment. You do not want total darkness; you do not want too much light. You want just enough to be able to see your way about without impairing the brilliancy of the picture.

Sometimes you are allowed to find your seat as best you may; then you run the risk of treading upon a man's corns or a lady's dress, and then are proportionately cursed. As a rule, however, it is to the credit of moving picture theater owners that they have courteous ushers and attendants. The more vigorous these latter are in excluding undesirable visitors, the better for the reputation of the house. We have more than once had to complain of the presence of people under the influence of strong waters or who go to sleep and snore, thus disturbing the enjoyment of their fellow visitors. But moving picture theaters are rising so much in popular esteem that this sort of thing is rapidly becoming a feature of the past. Many picture theater exhibitors are vying with each other in the proper care of their audiences.

Too much attention cannot be given to the cleanliness of the house; to its proper ventilation, and, then to the preservation of quiet and order amongst the audience. Again the sale of candies, with the noisy vocal accompaniments of the vendors is, we think, generally to be deprecated. Many high class moving picture theater exhibitors refuse to do this on the ground that the better kind of visitor is excluded by these cheap jack methods. Others again have objected to the lantern slide advertisements of candies which are put on the screen. Personally, we object to this sort of thing, as we think it tends to lower the dignity of a moving picture theater.

The eternal feminine hat is always a source of much irritation to mere man. It is difficult to see how the admonition to the fair creatures to remove their hats can be dispensed with, for in this regard the average woman is quite a savage person. It is a matter of pure indifference to her as to how much inconvenience the person sitting behind her may be put to by the wearing of her hat. She bought it to wear; to be looked at; to be admired and envied on all and any occasion, and if she has to remove it "hell hath no fury like a woman" deprived of her pet hat.

Excerpted from "Handling the Visitor." *Moving Picture World* 5 (October 9, 1909), 482–3.

We have sat behind rows of these things in a church, as well as in a moving picture theater, and our profanity has been too deep for vocal expression. Clergymen anathematize them; caricaturists make fun of them; men curse and criticise them. So what are we to do, except suggest that wherever possible before a woman enters a moving picture theater she must be made to understand that she must remove her hat. He will be a brave moving picture exhibitor who always successfully does this.

On general principles, therefore, we put it that the less advertising matter there is thrown on the screen, the less an audience is made to feel that the object of a moving picture theater exhibitor in getting them into his house is to extract something more than the admission money from them, the more likely that house will find public favor and continuous support. It is annoying, to say the least of it, to an average person of refinement to have a considerable part of his time taken up in reading announcement slides about ladies' hats, candies and the like. What we are insisting upon is the exclusion as far as possible of the mere huckstering element of a moving picture entertainment, and the mak-

ing for everything possible in the way of orderliness, neatness, good sanitation, plenty of light, but not too much of it, courtesy on the part of the ushers and in short the general atmosphere of comfort, if not luxury, which the public at large always looks for in a place of entertainment and pleasure.

There is one little convenience which we think the public would always appreciate, and we are surprised that it is not taken up, namely the circulation amongst the audience of synopses of the stories of the films shown. Of course, these things could not be read in a dark house, but there is no reason why even in a continuous performance there should not be brief intermissions when the programme, if such we may call it, could be read by the audience. Some moving picture houses we know supply programmes, but none that we are aware of print anything about the stories of the films. This is a point we commend to the enterprising moving picture exhibitor. Anything which makes for the comfort of an audience is bound to result in a continuous patronage and the building of the family support which is one of the surest roads to success in conducting places of public entertainment.

8

Posteritis (1910)

F.H. Richardson

Here in New York City a new and startling disease has sprung up. Applying a descriptive name to it seems something of a task since one will insist it should be "Color-Madoritis," another will suggest "Poster Bug," while a third will insist that just plain "Damphool" best describes the malady.

The writer, however, is inclined to think that "Posteretis" [*sic*] fills the bill better than anything else as a descriptive term to be applied to the new, strange affliction that is rapidly fastening its fangs on New York City moving picture theater managers.

It must be admitted that one or two neatly printed, framed posters adds to the attractiveness of the average theater front, besides giving the prospective patron an idea of what particular brand of joy awaits on the inside. It does not follow, however, that because one or two posters look well, half a dozen or more are going to thrill the passing throng with admiration or cause them to be bitten by the Buy-a-ticketus bug. Nay, nay, Pauline! Not so! On the contrary, a front plastered over with posters – posters on the walls, on the ticket office, on easels and on a line extending across the front, presents almost anything else than a pleasing, attractive appearance.

In the amusement world the great spread or [*sic*] banners almost invariably proclaims the sideshow – the fake. At any rate such a display immediately predisposes the average man or woman to look askance and wonder when he or she buys a ticket whether or no they will, later on, have cause to remark sotto voce to themselves, "stung!"

The writer has heretofore pointed out in these columns the fact that it is the quietly rich, dignified front that predisposes the passer-by to enter; not the garish, poster-plastered, cheap-looking, tawdry get-up, supplemented by a shrill phonograph or leather-lunged barker. If the show is really good the regular patrons will very soon discover the fact and the casual passer-by will enter more readily if the front be decorated in a quietly rich way, than if it be plastered with cheap looking posters in all the colors of the rainbow.

The writer has, here in New York City, on Fourteenth Street not far from Broadway, counted sixteen posters on one front at one time. Nor was this all, since, in one instance at least, but three of the posters really had any connection with the films that made up the programme. The rest of this marvelous color display was a lie! Time, time and again have I passed fronts carrying five, six and eight posters, some on the walls, some on a line strung across the front and others on easels. How awful it looked! Whether the show inside was a fake or not the front said it was plainly enough! Had these posters been well and neatly framed, under glass, the effect would not have been so bad, though even then it is doubtful if more than two posters

Excerpted from F.H. Richardson, "Posteritis." *Moving Picture World* 6 (1910), 987.

can be used to advantage on any storeroom theater front or more than four on a front of larger size. Nor is there need for multiplication since four will usually cover the show pretty well. Be that as it may, the displaying of posters of subjects not being shown, unless plainly labeled as a future programme, is a rank swindle. Petty tricks of this kind will injure the business of any house in course of time and not only will it hurt the individual house but it will injure the business as a whole.

9

Swelling the Box Office Receipts (1911)

George Rockhill Craw

While, as pointed out last week, the welfare and comfort of the audiences are important elements in the building of the box office business of a theater, still the most scrupulous regard for these two important essentials will not make a theater popular unless it furnishes a first-class entertainment.

Indeed, the program's power to please is the most direct factor in the popularity of a playhouse, although welfare and comfort facilities are no less important because of their more indirect bearing.

But, with the audience, "the play's the thing." If it is good, they come again and tell others of its merit. If it is poor, they stay away, and go to the rival house. [...]

Guarding Against Rivalry and Loss

"Rough house" films that will please the audience of a theater located in a neighborhood made up of the laboring classes will not gain favor in a house situated in a high-grade residential district, but it is surprising how well the films that please in the exclusive neighborhood are received by the lower classes. I refer to high-class subjects, such as classic romantic dramas, travel subjects, etc. Theater owners will do well to cultivate the taste of their audiences by gradually increasing the number of high-class film subjects, thus cutting down the demand for slap-stick comedy and cheap melodrama.

Besides the ethical side of cultivating the taste of the people, there is a box-office reason for so doing. Suppose a theater, located in a neighborhood of the "hoi-polloi," has a very profitable business. We will say it runs the slap-stick comedy and the cheap melodrama. Because there is no other playhouse in the neighborhood, the audience, which is easily entertained, accepts the show and is faithful in its patronage.

The management, content to let well enough alone, makes no effort to ascertain whether higher-class films would not please better. All goes well until another theater opens as a rival. Its owner, believing the neighborhood would appreciate high-class film subjects, puts on a choice program. Its business grows, but the other theater holds its own with its lower quality of films. It is evident the people of the neighborhood are attending both shows – doubling the amount of money they formerly spent for moving pictures.

But gradually the lower grade begins to lose business, and then, suddenly, it realizes that its former prestige is gone, that it has lost its patronage to the higher grade house, and as its managers are probably not resourceful, they sell out, knowing that it is the most

Excerpted from George Rockhill Craw, "Swelling the Box Office Receipts." *Moving Picture World* 8 (May 13, 1911), 1059–60.

difficult and expensive thing in the world to regain the patronage of a house that has "gone dead."

Box Office Insurance

The taste of an audience improves as the days go by. If the losing theater's management had itself cultivated this taste by running the better-class films occasionally, trying them out on its audience, and ascertaining the effect, it would have built up the quality of its own show and the taste of its audience, leaving no demand for another theater, and holding its own in the face of any competitive house that might have been established in its neighborhood.

Indeed, proper film selection amounts almost to box office insurance. It is the best protection against competition and loss.

One bright theater owner, who keeps a watchful finger ever upon the pulse of his audience, has slips of paper passed about, once each week, before the beginning of the program. He announces that it is his desire to show the kind of films that his audience likes best; therefore he has had the slips of paper passed around so that the members of the audiences may write down the films they like best, and the ones they dislike, giving their reasons briefly.

As the audience passes out, the slips of paper are dropped into boxes held by the ushers. The owner then tabulates the result, which shows the most popular film of the performance, the next popular, and the least popular. At the end of a month, he has a pretty accurate knowledge of the class of films his audience likes best, and is able to please all his patrons in the selection of his films. [...]

Box Office "Pays the Piper"

And now we come to that much discussed subject, the music of the film theater. That it has a most important part in the building or killing of business is obvious. We are all familiar with that particular brand of cacophony, which Mr. Harrison has so patly and humorously labeled "Jackass Music." Not only does the term suggest the bray of an ass, but its brains as well.

However, perhaps the term is a little harsh and undeserved by many of the embryo musicians to whom it is applied, as they are probably doing the best they can to earn the pittance that must reward such meagre talent. Rather, I should say, are the managers to blame for permitting such horrisonous orchestras to drive away trade, and if it came to a contest as to length of ears, it would be difficult to determine who should win, the dissonant musicians or their employers.

The orchestra is the voice of the picture. Rather have one good pianist than a full orchestra of poor players.

A beautiful picture accompanied by "Jackass Music" is as shocking as a lovely girl with a boiler maker's voice. There are many photo-play orchestras that are made up of fair musicians, but who lack the guiding mind to play a picture understandingly. All musicians have not the dramatic ability that must always guide in the proper selection of music for photo-plays, and the proper way to play it. A little coaching is all that is needed to greatly improve most of the film theater musicians of the country who really understand their instruments and their music, but who lack the knowledge of its proper application to photo-plays. Theater managers everywhere are giving more and more attention to their music, realizing that it is the box office that "pays the piper," and in more senses than one.

Illustrated Songs and Vaudeville

The formative stage through which the film theaters are passing will probably make the illustrated song an institution and will eventually discard cheap vaudeville. The two forces working to accomp[l]ish this are economy and taste. The half-baked "actors" who smirk and wiggle and clog-prance about the stage are an expensive proposition, partly because of the number of them required for a vaudeville program, and partly because they do not build up a substantial, desirable business from the box office standpoint.

However, there are in every town and city many young people who sing well and who are not averse to earning money in refined film theaters. In fact, many who have marked talent are paying for a musical education in this way.

The tendency of the song slide manufacturers is toward improvement, both in the selection of the songs and in the illustration of them. The bright dashes of color in these slides furnish a pleasing contrast to the monochromatic picture plays, and the softer vocal music of the song relieves the orchestral stress of the accompaniments played to the motion pictures.

Coon shouting should be tabooed in theaters wishing to build up a refined, substantial patronage, but there is nothing more effective than a good, clean comic song, of which we have only too few to which colored slides have been set. Pretty colored slides and a sweet melody will carry through a sentimental song, the words of which may be absolutely inane in their "mushiness."

The same careful study and good judgement necessary in the selection of picture play films should be exercised in the choosing of illustrated songs, while every effort should be made to obtain singers with good voices and who have enough vocal technique to know how to use them. There are plenty of good singers to be had if the theater management will seek them intelligently and unceasingly, until it gains the proper quality for its vocal requirements. It should be remembered that the soloist is an important factor in building up box office receipts.

10

The Murder of Othello (1911)

H.F. Hoffman

[...] The public have a right to expect good operating, instead of a lot of breaks and stops and flickers and ghosts and burning reels, and when these things happen it is up to the men who gather news to say something about it.

Now then, having brushed away opposition from all sources, let us proceed with the Murder of Othello. He was murdered by an operator last Friday night. They took him out of his tin armour and placed him on the operating table in the operating room. They made a diagnosis, gave him an anasthetic, then put him through a sausage machine and when the poor fellow came out of the other end he was mangled beyond recognition.

I had been talking just before with the manager. He said, "Yes, I take the Moving Picture World. A manager should not be without it because it is so full of valuable advice. Have you noticed our solid brick operating room?" I then took notice. The place was an airdome seating at least 1,500, with loads of room to spare. Behind the rear seats was a promenade fifty feet wide, and there at the end of the middle aisle stood the solid brick oven on four legs. It covered an area about six feet square or 36 square feet. He could have built a two-story residence there without interfering with anyone's view, and yet he who took the World for its helpful hints had con[s]tructed this 6 × 6 oven and called it an operating room. [...]

The Othello picture began with the usual chorus – "What's the name of this?" "I wonder what this is." "Mamma, who's that man?" "Did you get the name?" "I beg pardon, sir, did you notice the title of this?" "I wish I knew what this is all about." "What is it?" "I don't know, looks like something from the Bible." "What did it say?" "Excuse me, was there any name to this?" "No, I didn't see any," etc. Now in the name of just plain common sense, I am going to ask why this thing is done, day after day, in so many places. Is it possible that a man can have the nerve to call himself a manager or an operator, and still show such indifference to the one thing of all that brings the people to the place – the picture?

I would like to have a photograph of the mind of such a man to see by what mental process he concludes that the audience knows what it is looking at. After the first offense, if that party were in my employ, he would last about as long as a June frost. All this talk about reels coming from the exchange without titles is a lazy man's excuse. Cover glass is cheap and title slides can be written in half a minute. Fancy lettering is not necessary and takes up too much time. There is nothing in a temporary slide that looks any better than good plain handwriting, especially if the slide is tinted and the principal words are properly capitalized and underscored. Try it and you will find it better

Excerpted from H.F. Hoffman, "The Murder of *Othello*." *Moving Picture World* 9 (1911), 110.

than most of these horrible hand-printed affairs.

The big laugh in Othello came with the first scene when the title and sub-titles came through reading backwards. It was the same laugh you hear when a song slide gets in upside down. But the fun didn't end there. Instead of clipping his film at once and reversing the upper reel, the operator let the whole thing go through the way it was. We are all aware that Othello is not the easiest subject in the world to follow, even under the best of circumstances. The title and all the sub-titles are extremely necessary, even to those who know it, and a good lecture should go with it for those who do not. Imagine the audience then, for the most part in utter ignorance of what they were looking at. The light was vile. The patrons had their choice of two things to look at. On the sheet the spectacle of a white woman smearing her love upon a colored man, or in the operating room, the operator who had attracted their attention.

It seems that in his dilemma he had hit upon the idea of hiding his mistake by speeding up his machine when the sub-titles appeared, so as to get them over with quickly. But the racket of it only made matters worse by drawing their attention to him. All thought of how the audience was enjoying the picture was far from his mind, but they were enjoying it just the same. They quickly saw that he was trying to pull the wool over their eyes so they began to watch for the sub-titles. When these appeared and he put on the high speed the audience would howl with delight. He was greeted with mock applause, laughter, cat calls and other noises. Nobody felt bad when Othello breathed his last. The program was short on comedy anyhow, and this filled the bill very nicely. On my part, for a long time to come, I will remember the murder of Othello.

11

Projection (1912)

F.H. Richardson

Projection is a term which, taken as a whole, involves much. To put perfect projection on the screen and maintain it thus requires ability of high order, as well as constant vigilance and some degree of artistic sense. In the first place the light must be distributed over the sheet with perfect evenness, so that there is no shadow, other than that of the photography itself, and no discoloration except that caused by some fault in the film.

To be able to determine accurately, at a glance, whether a faint shadow, or discoloration of the light, is due to the light itself, or to some fault in the film, requires close study and considerable experience. The operator should observe and compare closely. He must study his projection. He must never arrive at the point where he imagines there is nothing more in this connection for him to learn. The high-class operator who produces high-class results can seldom tell you, except in a very general way, what a film portrays, even after he has run it several times. He has his whole attention taken up in constantly watching for faults in the light and in gauging the matter of speed. [...]

Speed at Which the Film Is Run is a matter deserving of the closest study and attention on the part of the operator. In this is involved one of the finer points of projection. It is this which lifts the real operator out of the class of the ordinary mechanic and

makes of him something of an artist. Lack of preception in this matter, or lack of attention to it, stamps the ordinary operator as ordinary, and advertises the fact to the world at large. It lies in the power of the operator to govern absolutely the speed of all moving things on the screen. He cannot change the actor's gesture, or movement, but he can vastly alter its speed, merely by altering the speed of his machine.

The actor may, in fact, bring his fist down on a table as a clincher to an argument, slowly. Run at ordinary speed the fist would come down exactly as the actor's fist did come down. But the actor may have misjudged the action and the operator has it in his power to bring that fist down at the speed to look best and correspond best with the other movements of the subject at that point. He can bring it down with apparently table-splitting force or he can slow the movement until the blow is a gentle tap. In an automobile race he can speed up the machine until the cars seem almost to fly; also he can slow them down until the race is a howling farce. But when it comes to animal or human action he must study each subject closely. He must make the man, woman or animal, as the case may be, act naturally. If the speed is too great the movements are jerky and impossible; if too slow, the other extreme is reached and the figures appear to float along.

Excerpted from F.H. Richardson, "Projection." In *Motion Picture Handbook*, 2nd ed. (New York: Moving Picture World, 1912), 318–20.

The operator may not think the possible improvement is great enough to justify close attention to these details. All I can say of the man who takes this view is that he will never, never, in this world, make a high-class operator. It is true that in the ordinary dramatic film the possible improvement in action through speed regulation is not great. Usually the scene is well acted and the camera run at reasonably regular speed. It is nevertheless the fact, however, that there are very few films in which some improvement is not possible, and the man who persistently and consistently bends his entire energy to improving his projection in every possible way is bound to win out sooner or later. Such work cannot but be noticed. It may take time and it may be discouraging, but success will come, and with it, in some degree at least, reward.

In general, aside from the action of separate figures in various scenes, it may be said that as a rule solemn scenes will be improved if the machine turns slowly. Take, for instance, a death bed scene. It is solemn. The figures should move as slowly as is consistent with naturalness. Again, take the Pathe Passion Play; probably the Bible patriarchs in real life actually moved as fast as anyone else. They may have, upon occasion, even run. Nevertheless rapid action does not suit our preconceived notions of such things. I have often seen the Pathe Passion Play run at such enormous speed that the characters were jumping around the screen like a lot of school boys. Such an exhibition was disgusting to the audience and offensive to those of deeply religious inclination and who revere those characters.

Overspeeding the Machine is reprehensible in the extreme. This is an all too common fault and is attributable to managers of theaters who have no respect for the property intrusted to their care by the film exchange, and no adequate conception of the business of exhibiting motion pictures, or their duty to their patrons. [. . .]

Managers seek to excuse this practice on two grounds, viz: "There is a crowd waiting to get in and we must rush 'em through and get the money," and, "My patrons demand a certain number of pictures and I cannot run that number at the right speed and make a living." Neither of these excuses is good. The first one is no excuse at all. The manager making it simply admits his willingness to swindle the patrons who have already paid admission in order to get the money of those who are waiting. The second excuse is puerile, since it is the managers themselves who have educated their patrons to expect more than can be profitably supplied. Managers, instead of working together, have, in a senseless endeavor to best each other, increased their programmes beyond all reasonable limits. But, aside from this, I do not believe the audience exists that would not prefer to see three reels properly projected, than four or five run through at break-neck speed. Managers claim this is not the fact, but I flatly dispute them. The fact is that they are afraid to try the matter out, putting on first-class projection at proper speed.

But this is not all of the story of wrong. The manager who compels this running at high speed injures the film. The sprocket holes are strained and weakened. Every manager who receives that film thereafter must suffer from the work of the speed maniac. He has injured the show in perhaps fifty other houses that must use that film thereafter, and he has lessened the enjoyment of perhaps 75,000 people who will afterward see that film as a part of an exhibition they have paid money to see. Exchanges certainly ought to take drastic measures to put a stop to overspeeding, and overspeeding may be defined as anything less than 15 minutes for a 1,000-foot reel, or 13 minutes for a 900-foot reel.

12

The Regulation of Motion Picture Theaters (1912)

Boyd Fisher

Regulation of motion picture theaters by civic authority is necessary for three reasons. First, the danger from fire, or the danger from panic arising from the fear of fire, is very great. Second, the moral danger to children and young people is in some conditions very great. Third – a reason not wholly to be neglected – the intellectual dangers are often great.

The attendance at motion picture theaters – reaching toward seven million daily in the United States – is so large that where dangers beset the people in attendance, strict regulation is inevitable. Every city has to face the problem, and when officials begin to regulate, they may as well do it right from the start.

The danger from fire is the one most feared. It is so greatly feared that the danger from panic becomes actually the greatest danger. The lives that have been lost in motion picture theaters have been sacrificed to panic, usually from false alarms.

To guard against panic deaths, regulation must provide that all picture theaters shall be on the ground floor and that exits shall be large, shall open outwards, shall remain unlocked during performances, shall be accessible on at least two sides of the theater, shall lead into streets or into alley ways, and that they shall be plainly labeled with electric sign boxes operated upon an entirely separate circuit. The aisles must bear a specified ratio, as to width, to the size of the theater. No aisle should be less than three feet wide in the clear. The chairs should in every case be securely fastened to the floor, and no camp chairs or other obstructions should be allowed in the aisles.

The danger from fire, however, demands additional precautions. First, the theater should either be in a separate building or cut off from the rest of its building by absolutely fireproof, unpierced division walls. The walls and ceilings should be covered either with metal lath, metal, or plaster boards with joints covered with mortar. The ceiling of a basement under an auditorium should be absolutely fireproof. Fire apparatus should be in every case required ready for use, electric wiring must be scientifically correct. Finally, and most important, the motion picture machine must be enclosed in a fireproof booth, but no booth should be constructed wholly of iron. Booths must have vent flues leading to the open air. All openings in the booth must be fitted with shutters arranged to drop instantly in case of fire in the booth, and the door to the booth must be arranged to close by the action of gravity. Films must be kept in a metal box and must be rewound only in the booth.

All but the last of these provisions relate to the initial construction of a theater, and should be observed before a license is granted to operate the theater. The operator himself must also be licensed, and suffer the

Excerpted from Boyd Fisher, "The Regulation of Motion Picture Theaters." *American City* 7 (1912), 520–1.

revocation of license in case of failure to observe the rules of safety. This provision is the most important and potent one to guard against both panic and fire. The handling of inflammable films in close proximity to a kindled arc lamp requires constant watchfulness, and only by providing that the city itself may at any time take an operator's job away from him, can the municipality assure the same coöperation from him as from the manager. A whole code of rules, which need not be set down here, is necessary for the guidance of operators.

Provisions for Moral Safety

So much for panic and fire dangers. The chief provision for moral safety that has been adopted in most cities is the law requiring that no child under sixteen years of age may attend a picture theater without parent or guardian. This law is unwisely sweeping. It is systematically evaded because impossible of enforcement. A better provision is to permit children unaccompanied to attend theaters after school hours and up to seven or eight o'clock. This decreases evasion of the law, allowing the child an easy escape from its discomforts while getting him home before the dangerous hours.

The dangers from films themselves have practically passed. The work of the National Board of Censorship of Motion Pictures is increasingly effective, reinforced as it is by crystallized popular opinion and moral taste. The moral quality of motion pictures exhibited through the regular channels is vastly superior to that of any other form of popular entertainment. It is, on the whole, of great educational value, superior for children in this respect to the newspapers or even books when unaccompanied by teaching. In spite of these facts, however, occasional objectionable films get into the regular and irregular channels of film distribution and the municipal authorities must have power to shut them off absolutely. There need not be a continuously active censorship to see to this. This

should be a reserved power of the regularly constituted license authorities. Kansas City manages it admirably by giving the Welfare Board power to revoke licenses for showing objectionable films. The phrasing of the Kansas City law, however, is hypercritically drastic.

A provision for moral management that ought to be in every license law grants a license to a place and not to a manager. This puts it up to the property owner to see to it that the theater is morally conducted, because if a license be revoked for immoral management it cannot then be taken out by a relative or partner of the first license holder. This provision legislates against managers who allow their theaters to become demoralizing to the young, and it renders unnecessary provisions of undue stringency in other directions.

Two regulations that may be classed as partly moral, partly physical, deal with lighting and with ventilation. An indirect lighting system should be encouraged, and a sufficient lighting during performances should be required. Indirect lighting diminishes eye strain, and some light is necessary for moral safety. Ventilation should be regulated, but it need not be rigid. Adequate ventilation is secured by the introduction of only fifteen cubic feet of air per minute for each person in the audience, if it be kept in gentle motion by fans, and be kept at a temperature of 62 to 66 degrees Fahrenheit with a relative humidity of 50 to 75 degrees. Audiences should not be kept too hot, nor should they be allowed to sit in rooms where the air is too dry. Summer and winter the air should be kept in motion by fans and properly moistened.

Regulating Intellectual and Artistic Quality

The remaining provisions are important. They have to do with the indirect regulation of the intellectual and artistic quality of shows. First, the license fee should be not less than $100 and should be determined in any event so as to keep down the number of theaters, limiting them to more skillful management which will not need to resort to debasing and cheap expedients for profit. Second, vaudeville should be expressly barred from picture theaters. At the prices charged by distinctively motion picture theaters, vaudeville can not be profitably furnished unless it is either immoral and cheap or simply inferior and cheap. To rule it out of all except vaudeville theaters is to safeguard the moral and intellectual quality of picture theaters.

Finally, there should be no limitation of seating capacity in picture theaters unless it be to provide a minimum seating capacity. A small show is a cheap and unworthy show.

The sum of all wisdom in motion picture theater regulation, however, is the concentration of all regulative authority in one department, and that department the one which has power to grant and revoke licenses. Inspection by this plan can be thorough and expert, with no twilight zones of authority for theater managers to take refuge in.

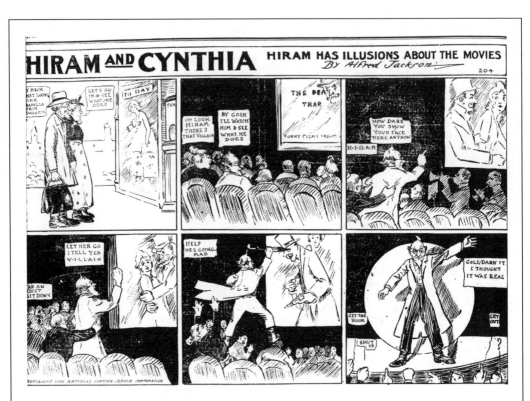

Alfred Jackson, "Hiram and Cynthia" (1916)

13

Architectural Treatment of the Moving Picture Theatre (1914)

Aymar Embury II

The growth of the moving picture business has been extraordinary and unprecedented, the daily exhibitions are attended by millions of people, and the business bears to-day every indication of being permanently established on an enormous scale. [...]

[...] [T]he business has grown to such vast proportions that a theatre in New York has been erected especially for moving pictures, with the second largest seating capacity in the city, and there is no public avenue in a town of any size at all in the United States which does not contain one or more buildings especially constructed for the showing of moving pictures and designed to some extent at least with an intelligent eye toward the requirements of the business. To recapitulate them briefly, they are safety first; ample exits and a fireproof booth for the film and machine; good bill-board space, and a design so expressive of the purposes of the building that signs are unnecessary. It is the last of these requirements which is most truly an architectural function, and which most interests me, because there has been no floundering around in search of an appropriate type, but almost all the designers seem to have reached independently about the same conclusion, which may be, and most usually is, extremely bad architecture, but can be, and occasionally is, very handsome indeed. The style is, of course, of a sort of Art Nouveau,

and there does seem to be pretty good logic back of the sentiment which expresses an invention recently unheard of in forms equally new.

Art Nouveau has by no means reached its final form; it is still more or less embryal and confused, although it really does seem to have something in it which is vital and of influence, even on our Classic architecture, although it will probably not be completely amalgamated with that historic style. I rather expect to find it flourishing as an independent style, much as the Classic and Gothic styles of to-day are being used, although in a subordinated position.

The material most commonly used in these moving picture theatres is also something, in a sense, new, and like the style is singularly well adapted to expressing the moving picture house. Terra cotta is, of course, the material in mind, and while it is perfectly true that the Greeks used terra cotta for small ornamental portions of their masonry structures, terra cotta as a means for facing whole buildings is (with a few exceptions) a modern development. Terra cotta is besides a very useful building material of sound structural value, and should be employed without disguise.

Unfortunately, terra cotta has been pushed too much as a substitute for stone where it should be promoted as a material worth using on its own merits, and curiously

Excerpted from Aymar Embury, "Architectural Treatment of the Moving Picture Theatre." Supplement to *The Brickbuilder* 23, no. 2 (February 1914), 37–9.

enough it is in these Art Nouveau moving picture theatres that the material has been treated with the greatest frankness. This probably arises from two reasons, the first being that the decoration in Art Nouveau is essentially plastic, and the second being that a very free use of color has been desired by the proprietors of these theatres to make them attractive to the public, and one can hardly imagine stone forms duplicated in colored ornament. A third possible reason is that both the material and the style are excellently adapted to the treatment of large, plain surfaces, and the fact that moving picture houses are dark inevitably results in façades without window openings and with large surfaces to be decorated. Buildings, then, for the movies are tremendously well adapted, both sentimentally and practically, to the use of terra cotta, and I think it is more or less creditable to the American architectural profession that they should have realized this far in advance of their European contemporaries. I have seen in England and France many amusing designs for the movies, but terra cotta was not used in any of them, and in consequence most of them looked like a cross between a small bank and a sublimated store. It is interesting, too, to find that this new type of building has been so well handled in principle at least, whatever we may think of the particular examples, since the other new type of building with which American architects have had to deal, the sky scraper, has not yet arrived at any definite conclusion. [...]

[...] The street architecture in our American cities is not monotonous, whatever else can be said of it, and perhaps we have been able to develop the style here, rather than importing motives ready made for this very reason, although we all of us realize that there is far too little attention paid in the design of our American buildings to those nearby, partly because we are individualistic, not to say selfish, and partly because our structures are so impermanent, and we therefore find it unnecessary to conform our architecture to that of a building which probably will not be in existence more than a few years. Therefore what would in a European city have been aggressive daubs of color in a monotone street, are here only a little gayer and a little more cheerful than the buildings with which they are surrounded, and very appropriately express their purposes.

Colored terra cotta is so easy to obtain, so little liable to deterioration in weather conditions, lends itself so readily to interesting forms, and is above all so inexpensive, that it has succeeded where stone or plaster would have failed; and while the vast majority of our moving picture theatres have been designed by incompetent architects, these men at least have found a scheme which is successful and delightful, and if the interest in the movies continues to grow and the receipts therefor continue to demand larger and better buildings, it will not be long before we will find the best of our architects, painters, and sculptors working in collaboration to design and to color façades of permanent artistic value, and I think also that we will find them deriving the motives for these buildings, not from Classic or from Gothic art, but from the current and colloquial architecture of the movies, designed not from above downward, but which has sprung up instinctively from the efforts of humble and unappreciated men. Architecture like this, which is in a way indigenous, is bound in the end to be the most satisfactory, since in it we find the nearest thing to a complete realization of needs, and not adaptations of motives designed to express purposes completely different, and the educational value of the moving picture theatre may prove to be as great to American architecture as the movies have been in broadening the people who see them.

★ ★ ★ ★ ★ ★ ★ ★ ★ ★ ★ ★ ★ ★

PART II

Palatial Palaces and
Everyday Practices:
1916–1930

★ ★ ★ ★ ★ ★ ★ ★ ★ ★ ★ ★ ★ ★

Introduction

Part II features material primarily concerned with the later silent era in American cinema, which saw the rise of both the picture palace and the vertically integrated motion picture company that owned theaters as well as had the capacity to produce and distribute films. Kathryn H. Fuller, in the selection reprinted here from her book, *At the Picture Show: Small-Town Audiences and the Creation of Movie Fan Culture*, charts the growth of the urban middle-class movie audience through the 'teens, and, specifically, the courting of this audience in Paramount's national advertising campaigns. The result, she argues, was a widening gap between urban and small-town theaters in the 1920s, exacerbated by the construction of increasingly elaborate picture palaces. This hierarchical stratification of exhibition sites put more and more of a premium on the grand, first-run, studio-owned, metropolitan theater. The effects of such stratification on the small-town exhibitor, the neighborhood theater audience, and the production studios register throughout the next 30 years of American film history, as we will see in a number of selections in Parts III and IV.

The view of and from the palace, as it were, is represented here by three selections from *Architectural Forum* (1925), including a statement from renowned showman Samuel L. ("Roxy") Rothafel, who would in 1927 open his self-styled "cathedral of the motion picture," the 6,214-seat Roxy Theatre. The accompanying pieces come from E.C.A. Bullock, who worked in the firm of Rapp and Rapp that designed opulent palaces like the Chicago Theatre, and influential architect John Eberson, responsible for "atmospheric" theaters, like the Capitol, which he describes in his article. All three commentators uncritically celebrate the picture palace, which is for them less a venue for moving pictures than a larger-than-life, transformative experience, suffused with high-cultural associations.

Once again, popular manuals offer a much different perspective on the industry. The selections from *Building Theatre Patronage* (1927) and *Motion Picture Theater Management* (1928) instruct the exhibitor in how to train his [sic] staff, maintain good public relations, and satisfy the "preferences" of his regular patrons. The goal is for the theater to remain or become an efficiently managed centerpiece of the community, visible and active. The image in these manuals of the movie theater as an autonomous small-business enterprise strikingly contrasts to Douglas Gomery's account of chain-store operating practices in "Fashioning an Exhibition Empire: Promotion, Publicity, and the Rise of Publix Theaters." Gomery relies primarily on the trade press (and on the in-house publication, *Publix Opinion*) for his sources. He focuses not on architecture and localized micro-management, but on the national promotional strategies that were so crucial for the success first of Balaban & Katz and then of the Publix chain of theaters. These readings raise basic questions about the autonomy, design, community role, and operating principles of the movie theater in the 1920s, apart from any consideration of just what appeared on screen or was performed live as part of the quite variable "balanced" program.

Three selections sample the contemporary discourse on the important role of musical performance in movie theaters, a discourse that in some ways replays the arguments for cultural uplift and the concerns about audience behavior that we saw in certain selections in Part I. Writing in *The Musician*, a monthly magazine for music teachers, K. Sherwood Boblitz complains about inept "movie playing," which is all the more condemnable, he insists, since the movies serve as many children's prime introduction to live music. George Beynon similarly calls for the continual "uplift" of "photoplay music" in his *Musical Presentation of Moving Pictures* (1920), a guidebook featuring detailed instructions for moving picture theater orchestras. John F. Barry and Epes W. Sargent, in contrast, advise the theater operator to keep the taste of his patrons in mind and forego any "high-brow" music. Of course, such debates would become something of a moot point with the coming of sound films only a few years later. The selection reprinted here from Warner Bros. president Harry M. Warner's presentation at Harvard University in 1927 gives some indication of the issues raised by the substitution of "canned" for live music.

The coming of sound did nothing to waylay other continuing anxieties, specifically concerning children at the movies, as detailed here by J.J. Phelan in his comprehensive 1919 survey of motion pictures in Toledo, Ohio. Orrin Cocks, speaking at the 1920 National Conference on Social Work, is more optimistic about the potentially beneficial role of local movie theaters. The sort of fears voiced by Phelan were reaffirmed more than a decade later in Henry James Foreman's *Our Movie Made Children* (1934), a "popular summary" of the findings of a group of academic social scientists (the Motion Picture Research Council) supported by the Payne Fund. The anxieties that run so deep in Foreman's sensationalized account of adolescent moviegoers in crowded tenement districts of New York City resonated deeply in America during the 1920s, as Richard deCordova shows in "Ethnography and Exhibition: The Child Audience, the Hays Office, and Saturday Matinees." This essay combines a critically sophisticated look at ethnography as a method for exploring film spectatorship with a well-documented account of specific attempts to use the Saturday matinee to manage (and constitute) the "child audience." In both respects deCordova opens up important lines of investigation, concerning, on the one hand, the discursive construction of movie audiences and, on the other, specialized exhibition occasions like the Saturday matinee.

Ahern, "The Crazy Quilt" (1912) and "Our Boarding House"

14

"You Can Have the Strand in Your Own Town": The Struggle between Urban and Small-Town Exhibition in the Picture Palace Era

Kathryn H. Fuller

"There are so few moving picture houses here [in Manhattan] which attract the most desirable classes," lamented a *Moving Picture World* editorial writer in 1911. "The proud and just boast of many Western and Southern exhibitors, that their patrons come in automobiles, is miles away from being realized in the city and county of New York." Film exhibitors in small towns and medium-sized cities in other sections of the country claimed that there was little comparison between New York City's Lower East Side "nickel dumps," which received all the bad publicity, and their own tidy theaters and respectable audiences. While such comments provided critics with excuses to vent their xenophobic prejudices, they did have a point. Most small-town exhibitors did attract a steady contingent of middle-class patrons along with workers and their families, whereas big-city nickelodeons were perceived to have almost no respectable patronage.[1]

The differences between rural and urban moviegoing expanded dramatically at the end of the nickelodeon period. Small-town exhibitors, social critics, and producer-distributors all thought that the rise of feature films and picture palaces drove a wedge between city and country moviegoing.

Such changes, though, could not be attributable to feature films, since the same films appeared in both locations; the picture palaces, however, made quite a difference. In the itinerant and nickelodeon eras, small-town and urban moviegoing experiences had coexisted peacefully (if sometimes grudgingly). Film exhibition had been a disorganized, independently owned and operated small-business field. At the close of the nickelodeon era, however, the maturing film industry built an interconnected system of production, distribution, and exhibition. Now structure and hierarchy entered the picture business, and the balance of equality between urban and small-town film exhibition shifted noticeably, and quickly. The film industry belatedly began to take note of the urban middle class's previous, guilty patronage of big-city nickelodeons and regular attendance at "small-time vaudeville" film programs. The industry only then began to discover the new, more upscale movie theaters and customers. The movie business began to invest in these theaters and to promote them to the public as the new ideal in film exhibition. As one moviegoing experience was promoted as the most desirable, the others inevitably became

Kathryn H. Fuller, "'You Can Have the Strand in Your Own Town.'" In *At the Picture Show: Small-Town Audiences and the Creation of Movie Fan Culture* (Washington, DC: Smithsonian Institution Press, 1996), 98–114, 219–21. Copyright © 1996, by the Smithsonian Institution. Used by permission of the publisher.

regarded by the public as inadequate or less preferred.

By the early 1920s, the public saw the small-town moviegoing experience as second-rate when compared with taking in a show at a big-city picture palace. Paramount's advertising propaganda fueled a perception that newer, larger, more elegant theaters naturally offered a better movie show. Certainly the picture palaces offered a richer sensory experience. In most cases, however, the films shown in palaces were still the same as those shown in the older, small-town movie theaters. New films were just shown at palaces sooner, with the organization of the "end-run" distribution system that favored the larger, urban "first-run" theaters. Picture palaces embroidered the moviegoing experience with many nonfilm elements, bedazzling their patrons with impressive stage shows, vaudeville acts, large orchestras, Wurlitzer organs, gloriously opulent decorations, corps of ushers, and all the amenities of theaters with two thousand to five thousand seats. Small-town nickelodeons with three hundred seats could not hope to match such a show, although a new generation of more upscale movie theaters and small-time vaudeville houses that would be the pride of their communities was being built in small towns and medium-sized cities. The small-town moviegoing experience still had a great deal to offer audiences, but big-city picture palaces got all the publicity and attention in the 1920s.

"People Who Do Not 'Need to Go' to the Picture Show": The Urban Middle Class

From the start of the nickelodeon era, New York City had served the film industry as a model of film exhibition and audience demographics. The rationale for this decision was simple; not only was New York the largest city in the nation, but it was the center of the amusement industry, and most film producers and the trade press were then headquar-tered in Manhattan or its boroughs. New York City's immigrant and working-class nickelodeon patrons monopolized what little attention the film industry had shown its audiences, even though the number of film exhibitors and moviegoers in the largest cities represented only about 25 percent of the national total. Nevertheless, to the film business, the urban segment was the most visible 25 percent of the audience, or the tail that wagged the dog. Like the theatrical and vaudeville worlds, the movie business considered the rest of the country a vast backwater that followed New York's lead.

Most film industry leaders were therefore inclined to pay little heed to the particular situations of exhibitors elsewhere. *Exhibitor's Trade Review* editor W. Stephen Bush, returning from a tour of southern theaters in 1917, chided his colleagues: "We in New York do not always appreciate conditions in the South. We are apt to forget that New York, interesting, picturesque and dominant as it is, after all is only a part of the United States. We fail to get the viewpoint of the 'man in the provinces.'"[2] While Bush's comments found few listeners in New York City, small-town movie theater owners heard him; they were all too cognizant of what one suburban Stamford, Connecticut, exhibitor derisively termed the film industry's "East Side Standard." He claimed the industry myopically geared film production to cater solely to the interests of New York's tenement-district nickelodeons. "The East Side exhibitor has had altogether too much to say in deciding what the public wants and what it does not want," complained the Stamford exhibitor. He charged that so many movie theaters were massed together in New York City's boroughs – 450 in one estimate – that they had become "the commercial factor" in film industry decision making. He reminded film producers that the New York film exchanges "supply many out-of-town customers who cater to an intelligent educated trade" in suburbs like his own town, in Rutherford, New Jersey, and even on 116th Street in Manhattan. And he blamed the lack of more suitable films for his middle-class viewers on "The East Side exhibitor [who] has placed the ban on educational or scenic stuff" and who wants only "blood and thunder melodrama."[3]

According to the film industry trade press in the nickelodeon era, the middle-class people of big cities like New York, Boston, Philadelphia, and Chicago stayed away from movie shows, leaving urban nickelodeons to working-class and immigrant audiences. Progressive Era muckraking journalist Mary Heaton Vorse, exposing the horrors of lower Manhattan's tenement district nickelodeons, addressed her urban middle-class readers as "people who do not 'need to go' to the picture show."[4]

Evidence, of course, shows that most of the urban middle class did not ignore motion pictures in the nickelodeon era. In the South, Midwest, and West, the urban middle class attended nickelodeons with enthusiasm. Even in the eastern cities, women on shopping trips and businessmen on their lunch hours were hesitatingly venturing into movie theaters. Cementing the attraction between the urban middle class and motion pictures was the fact that their children attended nickelodeons in droves. The urban middle class acquiesced to the seductions of consumer culture found in the movie theater, but often with guilty hesitation stemming from misgivings about the propriety of nickelodeon attendance and fears about movies' promotion of loosened standards of public morality and behavior.

For all the New York-based film trade press's supposed attention to New York's nickelodeons, the success of small-time vaudeville shows and the opening of elegant picture palaces in Manhattan in 1914 caused a great stir in the local newspapers and in the exhibitors' trade journals. "New Strand Opens; Biggest of Movies" announced the *New York Times*:

The Strand Theatre at Broadway and 47th Street, the largest and most elaborate moving picture house in New York, which is to be opened to the public this afternoon, threw open its doors last night to a great crowd of invited guests who inspected the theater top to bottom.... The seating capacity of the new theatre, which was originally intended to be a home for big musical productions at popular prices, is almost 3,500 and marks the rapid growth from the rebuilt store moving picture theaters.

S.L. "Roxy" Rothafel, soon to be the king of movie palace managers, was the first program director of the Strand. During the spring of 1914, it was also announced that Proctor's Fifth Avenue Theater would switch from vaudeville to movie shows and that the Metropolitan skating rink, on Broadway and Fifty-second Street, would be renovated into a "cinematograph playhouse with an expensive pipe organ and private boxes intended to attract society patrons"; it would show D.W. Griffith films and other "elaborate photoplays." On the other hand, in March 1914, theatrical impresario Oscar Hammerstein won an injunction (on appeal) to keep movies out of his Republic Theater. The court ruled that it was "an open question whether motion pictures were not a lower form of dramatic art than high class drama for which the theatre had been leased, and whether the presentation of a film play did not damage the theatre as a place of dramatic presentations."[5]

The New York press and the film industry reacted as if middle-class urban audiences appeared out of nowhere, fully fashioned, at the Strand, Rivoli, Rialto, and other pioneering picture palaces in Manhattan. The picture palaces offered New York City's middle-class audiences what Ben Hall has described as "an acre of seats in a garden of dreams." The palaces also offered middle-class New Yorkers the opportunity to "come out of the closet" and admit their movie patronage in a public manner, the way middle-class moviegoers in medium-sized cities and small towns had been doing all along.[6]

The widely perceived "suddenness" of the shift in the class composition of New York City's movie audiences was due in part to the trade press's shortsightedness. Russell

Merritt and Douglas Gomery have demonstrated that the already existing, steady patronage of urban middle-class moviegoers at city nickelodeons spurred film exhibitors' expansion into the larger and more elegant theaters. As a few observers at the time also noted, New York's pattern of film exhibition may have been an atypical case study for middle-class entertainment. Entrepreneurs in Denver, Milwaukee, and dozens of other sizable cities had been encouraged by excellent box-office receipts at local nickelodeons to build upscale motion picture theaters with one thousand or more seats. New York City, however, had a larger and more visible concentration of working-class nickelodeons for critics to disparage and a smaller supply of middle-class and mixed-class movie theaters than any other city in the country.[7]

Film historians have identified a variety of factors that caused the urban middle class to adopt the moviegoing habit in the mid-1910s, including the opening of elegant movie palaces; the establishment of higher ticket prices in palaces, which made their audiences more class exclusive; the release of spectacular and costlier feature-length films; and the emergence of movie stars with "respectable" images, such as Mary Pickford and Douglas Fairbanks. As Merritt, Gomery, and Robert Allen have argued, however, if some segments of the urban middle class had not attended big-city nickelodeons in steadily rising numbers from 1907 and 1908 on, film exhibitors would hardly have begun to finance and construct the second generation of larger and more opulent small-time vaudeville movie theaters and picture palaces in city commercial centers and middle-class residential neighborhoods.[8]

The urban middle class's attitude toward nickelodeons and moviegoing exposed its deep ambivalence toward commercial amusement and the encroaching consumer culture. Urban middle-class adults claimed to be chagrined when caught entering movie shows. Nevertheless, even big-city, middle-class audiences had been attracted to the educational, "uplifting" exhibitions of scenic,

religious, and industrial motion pictures held in more respectable settings like lecture halls and churches. Their continued interest in motion pictures inexorably drew them into film exhibitions in the cities' vaudeville theaters and nickelodeons.

Unlike the more constricted social world of the small town, the social milieu of the urban middle class provided plenty of class-specific entertainment and activities for enjoyment besides movies. Since the mid-nineteenth century, an increasingly wide range of amusements had become available to the middle class in urban areas such as New York City, from public parks and private clubs to restaurants, cabarets, Broadway shows, the symphony, the opera, and the spreading realm of department stores and other emporiums of consumer goods and luxuries. Middling-level amusement seekers in New York may have cared less for the city's movie theaters because there was so much else to do.[9]

In 1909, *Moving Picture World* published a series of articles for the prospective nickelodeon investor. In "Selecting a Theater Location," author F.H. Richardson clung to older, class-segregated ideas of popular entertainment, writing that "if the neighborhood is a very wealthy one, a nickel house will likely draw no considerable patronage except children, servants and transients." In Richardson's opinion, the urban middle class had not yet become "accustomed to purchasing their amusement" and would need to be "educated to do it." But as an afterthought he wrote that middle-class children could be counted on as steady movie patrons. Another *Moving Picture World* columnist in 1910 fumed in exasperation at the urban middle class's reticence at acknowledging its nickelodeon attendance, "not that educated people do not go to moving picture shows; they do, as we know by actual observation." He suggested that urban exhibitors should promote educational films to make middle-class adults "see that the picture is something more than a mere trick for entertaining young people."[10]

Michael Davis's 1911 survey of commercial recreation in New York City found that despite their spoken prejudices against going to the movies, middle-class New Yorkers were mixing with working-class audiences in the city's various entertainment venues. Davis estimated that nearly 40 percent of the vaudeville audience, 33 percent of the audience for small-time vaudeville (a combination of variety acts and films, a newer upscale form of movie show), and 25 percent of the nickelodeon audience in Manhattan were white-collar men and women.[11]

Perplexed by the extent of middle-class patronage he found at movies and vaudeville shows, Davis looked more closely at the amusement habits of urban middle-class children. He conducted a survey of middle- and working-class children attending public schools which showed that 62 percent of those children attended the movies once a week or more often. These findings he compared to a survey of fifty-nine upper-middle-class girls who attended "expensive private schools." Of these young women, he reported, forty-four, "or 74 percent, declared they never went to moving picture shows, 10 percent [six students] went 'rarely,' and half of the remainder [nine students] 'often.' The latter were mostly girls under 12, few of the older girls declaring attendance. All these children, however, went to high-priced theatres, the elder girls frequently."[12] Davis had found that middle-class boys and men outnumbered girls and women in movie shows in New York City by a two-to-one ratio. The status-conscious young women he interviewed might have been loath to admit to any interest in the "common" nickelodeon show, but they were quite proud of their many excursions to Broadway theaters, where the middle class constituted almost half the audience. The younger girls perhaps felt less protective of social standing and answered Davis's questions with more forthrightness.

If there were so many other amusements in which the urban middle class could partake, did they need the movies? Part of the answer lies in the fact that not all members of the middle class were equally entertained. Indeed, children were relatively under-amused, and nickelodeon theaters exploited this new constituency. Urban middle-class children had parks and school playgrounds in which to play, and toys and libraries and social clubs. But, compared with their parents, they did not enter the work force as early, endured more years of schooling, had larger amounts of after-school time on their hands, and were less burdened with chores in their "modern" households. Urban middle-class adults had an expanding realm of commercialized leisure to entertain them, including restaurants, department stores, theaters, cabarets, and vacation resorts, but these were not places for children. Middle-class youngsters, however, had increasing amounts of small change jangling in their pockets from allowances and gifts, and had a relatively crime-free social environment that permitted them the freedom to roam their urban and suburban neighborhoods unaccompanied. Urban middle-class children represented a wealthy new leisure market waiting to be tapped, and various retail concerns (candy stores, soda fountains, movie theaters) eagerly began to court these young consumers' business. Their movie attendance paved the way for their parents' acceptance of the movies.[13]

Meanwhile, New York City's middle-class families (especially if they were theatergoers) could not escape the frequent references to movies and nickelodeon theaters that surfaced in numerous Broadway musical comedies, reviews, and vaudeville skits. One example is the tune "The Cinematograph Man," from the popular 1909 Broadway review, *The Beauty Spot*. In this song and skit, a Park Avenue swell, feeling run-down and blue, goes to his doctor. The doctor recommends regular visits to the cinematograph (nickelodeon) to see the comedies. The man goes and is so affected by the jerkiness of the poorly projected films that he contracts a kind of St. Vitus's dance. In the song's chorus, the cinematograph man "flickers" across the stage. Irving Berlin contributed the number "At the Picture Show" to the 1912 production starring Eva Tanguay, *The Sun*

Dodgers, and dancing girls frenetically performed the jerky, syncopated "Moving Picture Glide" in the Winter Garden Theater's *Passing Show of 1914*. Tin Pan Alley lyricists and Broadway show producers often wove songs dealing with the latest American fads and foibles into their shows, and we can assume from the regular appearance of movie-related songs that middle- and upper-class Broadway audiences were familiar enough with the movies to appreciate the topical humor.[14]

Outside New York City in the other large urban centers, nickelodeons were not as removed from urban middle-class experience as social critics contended. In Boston, Baltimore, and Milwaukee, movie theaters were located at transportation hubs in the downtown commercial districts that straddled the borders of working-class and middle-class residential areas. These nickelodeons were located next to department stores, hotels, smaller shops – the commercial outlets that middle-class women and men frequented. Certainly, an intriguingly decorated nickelodeon, beckoning with posters, music, lights, and decorations to weary shoppers or businessmen on their lunch break, was a temptation they could not resist forever. As Russell Merritt has noted:

Without feature films and refined theaters, it is unlikely that middle-class audiences would have long remained. But the nickelodeon and its one-reelers had in fact performed the initial task generally credited to imported features, movie palaces, and the First World War. The seduction of the affluent occurred not in the cushioned seats of the Roxy, Strand or the Fox Palace, but on the wooden chairs of the Bijou Dream and Theater Comique.[15]

A columnist in the *Boston Journal* questioned her middle-class readers in 1908: "Have you contracted the moving picture show habit yet? Most of the folks I know have, though for some reason they one and all seem loath to acknowledge the fact. Per-

haps it is because it seems a childish pastime and not just the form of amusement one would expect worldly men and women to patronize to any extent." She warned that readers' friends and neighbors might be movie patrons, but "you will not know it unless by chance you happen to see him or her buying an admission at the window, or after groping your way to a seat in the dark find one or the other filling the chair at your side." While waiting outside a Boston nickelodeon to meet a female acquaintance who also sheepishly admitted to the movie habit, the reporter encountered all manner of bourgeoisie – local merchants, businessmen, the butcher, a banker, mothers with their children, department store clerks, a doctor, and three women resting from their shopping – on their way into the nickelodeon. "I was just about to give my friend up and venture in alone when another figure loomed before me which made me feel quite conscious," continued the reporter. "It was that of a woman friend of mine who seemed to shrink within herself when she saw me. She felt as I felt no doubt – like a child caught at the jam-pot." Alluding to the middle class's affinity for nonfiction films, the reporter claimed she especially enjoyed "fascinating views of foreign shores, of mirth-provoking happenings and of events in the news which form the basis of the entertainment."[16]

New York theater critic W.W. Winters also noted the guilty pleasures experienced by urban middle-class moviegoers. He described parties of adventure-seeking folk who went downtown "slumming" to city nickelodeons, rubbing elbows in the darkened halls with the working class, and at least for an hour or two, pushing aside ingrained class prejudices. "Somehow you all enter into the spirit of the thing. Armed with a few stray nickels, a bag of peanuts, a good supply of patience and good humor, and oh! what a time we did have!...Don't you slip away from yourself, lose your reticence, reserve, pride and a few other things?" Winters recounted the continuing struggle amusement-seeking urban middle-class people felt between desiring pleasure and exercising restraint. "Of course, it's understood that you had not only no idea of ever going in the 'cheap' places, but, when you were finally inveigled in, that you would go once, but never again. But what's the use? Why not submit gracefully and admit that the five-cent theaters have a place all their own and that, after all, you are going again."[17]

The Urban Picture Palace's Consequences for Small-Town Exhibition

The film industry in the 1910s, like other growing consumer-product manufacturers, began vertical integration of manufacturing and marketing, expanding from film production further into distribution and film exhibition. Film producers became much more interested in film audiences and began to pay more attention to the "new" genteel urban movie audiences. Now that the big-city middle class admitted to itself that, "after all, you are going again," entrepreneurs began to build more elegant movie theaters for it to attend. In the same way that consumer-product manufacturers strove to attract many different types of customers in a nationwide market to their limited number of brand products, the film industry now also wished to have all the diverse kinds of moviegoers act like a nationwide audience. But it was not to be a nationwide audience of equal viewers. The urban moviegoing experience was promoted as the industry standard, and small-town viewers, a "silent majority," were left to follow behind, frustrated and envious.[18]

The evolution of the film industry's attitudes toward its audience, which in turn influenced the image of moviegoers in the wider popular culture, came with film manufacturers' efforts to achieve vertical integration within their industry. Begun hesitantly by studios such as Lubin and Vitagraph, who exhibited their films in their own theaters

(Lubin's chain of theaters in Philadelphia and Baltimore, and the Vitagraph theater in Brooklyn), film producers' efforts to control the distribution and exhibition of their own movies finally began to be realized in 1914, with the growth of the Paramount–Famous Players–Lasky Corporation.

Adolph Zukor and other Paramount executives sensed that large profits could be made in exploiting the urban middle class's interest in motion pictures. The company promoted spectacular, feature-length film adaptations of stage plays starring prestigious Broadway stars. It invested in the construction of a huge, elegant movie palace in the Broadway district of New York, the Strand Theater, which would be dedicated exclusively to the exhibition of Famous Players–Lasky films. Paramount then conducted extensive, nationwide advertising campaigns in prominent newspapers and magazines, which were some of the earliest and most prominent film advertisements ever addressed primarily to moviegoers and not just to exhibitors.

In 1917, Paramount inaugurated an ambitious program of advertising in nationally distributed magazines like *Saturday Evening Post* and *Ladies' Home Journal* to promote the benefits of moviegoing to the middle class. The campaign theme was "You can have 'The Strand' in your own town." Paramount appealed to the aspirations of middle-class, small-town dwellers to run in the same social circles and to be as culturally "current" as their city cousins through the movie theater's agency:

Last time you were in New York you went to 47th Street and Broadway and joined the big crowd of good-looking, well-dressed people that passed through the gay entrance of the Strand.... You sat in the loge and looked over the great orchestra, the sweep of faces in the wide balcony, and then you watched the best motion pictures you had ever seen .... You wished that you could have such a theatre at home – one with pictures like those and a crowd like that. You have the

Strand in your own town if you have Paramount Pictures! You have the good plays and the good audience.[19]

The same Paramount films would transform any Main Street theater into Broadway, Paramount pledged, and change sleepy villages into "centers of metropolitan animation during the hours that used to yawn." There would be "[n]o more 9 o'clock towns, and no more 9 o'clock people!"[20]

While Paramount proudly proclaimed in its 1920 advertising that Strand Theaters in Manhattan and Middletown "both show the same pictures," the company systematically denigrated the small-town theater in favor of the more opulent picture palace (which, not coincidentally, Paramount was building or purchasing by the score) as the site of the ideal moviegoing experience:

> Whether you attend a million-dollar palace of the screen in the big city, or a tiny hall in a backwoods hamlet, you will find that it is always the best and most prosperous theatre in the community that is exhibiting Paramount Artcraft Pictures.... A theatre cannot be better than the pictures it shows. Good music, wide aisles, luxurious seating and fine presentation have all naturally followed as the appropriate setting for Paramount Artcraft Pictures.[21]

Paramount began to build or purchase movie palaces in other major cities, and other theater-chain entrepreneurs, such as Marcus Loew and William Fox, followed suit. Interested in attracting only a portion of the nation's movie audience, the urban middle class, they nevertheless shaped the popular ideal of the moviegoing experience for viewers across the country.

Although movie audiences in Strand Theaters in small towns and big cities alike may have seen the same Paramount films, certain basic inequalities existed. For instance, they did not view prints of equally pristine quality. Small-town exhibitors had complained throughout the nickelodeon era, to little avail, about the dismal state of the heavily used prints they received from distributors. One Philadelphia exchange manager tried to mollify disgruntled rural theater owners in 1907 by describing the brief life of the fragile one-reel film. He explained that the largest city theaters claimed such a film the first week for a sixty-dollar rental; but only three weeks later, badly worn, it became the only film tiny small-town nickelodeons could afford to rent, at fifteen or twenty dollars. Prematurely old, streaked, and scratched prints were derisively labeled "junk films." One industry critic scolded the small-town exhibitors who screened these cheap but inferior prints, writing that "the audience thinks it's watching a combination snow and rain storm." In 1919, a St. Petersburg, Florida, exhibitor blamed exchanges, complaining that his audiences liked the same films as city folks, yet because his small theater could afford to rent only sixty-day-old prints, his patrons saw nothing but scratched, chopped, patched, and unpleasant-to-view films. The film industry, of course, tried to downplay or minimize these complaints when it was to its profitable advantage. It wanted its relatively small stock of films to be seen by the largest possible number of people in the largest number of theaters. Small-town theaters remained the "end of the line" in distribution.[22]

It became the height of civic responsibility and pride for any town or medium-sized city with aspirations toward big-city status to have a picture palace. In the mid-1920s, Cooperstown got a five-hundred-seat mini-palace, the Smalley, courtesy of onetime Cook and Harris company rival William Smalley, who had become a theater magnate controlling more than twenty movie theaters in central New York state villages. The Palace Theater in Canton, Ohio, was built in 1926 as a monument to successful local druggist and patent-medicine manufacturer H.H. Ink. The Palace was an "atmospheric" theater, its auditorium decorated to look like a Spanish garden in the twilight, its ceiling painted a deep blue and set with tiny lightbulb "stars"

95

that twinkled on cue. It cost one million dollars to build and seated 1,900 people. Just two months later, the Loew's Corporation opened an equally opulent theater, which seated 2,175 people, just across the street. With seating capacity suddenly increased by nearly 50 percent to 9,700, Canton's twelve movie theaters faced stiff competition for patrons.[23]

While the picture palaces, as inheritors of the nickelodeon movie theater tradition, possessed elegant and attractive exteriors, their interiors and attention to audience comfort drew the most notice and comments from audiences and social critics. The picture palaces in many ways built on trends in the decoration of hotels, restaurants, stage theaters, and imposing public buildings like train stations, post offices, and libraries. The picture palace had many things in common especially with the department store, and recapitulated in the 1910s and 1920s the department store's evolution from the dry-goods emporium of the mid-nineteenth century to the fantastical palace of consumption. Like rival department store owners, managers of competing picture palaces vied to introduce more and more luxuries for their clientele – women's retiring lounges, men's smoking rooms, baby nurseries, smartly uniformed ushers, and luxurious furniture, carpeting, and wall hangings for all to admire.[24]

The differences between urban and rural moviegoing intensified with the construction of ever more fabulous picture palaces like the Capitol, State, and Roxy in New York City, the Uptown and Chicago Theaters in Chicago, and those in other big cities in the 1920s. The several hundred first-run urban theaters were owned or controlled by producer-distributors like Paramount–Famous Players–Lasky, Loew's-MGM, Fox, and Warner Brothers–First National. Although they represented only about 20 percent of the nation's twenty thousand movie theaters in the 1920s, these enormous, opulent theaters soon generated the majority of film producers' profits. Producers found that by maintaining the leading outlets, they could exert a

profitable, oligopolistic effect on the mass of independently owned theaters.[25]

The local Bijou on Main Street was increasingly an insufficient outlet for consumer-culture-driven fantasies; as one Iowa exhibitor reported, people in small towns wanted the standards of movie presentation found in the big cities. Even setting their sights higher did not help, for no matter how elegant the large town and small city's minipalaces strove to be, they were continually outclassed by the ever more huge and overblown big-city palaces.[26]

In some ways this increasing disparity would be mitigated by the growing popular culture of film, which was fostered by the fan magazines and by the promotion of movie stars and was available to urban and small-town moviegoers alike. However, the cosmopolitan attitudes promoted in the glamorous society films produced by Cecil B. DeMille and starring Gloria Swanson and Norma Talmadge also contributed to some small-town viewers' sense of dissatisfaction. Theater critic W.H. Bridge, surveying the impact of movies on small-town life in 1921, had noticed that this dissatisfaction had a definite generational dimension. "Undoubtedly the outstanding element in the life of the young in a small town is the movie," he wrote. "It is the big emotion, the adventure, the escape .... Home life itself is a dull interval between shows, and must be enriched with perusal of a movie magazine or a practical simulation of the current heroine, with the help of a beauty box."[27]

Robert and Helen Lynd found that both age and class played a role in the small-town movie doldrums. They reported that even as Muncie's youth crowded into its nine movie theaters in the mid-1920s, teenagers constantly complained about the lack of entertainment opportunities and escaped whenever possible by automobile to Indianapolis's ornate picture palaces. Middle-class teens outnumbered working-class young people in the Muncie movie audiences, as the latter seldom had enough money to attend regularly. The Lynds concluded their study with concern that the movies and their sensationalist advertising campaigns emphasizing sexual titillation and conspicuous consumption wore away at the bonds of family, community authority, and small-town tradition.[28]

Having the Strand in one's own hometown seemed a broken promise for some small-town moviegoers by the mid-1920s. For most movie patrons outside the big cities, the small-town theater was an accepted compromise between urban and rural, whereas for others the picture palace remained an unrealized dream. At least in Paramount magazine ads and in the pages of the fan magazines, moviegoers in rural areas, small towns, and big cities appeared to merge into a nationwide audience, and it suited the film industry's needs to perpetuate this impression. The earlier distinctive forms of vibrant itinerant exhibition and genteel, mixed-class nickelodeon moviegoing available in small towns was subsumed by the growing film industry into what seemed to some critics a diluted, meager version of the favored urban picture palace experience.

But if only one type of exhibition was most sought after, how did the small-town movie theaters endure and not simply go out of business? The answer lies in the creation of movie fan culture. The proliferation of movie fan magazines, the evolution of male and female movie fans, the cults of movie star worship, the spread of movie references to other parts of popular culture, even the linkage of movie stars to consumer culture through product endorsements – all worked to compensate small-town movie fans for any perceived deficiencies in their local experience. One nationwide mass of movie fans shared a common moviegoing culture, whose creation reinforced similarities between the tiniest, most run-down, small-town nickelodeons and the most sumptuous big-city picture palaces.

Despite being overwhelmed by the picture palaces, small-town movie theaters still continued to offer, within a familiar community setting, the considerable pleasures of fantasy-inflected Hollywood movies, mysterious film stars, and movie fan culture.

Notes

1 "Facts and Comments," *Moving Picture World* 10:5 (November 4, 1911), 356.

2 W. Stephen Bush, "Trade Review Editor Surveys Motion Picture Conditions in the South after Successful Tour of Several States," *Exhibitor's Trade Review* 1:18 (April 7, 1917), 1220.

3 "The East Side Standard," *Moving Picture World* 7:13 (September 24, 1910), 698. Important questions and new evidence on the composition of New York film audiences are presented in Ben Singer, "Manhattan Nickelodeons: New Data on Audiences and Exhibitors," *Cinema Journal* 3 (Spring 1995), 5–35.

4 Mary Heaton Vorse, "Some Picture Show Audiences," *Outlook* 98 (June 24, 1911), 442.

5 "New Strand Opens; Biggest of Movies," April 12, 1914; "'Society' Movie Playhouse," February 16, 1914; and "Hammerstein Wins Injunction," March 7, 1914 – all in *New York Times* and reprinted in Gene Brown (ed.), *New York Times Encyclopedia of Film*, vol. 1 (New York: Times Books, 1984), April 1914.

6 Ben M. Hall, *The Best Remaining Seats* (New York: Bramhall House, 1961; reprint, New York: DaCapo, 1988).

7 Russell Merritt, "Nickelodeon Theaters, 1905–1914: Building an Audience for the Movies," in *The American Film Industry*, ed. Tino Balio, rev. ed. (Madison: University of Wisconsin Press, 1985); Douglas Gomery, "Movie Audiences, Urban Geography, and the History of the American Film," *Velvet Light Trap* 19 (Spring 1982), 23–9.

8 Eileen Bowser, *The Transformation of Cinema, 1907–1915* (New York: Charles Scribner's Sons, 1990), 255–6; Lary May, *Screening Out the Past: The Birth of Mass Culture and the Motion Picture Industry* (New York: Oxford University Press, 1980); Robert Allen, *Vaudeville and Film, 1895–1915: A Study in Media Interaction* (New York: Arno Press, 1980).

9 On urban middle-class amusements in the early twentieth century, see Lewis Erenberg,

Steppin' Out: New York Nightlife and the Trans-formation of American Culture, 1890–1930 (Westport, Conn.: Greenwood Press, 1981); Lois Banner, *American Beauty* (New York: Knopf, 1983); Lawrence Levine, *Highbrow/Lowbrow: The Emergence of Cultural Hierarchy in America* (Cambridge, Mass.: Harvard University Press, 1988).

10 F.H. Richardson, "Plain Talks to Theatre Managers and Operators, Chapter 24: Selecting a Theater Location," *Moving Picture World* 5:20 (November 13, 1909), 676; "The Educated Classes and the Moving Picture," ibid., 6:14 (April 9, 1910), 545.

11 Michael M. Davis, *The Exploitation of Pleasure: A Study of Commercial Recreation in New York City* (New York: Russell Sage Foundation, 1911), 30, 35.

12 Ibid., 30, 35.

13 Erenberg, *Steppin' Out.*

14 "The Cinematograph Man," words by Joseph W. Herbert, music by Reginald de Koven, copyright 1909 by Joseph W. Stern and Company, New York; "At the Picture Show," words and music by Irving Berlin, copyright 1912 by Watson, Berlin, and Snyder, New York (from a musical review called *The Sun Dodgers*, words by E. Ray Goetz, starring Eva Tanguay, produced by Lew Fields); "The Moving Picture Glide," words by Harold R. Atteridge, music by Harry Carroll, copyright 1914 by Shapiro, Bernstein and Co., New York – all in box 699, DeVincent Sheet Music Collection, National Museum of American History, Smithsonian Institution, Washington, DC. *The Beauty Spot* was a hit, running 137 performances.

15 Gomery, "Movie Audiences, Urban Geography, and the History of American Film," 23–9; Russell Merritt, "Nickelodeon Theaters: Building an Audience for the Movies," *American Film Institute Reports* (May 1973), 4–8.

16 "Picture Shows Popular in the 'Hub,'" *Boston Journal*, n.d., reprinted in *Moving Picture World* 2:20 (May 16, 1908), 433.

17 W.W. Winters, "With the Picture Fans," *Nickelodeon* 4:5 (September 1, 1910), 123.

18 Gomery, "U.S. Film Exhibition: The Formation of a Big Business," in *The American Film Industry*, 219.

19 "Advertising for You," *Exhibitor's Trade Review* 2:13 (September 1, 1917), 64–5.

20 "There Are No More Nine O'Clock Towns," *Saturday Evening Post* (April 10, 1920), 37.

21 "And They Both Show the Same Pictures!," ibid. (September 20, 1919), 39.

22 Charles W. Kohl, "A Few Suggestions," *Moving Picture World* 1:38 (November 28, 1907), 610; Bertram Adler, "How to Run a Moving Picture Show," *Nickelodeon* 2:3 (September 1909), 85; Thornton Parker, "Florida Exhibitor Enters Protest vs. Exchange Method of Palming Off Worn-Out Films on Small Audiences 'Out in the Sticks,'" *Exhibitor's Trade Review* 5:8 (January 25, 1919), 638.

23 Edward T. Heald, "Movies, 1926–1957," in *The Stark County Story*, vol. 4 (Canton, Ohio: Stark County Historical Society, 1958), 506–8; James Ink, interview by Edward Heald, n.d., in Motion Pictures Files, Stark County Historical Society, Canton, Ohio. See also Marianne Triponi, "The New Ironwood Theater in Context: Movie Palace as Symbol," *Journal of American Culture* 13:4 (1990), 1–7.

24 Lary May and Stephen Lassonde, "Making the American Way: Moderne Theaters, Audiences, and the Film Industry, 1929–1945," *Prospects* 12 (1987), 89–124.

25 Gomery, "U.S. Film Exhibition: The Formation of a Big Business," in *The American Film Industry*, 220–1.

26 "Adams Circuit Owner Says Small-Town People Demand City Presentation Standard," *Exhibitor's Trade Review* 7:17 (March 27, 1920), 1894.

27 W.H. Bridge, "The 'Movie' and the Small Town," *Drama* 11 (July 1921), 363–4. On film themes of the 1920s, see Richard Koszarski, *An Evening's Entertainment: The Age of the Silent Feature Picture, 1915–1928* (New York: Charles Scribner's Sons, 1990); David Bordwell, Janet Staiger, and Kristin Thompson, *The Classical Hollywood Cinema: Film Style and Mode of Production to 1960* (New York: Columbia University Press, 1985); Mary P. Ryan, "The Projection of a New Womanhood: The Movie Moderns in the 1920s," in *Our American Sisters: Women in American Life and Thought*, ed. Jean Friedman and William G. Shade, 2nd ed. (Boston: Allyn and Bacon, 1976), 366–84.

28 Robert S. Lynd and Helen Merrill Lynd, *Middletown: A Study in Modern American Culture* (New York: Harcourt Brace, 1929), 263–9.

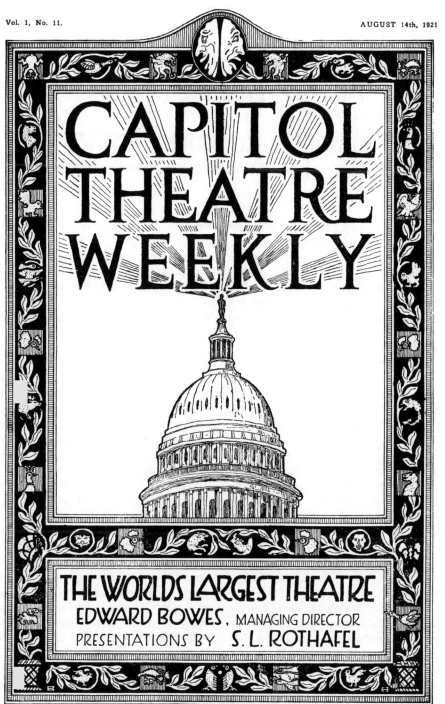

Vol. 1, No. 11.

AUGUST 14th, 1921

CAPITOL THEATRE WEEKLY

THE WORLDS LARGEST THEATRE
EDWARD BOWES, MANAGING DIRECTOR
PRESENTATIONS BY S. L. ROTHAFEL

Cover design by BERNARD HERZBRUN.

Cover of *Capitol Theatre Weekly* (August 14, 1921)

15

What the Public Wants in the Picture Theater (1925)

Samuel L. Rothafel ("Roxy")

People want primarily to feel that it is *their* theater. Their first contact with the house is by way of the cashier, the doorman, the house manager and the ushers who conduct them to their seats. One can readily realize, therefore, how important it is that this first impression convey all that the management desires in the way of courtesy and service. To this end the house staff should be under strict training, of almost a military character. The members should be drilled regularly, so that their movements and demeanor may be smart, snappy and precise. They should be taught the importance of personal cleanliness, so that their uniforms and general appearance at all times are immaculate. They should be given "institutional" talks which instill in them a sincere and wholesome interest in their work and a pride in the institution which cannot help but be reflected in the attitude that "the patron is always right."

One cannot over-emphasize the importance of "atmosphere." The Capitol Theater is fortunate in having an inspiring and beautiful interior, one which, on being entered, immediately fills patrons with interest and expectation. Fresh flowers are placed daily in the lobbies and promenades of the theater, on which one item alone are spent several thousand dollars a year. Superficially, this may seem like extravagance, but it is one of the ways in which we have helped to establish the atmosphere we desire to have in the theater. By creating this atmosphere, and making the patron feel that he is our special guest and that nothing for his comfort and convenience has been overlooked, we have won the first battle; after this everything is much easier.

I have said that the patron likes to feel that this is *his* theater. To that end we are guided in our advertising and showmanship by principles of sincerity and good faith. A policy of dignity, honesty and good taste, consistently adhered to, cannot help but reap its harvest in securing us the good will of our patrons. We are honest and sincere with them, and in return we shall have their confidence.

Behind the theater there should be an ideal, a living idea. Behind the programs there should likewise be an animate idea. It is that intangible something, that moving spirit, that makes the theater a living factor of local activities and a community center. One of the most amazing and awe-inspiring things I have ever felt is to be in the Capitol on a Sunday evening, when the house is crowded to the doors. Every seat in the orchestra and balcony is filled, with rows and rows of patient "standees" in the rear. And these thousands of people will listen, breathless, eager-eyed, and with all their senses focused on the stage, while the big

Excerpted from Samuel L. Rothafel, "What the Public Wants in the Picture Theater." *Architectural Forum* 42, no. 6 (June 1925), 361–4.

orchestra of 75 fills the house with the strains of an overture of Wagner. This is their program, conceived especially for them, somewhere close to the heart and yet not far from the mind. They love it and are proud of it and throng the house to hear it.

I should consider the success of any theater incomplete without the *esprit de corps* of the organization. There are over 350 persons connected with the active operation of the Capitol. The list includes people performing a wide variety of duties: members of the staff, heads of departments, artists, musicians, projectionists, electricians, property men, carpenters, painters, wardrobe women, engineers, managers, attendants, ushers, pages, cashiers, clerks, porters, cleaners and watchmen, while every individual from the highest to the lowest is inspired by the spirit of teamwork – the subordinating of personal prominence to the efficiency and welfare of the whole organization and to its upbuilding. [...]

We do not place ourselves on a lofty pedestal and from the exalted altitude of our position decide that the public wants this, that or the other thing. We make no attempt to "please the public," a phrase which is easily bandied about, for the simple reason that we do not presume to know what it is the public really does want. But we do know one thing. We try to keep faith with our public. We try to create a program based on the fundamentals of good taste, honesty and sincerity, and within the bounds of average intelligence. We have a critical standard of our own; we try, first of all, to please ourselves, and we are our own severest critics. The old-time showman, wearing a high silk hat and with a red carnation in his buttonhole, who placed his hand on his chest and shouted, "Give the public what it wants!" belongs to a long forgotten age.

I agree with the contention that "the picture is the thing." Of course the picture is important, and we could not do without it; but what we have tried to do is to build around it an atmospheric program that is colorful, entertaining and interesting. This type of program, with its ballets, musical presentations, stage settings and lighting effects, calculated to form a series of pictures sometimes contrasting and sometimes gracefully merging into one another, was originated by ourselves. It seems to please our patrons, and so we have no complaint to make.

Now as to the music. We have never advocated in this type of entertainment the presentation of operatic arias sung in foreign languages, which few enjoy and even fewer understand. We have tried to eliminate hokum and insincerities from our programs. By the same token we have refrained from presenting jazz numbers, which in themselves might be popular and successful, but which reviewed in the program in its entirety would be a jarring note in the harmonious effect of the whole. The music, in my opinion, should do more than merely accompany the picture. Its function is to *interpret* the action and character of the picture, to lift it up and carry it over the flat dimensions of the screen. It is interpretative music that supplies the body and foundation of the presentation. The music should not obtrude itself upon the patron. If it is interpretative in the full meaning of the word, it will become so integral a part of the picture that the lines of confluence will be hardly distinguishable, and such music we try to present.

The lighting, too, is most important. There is no miracle about it, no magic, although the gorgeous ensembles of color simulate the effect created by a magician's wand. Neither is it an indiscriminate or haphazard throwing together of colors, since behind each lighting effect there is an idea, consistently conceived and executed. Elemental passions and emotions have their counterparts in the primary colors – red, blue and green. They are the colors which best express the spirit of the Latin countries – Italy and Spain – and they are the colors which we use as the principal motifs in lighting such orchestral numbers as *Capriccio Italien* and *Capriccio Espagnol*. Russian music also deals with the elemental nature of the people. Tschaikowsky's music has its roots deep in the national spirit of the

Russian people; sorrow, suffering, privation, injustice are expressed by the use of primary colors. Pastels, on the other hand, represent the abstraction of the idealistic. In lighting an overture such as that of *Mignon*, we keep in mind the nature of the character portrayed, and the lighting should consistently describe that character. In lighting *La Boheme*, again, the important thing is the theme of the music – the gay, carefree atmosphere interpreted in terms of color, for both color and music aid interpretation.

It is my belief that the motion picture theater of tomorrow will aspire in its artistic endeavors to reach the standard of grand opera. We shall see theaters equipped and constructed along different lines, generally on one floor, and with stages of much greater proportions than those we now have. The decorative effects will be of a neutral character and free from ornamental properties or design. They will be created by light, thereby creating atmosphere appropriate for each individual production. Vast progress will be made in many ways.

Development of the present systems of lighting. I am convinced, will be the greatest stride made during the next few years. In this respect, too, the theater of tomorrow will be different. Projection of light from various parts of the house upon highly sensitized screens will be utilized to create effects. Color will play a most important part, and the control will be in the hands of a single operator, stationed somewhere in the orchestra, who will play upon a keyboard similar to that of the piano. By this means shades of color and intensities of light will be varied to suit the mood of the action. By combinations of the primary colors, pictures shown upon the screen will be suitably presented, while the music from a symphony orchestra, synchronizing with the acting, will aid in making a single impression upon the spectator.

PROGRAM

Week Commencing May 12th, 1918

1. **"LIGHT CAVALRY" OVERTURE**......Franz Suppe
   (Born 1820; died 1895)

   "Light Cavalry" is a two act opera by Suppe; libretto by Carl Costa. It was produced for the first time, March 21st, 1866, in Vienna, and proved to be very successful.

   STRAND SYMPHONY ORCHESTRA

   OSCAR SPIRESCU Conductors CARL EDOUARDE

   NOTE.—The above number will be rendered at the performances starting at 2, 4, 7.30 and 9.30 P. M.

2. **STRAND TOPICAL REVIEW**
   Selected and compiled by the Management as fast as modern equipment can deliver.

3. **SCENIC**
   The Management of the STRAND takes great pleasure in presenting the third of a series of OUTING-CHESTER travel-scenics, subjects of which have never been photographed before.

   "A MOUNTAINEERING MEMORY"

4. **VOCAL**
   (A) "THE STAR" ....Rogers
   (B) "WHEN YOU'RE AWAY" (From "THE ONLY GIRL") ....Herbert
   IRENE AUDREY, Soprano

   NOTE.—Miss Audrey will appear at the performances starting at 2, 7.30 and 9.30 P. M.

FRANZ SUPPE

PROGRAM

Continued

5. SCREEN CLASSICS, INC.
   presents
   MME. NAZIMOVA
   in
   "TOYS OF FATE"

   CAST

   AZAH ....MME. NAZIMOVA
   HAGAR ....CHARLES BRYANT
   Henry Livingston ....FRANK CURRIER
   Pharos, the gypsy chief ....IRVING CUMMINGS
   Greggo ....DODSON MITCHELL
   Bruce Griswold ....EDWARD J. CONNELLY
   Howard Belmont ....
   Blanche Griswold ....NOLA MAC

6. **VOCAL**
   (A) "GOD BE WITH THE BOYS TONIGHT" ....Sanderson
   (B) "THE ROSARY" ....E. Nevin
   HENRY MILLER, Bass

   NOTE.—Mr. Miller will appear at the performances starting at 2 and 7.30 P. M.

7. **COMEDY** FIRST NATIONAL EXCHANGE
   presents
   "HERE COMES THE GROOM"
   A Christie Comedy

   CURTAIN

8. **ORGAN SOLO**
   MARCH MILITAIRE ....Gounod
   RALPH H. BRIGHAM, Organist
   HERBERT SISSON, Organist
   Steinway Piano used exclusively.

   NEXT WEEK
   ADOLPH ZUKOR
   will present
   PAULINE FREDERICK
   in
   "RESURRECTION"
   From the famous story by Count Leo Tolstoy

Strand weekly program (May 12, 1918)

16

Theater Entrances and Lobbies (1925)

E.C.A. Bullock

The people of today's hurly-burly, commercialized world go to the theater to live an hour or two in the land of romance. So it is that the sophisticated playgoer must be taken up, on the architect's magic carpet, and set down suddenly in a celestial city of gorgeous stage settings, luxurious hangings and enchanting music. The atmosphere of a king's palace must prevail to stimulate the imagination of those who come within its doors. Yes, even before the patron enters the theater, the architect must stress first impressions through one of the most important architectural problems, – entrance and lobby appeal. The successful theater architect must master the psychology of the theater-goer. He must understand the patron's love of adventure and be able to excite his spirit of romance.

Giving first consideration to the entrance of a playhouse, an attractive theatrical appearance should be sought. An exterior design in which the curves of graceful arches predominate, but are not overdone, provides a pleasing contrast to the cold, straight and commercial lines of the usual surrounding buildings. The entrance motifs above and below the canopy, if there is one, should be made up of large and broad unobstructed openings, providing generous and alluring glimpses of the interior. With a flood of direct, indirect or outline lighting, to blaze the trail to the theater through many blocks, the entrance must be compelling, it must be inviting, and it must overshadow everything in its immediate neighborhood. It must actually be a magnet to draw the people on foot and in vehicles toward its doors.

Electric signs should be designed at the same time as the theater front, thus avoiding what has occurred in so many instances, – the obscuring entirely of a fine terra cotta front or stone exterior by huge and ugly electric signs. If it is necessary for the sake of advertising to cover the front of the building with a superabundance of signs to meet competition, the entrance should be so designed that it provides a simple background for the signs and not be a thing of beauty in itself to be covered and concealed. Sign makers, owners and architects should coöperate more closely to this end.

It is generally agreed that the box office should be placed at the center of the entrance, as near the street as is possible, and under no circumstances should it be necessary to pass through doors or by other obstructions before a ticket may be purchased.

This is the day of the unusual in theater design, and the new Paramount Theater on Times Square, New York, now under construction for the Famous Players–Lasky Corporation, contains several innovations which it is believed will arouse exceptional interest. The main entrance on Broadway will give

Excerpted from E.C.A. Bullock, "Theater Entrances and Lobbies." *Architectural Forum* 42, no. 6 (June 1925), 369–72.

into a grand lobby 200 feet long and 47 feet wide and rising five stories. Finished in imported marbles and bronze, the lobby will be similar in many ways to the foyer of the world famed Paris Opera House.

The Rialto Square at Joliet, Illinois, now under construction, has a fair example of the niche type of entrance made necessary by commercial and office building requirements. In place of the usual commodious lobby, the great recess or niche has been transformed into a veritable miniature and beautiful stage, which will possess immense drawing power. This is of course an unusual treatment.

Equally important to the success of the entrance is the design of the lobby. In reality the lobby must be a place of real interest, a place where the waiting throng may be transformed from the usual pushing, complaining mob into a throng of joyous and contented people. The walls and surfaces of the lobby should be as open in treatment as possible, permitting the theater-goer to get one vista after another, which will produce a decided spirit of adventure and a desire to gain admittance to the other parts of the house. In other words, the lobby should be so designed and so equipped that the fascination resulting from it will keep the patron's mind off the fact that he is waiting. It has a psychological importance.

The stairway should be genuinely enticing, a beckoning magnet and invitation to the upper levels. In the matter of lobby railings for segregating the patrons, it can be said that when the lobby is crowded they cannot be seen, and that when the lobby is not crowded they are not needed. The lobby should be spacious, providing comfortable standing room for the crowds on holidays, and also room for the audience inside to leave with ease.

Our better theaters have done much toward making the lobby appeal to the crowd. Fine paintings, impressive statuary, costly rugs and beautiful tapestries, used for decoration, have a marked effect on the waiting patron. A feature of both the Chicago and Tivoli Theaters in Chicago is the furniture, especially the rich gold grand pianos situated on the mezzanine promenades. The musicians in charge render light, airy selections which make the waiting minutes fly by quickly. [...]

17

A Description of the Capitol Theater, Chicago (1925)

John Eberson

Most of us can remember "way back when" in the history of the motion picture industry. We recall, more or less vividly, the type of buildings that housed a form of entertainment the provision of which in a comparatively short time has grown to form the seventh largest of the country's industries. One cannot but marvel at the progress that has been made, both in the production of pictures and in the creation of modern edifices for their presentation for the public's benefit.

A striking fact, however, is that in the architectural treatment of places of public amusement we have built along lines of pronounced similarity. This tendency toward sameness does not apply only to theater construction; we see it in modern office buildings, hotels, and other structures now rising. Accepted lines, styles and treatments are followed. The proportions of the project and its embellishments generally constitute its outstanding claim to what distinction it may possess. It is not surprising, therefore, that a theater entirely different from the traditional should be viewed with speculative interest. The Capitol Theater, Chicago, represented a new thought and a new idea in motion picture theater design. [...]

Since variety is the primary demand of an amusement-loving public, it is reasonable to assume that such variety will be appreciated in the place of entertainment as well as in the entertainment itself. The opening performance in one of our gorgeous picture palaces of gold, glitter, silk and satin, rich ornament and glaring decorations, is truly an inspiring sight; but it has been observed that the rapture of the audience is not particularly lasting. Surroundings soon become something akin to oppressive and embarrassing to the steady patron, and with the multitude of new theaters opening, differing from their predecessors only in point of decorative splendor and novel garnishment, it is apparent that the public mind has an idea of what may be expected.

With an appreciation of these facts in mind, the "atmospheric" type of theater suggested itself to the architect of the Capitol Theater. He visualized a magnificent amphitheater set in an Italian garden; in a Persian court; in a Spanish *patio*, any one of them canopied by a soft, moonlit sky. He borrowed from Classic, ancient and definitely established architecture the shape, form and order of house, garden and loggia with which to convert the theater auditorium into Nature's setting. It became necessary to study with utmost care the art of reproducing ancient buildings in form, texture and colors; it was more important to intelligently, appreciatively and artfully use paint, brush and electric light, tree ornament, furnishings, lights and shadows to

Excerpted from John Eberson, "A Description of the Capitol Theater, Chicago." *Architectural Forum* 42, no. 6 (June 1925), 373–6.

produce a true atmosphere of the outdoors without cheapening the attempted illusion by overdone trickery. The auditorium thus created seemed to please. Despite its vastness and expanse it offered an atmosphere of intimacy, – a highly desirable feature in theaters, – and – most important of all – the atmosphere is always new, fresh and alive.

The Capitol Theater, Chicago, owned by the National Theaters Corporation, has a strictly Italian Renaissance exterior executed in glazed polychrome terra cotta for the main body and rich polychrome glass in ornamental enrichments, strictly representative of the modern revival and rebirth of antique and classic Roman architecture. Lobbies and foyers are adorned with modified replicas of ornament and designs, typical of the work found at S. Miniato, and done by Niccola Pisano. The entrance lobby has a faience tile floor, imported marble wainscoting and a richly ornamented ceiling with motifs taken from the Villa Cambiasco, and doorheads studied from one of the galleries of St. Peter's. The main lounge or grand staircase hall is four stories high, representing an Italian *cortile* with clear sky overhead and rich, palatial garden walls adorned with carved niches and statuary. The promenade back of the amphitheater is a replica of an old stuccoed cloister arcade, embellished with wrought iron gates, lanterns and iron-framed mirrors.

The proscenium arch of the Capitol was conceived as a triumphal arch, supported on columns and roofed with a Roman tile roof surrounded by a stone balustrade. The auditorium of the Capitol might briefly be described as representing an Italian garden under a Mediterranean sky, featuring a moonlight night. On the left side of the auditorium is an Italian palace facade. The right side of the auditorium represents a terraced roof garden with a small temple building. Surmounting the whole is a representation of a deep blue sky with moving clouds and twinkling stars, creating a completely out-of-door setting. The cupola of the temple was modeled after one of the many examples of architecture found in Milan, and in the Certosa of Pavia. The openings to the boxes, representing entrances through the palace garden walls, are Ponzello arches.

The pilaster ornament of the great columns, and the pilasters supporting the triumphal arch, are exact reproductions of carvings in a collection of reproduced pilasters in the Academy of Fine Arts in Verona. The door friezes of the main auditorium represent a double gallery and promenade, separated from the auditorium by rich archways carried on marble columns; thus extreme depth and distance are added to the huge interior, and in doing so every aisle and seating requirement ordained by the law has not only been met but the spaces usually allotted to aisles and cross aisles have almost been doubled in size. All of the theater interiors were decorated in rich polychrome. The installation of a very elaborate and specialized lighting system made it possible to add to the illusion and to the patrons' pleasure.

Modified caryatides, sculptured human female figures, are used as column supports of the pergola which conceals the two main ramps leading from the gallery to the balcony. The rustication of the stonework on the palace and garden walls is as found in Renaissance buildings in Florence. The entire decorative scheme of the exterior ornament on the building is carried out in fresco.

The stage setting carries the architectural vision from the auditorium onto the stage without any visible line of demarcation: The entire stage is designed as an Italian formal garden, with towering hedges, practical fountains, and containing a production stage which has a false proscenium resembling a Classic temple. The illusion created by the open air treatment of the auditorium and the intricate scenic and lighting effects of stage setting gives perfect harmony. An interesting detail of decoration is the use of roughcast plaster, in an antique finish.

The Capitol Theater has a reinforced concrete foundation, steel skeleton frame, and reinforced concrete amphitheater. The commercial portion of this structure is of reinforced concrete. A very interesting feature is the use of the reinforced concrete proscenium girder spanning 65 feet, being 4 feet thick and 12 feet high. All stairs are of reinforced concrete, covered with marble. A complete, scientifically controlled heating and ventilating plant was installed, containing refrigerating apparatus, by the use of which fresh tempered and treated air is delivered to all portions of the building – warmed, washed air in winter and cooled, washed air in summer. The distribution of this air is accomplished by both side wall and floor openings, and an automatic, controlled system will assure patrons at all times of proper and agreeable atmospheric conditions.

The sub-stage floor of the Capitol contains a very large rehearsal room, a screening room, a musical director's library, toilet rooms for employes and all possible mechanical equipment, such as hydraulic curtain machine, vacuum cleaners, remote control board, organ blowers, ozone machines, electric air scenting machines and tanks, fire pumps, oil-burning heating equipment, transformer vault, refrigerating machine, motor generator, etc. A vestibule, 20 by 50 feet, contains a box office built of marble and cast bronze, permitting easy access to the main entrance and accommodating patrons at two windows. This vestibule and the 100-foot canopy which protects its entrance are illuminated with hundreds of incandescent lamps, giving the brilliance of daylight. Six sets of standard theater exit doors lead from this vestibule into the outer lobby, a room 50 by 60, having an Italian faience tile floor, walls covered with red damask, and a most interesting wood ceiling.

Festive torches cast interesting shadows on the loggia, which forms the portal to the circular foyer which is 36 feet wide and 115 feet long. The loggia contains a grand stairway executed in marble with hand wrought railings, surrounded by garden walls and covered by a domed sky ceiling illuminated in polychrome effect with Italian lantern ceiling fixtures. Another set of exit doors separates this outer lobby from the grand staircase, the imitation Italian limestone walls creating an unusual feeling of distance and grandeur. The circular foyer, which leads directly to another set of exit doors, represents an arcade with rough plastered walls, faience tile floor and an all-over pattern arched ceiling, decorated in richest polychrome and lighted with special fixtures.

Adjoining the foyer and separated by open hand-wrought iron gates is a large smoking room and men's retiring room with vaulted rough plaster ceiling and black and yellow tile wainscot.

In one of the interesting corners of the foyer is a gateway, leading out into what seems to be an open garden, a bit of interesting illusion created by the painters' and property makers' art; through a semi-open gate one perceives an Italian rose garden, adding depth and preparing the guests for the surprise which they are to experience when entering the house.

Promotional giveaway, Chicago Theatre

18

Building Theatre Patronage (1927)

John F. Barry and Epes W. Sargent

Patrons

The leading motion picture theatres now rank with the most imposing structures in every community. All the arts – painting, music, sculpture and architecture – combine to complete their beauty. Those who do not understand the motion picture theatre, have been puzzled by the architecturally splendid structure, the palatial foyer, the luxurious touches which typify the leading theatres. Impatiently they ask, "What's all this for?"

If you understand why patrons visit the motion picture theatre, you understand why architects plan as they do. People come to the motion picture theatre to live an hour or two in the land of romance. They seek escape from the humdrum existence of daily life. There are few other places in the present commercialized world where they can get mental rejuvenation and imaginative play at so small a cost. The fireside has been replaced by unromantic radiator pipes. Other meeting places have disappeared. People realize that for a small charge they can be lifted up on a magic carpet and set down in a dream city amidst palatial surroundings where worry and care can never enter, where pleasure hides in every shadow.

Watch the bright light in the eyes of the tired shop girl within the modern motion picture theatre as she sighs with satisfaction walking amid furnishings that once delighted the hearts of queens. See the tired toil-worn father whose dreams have never come true. Look inside his heart as he finds strength and rest within the theatre. Here we have an institution of recreation and rest, of imaginative release, all in the spirit of playland. Here is an economic necessity. Here is a shrine of democracy where there are no privileged patrons. All the decorative details are elements that make up the atmosphere of a palace, to stimulate the imagination of tired minds and re-create the strength of weary hearts. The architect has mastered the psychology of the theatre-goer. He understands the patrons' love of adventure and the craving for the beautiful and the luxurious, and with deft touches excites the spirit of romance by the very structure and decoration of the theatre.

The entrance arouses the patrons' spirit of adventure, for the graceful lines of the theatre are in contrast to the cold straight commercial lines of nearby buildings. The lobby is so designed that its fascination makes waiting a pleasure – because of rare paintings, impressive statuary, costly rugs and beautiful tapestries. Even the electric signs, that for the early theatre were crudely designed by tinsmiths, are now carefully studied to blend with the architectural treatment of the whole. The great stairways are enticing where an ugly

Excerpted from John F. Barry and Epes W. Sargent, *Building Theatre Patronage: Management and Merchandising* (New York: Chalmers Publishing Company, 1927), 11–14, 24–5, 79–81, 91–5.

staircase would suggest only a tiring climb. The theatre itself is an entertainment. [...]

The Theatre as an Institution

No theatre should depend for patronage exclusively upon the program which is booked. Programs come and go. The theatre alone remains. A motion picture theatre offers 52, or 104, or 156 or more programs a year. If the program alone is relied upon for patronage, if the program alone is advertised, then every time the program changes, the theatre is just where it was before any advertising expenditure was incurred. No permanent business builder has been established. The permanent business builder, irrespective of any particular program, is *the theatre as an institution.*

Practically every detail of theatre operation can be an influence for building patronage. Do not confine building theatre patronage to the programs. Consider every detail of your operation as an influence that builds patronage. Supervise every detail from that viewpoint. Bring to the attention of potential patrons other things besides the program. Because the theatre remains while programs come and go, develop your theatre's reputation as something with permanent influence.

At a time when the motion picture theatre was a seemingly temporary enterprise, when equipment, service, lighting and other details of operation were not worthy of consideration or mention, it was natural that the program alone was relied upon for patronage. Even to-day when the program is exceptional, the program primarily will be responsible for business.

But exceptional programs are relatively rare. Regular attendance must be built with other things which go to make the theatre an institution. They include every detail of operation – admission price, location, accessibility, seating comforts, projection, music, personnel, ventilation, patron conveniences, starting hours, program management no matter what the program is, distinctive novelties of every kind. The theatre as an institution, is the permanent factor that makes regular patrons. When there is little to choose between the entertainment values of programs at competitive theatres, patrons attend one theatre rather than another because of its institutional reputation. [...]

Your Community

The theatre manager cannot know too much about his particular community and his potential patrons. Potential patrons are all those who are possible customers of the theatre. There is practically no theatre that has reached its maximum in attendance. Theatre records are broken even at the theatres that seem to have reached their maximum. Therefore, no manager should ever sit back satisfied with results. The minute he ceases to improve his operation and to draw new patrons by further ingenuity and clever merchandizing, an active competition will cut into his patronage. If there is no active theatre competition, those patrons who were attracted by intensive effort begin to slip off and lose the habit of theatre attendance because other forms of entertainment make a stronger appeal.

Two things are necessary – maintaining existing regular patronage – and – attracting new patrons. In the community served by any theatre, there is a potential patronage including those who are not regular patrons of a particular theatre that can be won by skillful merchandising. Within the limits from which the theatre draws, there is what might be called untouched soil from which new patrons can be developed. These include those of theatre-going age who seldom or never visit your theatre. Besides these, there are children who will soon reach the theatre-going age. In these children the manager can develop not only a love of motion picture entertainment, but also a fixed preference for a particular theatre. A large percentage of your present theatre attendance is below the age of twenty-one. Each new year many others become of theatre-going age. You should do something to win these prospective patrons.

Retailing

The theatre manager is a retail salesman. Retail selling in every business requires analysis of the product, analysis of the customer traffic within the neighborhood of the institution, and the use of those advertising means most efficient for reaching potential customers. We are considering here the community as a center of theatre patrons and also patron traffic within the neighborhood of the theatre.

The closer any theatre operation is to the preferences and habits of a particular community, the more likely it is to succeed. Every community is different. Every manager faces problems which are unlike the problems of other managers. Even the very same program must be sold differently to different communities. Thus it is evident that knowledge of the community is most important. This knowledge is not acquired over-night. It is not a knowledge that is learned once and for always. Even managers who have lived in a community over a long period of years must constantly keep pace with new developments. Many a successful manager when moved to another theatre fails to succeed there because of his ignorance of the new community.

Analysis

Analysis of the community is important for every retailer. It is especially important for the theatre manager because of the nature of what he is selling. Other retailers sell standard products which appeal to the same taste and the same appetite everywhere. The same can of beans sold over the grocery counter satisfies the same appetite everywhere. So do standard products like butter, bread, candy, canned goods, etc. With such standard products and so many others that are retailed, it is very often price and not preference or taste

which makes the sale at one store rather than at another.

Preferences

But entertainment depends on the particular preference of the community. It is most effectively merchandized when advertising emphasizes those features which appeal most to the community's preference. Merchandizing of entertainment is often successful because it is tied-in with something of particular interest to the community at the time. Originality and novelty of appeal that will be effective locally can only be decided upon with an understanding of the particular community. Even the style and wording of advertising must be suited to the individual community. Words and phrases that are effective in some communities are not effective in others. This is why stereotyped general statements are never as effective as those prepared in the language of the community and focused on sentiments in which the community is particularly interested. [...]

A necessity

The problem of selling motion picture entertainment is different from any other. Many of the appeals used for other products would be ineffective. It has been said that motion picture entertainment is a luxury and consequently the luxury appeal should be used. But as far as the manager is concerned he should feel that he is selling not a luxury but a real necessity. People need what he has to sell almost as much as they need food. The motion picture theatre today is an economic necessity. It answers a modern need. Conditions of living today are so confined, modern industry is so exacting in its demands, and modern living is so intense that people more than ever before need imaginative and emotional relaxation. Places where this relaxation was possible under other conditions of living no longer exist. Even the home has become confining – consider living conditions in the modern apartment. Consequently, there must be a place for relaxation that is within the family budget. The modern motion picture theatre is the answer to a real need. It fits right into modern conditions. It came at a time when there was a new public able to afford the entertainment it could give, requiring that entertainment not as a luxury but as a real necessity.

Of course motion picture entertainment cannot be considered a necessity for the wealthy who can afford other diversions. But for those who are not wealthy it is a necessity. While present conditions of living exist it will continue to be a necessity. The routine of daily life develops boredom. The human being is not a machine that can go on working without diversion. Change from the familiar routine is needed. The imagination must have a chance to play. Mental strength must be renewed. The quiet reading of fiction as a regular diet as an answer to the need for diversion is not sufficient. The motion picture theatre offers the most welcome escape from the humdrum existence of daily life. People go there to be entertained because they cannot entertain themselves or because other forms of entertainment are not accessible or not within their means. If there is any doubt about the necessity of motion picture theatre entertainment, consider what would happen if the motion picture theatres of the country were suddenly closed. The man who sells a necessity has more confidence in the number of sales possible than the one who sells a mere luxury. Consequently, the theatre manager should feel that what he is selling is a real necessity. This realization puts a certain confidence and a certain conviction into his efforts.

General appeals

If motion picture entertainment is a necessity, with what appeal should it be sold? The old appeal on the curiosity basis "pictures that move" is no longer effective. It is incorrect to state that motion picture patrons generally are interested in "acting" – meaning

histrionic ability. The stars are known personalities, real "acquaintances" of whom actions consistent with their known personality are expected rather than "playing a part."

It does not suffice to say that the appeal of motion picture entertainment is "sport and adventure for the men, romance for the women" or "life, love and laughter." This general appeal, like any other general appeal, is less effective than the specific, detailed appeal. Besides, there is no general appeal that will be equally effective for every program.

Every advertising appeal can be traced to certain primitive human instincts such as curiosity, the social instinct, the desire to excel, self-preservation, the instinct to be admired, the instinct for personal gain. But besides these basic instincts to which appeal can be directed, there are others with which the manager should be familiar.

Reasons why

A manager was asked why people attend his theatre. He answered: "People like to see a show and they get it here." But how many different reasons for attendance at a particular theatre might be given? How many reasons are there which account for attendance? If the manager could be familiar with the innermost thoughts of theatre patrons he would find reasons for theatre attendance that he never suspected. If he were familiar with these reasons he might then make a more effective choice of the advertising appeal to be used for different programs.

It is impossible to list completely the reasons for theatre attendance, nor is it correct to state that they can all be reduced to "sport and adventure for the men, romance for the women."

Here is a brief list of reasons selected at random from over two thousand that might be given:

The desire to see the latest styles; to learn a new dance step; to see a photoplay of a novel that was read; to see how people live in other parts of the world; to get ideas for new styles of home furnishing; to see the photoplay of a stage success that was enjoyed or that was not seen but very much discussed; to learn etiquette; to study character; to learn to make love; for self-improvement; to hear the music; to enjoy comfortable surroundings such as are not in the home; to study character, to imitate a star who is a model; to escape the heat; to escape the cold; to see the latest news on the screen; to study the work of a director; to study how a star wears her clothes; to spend two hours in the company of a friend; to keep the family together at entertainment that will bring enjoyment to all; to learn screen technique or amateur camera work; to entertain guests; to re-live youth; to see a new screen face; to sing with the organ slides; to see phases of life which interest; to see a period of history which interests; to see how a mystery is solved; to see a new style of hair dress; because the theatre is close to home; to dream dreams that never came true; to laugh; to get the solution of a problem which is similar to an individual's own problem; interest in a type of story.

It is evident that all these reasons do not apply to any individual. Nor do all these reasons determine attendance at a particular program. Nor do these reasons include the many details of theatre operation which are considered by patrons in their decision to visit one theatre rather than another. But the reasons given at least indicate some vague desires which skillful advertising can convert into the purchase of theatre tickets.

The point to be made is that careful selection of the advertising appeal must take into account the fact that people differ, and from a wide variety of appeals selection should be made according to two things: the type of program which is to be merchandised and the type of prospective patrons for whom the advertising is intended. Thus the most effective appeal for each type or class of patron should be selected rather than a vague, general appeal. It must be remem-

bered that the same appeal is not equally effective for all prospective patrons because they vary in age, in sex, in racial characteristics, in education, in reading habits, in their environment, in buying power, in experience and even in language limitations.

Preferences

Patrons like to feel that they have some part in the selection of programs and that their preferences are considered by the management. These preferences can be learned by conversations with patrons and by reports from the staff concerning patron comment. It is a wise policy to listen carefully to the opinion of patrons concerning a program. The tactful manager who listens to the patron's opinion can very often call attention to some good point in the program which the patron might have overlooked. At any rate the patron feels a certain satisfaction in knowing that his opinion is carefully considered and that some assurance was given that in selecting future programs the patron's opinion would be considered.

A questionnaire concerning patron preference can be used to good advantage. This questionnaire can be distributed to patrons at the theatre or sent to their homes by mail. To encourage the careful filling out of this questionnaire fan photos or souvenirs can be offered. These will be mailed upon the receipt of the questionnaire or given to the patron who leaves the questionnaire filled out at the theatre. It is suggested that a personal letter accompany the questionnaire calling attention to the fact that the management is anxious to comply with the preferences of patrons and perhaps mentioning some of the outstanding productions that were well received by the community as indicative of the attempt made to secure the best. The headings of the questionnaire depend on the policy of a particular theatre. Even if the opinions given on the questionnaire were not used by the management, the distinction of the questionnaire has the advantage of creating a favorable impression. But the fact of the matter is that helpful information is very often secured by these questionnaires and details are brought to the attention of the management which might otherwise be over-looked. A questionnaire is found in the appendix.

Audience reaction. – A record should be kept showing the reaction of audiences to each program, indicating what it was that the patrons seemed to like about the theme, the locale, the direction, the cast, the title, sub-titling, new faces, the suitability of the story for the particular star, etc. This record should not be used only for feature photo-plays. It should be used for short subjects, overtures, organ solos, scenics and novelties.

19

Motion Picture Theater Management (1928)

Harold B. Franklin

The Place of the Motion Picture Theater

There is hardly any need to define what is evident to all. To the general public, a motion picture theater is devoted to entertainment by means of films, where all may attend who pay for admission in accordance with a scale of prices posted at the box office, provided they conduct themselves properly. On the other hand, it is equally obvious that such an institution is a business, an enterprise offering to the community a highly desired commodity in exchange for income that must, naturally, include a profit. Any cinema, anywhere, is both of these things, and succeeds in measure as it accomplishes the double aim of amusement and financial return.

In another sense, each theater might require separate characterization. We are not likely to confuse the simple structure at the country crossroads with the mammoth edifice that towers above the crowded city thoroughfare. The problems, the possibilities, the ingenuities of management will show a thousand and one distinctions between this house and that, one manager and another – to say nothing of the manifold differences of music, advertising, service, and even sanitation which set off one amusement center from all the rest. A theater, like a man, is a personality – for better or worse – by itself; and each

one defines itself to the locality in its own way.

Yet between the general definition and the particular, there still lies the possibility of making certain classifications according to certain similarities. The trade does not pretend to cater to all alike, or to each entirely on the basis of special need. A number of types are recognized; and while their function is the same anywhere, and their needs different everywhere, they are found to group themselves naturally according to broad similarities determined by experience.

The better sort of theater, for example, is known as the "De Luxe First Run," a title which indicates a richness of display, a priority in the showing of recent pictures, and, of course, a great income. This kind of house caters to the pleasure of an entire metropolis. Accordingly, it is situated in some central district, such as the main business or shopping zone. On its program will be found a feature, which consists of five to seven reels of a thousand feet of film each; a number of short subjects, generally comprising a one- or two-reel comedy, and a news weekly; or sometimes a travel scenic or other novelty subject. In larger cities, there may be also one or more of the following stage presentations: a revue, a prologue inspired by the feature, a dance divertissement, soloists, or some number specially produced by the man-

Excerpted from Harold B. Franklin, *Motion Picture Theater Management* (Garden City, New York: Doubleday, Doran, and Company, 1928), 26–33, 128–38, 325–9.

agement. Frequently, well-known actors or actresses appear before the patrons of a De Luxe Theater.

"Neighborhood Theaters" are located in residential sections, and are thus to be distinguished from the first type. They may seat three or four hundred, and be of simple design; or they may vie with the finest class of downtown institution. The size and magnificence are determined by the size and character of the surrounding population. Such theaters usually play motion pictures after the first showing of the more centrally located houses, and are therefore distinguished from them by the name "second run." The type of program, otherwise, is practically the same as that of the De Luxe, except that in smaller and smaller communities the auxiliary elements are fewer and less elaborate. For instance, the full-sized symphony orchestra dwindles by degrees to a solo organist as we go down the ranks; and the elaborate changes of scenery are in some places reduced to one permanent stage design, and in most are not to be found at all. Yet in cities of great size the neighborhood theater may present a program in every way as ambitious as the one downtown; excepting that the orchestra seldom exceeds thirty pieces, and the showing of the "second run" feature is made "simultaneously" with that of other neighborhood houses.

Third, fourth, or fifth run theaters are to be found wherever the population warrants the type. The importance, naturally, diminishes with the run. Among these are to be found the so-called "sensational" houses. They are generally small places that cater to the element which craves "action" pictures, that is, not only western subjects, but others that may be called melodramatic in the extreme. They can best be characterized as being of the "Nick Carter" type. They help fill the place left by the "ten-twenty-thirty" stage show of the last decade. There is a sharp line of division between the conduct of the "sensational" type of picture theater and the others.

Another kind that may properly be classified with motion picture theaters is the vaudeville-picture house. This type is found mainly in the large cities. The program consists of a feature and five or six acts of vaudeville. The pictures exhibited are either second run, or first run products of secondary importance. This type of theater reached its highest development under the policies established by Loew's under the supervision of Nicholas M. Schenck.

In some parts of the country there is a type known as the "double feature" house, because the program consists of two features instead of one. The purpose, obviously, is to entice the "bargain" instinct of patrons. Yet there are distinct disadvantages in such procedure. It is like asking a person to read two novels in the same evening. The operation of these theaters seems inadvisable to the most constructive minds of the industry, and is discouraged as much as possible.

In the smaller towns the local theater often houses the motion picture as well as the vaudeville, legitimate, or concert attractions, playing each for a day or two, according to bookings. A community of this size is willing and able to patronize a variety of amusements, but is not large enough to support a run of any continuance. The theater therefore is a kind of cross-section of the world of entertainment; and it is significant that even here the new art is giving more than a good account of itself among its elders.

No classification of motion picture theaters would be complete without mention of the greatest type of all – the type which I shall classify as the "Super." It is the last word in architectural treatment. It seats, usually, from 3,500 to 6,000 patrons – a city under one roof! It contains lobbies and public rooms of grand scale, whose proportions are comparable with those of great public buildings. In most instances, too, the super-theater equals the best of contemporary structures in decorative effect. It has the spaciousness, the luxurious appointments, of an elaborate mansion. Of this type the best instance to cite is the Paramount Theatre, New York. [...]

Since these various groups are well defined in the industry, it stands to reason that management of a given theater must bear in mind the kind of patronage to be attracted, and must act accordingly. Care must be taken to insure the surroundings and accommodations which will attract the desired patronage. If, for example, the clientele desired is of the steady, self-respecting middle class, the lobby and other portions of the house should be as clean and cheerful as the home standards of patrons naturally would demand, and displays should be bright and attractive, but not cheap or sensational. It is generally conceded that a theater personality will attract a particular class of people.

Sometimes, of course, changes of neighborhood and of population will dictate a distinct alteration in the personality of the house. Managers must take cognizance of such shifts, and be guided by them. For example, 125th Street in New York was for a long time considered the "Main Street" of people living above 110th Street. In recent years, however, the colored belt of this section of Harlem has come down so close to 125th Street that the thoroughfare no longer attracts white residents living to the south of that line. There has consequently arisen, for the managements of theaters located on the street, a problem requiring the most alert judgment and resourcefulness. In the same manner, a new class of people will often encroach on a district of established character, and inevitably the whole personality of the local theater will undergo marked change. It is therefore sound policy to make a careful study of conditions that will insure the attraction of the desired clientele. The factors here are location, design in structure, service, and quality of entertainment. [...]

The hundreds of thousands who congregate nightly under the exhibitor's roof are indulging in a luxury only in a secondary sense. Truly, they gather here as they go elsewhere for bread; because here, as nowhere else, is to be found the civilized man's great necessity – release from the day's routine – an alternation from perhaps tedious reality to liberating romance. They turn their faces to a blank wall which, at the operator's command, becomes a window upon the variegated globe of the actual, or a magician's crystal into which frustrated hearts may gaze and find of moment for the recognition of life's dreams and ecstasies. Lost from the humdrum, they thrill to adventure, melt in love, or throb with sympathy. This is no luxury, this hour of recreation that falls like manna on the hungry spirit; and just as housekeepers go by habit to those shops that best supply them with the bread and meat of daily subsistence, so the steps of the hungry for romance may be drawn to the door of the exhibitor who knows his mission and performs it truly. [...]

The Service Staff

Instructions to ushers

Loyalty to your work requires that you help in every way to maintain the standard of the theater.

The purpose of these instructions is to set before you the standards of action which will be of service to the patron, the theater, and your fellow employees.

Good manners, courtesy, and consideration for others should be noticeable in your conduct.

Ushers or other employees should never exhibit haste or impatience to a patron. A quiet attentive manner will go a long way toward convincing a patron that employees are trying to please.

Employees should always be ready to render little courtesies, such as picking up articles dropped, assisting with wraps, etc. [...]

It is advisable to establish uniform expressions which ushers or other employees may use in guiding patrons, in the interests of uniformity and simplicity in handling large crowds. These may include such expressions as "Seats two aisles to the right, please," or "Seats this way, please," etc. A system of signaling may be established so that ushers in aisles may indicate available seats to

USHER   FLOOR MANAGER   CHIEF USHER

Uniformed Staff

ELEVATOR OPERATOR   PAGE BOY   DOORMAN   STREETMAN   FOOTMAN

SERVICE EMPLOYEES

Illustrations from Harold Franklin, *Motion Picture Theater Management* (1928)

ushers at the head of aisles – such signaling must not be noticeable by patrons, and must be carried out without any noise, but rather by the position of the usher and the manner in which he holds his hands. The right hand across the breast may indicate that there is room for one. Accordingly the usher at the head of the aisle invites one patron to pass down the aisle. Placing the right hand behind the back may indicate that there is room for two; both hands behind his back would mean there is room for three; placing the left hand on the breast, room for four. Ushers must be drilled repeatedly and carefully so that such signals become automatically correct. Flashlights are sometimes used by ushers to direct the way in seating patrons – modern theaters, however, equip their aisles with aisle lights under the arms of chairs, making the use of flashlights unnecessary. [...]

No one must leave his post without specific permission of floor manager. Proper drills of a military character give the uniformed staff suitable bearing and appearance. Such drills should include the "attention" position, "marching," "facing" both to right and left, and "dressing" into position. Such drills may be suggested by the infantry drill manuals. Uniforms must fit employees if they are to look well, and if employees are expected to have sufficient pride in their appearance. Workers must be careful of their speech in addressing patrons, or replying to inquiries. The tone of voice must be in keeping with the atmosphere of the theater. Patrons must always be approached with respect. Ushers must render whatever service they can to help patrons, but must *not* leave their posts. They must not obstruct the view of patrons by standing in aisles unnecessarily. In case of objectionable conduct on the part of any patron, they should report such situation to floor manager. They must keep aisles clear of rubbish, picking up papers or other material and placing them in a box in the rear. Employees stationed near doors should always open doors for all persons approaching them. Members of the uniformed staff are not to smoke on the premises. [...]

Elevator operators

The elevator operator must run his car with the maximum of safety, and is held strictly responsible for closing all doors and safety gates. The liability for accident because of an open gate is too great to be overlooked. Any defect in the closing of gates or doors should be immediately reported to the manager.

The elevator operator must never leave his car while on duty. He must be watchful of floor signals. Smooth running of the car is essential. There must be no "jerky" operation. Stopping at the exact level of each floor is insisted upon. It should never be necessary to suggest to passengers to "Step up" or "down." Operators should always announce floors in a clear tone. Politeness, alertness and courtesy are essential to the proper performance of the operator's duties. Operators can be of service in answering patrons' questions and should be well informed as to the location of the public rooms in the building. They must not enter into lengthy conversation with any one, but must reply briefly, yet pleasantly, to all queries.

They are responsible to the floor manager in carrying out their work. When on duty, they must report any defect in the running of the car. Operators shall be suitably uniformed.

Page boys

Page boys are under the direction of the floor manager. These boys are used as messengers within and without the theater building. In some theaters they assist in the checking of articles, umbrellas, etc., when there is a check room service. Special boys are assigned for this work.

Page boys are used to direct visitors to the office when so ordered, and also to direct patrons to their destinations. The instructions issued to ushers should govern the conduct of the page boys. The uniforms should distinguish the page boys from other employees.

Doorman

The Doorman shall be responsible to the house manager. He holds a post of great importance. Coming in contact with every patron who enters the theater, he must be a man of good breeding and of pleasant personality. He should be a patient type, and possess tact and a smiling countenance. He should be familiar with the program schedule in order to give information, when asked, regarding the starting time of various parts of the program.

Each person who enters the theater must have a ticket – this rule must be carried out without exception. Intoxicated persons must not be permitted in the theater. Tact is necessary to prevent such persons from making themselves obnoxious. Pets or animals should not be admitted to the theater.

The Doorman shall be uniformed so that he may be distinguished from other employees. A theater generally has two doormen, so that proper relief shifts may be arranged. [. . .]

Streetmen

In some theaters of large capacity, streetmen supervise the crowds in the outside lobby and on the sidewalk. These employees are uniformed for the occasion and assist in the handling of the crowds. They are under the supervision of the floor manager.

Footman

This employee caters to the automobile and carriage trade. He opens and closes the doors of all vehicles. He should be in a position to give information to patrons as to the program schedule, and as to garage and parking facilities. The footman's manners must be extremely courteous. A good impression is made if the footman bows slightly, raising his right hand to his cap in the form of a salute, before opening or closing a door. Under no circumstances should a footman touch a patron, unless asked to. In rainy weather the footman shall have a suitable umbrella, to protect patrons from the rain in coming from or going to cars. He shall likewise have facilities at his disposal for calling when requested.

Vehicles of all descriptions must be kept from the curb of the theater entrance. The management will provide No Parking signs, through the coöperation of the police department. The footman should be properly uniformed.

Feminine Personnel

The girl in the box office

The cashier should be of pleasant personality and refined appearance. The better theaters furnish cashiers with silk blouses. Another little touch which has a splendid effect on the cashier, and makes a good impression to the public is always to have a flower or two in a vase on a shelf, or in a cone shaped hanging receptacle in the box office.

Naturally, the person selected for this work should be trustworthy.

She must answer all questions cheerfully, and when a patron approaches the box office, the cashier should ask "How many, please?" and should always say "Thank you!" after each sale. When business moves so fast that this is not possible, the cashier's manner must indicate the spirit which a "Thank you" might convey.

The price scale must be indicated clearly at the box office window so that a patron may easily read the sign. Any regulations as to the admission of babes in arms, or other children, should also be prominently posted. [. . .]

Nurses

Nurses are in attendance in theaters that are equipped with first aid rooms. Such rooms should be provided with an adequate first aid kit. Naturally, nurses are in full charge of the first aid room and its appearance. They wear appropriate uniforms, and are considered part of the uniformed staff, under the supervision of the house manager.

Matrons or maids

These women are in charge of ladies' rest and toilet rooms. In the absence of a first aid room, a matron shall be in charge of the first aid kit.

The matron shall see to it that the theater's rules are obeyed in all the rooms devoted to women patrons and children. She shall be fully responsible for the appearance of the room while the theater is open to the public. All furniture and art objects must be cleaned and dusted. All wash basins, drains, and faucets must always be kept clean and be in good working order. Cleaning equipment must be placed in a closet provided for the purpose.

The management should furnish for its patrons suitable dressing table articles, such as combs, mirrors, brushes, powder, etc. The name of the theater may be embossed on these, and the maid is responsible for them.

Conclusion

Employees should be trained to consider each other, as well as patrons. Every one in the staff is an integral part of the organization. There can be no room for those who are out of step or out of tune. Loyalty and service are to be linked to coöperation in the developing of the splendid morale which every unit must have if it is to prosper. There is no better way of appraising the value of the individual than by observing the desire and the effort he shows to establish and foster the unity of the whole. [...]

The Public: Good Will and Ethics

The old saw, "Keep your ear to the ground" has an interesting little side-phase, if one is willing to be imaginative for a moment. It seems to raise old Mother Earth to the personality of an informant or an advisor. Coming back to industry again, let us by the same token reconsider the part played by our guests. How can we keep our ear to the ground in our own pasture?

For the public is really the most important expert of all. It is an authority on what it wants, to begin with; and it is the final judge in that regard. For one thing, as I pointed out in a very early chapter, it doesn't want "high brow stuff." The result? No high brow stuff. It doesn't want to see pictures acted by people whose conduct is scandalous. The result? Is there any need to state it?

Such pressure cannot be exerted entirely in a negative fashion. It is true that mere lack of patronage or falling off of attendance is not directly expressive. Furthermore, if people do not applaud a thrilling scene or laugh at a comic one, the criticism is obviously impassive. Yet, though pressure by negation exists, and is powerful, there are more direct ways in which patrons get their wishes known.

They are not always – they are rarely – unresponsive in some way. They very frequently applaud, for instance, or rock the house with vocal mirth. Tragic situations produce the sounds of sympathetic weeping. The swift intake of many breaths is better than clapping as a praise of some realistic representation of peril. Even in the darkened auditorium, the astute manager, with his "ear to the ground," can catch positive reflections of the moods of his audience. And his eyes, accustomed to the dimness, can tell at a glance whether whole masses of patrons are raptly attentive, or bored to sleep or conversation. Patronage may know it or not, but management is advised.

Especially is this so after the performance, when the crowd streams across the lighted lobby, clear to view. If there are repeated commendations, or even comments, the film has pleased, or at least interested. If the patrons seem merely wearied, or in a hurry to get away, or resentful – something is wrong. Perhaps there will even be a few direct complaints, spoken to or audible to the doorman, the captain, an usher. Do not overlook these. The public is conferring its expert advice, free of charge – if not free of possible loss or profit!

The same is valid in connection with service, equipment, or any other element. If a patron speaks angrily to an usher – why? If he comments sarcastically about the absence of drinking cups in the container – look out! And look out especially for the anger that is repressed, the sarcasm that only the eyes speak. The public is denoting or hinting a priceless appraisal. Some one should be there to listen, to see, to remember, to correct. Contrarily, a pleasant smile, a word of thanks, mean that the patron is delighted with the service or some other feature. Management should approve as keenly as the opposite, and check up in favor of the element that produced it.

Similarly, the house should note its external relations with an eagle eye to advantage. In the operation of theaters, management is brought in contact with many different business institutions as well as organizations of civic and social caliber; and its contact with the public of course is of great importance.

The motion picture theater is the most representative building in many communities and probably entertains within its walls more persons than repair to any other. Over 47,000,000 persons attend picture shows every week in the United States. With such responsibility, its duty and obligation to the public is quite clear. Those who are privileged to operate theaters have within their power the handling of an instrument of great possibilities for good. The motion picture can be made an agent of untold community value, if guided intelligently and controlled by persons who recognize their moral responsibility.

All this should be an influence affecting the dignity of the motion picture theater. Since these houses are everywhere contributory to the welfare of their communities, it cannot be denied that there is a certain dignity and importance to the profession of theater management. It should continue to be governed by the highest ideals of American business. Therefore the social and industrial activity of the house is of great importance in the community. [...]

Management should keep in close contact with every civic organization through membership, taking an active part in its affairs and also coöperating with every worthwhile civic, social and business event. The Chamber of Commerce, Rotary, Kiwanis, Lions and other local associations are brought in close touch with theaters because of events which they arrange periodically. Every valid public undertaking should be supported wholeheartedly. Management will use every possible means to advance the interests of theater operations, and create the best understanding of this business. Such active contacts will do much to make friends and to be of material value in attacking attempts at unfair legislation. In recent years those in public office have shown a fuller appreciation of the important niche the motion picture theater fills in community life. Those within the industry have demonstrated that they can conduct their business without outside interference, and the spread of censorship regulations has been arrested and found unnecessary.

20

Fashioning an Exhibition Empire: Promotion, Publicity, and the Rise of Publix Theaters

Douglas Gomery

During the 1920s national theater chains, led by Paramount's mighty Publix theater chain, captured and dominated movie exhibition in the United States. Formed during the fall and winter months of 1925–6, before the decade was out Publix would come to represent the largest and most influential theater empire of the pre-multiplex era. In September of 1925, Paramount (then formally titled Famous Players) took over the Chicago chain, Balaban & Katz, and then Adolph Zukor moved Sam Katz to New York City to build the Publix empire based upon the principles which had worked so well in Chicago.[1]

From the spring of 1926 through the early days of the Great Depression, Sam Katz (never Samuel, except to his mother) and his New York City-based management team of efficiency experts acquired and merged, so that by 1930 Publix controlled nearly 1,200 movie theaters. At its acme, during the heady days of 1929 and 1930, Publix completely dominated American moviegoing in three regions: one in cities which formed an arc from North Carolina to Florida to Louisiana to Texas; the second in an urban arc across the upper Middle West, from Minnesota through Illinois and Iowa to Michigan; third, Publix also owned and operated Famous Players Canadian, the dominant chain in the nation above the northern border of the United States. Attendance was claimed to be two and a half million patrons per day.[2]

Sam Katz sought to make Publix the Woolworth's of moviegoing. Like other retail chains of the day, he employed the then new, modern methods of the efficiency operation that were being developed and recommended by university experts from Harvard to Stanford Schools of Business. Through the methods of the chain-store organization and operation, Publix became the equivalent of A&P in the grocery field – the nation's most profitable retailer. Indeed, on April 24, 1930 the Paramount Famous Lasky Corporation officially recognized the importance of Katz's creation, becoming the Paramount–Publix Corporation.[3]

The key tool in fashioning this movie exhibition retailing giant was its innovative use of advertising and promotion. No longer was it simply enough to tack up posters near the theater. A national operation needed to employ the latest tools of the mass media to tempt middle-class, urban customers. To better understand the creation of Publix and its advertising and promotional methods, in this essay I take a two-step approach: (1) First, I examine the various means by which Publix rose to power; (2) second, I analyze how it innovated modern tools of advertising and publicity to sell the movies. Only through this two-step process, I argue, can we analyze and appreciate the importance of Publix theaters in establishing the idea of national moviegoing using chain-store business operations which continued to the end of the twentieth century, and beyond.

Building National Chains

Movie theater chain exhibitors followed the lead of department stores and grocery stores in pioneering significant changes in mass selling in the United States. During the years preceding the First World War, innovations of chain-store retailing were established. With branches throughout the nation a company could increase sales volume, introduce faster delivery of services, fashion standardized product offerings, nationalize promotion and advertising, and create ever-rising profits. During the first two decades of the twentieth century, retail chain successes came with grocery stores (A&P, Grand Union, and Kroger), and variety stores (Woolworth's, McCrory, and Kresge's), and thereafter chains of pharmacies, gasoline stations, and department stores followed – as did movie exhibition. Chain-store operating methods, so commonplace as the twentieth century ended, were nothing short of revolutionary as the twentieth century commenced.[4]

In short, chain-store operating techniques kept costs low, revenues high, and thus profits at their maximum. Costs were minimized by taking advantage of economies of scale. Fixed costs were spread over more and more operations, so the cost per store would be far lower than the competition across the street. For example, A&P maintained but a single centralized accounting department that handled all financial records and inventory control for its growing collection of stores. A&P store managers needed only to send in the basic information; experts at the central office entered the data and maintained the records. To milk all possible cost savings, chain executives relied on what was then termed "scientific management." Executives pressed each department of the modern chain-store enterprise to optimally perform its specialty – at maximum speed. Employees learned only those tasks necessary

to deliver the product or service, while owners and operators of single-store outlets had to be jacks-of-all-trades. Family operation, for example, may have best characterized the running of a nickelodeon; more than 100 employees, led in number by ushers and musicians, operated a 4,000-seat movie palace.

Chains also secured discounts in buying supplies of all sorts. This monopsony buying power of the chain, that set of economic advantages which result when a firm is one of a limited number of buyers of a necessary input, kept costs low. For example, as A&P grew to become the dominant grocery chain, it could seek and secure discounts from its suppliers, be they farmers or mass producers of household items. A&P would buy in bulk, at lower than normal unit prices. Movie theater chains would do the same in booking films, building several massive picture palaces based on the same designs, and mounting stage shows.[5]

On the demand side, chains used experts to take advantage of national advertising and garner the lowest rates for "ad buys" to promote moviegoing. Chains maintained research departments to study their markets and create advertising that reached its target customers. In general, chain operations of all types pioneered national advertising and promotion in the retail field. For the movies, Publix led the way to the use of newspapers, magazines, and radio to draw more and more customers into their cavernous palaces of spectacle.[6]

The men and women who owned and operated movie chains around the country may have come late to the chain-store revolution, but by the mid-1920s were working furiously to catch up by copying the efficiencies and promotional tactics of their retail cousins down the street. And like the chain-store revolution in general, national chain stores for the movies functioned as an urban institution, where the middle class, with ever-growing discretionary monies to spend, lived and played. Simply put, the chain-store revolutions must be placed at the core of the creation of the movie exhibition institutions known as "Hollywood."[7]

Movie Chain Basics

Publix led the way to national chain-store operation for the movies. To create any national retail chain operation, one needs a set of tactics. On the level of motion picture exhibition, Sam Katz and Barney Balaban pioneered such a system in their Chicago-based Balaban & Katz operation. Commencing in 1917, Balaban & Katz pioneered a five-part approach to movie house operation. By 1924 Balaban & Katz had become the most profitable movie theater chain in the business. The Balaban & Katz five-part strategy meant a movie show which was close to the patron's home, offered in a cathedral of entertainment, with services unmatched for middle-class citizens of the United States, complete with live stage shows (later on film), and a cool climate to promote summertime moviegoing. Sam Katz and the Balaban brothers redefined the movie business, and innovated the tactics that made possible national chains of motion picture theaters.[8]

Balaban & Katz's path to profits started with the scientific determination of optimal location. No need to have a cinema in every neighborhood; make sure no patron was more than 20 minutes from a grand picture palace, taking advantage of Chicago's new mass transit system. With fewer than a dozen 4,000-seat cinema cathedrals Balaban & Katz could serve "all" of Chicago. Balaban & Katz promoted this cinema propinquity on billboards, in newspapers, and through posters – particularly posted on the sides of trolley cars – all across the city of Chicago.[9]

Location represented but the first step in dominating Chicago moviegoing. Katz (and his partner Barney Balaban) instructed employees:

We cannot afford to build up a patronage depending entirely upon the drawing power of our feature films as we [exhibit] them. We must build in the minds of our audience the feeling that we represent an institution taking a vital part in the formation of the character of the community.[10]

Balaban & Katz did not simply rely on ease of access. It was not enough to select the optimal crossroads to locate a theater; a chain had to offer a good show. Balaban & Katz entertainment commenced with the *building* which housed the motion pictures – a plaster-coated palace for motion picture viewing. Balaban & Katz sought to make their buildings attractions unto themselves. Sam Katz told an audience at Harvard University's Business School that:

After the location has been determined, [a study is made] and from that we determine the type of architecture that ought to go into that particular theater. If the community has already a theater in the style of the French Renaissance or the Italian Renaissance, we will probably take an entirely different type of architecture of our theater, so as to make it distinctive.[11]

Balaban & Katz spared no expense outfitting a movie palace. For its 5,000-seat Uptown theater in Chicago, Balaban & Katz laid out nearly $25,000 on furniture, and double that amount on drapes and carpets. The restrooms, hidden in the basement or in the balcony foyers, were larger and more splendid than any person's house or apartment. In newspapers and magazines Balaban & Katz promoted the image of class with its picture palaces. They were spacious, clean, and decorated with their own set of drapes, furniture, paintings, and mirrors. The patron could only wonder if the well-to-do had such facilities in their country clubs or board rooms, and with drawings in newspapers and magazines Balaban & Katz promoted this image of class.[12]

But the best publicity was that fans could see their theaters light up from miles away as they rode the trolley to the "picture show."

Thousands of lights transformed simple marquees and upright signage into beacons seen throughout sectors of the city. One film professional trade paper, *Exhibitor's Herald*, noted that the outside lights from the Uptown theater collectively proved so intense that their heat could be felt from 100 feet away. And Sam Katz reminded his employees: "Every light brings in a customer."[13]

Balaban & Katz had a stated policy of treating the movie patron as a king or queen. It offered free child care, attendant smoking rooms, foyers and lobbies lined with paintings and sculpture, and organ music for those waiting in line. In the basement of each Balaban & Katz movie palace was a complete playground, including slippery slides, sand boxes, and other objects of fun awaiting youngsters. For no extra cost, nurses looked after the children while parents attended the show upstairs. Ushers maintained quiet and peaceful decorum throughout the picture palace complex. Balaban & Katz widely advertised its service as part of what made its moviegoing experience distinctive and different.[14]

At all picture palaces, Balaban & Katz offered live vaudeville with motion pictures. This hardly represented some new mass entertainment concept. Samuel ("Roxy") Rothafel and Sid Grauman had made big names for themselves in New York City and Los Angeles through their pioneering stage shows. Balaban & Katz, more than any other company, fully exploited the special added attraction of their stage shows and made its stars obsessions for moviegoing fans. Motion picture exhibition expert Harold Franklin recognized that:

Another type of motion picture presentation has been evolved during the past few years [by] Sam Katz...This has resulted in a form of entertainment that is somewhat of a "revue" or "musical comedy" character, and is of a lighter vein than the prologue or "concert"...It may take the form of a "Syncopation Week," "Beauty Revue," "Take a Chance Week," "Jazz Idea," "Hello,

Lindbergh," or whatever may have box office possibilities.[15]

Balaban & Katz offered stage shows to celebrate holidays, fads of the day, and heroic adventures. It developed shows around all the popular culture highlights of the Roaring '20s – from celebrating the Charleston dance craze to poking fun at its electronic rival, radio. Through promotion and publicity the Balaban & Katz stage show became so attractive and of such a high quality that the occasional dissatisfied customer demanded their money back – even before the movie portion began![16]

Sam Katz exploited the star system and developed local stars. One best symbolized the appeal of the Balaban & Katz live entertainment. Paul Ash was a red-haired, flamboyant band leader from California. Ash may now be but a mere footnote in the history of popular music, but for Balaban & Katz during the 1920s, Ash and his Merry Gang engaged the audience by sprinting up and down the aisles, conducting sing-alongs, and offering smoothed versions of innovative jazz styles then originating in clubs on Chicago's southside. Ash fostered hokum-filled jazz stylings that produced critical newspaper commentary, and seemed the source of lines of patrons which stretched around the corner starting at ten in the morning. Sam Katz made sure no one forgot that Ash and his gang were only available in B&K theaters by taking out regular newspaper advertisements for his stage star.[17]

Optimal locations, beautiful buildings, splendid service, and live stage show stars could and did attract fans throughout the then traditional moviegoing season – September through May. But Katz also wanted to fill his cinematic cathedrals throughout the Midwest's brutal summers. Here partner Barney Balaban found an innovator of air conditioning, based in Chicago's meat-packing industry. Balaban & Katz's Central Park, opened in 1917, stands as the nation's first mechanically air-cooled motion picture theater, developed by Chicago's Kroeschell Bros. Ice Machine Company, which transformed a carbon dioxide refrigeration system into a two-room unit that could efficiently and effectively cool 5,000-seat auditoria. Balaban & Katz in all its advertisements constantly reminded the public that its theaters were the only sites of wonderland summer cool fun. By 1924, with icicles hanging from every newspaper advertisement and from the marquees of all theaters, Balaban & Katz's cooled movie theaters were the talk of the movie exhibition business across the United States, and formed the fifth principle of the new movie-chain economics.[18]

With its five-point strategy Balaban & Katz kept theaters full year round, and costs of operation low. Workers were not paid much, as many would have paid to work "in the movies." Only projectionists and musicians were unionized, and they represented half the average picture palace's staff. The buildings were expensive to construct, but as they were filled from morning to night, every day of the week, mortgages were quickly retired. Katz even sometimes demanded and got well in excess of one dollar for admission – the best seats on Saturday and Sunday nights when Paul Ash was on stage.

Per seat Sam Katz calculated that his Chicago chain ranked as the most profitable motion picture theater circuit in the United States. It is no wonder the major Hollywood companies scrambled to ally themselves with Balaban & Katz. Midway through 1925 Hollywood – in the person of the legendary entrepreneur Adolph Zukor – came to call. The alliance of Zukor's Hollywood movie company, Famous Players–Lasky (later called Paramount), with Balaban & Katz linked Hollywood's top films and stars with the most innovative and profitable chain of motion picture theaters. A national chain would be the logical extension of this alliance.[19]

The Formation of the Publix Empire

This national chain would be called Publix. Sam Katz transferred the Balaban & Katz sys-

tem to Paramount's then chain of 500 movie theaters. Within two years Katz's newly christened Publix chain stood atop the film industry as the world's largest, most profitable, and most imitated. By 1930 millions of patrons streamed into Publix theaters each and every day. Once Sam Katz had his Publix operation up and running, he acquired regional theater chains to transform them into Balaban & Katz-style extensions of his Publix chain. Katz's takeovers of small regional chains were the regular headlines of the movie business press. In rapid fashion Katz took control of motion picture theaters in Minneapolis, Minnesota, across the states of Iowa, Indiana, and Ohio, in Detroit, Michigan, through the states of Louisiana, Maine, and Pennsylvania. No period of movie theater consolidation during the prior 30 years of movie history came close to matching what Sam Katz wrought during his build-up of the Publix chain.[20]

Katz had air conditioning installed in all Publix picture palaces, and set in motion the Balaban & Katz policy of live stage shows. All stage show units were created in a central studio in Long Island City, New York, across from Manhattan, and then sent out on a regular rotation around the growing Publix circuit. Katz then pro-rated the cost of mounting his stage shows across dozens of picture palaces along the circuit, which at the beginning of May of 1927 included theaters in New York City, New Haven, Boston, Buffalo, Detroit, Chicago, St. Louis, Kansas City, Omaha, Des Moines, Dallas, San Antonio, Houston, New Orleans, Memphis, and Atlanta. This meant that 16 separate units were out on the road at any one point in time. At the acme of the silent film, in 1927, Publix employed more musicians and vaudeville performers than any other theatrical organization in the nation.[21]

Sam Katz centralized Publix corporate power in his New York City office, high atop the Paramount building at 1501 Broadway on lower Times Square. Katz and his assistants made all decisions, from approving carpet patterns to what was the best music to accompany silent film offerings. Because of this centralized management, Sam Katz had more power and influence in moviegoing than any figure in the movie exhibition business. He took movie exhibition out of a "seat-of-the-pants" era and into 1920s-style "scientific management." Under Katz the movie show became yet another chain store on Main Street, invariably found just down or across the street from its inspiration – F.W. Woolworth & Company's five-and-dime stores.[22]

Sam Katz and his assistants obviously gave preference to booking Paramount films, yet Paramount hardly produced enough "product" to meet Publix's rising demand. He knew he controlled so much of the market that the other Hollywood studios would bow to his booking demands. In 1927 Sam Katz himself best summed up what he and his colleagues had innovated when he remarked on the record: "Publix Theatres are service stations for each other, for the benefit of the public that makes our investments safe."[23]

Katz set up the Publix school for training managers to follow his orders and know his system. Katz told an audience at Harvard University's Business School in 1927 that:

> There are ... fundamentals in the training of our men that are applicable to each and every theater on our circuit. In the first place, we are attempting to interest [in] our business the college graduate. ... We have found that the background of their academic training in college has prepared the men to think in orderly and well organized terms and in a systematic manner.[24]

Publix training sessions, supervised by John F. Barry, were conducted in the Paramount theater 20 stories below Sam Katz's office. Each class of about 50 learned the system, and options for local promotion and publicity. They were told to expect to create an event a day so as to draw free media attention. Publix experts taught neophytes how to plant pre-written stories in the newspaper. Many motion picture insiders scoffed at the idea

that the skills of show business could be taught, but Sam Katz had no doubts. He knew his Publix system depended on a trained, skilled class of managers on the local level, and the investment in training them would pay off many times over in the long run.[25]

The Coming of Sound

The coming of sound caused hardly a ripple in Sam Katz's Publix chain-store efficiency tactics. Filmed stage shows – short recordings of the top vaudeville acts of the day – were simply substituted for the far more expensive live stage shows in all but the largest motion picture theaters. A headline in the confidential in-house publication, *Publix Opinion*, summarized the situation: "Stupendous Sound Shows Now Put Every Publix Theater in Deluxe Class." On May 18, 1929 Sam Katz declared that only a handful of special movie palaces – in the biggest cities – would continue to offer live stage shows. Costs fell; profits soared.[26]

The process took only a couple of years. On February 17, 1927 Paramount Famous Players, along with Universal, Loew's, First National, United Artists, and Producers Distributing Corporation, signed an agreement to jointly select one sound system. Adolph Zukor and Sam Katz reasoned only standardization would lead to lower costs; it was in their best interest to collude. They selected Western Electric, and all signed on May 11, 1928.[27]

Moreover, as negotiations were going on, the overall US economy began to turn up; theater attendance, particularly at chain cinemas, began a dramatic double-digit rise after Labor Day, 1927. Sam Katz delivered the best quarter in Publix history. By the end of 1927, Paramount had accumulated the greatest profits in its corporate history, an increase of 44 percent for the year.[28]

Paramount and its allies had negotiated well with Western Electric. After May 1928 chain cinemas were delivered sound equipment as rapidly as Western Electric could make and ship the necessary parts. Unaffiliated theaters simply waited. Indeed, for a short time, unaffiliated theaters counter-programmed. During 1929, as the major theaters systematically abandoned stage shows in all except their largest houses, non-chain theaters began to *add* live vaudeville stage shows. But this did not help. Customers drove to the nearest major city to attend wired chain theaters. Big-city residents simply took the trolley downtown to a wired picture palace. The Hays Office suddenly had a new duty: arbitrate disputes and grant relief. By the spring of 1929 conditions had settled, and the exhibition side began to operate normally again. The cost of an installation, even in a 5,000-seat picture palace estimated to be about $20,000, proved trivial compared to the additional receipts that came about as customers lined up, day and night, to see the new talkies.[29]

The greatest problem lay with the opposition by the American Federation of Musicians (AFM). Sam Katz and Publix began to lay off orchestra members during the summer of 1928. The AFM took a stand that July when Sam Katz ordered the orchestra of 12 removed from Publix's McVicker's theater in downtown Chicago. James C. Petrillo, president of the Chicago local, protested and conferred with Katz. Katz refused; he was already counting up the savings. On July 22, 1928 Petrillo gave up and journeyed to New York to meet with AFM national president Joseph Weber. On August 28, 1928, Weber and Petrillo announced that there would be a strike unless all of the new contracts provided for at least six musicians for 44 weeks. In addition, the union demanded guaranteed employment for one organist per house. The contracts expired with no signed agreement. On September 1, 1928, Publix went to United States District Court and secured four temporary injunctions restraining the union leaders from calling a strike. The AFM immediately engaged Clarence Darrow as outside counsel, and sought help from William Green, president of the American Federation of Labor. By

September 5, 85 percent of Chicago's theaters had no music; 700 musicians had walked off their jobs.[30]

Three days of hard bargaining commenced, and an agreement was signed. Although both sides claimed victory, the union's power had decreased significantly. Four musicians would be used for one year, but then contract negotiations would be opened again. This contract ran but one year, not the usual three. The required number of weeks of employment for the year also fell from 44 to 36. We now know this strike signaled the beginning of the end for the musicians. Only the power of a sympathy strike by stage hands and projectionists kept the exhibitors from instantly releasing all musicians. The AFM turned in earnest to radio for new work.[31]

Publix profits indeed caused Paramount to expand. In June, Zukor made his strongest move as Paramount acquired 50 percent of the newly formed Columbia Broadcasting System. No cash exchanged hands. Paramount simply traded 58,823 shares of Paramount common stock, then worth over $3,800,000, for the 50 percent interest of CBS common. The radio network with 54 affiliates would use Paramount film personalities as NBC used RKO's stars. Paramount in turn could employ its presentation talent on CBS stations. In exchange, CBS acquired the talent necessary to compete more strongly against NBC. But radio investments simply signaled how well Publix was doing. In September 1929, Publix controlled 700 theaters, by May 1930 it owned over 1,400 in number. No one knew the exact total on any one day, for Sam Katz was always trading and contracting.[32]

Chain-Store Promotion and Publix Techniques

Throughout its growth, advertising remained key to Publix's continuing success. Katz told all new employees:

130

Advertising is Selling. This selling, as far as it applies to the theater, exerts its influence in activities which are practically countless. It is your job to master every one – to understand the possibilities and limitations of each. Every one of these activities can bring dollars to the theater you manage.[33]

Sam Katz rode the innovation of mass marketing and constantly promoted moviegoing in general, and the current Publix show in particular. On a daily basis Publix's New York City-based advertising department purchased space and sent off copy to hundreds of newspapers and dozens of national magazines. Publix promotion always aimed to expand moviegoing demand. Yet with the run-zone-clearance system setting fixed prices, ever lower as one awaited the next run, the Publix promotion staff could not herald what most chain stores did: lower prices. Instead they sought to induce the potential patron to pay top dollar to attend a first-run motion picture, and thus maximize Publix's revenues.[34]

Publix employed all the then available tools of modern 1920s advertising and promotion. Their daily ad buys were so large and frequent that it made sense to set up an advertising department rather than employ an outside advertising agency. Experts in the Publix central office constructed national advertising campaigns, and then local managers suggested means by which to tailor these national plans to special local needs and customs.[35]

Advertising, publicity, and exploitation – in the 1920s – were divided into seven categories by Sam Katz and his assistants.

First, Katz and his staff sought free newspaper and magazine stories. When possible, Publix would write the story, and the newspaper or magazine would run it as written. Such stories, written by Publix experts in the central office, were regularly offered to newspapers and magazines free. Tied to an upcoming motion picture, the local newspaper and/or national magazine would print a prewritten profile of the star or a behind-the-scenes exclusive account of the making of the film.

In a major city a daily newspaper offered means to communicate to millions of persons at a single time; national magazines, weeklies, also were read by millions. Fan magazines were particularly good vehicles to reach a growing number of movie devotees.[36]

But even Publix experts could not always count on newspapers and magazines accepting their free publicity. The fallback second option came with the Publix office purchasing an advertisement in the newspaper or magazine. During the week this meant paid space in a newspaper's motion picture theater directory, while on the weekends, the principal time for going out to the movies, display advertisements were bought. Magazine space was also purchased on a weekly basis. Generally, the rule of thumb told Publix to spend from 5 to 10 percent of expected gross revenues on paid advertising. Such advertising campaigns were planned months in advance, in almost military fashion. Here the regularity of the studio system proved a great assistance to Publix's planning of publicity, advertising, and promotion.[37]

Third, there was what was then called bill posting, now labeled outdoor advertising. The central tool was the poster, an inherited tradition from vaudeville and live theater in the days before the movies. Coming in a variety of sizes (from window cards to vast "twenty-four-sheets"), posters could be found throughout the community during the days before the film was booked to appear. By 1928 the typical Publix campaign called for nearly 10,000 posters, of all sizes, printed in bulk at discounted prices.[38]

Fourth, there were special stunts. If the film had a foreign theme, then the ushers were instructed and dressed in appropriate costumes. If the movie involved a steam locomotive, then a cardboard display of an engine might be constructed next to the box office. Multiple ideas were sent down to managers, who then would select what might best work in their local market. For films booked for June of 1929, for example, Publix executives recommended tie-ins to school graduations, links to summer vacations, or to buying a new home, events inspired by baseball, flag day, weddings, the longest day of the year, father's day, and even in its Southern cities something about Jefferson Davis' birthday on June 21. Publix regularly offered prizes for the best ideas for stunts, typically several hundred dollars in the clever manager's pay envelope.[39]

Fifth in line as to preference for use for advertising and promotion was radio. So for the November 1927 opening of new Publix theaters in Denver, Fort Worth, Texas, and Birmingham, Alabama, the main office set up radio remote broadcasts from the theater premieres and asked listeners to telephone their local newspaper if they had heard the broadcast. In 1929 Publix's parent company, Paramount, became part owner of CBS radio, and so even before Paramount released *The Virginian* (with Gary Cooper) the CBS radio network – at 10:00 p.m. (EST) on November 2, 1929 – presented a radio play version. CBS offered Publix numerous possibilities for national network exposure, and by 1930 Publix regularly saluted its new picture palaces with radio network special productions.[40]

Sixth came one means of promotion not available to other chain operations – trailers – industry jargon for previews of coming attractions. Publix experts loved to herald forthcoming films using the theater's own movie screen and a "captured" audience. While trailers had on occasion been used by other exhibitors, Sam Katz made this particular means of promotion a cornerstone of the theatrical exhibition business. Indeed, Sam Katz deemed trailers so important that he was willing to have Publix make its own – even for non-Paramount films. He did not trust what the other Hollywood studios sent him.[41]

Finally, at the bottom of the rank order of preferred options, there was local innovation. Managers were urged to innovate, but only after they had covered the six options outlined above. Some local operators employed direct mail by sending flyers to possible patrons who lived in sections of town known to have the greatest concentration of movie fans. Publix also found success with advertisements posted on the sides of street cars that ran through these sections of town, often directly to or past the Publix theater. Sam Katz and Barney Balaban knew why: "Because [of] the type of theaters we operate we depend upon appealing to a great number of people of a class who ride in street cars."[42]

To push these seven techniques, Sam Katz established a publicity and promotion department by hiring experts from up and down Madison Avenue, and from America's top universities. Publix supplied its own press kits, not relying upon Hollywood studios. The typical Publix promotional manual contained model advertisements, sketches, and photographs to send to local newspapers, suggestions about how to place advertising, and ideas for stunts. Local advertising budgets were balanced once a month and within those 30 days the local manager had some flexibility. In A.M. Botsford Katz had an experienced advertising manager, a former newspaper editor, but no one doubted that Katz, not Botsford, approved all decisions from his office high atop the Paramount building.[43]

At the core of the Publix promotion policy was institutional advertising, not aimed at selling any single film but directed at increasing demand for the complete Publix product. In national magazines and large city newspapers Publix heralded: "You don't need to know what's playing at a Publix house. It's bound to be the best show in town." Connected images envisioned a picture palace paradise, with well-dressed spectators and ushers, in plush buildings, enjoying stage shows and air conditioning. Publix regularly spent in excess of $1 million per year for institutional advertising in national magazines such as *Saturday Evening Post*, *Ladies' Home Journal*, and *Cosmopolitan* as well as 300 newspapers in 80 key cities across the USA.[44]

Publix experts carefully tracked the circulation of the newspapers and magazines used for advertising and promotion. For one company campaign *Publix Opinion* heralded "10,000,000 Persons Know of Opportunity," and then tallied the 16 newspapers with more than 2,000,000 circulation used. The writer estimated that at least five persons read every newspaper, and so simple multiplication meant 10,000,000 had learned of this Publix promotion. Newspapers used included the *New York Graphic*, the *Detroit News*, the *Boston Traveler*, the *Chicago Daily News*, the *Buffalo Evening News*, the *St. Louis Star*, and the *Atlanta Constitution*, all with circulations above 100,000.[45]

Sam Katz did what guidebooks on advertising of the day suggested: promote the special qualities of his product. This is where the five facets of Balaban & Katz entertainment (now credited to Publix) came into play. Publix advertising heralded its comfortable seats and impressive buildings. Campaigns applauded the service and courtesy of the ushers and other personnel. They detailed the special stage shows. These traits made Publix distinctive and that is what the company's New York City advertising women and men promoted.

For example, a series of advertisements preceding the summers of the late 1920s and early 1930s praised Publix air conditioning. While industry insiders were worrying about the coming of sound, Publix told anyone who might listen, over all possible media, that it had already set in motion that wonder of technical marvels – air conditioning! The company told the world that it had spent millions installing this apparatus for comfort. By 1928 newspapers generated article after article noting that Publix was the largest buyer of air-conditioning equipment in the world.[46]

Advertising ideas formed the core of the confidential internal in-house publication sent to all managers entitled *Publix Opinion*, which Katz started in late April 1927. Sam Katz sent out this warning with the first issue: "[*Publix Opinion*] is the property of PUBLIX THEATERS CORPORATION. Its contents are confidential within the Publix and Paramount organizations. It is not to be cut or

mutilated in any manner, nor removed from the custody of the individual in whose care it is entrusted. Signed: Sam Katz, President." A.M. Botsford, Publix advertising chief, functioned as the editor of *Publix Opinion*. In essence this was a means of sending ideas down the line, the functional equivalent of the bulletin board for clippings found in the Publix managers school. For promotion and publicity the season began in the fall, after Labor Day. Like launching the familiar beginning of the new television season during the latter third of the twentieth century, Publix set in motion a publicity wave to induce added demand for the new season of moviegoing.

"Publix Harvest Month" offers a typical campaign. Beginning in September 1927, following the usual pre-season blitz to time with Labor Day, Sam Katz and his assistants targeted (to use a modern term) 200 of Publix finest (urban) movie palaces. Local managers were prompted to seek a Harvest Queen. Special advertising, with a "Wheat Stack" or "Horn of Plenty" in the corner, filled all newspaper and magazine advertising copy. The theaters received special trailers. Fans could win prizes such as a pair of cufflinks from Adolphe Menjou or a gold watch from Bebe Daniels.[47]

And during October 1927 this marketing blitz worked. Publix theaters from Atlanta to Boston to Texas to Iowa broke existing house records. Publix had cleverly spiked up demand for its package of services – from stage shows to well-dressed ushers to palatial picture palaces. Interestingly absent from the campaign was mention of particular motion pictures. Even in the confidential in-house publication, *Publix Opinion*, there came but a line or two noting the actual films shown at Publix theaters during October 1927 – *Underworld*, *The Way of All Flesh*, *Romance*, among others. No, the accent for advertising and promotion was on location, architecture, service, and stage shows. Publix sold a continuous package of pleasure, not any single motion picture, and its promotion and publicity were based on that flow. The image and brand of gratification was the basis of drawing customers into the Publix theaters.[48]

Conclusions and Implications

Publix functioned as a chain operation, pure and simple. Sam Katz stated this directly, in a confidential speech to managers of his New England theaters: "We set about establishing an organization which we like to term a service station. . . . [In the New York office] we review, daily, and every hour of the day, the activities of all kinds of operations all over the United States."[49] Here the movie industry simply took up techniques innovated by others, and offered nothing special save more publicity and promotion than had been seen up to that time.

Katz relied on a changing urban nation. Chain operations held their most distinctive advantage in cities since such a large company like Publix could expend considerable sums on expensive newspaper advertising. The independent theater owner down the street found such liberal use of newspaper space cost-prohibitive. But poster art worked as well, as the potential audiences embraced written and visual promotions.[50]

But as powerful as Sam Katz was and how well his system maximized profits, he could do nothing to wipe away the effects of the coming of the Great Depression. As early as October 1929, after years of positive headlines, something began to seem amiss. Katz's confidential in-house publication, *Publix Opinion*, headlined: "Mr. Katz Orders Drive to Remedy Box-Office 'Blue Monday' Slump." Katz himself wrote (in the form of a telegram to all managers) that "Have noticed tendency severe drop in grosses class 'A' theaters on Mondays all over circuit . . . Monday proving recently to be disastrous day for houses every where. Something must be done immediately."[51]

This seemed like a temporary detour on a march to ever-greater power and profits. But we now know it was simply a foreshadow of the greatest economic downturn of the twentieth century. At the time, Katz simply never saw the Great Depression coming. Indeed, he continued to borrow extensively so as to keep buying more theaters, and keep his theater empire ever growing. As the 1930s commenced, Publix's debt rose steadily into the hundreds of millions of dollars, and Katz resisted any change in the methods that had worked so well through the 1920s. He had fought hard to create an empire based on scientific chain-store methods; only in 1932, voted out by outside directors, did Katz resign. And with his departure the first great era in the history of moviegoing in the United States had come to an end.[52]

But his legacy continued. Publix, copied by all the other major chains, took the localism out of movie exhibition. Gone was the power of the local manager. Under Publix control they became glorified janitors. Power would forever go to the national office. The coming of sound really altered the movie business little; the coming of chain motion picture theater operation did. Here we find the considerable effect of the Great Depression as well. No doubt Sam Katz would have kept Publix expanding had the economic downturn not come. But hard times ended Publix expansion, and signaled the commencement of the economic structure in place. We now know that meant the beginning of what we call the studio era.

Notes

1 *Motion Picture News*, July 31, 1926, 396; *Motion Picture Herald*, November 5, 1932, 9–10.
2 *Variety*, August 7, 1929, 3. The profits and power extracted from control of the Canadian motion picture market should not be discounted. This meant an additional 2,000,000 patrons per week. See *Motion Picture Herald*, January 20, 1945, 10.
3 *New York Times*, April 25, 1930, 28.
4 Alfred D. Chandler, Jr., *The Visible Hand: The Managerial Revolution in American Business* (Cambridge: Harvard University Press, 1977), 209–84; Richard S. Tedlow, *New and Improved: The Story of Mass Marketing in*

America (New York: Basic Books, 1990), 1–21; Daniel Bloomfield (ed.), *Chain Stores and Legislation* (New York: H.W. Wilson, 1938), 72–4.

5 Theodore N. Beckman and Herman C. Nolan, *The Chain Store Problem* (New York: McGraw Hill, 1938), 42–74.

6 Walter S. Hayward and Percival White, *Chain Stores*, 3rd ed. (New York: McGraw Hill, 1928), 1–14; Beckman and Nolan, *The Chain Store Problem*, 19–28.

7 Chandler, *The Visible Hand*, 233–7; Tedlow, *New and Improved*, 186–214; Beckman and Nolan, *The Chain Store Problem*, 38–9.

8 For details of the history of Balaban & Katz see *Publix Opinion*, April 30, 1928, 1–2. Note: *Publix Opinion* was the confidential, in-house publication for officials and managers of the theater chain.

9 *Motion Picture News*, April 5, 1919, 4; *Exhibitor's Herald and Motography*, April 31, 1919, 37; *Motion Picture News*, May 31, 1919, 3574; *Exhibitor's Herald and Motography*, September 6, 1919, 46; *Motion Picture News*, December 6, 1919, 4065; *Motion Picture News*, January 24, 1920, 1038; *Motion Picture News*, August 6, 1921, 759; *Variety*, May 26, 1922, 39; *Motion Picture News*, June 24, 1922, 3321; *Variety*, June 23, 1922, 38; *Variety*, July 7, 1922, 61; *Motion Picture News*, July 8, 1922, 178; *Variety*, July 12, 1923, 20; *Variety*, April 9, 1924, 16; *Variety*, July 23, 1924, 24; *Motion Picture News*, November 15, 1924, 2482; Joseph P. Kennedy (ed.), *The Story of the Films* (Chicago: A.W. Shaw, 1927), 265.

10 Barney Balaban and Sam Katz, *The Fundamental Principles of Balaban & Katz Theatre Management* (Chicago: Balaban & Katz, 1926), 54.

11 Kennedy, *The Story of the Films* 265. This book, edited by the former president's father, is a collection of speeches, one of which is by Sam Katz. See also *Publix Opinion*, April 30, 1928, 2.

12 *Publix Opinion*, April 30, 1928, 2.

13 *Exhibitor's Herald*, June 19, 1926, 50; *Publix Opinion*, April 30, 1928, 2.

14 *Motion Picture News*, July 31, 1926, 395; Harold B. Franklin, *Motion Picture Management* (New York: George H. Doran Company, 1927), 124–38.

15 Franklin, *Motion Picture Management*, 299.

16 *Variety*, September 22, 1922, 1; *Variety*, June 14, 1923, 21; *Variety*, January 31, 1924, 21; *Variety*, March 11, 1925, 39–40; *Motion Picture News*, July 31, 1926, 395–6; Kennedy, *The Story of the Films*, 276–7.

17 *Variety*, July 22, 1925, 27; *Variety*, August 5, 1925, 27; *Variety*, August 19, 1925, 32, 35; *Variety*, October 28, 1925, 30; *Exhibitor's Herald*, November 21, 1925, 53; *Variety*, May 26, 1926, 23.

18 Fred Wittenmeyer, "Cooling of Theaters and Public Buildings," *Ice and Refrigeration* (July 1922), 13–14; "Air Conditioning," *Ice and Refrigeration* (November 1925), 251; Franklin, *Motion Picture Management*, 305–12.

19 *Motion Picture News*, May 10, 1924, 2085; *Variety*, January 14, 1925, 21; *Motion Picture News*, February 14, 1925, 708; *Motion Picture News*, March 14, 1925, 1150; *Variety*, September 2, 1925, 33; *Variety*, November 4, 1925, 29; *Variety*, December 16, 1925, 29; *Variety*, April 7, 1926, 24, 28; *Motion Picture News*, July 31, 1926, 396.

20 *Exhibitor's Herald*, October 3, 1925, 25–7; *Motion Picture News*, July 31, 1926, 395; *Motion Picture News*, July 31, 1926, 395; *The Magazine of Wall Street*, April 23, 1927, 1178; *Commercial and Financial Chronicle*, April 21, 1928, 2490; *Variety*, August 7, 1929, 10.

21 *Motion Picture News*, January 9, 1926, 203; *Publix Opinion*, April 24, 1927, 1; *Publix Opinion*, May 1, 1927, 1; *New York Times*, July 10, 1927, 24; *Publix Opinion*, March 12, 1928, 5; *Film Daily*, April 8, 1929, 1.

22 *Publix Opinion*, April 24, 1927, 3; *Publix Opinion*, April 30, 1928, 2; Kennedy, *The Story of the Films*, 275–7; Howard T. Lewis, *Cases in the Motion Picture Industry* (New York: D. Van Nostrand, 1930), 516–21.

23 Quotation from *Publix Opinion*, April 30, 1928, 2. See also *Publix Opinion*, April 24, 1927, 3; Kennedy, *The Story of the Films* 275–7; Lewis, *Cases in the Motion Picture Industry*, 516–21; *Variety*, August 7, 1929, 2–10, 189.

24 Kennedy, *The Story of the Films*, 266–7.

25 *Exhibitor's Herald*, September 12, 1925, 8–9, 26–7; *Film Daily*, January 14, 1926, 1; *Film Daily*, February 26, 1926, 1; *Film Daily*, July 30, 1926, 1–2; *Moving Picture World*, March 26, 1927, 32–3; *Publix Opinion*, January 28, 1928, 2; *Publix Opinion*, February 4, 1928, 1; *Publix Opinion*, May 29, 1929, 5; *Publix*

Opinion, May 11, 1929, 10–11. See also Kennedy, *The Story of the Films*, 267; Arthur Mayer, *Merely Colossal* (New York: Simon & Schuster, 1953), 106–11 and 516–18; Howard T. Lewis, *The Motion Picture Industry* (New York: D. Van Nostrand, 1933), 348–50.

26 The headline is taken from *Publix Opinion*, April 27, 1929, 1. See also *Film Daily*, April 8, 1929, 1; *Film Daily*, April 16, 1929, 1, 4; *Publix Opinion*, May 11, 1929, 1; *Variety*, May 29, 1929, 30; *Variety*, May 14, 1930, 4.

27 *General Talking Pictures* v. *Western Electric*, 18 F. Supp., Exhibit 105.

28 *Barrons*, September 19, 1927, 19; *Barrons*, April 30, 1928, 14; *Barrons*, October 8, 1928, 14; *Barrons*, May 28, 1928, 22.

29 *Variety*, February 8, 1928, 4; *Variety*, July 18, 1928, 23.

30 *Variety*, July 11, 1928, 17; *Variety*, July 18, 1928, 19; *Variety*, August 1, 1928, 14; *Variety*, August 29, 1928, 16.

31 *Variety*, September 12, 1928, 11; *Variety*, November 21, 1928, 57; *Variety*, January 9, 1929, 27; *Variety*, May 8, 1929, 71; *Variety*, May 15, 1929, 64; *Variety*, May 22, 1929, 6; *Variety*, September 18, 1929, 70.

32 *Variety*, September 12, 1928, 57; *Variety*, July 11, 1928, 4; *Barrons*, October 21, 1929, 15; *Variety*, June 19, 1929, 65; *Barrons*, October 21, 1929, 15; *Variety*, September 11, 1929, 5.

33 *Publix Opinion*, May 11, 1929, 10.

34 Chandler, *The Visible Hand*, 209, 227–8, 233–7.

35 Glendon Allvine, "Mass Movements in the Movies," *Commerce and Finance* 22, no. 14 (June 3, 1925), 1083; *Publix Opinion*, May 8, 1927, 1; Hayward and White, *Chain Stores*, 152–68, 198–236.

36 *Publix Opinion*, December 22, 1928, 4; Frank H. Ricketson, Jr., *The Management of Motion Picture Theaters* (New York: McGraw-Hill, 1938), 216–21.

37 Balaban and Katz, *The Fundamental Principles of Balaban & Katz Theatre Management*, 86; *Moving Picture World*, March 26, 1927, 309; *Publix Opinion*, August 25, 1928, 5; *Publix Opinion*, December 22, 1928, 4.

38 *Moving Picture World*, March 26, 1927, 348, 422; *Publix Opinion*, August 25, 1928, 5; *Publix Opinion*, December 22, 1928, 4.

39 *Publix Opinion*, May 8, 1927, 1; *Publix Opinion*, February 18, 1928; *Publix Opinion*, December 22, 1928, 4; *Publix Opinion*, May 25, 1929, 4–5.

40 *Publix Opinion*, November 7, 1927, 1; *Publix Opinion*, December 22, 1928, 4; *Publix Opinion*, January 5, 1929, 5; *Publix Opinion*, February 16, 1929, 1; *Publix Opinion*, November 1, 1929, 1–2.

41 Balaban and Katz, *The Fundamental Principles of Balaban & Katz Theatre Management*, 85; *Publix Opinion*, December 22, 1928, 4; Lewis, *The Motion Picture Industry*, 242–5.

42 The quotation is from Balaban and Katz, *The Fundamental Principles of Balaban & Katz Theatre Management*, 87. See also Franklin, *Motion Picture Management*, 243–57; *Publix Opinion*, December 22, 1928, 4; Ricketson, *The Management of Motion Picture Theaters*, 216–44.

43 *Motion Picture News*, July 31, 1926, 396; *Moving Picture World*, March 26, 1927, 309; *Variety*, August 7, 1929, 10, 189.

44 Allvine, "Mass Movements in the Movies," 1084; *Moving Picture World*, March 26, 1927, 309; Lewis, *Cases in the Motion Picture Industry*, 516–18; *Variety*, August 7, 1929, 2–8, 189; Kennedy, *The Story of the Films*, 280; Franklin, *Motion Picture Management*, 242–5; Lewis, *The Motion Picture Industry*, 237.

45 *Publix Opinion*, June 5, 1927, 1.

46 *Publix Opinion*, April 16, 1928, 1.

47 Keep in mind that the core of Publix theater holdings was in the South and Middle West, and so advertising campaigns of the late 1920s were often aimed at city folks who had just moved into urban America but missed their rural roots.

48 Sam Katz had the staff temporarily rename *Publix Opinion* as *Publix Harvester*. See such titled issues of September 19, 1927, September 26, 1927 (with two separate issues), October 3, 1927, October 10, 1927, October 17, 1927, and October 24, 1927. See also *Publix Opinion*, August 6, 1928, 1.

49 *Publix Opinion*, March 12, 1928, 1.

50 Geoffrey M. Lebher, *Chain Stores in America, 1859–1962* (New York: Chain Store Publishing Corporation, 1962), 85, 222–38; Hayward and White, *Chain Stores*, 222–32.

51 *Publix Opinion*, October 11, 1927, 1.

52 *Barrons*, October 28, 1929, 15; *Film Daily*, November 18, 1930, 1, 4; *Film Daily*, April 10, 1931, 1–2; *Film Daily*, August 20, 1931, 1; *Motion Picture Herald*, November 5, 1932, 9–10; *Barrons*, November 7, 1932, 16.

Promotion of *American Tragedy* at a Publix theater (1931)

21

Where "Movie Playing" Needs Reform (1920)

K. Sherwood Boblitz

The movies' period of probation is over; they are with us now to stay, to be a factor either for good or evil as the public demands and the producers fulfill, to educate our children or to be a detriment to them, to uplift our morals or to degrade them. We have accepted the motion pictures as a fixture, and we recognize their possibilities. And on the whole we are glad they are with us.

But there is one phase of the situation which is comparatively unnoticed, and which is, nevertheless, one of the most important points not only in relation to this specific field but to the entire scope of art. This is the piano playing furnished by the "parlor" for the joy and delectation of its patrons.

Before proceeding to a critical analysis of the music itself, let us look for a moment at the conditions that surround the player. The instrument itself is generally old, out of tune, strings dusty, and incapable of producing the correct vibrations. The stool has no back and the pianist plays for hours with the muscles of her back becoming constantly more strained. The light, both night and day, is poor and inadequate, forcing the pianist either to play by memory, ear, or incorrectly by the notes which she strives to make out.

The ventilation is insufficient even in the best regulated of the houses, and after the first hour it is not surprising to find a racking headache installed, which, of course, directly affects the spontaneity and quality of the music that is produced. The sheets of music cast over the piano in disorderly array are dirty, badly printed, pasted, and dog-eared, nor is there any system for keeping music where the player can easily lay hands on it. One particular piece must take its chances buried under a hundred others.

There are many distractions to the pianist that are even more annoying than the inadequate facilities. The front row is invariably filled with children kicking their heels, giggling and talking for the pictures. The audience as a whole indulges in fervent hand-clapping at frequent intervals. The boys love to whistle accompaniments to the music, regardless of either tune or time.

But more important than all else are the long hours of the performer unbroken by rest or recreation. With muscles weary and tired, with hands strained and eyes worn, she yet must sit bolt upright on her uncomfortable stool and hammer foolish tunes out of her poor instrument – and all for a paltry salary that is scarcely sufficient to hold body and soul together.

But we should concern ourselves little, however, were it not for just this one fact, which is too vital and glaring to longer go unnoticed or uncommented upon: the only music that many children and adults are ever able to hear is in the movie parlor. It is

Excerpted from K. Sherwood Boblitz, "Where 'Movie Playing' Needs Reform." *The Musician* 25 (June 1920), 8, 29.

practically impossible to take children to musicales and concerts, and unless they are studying at the right kind of a school where the principles of good music are instilled in them, they are compelled to form their impressions, not only of American music, but of the entire field of musical art, from the tunes played on a hurdy-gurdy and at the motion pictures.

The criticism is made – and with some justice, too, it may be – that Americans fail to have the proper love and appreciation of music. Is it not just possible that these very facts have something to do with the matter? In Germany, for example, children may hear their national music well played by a well-trained band every day, if they will. But in America there is nothing in any way similar to this, and we are fast awakening to the fact that if we would have our children love the things of our heart we must take some steps in the matter.

Let us analyze the music which to them represents the art. The lights go out, the first picture appears on the screen, accompanied by a loud pound from the piano; then a series of runs through which the loud pedal is weighed down to its utmost; this bad pedaling is now quite a feature; the pedal is put down at the beginning of a piece and it is safe to say that it is released scarcely half a dozen times, and then more through accident than intention; there is not the remotest effort at phrasing of any nature.

Too frequent, too jerky, and too inaccurate scales predominate. Indeed, they are quite a favorite with the youthful portion of the audience, and they would feel quite neglected were there not great sweeps up and down the piano punctuated by crashing chords in the bass.

The choice of music is uniformly cheap and inartistic, generally rag-time, and tawdry at that. It does no one good to write it, to play it, to hear it, and there is an appalling lack of variation. Transition is made with a certain amount of cleverness from one rag to another, to the loss of the "accompanists" who are merrily whistling and clapping their heels.

At times, it is true, we find sacred pieces, classical music, and even operas rendered, but these are performances to turn away from with horror – for they are "ragged," out of tune, out of time, out of key until their original tenor is lost, and were we not more than familiar with them we should not have recognized them. Lack of time and rhythm prevails not only here but in all the playing, due partly to the rapid turning of the reel by the operator with which the pianist must keep up, whether or no.

Another fault which is prevalent not only with picture players but with all beginners is what is known popularly as "slap-stick playing" – that is, the hands do not strike the keys together, but one follows the other by a perceptible pause. Aside from being inaccurate, it is death to any good playing.

Yet, after all, is this the case against the child or for the pianist? Is it quite fair to expect excellent instructive playing under such conditions and for such pay? How can we expect to find an efficient player? Is it possible that good playing could ever exist temporarily or permanently with such hours and lack of rest or recreation? [...]

The owners of the theaters express complete satisfaction with the present arrangements. And why should they not? They receive service for almost nothing, and their patrons are charmed with what they are giving. But how about the children who are growing up on such diet? Are we willing for their conceptions of music to be so maltreated and distorted? It would seem that we are.

Goods delivered are created by popular demand – the public gets what it wants when it asks for it. Hence it is not fair to blame either the producers or the players, but just our own selves. If we wish our children to hear good music and thus learn to recognize it and appreciate it, let us insist upon better pay, easier and shorter hours for the pianist, and more adequate surroundings.

It is the only music that many children ever hear.

Why not make it good?

139

22

Musical Presentation of Motion Pictures (1921)

George W. Beynon

Fitting the Pictorial

Through the constant and consistent efforts of those musicians who are striving to uplift photoplay music, we have arrived at a stage where every picture must receive a suitable accompaniment. Patrons have become familiar with the art of picture fitting through attending those theatres where large orchestras are maintained and high-priced conductors interpret the scenes. No slipshod methods are any longer tolerated by those who pay admission to see and HEAR.

Fundamentally, there are no set rules for fitting the animated magazine, and for that very reason no definite class of music can be selected beforehand. It is as necessary to preview a Pictorial as it is compulsory to prepare the Feature. In fact, as no cue-sheets are distributed for the former, it really becomes more essential to note its requirements. It is not always wise to run the pictorial as released. Frequently, by changing the positions of certain scenes, a better musical setting is procurable. This means that the orchestra leader and the house manager should confer on the matter, and often the operator can be of valuable assistance in giving suggestions. In order to suggest the possibilities in this science, it is necessary to work from a positive hypothesis. Suppose that there is a Screen Telegram showing the

following subjects in the order named: 1. DUPONT POWDER MILLS. 2. RED CROSS PARADE. 3. BAN JOHNSON AT THE BASE- BALL PARK. 4. GENERAL PERSHING REVIEWING THE FRENCH SOLDIERS. 5. COMMENCEMENT EXERCISES AT YALE. 6. THE ARRIVAL OF PRESIDENT WILSON. 7. THE AMERICAN ARMY IN FRANCE. 8. COLORED PARSON IMMERSING HIS BAP- TIST FLOCK.

It can readily be understood that these scenes must be shifted, as it would be folly to finish the review with the baptismal picture. The scenes should work up to a climax of hearty applause. To get this effect, close with one of the patriotic scenes, or that of President Wilson. At the same time, it would not be good showmanship to group all the "hand-getters" together. There should be a breathing space between to allow for greater effectiveness. Try arranging the scenes in the following manner: 1, 3, 4, 5, 8, 2, 6, and 7.

This grouping will give ample variety of tonal color and change of tempi. The first item, showing how gunpowder is made and delivered to the army, is largely educational and neutral in atmosphere. A light Moderato with a pleasing melody and of considerable length can be used. This gains the interest of the spectators at once. Number three gives the opportunity of playing that

Excerpted from George W. Beynon, *Musical Presentation of Motion Pictures* (New York: Schirrmer, 1921), 95–100, 144–8.

old favorite, "Take Me Out to the Ball Game." It will probably be short, and the chorus once through will fill the time-allowance.

In number four, there is only the choice "Marche Lorraine." This is the official march, always played when French troops are on field review. Do not make the mistake of playing an American patriotic number for General Pershing; because, even though one may desire to be courteous, there must be accuracy in the portrayal of the atmosphere.

In order to vary the music slightly for number five, a light waltz could be played if the action permits it. There is no chance to go wrong if the "Boola-Boola Song" is used, because it is typical of Yale University. If the scene is one where diplomas are presented, play the air *pp* only as suggested. Of course, a scene of this sort would naturally be short and could easily be finished at the cadence.

Number eight has many possibilities in the way of interpretation. If the orchestra can afford to take the risk, it may bring a laugh to burlesque this portion by playing "It Takes a Long, Tall, Dark-Skinned Gal to Make a Preacher Lay His Bible Down." A strong darky spiritual would certainly be appropriate, while some plaintive Southern coon song would not be amiss. Do not play "Mighty Lak a Rose."

After this bit of quiet humor, the audience is ready for number two; and, when they hear the strains of "Onward, Christian Soldiers," they are bound to break forth in rounds of applause. This number should not be played as a quickstep, but with the natural dignity which befits it. The interest of the auditors is now running high and their patriotic spirit has been aroused to the point where the appearance of the President brings them to their feet.

For number six, another march of grandiose quality or some patriotic air that will fit the situation should be chosen. It will naturally be very short, so the change can quickly be made into that most popular of all present-day songs, "Over There," for number seven.

Care must be taken that, when the marching soldiers appear, the music is kept in perfect time with their step. This is extremely important to enhance the effect, and is an art in itself. This number can be played when our army is shown marching in France, and is a fitting finish to a fine pictorial. The interest has not been allowed to lag nor have the climaxes been overshot.

All selections should be started softly and be continued *p* while the subtitle is on the screen; then break into the required volume of sound immediately upon the appearance of the action. If further subtitles appear in the same scene, the music can quiet down until they fade out. For neutral scenes, like number one, for instance, the orchestra should be kept down and the brass cut out altogether. At no time play *ff* before reaching the climax. The volume should be graded according to the action; then, when the big moment comes, there is power with which to emphasize it.

Clap-trap effects should never be used in the Pictorial. The fact must not be lost sight of that it is news, not melodrama, that is being shown. It must be taken into consideration that the patrons of the theatres have doubtless read all about what they are seeing, and they have associated the facts with ideas of dignity. Their sense of news propriety must not be jarred by the clanging of cowbells. [...]

It has been said that genius is the art of taking pains. Every theatre can have a genius if the leader so desires it. A genius in the orchestral pit means a full house, a full house means a successful business and a satisfied employer, and the last two mean a raise in salary. It pays to be a genius.

No picture can be fitted at one viewing without missing many vital details or sacrificing some important changes in the music. Picture fitting is no longer a question of throwing together indiscriminate selections, but has become an exact science. The day has arrived when producers fear improperly arranged music because of its power to ruin their feature. Music is the fulcrum on which,

141

by the lever of good musical sense, a picture may be raised to great heights. [...]

Futurity

Comparisons may be odious, yet it seems necessary to go back to the piano and drum period of picture presentation to illustrate the strides in the profession. Just as the picture industry has advanced step by step, so has music kept pace, providing a higher form of entertainment with each upward rung. Its mission has been identical with that of better pictures – to draw a better class of patrons – and it is fulfilling its destiny. In the infant days of photoplays, the people who patronized the "movies" cared little for music but appreciated the noise. The banging improvisations of a piano player, augmented by the cymbal-crashing drummer, delighted their ears and provided opportunity for loud chatter or louder guffaws. [...]

To-day we have in America probably sixty picture theatres with thirty or more men in the orchestras; hundreds of houses have large organs and thousands small orchestral combinations. All this in spite of the expense incidental to gathering together a good orchestra, the difficulty in procuring proper musical service from producers, and the loss of seating capacity by staging the orchestra or placing the organ.

What does the future hold?

Judging from the rapid strides already made, we fear even to speculate, lest our prediction fall far short of the ultimate mark. A review of a few pertinent facts may give some inkling of the possibilities.

To-day every producer realizes the worth of a proper musical setting to his picture, and to the best of his ability strives to meet the needs of the exhibitor. Many are providing cue-sheets, while some go to great expense in arranging orchestral scores. No longer is there any apathy shown in the executive offices of the big film magnates when the subject of music is broached. Their house organs are giving music wide publicity.

Music service departments are becoming a large factor in the selling of pictures, and what the other fellow is doing in this line is closely watched, lest he forge ahead of them.

In the theatres the audience is more conversant with the dual art of pictures and music, continually demanding a better musical performance. The exhibitor keeps in close touch with his orchestral leader. What was good enough a year ago is decidedly poor now. The work of fitting pictures has become more exacting in its details than ever before. Frequent repetitions of a number are frowned upon, and woe betide the leader who in a moment of carelessness uses inappropriate music. It is nothing unusual to have people request the musician to give them the name of a particular selection played during a specified scene. This demonstrates the musical educational value of picture music. [...]

Musical scores are receiving more and more consideration from the producers. The advantages derived from this form of musical accompaniment are manifold. The use of themes arranged in varied forms for the different characters has proved to be the highest form of setting, but has suffered somewhat at the hands of poor arrangers. This form is in its infancy, and no doubt will be developed to Wagnerian proportions as time goes on. The fitting of features by the process of suiting the dominant emotional scenes is also good and has reached artistic heights. Flash-backs are no longer regarded musically unless their bearing on the plot is essential.

We feel that the music of the future will be a score that combines both forms of treatment. Each score will be fitted for its atmosphere, dominant feeling and tempo, synchronized and properly keyblended, while interwoven will be found the themes significant of the characters in the foreground. Close attention will be paid to orchestral coloring, light and shade, depth and shallowness. Above all, variety will be the keynote of the entire composition. Orchestras everywhere will be enlarged, better organs and more capable organists will be used.

The fifth largest industry will become the fourth and gather within its fold the greatest composers, musical directors and virtuoso players of the day.

Though great has been the advance of the silent drama, greater yet has been the progress in its music; and the future holds a promise, stupendous in its magnitude, that picture music will rank favourably with grand opera and symphony.

23

Music (1927)

John F. Barry and Epes W. Sargent

Importance

Good music enhances the entertainment value of any program. The most exceptional program can be spoiled by poor music; but it should be remembered that, important as music is, the musical accompaniment of the photoplay is secondary and not paramount. Music should accompany and not predominate. It should never distract. An accompaniment that is too noisy is distracting. The influence of the music accompaniment should be subconscious. The closer it is to perfection, the less direct attention it attracts, because it is so close to the movement and the spirit of the photoplay that it brings the audience along with the action to an even greater emotional response. A conflict between the music and the screen, or the evident effort of musicians to attract attention to themselves or to their music, is detrimental.

Recreation

People do not visit the motion picture theatre for a musical education. The motion picture theatre is not a rival of the concert hall. The majority of people in the audience are tired after a hard day's work. They want recreation and entertainment. Remember that the majority of patrons are not "high-brows."

Classical music which is beyond their appreciation should be avoided. Classical music lovers who appreciate fine technique are in the minority. Music can be melodious and simple and generally understandable – and yet be classical. The long, heavy classical selections may be endured peaceably by the audience; the audience may not fidget; they may not talk; they may even try to applaud politely. But notice the very evident sigh of relief when the long, heavy classical selection is over. It is reactions like these which the theatre manager can notice. He is interested in details of operation as they relate to the box office.

The musicians may be interested in music as an art, rather than in its influence upon attendance. Therefore, the tactful manager can make suggestions based on his knowledge of patrons' preference, and if he does it tactfully, the music will be what patrons want. After all, showmanship depends upon giving people what they want, and not upon giving them what they should want according to some theoretical principles of music.

Orchestra Combinations

Small orchestras so common in theatres should not attempt to play selections which

Excerpted from John F. Barry and Epes W. Sargent, *Building Theatre Patronage: Management and Merchandising* (New York: Chalmers Publishing Company, 1927), 383–92.

have been arranged for symphony orchestras. Many defects can be traced to the failure to realize that the music rendered is not orchestrated for the size and combination of orchestra which is playing it.

Another cause of defect is improper combination. For the three-man orchestra, the best combination is piano, violin, and cello. Variety can be secured by using the violin for solos. Further variety is possible by playing the instruments on mute, then the pianist can solo with a countermarch by the violinist. The cello can also solo. Thus, with a three-piece orchestra, variety is possible. The same variety is possible with other combinations indicated here. If a cello player is not available locally, the clarinet can be substituted. For the four-piece orchestra the best combination is piano, violin, cello, and clarinet (a flute can be substituted for the cello). For the five-piece orchestra the best combination is piano, violin, cello, clarinet, and drum. A drum with a complete set of traps proves very useful for novel sound effects if not overworked. With the above combination it is preferable to have the leader play the piano or the violin, rather than any other instrument. For the six-piece orchestra the combination suggested is piano, violin, cello, clarinet, drum and cornet (a flute can be substituted for the clarinet). A cornet in so small a combination should be muted. For the eight-piece orchestra a bass can be added. For the nine-piece orchestra a trombone can be added. For the ten-piece orchestra, another first violin can be added.

The combinations suggested above are suitable only when vaudeville is not shown in addition to photoplays. Evidently, brass and drums are necessary in the orchestra which accompanies vaudeville.

Library

Synchronization of music for the photoplay is possible by following the standard cue sheets. However, a sufficiently equipped music library is necessary. [...]

The cataloguing of the music library is important. The most generally used method is that of filing selections according to moods. A cross-reference system can be used when parts of the same selection are suitable for different moods. The following headings are suggested for the mood file:

agitato for fire	dramatic	marine
agitato for storm	English	mystery
agitato for battle	festival	nocturne
agitato for crowd movement	fox trot French	oriental pastoral
American	gallop	pathetic
andante	German	Polish
bacchanale	grotesque	pulsating
ballet	Hawaiian	reveries
blues	humorous	romance
caprice	Hungarian	rube
children	hunting	Scotch
Chinese	hymns	sentiment
collegiate	Irish	Spanish
conversational	Italian	tango
dance classic	jazz	valse
descriptive	marches	western

It is well to mark music with the date of purchase and the dates of use, so that the same pieces will not be played too often. Variety is essential. [...]

The Organ

The organist should not be permitted to improvise. He should have a library at his disposal. If monotonous repetition is to be avoided, this library should include a number of pieces which will make it possible to prevent repetition within a reasonable period. Sufficient time for relief should be given the organist so that his playing does not become mechanical. The organist should give the same attention to previews and cueing that the orchestra does. An organ score should be used as far as co-operating with the orchestra is concerned. Such matters as proper co-ordination, so that the changes always are made in the same pitch, depend upon tactful suggestions from the manager.

Possibilities

Very few organs are used in a way which brings out all their possibilities. Comedy numbers, especially, give the organ many opportunities to use percussion devices and traps; yet how often do we find meaningless waltzes slovenly following the comedy. Comic effects can be interpreted with whistles, organ horns, sirens, sleigh bells, gongs, tom-toms, drums, tambourines, etc. When a skillful organist played the instrument which in a certain theatre had seemed so monotonous, the manager said, "What trick did you use? I didn't think my organ had all that." The answer was, "You don't really appreciate an organ until you understand all that it can give when used by one who understands its fullest possibilities." You have paid for this equipment – get your money's worth.

Home-made sound devices for accompaniment can be cheaply built for use back-stage or in the pit.

24

Future Developments (1927)

Harry M. Warner

Question Period

Mr. Kennedy. Mr. Warner, I have been handed several questions which I think those that are here would like to have you answer.

Mr. Warner. I shall be very glad to.

Mr. Kennedy. Do you lease or sell the vitaphone?

Mr. Warner. I said that was a problem that we are confronted with. At this particular time this is what we do. We take the cost of the machine and we lease it on that basis to the man who runs the theatre. If he does not want to pay cash, he pays in installments extending over twelve months; possibly twenty-five per cent cash and the balance divided over twelve months. Then we charge him a tax of 10 cents a seat a week. If the theatre has two thousand seats, he pays us $200 a week for forty weeks in the year, figuring that he may close his theatre twelve weeks in the summer time. That does not mean that that is the way it is ultimately going to be done, because I personally believe that the man who has a small theatre in a small town will not be able to pay that much money. If he has nine hundred seats and we charge him $90 a week in addition to the price of the machine, I think ultimately the burden will prove too heavy, and we shall have to modify our policy to meet the requirements of the situation.

Mr. Kennedy. What approximately does it cost to install?

Mr. Warner. We have got it down to the cheapest figure. In a theatre of nine hundred or one thousand seats, it costs $16,000; in the next size, the theatre of about fifteen hundred seats, $18,000; in the larger theatres, $22,000; in a theatre like the Roxy, $25,000. That is the actual cost to us. [...]

Mr. Kennedy. Describe how your method differs from the Fox method, the other so-called "talking picture."

Mr. Warner. In the Fox method you take both picture and music on a film instead of taking the picture on a film and the music on a record and running both off so that they correspond exactly. When we first started, this was the way the mechanical end operated. A camera and a vitaphone instrument were placed in one little sound-proof room. They were connected with a rod and cog wheels on each side and both worked automatically. But the grind of these two wheels was heard in the audience. After we got the picture people in it, they developed it so that the camera could work on one floor and the recording man on another. We now have them six stories apart, and in the building we have bought in New York, where all our work will be done, known as the Cosmopolitan

Excerpted from Harry M. Warner, "Future Developments." In Joseph P. Kennedy (ed.), *The Story of the Films* (Chicago: A.W. Shaw, 1927), 330–5.

Studios, we shall be able to operate still farther away.

The time is not far distant when you will be able to see and hear the inauguration of the next President. His address to the American people will be spread everywhere through the theatres on the vitaphone perfectly because by that time we shall be able to record in New York the address delivered in Washington.

We have developed our machine with an extra attachment that costs less than a thousand dollars, which enables us to use also the Fox movietone method. So that a theatre putting in a vitaphone can use either the method now used by us or the one on the film. Remember that the other system does all the work by a ray of light that penetrates and marks the film. I heard a demonstration not long ago, and it is very good. In order to protect ourselves in the future, we obtained all the rights and interest in the movietone method. The arrangement was a mutual one. Mr. Fox also has the right to manufacture his own numbers and his own pictures to be run on our machine. We gave him the right to manufacture either way, so that he can manufacture pictures by installing our apparatus or continue the way he is doing at the present time.

Question from the audience. What is the attitude of the organ manufacturers?

Mr. Warner. It is very hard to prophesy just what the vitaphone is going to eliminate ultimately. It is true that, if machines once become established in enough theatres and there are enough pictures synchronized to run those machines, there will be no need of organs, but I think that will not happen until a long time from today. Here is a town, let us say, of thirty thousand inhabitants, and there are five theatres. Each of these theatres possibly changes three times a week. That would be a fair average for a town of that size. That makes fifteen different and distinct shows in one small town. You can see that it is going to be a long time before there are enough pictures synchronized to eliminate the organ.

Question. Do you propose to sell the vitaphone at cost or less than cost and make the money from the use of it, or do you propose to make the profit on the sale of the vitaphone?

Mr. Warner. There are several things to consider there. If there is a competitive machine, that may influence our policy. As yet, I do not know of any effective competition. There are a great many machines being demonstrated, but one thing is lacking and that is amplification. There is only one company that has the telephone, and telephone amplification is that which is used with the vitaphone. I think ultimately the seat tax will be changed, but it is a little bit too new to say just how.

You do not mind if I get away from the question a little bit. What I am going to tell you has a bearing on the general subject. I went once to a certain theatre man who thought the vitaphone was too expensive and asked him, "How much money have you made in the last six weeks? Let's see your books." He had made somewhere around $1,500 in six weeks. Then I said, "If I can put a vitaphone in that will cost you $18,000 and give you a picture to play that can pay for the machine in one run, what do you care about the cost?" We made a deal with him on that basis. The division was fifty-fifty. We got $54,000 for our picture and he got $54,000 in six weeks.

There was another man who had a theatre. Ordinarily he could not pay us much. If we got $2,500 for a picture, that was high for him. He gave us $34,000 for our vitaphone picture on a fifty-fifty basis. So it is very hard to tell just how the income from this thing is going to be divided. You might take another picture and not do so well with it. We have not had enough time to go into all these things, and there is no set rule, except this – the man pays for the machine. Do not forget that we are doing this single-handed today. We are doing it with our own money because we believe in it. We honestly believe the vitaphone is going to do more good for humanity than anything else ever invented.

We all know that if you and I can talk to one another, we can understand one another. If Lincoln's Gettysburg Address could be repeated all over the world, maybe the world at large would understand what America stands for. We think that people read and know a lot of things, but when we get out into the world and see the masses of people and find out how many are working so hard to earn a living that they have not time to read, then we realize how much remains to be done in the way of bringing knowledge to them.

If we have a message of friendship or enlightenment that can be broadcast throughout the world, maybe the nations will be led to understand one another better. The vitaphone can do all that. There is a limited number of people who can go to the opera and pay seven or eight dollars to hear the great operatic artists of the world, but there are millions who cannot. Some of them want to hear good music, and the vitaphone makes that possible. These are the benefits and potentialities of this invention that honestly and sincerely make us fight on for it. If the issue was just money alone, I give you my word as a man that with the money I have put into the vitaphone already all four Warner brothers could live the rest of their lives without worrying.

American Federation of Musicians' advertisement (1931)

Fontaine Fox cartoon (1929)

25

Motion Pictures as a Phase of Commercialized Amusement in Toledo, Ohio (1919)

J.J. Phelan

[...][I]f the industry needs no control, why the antagonism of film producers and exhibitors against Federal Censorship? Surely a business dominated by the ideals it claims can have no consistent objection to a Federal control, which would aid in the furtherance and extension of those ideals.

In the light of the discussion and the evident need of control in some form, the following suggestions are submitted. They are not intended as a "cure-all," but as a reminder of the many ways social service can aid in one of the greatest problems confronting the American city. If unity of community action is secured in but one feature alone, the advisability and necessity of the others will become increasingly evident.

A Proposed Solution

1. The increase of parental responsibility, as seen in intelligent and sympathetic guidance, regarding the evils of promiscuous, excessive and indiscriminate attendance at picture-shows, burlesque and vaudeville – care to be exercised against "over-control" as well as "under-control."

2. The possible creation of a Department of Public Morals as a branch of the City Government. This department to supervise all of the public amusement places of the city; co-operate with the various charitable, philanthropic, social, religious and educational agencies, and enforce the present City Ordinance regarding the attendance of unchaperoned minors at theatres. To give it legal status, this department could be made a branch of the Department of Public Welfare or Public Safety.

3. The immediate appointment of a local Board of Film Censors, to co-operate with the Ohio Board of Film Censors as to the type of pictures most desirable for children. The number, personnel and all matters of detail to be worked ou[t] carefully by the Social Service Commission of the Inter-Church Federation, Catholic and Jewish churches. The censorship of all picture posters and advertising schemes outside of theatres and picture houses is also necessary.

4. The insertion in the local press (each week) of the bulletins issued by the Committee of Better Films for Young People.

5. The development of a Children's theatre in the city wherein clean, wholesome and proper plays may be shown to both

Excerpted from J.J. Phelan, *Motion Pictures as a Phase of Commercialized Amusement in Toledo, Ohio.* Social Survey Series III (August 1919), 120–2.

children and parents. A local theatre might be secured for the proper days.

6. Immediate instruction to be given to theatre managers and all employees regarding enforcement of present city ordinance as to attendance of unchaperoned minors.

7. Request for the appointment of a Federal Board of Film Censors. The only Federal control at present being the Federal Interstate Law, which prohibits the interstate transportation and foreign importation of prize-fight films by various states and local bodies. Hence, the need of a larger, more representative and adequate system of control.

8. The creation of a law to prevent children from attendance at shows after nine o'clock in the evening.

9. A reasonable and efficient method devised, whereby "movies" may be shown with comfort, little expense and safety in the home.

10. The need of co-operation between the educator and film-maker to build up a film library as complete and comprehensive as is the school library.

11. A civic awakening on the part of the public, that only the best pictures be allowed to be exhibited, and the determination to patronize only the best show-houses.

26

The Motion Picture and the Upbuilding of Community Life (1920)

Orrin G. Cocks

In most of the communities of the United States there is one motion picture theater for every 5,000 to 10,000 of the population. People flock to these places in such numbers that it has been estimated in the larger cities that a number totaling the entire population visits the theater every five to seven days. In spite of its attractiveness to the people, the motion picture, both as entertainment or instruction, is an unused social asset of American life. While it reaches more of the population than any other amusement agency, social workers have allowed it to develop almost entirely along commercial lines. Yet, here is a form of entertainment which attracts and which is understood by the people. They do not need to be urged to come. They not only attend willingly but pay their way on a self-respecting basis.

A strong and possibly impregnable argument can be presented for the wholesomeness of the motion picture for adults. Do you realize that it is the only national amusement which attracts the whole family, gives them change, relaxation, and thrill, and permits them to discuss life-problems in common at home following the evening's entertainment? Do you also realize that the majority of young people are drawn off the street at night and week by week are furnished an entertain-

ment which is satisfactory and which is more impersonal than the man or the girl they otherwise would meet on the darkened street? [...]

The one subject that commands our continuous attention is that of the effect of the ordinary dramatic motion picture on the minds of children. No one who is possessed with a grain of the common garden variety of common sense contends that the ordinary dramatic picture is satisfactory for the child. It was never meant to be. In most communities, however, parents allow their children to go freely to the motion picture theater. Evidently there is necessary to be built up here those "folk ways," manners, and customs which have been handed down through 1,500 years in connection with the spoken drama. I believe that nothing short of parental education, followed by parental control, will meet this situation.

It is useless to attempt to force a child to stay out of the attractive, alluring motion picture show if we offer him no substitute. Common sense would seem to suggest that we discover the kinds of pictures children like and those which are adapted to the world of the child, and furnish them freely in every city and town. Already the National Board has prepared such lists, and the pictures can

Excerpted from Orrin G. Cocks, "The Motion Picture and the Upbuilding of Community Life." *Proceedings of the National Conference on Social Work* (Chicago, 1920), 311–13.

be rented if there is sufficient energy and interest in local communities. This phase of children's recreation, however, should be considered as a part of the larger program for recreation, and increasing emphasis should be placed upon the primary value of outdoor active recreation, which stimulates inventiveness and the self-reliance of children. The motion picture at the best is a poor substitute for free and active play.

I would like to suggest to the social workers that the exhibitor also is an unused social factor in almost every community. Surprising and valuable results have been obtained by treating this citizen in a friendly manner, as a potential social servant and discussing with him the problems of the finer forms of community recreation. He has at his command great masses of material which can sway the hearts of men, women, and children, if he can be made to see that the people want this form of entertainment occasionally and that he can render a civic and patriotic service by doing his part. Do not ignore the motion picture manager as a powerful factor in the social life of your community!

27

Our Movie Made Children (1934)

Henry James Foreman

Movies in a Crowded Section

"The street, the sidewalks swarm with people, pushcarts stand along the curb; their proprietors hawk their wares to all passers-by. In the store windows bordering on the street is a bizarre assortment of dry-goods, cheeses, condiments and liquors, and from open doors issue a host of smells even more provocative. People elbow each other for passage along the sidewalk, while others pause to bargain loudly with the pushcart peddlers. The shrill notes of a hurdy-gurdy are heard down the street, and from somewhere overhead in the solid block of six-floor tenements comes the strident noise of a radio out of control. A street-car clangs its way along among the pushcart peddlers and their customers, and a moment later an elevated train roars by overhead. The traffic lights change and from another direction a heavy truck drags along, scattering the dust of the street in its wake. The boys in the street at their game of ball give way before it, but in the ensuing traffic are able in some way to continue their play. Through a nice judgment of distance and a dexterity in traffic born of long experience they continue their game – even though at the risk of life and limb. Such is the street world to which many of the under-privileged boys of a large city are exposed."

This is the setting as described by Thrasher and Cressey of the motion picture research in a congested area of New York City.[1] A number of large cities in America have areas somewhat similar to this one, though not in all respects alike. Even as New York communities go, it is among the most cosmopolitan. Its inhabitants, although predominantly Italians, include Porto Ricans, Negroes, Russians, Jews, Filipinos, Finns, Poles, Czecho-Slovaks, Yugo-Slavs, Turks, Irish, Lithuanians, Germans, Austrians, Rumanians, Greeks, South Americans, Scandinavians, Syrians, Armenians, a few Dutch and French and a tiny fragment of the older American stock left over in the wake of its own migration. It is neither a League of Nations nor a melting-pot. Or, if it is a melting-pot, there is hardly any knowing what will emerge from it as a final product. [...] In other words, it is largely a first generation immigrant settlement. Playgrounds are scarce and play life fills the teeming streets. The public school system is the chief Americanizing influence in the community. It is a community very little organized in the sense of neighborliness and neighborly responsibility, and the gang, the hangout, the poolroom, or the "private social club" and the taxi dance-hall are the ordinary methods of social cohesion. Speakeasies and bootlegging establishments abound, but the great and established source of entertainment is the motion picture and the movie theatre.

There are fifteen motion picture houses in the community, ranging from a large,

Excerpted from Henry James Foreman, *Our Movie Made Children* (New York: Macmillan, 1934), 251–61.

somewhat luxurious one, built fifteen years ago, to several dilapidated store compartments which have been converted into cheap movie houses. These the boys with a certain folk precision in nomenclature label as "dumps." Generally speaking, they do not go to them if they can help it, but the low price is a lure and to see a picture for a dime will take one even to a dump.

All varieties of films are shown in the region with the exception of what the researchers label as "intellectual pictures." For these the score is zero. Comedy and adventure are fairly represented, but the largest number of pictures shown, over sixty per cent, group themselves under the headings – *mystery, romantic love, crime* and *sexual impropriety*. Stridently advertised and loudly "ballyhooed" are these pictures, not only by "trailers," posters, local newspapers and all the usual means, but by such lobby displays as the use of stilettos, a hangman's noose, or a replica of an electric chair. A lurid drinking scene painted over a large expanse of beaverboard showing young girls in suggestive poses may be used to indicate that the photoplay is of a sexy nature. Various as is the motion picture diet, the proprietors of film houses in this region agree that gangland pictures draw the greatest number of young people. Sex pictures are a second choice and advertisements are not wanting to indicate that the picture is immoral, so that the natural tendency is to see it early – before the "cops" come along and close up the theatre. [...]

Judging by some of the attendance records obtained by the investigators, the motion picture theatres in this community should be highly successful. As one of them, the late Dr. R.L. Whitley, observes: "Second only to the time spent in the home, in the school, and on the street is the time the boy spends at the movie. Among 1356 boys examined on this subject, 627 declared that they go to the movies once a week, 455 twice a week, 137 three times a week and 57, four or more times each week. In other words, eighty per cent of

them go to the movies once a week or oftener. On an average, all these boys of various groups see over eighty-three programmes a year." [...]

[...][M]uch of the social interest of the boy in this region centers about the motion picture theater. Special contacts, special activities, and certain dark practices are made possible or facilitated by the dimly lighted movie house. Mothers can leave their children there knowing that they will stay until called for, as illustrated by the statement of the theater nurse in an earlier chapter. In rare instances a local criminal gang, whose members are known to the proprietor or attendants, may visit the motion picture in a body as a means of establishing an alibi. At times, during the cold months of winter, whole families may come and remain the entire day in order to save the expense of heating their rooms. "A complete inventory of the activities in the local theaters in this community," concludes the report, "would have to include everything from the 'spotting' and 'planting' of victims for gangland bullets to clandestine sexual activity in the darkened movie house – and even to childbirth." [...]

In a projected book by the late Dr. R.L. Whitley he presents some of the uses of the cheaper grade of motion picture theaters of the region in this manner:

"In a number of cases the motion picture house is much more important in relation to delinquency than is the material shown on the screen. The motion picture house is generally dimly lighted. Ordinarily there are some sections of the house where few people are sitting. The house in general is one of the most convenient spots in the community, for these reasons, in which boys may engage in a variety of sexual practices; especially during daylight, there are few spots in the community where boys may engage in sexual practices with girls without being apprehended and punished. Occasionally the boy is able to find a vacant or a secluded spot in the park, but ordinarily he confines his sexual activities outside the movie house to the night. As a consequence, a variety of sexual practices are observed by the boy ordinarily in the movie house, and occasionally he engages in various forms of sex activity in the house itself." Dr. Whitley cites a number of illustrative cases which cannot for a variety of reasons be quoted here. The following, however, is one of the cases:

" 'In the pictures you see guys necking. The —— Theatre is a dirty place. All the girls are cursing and the guys holler, 'Hey, any chance?' After the show is over they have a good time upstairs. They are drunk nearly every night up there. These ushers are always drunk.' The boy saw a man handling a girl intimately. He saw 'guys fooling around' with girls in a number of ways."

Cases are adduced in which the movie house of this area is used as a place of assignation. As a means of making acquaintanceships, the "pick-up" of the local movie house is known by most young people and utilized by many. So common an institution is it that the local theater proprietors and managers accept it as a part of the situation. As one of them explained it to the investigator:

"In most cases they (girls) either come for the express purpose of petting, in which case they do not disturb anyone, or else, if they come unattended, they are willing enough to receive attention from a stranger." He said, "The type of girls who come to the movies, in most cases, do not say no, and we don't bother with these cases in which both are willing."

Being unsupervised, in short, the motion picture theater in this region has in some cases noted made easy contacts for younger boys with older and more mature criminals. The researchers did not undertake to study this particular phase of the situation, and yet a number of cases spontaneously appeared showing several instances in which initial contacts were made with criminal or more hardened characters. There is a case on record in this research in which two high-school boys who became acquainted under these auspices subsequently engaged in a series of crimes which finally ended in the murder of one of their victims. The prestige of the criminal and gangster both on and off the screen in the community is curiously illustrated in a footnote to this study by the investigators. It is indicated that in certain cases the local theaters have asked notorious local gangsters to help in quelling by intimidation the boisterous conduct of some in the children's section of the theater. In cases where this has occurred, of course, it has enhanced the gangster's prestige in the eyes of the boys and on occasion has served to bring the youngsters to the attention of the local "big Shots." "And we have one or two instances on record," Mr. Cressey informs the writer, "in which a boy without a criminal record was interested in a delinquent career by other delinquents with whom he chanced to see a gangster picture." Fired by enthusiasm, in other words the boy laid aside his inhibitions and proceeded then and there to indulge in delinquent acts.

Note

1 This chapter and other references in the volume to the New York University study have been based upon a tentative and preliminary report prepared by Mr. Paul G. Cressey, Associate Director of the New York University investigation. His completed and final report was not available at the time to be used in the preparation of this book.

Theater front with youngsters and man on stilts (1933)

28

Ethnography and Exhibition: The Child Audience, the Hays Office, and Saturday Matinees

Richard deCordova

Everybody is talking about the movies, about what is wrong with them, what is right with them; whether they are moral or immoral. There are many who say they are the one and just as many who say they are the other, and in between there are those who say they are both and those who say they are neither. And there is always much talking and a very great deal of walking up and down on the platform.

These are grown folks.

They are talking about movies, especially about children and movies.

I listened a long time and then slipped away and went in search of the children to ask them what they thought about it all – about children and movies.

And this book tells you what the children told me about movies.[1]

So began Alice Miller Mitchell's 1929 book *Children and Movies*. Oddly enough, an article today might plausibly, or even predictably, start with much the same lines. It would only need to substitute "emancipatory" and "oppressive" for "moral" and "immoral" and stress other subordinate groups (women, workers, "ordinary fans") over children as the topic of all of the talk. Indeed, after years of a text-based criticism dedicated to determining the ideological effectivity of films, scholars are beginning to step off "the platform" in search of the concrete audiences that consume and make sense of those films.

This has all of the characteristics of a departure, but it is perhaps also, by some unexplored route, a return, a return to a set of interests and methods (though perhaps not goals) that characterized early research on film. Audience studies proliferated in the 1920s and 1930s, particularly those focused on children. Statistical studies of various sorts measured childhood attendance at the movies and the broad film preferences of boys and girls.[2] More properly ethnographic studies such as Mitchell's and Blumer and Hauser's *Movies, Delinquency and Crime* attempted to gauge the broad meanings children ascribed to the movies and moviegoing.[3] And more narrowly statistical and ethnographic studies of reading such as *Children's Responses to the Motion Picture "The Thief of Baghdad"* attempted to record and assess the meanings produced by a single film.[4] Although groups other than children occasionally fell under the researcher's gaze, the child's encounter with the moving picture constituted the primal scene of early audience research and, for that matter, social criticism of the movies. Film scholars have tended to ignore this scene, perhaps in order to distance themselves from the disreputable forms of research it engendered. However, an investigation of the practices through which researchers attempted to understand the child audience may tell us something about audience research today and the various power relations that subtend it.

The ethnographic impulse in recent cultural studies has arisen largely as a way of countering or complicating theories of spectatorship put forward in much of 1970s film theory. Within that theory an abstract, psychoanalytically inflected notion of the textual subject served to account for the role of the spectator. In effect, the textual subject permitted a way of theorizing spectatorship without straying from what was largely a theory of textual determinism. Textual processes placed a pliant spectator in a position from which sense could emerge.[5]

Ethnographic work has held a particular promise for contemporary researchers as a way of challenging this abstract and deterministic view with the concrete evidence of the ways audiences make sense of texts.[6] It has tended to shift the presumed source of meaning away from the text to the spectator and the social matrices within which s/he is inscribed. In doing so, it has stressed the variety of ways that people interpret texts and their activity in doing so. One of the avowed aims of this research has been the empowerment of spectators, not only by conceptualizing and stressing their activity, but also by allowing them to speak for themselves within academic discourse and escape their status as mere objects of research. The democratic, anti-elitist, non-paternalistic goals of this work exist in marked contrast to those implicit in traditional mass-culture research in this country, including of course, most of the work on children and movies produced during the 1920s and 1930s.

However, as much recent anthropological writing suggests, the methods that allow ethnographers to pursue these goals also militate against them to some degree, placing limits and posing a set of problems that are not, in any simple way, overcome.[7] Simply put, the researcher cannot have unmediated access to the readings of other groups; one is, from the start, involved in the interpretation of these readings as texts from a particular institutionally and culturally prescribed (and often privileged) position. It is not necessarily damning to say that these texts must themselves be interpreted. However, the point does raise certain questions about the extent to which the subjects of this research can escape becoming its object, constituted in an interpretive gesture by the researcher in relation to his/her agenda, identity, and desires. If identity is always, as psychoanalysis claims, "secured" on the rather difficult terrain of the Other, then the ethnographer, whose task has historically been the explanation of "other" cultures, is involved in no small way in an act of cultural self-definition – and perhaps self-legitimation. Such processes as displacement, transference, and projection are thus not simply unscientific aberrations but constitutive of the ethnographic act itself. These concerns have, of course, been central to the post-colonial critique of ethnography in recent years, a critique that has pointed to the complex ways in which the ethnographer's construction of an image of a native other has been implicated in the history of colonialism. At some level, this image has had more to do with the Western ethnographer's identity than with that of the subject whose identity and culture are ostensibly being explained. And, of course, the West had to construct a certain image of itself in relation to the other to make the colonialist venture possible.

I point to the constructedness of the ethnographer's subject not to ascribe any similar motives to recent work on ethnography of media audiences, but to call attention to an inescapable condition of audience (ethnographic) research. Mitchell seems to assume naively that the child's response to movies is transparently available to her and that she can make them transparently available to the reader of her book. That naiveté is perhaps misnamed, however; the illusion of transparency is what gives such work its authority, the sense that the researcher's interpretive role has become minimized and that the subjects are simply speaking for themselves.

Studies on the cinema and children in the 1920s and 1930s provide ample evidence with which to question such claims to transparency. Audience research of the day hardly existed in the realm of disinterested knowledge; it was connected to broader social and political imperatives, ones which in fact depended upon a certain conceptualization of the (child) audience as a necessary support. It is that connection which interests me here – the ways that the construction of the child audience in research was linked to efforts to construct the "real" child audience through the regulation of production, distribution, and exhibition, and linked more broadly still to efforts to construct children – childhood – in the society at large. If I focus on the constructedness of the child audience here, it is not to deny the unruliness of real audiences but to stress the researchers' and reformers' allied attempts – which were neither wholly successful nor wholly unsuccessful – to produce and place the audience in a certain way.

The problem of understanding and controlling the child was obviously not confined to the cinema. Indeed, the construction of children extends well beyond the bounds of audience research to the broader social and cultural processes through which notions of childhood are constituted and maintained. Historians such as Philippe Ariès have demonstrated that childhood is not an essence but an historical construction, a period of life defined differentially in relation to other periods of life by particular societies at particular times.[8] And Freud, in his investigations of fantasy structures, argued that childhood was not only the source of the psychic dynamics of adult identity but also something that the adult is always reworking, reimagining and refabricating according to the demands of repression.[9] Whether we take a socio-historical or psychoanalytic approach, the process of representing the child audience is always overdetermined by the analyst's frame of reference. What does it mean for us (adults) to understand the child at the moving pictures, to produce a particular image of him or her? In what complex ways and through what processes (displacement, projection, disavowal) is that image linked to adult identity? What, in short, is at stake in the system of differences through which our society attempts to constitute a boundary between child and adult?

Such questions are still with us today and are important in considering the continuing viability of arguments about the mass media's effects on children. Although these arguments did not begin in the 'teens and twenties, it is during this period that they were put forward most forcefully and were most closely tied to political and social action. Even the most cursory look at popular writing about the cinema during this time reveals the obsessiveness with which writers approached the problem of children and movies. Everyone with a complaint about the movies found references to the victimization of children their most powerful rhetorical tool. Denouncing the movies' harmful influence on children was a way of venting one's spleen on any number of perceived social ills – ills that in many cases extended well beyond the issue of childhood *per se*. So, for instance, as Robert Sklar has argued, references to children were often veiled attempts to deal with the problem of class – the immigrants and workers who were also enthusiastically embracing the movies.[10]

The concern over children and the movies was not merely a displacement of other concerns, however. To some significant degree, what was at issue in writing on the cinema in the 'teens and twenties was the preservation of a particular image of childhood that had its roots in the nineteenth century. During this time, childhood was set apart as a distinct stage of the life cycle and sentimentalized. Children were no longer encouraged to imitate adults so much as they were encouraged to behave like children, to exhibit precisely their difference from adults, their innocence and their disingenuous charm. Childhood became a period of life to be protected and preserved at all costs, and the supervision of childhood became much more rationalized as the church, the state, the schools, and families implemented changes to further order the child's life and establish a greater degree of control over it. As the family's economic and educational functions dwindled, its remaining function in the nurturing and maintenance of children was ascribed more importance. The family and the home themselves became sentimentalized and idealized, in Joseph Kett's words, as a "total environment united by ties of warmth and intimacy."[11]

This image of childhood was a historical construction. The writers and reformers in the 'teens and twenties undoubtedly viewed childhood as an essence at some level, but they also clearly realized that it was subject to historical forces, that definitions of childhood and the experience of childhood could change and, from their perspective, change for the worse. An article in *Playground* posed the question implicit in much writing of the period: "Are We Trying to Abolish Childhood?"[12] Such writing revealed an intense interest in preserving a certain image of children, and it followed from the claim that this image was in crisis.

This brief sketch provides a context through which to understand how people of the time could have conceived the cinema as a threat to definitions of childhood. First, in an era which increasingly worked to separate children from adults through institutions such as children's hospitals, juvenile court systems, and reform schools, the cinema mixed ages indiscriminately, providing the same entertainment for adults and children alike. The ideal of preserving childhood by maintaining a childhood culture distinct from adult culture was disrupted by the cinema as the boundaries between children's films and adult films became blurred. The fact that many children seemed to prefer the films aimed at their parents to the films made for them was particularly troubling because it called into question the difference between adult and child desire. Virtually everyone who wrote on the subject was interested in maintaining a traditional system of differences between child and adult. The cinema, because of its mixed audiences and adult films, was viewed as a threat to that system.

A second threat the cinema posed to the traditional image of the child revolved around the family's role in the supervision of the child's leisure. The view of the family as a "total environment" for the nurturing and supervision of children was no doubt a comforting one, but it was increasingly challenged by the changes of the nineteenth and early twentieth centuries. City life provided the child with a broader range of contacts, while parks, school activities, automobiles, and movies increasingly drew children away from the home. As Robert and Helen Lynd noted in their study of Muncie, Indiana, "the family was declining as a unit of leisure time pursuits."[13] Reformers viewed the cinema as a particularly strong threat in this regard because children regularly went to the cinema without their parents. Once there, they were outside the purview of adult supervision.

Around this perceived crisis, a veritable industry arose to "place" the child both symbolically and physically at the movies, to give children a particular way of looking at films that satisfied adult conceptions of childhood innocence. This attempt at placement took several forms – from the ethnographies previously mentioned, to debates and initiatives surrounding what would today be called the textual subject, to attempts to define and regulate the body of the child at the movies. An account of the full range of these forms and practices is well beyond the scope of this study. What I would like to focus on here is a specific set of initiatives that attempted to "place" the child at the movies – the children's matinee movements of the 1910s and 1920s, and particularly the Hays Office efforts of 1925.

A number of solutions to the problem of childhood movie attendance were in fact offered during these years. Many writers and reformers called for the censorship of all films that included scenes deemed harmful to children. The National Board of Censorship, and later the Hays Office, countered this argument by claiming that such a measure would reduce all adult entertainment to the level of "childish intelligence."[14] The prospect of child-like adults was perhaps as threatening as that of adult-like children; it was precisely the difference between the two that most were trying to maintain. Others called for laws prohibiting children from attending pictures unaccompanied by an adult. By the late 1920s, New York and New Jersey had such laws on the books, and six other states had slightly less stringent laws that restricted children's attendance at certain hours.[15] The difficulty of enforcing these laws was widely noted. A few states and cities had laws that prohibited children from attending certain films identified as harmful by censorship boards. There were calls for a specialized movie industry devoted exclusively to the production and exhibition of films for children; there were requests for special family shows that children and parents could attend together; and there were pleas to parents to reassert control over their children's leisure and restrict their moviegoing to only the most wholesome fare.

Children's matinees were thus among the least radical solutions offered to solve the problem of children and movies. Matinees involved no state censorship, no laws restricting children's access to films and no change in the basic structure of production and exhibition. They were preferred most by those people who believed that the power of the movies could be harnessed for the good of children. They were also favored by those most closely aligned with the industry, and, at least by 1925, by the industry itself.

It was in that year that the Motion Picture Producers and Distributors Association (MPPDA) began its campaign for Saturday morning movies. On April 25, 1925 approximately 2,700 children paid their dimes and entered the Eastman theater in Rochester, New York for a Saturday matinee. They had seen the posters advertising the show in their classrooms, and their parents had been encouraged, through the newspapers and through the local activities of such organizations as the PTA, the Federation of Women's Clubs, and the Daughters of the American Revolution, to have them attend it. The children were escorted to their seats by Boy Scouts, sang "America the Beautiful," and then viewed a film program made up of a short health talk, a Fleischer cartoon, a scenic short, an animal picture, and the feature presentation, *The Hottentot*. The program was, by all accounts, a great success – not surprisingly given the fact that the considerable forces of the MPPDA were behind it. The Rochester screening was carefully planned to inaugurate publicly the Hays Office drive for Saturday morning movies for children.[16]

Long before the Hays Office involvement, as early as 1913, children's matinees were a visible component of urban culture. In 1913, an organization called the Children's Motion Picture League began to organize children's matinees in six theaters in New York City. Although their efforts were almost certainly not the first, they drew national attention and, according to an article in *Outlook*, served as a model for similar ventures in the South, Southwest, and Puerto Rico.[17] At the beginning of the same year, a theater manager in Davenport, Iowa had organized a series of matinees that continued successfully for at least five years. By 1915, there were regular matinees in Boston, Louisville, New Orleans, Grand Rapids, New Rochelle, and probably many other cities in the country. The matinees during these early years were largely local efforts, initiated by community leaders as a way of dealing with the specific problems they sensed in their own neighborhoods. They were rarely organized by individual theater managers; in fact writers contended that matinees would not be successful without the broad support of the civic and religious organizations of the community. So, the organization of matinees was almost always conducted by local reformers, under the auspices of the PTA, the Board of Education, local Women's Clubs, or special committees formed from ad hoc groups of concerned citizens. In fact, it is probably fair to say that matinees remained local efforts through most of their history. However, in 1916, the National Board of Review's Committee on Films for Young People (formerly the Committee on Children's Pictures and Programs and later the National Committee for Better Films) began a concerted effort to organize the various local activities into a national movement.[18] Local groups active in promoting children's matinees and family programs were joined together as the Affiliated Committees for Better Films under the umbrella of the National Committee. The National Committee coordinated and organized the movement through four types of activity. First, they worked to recruit new affiliated committees. Mary Peck, a former University of Minnesota Professor, was sent on a speaking tour in late 1916 and early 1917 toward this end. The committee solicited national publicity and wrote letters to local groups throughout the country to encourage involvement. By October 1917, there were 99 affiliated committees spread throughout the country. Second, the National Committee published and distributed pamphlets and lists of suitable films for matinees and for family shows. These included "Principles Governing the Selection of Motion Pictures for Young People Under 16," "Films! Fine Films! Films for Youngsters!" and "A Garden of American Motion Pictures." Third, they published the monthly *Committee for Better Films Bulletin*, which served as a clearinghouse for information on community involvement in moving pictures, particularly special programs. Finally, they encouraged motion picture companies to produce films suitable for children and to keep those films that had already been produced in distribution.

The growth of the matinee movement during the middle 'teens is impressive, though the matinees did not always reflect the tastes of the child audience. The problems reported at a large New York City theater were not unusual:

> The program was planned for clean entertainment, making education secondary to the amusement that children need on Saturdays.... [It] included *Pigs is Pigs*, featuring John Bunny, Bostock's wild animals and a fine production of *Alice in Wonderland*.

> It seemed as if it would be a morning of rare pleasure for the boys and girls who were accustomed to attend the usual program of motion pictures.

> But the children would not attend on Saturday morning, nor on succeeding Saturday mornings. They wanted to pay more and see a sensational adult picture thrown on the screen. As one little girl of twelve expressed it: "We like to see them making love and going off in automobiles." And a boy explained, "There won't be any shooting or dynamiting in those kid pictures. What's the use of seeing them?"[19]

Despite such objections, the children's matinee became both a common and highly conventionalized form of exhibition during the 'teens. Local organizations publicized the shows and encouraged their members to have their children attend; some organizations and businesses bought up blocks of tickets to give to poor children or to their employees. Within the theater, Boy Scouts, Girl Scouts, or college women in caps and gowns served as ushers, and one or more matrons watched over the children. Stage presentations prior to the films often showcased local child talent or an adult storyteller. It was quite common to award a five dollar gold piece or a season pass to the matinees for the best essay written about the film viewed that day. And, in some cities, Public Library tie-ins encouraged children to read books related to the films. By 1925, a substantial body of knowledge had been developed about the conduct of children's matinees.

The Hays Office drive for Saturday morning movies was launched by the Committee for Public Relations, an advisory board that Will Hays had formed shortly after assuming his duties as head of the MPPDA in 1922. The Committee for Public Relations was made up of the leaders of over 60 national civic and religious organizations, including the National Council of Women, the American Legion, the National Council of Catholic Women, the Boy Scouts of America, the YMCA and the American Civic Association. The committee thus had access to and influence over most of the local organizations that had traditionally produced matinees in their communities.

During 1924 and early 1925, the committee completed a survey of the films in the vaults of the MPPDA's member companies. They identified those films that were suitable for children to view and constructed a series of 36 programs for special matinees. By the fall of 1925, 52 programs were available to any organization or theater – a full year's supply of movies for weekly matinees. Each program consisted of a feature film, a two-reel comedy, and what was referred to as a semi-educational short, usually a scenic or industrial film.

The films were re-edited and often re-titled to make them appropriate for the child's psychological needs. *The Hottentot*, the feature at the Rochester matinee, was cut by 1,500 feet. According to *Motion Picture News*, it was cut "not because of its objectionable business in its action, but because the reel in its original form was considered too long to sustain the interest of the young audience."[20] However, the *Pasadena Post* noted that the editing was also meant to have a moral function:

> There has been an effort to cut out everything that would puzzle or mislead the youthful spectator. Simpler captions have been substituted. Nothing tending to imply impropriety in the conduct of any character has been retained. If curiosity is aroused in the young mind, it is hoped that it shall be an entirely wholesome curiosity, the answering of it useful to the youngster.[21]

Apparently, the curiosity aroused by 1,500 feet in plot gaps was considered of the wholesome kind.

The films were shipped in "special metal containers" that held all eight reels, and exhibitors, in signing the standard contracts for the films, promised to show nothing but the movies included therein. This policy was designed to ensure that films appropriate for children would not be paired with inappropriate ones. But it also greatly reduced the burden on the citizens and theater managers interested in organizing children's matinees by providing a full, ready-made program of films. Those who organized matinees frequently commented on the many difficulties involved in securing a program of films. There was never enough children's fare produced to fill a regular schedule of matinees with current releases. Thus, organizers had to depend primarily on films that had long since had their first run, and because such films had often dropped out of distribution entirely, organizers had to write a number of exchanges to locate prints which were usually in poor condition. Moreover, to put together a single show they often had to deal with two or three exchanges, potentially a different one for each of the films to be used. One of the most significant aspects of the Hays plan was that it reduced the labor of choosing, locating, and securing prints by devising an incredibly streamlined system of national distribution for children's films.

Organizers of matinees only had to deal with one exchange for a steady supply of ready-made programs of such films.

In the late summer and early fall, the plan was set in motion on a national scale when 32 of the largest cities in the country began to exhibit the MPPDA-sponsored weekly matinees. When he announced the plan, Hays said that he expected it to extend everywhere, and in fact by the fall a number of smaller cities had also implemented the idea. He proclaimed that the arrangement was "the complete answer to the situation. Any really interested group anywhere, cooperating with the local exhibitor, may now obtain pictures proper for this purpose."[22]

The children's matinee movement was motivated by a number of goals. For the MPPDA, of course, the primary goal was always the protection of the economic interests of the industry. And, as always, Hays was quite successful in aligning himself with moderate reformers to protect the industry from more extreme adversaries whose agendas would lead to a reduction in industry profits. Censorship and child attendance laws were definite threats during the 1920s, and the MPPDA drive for Saturday matinees was an effective and apparently constructive way of countering those threats. However, the industry had other, related motives. Critics charged that Hays was interested only in turning children into movie fans. Little probably had to be done to accomplish that, but there is no doubt some truth to this claim. The matinee drive coincided with a broader drive called the Greater Movie Season, an elaborately planned set of festivities and gimmicks planned to foster further good will and involvement in the cinema. Additionally, the industry was concerned with what Hays called the "Free Movie Menace." Civic, religious, and educational organizations were increasingly showing films in auditoriums and courtyard squares, often without charging admission. Thus, an alternative mode of exhibition had arisen that bypassed the theaters and presumably hurt their business. Many of the early matinees were run pre-

cisely this way. In Hays' 1925 annual report, he noted the efforts of the MPPDA's Film Board of Trade to control this menace, while Jason Joy, in an early statement on the matinee plan, argued that it was unwise to show movies to children for free because it had the effect of lessening the child's estimation of the show's value.[23] In one sense, then, the matinee plan was an attempt to gain back a significant portion of this alternative business. However, there was also a more direct pecuniary interest in the industry's cooperation. Although Hays' publicity always claimed that the matinees were not money-making ventures but acts of good will on the part of the industry, the plan was, from the beginning, designed to earn profits. A plan submitted to Hays by Ward Wooldridge, the secretary of the Public Relations Committee, claimed that in the most conservative estimate, exhibitors would gross $1,620,000 and member companies $405,000 in the venture over a three-year period. Most of the latter figure would be eaten up by print costs and publicity, but for the member companies, any profit on these older films appeared as a windfall. The exhibitors, meanwhile, could make a tidy profit during a time of the day that the theater was usually dead.[24]

But civic organizations and reform groups were not simply being duped by the industry. They had their own complex set of goals, and the matinee movement appeared as a practical way to achieve them. First, the matinee movement addressed the widespread concerns that the mass media and modern life were destroying childhood; matinees were one means of attempting to reassert traditional distinctions between child and adult by identifying, producing, and preserving a children's culture within the cinema itself. The desire to segregate children from adults in the cinema was a strong one, and reformers felt that if provided their own Saturday movies, children would be less likely to go to the movies during the rest of the week. One study in Asheville, North Carolina reportedly found that the percentage of children in general audiences had been reduced from 28 percent to 3 percent since the establishment of Saturday matinees.[25] Reformers also hoped that the matinees would instill in children a heightened appreciation of films and a greater ability to distinguish the good from the bad, the wholesome from the unwholesome, and the highbrow from the lowbrow. The essay contests that were so frequently conducted through the matinees were certainly a part of this effort; they rewarded children for responding to movies along lines valued by reform-minded middle-class adults.[26] In addition, the matinee movement was designed to address certain fears about the relationship between the child and the space of the movie theater. The MPPDA matinees were placed largely in the theaters of "preferred exhibitors" – theaters that were large, lavish, well ventilated, and well lit. Thus, unlike the small, dark theaters that were seen as bad for both the health and the morals of the young, the matinees placed children in a healthy environment, under the watchful eye of a matron, a surrogate of parental authority.

The Hays Office drive for Saturday morning movies was abandoned in 1926, and the work of organizing and promoting matinees fell back into the hands of local organizations and the National Committee for Better Films. This drive was only a small part of a much broader history, a history not only of matinees but of social concern over the movies and children. But the Hays Office efforts were emblematic in certain ways, particularly in the ways in which they positioned the child at the moving pictures. First, through the selection and editing of films they attempted to produce a particular kind of textual subject, a symbolic position and mode of address that would ideally produce the spectator as a true child. Second, through essay contests, organizers tried to gauge the actual response of real children to the films of the week. If this was not exactly ethnography, it was only because of the explicitness of the aim of shaping that response; the response rewarded was the one deemed best from an adult perspective. Finally, the mati-

nees exerted a power over the child's body, both through the ways in which it worked systematically to separate the child from the adult and through the ways it placed the child in a system of surveillance within the space of the theater itself.

The concept of audience was really relevant only in two general contexts in the 'teens and twenties. First, it was used as a way of criticizing the cinema or some aspect of it. Those who did not like the cinema argued their cases most forcefully when they located a victim among those who did, and, as in all good melodrama, the villain's villainy rose in direct proportion to the victim's helplessness, gullibility, and lack of awareness. The cinema was evil because of what it was doing to a particular audience, and in such arguments, children often if not always made the best victims. Second, the concept of audience was relevant as part of broader efforts to survey and circumscribe the activities and attitudes of particular groups within society – groups such as women, immigrant workers, and children, who were marked both by their "otherness" and by their relative lack of social power. Attention to these audiences may have followed from a good-hearted concern for the victimized and helpless, but it was also inseparably linked to a form of surveillance designed to assure effects of power such as those described by Michel Foucault in *Discipline and Punish*. Ironically, in a world of surveillance, the darkened movie theater afforded the possibility of escape, and, insofar as it intensified the spectator's power to see without being seen, even reversal. Audience research and a set of related efforts attempted to combat this, to pierce the darkness of the theater, to place the spectator under the steady gaze of social scientists, reformers, and policy makers. Certain groups of spectators would not simply watch movies; they would be watched while watching them.

It seems odd that with the exception of Robert Sklar and Garth Jowett, film history has so completely ignored the obsession with the child audience, particularly if we admit

167

that it was the dominant feature of critical approaches to the cinema at the time. We might say more – that the image of the child at the movies has functioned as a precondition of audience research generally. If mass-culture research has historically been paternalistic, it is because it has been modeled on that image, an image that remains largely unexamined. An understanding of such attempts to constitute and control the child audience during the 'teens and twenties might give us a keener sense of the stakes of audience research today.

One might object that we are already beyond that now, that the paternalistic view of the audience has been discredited and cast aside and that we now finally have the opportunity to see how real audiences read and react. But in fact, I would argue, we are still firmly within the problematic established in debates around the cinema and children in the early part of the twentieth century. Recent work in film and cultural studies has certainly not yet dislodged this traditional view from dominance. And furthermore, that work, which relies increasingly on ethnography, remains stuck within the terms of this traditional debate, condemned to what may be a strategically important but conceptually limiting reversal of its terms. Where the audience was once passive, it is now active; where once gullible, now critical; where once manipulated, now manipulative, etc. I offer no way out of this bind, but suggest that a genealogy of the concept of media audiences and a consideration of the child's significance as the privileged site of audience research might give us a better sense of the present situation. Foucault asked "What matter who is speaking?" to call attention to the ways the concept of the author functions in a given society at a given time to limit, manage, and contain the proliferation of discourse.[27] "What matter who is viewing?" might be asked in a similar spirit, not as a way of denying the real experience of spectators but as a way of calling into question the conditions under which concepts of audience have entered into public discourse.

Notes

1 Alice Miller Mitchell, *Children and Movies* (Chicago: University of Chicago Press, 1929), xvii.

2 See, for instance, Harold O. Berg, "One Week's Attendance of Children at Motion Picture Entertainments," *Playground* (June 1923), 165; Harvey C. Lehman and Paul A. Witty, "Education and the Moving Picture Show," *Education* (Sep. 1926), 39–47; Clarence Arthur Perry, "Frequency of Attendance of High-School Students at the Movies," *School Review* (Oct. 1923), 573–87; "The Child, the Movies and the Censor," *Sunset* (July 1916), 31.

3 Herbert Blumer and Philip M. Hauser, *Movies, Delinquency and Crime* (New York: Macmillan, 1933).

4 Mary Allen Abbott, *Children's Responses to the Motion Picture "The Thief of Baghdad"* (Rome: International Educational Cinematographic Institute, League of Nations, 1931).

5 See John Fiske, *Television Culture* (New York: Methuen, 1987) for a useful elaboration of this point.

6 Prominent examples of this work include David Morley, *The Nationwide Audience: Structure and Decoding* (London: BFI, 1980) and Ien Ang, *Watching Dallas* (London: Methuen, 1985).

7 See, for instance, James Clifford and George E. Marcus (eds.), *Writing Culture: The Poetics and Politics of Ethnography* (Berkeley: University of California Press, 1986); George E. Marcus, "Rhetoric and the Ethnographic Genre in Anthropological Research," *Current Anthropology* 21 (1980), 507–10; George E. Marcus and James Clifford, "The Making of Ethnographic Texts: A Preliminary Report," *Current Anthropology* 26 (1985), 267–71; Vincent Crapanzano, "On the Writing of Ethnography," *Dialectical Anthropology* 2 (1977), 69–73; George E. Marcus and Dick Cushman, "Ethnographies as Texts," *Annual Review of Anthropology* (1982), 25–69.

8 Philippe Ariès, *Centuries of Childhood: A Social History of Family Life*, trans. Robert Baldick (New York: Vintage, 1962).

9 For an excellent account and application of psychoanalysis to the question of childhood see Jacqueline Rose, *The Case of Peter Pan: Or the Impossibility of Children's Fiction* (London: Macmillan, 1984).

10 Robert Sklar, *Movie-Made America: A Cultural History of the Movies* (New York: Basic, 1975), 122–40.

11 Joseph F. Kett, *Rites of Passage: Adolescence in America, 1790 to the Present* (New York: Basic, 1977), 138. Another particularly strong account of the new status of childhood in the late nineteenth century is Viviana A. Zelizer, *Pricing the Priceless Child: The Changing Social Value of Children* (New York: Basic, 1985). Related work in this area includes Bruce Bellingham, "Institution and Family: An Alternative View of Nineteenth Century Child Saving," *Social Problems* 33:6 (1986), S33–57; Philip Greven, *The Protestant Temperament: Patterns of Child-Rearing, Religious Experience and the Self in Early America* (New York: Knopf, 1977); Hilary Russell, "Training, Restraining and Sustaining: Infant and Child Care in the Late 19th Century," *Material History Bulletin* 21 (1985), 35–49; Robert Wells, "Family History and the Demographic Transition," in *The American Family in Social Historical Perspective*, ed. Michael Gordon (New York: St. Martin's, 1983), 372–92; Bernard Wishy, *The Child and the Republic: The Dawn of Modern American Child Nurture* (Philadelphia: University of Pennsylvania Press, 1968).

12 "Are We Trying to Abolish Childhood?" *Playground* (April 1923), 32.

13 Robert Lynd and Helen Merrell Lynd, *Middletown: A Study in American Culture* (New York: Harcourt, 1956), 272.

14 Lawrence A. Averill, "The Motion Picture and Child Development," *Educational Review* (May 1918), 398–409.

15 Roy F. Woodbury, "Children and Movies," *Survey* (May 15, 1929), 253–4.

16 *Motion Picture News* Oct. 16, 1925; *Rochester Times Union*, Apr. 17, 1925, Apr. 22, 1925, Oct. 2, 1925; *Rochester Herald*, Apr. 17, 1925, Apr. 20, 1925, Apr. 25, 1925; *Rochester Democrat Chronicle*, Apr. 18, 1925, unpaginated clippings, Will Hays Papers, Indiana State Library.

17 "The Children's Motion Picture League," *Outlook* (July 26, 1913), 643.

18 For general accounts of the activities of the National Board of Review see Charles Matthew Feldman, *The National Board of Censorship (Review) of Motion Pictures: 1909–1922* (New York: Arno, 1977); Garth Jowett, *Film: The Democratic Art* (Boston: Little, 1976), 108–39; Nancy J. Rosenbloom, "Between Reform and Regulation: The Struggle Over Film Censorship in Progressive America, 1909–1922," *Film History* 1 (1987), 307–25.

19 "Motion Pictures Specially for Children," *Rutland Evening News*, Oct. 31, 1916, unpaginated clipping, New York Public Library, Theater Arts Collection, New York.

20 "Hays Morning Show Tried Out," *Motion Picture News*, May 16, 1925, unpaginated clipping, Will Hays Papers.

21 *Pasadena Post*, Nov. 9, 1925, unpaginated clipping, Will Hays Papers.

22 Will Hays, "Motion Pictures and the Public," address to the Women's City Club of Philadelphia, Apr. 20, 1925, Will Hays Papers.

23 MPPDA Annual Report, 1925, Will Hays Papers; *Playground* (Sep. 1925), 345.

24 Ward Wooldridge, memo to Will Hays, Apr. 28, 1925, Will Hays Papers.

25 *Schenectady Gazette*, Oct. 3, 1925; *San Mateo News Leader*, Jan. 29, 1925, unpaginated clippings, Will Hays Papers.

26 As Jason Joy said in one of the announcements of the matinee plan, "best of all, the young people are taught to appreciate the really high-class sort of picture – and having acquired that taste in their youth will continue it as they grow up" (*The American City*, Sep. 1924, 246). Lea Jacobs discusses the related aesthetic ideology of the film education movement in "Reformers and Spectators: The Film Education Movement in the Thirties," *Camera Obscura* 22 (Jan. 1990), 22–49.

27 Michel Foucault, "What is an Author?" in *Textual Strategies: Perspectives in Post-Structuralist Criticism*, ed. Josue V. Harari (Ithaca: Cornell University Press, 1979), 141–60.

★ ★ ★ ★ ★ ★ ★ ★ ★ ★ ★ ★ ★ ★

PART III

**Picture Shows
and New Theaters:
The 1930s and 1940s**

★ ★ ★ ★ ★ ★ ★ ★ ★ ★ ★ ★ ★

Introduction

Part III looks at moviegoing, exhibition practices, and theater design in the first two decades of the sound era, from the industry's weathering of the Great Depression and its remarkable success during the late 1930s and Second World War years, through the precipitous decline in box-office revenues in the late 1940s. Certain major themes introduced in previous sections are replayed here, most notably in my selection, "Hillbilly Music and Will Rogers: Small-Town Picture Shows in the 1930s." Relying on local newspapers and oral history interviews, this essay looks at the civic and social role of the hometown picture show, as well as booking practices and live musical performances at movie theaters in several rural Kentucky small towns. Above all, this essay examines whether, after the increased standardization that came with the changeover to sound films, there are still important local or regional exhibition practices. What most struck me in exploring this question was the link between radio stations (both local and national) and movie theaters that featured live performances of so-called "hillbilly" music. This link underscores the interconnections between American cinema and other forms of commercial entertainment.

Entrepreneurial movie theater operation and extra-filmic attractions are also taken up in H.O. Kusell's account in the *New Republic* of the Depression-era phenomenon of "bank night" and the various contests and other "constructive simulations" catalogued by Frank Ricketson in his 1938 manual, *The Management of Motion Picture Theatres*. The actual day-to-day operation of a small movie theater is the subject of two journalistic profiles reprinted here: Carlie Beach Roney's first-person account in the *Saturday Evening Post* of owning and operating a theater in Milford, Michigan, during the Depression and *Fortune*'s feature article about an independent movie exhibitor in Galesburg, Illinois, trying to survive in 1948. These vivid profiles stand as good examples of the sort of coverage accorded film exhibition in the mainstream popular press and in more specialized business magazines of the period. Both articles pay particular attention to the independent theater operator's acquisition of product, the "buying" and scheduling of films. It is, in fact, surprising to see just how publicly prominent were the debates in this period over block-booking and other aspects of the exhibition business. Two examples from magazines are reprinted here: a 1935 article from *Christian Century* and a 1938 illustration from *National Parent–Teacher*. Mae D. Huettig provides a more scholarly view of these trade practices in her groundbreaking

1944 study, *Economic Control of the Motion Picture Industry*, undertaken with the support of a research fellowship from the Rockefeller Foundation. Block-booking and other trade practices, as Huettig claims, are worth attending to because "they shape moviegoing habits," determining why and when people see what they see in American theaters. Years of editorializing, government hearings, and federal anti-trust suits culminated in the Supreme Court's 1948 decision in the Paramount case, which required the major studios to end block-booking and divest themselves of their theater holdings.

The other line of inquiry represented in this part of *Moviegoing in America* concerns theater architecture in the 1930s and 1940s. This discourse, primarily conducted in specialized trade journals like *Architectural Forum* and the *Society of Motion Picture Engineers Journal*, is in many ways a reaction against all that the picture palace described in Part II represented. Ben Schlanger's 1932 call for accurately proportioned and maximum-sized movie screens stands as something of a manifesto for the "new theater," which he sees, above all, as a site for viewing films, not for being awed by ornate splendor or basking in atmospheric decor. Schlanger would continue to argue for, as well as to design, modern, well-engineered movie theaters over the next 20 years. His "Motion Picture Theaters," from *Architectural Record* (1937), considers not only screen dimensions and seating arrangements, but also the optimum location and size for a new theater. Schlanger's ideas inform two publications from 1948 that are also reprinted here: *Architectural Record*'s call for "A New Architecture for the Movie Theater," one that would more accommodate the coming role of television; and a volume published by the Society of Motion Picture Engineers, *The Motion Picture Theater: Planning, Upkeep*, which includes Walter A. Cutter's "Psychology of the Theater." Covering some 20 years of professional discourse, Part III's material on the design and function of the movie theater contrasts sharply with earlier selections on the nickelodeon and the picture palace. This material also looks forward to post-1980 exhibition sites, like the freestanding multiplex. Furthermore, to read the calls by Ben Schlanger and others for a "modern" movie theater is to be reminded again of the complex relations that link the screening site, the viewing audience, and the movies shown.

29

Hillbilly Music and Will Rogers: Small-Town Picture Shows in the 1930s

Gregory A. Waller

In his 1928 instructional handbook, *Motion Picture Theater Management*, Harold B. Franklin insists that "a theater, like a man, is a personality – for better or worse – by itself; and each one defines itself to the locality in its own way."[1] If this might have been in some measure true in 1928, how true was it several years later, after the conversion to sound had helped to regulate and perhaps standardize the exhibition and hence affect the reception of the movies in the United States? To what extent does it make sense to pay attention to locality and region as relevant factors in the cultural history of American film during the Depression?

The principal representation of American regionalism in the movies is to be found in westerns, particularly in the low-budget variety that were a mainstay Hollywood product during the 1930s. While there are many films set in the mountains of Tennessee, in ante-bellum plantation days, in the bayou or the swamp, the "Southern" does not exist in the same way that the western does. In his book *Hillbillyland*, J.W. Williamson set out to analyze "what the movies did to the mountains and what the mountains did to the movies." His discussion of the Depression focuses on the stereotype of the hillbilly fool,

as most influentially found not in the movies, but in *Esquire* magazine cartoons and Al Capp's *L'il Abner*.[2] There's also a take on Hollywood going hillbilly (via Broadway in this case) that Williamson somehow missed, an elaborately absurd production number from Fox's New Deal musical, *Stand Up and Cheer* (1934). "The country's crying for hillbilly tunes," declares the head of the newly created federal Department of Entertainment, and since "the public must be pleased," he concocts – or perhaps simply imagines – a song-and-dance extravaganza called "Broadway Goes Hillbilly." With "mountain music" the latest object of fickle, ever-shifting consumer taste, Broadway – and, by implication, Hollywood – must deliver the goods, which in this case results in a surreal re-combination and re-staging of already-known cowboy and hillbilly music and iconography: poverty becomes opulence, urban turns rural and back again, as chorus girls swap slinky satin gowns for gingham and straw hats and then for satin overalls and lariats. By the logic of *Stand Up and Cheer*, the regional is a conventionalized style – easily incorporated, readily exploited, ripe for parody and jazzy updating. By bringing together Broadway and Hillbilly (and the western), the

"Hillbilly Music and Will Rogers: Small-Town Picture Shows in the 1930s" originally appeared in Melvyn Stokes and Richard Maltby (eds.), *American Movie Audiences: From the Turn of the Century to the Early Sound Era* (London: British Film Institute, 1999), 164–79. Reprinted with permission from the British Film Institute.

Department of Entertainment stands up for and so reconstitutes Depression-era America, creating a producer-driven, topically minded, metropolitan-based national culture capable of performing regionality. *Stand Up and Cheer* reminds us that by 1934 (at least) mountain music and the rural, white South could no longer be taken *only* as sites of authentic, deeply rooted Anglo-American folkways.[3]

We cannot now know what audiences in Appalachia or the Ozarks did with "Broadway Goes Hillbilly," but certain aspects of the local or regional moviegoing experience are somewhat more accessible to the film historian. There is, to use Harold Franklin's word, the "personality" of the movie theater itself, which I take to include management style, architectural design, interior decor, booking policies and promotional strategies, as well as

the theater's civic and social role, or what we might call its public persona in the community or neighborhood. Douglas Gomery and others have written on the practices and policies of first-run picture palaces and studio-owned theater chains during the 1930s.[4] By way of contrast, the theaters I use as my examples in this chapter were small-town (or very small city) venues located in the agricultural region of south-central Kentucky, a state that had not enjoyed the economic prosperity of the 1920s before things got much worse during the Depression. My study focuses on the theaters listed below, which also details seating capacity, if known, and the size of the local population according to the 1930 Census. All these theaters, however, drew their patrons from well beyond narrowly defined town or city limits.

Campbellsville (population: 1,923)	Alhambra (500 seats)	Cozy (200 seats)	
Clay City (population: 1,551)	Ace		
Columbia (population: 1,195)	Paramount	Rialto (300 seats)	
Glasgow (population: 5,042)	Trigg	Plaza (1,700 seats)	
Greensburg (population: 770)	Bowen	New Mossland (700 seats)	Fort Airdrome
Jamestown (population: 410)	Mary Agnes		

By way of comparison, I also examined the motion picture business in the Appalachian coal-country of eastern Kentucky, using as a test case the Family (200-seat) and Virginia (600-seat) theaters, both of which were located at Hazard, which had a population of 7,085 in 1930.

Local newspapers, oral-history interviews, antiquarian collections, and paper ephemera reveal much about these theaters as examples of small-town film exhibition in the United States during the Depression. Needless to say, such sources are not absolutely reliable nor even remotely comprehensive. But they offer a body of information often unavailable

elsewhere concerning theater design, advertising, viewing habits, and promotional activity. For example, even the relatively small collection of flyers and posters kept by the daughter of a theater owner in Campbellsville, and now housed in the University of Kentucky Special Collections Library, vividly demonstrates this exhibitor's reliance on contests, ticket give-aways, and promotional tie-ins to local merchants, and – more importantly – it helps to explain how segregation operated in terms of special "colored" screenings. This sort of material, particularly newspapers and oral histories, also offers crucial information about three specific areas: the

Handout flyer (later 1920s) and newspaper advertisement (1935) for the Alhambra Theatre civic role of the theater, the exhibitor's booking patterns, and the performance of live music in these movie theaters during the 1930s.[5]

First, there is a marked emphasis in the local press and in anecdotal accounts on the entrepreneurial acumen, initiative, and sense of civic responsibility shown by hometown exhibitors. All of the Kentucky theaters I examined were independently owned and operated by local residents. Some of these venues had been open since the early 1920s, others were newly constructed in the midst of the Depression. For the most part, they were near the tail-end of the run-zone-clearance distribution system, but that fact hardly seemed to have registered with local residents, who were more inclined to admire the way their hometown exhibitors had managed to thrive in the midst of hard economic times.[6] When one theater owner undertook a major redecoration of his venue in 1931, the town newspaper praised him for his "brave move in the face of all the moaning and groaning. It is an expression of faith in the community."[7] Indeed, each new theater or costly updating was likely to be perceived as a "distinct contribution to a bigger and better" hometown.[8]

The exhibitor's commitment to place and his standing as praiseworthy civic booster extended well beyond his "brave" investment in the economy of Main Street. For example, in 1936 Bruce Aspley, owner of the two theaters in Glasgow, received the American Legion award for "fine and upstanding citizenship." Aspley, the local newspaper effused, "is very public spirited – no call has ever been made upon him for any civic, benevolent or religious cause but he has responded willingly and cheerfully. He has thrown open the doors of his theaters for religious meetings, for the use of the city schools, for public gatherings, and even for charitable entertainments."[9] For theater owner Paul Saunders of Campbellsville, this sense of "public spirit" (and good public relations) meant screening special motion picture programs for groups like the Parent–Teachers Association and the American Legion. Saunders also allowed his theater to be used for meetings of the Rotary Club and the Sportsmen's League and arranged benefits for the Cancer Prevention Drive, the Red Cross European Relief Fund, the high-school band, and local flood victims.[10]

During the 1930s, this type of civic activism directed toward such non-controversial goals was itself, of course, a political position as well as a way of demonstrating that the movie theater was committed to the community at large. These uses suggest that the small-town movie theater (which likely occupied a central spot on Main Street) carried on the work and took over the civic role filled by the multi-purpose opera house earlier in the century. "Make the [movie] theater a community center," declared a 1926 advertisement for the Paramount Theater in Columbia, and this advice seems to have been followed in all the localities that I examined.[11] The ready availability of picture shows for meetings, benefits, and sponsored screenings also underscores the working relationship between the exhibitor and certain primary institutions of the small town: churches, schools, and service organizations. In more rural, predominantly Baptist areas, there was still substantial opposition not only to specific films and Sunday screenings, but to picture shows in general. Not surprisingly, there are also many examples of small-town Kentucky exhibitors adjusting their schedules with local churches in mind. The Rialto, for instance, made clear in its advertisement for *Snow White* (1937) that, although its contract with the distributor called for a Sunday screening, "the time has been arranged so that it will not conflict with any of the church services."[12]

There seems to be no question that theater owners like Aspley and Saunders were highly responsive to the civic and charitable concerns of their communities. To what extent did the booking policies of small-town exhibitors also reflect a sense of specific locality or what could be seen as a regional orientation and affiliation? One especially striking example in this regard was the use of locally produced newsreels or slides, though it is impossible to tell just how widespread this practice was in the 1930s. The first instalment of the Plaza Theater's in-house newsreel in 1938, for example, offered footage of the arrival of mail at the local airport, as well as pictures of "well-known professional or business men," and "candid camera shots."[13] A decade earlier, L.O. Davis had begun screening his own motion pictures of area festivities and news at his Virginia Theater in Hazard.[14] In addition, advertisement slides for local merchants and brand-name products were apparently standard components of the movie show, and, on at least one occasion, theaters in Campbellsville and Greensburg screened slides of townspeople (mostly children) and Main Street stores, in all likelihood shot by an itinerant photographer.[15]

Such instances suggest that exhibitors could quite literally localize their programming, but slides and in-house newsreels accounted at best for but a fraction of what was screened in small-town picture shows. The question remains: how much choice was available to an exhibitor in Columbia or Hazard in terms of selecting, arranging, and programming Hollywood product?[16] I have yet to find business records for any of these theaters, but anecdotal evidence suggests that Saunders, for one, dealt directly with regional booking agents, at least until about 1940, and thus, in principle, he was able to gear his offerings to local tastes, assuming that there were movies pitched toward such tastes. Judging from his advertisements for the Alhambra, this meant three things: holding over certain films for longer than usual runs, as was the case, for example, with almost all Will Rogers films; occasionally bringing back a title, for example, *It Happened One Night* (1934) or *Jesse James* (1939), for a return engagement; and arranging weekly schedules so that, at least two-thirds of the time, westerns filled the prime Friday and Saturday slots, when downtown was crowded with rural folk. In the rare instances when a movie had something of an explicit Kentucky

connection, it might be held over, as when the Rialto scheduled several extra (sold-out) performances of *In Old Kentucky* (1935) with Will Rogers. Or the film might be re-booked, as was the case with *The Trail of the Lonesome Pine* (1936) – based on the bestselling 1908 novel set in Kentucky by John Fox – in January and March 1937.

For a sense of one theater's bookings for an entire year, consider the Rialto's 1935 schedule, which included some 150 movies designed to fill three changes of program. There were matinées on Saturday and sometimes on Thursday, but no screenings on Sunday. During 1935, the Rialto's bookings included *The Thin Man* (1934), *The Bride of Frankenstein* (1935), *The Devil is a Woman* (1935), *It Happened One Night* (1934), and *Black Fury* (1935), though the schedule was dominated by musicals, comedies, college pictures, and B-westerns. The only films accorded return engagements were *Imitation of Life* (1934) and Shirley Temple's *Curly Top* (1935), together with Will Rogers' *Judge Priest* (1934) and *Life Begins at 40* (1935). This schedule seems relatively typical of the theaters under consideration here, though it is possible that there was more variation and programming "control" in terms of which shorts (particularly serial episodes, cartoons, and newsreels) were on the bill at each theater. Judging from the bookings at the Rialto and these other small-town Kentucky theaters, it is difficult to see any striking regional or local patterns at work, beyond the appeal of the folksy humor of Will Rogers, the drawing power of patently Kentucky-related movies, and the prominence of certain genres, notably westerns. These trends are surely worth noting, though the major impression left by a survey of advertised playdates is that the film-booking practices at the Rialto and the Alhambra are best understood not in terms of a particular region or locality but in terms of their status as small-town, provincial theaters far removed from first-run venues.

In fact, more than any of the specific films shown, what stands out in the 1935 schedule

179

at the 300-seat Rialto is that it included seven live performances, each co-billed with a regular film program. All but one of these shows featured what was advertised as "hillbilly" or "mountain" or "cowboy" music by the likes of Fiddlin' Abner Smith, the Georgia Wildcats, and the Northwest Mounted Police Company. These live shows typically had nothing much to do with the co-billed feature film. On January 21–2, 1935, for instance, the Rialto paired the costume drama, *Marie Gallante* (1934), starring Spencer Tracy, with the string band tunes and rural clowning of Uncle Henry and His Original Kentucky Mountaineers, who had also appeared at the theater two months earlier on the same bill as *Strange Wives* (1934). And, conversely, none of the material I have examined indicates that any Kentucky exhibitors tried to package hillbilly music with a seemingly more "appropriate" movie, like a Will Rogers vehicle or the Wheeler and Wolsey comedy, *Kentucky Kernels* (1934).

There was, however, considerable variety among the theaters surveyed in how often and what type of live performances were booked as the 1930s progressed. Somewhat surprisingly, however, I found no direct correlation between the size and standing of the movie house and the reliance on amateur as opposed to professional talent. For example, soon after the New Mossland Theatre opened in Greensburg in 1937, it tried to outdo its competition in the surrounding counties by bringing in well-known country music performers almost every other week, including fiddler extraordinaire Curly Fox and Grand Ole Opry regular Uncle Dave Macon.[17] In contrast, Glasgow's Plaza Theatre – by far the largest and most palatial of the venues surveyed – favored local performers for its elaborate amateur talent contest, which lasted for six consecutive weeks in 1936 (and was held again in 1938). This contest drew a range of different entrants: tap dancers, singers, acrobats, tuba soloists, and Hawaiian guitar players, as well as more recognizably regional acts, including the prize-winning Kentucky Ramblers, a string band decked out in overalls, blue shirts, and red bandannas.[18]

In the early 1930s, patrons at the Rialto could sometimes see a small-time touring vaudeville troupe or a group of local white citizens don blackface for a benefit minstrel show, and, on occasion, a theater might book a ventriloquist or hypnotist or some other novelty act. But for all purposes, as the Depression continued, live professional entertainment in these venues meant hillbilly/mountain/country-and-western music, which was likely to be already familiar to anyone with a radio in Kentucky in the 1930s. What exactly was this music? How did it figure in the ongoing relationship between commercial culture and regionalism in the United States? And did booking these musicians somehow mark the theater as "regional" or complement the role of the picture show as "community center?"

According to Bill C. Malone, the most prominent and influential historian of country music, the 1930s marked a crucial transition in this genre. What began as devalued, regionally circumscribed "hillbilly" music became something called "country-and-western," a legitimated, marketable quantity for the commercial music industry at large. Several factors figured in this transformation: the immense popularity of singing cowboys like Gene Autry and Tex Ritter; the new electrified hybrid style of Texas musicians like Bob Wills and Ernest Tubbs; the influence of mass-marketed catalogue stores like Sears–Roebuck (which sold sheet music, recordings, and inexpensive instruments); the revival of the recording industry after 1934, with the introduction of low-priced records and the spread of the jukebox; and, above all, the immense popularity of radio.[19] During the Depression, the appeal of country music increasingly stretched well beyond its origins in the southeastern United States; something resembling a full-blown country music industry began to take shape; and hillbilly music, in Malone's phrase, "took great strides toward national dissemination and eventual national homogenization."[20]

My point is not to argue with this master narrative (one that is familiar enough in the historiography of other popular musical genres and, indeed, of Hollywood) – a story of consolidation and standardization which seems inevitably to call forth a compensatory or corrective celebration of heterogeneity and difference, as Malone's own richly detailed work demonstrates. Yet any claims for the "regionalizing" or "localizing" significance of live country music in small-town movie theaters in the 1930s must acknowledge that these very musicians participated in a commercial entertainment form then in the process of going national, borne on radio's airwaves.

For it is via radio that movie theaters enter the hillbilly picture, which should remind us that the relations across and between media and entertainment forms are crucial in understanding the cultural history of film in the United States. By 1931, 40 percent of American homes had radios; by 1938 that percentage had doubled. The airwaves were a prime commodity, and radio became the dominant medium for music during the period, broadcasting recordings, live in-studio or remote performances, and "transcriptions" of live shows.[21] The effect on regional music was quite varied. In the Northeast and upper Midwest, for example, ethnic programming flourished, helping to promote the popularity of both polka bands and also hybrid outfits like the Minneapolis-based Skarning and His Norwegian Hillbillies.[22] Elsewhere in the Midwest and throughout the South, and eventually across the United States and into Canada, radio proved to be essential in what Malone calls "the discovery, refinement, modification, and eventual standardization of southern country music."[23]

Soon after the Sears–Roebuck-owned station, WLS, began operation in Chicago in 1924, it premiered its National Barn Dance, a blend of down-home music, humor, and advertisements that soon became a nationally available Saturday evening mainstay for the NBC network and a programming model followed by countless other stations large and small.[24] One such imitator was WSM in Nashville, which renamed its own barn-dance show the Grand Ole Opry in 1927. By the early 1930s country musicians – not only singing, but also telling jokes, performing skits, and hawking their own songbooks and personal appearances – were regularly featured on a range of Saturday night barn dances as well as early morning and noontime shows, mostly sponsored by flour, drug, or laxative companies.

WSM and WLS gained particular prominence because they offered strong broadcast signals, up to 50,000 watts, as did WWVA from West Virginia, whose own barn-dance show – the World's Original Jamboree – could be received all over the northeastern United States and parts of Canada.[25] So-called X-stations, broadcasting from just across the Mexican border, transmitted with even greater power, enough to cover almost the entire US with programming that included evangelists' exhortations, patent medicine advertisements, and live (via transcription) country music by, among others, the Carter Family, who performed twice daily in 1938–40 from a station near San Antonio.[26] The growth and influence of these powerful stations – not to mention the spread of national networks – emphasize commercial radio's capacity to transcend locality and regionality as defined by, say, Campbellsville, Kentucky, Appalachia, or the South. Yet, at the other extreme (and loosely analogous to the small-town picture show), limited-market radio stations featuring country music also thrived. These included, for example, WLAP in Lexington, Kentucky, which by 1938 was daily offering live shows with Uncle Henry and His Kentucky Mountaineers at 7.00 a.m. and the Bar X Boys at 4.30 p.m. All told, one estimate has it that, by the late 1930s, "there were approximately 5000 radio shows in the United States using live country music," including about 500 "large-cast barn dances," at least ten of which were aired on national networks.[27]

Regular radio airplay meant that country musicians had a large potential audience for live performances, which usually took the form of one-night stands, always advertised with the imprimatur of the home station's call letters. According to Bill Bolick, who with his brother made up the Blue Sky Boys (one of the major influences on what would later be called bluegrass music), personal appearances were crucial sources of livelihood for country musicians, since only the very largest radio stations paid their performers a regular salary. Bolick recorded for RCA's Bluebird label and had much success in the later 1930s at small radio stations in North Carolina and Georgia. This led to countless live shows, usually staged at rural or small-town schools, courthouses, or churches. The Blue Sky Boys occasionally also played movie theaters, which required more time on their part, since the musicians did a half-hour show before each screening of the feature film. For these movie theater bookings the brothers received 50 percent of the total box office, after the $12 or $15 for the film rental fee had been taken off the top.[28]

The Blue Sky Boys' shows were prime examples of what Richard A. Peterson calls the "barnstorming" practices that lasted through the Second World War. Such acts commonly performed on small, independent radio stations supported by local sponsors, and worked as many one-night stands as possible in the listening area before moving on to another station. These working conditions favored small ensembles, often what Peterson calls "multi-talented and sober sibling groups" like the Blue Sky Boys, Bill and Charlie Monroe, and the Girls of the Golden West.[29] In the Kentucky theaters I surveyed, however, the live country music performance almost always involved a larger group or a multi-artist entourage, which turned the show into more of a special event. This is significant since "sibling groups" were also likely to specialize in "traditional" (read: hillbilly or mountain or folk-rooted) music. Perhaps more important, the booking of larger shows underscored a theater's status as the multi-functional centerpiece of Main Street, capable of meeting civic needs as well as fulfilling the demand for big-time, if not necessarily big-city, entertainment.

As was apparently the case further south, live country music performances in Kentucky during the 1930s were held at a number of different venues in addition to movie theaters: county fairs, schools, armory halls, even at courthouses or public squares. Sometimes the chief drawing card would be an "old-time fiddle contest," which might include local talent. More frequently, these well-publicized performances relied on the standardized format of the radio barn dance, which, as Peterson notes, was quite similar to vaudeville "because of the fast-paced sequence of diverse acts" providing an eclectic mix of musical styles and comedy turns.[30] For example, publicity photos (c. 1938) for a Columbus, Ohio show by the touring Renfro Valley Barn Dance suggest something of the range of talent involved, which included: Dolly, a "real cowgirl" in leather skirt, fancy boots, and cowboy hat; comedians Little Clifford and the Duke of Paducah, whose outfits call to mind silent-film comedians; Aunt Idy and the Coon Creek Girls in bows and gingham; and the Callahan Brothers and Fiddlin' Slim Miller in more stock male hillbilly attire.[31]

The Renfro Valley Barn Dance merits special attention here because it was an extremely successful Kentucky-based operation that made much of its rural, regional identity. The guiding force behind Renfro Valley was native Kentuckian John Lair, who left the insurance business to work at WLS developing what was at first called "hill-billy" talent. This included the Cumberland Ridge Runners, a group he created and managed. Lair thus knew first-hand what Mary A. Bufwack and Robert K. Oermann call the "acute image consciousness and superb publicity machinery" of WLS.[32] Lair relied on this experience when he began his own radio barn dance, the Renfro Valley Folks show, at WLW in Cincinnati in 1937. Two years later, the show moved to a site in Renfro Valley, Kentucky, where Lair constructed a self-styled "pioneer settlement," complete with a 1,000-seat barn auditorium, country store, lodge, ample space for displaying sponsors' products, and 12 log cabins fitted with indoor plumbing and heating, soon to be followed by a small museum, stables, craft shops, and more parking lots and tourist accommodations. All-in-all, the new Renfro Valley was a sort of proto-theme park with live radio shows as its principal draw. While within easy driving distance of Ohio and Indiana, it was figuratively situated deep in what the entrepreneurial Lair called the "Valley Where Time Stands Still."[33] Unlike other barn-dance programs, Lair told prospective advertisers in 1939, the Renfro Valley Barn Dance offered performers "actually living the parts they play on the program," and thus audiences "will be convinced of the sincerity and truthfulness of the entire performance, and will be apt to give additional credit to any statement made in behalf of the sponsor."[34] Advertisers like Bugler Tobacco and the Allis-Chambers Company, manufacturers of farm machinery, stood to benefit from the radio broadcasts, the live shows at the Renfro Valley site, and the personal appearances that Lair booked for his barn-dance performers at small towns and cities throughout the region. Particularly in the late 1930s and early 1940s, moving picture theaters like the Alhambra in Campbellsville provided a prime venue for the traveling Renfro Valley Barn Dance.

Headlining these shows were the Coon Creek Girls, one of several popular groups frequently booked at Kentucky movie theaters during the 1930s that looked – and may have sounded – the part of "authentic" regional talent. Acts like Sunshine Sue and Her Rock Creek Rangers, Uncle Henry and His Kentucky Mountaineers, Uncle Abner's Radio Stars, the Kentucky Ridge Runners, and the Tennessee Ramblers exemplify one variation on what Peterson calls "the theme of rustic authenticity" that was formative in the history of country music from the 1920s into the 1950s.[35] In *Creating Country Music*, Peterson argues that authenticity was imaged in three sometimes overlapping constructions in the 1930s: as the old-timer, the hillbilly, and the cowboy with a hybrid combination of hillbilly music and the visual image of the cowboy emerging as dominant by the end of the decade. (Compare the more "unstable" and patently fabricated images of chorines becoming mountain gals becoming cowgirls in the song-and-dance number from *Stand Up and Cheer* mentioned earlier.) Impresarios, performers, audiences, and media industries all participated to different degrees in the ongoing joint process of "fabricating authenticity" and institutionalizing this commercially successful genre of popular music.[36]

We can readily find this process of fabrication at work in terms of the musicians who played Kentucky movie theaters. For example, Lily Mae Ledford of the Coon Creek Girls admitted that John Lair "discouraged my buying clothes, curling my hair, going in for make-up, or improving my English. 'Stay a mountain girl ... plain and simple at all times,' he said."[37] And, as early WLS star Bradley Kincaid, renowned as the "singer of mountain ballads," explained to a fan who was upset that Kincaid wore a hillbilly get-up for his live shows: "the theater people everywhere demand that you wear the costume in keeping with the type of program you give. The costume that I wore is their conception of what the average mountain boy would look like. Personally, I would have preferred to come out on the stage in a nice new suit."[38]

Peterson is correct in emphasizing that "mountain" authenticity was but one marketable performance style available to radio musicians. In fact, the country performer who appeared most frequently at the theaters under consideration, fiddler Clayton McMichen, did not enact this form of rustic regionality. While appearing regularly on WHAS in Louisville, Kentucky, McMichen brought his Georgia Wildcats to, among other venues, the Rialto Theatre in Columbia in 1933, twice in 1934, and again in 1937 and 1938, playing jazz-inflected country swing music.[39] Would small-town theater audiences in the 1930s have taken McMichen to be a regionally rooted performer because of (or in spite of) his particular brand of country music or because of his ties to a Kentucky-based radio station? Here, again, it seems to me that we need both to note the importance of live, radio-driven, country-music performance in small-town movie theaters and to acknowledge that such music in all likelihood did not always signify a certain construction of regionalism or a localized alternative to mass commercial entertainment.

This point becomes still clearer when we realize that – in addition to Clayton McMichen and the Coon Creek Girls – screen cowboys and other "western" acts also performed live in Kentucky movie theaters. For example, Tom Keene, the Sons of the Pioneers, and Tex Ritter and his Musical Tornadoes appeared at the Virginia Theatre in Hazard.[40] The dean of singing cowboys, Gene Autry, played a well-publicized one-night stand at the Plaza Theatre in Glasgow in 1938.[41] Making available these touring shows reaffirmed the movie theater's prominent role in the community, a role here measured not by the strength of hometown ties, but by what looked to be a direct, privileged link to Hollywood. This connection to the far-distant mythicized center of national entertainment had always been a major selling-point for the small-town exhibitor, who could promise his customers the best and most popular films even as he sought to mollify local ministers, shoulder his civic duties, make the most of Will Rogers and B-westerns, and prove that there was money to be made in the midst of the Depression.

It is precisely the contradictory, or at least multiple, functions and roles of the small-town movie theater in the 1930s that are its most telling characteristic. In Hazard and Columbia and Campbellsville, the picture show occupied a central place on Main Street (symbolically, perhaps, it *was* Main Street) as entrepreneurial business, public meeting place, and community benefactor, as target of sermons and source of civic pride, and as provider of Hollywood product that was sometimes and in some ways tailored for local consumption. This picture show entered into the community's daily life to a degree that would not have been likely in the metropolis, even for the grandest picture palace.

Although we will never know precisely how exhibition affected reception, I am convinced that the Plaza and the Alhambra significantly informed and authorized what their regular patrons made of the movies. And, on the basis of reminiscences and oral-history interviews, I cannot but believe that the pictures and the picture show meant something different for the teenager, the old timer, the farmer, the housewife, and the African American citizen.

As well as what these particular theaters suggest about the role and place of the small-town picture show in its home community, what may be most intriguing about these Kentucky venues in terms of film history is that they frequently served as sites for live musical performance – well after the introduction of the sound film and well into what Giuliana Muscio, among others, has argued was the continuing trend during the Depression toward the "nationalization and homogenization of the American experience."[42] That the performers were by and large professional entertainers, barnstorming or on radio-sponsored tours, does suggest some degree of homogenization across these theaters (in contrast to, for example, the local musician playing daily at the same picture show during the 1910s or 1920s). That these traveling entertainers were offering some type of hillbilly/country-and-western music, which had already proved commercially viable, further complicates the issue.

Most obviously, appearances by the likes of the Golden West Cowboys and the Georgia Wildcats at small-town Kentucky movie theaters attest to the interaction between the film and radio industries, broadly understood, and to the sheer cultural power of radio during the 1930s. We might consider the independent exhibitor who booked such acts as simply one part of a radio-driven loop, who thereby promoted the standardization of entertainment. (Such a claim is persuasive, however, only if we downplay what could have been significant differences between live musical performance on the radio and in the movie theater and if we reject the possibility that performances in movie theaters could reinforce or evoke the various roles music had traditionally played in small-town life.) This explanation fits well with the argument, offered by Susan Smulyan in *Selling Radio*, that by the early 1930s, radio had become a commercialized, advertiser-driven, truly *national* medium controlled by a few all-powerful networks.[43] Yet, as noted earlier, while Depression-era country music radio was nationally available, it was also diverse and varied in terms of the power of individual stations, the music featured, and even the barn-dance format it preferred. If the booking of the Renfro Valley Barn Dance or Uncle Henry and His Kentucky Mountaineers by a small-town exhibitor was a smart way to make the most of commercial radio's growing presence, it was, at the same time, a means of reaffirming the movie theater's local status and even claiming – if indirectly – some sort of regional affiliation.

What has come to seem most problematic and intriguing to me in the course of investigating the ties between picture shows, radio stations, and country music is the notion of "region" as a category, as something distinct from but related to the local and the national. Three ways of understanding the fate of the regional in America during this period are particularly germane to my considerations here. First, in assessing the "commercialization of American broadcasting" between 1920–34, Smulyan notes that a crucial shift in early radio occurred precisely when "broadcasters began to think of themselves as regional rather than as local outlets". So began a process that led, she argues, to the hegemony of national networks at the expense of "regional needs," which for Smulyan are associated with "ethnic and racial diversity."[44] Second, focusing more specifically on what he calls "southern music," Malone argues that the emergence of country-and-western as an institutionalized form of pop music was a victory for "deregionalization," that is, for the "obliteration of regional differences within country music."[45] Finally, *Stand Up and Cheer*, as suggested earlier, presents what passes for the regional – here

"mountain" and "hillbilly" – as already merely a style, ripe for plucking and parodying by Broadway and Hollywood, more fodder for the all-consuming Department of Entertainment. Why then even bother with region and, in particular, with the hillbilly or southern mountain region? Because, even after the ostensible silencing of regional voices, the homogenizing of regional difference, and the recycling of regional style, the cultural politics of region still mattered in 1930s America – as evidenced in the ongoing construction of region. If the *Glasgow Times*, in a 1940 editorial, could sarcastically declare that "hillbilly radio stations should be so classified and given time on the programme between 3:00 and 3:01 in the morning,"[46] then "hillbilly" remained something to be reckoned with, as a type of music, a familiar radio program format, and a category to be marked and banished. I take this also to suggest that communities like Glasgow participated in an ongoing, contested process of self-definition, wherein certain versions of the local, the regional, and the national might be actively resisted or embraced, certain lines of affiliation strengthened or cut, all at the same time. And the picture show could not help but be at the center of this process, bringing Hollywood to town, taking a highly visible place in local civic and business affairs, and occasionally even letting Main Street go hillbilly or some facsimile thereof.

Notes

Thanks to Brenda Weber for her careful reading of this essay, to Bill C. Malone for his encouragement and concrete suggestions, and to the helpful staff at Berea College Archives.

1 Harold B. Franklin, *Motion Picture Theater Management* (Garden City, New York: Doubleday, Doran & Company, 1928), 29.

2 J.W. Williamson, *Hillbillyland: What the Movies Did to the Mountains and What the Mountains Did to the Movies* (Chapel Hill:

University of North Carolina Press, 1995), 37–50.

3   For my purposes the key companion text to *Stand Up and Cheer* is David E. Whisnant, *All That Is Native & Fine: The Politics of Culture in an American Region* (Chapel Hill: University of North Carolina Press, 1983).

4   See, for example, Douglas Gomery, *Shared Pleasures: A History of Movie Presentation in the United States* (Madison: University of Wisconsin Press, 1992), 34–56; Tino Balio (ed.), *Grand Design: Hollywood as a Modern Business Enterprise, 1930–1939* (Berkeley: University of California Press, 1993), 26–30.

5   In particular, I have examined all extant newspapers for this period published in Hazard, Campbellsville, Greensburg, Glasgow, Columbia, and Cave City, Kentucky, as well as any relevant country newspapers. See also the oral-history interviews housed in special collections at the University of Kentucky library. I have also relied on interviews that were conducted for my documentary film, *At the Picture Show* (1993), a look at moviegoing and film exhibition in Campbellsville, Kentucky, from the 1920s to the 1940s. For information on exhibition in the silent era in Kentucky, particularly in Lexington, Kentucky, see my *Main Street Amusements: Movies and Commercial Entertainment in a Southern City, 1896–1930* (Washington, DC: Smithsonian Institution Press, 1995). Special thanks for the superb work done on Hazard, Kentucky, by my research assistant, Katherine Ledford, who was funded by a grant from the College of Arts and Sciences at the University of Kentucky.

6   For an overview of the political and economic situation in Kentucky during the Depression, see George T. Blakey, *Hard Times and New Deal in Kentucky, 1929–1939* (Lexington: University Press of Kentucky, 1986).

7   *Campbellsville News-Journal*, May 28, 1931, 2.

8   *Adair County News*, January 6, 1931, 1.

9   *Glasgow Times*, June 4, 1936, 1; January 23, 1936, 1.

10   *Campbellsville News-Journal*, April 27, 1927, 6; April 21, 1938, 1; February 2, 1939, 1; June 13, 1940, 1.

11   *Adair County News*, September 28, 1926, 1.

12   *Adair County News*, March 30, 1938, 5. This sort of accommodation had long been the rule in Columbia. In August 1926, for example, the Paramount Theatre canceled Tuesday, Thursday, and Friday screenings so as not to interfere with a Baptist revival meeting (*Adair County News*, August 10, 1926, 1).

13   *Glasgow Times*, June 30, 1938, 1.

14   *Hazard Herald*, June 1, 1928, 1.

15   An extensive collection of glass-plate slides that were screened in Campbellsville is now part of the Saunders collection at the University of Kentucky library.

16   Brian Taves, "The B Film: Hollywood's Other Half," in Balio, *Grand Design*, 326, briefly describes the "states rights" distribution system in the 1930s that served many "small or rural theaters."

17   *Adair County News*, December 22, 1937, 4.

18   *Glasgow Times*, March 5, 1936, 2.

19   Bill C. Malone, *Country Music, U.S.A.*, rev. ed. (Austin: University of Texas Press, 1985), 78–175. See also Malone's *Southern Music American Music* (Lexington: University Press of Kentucky, 1979) and *Singing Cowboys and Musical Mountaineers* (Athens: University of Georgia Press, 1993); Charles K. Wolfe, *Kentucky Country: Folk and Country Music of Kentucky* (Lexington: University Press of Kentucky, 1982), provides invaluable biographical data about performers of the 1930s. For some sense of how the history of early country music – so inevitably bound up with issues of authenticity, origination, and commercialization – is told outside of an academic framework, see Turner Broadcasting's six-hour TV documentary, *America's Music: The Roots of Country* (1996).

20   Malone, *Country Music, U.S.A.*, 94. Victor Greene argues in *A Passion for Polka: Old-Time Ethnic Music in America* (Berkeley: University of California Press, 1992), 113–79, that the fate of so-called "old-time ethnic music" in the United States was very similar to what happened to hillbilly music. During the 1930s, Italian, Czech, Polish, and Finnish musicians, according to Greene, became more commercial-minded and less locally and mono-ethnically oriented. By 1940, this popular "cross-over" style – dubbed "international" music by the trade press – had taken its place in the mainstream popular music industry alongside country-and-western.

21   Transcriptions were direct recordings of live radio broadcasts on wax discs, which could

be duplicated and re-broadcast. See Susan Smulyan, *Selling Radio: The Commercialization of American Broadcasting, 1920–1934* (Washington, DC: Smithsonian Institution Press, 1994), 122–3.

22   Greene, *A Passion for Polka*, 122, 149–52.

23   Malone, *Country Music, U.S.A.*, 32. See also Richard A. Peterson, *Creating Country Music: Fabricating Authenticity* (Chicago: University of Chicago Press, 1997), 97–155.

24   One way to trace the history of WLS as it attempted to find/create a radio audience in the 1920s is through the elaborate ads (complete with photos) it ran in local newspapers. See, for instance, *Adair Country News*, April 28, 1925, 2; December 28, 1926, 3; January 4, 1927, 3. On the entire radio barn dance phenomenon, see Peterson, *Creating Country Music*, 97–117, and Mary A. Bufwack and Robert K. Oermann, *Finding Her Voice: The Illustrated History of Women in Country Music* (New York: Henry Holt, 1993), 74–107.

25   Ivan M. Tribe, *Mountaineer Jamboree: Country Music in West Virginia* (Lexington: University Press of Kentucky, 1984), 43–72.

26   John Atkins, "The Carter Family," in Bill C. Malone and Judith McCulloh (eds.), *Stars of Country Music: Uncle Dave Macon to Johnny Rodriguez* (Urbana: University of Illinois Press, 1975), 107–8.

27   Bufwack and Oermann, *Finding Her Voice*, 107.

28   Telephone interview with Bill Bolick, January 6, 1998.

29   Peterson, *Creating Country Music*, 130–6.

30   Ibid., 98–106.

31   *Columbus (Ohio) Star*, March 27, 1938, 10, in Berea College, John Lair Collection, Box 59, Promotional Material. Note that this mix of performers was still much less eclectic and "pop" oriented than what Timothy A. Patterson has found to be the case at the WLS *National Barn Dance* and the WHO *Iowa Barn Dance Frolic* earlier in the 1930s ("Hillbilly Music among the Flatlanders: Early Midwestern Radio Barn Dances," *Journal of Country Music* 6, no. 1 [1975], 12–18). For some sense of the diversity of talent grouped under the "barn-dance" banner later in the decade see, for example, Tribe's encyclopedic survey of the acts booked on West Virginia country radio stations. Even the publicity photographs Tribe includes suggest the wide range of performers who became regulars on such stations in the 1930s and early 1940s, including rustic types, cowboy singers, juvenile and family acts, mountaineers, farmers, Indians, and city slickers (*Mountaineer Jamboree*, 42–109).

32   Bufwack and Oermann, *Finding Her Voice*, 96.

33   Malone, *Country Music, U.S.A.*, 96–7; Wolfe, *Kentucky Country*, 76–84; *Renfro Valley 50th Anniversary Keepsake* (Renfro Valley, 1989), 1–12; "History of the Renfro Valley Barn Dance" in *Renfro Valley Keepsake* (1940), 3–4 (Berea College, John Lair Collection, Box 59).

34   John Lair, "The Renfro Valley Barn Dance" (Berea College, John Lair Collection, Box 1: Correspondence, Freeman Keyes file). Complicating the notion of fabricated authenticity here is the fact that, as Wolfe notes, the *Renfro Valley Barn Dance* did serve as a "local clearing house for talented Kentucky musicians" (*Kentucky Country*, 84).

35   See Wolfe, *Kentucky Country*, 66–95 for biographical information on these and other Kentucky-based performers.

36   Peterson, *Creating Country Music*, 3–11, 55–94. See also *Readin' Country Music: Steel Guitars, Opry Stars, and Honky Tonk Bars*, ed. Cecelia Tichi (Durham, NC: Duke University Press, 1995).

37   Bufwack and Oermann, *Finding Her Voice*, 104.

38   Bradley Kincaid, letter to Emma Riley Akeman (April 14, 1931). Berea College, Bradley Kincaid Music Collection II, Box 13–1: Correspondence, personal 1931–1932.

39   On McMichen, see Malone, *Country Music, U.S.A.*, 52; Wolfe, *Kentucky Country*, 89–92. A similar point could be made about another group that regularly played Kentucky movie theaters: Milwaukee-born Pee Wee King's Golden West Cowboys, who for a time had a daily 7:00 a.m. show on WAVE in Louisville. King shortly afterwards became a mainstay on the *Grand Ole Opry* (*Adair Country News*, March 24, 1937, 5).

40   *Hazard Herald*, April 13, 1939, 8.

41   Soon after, Autry would be touring extensively over the United States in shows that featured one of his own films and a stage performance based on his nationally available *Melody Ranch* radio show, another step in a remarkable career that, according to

historian Douglas B. Green, "helped to bring hillbilly music out of its backwater, gave it a new life, a deserved and long-needed dignity, and national exposure" ("Gene Autry," in Malone and McCulloh, *Stars of Country Music*, 154).

42 Giuliana Muscio, *Hollywood's New Deal* (Philadelphia: Temple University Press, 1996), 21.

43 Smulyan, *Selling Radio*, 7–10.

44 Ibid., 21, 63.

45 Malone, *Southern Music American Music*, 85.

46 *Glasgow Times*, August 29, 1940, 1.

30

Bank Night (1936)

H.O. Kusell

Bank night, like many other economic pana-
ceas, stems directly from the depression.
There is perhaps no better barometer of
the public's financial status than its attendance at movie theatres, an attendance now
estimated at between 80,000,000 and
85,000,000 weekly at an average admission
price of 23 cents. This business is normally
split between the large chain operators and
the independently owned theatres. It was
when the former tried to corral the bulk of
this business that drastic measures became
necessary to keep the independent exhibitors
in business.

On January 29 of this year in St. Louis,
Missouri, the government, for lack of evidence, withdrew its charges of conspiracy
against three major movie companies. That
trial was an attempt on the part of the government to prove that Warner Brothers,
Paramount and RKO had conspired to eliminate the independent exhibitor entirely by
the simple expedient of refusing to supply
him with pictures. Since most of the major
companies have subsidiaries which operate
movie houses with first-run pictures, the government alleged that these major companies
had conspired to exchange their product
among themselves, thereby ensuring for
their own theatres the first run of pictures in
their respective communities. It was a material blow to the independent exhibitor when
the government failed to sustain its charges,
for whether or not the conspiracy allegation
was true, the fact remains that the independent exhibitor must still play all pictures from
four to ten weeks later than their initial
showing in first-run theatres.

Until four years ago the major companies,
feeling financially secure in their monopoly of
first-run pictures, looked upon the independent exhibitor with quiet disdain. The difference in admission price between these two
types of operators averaged 20 cents a ticket.
In pre-depression days the public was willing
to pay that much more to see its favorite
movie star as soon as his picture was released. But when the movie-goer began to
budget his entertainment expenses, the
chain, or first-run, operators found that
their box-office receipts were dwindling. It
was then that they took the first step toward
shutting out competition. They reduced their
admissions in the majority of cases to within
five cents of the scale charged by the independent. Their business immediately revived.
While gross receipts were not so large as formerly, their theatres were playing to more
people and creating good will for the future
– and at the same time strangling the small
exhibitor.

The small exhibitor's position was now
precarious. He was already running double
features, and an additional picture was out of

Excerpted from H.O. Kusell, "Bank Night." *New Republic* 86 (May 6, 1936), 363–5. Reprinted with permission
from the *New Republic*.

the question. There was not enough available product. His need for an attendance-stimulator was obvious and immediate. The first restorative used was "give-away" or "premium" night. A piece of chinaware was given free to every woman attending the theatre on a designated night each week. If she went regularly and consecutively she could in time amass a full set of dishes. At once the feminine patronage increased from 20 to 25 percent on these nights. The women window-shopped the various theatres and finally gave their steady patronage to the theatre having the pattern they liked best. The picture was a secondary consideration. It was no uncommon thing for theatres to advertise "Tonight Is Dish Night – Also a Feature." And there was the Philadelphia exhibitor who walked into the film exchange one day and laid a platter on the booking manager's desk. "Look," he said, "have you got a feature that will go with this?" The efficacy of this advertising device can be measured by the fact that one New York distributor of chinaware supplied the theatres in his territory with from three to five carloads of dishes daily.

The major circuits did not adopt this premium policy. They felt that such competition in gifts would soon kill its own effectiveness. And they were right. In a few months dishes were no longer enough to pull the public to the movies. The independent theatre-owners then tried other lures, the most popular of which was giving money to the holder of a lucky number. This practice was soon prohibited as a violation of the lottery law.

Then Mr. Charles U. Yeager, a manager for the Fox West Coast Theatre Circuit, conceived the idea of Bank Night. He organized Affiliated Enterprises, Inc., copyrighted the name Bank Night and its form of operation, and tried it out in a small town in the Rocky Mountains. Its success was immediate and unprecedented; it swept the West more quickly than the Townsend Plan.

Here is how Bank Night works. The exhibitor contracts with Affiliated Enterprises to furnish him with a reel of film, known as a trailer, which advertises and announces the introduction of Bank Night, together with a register for signatures, record books and a set of numbers, or foils, which are used in the drawing of the lucky number. The register is set up in the lobby of the theatre and anyone may sign it without being obliged to buy a ticket. The participants need only sign once to be permanently listed for all future drawings (the duplication of signatures has been eliminated by an elaborate system of cross-indexes). The number opposite the signature is dropped into a drum and on the night chosen for the drawing someone (preferably a little girl) is selected from the audience to draw a number from the drum. The rules require that the holder of this lucky number must claim the prize within five, ten or fifteen minutes from the time the number is called (the time limit being at the discretion of the theatre manager). It is not necessary for the winner to be in the auditorium. He may be in the lobby, on the sidewalk, or at home. So long as he can get inside the theatre within the alloted time he may claim the prize. Those outside the theatre are informed of the result by a loud speaker, or by the name being posted in the box office. If the winner does not appear to claim his prize, the money is added to the next week's award. In many cases several weeks have elapsed before a winner has appeared.

The prizes range from $25 to $1,000, depending upon the size of the theatre and the degree of local competition. This money is held in escrow by the theatre's bank. After the theatre manager and the judges of the award have verified the winner's signature, and he has been further identified by someone in the audience, he is all ready to receive his reward, which he gets at the bank the following morning. Since it is unnecessary for the winner to purchase a ticket in order to claim the award, and since Mr. Yeager does not permit Bank Night to be advertised in the newspapers, he has been able to circumvent the lottery law in most states.

Bank Night has been operating for eighteen months and is now used in 4,300 theatres, each of which pays a royalty to Affiliated Enterprises, Inc. These royalties are determined by the size, location and admission scale of the theatre. They range from $15 to $75 a night per theatre. Affiliated's weekly income has been estimated at from $100,000 to $125,000. Deducting 50 percent for overhead and operation charges, this leaves Mr. Yeager and his associates, Claude Ezell, the national organizer, and Rick Ricketson, the original backer, a sizable piece of change. But there are penalties for its popularity. Hundreds of variations and infringements have been attempted, and Mr. Yeager is kept busy prosecuting them. Exhibitors create their own versions, using such names as Prosperity Night, Movie Sweepstakes, Treasury Night, Cash Award Night, Buck Nite, Parlay Cash Night and many others. But call it what you will, Bank Night and its imitators have caused more theatres to open during the depression than any other device. There are cases on record showing that circuits operating as many as sixty theatres have been saved from bankruptcy by this system. The fact that it has made converts of a great many former non-movie-goers can be checked by small-town exhibitors, who know the majority of their audience by sight. Box-office receipts increase on Bank Night from 100 to 400 percent over normal grosses. In some communities civic and social clubs have changed the dates of their meetings to avoid conflicting with Bank Night.

With this evidence of the independent theatre owner's new prosperity, the chain operators quickly lost their former indifference. The new slogan was now: "Live and let live... but not for long." They found it expedient and necessary to adopt the double-feature policy as well as some of the business-pulling machinations first put into use by the small competitor, so much so that current estimates show that more than 60 percent of the 15,300 movie houses in the country are now using some form of give-away night. The percentages run higher in various communities. In New York City, for instance, more than 90 percent of the movie theatres give prizes. In one section of Detroit, in which ninety theatres are located, all were found to be operating on the "Give-away night" system, some using the process as many as two, three and four times a week. [...]

How long can the appeal of Bank Night or some similar device last? Just so long as the public feels the scheme is honestly run and until the exhibitor finds more participants on the sidewalk than in the theatre. In spite of the huge increases to box-office receipts of these give-away nights, exhibitors are not too sanguine about their benefit to the business, since they have created a precedent that will become increasingly difficult to maintain. The independent exhibitor's salvation lies in one or all of the following propositions: (1) economic conditions throughout the country improving sufficiently so that major chains can revert to their former admission prices; (2) outlawing the double-feature policy in the first-run houses, thereby releasing a larger available supply of pictures for the independent; (3) eliminating give-away nights in the major circuits; (4) an increasingly better, and hence more salable, output of films.

31

The Management of Motion Picture Theatres (1938)

Frank H. Ricketson, Jr.

Constructive Stimulation

[...] Business stimulators seem to fall into seven [*sic*] classifications. The divisions are something as follows:

1. The old-fashioned give-away.
2. Bank Night.
3. Benefits.
4. Scrip.
5. Games.
6. Contests.
7. Premiums.
8. Good-will service.

The Old-Fashioned Give-Away

Small houses, where crudity of operation was expected, had the exclusive use of the give-away for some time, but gradually it has become an element of rising importance and is not uncommon now in large de luxe theatres. Any business stimulator that is not a part of the prescribed entertainment for the theatre is termed a give-away or a "racket." It is any kind of artifice designed to stimulate extra business.

Scope. It consists of premiums, drawings for prizes, merchandise furnished by manufacturers to be donated to patrons to advertise their products, special bonuses or rewards which go with the sale of theatre tickets, the redemption of labels and trade-marks or any evidence of trade in exchange for theatre tickets, or any form of inducement to encourage patrons where the entertainment and the theatre and its service are not the only considerations.

A few years ago the give-away was not considered show business, and even now it is a subterfuge that every exhibitor dislikes to employ. The depression and poor pictures have made it a necessary adjunct in certain types of houses. Whether the improvement in pictures will abolish it is a matter that the future will have to decide. My hunch is that the give-away is here to stay, or at least until something better comes along.

Handsome profit is the only consideration warranting a theatre manager's resorting to stimulators. If there is any doubt as to the returns it will bring to the box office, then do not try the "racket." If the theatre is standing the entire expense and effort, the same amount will often be more profitable if divided between entertainment and advertising.

The successful stimulators have been those which the theatre can promote without expense or through the cooperation of merchant, manufacturer, or civic group. Like so many other phases of the business, a give-

Excerpted from Frank H. Ricketson, Jr., *The Management of Motion Picture Theatres* (New York: McGraw-Hill, 1938), 248–66.

away may be successful in one place and a failure in another.

Bank Night is an exception. Ordinary give-aways cannot be considered in the same category with Bank Night as a business stimulator. It was an innovation which helped lift the industry from the depression. Bank Night added literally hundreds of thousands of new theatre patrons, and many showhouses which as a policy did not feature a give-away opened their doors to it. [...]

The capital prize determines the value to the box office. The prize must be big and must have a universal appeal. Many exhibitors have found this difficult to understand. Time and again, exhibitors with cash nights have tried to give away ten cash prizes of $10 each instead of a single $100 prize. The receipts have always been favorable to the latter. A few consolation gifts of unimportant value are helpful, but it is the big prize that sells theatre tickets. The same holds true in every form of gift or de luxe prize. In the old country store, which probably started all theatre give-aways, the exhibitor discovered that it was better to bring ten or twelve winners on the stage and load them with all the groceries they could carry than to distribute fifty or sixty packages, one to a person. [...]

Benefits and Scrip

Benefit shows in which educational, religious, fraternal, or social organizations in a community sell the theatre tickets for a given performance or day are a source of excellent revenue for either attractions or days of the week that will not do average business. Benefits follow two plans:

1. An organization takes over the theatre for one night, or
2. The organization sells tickets and receives a nominal percentage from the first few hundred sold and a larger percentage as the sale increases.

Under the first plan, the theatre is guaranteed a definite sum and turns over the entire box-office receipts for the given period.

The second plan is the one generally used and forms the basis of our discussion here. Under this plan, the organization receives credit only for tickets actually sold by it before the show day. The percentage is graduated until the organization often receives as high as 50 per cent for large sales. A special ticket is printed and it is exchanged at the box office on the night of the benefit for theatre tickets. [...]

Preference is given to schools first, churches second, then charitable organizations, lodges, and groups that will work. Where the benefit performances have been capably handled, they become annual affairs of the organization and bring both profit and good will to each party of the contract. Benefits should be so spaced that solicitations do not become a nuisance. In small towns, one benefit a month is enough, but some theatres in larger communities with widely diversified groups find as many as two benefits a week profitable.

Scrip. In many communities, scrip-book sales can be furthered profitably by a theatre during the holidays and for seasonal contests. The popular style of scrip book is of $2.50, $5, or $10 value. The book contains scrip which is exchanged at the box office for theatre tickets and is usually sold at a 10 per cent discount. The result of various surveys on scrip sales show that where it is sold in contests and for seasonal gifts, about 80 per cent is eventually redeemed, but where it is sold to customers as a standard policy of the theatre, it is used 95 per cent to 100 per cent. Scrip books make ideal Christmas presents and will add extra revenue during the pre-Christmas slump. Scrip campaigns are also suitable for any kind of popularity or employees' contest. An objectionable feature to scrip as a standard policy of the theatre is that it undersells the box office and permits petty irregularities in the handling of theatre funds. Many circuits have abandoned scrip, except on special occasions, for this reason.

Games, Contests, and Premiums

Games

A variation of the old and ancient game of Lotto has been revived in over 2,500 theatres. A few new twists and a multitude of names have been given to this development in business stimulators. The idea gets away from the deck of Lotto cards or the grab-bag disks used in the days of the game's early popularity and substitutes one of two methods: projection on the screen or the actual placing of a large wheel on the stage.

The latter is a roulette type of contrivance with numbered strips and an arrow indicator, and provides a practical method for large-audience participation. The complete paraphernalia consists of the wheel, audience cards, and stage blackboard for verification. The prizes are cash, groceries, candy, or whatever the theatre managers feel will attract patrons.

When the play begins, the patron has a card. The indicator on the wheel is spun and any number on which the indicator stops, is checked by the patron on his card. When a patron fills a consecutive row of five numbers, he rises from his seat, calls "Lotto" (or whatever name is given the game), and goes to the stage or the front of the theatre, where the attendant verifies the numbers and the patron receives a prize. [...]

Contests

Contests cover a broad field of interest stimulators. It is not our intention to outline all conceivable ideas or to detail their activities, but rather to touch on the varieties. The magnitude of the contest will depend upon the original idea. It may be limited to a small lobby effort, a daily front-page feature of the newspaper, or the headline stage attraction of the theatre. The purpose and the avenue selected for the event decide the size and importance.

Popularity contests. The most usual forms of popularity contests are baby, beauty, bathing beauty, mother, and athlete contests. The theatre sponsors the contest alone or in co-operation with the newspaper or a group of merchants. Best results are obtained when the contest does not run too long. Voting can be by ballot at the theatre or by audience acclaim with the contestants on the stage. Prizes are generally solicited from merchants. Contestants are chosen from a wide group of citizens to create as much interest as possible. They should be selected with great care. Leading citizens are selected as judges. They should not be connected with the theatre and their decisions should be final. A theatre cannot afford to sponsor a contest in which it is the judge. Prizes are arranged and rules prepared in advance.

Literary contests. Any controversial subject concerning the picture itself is suitable for a literary contest. Cooperation may be had from schools, with prizes offered for the best essay of any class. A newspaper may offer prizes, often furnished by the theatre, for the best hundred-word article written by a subscriber. Variations of the literary contest are missing words, local advertisements, jumbled words, coined words, dialogues, criticisms, cartoons, advertisements, or solutions to a problem of the picture.

Impersonation contests. Impersonation contests are on measurement, likeness, perfect features, make-up, age, or characteristics. Contestants appear in person or submit photographs, whichever the theatre may decide better serves the purpose. When a tie-up is made, it is with the newspaper, which publishes the pictures of the different contestants.

Feats of skill. Displays of skill suggested by some particular feature which the picture exploits are held on the stage of the theatre. Popular types include fiddling, dancing, singing, eating, drinking, winking, cow milking, climbing greased poles, and any of a thousand

194

other stunts that will create comedy or excite curiosity and have entertainment value.

General contests.   General contests are suggested by the picture, or for institutional value. Careful drivers, most worthy citizen, puzzle solvers, gardeners, golfers, doll dressers, dogs and other pets, scholarships, radio tryouts, mileage estimates, or any deeds of skill which attract attention may be used. The manager offers a prize for the fisherman in the county making the biggest catch during the season and exhibits the trophy in his lobby. Another showman will have a prize for the largest ear of corn grown in the county or the cow giving the most milk or the largest family or anything that has human interest and is certain to attract.

Premiums

The premium is probably the most unsuccessful business stimulator used. All other box-office schemes can be bait for the attraction that is offered. The premium is a bribe to attend the show, and no theatre manager has been able to find a compensating prize to overcome a poor show. Premiums are also the most expensive type of stimulators. Seldom can merchandise of any value be given to each patron and the cost kept within the price of the ticket. A favored plan is for the woman patron to receive a piece of china or silver or linen. The hope is that she will keep coming each week on a given night until she has completed her set. The cost of the article usually offsets the benefits. Trading stamps occasionally are used in small towns in co-operation with merchants. [...]

Good-Will Service

Good-will stimulators can be planned to touch everywhere, and may be of great value. They are numerous and entwine themselves into every mode of life. One showman may advertise "call the theatre for correct time." Another may have a bulletin news service in his lobby or encourage the habit of calling the theatre for football, basketball, and other results or for current news events. These are all good-will stimulators. The sponsorship of a basketball team, bowling team, or scholarship award, orphan shows, food and clothing matinees for the poor, previews for certain societies, free tickets for children living in rural districts when accompanied by adults are some suggestions. In fact any tie-up or publicity in which the policy is to establish good will becomes a stimulator. [...]

Every theatre has a personality. Around each house, or the manager who operates it, weave romantic tales of virtues or faults. Good will plays its part in proper stimulation. The theatre is in the public eye and its good qualities or its faults become in time legendary. This book is not large enough to detail all gestures that might fall into the specification of good-will stimulators. They are the tricks of advertising and call for the keen discernment of the management. Here are just a few:

For youngsters: stamp clubs, swimming classes, juvenile bands, scout propaganda, kid parties, birthdays, airplane modeling, hobby clubs, outings.

For adults: free health and accident insurance, identification tags for key rings, pocket pieces, calendars, desk pads, tire covers, matches, golf tees, and any kind of souvenir or novelty. No list is complete. New ideas are being born daily, and new needs are found hourly.

Parade float for the projectionists' union (ca. 1932)

32

Show Lady (1939)

Carlie Beach Roney

I had been a housewife for ten years. Then I was alone and had to start to earn my own living. With a capital of $2000. I hoped to buy a business which would be interesting as well as income producing.

I looked at "business opportunities" – everything from rooming houses and tearooms to cigar stands and commercial photography, before I met the man who sold theaters for a Detroit business-brokerage firm. His brisk talk of block booking, box-office appeal, and S R O signs made owning a picture show sound attractive, but I was frightened at the prospect of managing any of the first places he showed me – neighbor-hood theaters in Detroit and one in Saginaw. When he spoke of small towns, I felt on more familiar ground, for I grew up in a Michigan village and liked the idea of going back to one. Milford, he explained, was only forty miles from the Detroit film exchanges, which distribute film to most of Michigan. Its only theater could be bought for $1500 down, and was a sure-fire money-maker, a cinch for a smart woman. He would help me with everything – bookings, advertising and exploitation – until I learned the ropes.

That was on a Monday in October. I didn't understand – not then – why he waited until Saturday night to take me to see the theater. The place was packed, with a line-up at the box office. Later I discovered that Milford is a typical Saturday-night town, with all the farmers of the community making weekly trips for shopping and diversion.

So I decided to buy the Star Theater in Milford, Michigan – property, equipment and goodwill. The following Wednesday I met the owner in Detroit to sign a land contract and pay $100 to clinch the bargain. The balance of the $1500 was to be paid when the keys were turned over to me. The price was $7500; terms: the down payment, an additional one of $1000 in cash at the end of the first year, and monthly payments of seventy dollars.[. . .]

[. . .] Five dollars covered my necessary daily pay roll – three dollars for the projectionist, a dollar for a boy to relieve him and sometimes take tickets, and fifty cents each to the popcorn girl and a regular ticket taker. I sold tickets – usually done by the exhibitor's wife or daughter – in addition to my duties of management, and I also did the janitor work. I got acquainted with every inch of that house and learned the peculiarities of the furnace. By Christmas I was glad to turn the sweeping and coal shoveling over to a school-boy for three dollars a week.

On the Monday after I bought the theater I drove to Detroit to learn how to keep it. On my carefully tabulated list of things to do, the first item was to join the Michigan Theater Owners Association. Their manager spent two hours telling me how to go about my

Excerpted from Carlie Beach Roney, "Show Lady." *Saturday Evening Post* 211 (February 18, 1939), 23, 36, 38–40. Reprinted with permission of the *Saturday Evening Post*.

job of being an exhibitor. He examined the existing picture contracts for Milford and advised me to assume them. There weren't many; they were what my town was used to; it would give me a good start with the film exchanges if I did not disturb their bookings.

Then I proceeded to learn the law of movies by joining the Film Board of Trade, whose membership is open to film producers and distributors as well as exhibitors. Their secretary explained the board's chief function – a neutral board of arbitration for out-of-court settlement of disputes between members. This not only saves theater owners and exchanges the expense of litigation but also avoids the unfavorable publicity of airing theater troubles in court. I was told that defective film is a common cause of complaint. I would be entitled to a rebate of film rental from an exchange which sent me film with broken or weak edges that broke in the projector[...]

I spent the balance of that first day in the various film exchanges. Most of the managers had heard that the new owner of the Star of Milford was a woman. They ushered me into their private offices to sign the contracts I agreed to assume. Some of them offered me drinks, which, I gathered, is customary. Then they tried to sell me new contracts. I declined both drinks and contracts.

A Movie First Night

I returned to Milford in time to open the Monday-night show and smile at my new patrons from the box office. I did smile, but I wished there were more customers to smile at. My little stack of quarters and dimes just covered film rental on the feature.

The movie business has the advantage of being a strictly cash affair. Customers pay before they see the show, and film rental must be paid in advance. If your check has not reached the exchange before the film leaves, the cans come C. O. D.

On Monday of that first week my receipts were $7.50; Tuesday, $9.00 – a total of $16.50 for a show with a feature at $7.50 and a comedy at $3.00. Thursday and Friday were a little better – $28.50 receipts against a $10.00 feature and another $3.00 comedy. My Saturday show was a $7.50 Western, with $4.50 worth of short subjects, and I was able to smile gratefully at the farmers who shoved $82.50 through the window of my box office. I met my pay roll of $25.00 and paid $12.00 for express charges on film delivery. I figured $10.00 for advertising and lights at $4.50, and had a net of $40.50, of which $20.00 must be set aside for that extra $1000 payment at the end of the year.

I listed my yearly overhead expense as follows:

Payments on Property:	
12 Months at $70 a month ...	$840.00
Extra payment, end of year....	1000.00
Insurance	120.00
Taxes	70.00
Fire inspection	20.00
Association dues	10.00
Film Board of Trade	10.00
Fee covering use of copyright music	10.00
Annual total overhead......	$2080.00

Dividing that amount by fifty-two, I had the round figure of $40.00 overhead against my week's net of $40.50, and knew I had to continue my janitor duties.

Later I realized that this week suffered the natural slump following the run of a widely advertised special the week before I became the owner. I couldn't blame my patrons for staying away from the pictures I was showing – from what I could see of them at odd moments. I never saw a complete show.

A study of my contracts bookings convinced me I had to do something about the situation, and do it quickly. The town expected a change of policy from a new owner, which offered an opportunity to make a favorable first impression. I concluded I had to gamble on some good specials, and the time was fortunate, for October and November are among the best show months of the year in a farming community. I decided to put on a gala Opening Night with a super-special. The one I selected cost forty dollars, a record price for Milford, but I cleared $100 on it, and thought I had found the answer to all my problems. Twenty-five dollars had been my predecessor's top price, so there were several good specials available at slightly higher prices. For a time I ran two of them each month; later I spaced them farther apart. My film rental increased to an average of fifty dollars a week, box-office receipts to $180.

Naturally, I did not have the $1000 extra payment to make after the first year, but I spent various amounts on improvements so that my overhead over the whole period of 134 weeks came to only slightly less than my first estimate – that is, overhead cost me $40.00 a week during the first year, but only $35.00 a week over the whole period.

WEEKLY AVERAGE OF EXPENSE

Operating Costs:	
Pay roll	$25.00
Advertising	15.00
Express on film transportation	12.00
Lights	4.50
Coal and wood	2.50
	$59.00
Overhead	35.00
Weekly expense without film rental	$94.00
Average film rental	$50.00
Total weekly expense	$144.00
Average income over period of 134 weeks (Including peak week of $260.00 and low one of $95.00)	$175.00
Average net per week	$31.00

While my receipts varied widely my expenses were almost static, except for film rental. With $7.00 a day for overhead and around $12.00 for other costs of operation, film rental brought the minimum cost of any night's show to about $25.00, whether or not I sold the 100 quarter admissions I needed to break even. A February night of zero temperature and piercing wind set my record for low attendance at twelve. Cold and storm were not always liabilities. Sometimes the people who habitually drove to near-by city theaters were unable to make these trips over drifted icy roads and patronized my little movie – especially if I was showing a better-than-average picture. Specials still justified their extra cost.

Film rentals are based on the number of seats in your theater and the population of your town. I had 250 seats, Milford had 1600 people, so I was entitled to minimum rates.

The value of a picture depends on the number of paid admissions it will bring.

First-run theaters in large cities pay thousands of dollars for a feature which may run several weeks. In a small town, where everyone would see it in two days, the exhibitor may pay as little as $7.50 for the same can of film, whether he used it one day or three. First-run theaters get an extra value in a protection period during which that picture may not be shown in other theaters within a certain radius. [...]

My minimum film rental for features was $7.50. At that price I got program pictures – the ordinary, run-of-the-mine pictures needed for the bulk of programs in movie houses making several changes each week. For specials and some of the popular stars I paid from $25.00 to $100.00. Most prices are subject to bargaining with film salesmen.

Film salesmen are high-pressure boys. I remember one I met on my first trip to the Film Building. He was young, good-looking and very smooth. He extolled the merits of his pictures, but didn't urge me to buy. He said I was so wise not to sign new contracts until I became adjusted. He was very complimentary. He admired my furs. He told me it was a pleasure to meet an attractive woman with a talent for business. When I left, he said he would call on me soon. A little gleam in his eye betrayed that he thought a woman would be easy picking. I learned about salesmen from him.

I had to buy about 200 features a year, and two or three times as many short subjects. Few contracts cover less than five pictures, but once your signature is on the dotted line, every item listed above it must be paid for. If some prove to be too bad to use, your only alternative is to pay for them and not run them. The only way out is through the exchange offering to cancel a few unused pictures as an inducement to sell a new contract, which puts you in a bad position to bargain.

Film is perishable not merely because of its brittle composition. Once a year, when the producer has his twelve-month schedule outlined, a salesman tries to sell you the whole works. Failing in that, he makes frequent calls as long as any of his pictures are open for your town. All are ready to sell to small theaters as soon as one or two are made and have had first runs in your key city. I signed one contract which totaled more than $1000 for features and comedies, and was glad to get it, although few of the pictures were completed. It included most of my sure-fire stars, and all I needed to know was the name and the price.

On Saturday nights the farmers came to town and brought the biggest part of my week's income. My farmers liked Westerns and action pictures with real he-man actors. Most of these stars make from five to nine pictures a year, few of which cost me more than ten dollars film rental. The exchanges know which ones you need and increase the price each year. Cheap stars who are popular with your patrons can be built up with special exploitation. The exchanges furnish inexpensive souvenirs, paper sombreros, and so on, with which to exploit these pictures.

Juggling Stars

I don't think the word "exploit" has a sting the way exhibitors use it. The dictionary gives a first meaning of the verb, "to put to use; use selfishly, as workingmen," a common understanding of the word. You come closer to what exploitation means in the movies if you think of the meaning of the noun, "an

act marked by heroism, daring, skill or brilliance." Theater owners put their pictures to use, perhaps selfishly, but they do not exploit their patrons. They exploit exploits.

When the price of one of my best Saturday-night stars was boosted to fifteen dollars, I changed him to a mid-week run which brought seventy-five dollars. As dates to exploit this actor's deeds of daring, I booked his next picture to start on a Monday in June which happened to be my birthday. I gave a matinee birthday party for all the kids of the locality. Free admission, popcorn and suckers, with an added prize attraction of a pass to the theater good all during vacation. For the coveted prize I conducted a drawing in a spotlight on the stage.

Except for popcorn and candy, my only other expense was extra pay for my operator, as I never ran in the day time. Few small-town theaters do. The pass cost less than nothing, because any person with a theater pass generally brings at least one paid admission. With children this is apt to mean both parents – and quite often. My first idea about the party was to make friends with the kids. They can make plenty of trouble if they don't like you. Anyway, I like kids, and that was the nicest birthday party I ever gave. Afterward I got a great kick from the special smiles they gave me.

School had just closed and I ran a Standing Room Only matinee. And the funny thing about it was that every child came back to the show in the evening and brought most of his family with him. For an expenditure of less than ten dollars my receipts increased from the usual seventy-five dollars on that star to $135 on these two nights, and each of his later pictures cleared an extra twenty to twenty-five dollars. I was sorry he made only seven pictures a year. That's exploitation that doesn't hurt anyone.

An Easter Program

New ideas are usually worth money. In the movies it pays to work out almost any original idea. Naturally, a woman's ideas are different from the ones men have been working on for years, and a woman exhibitor may find it profitable to carry out any stunt she originates, no matter how unprecedented it may be.

During the week before Easter I ran a religious picture called Manger to the Cross. In itself that idea is not new. In fact, I had to book it in January to be sure of having it for Easter. Churches often run it at Christmastime, and it is not a subject to be handled lightly. I did not use ordinary advertising, posters and window cards, for the excellent reason that the exchange didn't have any. I worked through the local churches, including the little crossroad ones. I gave them free tickets for their Sunday-school children and adult tickets to sell on 40 per cent commission. For a short subject I used a one-reel floral travelogue, and then ran the five-reel feature as slowly as possible. I raised adult admission from my usual twenty-five cents to forty cents.

The picture was a silent one with a cue sheet for appropriate piano music and suggestions for vocal numbers. Soloists from the church choirs were glad to do these without pay. They sang Holy Night during the Bethlehem scenes, a solemn hymn during the crucifixion, and at the end, the one which has that triumphant "Up from the grave He arose!" Not in any church have I ever seen a more impressive Easter service than the one I staged in a movie. I'll never forget the exalted, rapt expressions on the children's faces as they came out of that show.

I paid twenty-five dollars for this picture, and my profit on it was about the same as on any special, but its value to me went further than that. It established my theater with the church people and offset talk of possible harmful influence of movies. It brought in people who had never come before. One very old lady told me it was the first movie she had ever seen. I followed up by running complimentary slides on Saturday nights announcing Sunday church services. Altogether, this church affiliation helped to put

me, as a woman theater manager, the "show lady," in a much better light in the town.

Schools and other local organizations were more than willing to co-operate on special occasions. When I ran a picture which tied in with their activities, I gave them 40 per cent on tickets they sold, 20 per cent of box-office sales, and they provided amateur acts between shows. Once a week the band played in front of the theater before the first show, again on the stage before the second, and their share of receipts helped them to buy new uniforms. The American Legion brought out a good crowd for a patriotic picture on Lincoln's Birthday. The high school put on playlets. Boy Scouts turned out in a body and helped put over a picture which was weak in box-office appeal, but an excellent show for them to see. For all these occasions I used extra care in selecting features.

This is an effective way in which exhibitors accomplish practical censorship. Theater owners cannot eliminate sensational pictures as long as some of their patrons want them, but they can, and very often do, use sense in setting the dates on which such pictures are shown. Children attend in largest numbers on Friday and Saturday nights, so the other days are more suitable for sophisticated pictures, even though young patrons may have a yen for the stars in those pictures.

Many exhibitors make an honest effort toward this sort of censorship. Most of theater-owner associations advocate it. Theaters know better than to advertise such a policy, but mothers can easily discover a general trend in Friday and Saturday shows.

When I sold out, the very conservative local paper surprised me with a laudatory front-page write-up. They spoke particularly of the better pictures I had brought to Milford, which gave me a laugh.

With some exceptions, I ran much the same pictures any exhibitor would. I hadn't much choice. I used caution in setting dates, and the different elements in town saw what they wanted to see. The community believed I gave them "better pictures" because I persistently told them so.

I started using the phrase as soon as I decided I wanted better pictures. I hoped to be a better exhibitor than my predecessor, who had been in the business for thirty years. In my inexperience I thought that wanting better pictures meant only that I was willing to pay higher prices for them. I suppose that was "just like a woman."

Telling the World

Before I put on my Opening Night I had the newspaper shop print 500 large pink cards with the words BETTER PICTURES in huge block letters, and a line below, STAR THEATER, MILFORD, UNDER NEW MANAGEMENT. I tacked those cards all over the countryside. I hammered on the words in all my advertising. Evidently I put it over. When that editor praised me, after I had left his town and he'd never get any more advertising from me, I know he believed what he said.

Notice that I said I tacked up those cards. I did. I put up all my advertising. Each week I covered the area, distributing handbills and tacking up cards which advertised my next special feature. I started because I knew I would do a better job than anyone I could afford to hire. I kept it up because of the showmanship value in a woman doing that work. Besides, it was a lot of fun. [...]

33

What's Playing at the Grove?
(1948)

Fortune

The women came slowly out of the theatre into the soft summer air and stood a moment under the marquee before they drifted along the shady street to their homes. "A marvelous picture," they said. "It was beautiful." (1ST GALESBURG SHOWING – DEBORAH KERR AND SABU IN BLACK NARCISSUS) A group of college boys shoved through the popcorn-smelling lobby and headed for Main Street. "I've seen pictures, but ——! Who the hell picked this one?" A young woman joined her friends at the parking lot. "I'm glad I didn't bring Fred. He wouldn't have gone to the movies again for two weeks." And a couple of bobby-soxers stopped at the counter on their way to the second show. "Two corn, please."

Weldon Allen, owner of the Grove theatre in Galesburg, Illinois, hadn't been sure how *Black Narcissus* would go over. He can no more tell exactly what pictures his customers are going to like than a book publisher can predict sales accurately. "You go nuts trying to figure it out." Even if he knew the sure-fire hits, he could by no means be sure of getting them for exhibition. The Grove is a small (390 seats) independent theatre four blocks from Main Street, and until last year Allen got only second-run product with a sixty-day clearance – that is, he could show only films that had played two months earlier in Galesburg's two first-run, circuit-owned, Paramount-controlled houses. In January, 1947,

through an arrangement with United Artists, he began to get new pictures and he had enough to play twenty-seven weeks of the fifty-two last year. Most of them were from United Artists, a few from other big distributors, but he had to take what they would give him.

Black Narcissus was a case in point. From what he knew about the picture he didn't think it would go over big in Galesburg. (He couldn't take time to go up to Chicago to see a screening at the exchange, but he had read trade-journal reviews.) Universal-International, however, had offered him the picture on a flat rental basis and, for the first time, suggested that he bid on a group of films, including *Casbah*, *A Double Life*, *The Naked City*, *Are You With It?*, and four English films. He bid high (for him) on the first three and low on the others. ("An English picture starts with two strikes against it here.") He lost out on *Casbah*, *A Double Life*, and *Naked City* – they went to the Paramount-controlled theatres up the street – but he got the other five. He played *Black Narcissus* seven days, single feature, because it was first-run, and it brought in about $1,200 gross for the week. He paid so little for it, about $250, that the profit was good in spite of the below-average attendance.

If it had been a first-run action picture or a top western, the kind Galesburg likes best, he

Excerpted from "What's Playing at the Grove?" *Fortune* 38 (August 1948), 95–9, 134, 136–8. Reprinted with permission from *Fortune* magazine.

would have paid much more and grossed much more. The rental price of *Body and Soul*, a prize-fight film starring John Garfield, for example, was 40 percent of the gross. He grossed $2,500 in nine days and had to pay $1,000 film rental. Since his overhead stays about the same, around $550 a week, whatever picture is showing, he cleared $785 on *Body and Soul*, $400 on *Black Narcissus*. Of course, if he could always run pictures like *Body and Soul* he'd be on top of the Galesburg world. Even if he could always run pictures that did as well as *Black Narcissus*, he'd be getting along all right. But so far he hasn't been able to do anything like that. The choice of pictures has been limited not only by the rental he can afford to pay but, he is convinced, by a tie-up between the distributors and circuit theatres.

There are five theatres in town. The two largest, the Orpheum and the West, are first-run houses owned by Publix Great States, the downstate circuit of Balaban & Katz of Chicago, which in turn is controlled by Paramount Pictures. Mr. Allen's independently owned Grove, although smaller, is in direct competition with the Orpheum and the West. The Colonial is a second-run house, allied to the circuit theatres. The Bond is a small independent, showing sometimes second-run but more often third or subsequent-run pictures.

Until 1947, the Orpheum and the West got all the first-run pictures, and even now they get almost all of them. Top pictures play at the Orpheum (1,105 seats), B pictures at the West (644). The Orpheum runs single features and changes twice a week, the West runs double features and usually changes the bill three times a week. In that way they can consume almost all the output of the producers. (Last year 487 pictures were produced in the U.S.) Allen is riled at this practice, which results in his getting few first-runs. "They don't try to get the most out of a picture," he says with some bitterness. "They'll slough it off on a Thursday-Friday double feature."

Obviously the distributors want to rent their product to the exhibitor who can and will pay the most for it, and the usual economic equation includes size of theatre, location, number of performances, and admission price. Allen insists that he can often do a bigger gross than the Orpheum or the West on a single picture by booking it for seven days even though he has only 390 seats. No one can prove or disprove this without access to the books of all the theatres in the town. In any event United Artists changed its distributing policy late in 1946 and started giving the Grove first call on its pictures. That break and the recent court rulings against producer-distributor-exhibitor monopolies have given Allen hope for an all first-run and consequently a money-making theatre. If he gets it, and he thinks he will, his chief limitation will be the size of his theatre.

Last year Allen did a gross business of about $63,000 and made a profit, before taxes, of around $14,000. (Like most independent theatre owners, he does not want his circuit competitors or his suppliers to know the exact figures of his business. The amounts given here are reasonable approximations.) His 22 per cent profit was higher than the average U.S. theatre's 17 per cent, chiefly because his overhead is unusually low: he employs only one union operator in the projection room and a part-time cleaning woman. The ticket seller, ticket taker, and popcorn girl are college or high-school students.

His two biggest expenses are film rental, around $18,500 a year or 29 per cent of the gross, and wages, which account for 17 per cent. He spends 5 per cent on advertising – about $80 a week to advertise a first-run picture in the local *Daily Register-Mail*, $25 or $30 on a second-run. He must also buy the posters and cards that go into the showcases in front of the theatre and the lobby. His other expenses include utilities, repairs, taxes, insurance, business trips, and supplies such as popcorn and candy. The popcorn-candy-coke stand at the Grove is an important element in Allen's business. Half the movie customers buy his Puffy Pete corn, at 10 cents a box, and children, although they pay low admission prices, make up for it by all the 6-cent Oh Henry's, Snickers, Power Houses, Nutty Fudges, and Tootsie Rolls they buy. About 10 per cent of Allen's gross comes from the stand and it makes a net profit of about $3,000 a year.

The theatre is open only at night during the week (admission 55 cents for adults, 18 cents for children), but on Saturdays and Sundays Allen runs three or five shows a day (depending on whether he is showing a double feature or a single) and expects to make as much money as he does the rest of the week. On crowded days he takes the tickets or doubles as usher, and he does practically all the chores and repair work himself. The profit for the year was certainly nothing to complain about, but the point is that it almost all came from first-run pictures. When he was forced to play seconds (as he was half the time last year and all the time in previous years), he barely broke even.

The position of Weldon Allen is not unique in the motion-picture business. Despite years of litigation and court rulings, discrimination against independents has not been eliminated. Wherever an independent theatre owner competes with a circuit there is likely to be a variety of what the Supreme Court has called "unwholesome practices." Competitive bidding for films, ordered by the District Court for the Southern District of New York in 1946, was hailed at the time as a boon to the independent. Under it each picture was to be licensed to the highest bidder in each competitive area. But the system was open to wide abuse – by both distributors and exhibitors – and the Supreme Court in its decision (the *U.S. v. Paramount et al.* case) of May 3, 1948, held that competitive bidding was no solution to restraint of trade. The judiciary, said the Court, could not involve itself in policing a nationwide business, and it was unwise to leave the management of the system to "those who had the genius to conceive the present conspiracy." After upholding most of the District Court's other rulings, the Supreme Court returned the case for a new study of the fundamental question of whether or not the major producer-distributors should be allowed to own theatres. If the courts do divest the majors of their theatres, the independents obviously will have clearer sailing. That does not mean that all will show first-run pictures (there will continue to be many successful second-run houses), but that theatre owners will have a chance to compete for first-runs in an open market.

In the meantime, independent owners like Allen will have to go on fighting for better clearance rulings and the right to bid for first-run pictures. It is true that if Allen could be sure of all United Artists first-runs and get a shorter clearance (say two weeks) on seconds from other distributors, he could make a pretty good living out of the Grove. But he can hardly be satisfied with that when he sees what he could do if he had all first-runs. He calculates that he has lost $100,000 profit in his seven years of operation because he was deprived of first-runs.

On Location

Galesburg is a city of 30,000 population in west central Illinois, 160 miles from Chicago. The sun-baked business blocks down-town give way quickly to quiet residential sections where the porte-cochered, verandaed houses of the well-to-do stand back from elm-shaded, brick-paved streets. White-collar workers and laborers live in smaller frame houses farther from the heart of the city. (Carl Sandburg was born in a little house near the railroad yards.) And beyond them all lie the fertile fields and farms of the corn belt. Knox College, as old as Galesburg itself, is in the center of town just back of the Knox County courthouse, and Old Main looks about as it did when Lincoln and Douglas debated there on a raw October day in 1858. The Burlington and Santa Fe main lines run through Galesburg and the Burlington has its largest division headquarters there. There are more than a score of factories – paving bricks, overalls, casket hardware, paints, and soybean products – in Galesburg, but it is still primarily a country town, the trading center of the rich, flat grainland that surrounds it.

In the winter the people of Galesburg go to concerts, club meetings, student plays, and basketball games. In the summer they find recreation in golf, swimming and boating out at pleasant man-made lakes nearby, picnics and baseball and passing carnivals. But all year round the most popular form of entertainment is the movies.

Weldon Allen was brought up in Galesburg, went to school there and then to Knox College. He had intended to be a chemist, but when he graduated in 1932, jobs were scarce and he couldn't find steady work anywhere. After his father lost his job with the Burlington in 1935, Allen and his family were really caught in the depression. Allen had always liked the movies and had taken courses in photography and stage technique. With the family's last $600 he leased the little deserted Gala theatre (now the Bond) near the old square and bought enough equipment to start showing westerns and serials. His prices were low and he got the depression trade that couldn't afford the big houses. (Theatres with low admission prices generally have done well in depression periods.) By 1939 he had accumulated enough capital to think of building a theatre of his own.

Being sure he would never get anything better than second-run pictures, he figured he couldn't fill more than 400 seats, and he couldn't afford to build a larger theatre anyway. He also figured that the best location would be just outside the business district, where customers could find room to park. A zoning law was before the city council at the time, but before it passed Allen bought the corner at Kellogg and Grove and started to build. There was a howl of anguish from homeowners in the quiet neighborhood. However, in spite of protest meetings and petitions the theatre was built and equipped. It opened in August, 1941, and even the old residents, who still complain that the value of

their property has deteriorated and that the noise of cars keeps them awake until after eleven at night, are regular patrons of the Grove.

The cost of building the theatre would normally have been $25,000, but Allen cut some corners by doing some of the designing and part of the actual work himself. He bought about $15,000 worth of equipment – projectors, soundheads, screen, seats, etc. – on the installment plan. He now owns the theatre and equipment clear, and he thinks its present value is practically double the original cost. He is putting in an air-conditioning system this summer, and he wishes there were some way of enlarging the seating capacity without destroying the visual and acoustical balance of the theatre. If he is able to get all first-run pictures he will be able to fill more seats. And if he had more seats he thinks that distributors might be inclined to give him more first-run pictures.

What's the Feature?

Movie-goers in Galesburg, like movie-goers in every U.S. city and town, don't see why the local theatre doesn't always play good pictures. Their definitions of "good" vary, of course, with their ages and tastes. Galesburg favorites, Allen says, are action pictures, "true romances" like *If Winter Comes*, super westerns like *Ramrod* and *Albuquerque*, and top comedies. Stars make a difference, of course, and Technicolor draws people. To Allen a "good" picture is, naturally, a picture that does well at the box office, although he refuses to play films like *The Outlaw* and *Duel in the Sun* (which, he says, are popular but too sexy and sensational) because he wants to keep the Grove a family theatre. At the request of members of the college faculty and students he played both *Henry V* and *The Great Mr. Handel* last year (he did well with *Henry*, not so well with *Handel*), but he is not bent on bringing culture to Galesburg. Arty pictures, documentaries, and foreign films may get rave reviews in class magazines and city papers, Allen says, but that doesn't mean that people will like them. "You can't convert the public," he says. "They don't want realism – they want entertainment and escape."

Allen had to learn the local tastes by experience. He reads the *Showmen's Trade Review* and *Box Office* carefully, but does not subscribe to the more influential *Variety* or *Motion Picture Herald*, and he pays no attention to the movie magazines that crowd the Galesburg newsstands. He says he can often tell that a picture won't click just by the title, but it's harder to tell what will click. The time of year makes a difference in the attendance ("October's bad for some reason, and just before Christmas"), and the weather ("a bad storm will keep them away or a very hot night"); daylight-saving time hurts business and so does a high-school basketball game. Along in May this year attendance dropped in all Galesburg theatres and even the merchants complained of falling sales. Maybe the beginning of a recession, some said, or spring fever. Allen has owned a theatre long enough to expect the unpredictable.

Running through the list of pictures he played last year, Allen could check on some of his successes and failures: "*Anna and the King of Siam*, although a second-run, did an outstanding business. I should have played it Sunday-Monday-Tuesday instead of Wednesday-Thursday. *The Kid from Brooklyn* did only fair but *Three Little Girls in Blue* was very good all three days. *The Macomber Affair* was first-run and on the opening Friday the gross was bigger than any Sunday second-run. *Gallant Bess*, a war-horse story, did even better. *Rage in Heaven* was a reissue but it did better than most seconds. *Boom Town* did fine and *Ramrod* was one of the biggest we ever had. *The Private Affairs of Bel Ami* was a stinker, a cluck, but because it was first-run it opened well. *Copacabana* opened slim, maybe due to warm weather. *Carnegie Hall* was strictly a class picture and business was below normal. *My Darling Clementine* opened well Sunday and dropped clear through the floor Monday. I played *Wake Up and Dream* on Thanksgiving

Day and lost money, and *Boomerang* fizzled all the way through. *Temptation* smelled to high heaven and the grosses proved it. *13 Rue Madeleine* played to only ninety-eight people on Monday night. *The Best Years of Our Lives* (second-run) ran at advanced prices and we had over 300 adults the first night. *Cloak and Dagger* did fairly good but I paid too much for it. *The Big Sleep* was no good. *The Roosevelt Story* was below average for first-run and I pulled it after four days. *Monsieur Verdoux* was one of my worst flops. It opened punk on Thursday, was way down Monday, very low Tuesday, ditto Wednesday. People just don't like Chaplin any more. I paid a lot for *The Late George Apley* and did all right with it. *Miracle on 34th Street* did above average right down the line. *Humoresque* fizzled and I'd paid top money. *Pursued* had a good Sunday and I grossed $264, but it fell to about $45 on Monday and Tuesday. The gross on a first-run is usually just about twice what it is on a second."

The procuring of second-run films is not too difficult for Allen. Salesmen from the distributing exchanges in Chicago come to call on him automatically with a fairly wide choice of product. Prices are more or less stable and there is no competitive bidding or guarantee against percentage-of-gross as there is on first-run. The rental, or licensing, price of a second is usually from $25 to $100 and Allen's average gross on a week's run is between $600 and $700. One difficulty of second-run bookings lies in competition from the circuit-owned Colonial, and from the Earl Theatre in Knoxville, five miles from Galesburg, which has a shorter clearance rule because it is in a different town. Another difficulty is the pressure from salesmen to take groups of pictures. Compulsory block booking, i.e., offering a feature on condition that the exhibitor takes another picture or block of pictures, poor along with good, has been outlawed by the courts. Salesmen, however, still come around with arguments for group booking that can be extremely persuasive. But the major difficulty is the sixty-day clearance. Allen has never taken his clearance troubles to arbitration in Chicago because he thinks it would take too long and cost too much, but he has often complained to distributors. If he could run a good picture a couple of weeks after its first appearance, particularly if it had been shown for only two or three days, he is sure it would do better than it does two months later when people have forgotten about it. "Sixty days," says Allen, "is not much better than one hundred and sixty."

Even in group booking the price of each film is the result of bargaining between salesman and exhibitor, based on the original cost of production, the age of the film, its first-run popularity, the stars, the trade-journal reviews, etc. Once the rental price is agreed upon, the dates are set and the films booked with the exchange. The films are delivered by truck from Chicago on the morning of opening day and Allen pays for them when they are picked up after the run. Ordinary pictures, "programmers," are usually run two or three days, perhaps as half a double feature, along with a newsreel, a short, trailers (prevues), and the ads of local merchants. Allen has never gone in for "bank nites," give-away dishes, bingo, or any of the other tricks to lure customers. "I'm only in the theatre business."

The rental of first-runs is both difficult and crucial for Allen. He is on a regular-customer basis with United Artists, and some of the other distributors have from time to time allowed him to make competitive bids or voluntary offers on certain pictures. Unlike many exhibitors who think it runs prices up too high, Allen prefers competitive bidding and believes he could make a good showing against the Orpheum and the West, but he has no such arrangement with the distributors, no assurance of a continuous supply. Paramount, of course, is out of the question – all product goes to the affiliated Great States houses. As for the other distributors, Allen has had invariably discouraging experiences that fill him with dark suspicions.

A Day on Film Row

Once or twice a month Allen goes up to Chicago to try to get commitments on first-runs. On a typical trip he left Galesburg on the 8:00 a.m. Burlington train, got to Chicago at ten-forty-five, and was in the South Wabash Avenue motion-picture district by eleven. He telephoned R.K.O. to make an appointment. The manager said it would just waste his time to come in since his letter was on the desk and would receive careful attention. He had a notation of Allen's offers for *I Remember Mama* and *The Miracle of the Bells*. The pictures weren't open for bids yet, but as soon as they were he'd let Allen know whether he could get them. Thanks for calling. Allen decided not to telephone again but to go directly to the next office. His first call was on the branch manager of Twentieth Century-Fox. The manager, in his paneled office, was delighted to see Allen and glad to talk over the situation frankly. Of course, most of their new pictures were already allocated to Great States, but... Allen would probably do best with regular competitive bidding. Why didn't he sit down and write a letter when he got back to Galesburg so they'd have it all down in black and white? In the meantime he'd talk it over with Great States and see what they could do. If he couldn't get Allen on regular bidding, he'd at least arrange to get him a few pictures. It was good to see him, and don't forget to write that letter. (Allen had called and written many times before and never got a definite answer.)

At M.G.M.'s offices the manager came out to the lobby where the bookers sit in glass-fronted booths and stood talking to Allen. He said he thought Allen would do better not to go in for competitive bidding because, with his 390 seats, he couldn't afford to outbid the Orpheum's 1,105. Allen said he thought he could if he ran a week against the Orpheum's two or three days. With *If Winter Comes*, for example, he'd grossed $1,900 and M.G.M.'s 35 per cent had been $665. That wasn't bad, was it? Anyway he'd like the chance to bid.

The manager suggested that he write. "Get it down in black and white." And he'd take it up with New York. He'd like to help him.[1]

Slightly discouraged but not surprised, Allen had a quick lunch at a corner restaurant and went around to some of the equipment houses on Film Row, to the National Theatre Supply Co. to ask when they could deliver the air conditioner, to Manley's to tell them they'd sent the wrong part for the corn popper, to another supply house to look at a drink-dispensing machine. The machine was brand new and "its novelty appeal is terrific – you can make 9 cents profit on every 10-cent drink." To Allen the price would be $500 – he would make it back before the summer was over. Allen said he'd think about it.

Allen dropped in at National Screen Service to pick out the mats he'd need for advertising his next pictures in the local paper. *Frieda, Captain Boycott, Are You With It?* were coming up and he picked out four or five mats for each.

His next call was on another producer-distributor and after a short wait he got in to see the assistant manager. Some months earlier Allen had had a letter from the company offering him a chance to bid on several pictures. He wanted to know why they hadn't sent him another list. The assistant manager said it had never been their permanent policy to offer him regular bidding, but he'd work on it. "I'm all for the little fella myself and I'll see what I can do." In the meantime why didn't Allen keep track of their pictures and send in voluntary offers? Of course, he couldn't promise – Great States was an old customer – but he'd take it up with the district manager. Since the Supreme Court had said that competitive bidding was no solution to the problem of allocation, the assistant manager said, they didn't know where they were at. Everybody knew that a crooked distributor could rig the bidding. All he had to do, for instance, was tell an exhibitor over the telephone what his competitor had bid and get him to go higher. Or the distributor allied with a circuit could take the low bid in a situation where there was independent competition and make up for it in closed situations where all the houses were circuit-owned. He wouldn't say they did, of course, but they could.

Allen wasn't impressed by the suggestion of rigged bidding; it sounded more to him like the old alibi. He'd gladly take his chances on competitive bidding, he said; what made him sore was that he didn't even have a chance to bid most of the time and when he did it was only on B pictures or "nervous A's" (pretentious but unsuccessful pictures). Why, right now he had bookings only for the next two months, and he didn't know what he'd do after that. All he wanted to find out was where he stood so he'd know whether he could be sure of first-runs or have to fall back on seconds and reissues. The assistant manager said he knew just how Allen felt, he'd been an exhibitor himself, and he'd work on it and let him know – by next week sure. Well, Allen said, he hoped he would. He was beginning to get fed up with the runaround and he was even thinking of bringing suit if he couldn't get action. The assistant manager said it might be a good idea if he did bring suit – if he had a good case. If he won, he'd be all set. But in the meantime, make us some offers. Just study the list and write a letter.

Allen's last call was at United Artists, his one steady source of supply. He wanted to check on his bookings and go over his schedule of dates, but the managers were out of the office. When he got through there was just time to make the six-thirty back to Galesburg. It had been a long day. He had a headache. And he didn't know whether he was any better off than when he started out in the morning. He knows, however, that he is better off than a lot of other independents. Many of them are lucky if they break even on pictures and pick up a living from their popcorn stands. By those standards Allen is doing fine. But his enthusiasm for the movie business is somewhat dimmed by the constant bargaining and maneuvering for the right to do business on an equal footing with his competitors. "I still like it," he says, "but it gets me kind of nervous."

Holiday in Technicolor with Mickey Rooney and *The Search* (made in Germany). He was happy to get *Summer Holiday*, not so happy with *The Search*.

Note

1 Two days later an M. G. M. salesman came down to see Allen and offered him *Summer*

34

Give the Movie Exhibitor a Chance! (1935)

P.S. Harrison

Sentiment in favor of the Pettingill bill (H. R. 6472) which would outlaw the block-booking and blind-selling of motion pictures, is spreading so rapidly that the Hays association, to offset it, has put out an anonymous pamphlet entitled, "What Do You Know About Block-Booking?" This is supposed to give the producers' side of the block-booking question. What it really does is to resort to the use of irrelevant and misleading statistics to try to confuse those who are honestly interested in the cause of better movies, while at the same time it makes a vicious and unwarranted attack on the local moving picture exhibitor.

The author of this new pamphlet begins by defining block-booking as "the wholesale renting of pictures by which the exhibitor contracts to take two or more or all of the pictures offered by a certain distributor, thus securing them more cheaply than if they were rented singly." The statement is erroneous. There is no such buying as "two or more"; it is *all or none*, except in a few instances which it would take too long to set forth in the present article.

Heads I Win; Tails You Lose

For example, the Fox contract for "the year commencing August 13, 1933 and ending July 31, 1934" offers to license for exhibition *a maximum of fifty-two and a minimum of forty* pictures, the only exception being (copying from the contract) "such photoplays as distributor is required by contract to obtain the consent or approval of the producer or other party to the terms and conditions of licensing the exhibition thereof." But what this supposed exception really means, in plain language, is that when a producer thinks that he has a picture which is worth a lot more money than usual, he can take that picture out of the regular "block," for which the exhibitor has already contracted, and force the exhibitor to sign another contract for that single picture at the increased "ante." Yet if the exhibitor is not willing to pay this increased price, he is still bound by the block-booking contracts for all the other pictures of that producer, unless he has been wise enough, by inserting a special provision in all his contracts for purchases from that distributor, to make his acceptance of the pictures on all the other contracts conditional, depending upon the approval of the contract for that particular picture. In other words, this "exception" to block-booking turns out to be a "heads I win, tails you lose" proposition for the exhibitor. It operates only when it is of advantage to the producer and distributor; it affords no protection, but loss, for the local exhibitor.

So much for the fundamental fallacy beneath this whole defense of the block-booking system. The rest of the pamphlet is devoted to answering the questions: "Is block-booking compulsory?" and "Does the exhibitor choose only the socially desirable pictures?" The answer to both, according to the Hays office, is "No." Well, let's see. [...]

Block-Booking – The Reality

In the 1934–35 picture season, for example, the Fox Film corporation sold "The Cat's Paw," with Harold Lloyd, on an individual contract. If the author of this bulletin meant to convey the impression that, because this contract contained only one picture, there is no block-booking, he certainly was not conveying the correct information, for the exhibitor had to buy all the other pictures (minimum 40, maximum 52) in order to obtain "The Cat's Paw." In the season the author of this bulletin mentions (1933–34) RKO sold seven pictures – "Ann Vickers," "Wild Cargo," "Flying Down to Rio," "Of Human Bondage," "The Son of Kong," "Little Women," and "Green Mansions" – on an individual contract. No doubt the author of this pamphlet included this contract for the seven pictures in his statistics to prove that there is no block-booking. But there is not a single exhibitor in the United States who bought these pictures unless he bought also all the other feature pictures RKO sold that season – more than forty!

I could bring other such examples to prove that the theater owner is unable to choose the pictures he feels the people of his community want, or which he wants. No compulsory block-booking? Why, not only is there block-booking; it exists with a vengeance, for in many instances the exhibitor must buy all the short subjects – one-reel, two-reels, newsweeklies, and even trailers – before he can obtain the features. [...]

In answering his second question as to whether local exhibitors show good pictures the author of the pamphlet endeavors to prove to the American public that the exhibitor is interested not in the pictures the "socially minded" consider good, but in pictures that will bring him profits, regardless of their moral fitness. In no other industry that I ever heard of has it occurred that the leaders have attempted to discredit their customers in order to prove that their selling policy is correct. It has remained for the motion picture industry to do that. But for years past, the Hays association has been endeavoring to prove to the American people that filthy and demoralizing pictures are not due to the policy of the producers, but to the exhibitors, who demand them. [...]

If indecent and generally demoralizing pictures flourished in the past, until finally the American people rose in angry revolt against the industry, that was due to nothing but the block-booking and blind-selling method of selling pictures. The exhibitor has had no voice, and he still has none, in the production of pictures. He must accept whatever pictures are delivered to him regardless of how demoralizing some of them may be. Where is, then, the injustice when the exhibitors demand that they be given a voice in the selection of entertainment for their people?

But the producers do not want to grant the exhibitors such a right, for they know that it will mean the end of their monopoly, the end of the despotic power they have been exercising over the industry. The question now is whether the American people will continue vesting in a small clique of picture producers the right to control a medium which has so much influence upon the lives and minds of the people, particularly upon the minds of our young men and women. I appeal to the readers of The Christian Century for justice for the local moving picture exhibitor. To that end, I urge them to write to their congressmen asking them to vote for the Pettingill bill, thus making it possible for the citizens of a community to work together with the exhibitors in the presentation of the proper kind of entertainment. The problem of proper pictures can never be solved permanently unless local self-government is established in their exhibition.

Illustration from *National Parent–Teacher* (March 1938)

35

Economic Control of the Motion Picture Industry (1944)

Mae D. Huettig

The Principal Trade Practices: General Description

The market for films is affected by two groups of trade practices: those governing the sale of films by distributors to exhibitors and those governing exhibition. In the first group are the highly controverted practices of block-booking, blind buying, and designated play dates. In the second group are the inter-related restrictions known as protection, or clearance, zoning, and over-buying. (The term "protection" was given up by the industry when gang racketeering began using it in conjunction with shakedown practice.) There are other trade practices of lesser importance, such as the forcing of shorts and newsreels, etc. These are essentially part of block-booking, however, and are included in the discussion of that practice.

At first glance this esoteric terminology may seem wholly irrelevant to the movie-goer. Yet these are the practices that shape movie-going habits, that explain what becomes of pictures missed during the first-run, why it takes so long before pictures reappear at neighborhood houses, why they may suddenly turn up simultaneously at six or eight different the-atres on identical double bills, and why the double bill must be suffered at all.

Before describing the trade practices in detail it should be noted that they have a compulsory quality not usual in other industries. They operate with an impressive uniformity which grows out of the interdependent relationship of the major companies. Any attempt on the part of one major to deviate from the accepted method of doing business involves the danger of reprisal in the form of joint action by the other majors. [...]

Block-Booking

Block-booking may be defined as the simultaneous leasing of groups of films at an aggregate price fixed upon the condition that all the films in the given block be taken. In practice this meant that the unaffiliated exhibitor had to take the entire block as offered or none at all, since the price of the pictures on an individual basis was usually prohibitive. Although this practice is temporarily modified by the consent decree, it merits some detailed attention because of its importance in the past and the uncertainty of its future.

Almost everybody in the industry has taken a position for or against the practice. Outside the industry, too, consumers, legislators, women's clubs and other organized groups long carried on a running battle against block-booking on the doubtful theory that it was responsible for the unsatisfactory films to which they were exposed. Neighborhood exhibitors defended themselves against complaining customers with the reply that they were under compulsion to take whatever films were offered by the distributor in order to receive any product whatsoever at a reasonable price.

The Federal Trade Commission investigated block-booking from 1921 to 1932. It collected some 17,000 pages of testimony and 15,000 pages of exhibits, concluding in 1927 that it was an unfair trade practice. A cease-and-desist order was issued and completely disregarded by the majors. The United States Circuit Court of Appeals reversed the decision in 1932 whereupon the Federal Trade Commission announced, probably somewhat wearily, that the entire matter would be dropped. Since then hardly a year has passed without an investigation into the matter by a House or Senate committee or the anti-trust division of the Department of Justice. A number of anti-block-booking bills were unsuccessfully introduced into Congress and state legislatures.

In 1938 an anti-trust suit was instituted against the eight majors. An avowed aim of the Department of Justice was the divorcement of exhibition from production and distribution. However, the case was never really tried. After the opening week of the trial in June of 1940, negotiations were begun which culminated in the consent decree. This incidentally served to avoid recording the mass of evidence collected by the Department of Justice on the trade practices of the industry. Among the changes for which the decree provided was a modification in block-booking. [...]

If block-booking were, as its proponents argue, simple wholesaling, why has it aroused so much opposition? In other lines of business, the principle of discounts for quantity purchases is generally accepted as equitable and constructive. The answer is to be found in knowing what block-booking means to the different groups in the industry and how it works. This, in turn, requires an understanding of a closely related trade practice, "blind buying."

Blind buying refers to the leasing of films sight unseen, usually in advance of their actual production. It was an integral part of block-booking because distributors do not generally carry a stock of finished films to be offered to the exhibitors. In order to sell in blocks, it was necessary to sell films as yet unmade.

When a film salesman called on an exhibitor, he had no samples with him. What he had was a prospectus, a schedule of planned productions based on what his company had or hoped to have in the way of prepared stories and talent. Some of the productions were described in considerable detail, particularly those based on popular stage plays or novels. Many, however, were merely assigned a production number by way of identification. [...]

For example, an independent exhibitor gave the following description of the supply of product offered him:

Columbia promises to make a minimum of 32 and a maximum of 40. The contract gives no information whatsoever, but the work sheet states that the program will be selected from properties of the company and from additional outstanding stories acquired during the year. First National-Warner Bros. Pictures will make 27. Only numbers will appear on the contracts and work sheets. If you buy from First National you get number 951 to 977. If you buy from Warner Bros. you get number 901 to 927. And the distributor also reserves the right to alter the prices and terms of four pictures, by merely giving a notice to the exhibitor before the available date of each picture. A blank space is provided for inserting the percentage and new terms to be charged. The Fox pictures will make a maximum of 50 and a minimum of 40. There are no work sheets. The names of features will be given in the trade papers during the year. You do not have that information at the time the contract is signed. Metro-Goldwyn-Mayer will make 50 pictures. It gives the names of the stars, plays, books, and stories. Paramount will make 65 pictures; work sheet contains the names of only 14 novels, plays and magazine stories. R.K.O. will make 45 pictures, identified only by numbers, 601 to 646. No description of the subjects. Universal will make 36 pictures, founded on published works. United Artists, because of the fact that it sells pictures individually, prepares at the beginning of every season a complete announcement of its products. It lists the proposed pictures by name, author, book, its stars, and cast, and gives a complete synopsis of each picture.[1]

From the distributor's point of view, block-booking and blind buying had a number of advantages. In the first place, this method of selling provided a minimum assured market for all grades of product. It was like insurance which paid in advance of any risk incurred. In the second place, the uniform practice of block-booking by the independent exhibitors effectively closed that section of the market to independent producers by the simple expedient of absorbing all or nearly all of the available playing time. One of the unlaid ghosts haunting the major companies is the fear that independent exhibitors may combine with independent producers to undermine or circumvent control.

Block-booking operates to close the market to independent product because the amount of playing time an exhibitor has is limited, even with a policy of double features, morning performances, midnight shows and frequent changes of program. Consequently, if the exhibitor buys blocks of films from three or four major companies in order to get the relatively few essential films, he frequently finds himself oversupplied in relation to the amount of playing time available. Since the pictures must generally be paid for whether used or not, he has little use for additional product.[2]

A third advantage of block-booking to the distributors is the undoubted economy of marketing. Selling each picture individually, after its completion, requires repeated calls on exhibitors and much more intensive sales effort. [...]

The principal opponents of block-booking are the small independent exhibitors. Their arguments are directed against two phases of the practice: first, its compulsory nature, and second, its use as a discriminatory weapon. Small exhibitors maintain firmly (and the evidence is strongly in their favor) that neither affiliated theatres nor the large independent theatre chains are compelled to buy in blocks. Both of these groups may buy in this manner if they consider it advantageous to do so, but the arrangement is voluntary. They are not forced into it under threat of being deprived of the better pictures. [...]

Designated Play Dates

Closely allied to blind buying and block-booking is the practice known as "designated play dates." It resembles the other trade practices in that it is uniformly applied by the major distributors against the less powerful exhibitors.

The term "designated play dates" refers to the practice of designation by the distributor of the days of the week on which certain pictures must be shown. The point of this arrangement is that movie attendance on Saturdays, Sundays, and holidays is generally from two to three times as heavy as during weekdays. Consequently, it is to the advantage of the distributor to select the pictures which he expects to be most successful, require payment from the exhibitor on the basis of a percentage-of-the-gross, and insist that those pictures be played during the days of peak attendance.

The exhibitor's argument against this practice is as follows: first, it definitely interferes with his right to manage his theatres in accordance with a policy he may consider more suitable. For example, theatre operators might reason that since attendance is higher on weekends than during the week, it might be wise to exhibit less important pictures in an attempt to attract additional attendance during the week. Second, almost all the pre-ferred playing time is taken up by the major companies. Consequently, the productions of smaller companies are exhibited on the days of lowest attendance.

As is true with both block-booking and blind buying, the designation of play dates by the distributors is limited to their dealings with the independent exhibitors. Neither the affiliated theatres nor the large independent chains are compelled to agree to such terms.

Protection

In exhibition the most important trade practices are these which have come to be grouped together under the heading "protection." The term is an apt one. It means just what it says in that the objective is protection of one group of theatres against competition from others.

Protection refers to the division of the theatre market with respect to clearance and zoning. First, theatres are classified with respect to their run, or the order in which they have access to films. Second, each theatre is given a certain amount of clearance over competing theatres. This states the length of time required to elapse before other theatres may show films exhibited in the earlier runs. Both runs and clearance operate in a given zone, the area defined as containing competing theatres.

Although the principle of protection may be found in the restrictive practices of other industries, its uniqueness in the motion picture industry rests on the fact that protection exists and functions by mutual agreement of all the majors. The very essence of protection is uniformity of operation, as will become apparent in the description of its operations.

Protection is vital to the exhibitor because the earning power of a given theatre depends almost entirely upon its status with respect to run and clearance. Other theatres in a given neighborhood may be newer, more attractive, or more comfortable than the preferred

runs, i.e., the first, second, and third runs. However, there is generally no effective competition between the preferred runs and the later runs, no matter how attractive the theatre may be. The advantage of prior run outweighs almost all other considerations.

The distributors defend the system of runs, clearance, and zoning with the classic argument of the "right to sell," i.e., the right to choose their customers on any basis that suits them. The fact that most of the major companies apparently make the same choice is fortuitous circumstance.

The importance of run is derived from the nature of the demand for films. For numerous reasons, movie-goers as a class attach great importance to the newness of a film. As we have seen, this has been true from the very beginning of the industry. Exhibitors have always been willing to pay premiums for early showings. In the process of bargaining, theatre men first demanded and received from the distributors protection against competing theatres in exchange for the higher film rentals paid. Originally this protection was limited to withholding the film from rival houses until after it had completed its showing in the first-run theatre. Later, however, an intervening period between first and second run was demanded. This was clearance. A necessary accompaniment of exclusive runs and clearance was zoning, or the definition of the area within which the restrictions were operative. [...]

Classification of theatres with respect to run, clearance, and zoning is generally uniform and definitive as far as all the major distributors are concerned. This means that the status of each theatre with respect to run and clearance is the same regardless of the distributor with whom he deals. There is no legal basis to this uniformity and there are occasional deviations from the established pattern; but, on the whole, the system of protection is regularly enforced. [...]

The foregoing examination of trade practices reveals that they operate not without some hardship on the independent exhibitor. The way one exhibitor feels about the situation can be gathered from the following statement:

> Perhaps the plight of the independent exhibitor can best be explained by using some more familiar business as an illustration. Let us assume, therefore, that A, a dealer in men's clothing, should apply to the several clothing manufacturers for a stock of specified models of suits and overcoats and receive the following reply, not from one but from all: You may have our line of suits and overcoats but we have no samples or descriptive matter and you must agree to take all of the garments of whatever design we see fit to make during an entire year. Not only must you take all of our suits and overcoats but all of our shirts, neckties, and collars as well. Also, you must buy all of your advertising accessories from us. We have or may have a store of our own in the same town with you and you will be permitted to offer our styles to the public within 30 to 365 days after they have been introduced in our store. Of course you will have to guarantee us a minimum price, as we are willing to share your profits but not your losses. We reserve the right to designate the particular day or days of the week on which you may sell certain models, and we will regulate the prices charged so as to protect our store against your competition. Some models may be reserved for our store exclusively. If we decide to expand in your territory, or someone comes in that we like better than we like you, we will take the line away from you altogether.

> This may sound fantastic but it illustrates the conditions under which independent exhibitors are forced to do business at the present time.[3]

Notes

1 Hearings before the Committee on Interstate Commerce, House of Representatives, 76th Congress, Third Session, *Motion Picture Films*, p. 163. Statement of Jeannete Willensky, secretary, Independent Motion Picture Theatre Owners of Eastern Pennsylvania.

2 The contract form usually contains the following provision with respect to pictures contracted for but not exhibited:

> If the Exhibitor shall fail or refuse to exhibit during the term hereof, any of said motion pictures, the Exhibitor shall pay as liquidated damages a sum equal to the fixed sum or sums herein specified as the rental for each such motion picture.

3 Hearings before the Committee on Interstate Commerce, House of Representatives, 76th Congress, Third Session, *Motion Picture Films*, p. 240.

36

New Theaters for the Cinema (1932)

Ben Schlanger

Screen Size, Proportion and Third Dimension

The screen is the motion picture stage. It is the nucleus of the whole theater design, the point around which the whole theater should be built. The dramatic effect of the screen performance on the spectator has yet to be thoroughly analyzed. The screen as it is presented in today's cinema is still an obviously framed picture instead of a space into which we peer, seeing the projected other world of the cinema. To achieve this much-desired effect, the scientific development of the third dimension effect on the screen is a primary necessity. This, however, implies many technical difficulties, and until they are overcome, other means at present more available must be used to increase the screen illusion of space reality. Upon these means, namely, the proper size, proportion and framing of the screen, depends the effective delivery of the performance to the spectator.

A maximum size screen is desirable. It should, if possible, dominate the whole forward portion of the auditorium. The spectator can thereby be made to feel that he is actually encompassed in the action which he views. The maximum size screen also enlarges the scale of images and backgrounds in relation to the spectator, thereby heightening the dramatic effect.

The size of the screen is dependent upon (1) the width and depth of the auditorium; (2) distance sacrificed between the screen and the first row of seats; (3) distance from the screen to the row of seats furthest from the screen: (4) the location of the balcony facia or facias fixes the maximum height of the screen (the usual large overhanging balcony limits the height of the screen): (5) the shape of the screen; (6) the width of the motion picture film (at present 35 mm.; a 50 mm. width is now being considered); (7) projection lens size; (8) length of throw from projector to screen.

The present type of theater structure cannot accommodate a large screen. There may be sufficient space in the proscenium opening, but balcony obstructions and unsuitable floor slopes afford vision characteristics which are adaptable only to the smaller screen now in use. A maximum size screen is very readily usable in a theater with reverse slope floor.

The proportion of the screen is an important factor in cinema design inasmuch as it controls the size of the screen. For example, the height of the screen should determine the slope and position of the floors and balconies, the shape of the auditorium, the location of the projection booth, the seating arrangement, and the chair back pitches. [...]

Excerpted from Ben Schlanger, "New Theaters for the Cinema." *Architectural Forum* 57 (September 1932), 257–60.

Screen Framing

Motion picture screens are commonly framed with a black velvet masking placed directly in front of the white sheet to insure a steady, sharp edge for the picture. The fuzzy edge of a magnified light source and the slight shifting of the picture due to vibration in the projection machine is invisible to the spectator because the black masking absorbs a few inches of spilled light all around the screen. However, because of contrast, the eye is always somewhat conscious of the frame, instead of the picture image only. The result is distraction and eye fatigue. In addition, the obvious frame of this type of masking destroys the illusion of space realism so much desired.

The illuminated screen and its surrounding surfaces should appear as an even tone of light stretching from side wall to side wall. The screen image in effect should blend into the side walls and ceiling, for the obvious architectural proscenium frame is useless and detrimental to the screen performance.

37

Motion Picture Theaters (1937)

Ben Schlanger

There are two types of motion picture audiences each of which should be considered separately in determining the need for new theater construction. One type is the audience evolving from a given neighborhood or township, where the patronage is the same most of the time. The other type is located in popular busy shopping or theatrical districts, where the patronage is more transient. The number of transient patronage type theaters in a given location is subject largely to the importance of the locations, and the number of entertainment-seeking transients found therein. However, in the case of the community patronage type, feasibility of the erection of an additional motion picture theater is determined by taking several factors into consideration.

Since the community patronage theater is the most prevalent and most popular, it should be given most study. Here, too, a distinction should be made between the city neighborhood and the small town theater, a distinction, however, which is lessened to a certain extent by the automobile. For example, smaller and more frequent theaters would be necessary in small towns, were it not for the popular use of the automobile.

Basically, the need for the erection of new community patronage theaters can be determined by consulting these factors:

a. Density of population for a given area. 100 seats for 1,000 persons (based on attendance for 1936) is recommended.

b. Availability of suitable film product.

c. Frequency of attendance (increases with quality and quantity of available film product and reduction in admission prices).

d. Obsolescence of existing theaters.

e. Proximity of other theaters.

In the matter of type and number of motion picture theaters desirable, the patron and the exhibitor naturally have entirely different points of view. If the theater-owning exhibitor had his choice, there would not be much new theater construction. He would much prefer exhibiting films in a centrally located, large seating capacity unit, regardless of how inconvenient it would be for the patron to reach the theater or how obsolete and unsuited the theater might be for the effective enjoyment of the film.

On the other hand, the theater patron would rather have at least two theaters of more intimate capacity (of about 600 seats instead of one 1,200-seat house) convenient to him and offering more choice in film selection. Owing to the increasing number of desirable new films and the reservoir of good films made in the past, suitable for revival, a new attitude in motion picture exhibition has come about, popularizing the community intimate motion picture

Excerpted from Ben Schlanger, "Motion Picture Theaters." *Architectural Record* 81 (February 1937), 17–20. Reprinted with permission from *Architectural Record*.

theater, located as closely as possible to the patron.

Choosing a Site

In choosing a location for the neighborhood or small town motion picture theater, first consideration should be given to the convenience of the patron in reaching the theater. Most desirable would be a location in the center of the population to be served.

While it is of some advantage to be located on the chief business street of the neighborhood or town, it is not most essential. Usually, a location immediately adjoining the more valuable property should be chosen. Where property is excessive in cost, it is quite common to find the more valuable part of the property devoted to shops, locating the theater by means of an entrance from the important street, having the bulk of the building in the less costly area to the rear. As the importance of the motion picture itself increases, however, the use of costly land becomes less necessary. The tendency is towards a building which may have in it, at the most, a few small shops to help reduce the rental of the theater portion. Wherever possible, the use of minimum-cost land, eliminating the need for shops, is desirable, thus permitting full architectural advertising value for the facade of the theater building.

In selecting a site, a corner plot or an inside plot having a public street or alley immediately to the rear of the plot is most desirable for the arrangement of emergency exits, controlled by local ordinances. In the small town theater where automobile patronage prevails, parking space adjoining the plot is quite essential. A secondary entrance to be used by persons alighting from automobiles should be considered. [...]

Financing

The amount of money that may be justifiably invested in a motion picture theater structure and equipment is controlled by the necessary rapidity of amortization of original costs. Most investors feel that the highly specialized nature of the motion picture theater structure calls for a short amortization period. There is only one justification for this attitude and that is the possibility of a drastic shift in population from a given community. Large-scale housing study and developments, and city and town planning tendencies obviate the necessity for considering this aspect. However it is logical to assume comparatively short amortization periods varying from three to ten years for the equipment of the theater. Ten years is a fair amortization period for the construction cost. But for three important considerations which cannot be overlooked, home television may be offered as an argument to reduce this amortization period. Firstly, the technical difficulties encountered in producing a suitably large enough home television screen have not as yet been overcome. Secondly, people still prefer to congregate in seeking entertainment, as may be evidenced by the continued popular demand of the motion picture in spite of the home radio. Thirdly, it is also quite possible that the motion picture industry would play a large part in the control of home television, distributing full length entertainment to public assembly buildings and shorter programs to the home.

Economical land and construction costs, and simplification of interior architectural treatment should be stressed to reduce the initial investment. This does not preclude carefully studied planning which will afford proper functioning of the structure and ample comfort conditions for the patron.

Desirable Seating Capacities

The small town or city neighborhood motion picture theater minimum seating capacity is, on one hand, correctly determined by the technical problems involved and, on the other hand, by the commercial aspects of motion picture film distribution. From a technical standpoint, considering ideal viewing conditions, no motion picture theater should have more than approximately 1,000 seats; preferably, nearer to 600 seats. Commercially, the chain-exhibitor prefers to control the first run of a given film and drain as much of the community population into one sitting as is possible. Recent construction of the more intimate motion picture theater by independent exhibitors, showing in most instances second and third-run films, has proven by the patronage enjoyed that the quality in film presentation is important, and that the patron prefers the theater having nearer to 600 seats. The intimate motion picture theater is more technically perfect for exhibiting films. This may be fully appreciated when the following data on maximum conditions advisable for viewing motion pictures are analyzed.

Film and Audience Size and Shape

The limiting factors in determining the maximum seating capacity from a standpoint of correct screen portrayal are: (1) physical width of the film, and (2) the proper relationship of the resultant maximum size screen to the audience shape and size.

The width of the film for professional use is 35mm. The absolute maximum size of screen to be projected from this film width is 35 ft. Further magnification of the film will produce (1) the visibility of the grainy structure of the film material, and (2) a tendency to destroy the contrast values in the photography. A 35-ft. screen necessitates a magnification of the film image to about 400 times its size. It is highly preferable to reduce this rate of magnification to achieve good pictorial quality. Where a good screen image is desired, the screen width should not exceed 25 ft.

The proper relationship between the screen size and the audience size and shape is determined by:

1. Avoidance of seating positions from which a distorted view of screen images occurs, distortion being due to the two dimensional characteristic of the screen surface. [...]
2. Fixing minimum distance between screen and first row of seats. The maximum angle for horizontal range of vision, being about 60 degrees, determines this dimension.
3. Fixing maximum distance between the screen and the row of seats furthest from the screen by
   a. Visual acuity, that is, the ability to discern details of photography.
   b. Proper subtended angle formed by the screen to the viewer's eye, insuring undistorted perspective of screen images.

[...] While the close-up shot used in motion picture photography is effective and, to a great extent, helps vision from the remote seats, it must be remembered that for effective motion picture portrayal the photography must consist of a large proportion of what is known as middle and distance shots upon which the details to be discerned are smaller.

Limited viewing distances are essential to maintain a more intimate relationship of the spectator to the screen action. The screen area should, as much as possible, predominate the field of view of the spectators' eyes, thereby eliminating distracting excessive wall and ceiling surfaces and intervening audience area. The viewing distance limits and tolerable viewing angles [...] have been arrived at from such investigations as have been carried on by the Society of Motion Picture Engineers and the author. Determination of preferable seat locations was made both from actual tests of tolerable distortion with a picked audience, recording their reactions, and observing the preferred seat locations as they became occupied in theaters in operation.

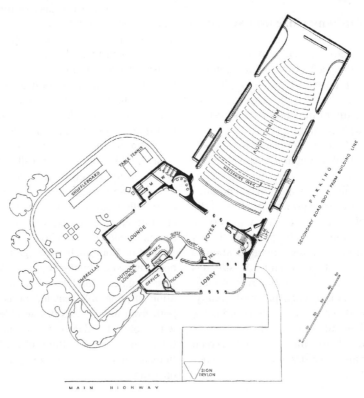

Ben Schlanger, "Design for a Theater for Motion Pictures," *Architectural Record* (June 1944)

38

A New Architecture for the Movie Theater (1948)

Architectural Record

The moving picture theater, now just about entering its second generation, looks to be due for some changes. The new generation will have to improve on the old, or the race may find itself dying out.

For science is right now giving the movie industry its worst scare since the movies began, with television making movie patrons "stay home in droves." The theater will have to, and should be able to, enlist science in its own behalf, and there are indications of important changes in the concept of a theater.

These changes should prove to be directly within the bailiwick of the theater architect. They certainly will not be mere dolling up of the theater; in fact they will probably be strictly in the functional order. And the progressive architect, with his eye on purpose and with science at his elbow, should be just the man for the job.

The basic weapon of the theater is "theater." The race with television will eventually settle down to a matter of real entertainment values, of dramatic impact of offerings, of intensity of illusion created.

Here the theater is still out in front of television. Its task is to remain ahead, to heighten its dramatic quality, to lure the television owner out of his home for better entertainment value.

So far the television set provides sight and sound, but not much "theater." It has caught on and is rapidly gaining new converts, but it is still an amazing new scientific toy. One still sits in a living room, amidst all the distractions of the home, and sees his show on a little screen. It is fine for sports and news events and perhaps style shows, but not for dramatic entertainment. As one man said recently, "I bought a television set almost a year ago, and hadn't been to a movie since, until last night. I guess I had forgotten how good the movies were."

Well, the movies are good, but they will have to be better. And while much of the improvement will have to come from Hollywood, the final battle will be in the local movie house, which must be redesigned for a better dramatic value.

To Free the Movie Art

Suppose, for example, that the movie industry were to accept a progressive suggestion that comes from the theater architect, Ben Schlanger. He points to the restrictive effect of a picture always of the same proportions, the same size, always seen in a dark frame. Why not, while reaching for dramatic impact, break completely away from this

Excerpted from "A New Architecture for the Movie Theater." *Architectural Record* 104 (November 1948), 121–3. Reprinted with permission from *Architectural Record*.

photo-album prison, and make the screen a fluid medium of art?

One step he suggests is to increase its size; it could easily be made 20 or 25 per cent larger. Already, it will be noted, there is a major change for the theater.

The larger screen would not mean simply a larger frame. The frame would be eliminated. In making the picture, the cinematographer would assume freedom within the larger area to use whatever picture size – or picture shape – best suited his subject matter. He might spread his picture to full width for a great mob scene, or for a chorus line. He might vignette a more intimate scene at relatively small size. The canvas broadens or closes in, brightens or darkens with its subject. Or the scene might move across the screen area to heighten the illusion of motion, which now is achieved only by having the background in motion.

To understand the effect on the theater itself, it is necessary to look into the vignetting idea. A year ago Ben Schlanger told the Society of Motion Picture Engineers:

"For the motion picture, where it may be better to present more realism, the vignette may well be a suitable representation of the peripheral portion of our field of vision. In real life there is no opaque masking frame in front of us all the time. The vignette is more like what one experiences visually.

"In still photography the vignette commonly fades to pure white at the extreme edges of the picture. This type of vignette would prove disturbing for the motion picture because of the competition created by stronger light at the edge. The vignette recommended here is one that diminishes the light value toward the edges of the picture. Light and color values seem to dim out in the visual peripheral. Colors do not change in hue, rather they seem to become grayer. The reduced light value proposed for the peripheral vignette is also the means of creating transitional light intensity between the bright picture and the picture environment...."

Schlanger has even considered that the vignetted light might extend beyond the screen itself to the surrounding surfaces in the theater. Obviously, then, we should need something different from the gargoyled proscenium arch of the first-generation movie house.

The lighting of the screen surround is an immediate problem, not waiting for the adoption of Schlanger's idea of vignettes. And so is the architectural phase of the auditorium as a housing for dramatic entertainment.

A florid architectural style only competes with the illusion on the screen; here certainly is a place for modern functional design.

Its functionalism might begin with a better surround for the screen, one which would contribute toward the solution of a really pressing lighting problem. Experts have told the RECORD recently that no movie theater in the country is well lighted.

The science of seeing tells us how violent are lighting conditions in the typical theater. The eye dislikes the brightness contrast of the lighted screen in the darkened frame. Schlanger's vignette idea would soften the contrasts around the screen quite naturally. But that could, and should, be done right now, with present films. Schlanger has used textured ribbed surfaces near the screen to pick up light in an automatic relation to screen light values. Another possibility is a dimly lighted background behind the screen and extending beyond it. Still another [...] is keeping the auditorium better lighted while the film is running. The author makes what is really the first attempt to apply scientific lighting to the movie theater. Besides eye comfort, and therefore better illusion, better lighting would also improve convenience, simple safety, and perhaps propriety in the theater of today. Television set owners quickly learn not to darken the room completely, for the same reasons. Now perhaps television is telling theater owners something they might well have known long ago.

Acoustics is another major area for theater improvement. And most theaters, while having an adequate level of projected sound, leave much to be desired as to quality, particularly as regards that "intimate" quality of sound which makes it seem to come from the screen. Here again the second generation movie theater, seeking to enhance its dramatic quality, might well profit from the science of auditorium acoustics, which has been developed largely since most movie houses were built. [...]

Then, too, science has gone ahead in many other technical matters of design which can make their contribution to better theaters. Sight lines that permit the patron to see the action without being distracted by heads in front, air conditioning to make him unconscious of surrounding temperature conditions or even odors, seating to make him settle back comfortably to be entertained.

In considering the future of the movie theater, some have mentioned its community aspects, in the light of social appeal to lure the family out of the home. They are inclined to cite the social side of the old theaters of Europe, something that is still strong in the opera. Certainly the theater, even the movie theater of the modern age, is associated with "going out." And going out is not to be outmoded by the television set, even though the set in the home is highly regarded as a means of keeping the younger generation off the streets. Probably the younger generation, nevertheless, will be loath to desert the familiar movie entertainment, and perfectly willing to be lured out of the home.

How much of the social side of the theater can be translated into design is not readily discerned. Obviously, however, there are many matters that bear on the appeal to the patron. The cheerful, bright theater marquee has always been a tradition of the theater, is still highly regarded by theater people. It can be vastly improved in design certainly, perhaps also in advertising appeal. The lobby and waiting rooms and washrooms might all be subjected to some scrutiny, now that patrons need to be lured instead of herded into the theater. All of these are clearly related to social aspects of the theater as an institution.

Perhaps also the new science of community planning may offer something to the theater. The movie house is a logical nucleus for an entertainment center that might offer many other varieties of amusement and social activities.

At any rate it is very clear that the theater architect will be giving a newly serious attention to the true function of the theater, and that will lead him into a new consideration of all of the sciences and arts that will add something to the quality of entertainment. The theater owner will be thinking of these things, too; he certainly will get over any idea he may have had that the function of the architect is to design a shell to cover so many seats. He will need the architect as never before.

39

Psychology of the Theater (1948)

Walter A. Cutter

The question before us is, basically, how many theater managers, how many members of the Society of Motion Picture Engineers, how many other persons connected with the industry have a significant conception of what we are calling "the psychology of the theater." What *is* its meaning and significance? What is its rightful place *in* the community life? How can the character of this modern miracle be expressed in a personality which will walk on the same terms with other community enterprises? Is it possible that many persons in the industry, involved as they are in their own concerns, do not realize how really "big" this industry has become?

All of these questions are important! A manager, if he is to be an effective force in his community, must know both these questions and their answers. It is he who must interpret the psychology of the theater to the community. For the theater we think has a "psychology," just as every person who comes to it has a psychology. The theater's personality is a complex one. It is, first and foremost, a business. It is often a show place in itself. It is a center of entertainment. It is an important medium of education. It is a major factor in shaping customs, opinions, and behavior. It is a place of gathering for the community. It is, in all senses, an escape, for through its door pass those who are for a few hours free from care, from problems, from the monotony and the jangling voices of everyday life.

How many millions chained to one locality by circumstances, have passed through the theater door to the broad horizons of the wider world. They have sailed all the seas, have visited the capitals of the world, and have rubbed elbows with distant peoples and strange customs. The creations of artistry, the marvels of science, industrial processes, and travel pass across the theater screen, along with the explicit entertainment. Moreover and most important, the motion picture theater, be it in Times Square or in some remote village street, has become so interwoven with our modern social life that it has become indispensable. It is not too much to say that if tomorrow, through the operation of some almost unimaginable social cataclysm, every theater would be closed, on the next day there would be an almost universal demand for reopening! How true it is then that you men and women who are the stewards of the "colossal" force should have a real understanding of its significance.

The Manager

The individual theater is the outpost of the industry and the manager is the visible

Excerpted from Walter A. Cutter, "Psychology of the Theater." In Helen Stote (ed.), *The Motion Picture Theater: Planning, Upkeep* (New York: Society of Motion Picture Engineers, 1948), 14–21. Reprinted with permission from the Society of Motion Picture and Television Engineers.

representative. For all practical purposes the individual theater and the manager *are* the industry in their community. The manager must and should be one of the best salesmen of the community as well as of his product. He must never give the impression that he is in the community, but not of it. He should have sufficient latitude to enter into such community activities as will confer a mutual benefit – on the theater and on the community. Only a shortsighted management would forbid him from making such contributions of time and money as will lubricate good public relations. The manager is *there*. He knows what he must do, and what he can refuse to do if he is to maintain good community relations. His judgment must be trusted until it is found that his judgment in such matters cannot be trusted. A realistic fact to be kept in mind is that so many people have such a vivid idea of the gigantic size of the motion picture industry that the idea must never get abroad that the theater "takes" from the community without giving something back along with the entertainment.

Resourceful managers have done many different things to advance the legitimate cause of good human relations. They have joined service clubs. Every manager should have a membership in such clubs. They have co-operated in constructive community enterprises. All managers should do so. Some have opened their doors for church services, when for some reason other quarters were not available. Some of the largest Sunday school classes in the country meet in theaters. Managers have provided the facilities, both space and films, for visual education of school children. Public meetings have been held. Other uses have been made. The underlying thought is not that you have to do any or every one of these, but that you should publish a *willingness* to try to meet any legitimate request. It is as true for theater managers as for anyone else, in the words of the poet, that, "What you keep is lost. What you give is forever yours!"

Technical Advances

Technical advances, made very largely through the laudable work of the Society of Motion Picture Engineers, permit the alert manager to exhibit another interesting facet of the personality, the psychology of the theater, namely, the reduction of distraction in the modern show. We are so prone to take inventions and innovations for granted that we may be unmindful of the superb physical aspect of the modern theater. [...]

[...] Technical progress in projection, sound, comfort, and safety has been striking. In theater architecture great advances have been made. While it is still recognized that a certain opulence of decoration is part of the theater's appeal, we have tended to move away from the excessively baroque and what the author terms the "ro-cuckoo" styles of architectural embellishments. The Idle Hour of yesterday would hardly recognize its modern descendant.

Engineering Advances

But let us look at this idea which we have called the reduction of distraction in the theater made possible by striking engineering advances. And it would seem that the patrons should know what underlies the successful showing of a picture: Our measure of how successful is this reduction of distraction, is how completely the individual patron is enabled to concentrate on the picture without distraction by uncontrolled noise, faulty lighting, discomforts of any kind, or fears as to his safety if an emergency should come about. Continuous study is given to these matters by functioning committees of the SMPE, and theater managers have access to a wealth of technical information.

Let us look at a few of these innovations. How many persons know what comprehensive study is given to theater carpet, its quality, texture, "joints," and method of laying.

We are all greatly impressed by projection and sound equipment, but part of the benefits of these technical advances would be lost were it not for the correct pitch of the floor and the proper arrangement of seats. And what improvements have been made in seats and in indirect aisle lighting, in the skillful arrangement of gallery steps and in the marking of top or bottom steps whose height may differ from the others thus causing a tripping and falling hazard if uncorrected. Such a simple and effective device as the increasing width of the aisle from front to rear has been noticed by millions who have no conception of its significance in emptying a theater.

Safety

Consider safety measures, which, though unseen to a large extent, must be present. The speaker is vitally interested in safety and in the safety of persons in places of public assembly. So are you! He is interested in a beautiful entrance and lobby, but more interested in how quickly and safely the entire theater can be evacuated. It may be well to repeat a statement from a previous paper: that if by reason of lack of provision for preventive measures a panic should happen in a theater, 20 years of good management can be undone in 20 seconds. So we come to consider all the study that has been given to the number, the types, and the arrangement of exits, as well as the means which are used to inform patrons of exit locations. We are interested in proper lighting of outside exits, in the substitution of ramps for steps where possible, in the fact that all exits must lead to a safe place.

As fire is a leading cause of panic, you, the manager, and you, the engineer, give constant thought to fire prevention and to the training of staffs in the handling of possible emergencies. A constant correspondence is going on between the manager and the engineer in which questions are asked and answers given as to how the safety of a given theater may be increased. We do not often think of this, but in proportion to the millions of patrons handled, the motion picture theater is relatively one of the safest places in which to be! How many people know this fact? All of these advances come about through the teamwork of the engineer and the manager, with the public as the ultimate beneficiary. When a patron sits in a modern theater he is enjoying, consciously or unconsciously, a rich inheritance of technical and managerial excellence. Why not tell him more about it, as the manager moves about the community?

Conclusion

[...] [T]here is a psychology of the theater, but it is a psychology which must be studied constantly, and learned, and interpreted. This is no small activity with which you are connected. It is a "big" thing with magnificent opportunities and large responsibilities. It is an industry built on great technical proficiencies and artistic achievements. Its success will depend ultimately on the fullest co-operation among all concerned, the producer, the engineer, the exhibitor, and the patron. There must be the fullest awareness of the problems just as there is the great appreciation of the achievements. It is the managers, ultimately, the men and women at the distant outposts, who are the interpreters. On this comprehension, their perception, and their alertness, the personality of the theater will largely depend.

Let us take a brief journey, not to one of the great theaters in large cities, but to a small "house" on the streets of a town. This particular house is a "two-shows a night." It is dusk. As the sunlight fails, the twinkling lights of houses and storefronts come on. The townspeople are at supper. The manager of the theater stands in front for a moment. He has lived here for a number of years and some of his roots are already deep in the life of the town. He sees lights in stores which would otherwise be dark were it not for the theater which brings the townsmen through the evening streets. He looks up and down the street, greets a few friends, and then passes inside. In a moment the bright lights of the marquee are turned on. The manager looks over the house, checks his little staff, and soon the patrons begin arriving.

In this simple procedure, something really tremendous has happened. From all of their diverse occupations, with all of their problems, their tastes and their hopes and fears these people have come to be entertained. But to the manager they are not just people. They are his friends, his fellow townsmen. In a real sense, he is the steward of a wider world than these people see every day, the world of the cinema, both the world of make-believe and the world of reality. Like Aladdin, when he turns on the lights of the theater, he turns on also the lights, the varied lights, of human experience. Certainly there is a psychology of the theater, there is a personality, a meaning.

Do we *know* it?

Discussion

Mr. Ben Schlanger: There is one point that Dr. Cutter brought out which I think is worthy of a little further enlightenment, and that is the cinema-goer who comes to the theater to forget all his problems completely and be in the world of what he is looking at in the cinema. And that is what we need greatly, a theater auditorium where a person can sit down and look at what is ahead of him and not be conscious of the physical shelter in which he is enjoying that picture. He has to be able to look at that picture, lose himself in it completely, and have no reminder of the fact that he is in an enclosure and looking at a picture.

That is a pretty difficult thing to accomplish but I think it is worth striving for.

If you have auditorium walls with certain types of decorations, let us say Georgian and Colonial, and the picture that is being shown on the screen is a scene in the Sahara desert, they do not belong together at all. In other words, the auditorium has to be a completely neutral enclosure, to enable you to enjoy completely that which is being shown to you, and we have to try to make that picture that is ahead of us not appear as a picture, but as real life; in the motion picture it can appear even more like real life than in the stage theater, because in Hollywood the boys have a few tricks up their sleeves that can produce it.

231

★ ★ ★ ★ ★ ★ ★ ★ ★ ★ ★ ★ ★ ★

PART IV

Drive-In, Art House, Multiplex: The 1950s and Beyond

★ ★ ★ ★ ★ ★ ★ ★ ★ ★ ★ ★ ★ ★

Introduction

The penultimate section of *Moviegoing in America* explores developments and innovations in film exhibition since the 1950s, which is, in one telling, the story of the movie theater's survival through the Age of Television and into the Age of Video. Perhaps the most highly visible aspect of Hollywood's re-selling of the motion picture experience in the 1950s is the showcasing of "new" large-screen and widescreen processes, involving both the exhibition as well as the production of films. In a selection drawn from his authoritative study, *Widescreen Cinema* (1992), John Belton claims that these processes "transformed the relationship between spectators and the screen" in a manner not acknowledged in influential theorizations of the film spectator that gained prominence in film studies in the 1970s. To support this argument, Belton looks closely at the marketing and the actual physical configuration of widescreen technologies, most notably, CinemaScope. Such an approach would prove equally useful in examining other prime moments of innovation in motion picture technology – the initial introduction of film projectors, for example, or of sound recording equipment, or, more recently, of high-end audio systems for theaters.

The 1950s also saw the increasing prominence of two screening sites that in key ways differed from picture palaces or neighborhood theaters: the drive-in and the art cinema. Frank J. Taylor's feature article on the drive-in boom for the *Saturday Evening Post* in 1956 is typical of the bemused, half-ironic response to "ozoners" from the popular press, which remained fascinated by the exhibitor as entrepreneur and by the survival of the movies in the wake of television and suburbanization. The patrons and moviegoing practices Taylor sees at the drive-in are a far cry from what other contemporary commentators found at the art cinemas located in metropolitan areas and college towns across the United States. The article included here by film critic Alexander Bakshy from a 1929 issue of the *Nation* suggests the roots of this type of exhibition. Bakshy applauds the handful of "experimental theaters" then operating in New York City, which, he claims, satisfy a "demand for motion pictures of a superior artistic and intellectual appeal" and provide an outlet for "foreign pictures of outstanding merit." Stanley Frank (writing in *Nation's Business*, the magazine of the National Chamber of Commerce) and John Twomey (writing in the first academic journal in the field, the *Quarterly Review of Film, Radio and Television*) make comparable claims for art cinemas in the 1950s. All three discussions of this type of venue point toward significant issues about the stratification of film audiences and the vanguard role of specialized theaters. In these accounts the independent American exhibitor frequently emerges as a central figure who helps to set the parameters of cinematic art, often by operating almost in resistance to Hollywood's hegemony. Over the next 30 years art cinemas permutated into repertory theaters that scheduled Hollywood classics, new and old foreign films, and cult favorites, with bills usually changing daily. The schedules reprinted here from New York City during a week in June 1981 give a sense of the repertory format at its esoteric and diverse best.

Betsy McLane's 1983 discussion of the commercial screening possibilities for American independent feature films, like John Sayles' *The Return of the Secaucus Seven*, provides another view of exhibition outside mainstream venues and practices. There is, in fact, a range of alternative screening sites that have been important throughout the twentieth century: non-theatrical venues, including homes, churches, YMCAs, union halls, community centers, schools, and libraries; different manifestations of the "adult" theater; and theaters catering to particular audiences defined by ethnicity or first language or race. One of the best discussions of this last category is Dan Streible's history of the Harlem Theater in Austin, Texas, from 1920 to 1973. This essay helps to fill in our understanding of African American moviegoing outside of major northern cities during the long years of segregation. Streible's essay also exemplifies another way of approaching the history of film exhibition: the case study of an individual theater, charting changes over time in ownership, clientele, and programming policies.

The dominant mainstream screening site since the late 1960s has been the chain-owned and operated multiplex theater. In a piece first published in 1972, Stanley H. Durwood, then President of American Multi-Cinema, Inc., explains his company's approach to the "multiple-theatre complex," which, he suggests, results in more profits for the exhibitor and more variety for the patron. William Paul, writing in *Film History* (1994), examines the causes for and the consequences of the exhibition practices of companies like American Multi-Cinema. Using *Variety* as his major source, Paul argues that multiplex cinemas and saturation booking policies which have become dominant in the contemporary period have fundamentally altered what we think of as the movies and as the experience of moviegoing. Again, the view from inside the industry is far more sanguine, as Barbara Stones suggests in the final chapter of her *America Goes to the Movies*, an in-house history published by the National Association of Theatre Owners. Stones celebrates the technological refinement and the "sophistication" of the 1990s cineplex and remains confident about the "enduring appeal of moviegoing." Her optimistic boosterism should be read in the context not only of Paul's article, but also of the long tradition of industry self-promotion.

Robert Allen's "From Exhibition to Reception: Reflections on the Audience in Film History" serves as something of an afterword to this entire collection, arguing for the importance of exhibition in film history, suggesting a number of potential areas for further research, and speculating about the historiographical issues involved in trying to draw connections between the exhibition and the reception of the movies.

Illustrations from Freeman Lincoln, "The Comeback of the Movies," *Fortune* 51 (February 1955) (Artist: Roy McKie)

40

Spectator and Screen

John Belton

Cinerama, CinemaScope, Todd-AO, and other large-screen and widescreen processes redefined traditional notions of spectatorship. The changes that occurred call for a rethinking of the ways in which cinema studies has tended to theorize the spectator's relationship to the screen.

Contemporary theory has appropriated the motion picture screen as a metaphor, which it has used, in turn, to describe the spectator's experience of the cinema. The notion of screen-as-metaphor, which took hold – appropriately enough – in the English-speaking world at *Screen* magazine in the 1970s, was, however, not unique to film theory but emerged, rather as a deliberate rewriting of both André Bazin's realist notion of the screen-as-window and Jean Mitry's formalist rendering of the screen-as-frame.[1] Following the psychoanalytically informed work of Jean-Louis Baudry, which had earlier appeared in *Cinéthique* and *Communications*, *Screen* embraced Baudry's transformation of Bazin's window and Mitry's frame into a Lacanian mirror, in which the child, immobile and lacking motor coordination, (mis)recognized its own image as an Imaginary, ideal, unified, and more perfect reflection of itself.[2]

For Baudry in "The Apparatus," the transcendental subject which the spectator found reflected in the cinema's screen/mirror resembled the deluded spectator in Plato's Cave, who mistook the shadowy images projected on the cave wall for reality. Thus Plato's "apparatus," which consisted of chained, immobilized spectators imprisoned in "a cavernous underground chamber with an entrance open to the light" who could not see the outside world but only the shadows on the cave wall, served as an analogy for the film viewer's experience of the screen in a darkened movie theater.[3] As an ideological apparatus, the screen, in effect, constituted the spectator as subject in a programmatic, regressive way, rendering the spectator into an ideological construction – into a "subject,"[4] who/which invested the images on the screen with a certain "impression of reality," activating a mechanism that provided an "answer to a desire inherent in our psychical structure" for such an illusion.[5] The screen-as-mirror reflected back images "cut to the measure of" our own desire, thus functionary as a machine which reproduced the ideology that had initially produced it.[6]

Fixing Desire

In "On Screen, in Frame: Film and Ideology," Stephen Heath recast the metaphor of screen-as-mirror slightly, exploring its status as an ideological apparatus which, much like Althusser's state apparatuses, transformed spectators into subjects of a statelike institution – the cinema. For Heath, the screen did not so much "reflect" as "fix" desire, regulating the operations of desire and assigning prescribed positions to those who look to the screen for an answer to their desires. Heath insisted that the cinema was born not when the basic apparatus of silent cinema – consisting of camera, film, projector, and screen – was perfected, but when the spectator's relationship to that apparatus was fixed, that is, when "the spectators [were] no longer set on either side of a translucent screen but [had] been assigned their position in front of the image which unroll[ed] before them."[7] In other words, for Heath, the cinema was more than a mechanical apparatus; it was an ideological apparatus. As such, the cinema came into being only when the circuit implicit in the mechanical apparatus was completed by the addition to it of a spectator whom the screen fixed in place.

Heath then extended his argument from consideration of the screen, which positioned spectators in the theater, to that of the frame, which organized the spectator's vision, centering it in various ways on the contents of the frame. For Heath screen and frame functioned, along with certain spatial codes (such as perspectival space, which furthered the work of the screen and the frame in organizing vision) and narrative, to determine the conditions of spectatorship.

Heath insisted that these conditions of spectatorship have remained more or less constant from 1896 to the present. The film frame, unlike the frame in painting, for example, remained limited to a standard 1.33/7:1 aspect ratio or "to a number of such ratios."[8] In "Narrative Space," Heath made the same point again with a further qualification, noting that the frame was limited "to a very small number of ratios."[9] The implication of Heath's argument, especially his comparison of the standard film frame with the variety of frames found in painting, was that

the relative fixity of the film frame (which was determined by the cinema's technological base in 35mm motion picture film) defined, in large part, the conditions of film spectatorship. Heath's theory of the frame rested upon an assumption of its uniformity. But that uniformity did not in fact exist, at least not in post-1952 cinema.

Historicizing Spectatorship

The advent of widescreen motion picture production and exhibition in the early 1950s transformed the previous relationship between spectators and the screen, a relationship that had been established with the advent of projection in 1896 and with the rise of the small-screen nickelodeons in 1905, that was consolidated in the 1910s and 1920s with the introduction of the large-screen motion picture palace, and that continued to flourish in the 1930s and 1940s during the heyday of classical Hollywood cinema. During the years 1952–1955 the screen aspect ratio changed from the traditional 1.33/7:1 to various widescreen formats, which ranged from 1.66:1 (Vista Vision) to 2.77:1 (Cinerama), and the size of the screen dramatically expanded from an average of 20 × 16 feet to an optimum (in large downtown theaters) of 64 × 24.[10] Widescreen cinema, especially CinemaScope and Cinerama, which relied on peripheral vision for much of their effect, addressed spectators in a markedly different way than did standard, narrow-screen 1.33/7:1 films. The wide screen may still have been a symbolic instrument of Lacanian and Althusserian subject formation, but it clearly reconstituted that subject in dramatically new ways and had redefined the traditional conditions of spectatorship established by the narrow-screen cinema, which had served as the basis for Baudry's and Heath's theorization of the cinema as an "apparatus."

Heath treated spectatorship and subject positioning as unchanging, as an ahistorical phenomenon. Spectatorship, however, needs to be viewed in terms of the changes in the cinema's basic exhibition practices from one historical period to another. Yet both Baudry and Heath, who discuss spectatorship in terms of the cinema's "basic" technological apparatus and the codes of Renaissance perspective that determine cinematic space, maintained that, once the screen–spectator relationship had been established, it remained unchanged. For them, as long as the basic apparatus remained essentially the same and as long as screen space remained more or less perspectival, spectators would continue to be positioned in relation to the image in roughly the same way regardless of changes in the smaller signifying practices of the cinema (those practices which vary from film to film) and of changes in the social formation. The only variable in the system was the content of films, which was seen to address spectators in different ways. Discussions by Heath and others of spectatorship and subject positioning frequently explored the differences among kinds of address and kinds of larger signifying practices – the differing modes of address of the Western and the woman's film, the different signifying practices of classical cinema, of art cinema, of modernist films by Jean-Marie Straub and Danièle Huillet or Nagisa Oshima, but these practices and modes of address were rarely historicized.[11]

Heath, it would seem, minimized the historical changes in film aspect ratios for a variety of reasons. Heath, more than Bazin or Mitry, consciously used the notions of screen and frame metaphorically – as visible symbols of the way in which classical cinema "hold[s] the subject – on screen, in frame."[12] Since Heath's screen and frame were metaphorical, their actual size or shape was of less concern to him than their symbolic function as abstractions for describing the spectator–screen relationship.[13] At the same time, variability in the shape of the screen was far less significant for Heath than were certain constants, such as the codes of Renaissance perspective which informed the way in which space was represented on screen, the oper-

ations of narrative which transformed space into place, and, in particular, the operations of suture, which effaced certain absences or differences that might, if perceived, threaten the illusory subject-unity which narrative cinema aimed to create. The screen, the frame, linear perspective, narrative, and suture worked together to overdetermine, as it were, how we look at what we see.

Redefining Spectatorship

Yet the changes in viewing situations that took place during the early 1950s marked a crucial break with the past; a new form of spectatorship was introduced, and a new set of expectations governed moviegoing. Passive viewing became associated, in industry marketing discourse at least, with traditional narrow-screen motion pictures; widescreen cinema became identified with the notion of "audience participation," the experience of heightened physiological stimulation provided by wraparound widescreen image and multitrack stereo sound. Although in both situations the spectator still remained immobile in a theater seat, the perceptible difference in audience–screen relationships between traditional cinema and the new widescreen formats was exaggerated in an attempt to foreground the spectator's new relationship with the screen, which was now, if nothing else, no longer invisible. The wide screen came to represent difference; it marked a new kind of spectatorship. Something basic had changed in the motion picture experience that redefined the spectator's relationship with the screen, which now entered further into the spectator's space, and with the soundtrack, which reinforced this extension of the image and exceeded even the image's border through strategically placed speakers on the sides, ceiling, and rear wall of the theater, surrounding the spectator with sound.

During this period it was also clear that one form of spectatorship had not merely been replaced by another monolithic universal model of spectatorship. Rather, spectators were confronted with a variety of viewing situations from which they could choose, each of which engaged them in a different way, depending upon theater size and design, projection aspect ratio, and the dramatic content of the film. The cinema became a host of different cinemas; its traditional mass audience became, in turn, an assortment of highly diverse viewing groups.[14] For the spectator, watching a narrative film in black and white in the traditional 1.33/7:1 format at the neighborhood theater remained strikingly distinct from experiencing the colorful travelogues mounted in Cinerama on huge, deeply curved screens in large downtown theaters; viewing "flat" widescreen films in Vista Vision differed from being visually assaulted by 3-D films which exploited the technology's ability to create the illusion of emergence;[15] by the same token, CinemaScope's epics and biblical spectacles and Todd-AO's superproductions of theatrical extravaganzas gave viewers experiences that were different not only from flat, 3-D, regular widescreen, and Cinerama films but from one another as well. The spectator was not only beckoned by ads to "participate" in a new form of motion picture experience but also invited to choose from among a variety of different kinds of participation.

Motion pictures attempted to maximize their participatory potential by adopting two dramatically different models of recreational participation – the amusement park and the legitimate theater – around which they then constructed new definitions of spectatorship. The coexistence of these different models marked a break with the monolithic notions of spectatorship which had preceded this era.

Though this assortment of viewing situations resembled, in part, the montage of attractions available at the circus, carnival, or amusement park, only Cinerama and 3-D provided spectators with the visceral thrills associated with this kind of participatory activity. Cinerama was carefully marketed by a sophisticated public relations firm as a radical new motion picture experience for audiences, promoting what it did to spectators and ignoring the technical details which

produced its illusory sense of participation.[16] Ads for Cinerama depicted spectators sitting in their theater seats perched precariously in the bows of speedboats, "skiing" side by side with on-screen water skiiers, or hovering above the wings of airplanes, "flying" along with an on-screen aerial view of the countryside. The text for ads for *This Is Cinerama* promised, "You won't be gazing at a movie screen – you'll find yourself swept right into the picture, surrounded by sight and sound."[17] The film's program booklet proclaimed: "you gasp and thrill with the excitement of a vividly realistic ride on the roller coaster ... You feel the giddy sensations of a plane flight as you bank and turn over Niagara and skim through the rocky grandeur of the Grand Canyon. Everything that happens on the curved Cinerama screen is happening to you. And without moving from your seat, you share, personally, in the most remarkable new kind of emotional experience ever brought to the theater."[18] The second Cinerama film, *Cinerama Holiday*, was described as a picture about people and places – "where they go ... what they do ... and you are with them ... Cinerama ... brings you into the drama of people's lives."[19] Subsequent Cinerama releases continued to sell the way in which the format put the viewer into the picture. Thus *Battle of the Bulge* "turns the screen into the mightiest battleground ever as it hurls you into the most extraordinary days of World War II."[20]

The participation effect was reversed in the marketing of 3-D; instead of audiences' entering into the world depicted on the screen, the space on screen was represented in ads as invading that of the audience, resulting in "a lion in your lap" and "a lover in your arms."[21] But the copresence of image and audience remained a strong selling point in the marketing of 3-D.

Theater and Cinema

With CinemaScope, the appeal was less visceral. Though early ads, which announced

241

that CinemaScope "puts YOU in the picture," resembled those for Cinerama, CinemaScope extended a much more subtle invitation to audiences to enter into the screen space. CinemaScope and other widescreen processes sought a middle ground between the notion of passive consumption associated with at-home television viewing and that of active participation involved in outdoor recreational activities. The model chosen by these systems for purposes of redefining their product, however, was less that of the amusement park, which retained certain vulgar associations as a cheap form of mass entertainment, than that of the legitimate theater.[22] Thus the credits for *The Robe* play against a dark red theater curtain, which then opens to reveal the panoramic spectacle of ancient Rome. During the credits of the second CinemaScope feature, *How to Marry a Millionaire*, greenish-gold theater curtains part to reveal the Twentieth Century–Fox studio orchestra playing theatrical-style overture music to introduce the comic spectacle which follows.

The theater emerged as the one traditional form of entertainment that possessed the participatory effect of outdoor recreational activities and a strong sense of presence, and, at the same time, retained a strong identification with the narrative tradition in which Hollywood remained steadfastly rooted. In aligning itself with the experiential quality of the theater, widescreen cinema sought to erase the long-standing distinction between spectatorship in the theater and cinema, which viewed the former as active and the latter as passive.

In comparing the theater and the cinema, Bazin argued that the theater, featuring a live performance which is presented in a space shared by both performers and audience, elicited the participation of the audience in a much more direct and intense way than did the cinema, which separated the space of the performance (that is, the space depicted on-screen) from that of the audience (that is, the space of the movie theater). In Bazin's view, "theater is based on the reciprocal awareness

of audience and actor . . . The theater acts on us by virtue of our participation in a theatrical action across the footlights and as it were under the protection of their censorship. The opposite is true in the cinema. Alone, hidden in a dark room, we watch through half-open blinds a spectacle that is unaware of our existence. . . . "[23]

The cinema, as Jean Cocteau observed, was an event seen through a keyhole.[24] Widescreen cinema expanded the keyhole to a point where, though it did not quite disappear, it provided spectators with a spectacle that possessed an increased sense of presence, especially in theaters with curved screens, in which the image engulfed the audience. Participation was no longer a matter of absolute distinctions between active and passive spectatorship. Widescreen cinema had created an entirely new category of participation.[25] What widescreen cinema created was a greater illusion of participation, at least in comparison with the narrow, 1.33/7:1 aspect ratio of pre-widescreen cinema, in which that illusion, if it existed at all, was weaker.

James Spellerberg has examined both advertising and trade magazines in terms of their identification of CinemaScope with theatrical forms.[26] As Spellerberg points out, "In its new position in the late 1950s, Hollywood was more like Broadway. Hollywood was less a mass medium and more a specialized form of entertainment."[27] In other words, motion picture spectators were addressed in (what was for the cinema, at least) nontraditional ways, which emphasized the motion picture as a participatory experience comparable to recreational activities. This discourse clearly distinguished it, as a form of entertainment, from traditional or even nontraditional forms such as radio or television.

Advertisements for CinemaScope films told audiences that they would be drawn into the space of the picture much as if they were attending a play in the theater.[28] Advertisements for CinemaScope and Todd-AO (as well as Cinerama and 3-D) repeatedly depicted audiences together with the on-screen spectacle as if they shared the same space, as if there were an actual copresence between screen and spectator. These ads promoted not so much individual films, as in the past, as a new form of spectator/screen relationship that promised a radical new experience of motion pictures in the theater. In a number of these ads, the action on screen extended beyond the borders of the frame into the space of the audience, breaking down in an illusory way the traditional "segregation of spaces." In 3-D ads the screen action reached out into the audience, while in ads for widescreen films it extended beyond the top and side frame lines into the theater space but remained more or less within the horizontal and vertical planes established by the screen.

Publicists compared the panoramic CinemaScope image to the oblong *skene* (stage) of the ancient Greek theater[29] and insisted that "due to the immensity of the screen, few entire scenes can be taken in at a glance, enabling the spectator to view them ... as one would watch a play where actors are working from opposite ends of the stage," the widescreen format enhancing the sensation of the actors' presence and giving spectators the illusion that they could reach out and touch the performers.[30] Darryl Zanuck boasted that CinemaScope gave audiences "a feeling of being part of the action."[31] He insisted that with CinemaScope "members of the audience seem to be surrounded by the curved and greatly enlarged screen" and that "the increased scope of the production cannot fail to draw the audience into the action on the screen."[32] With widescreen it was "possible for the spectator to feel that things are going on 'all around.' "[33] In other words, the "participation effect" quite literally meant the creation of a strong sense of physical participation.

Even though CinemaScope remained associated with classical narrative films, it introduced a level of visual spectacle that often threatened to overwhelm the narrative. This threat could be contained only by a shift in terms of the kinds of films that were made – a shift to historical spectacle – which functioned to naturalize pictorial spectacle. Yet this shift also involved a change in traditional modes of address which, even in the genre of the historical spectacle, carefully regulated tendencies toward spectacular excess. With CinemaScope (and other large-screen processes), the situation was initially reversed. Spectacular excess carefully regulated the sorts of narratives selected. As Zanuck realized, the main value of CinemaScope lay "in the production of large scale spectacles and big outdoor films ... In time, we may find a way to use it effectively for intimate dramas and comedies but at the present time small, intimate stories or a personal drama ... would mean nothing on this system."[34]

Todd-AO combined the theatrical aspects of Cinerama presentation and marketing with the theatrical presence and dramatic narratives of CinemaScope. Todd-AO produced "a sense of participation which brings the spectator into the action on the screen for any type of scene whether a close-up, a wide shot, or distant scenic shots." This sense of participation resulted in "a quality of intimacy between the spectator in the theatre and the image projected on the screen ... [so] that the patron ... feels as though he is sitting in a living room participating in the action with the characters on screen."[35] Advertisements for *Oklahoma!* boasted that "You're in the show with Todd-AO" and emphasized the sense of presence produced by the system: "Suddenly you're there ... in the land that is grand, in the surrey, on the prairie! You live it, you're a part of it ... you're in Oklahoma!"[36]

The appeal made by the promoters of widescreen processes in the 1950s to theatrical notions of participation drew attention to the relationship between spectator and screen in ways that were reminiscent of earlier historical moments when spectatorship was dramatically redefined – the transition from peep show to projection in 1896 and the transition to sound in the late 1920s. Both of these earlier redefinitions were invoked by the industry in its marketing campaigns. Against the background of flat, narrow-screen cinema, widescreen cinema distinguished itself in terms of its greater sense of "presence," a comparison which similarly underlay these two earlier techno-logical transformations. Seen in this histori-cal context, "presence" emerges as a relative rather than an absolute term which is con-stantly subject to renegotiation by audiences and the industry.

Widescreen systems such as Cinerama, CinemaScope, and Todd-AO created a specta-tor–screen relationship that both exceeded and undermined that of traditional cinema. On a purely physical level, these systems lit-erally overwhelmed the spectator. All three relied on curved screens (Cinerama and Todd-AO on deeply curved screens) ranging in depth from five to fifteen or sixteen feet depending on the width of the screen. The ideal viewing position lay at the center of the theater auditorium, at a distance from the screen of two and a half times the height of the image. Cinerama, in particular, depended for its increased sense of audience participation on enveloping the spectator in wraparound image and sound.

The participation effect, however, was itself a radical departure from previous modes of spectatorial address, which involved no use of peripheral vision. Cinerama and Cinema-Scope, in particular, effectively transformed the notion of frame, expanding the horizontal angle of view to such an extent that there was, for all intents and purposes, no sense of any borders at the edges of the frame.[37] In contrast to the "distraction" which Siegfried Kracauer suggested characterized the specta-tor's experience in the 1920s movie palace, in which the architecture of the theater encour-aged the spectator's eyes to wander from the screen to the surrounding decor, Cinerama, CinemaScope, and Todd-AO relied upon curved screens and wraparound images and sounds to draw the spectator into the world depicted on-screen; distraction gave way to attention-grabbing participation. Changes in theater design in the postwar era mirrored this development. The ornate prosceniums of the movie palace were either torn down

or hidden behind panoramic screens. These extended into the space of the audience and transformed the front of the theater from an atmospheric frame within which a motion picture attraction was presented into an eye-filling, wall-to-wall display of image and sound, in which screens blended into the side walls of the theater auditorium and the film was experienced directly, as it were, unmed-iated by theater architecture. This transform-ation of the front wall of the theater into a borderless screen survives today in modern theater architecture. However, contempor-ary screens tend to be significantly smaller than those of the 1950s, reduced in size by the "twinning" of older theaters and by the creation of smaller multiplexed mall theaters.

Notes

1 Charles F. Altman, "Psychoanalysis and Cinema: The Imaginary Discourse," *Quarterly Review of Film Studies* 2, no. 3 (August 1977), 260–1.

2 For Baudry, see "Ideological Effects of the Basic Cinematographic Apparatus," *Cinéthique*, nos. 7–8 (1970), and "The Apparatus: Metapsycho-logical Approaches to the Impression of Reality in the Cinema," *Communications*, no. 23 (1975). Baudry's "Ideological Effects," trans-lated by Alan Williams, appears in *Film Quar-terly* 28, no. 2 (Winter 1974–5), 39–47. This translation and that of "The Apparatus," by Jean Andres and Bertrand Augst, are antholo-gized in Philip Rosen (ed.), *Narrative, Apparatus, Ideology: A Film Theory Reader* (New York: Columbia University Press, 1986). Page refer-ences are to the Rosen anthology. Although *Screen* did not publish either of the Baudry essays, the metaphor figures most centrally in *Screen's* publication, in an English translation, of Christian Metz's "The Imaginary Signifier," 16, no. 2 (Summer 1975), as well as in Laura Mulvey's "Visual Pleasure and the Narrative Cinema," 16, no. 3 (Autumn 1975), reprinted in Rosen. Page references for Mulvey are to the Rosen anthology.

3 Baudry, "Ideological Effects" and "The Appa-ratus," in Rosen, *Narrative, Apparatus, Ideology*, 294, 302–7.

4   John Caughie, *Theories of Authorship* (Boston: Routledge & Kegan Paul, 1981), 292, distinguishes a subject from an "individual with a personality," describing the former as "a 'place' which that individual may be called upon to occupy within a formation (social, political, textual)." The spectator before the screen is both an individual with a personality and a social-political-textual (as well as a psychical) subject, yet the spectator-as-physical-presence-before-the-screen remains distinct from the spectator-as-subject. Though the actual spectator in the theater remains somewhat distinct from the abstract subject of theory, the physical relationship of the spectator to the screen plays a role in the theorization of subject positioning, if only as the primary point of departure for the conceptualization of a theory of subjectivity, as the individual instance upon which the theoretization of spectatorship in general depends.

5   Baudry, "The Apparatus," 307.

6   Laura Mulvey ("Visual Pleasure," 208) specifies the nature of this ideology as patriarchal by defining the desire as "male"; Baudry (in "The Apparatus") and Metz (in "The Imaginary Signifier") do not identify it with a specific gender.

7   Stephen Heath, *Questions of Cinema* (Bloomington: Indiana University Press, 1981), 1.

8   Stephen Heath "On Screen," in *Questions of Cinema*, 10.

9   Stephen Heath, "Narrative Space," in *Questions of Cinema*, 35.

10   Gio Gagliardi, *Motion Picture Herald* (August 6, 1955), 14.

11   On the various modes of address employed by different genres see Stephen Neale, *Genre* (London: British Film Institute, 1980), 25–30. Though Heath does not explore the issue of modes of address as such, his discussions of classical cinema in "Narrative Space" and of Oshima in "The Question Oshima" sketch out basic differences in the way these cinemas position subjects. For a discussion of the different narrative strategies employed by classical cinema and art cinema, see David Bordwell, *Narration in the Fiction Film* (Madison: University of Wisconsin Press, 1985), 147–233. Bordwell's cognitive approach to the viewing process provides a radically different model of spectatorship within which there is no place for a "subject"; yet his discussion of various modes of narration suggests ways in which the psychoanalytic notion of mode of address might be articulated differently in different kinds of cinema.

12   Heath, "On Screen," 15.

13   Heath's discussion of subject positioning moves, as Noël Carroll has pointed out, through a series of metaphors, which suggest the ways in which the cinematic apparatus and the cinema's signifying system construct subjects. See Carroll, "Address to the Heathen," *October* 23 (Winter 1982), 117. The "screen" provides the initial metaphor for the fixing of subject position; the "frame" is then presented as a metaphor for the creation of a boundary that centers the spectator's attention, a centering that is completed by the compositional codes of Quattrocento perspective, which in turn functions as a metaphor for the way in which the cinema establishes a fixed station point for its spectators to occupy. Renaissance perspective is necessarily a metaphor for two reasons: because film images, unlike paintings, contain movement (of characters, objects, the camera itself), which redirects the spectator's eye; and because films, unlike paintings, combine a variety of different perspectival systems; that is, each shot presents a different compositional organization (not to mention possible shifts from lens to lens or within a lens – the zoom – that slightly alter the way in which space is represented). Thus perspective images bind the spectator in place, while suture contains the necessary shifts in perspective from shot to shot or changes that occur within a single shot.

14   Thomas Doherty discusses the transformation of the motion pictures from a mass entertainment medium to a tiered medium in *Teenagers & Teenpics: The Juvenilization of American Movies in the 1950s* (Boston: Unwin Hyman, 1988), 1–3. For an account of how certain widescreen (and 3-D) formats were marketed to specific class groups, see John Belton, "CinemaScope and Historical Methodology," *Cinema Journal* 28, no. 1 (Fall 1988), 34–8.

15   The term *flat* was regularly used in the industry to distinguish films shot and projected with normal lenses from those filmed in 3-D and CinemaScope (or some other anamorphic process). For a discussion of 3-D's emergence

effect, see William Paul, "The Aesthetics of Emergence" (Paper delivered at the Society for Cinema Studies conference in Bozeman, Montana, June 1988).

16 Lynn Farnol, "Finding Customers for a Product: Notes on the Introduction of Cinerama," in *New Screen Techniques*, ed. Martin Quigley, Jr. (New York: Quigley Publishing, 1953), 141–2.

17 Ibid., 143.

18 *This Is Cinerama* (yellow) program booklet, n.d. (ca. 1952).

19 *Cinerama Holiday* program booklet, n.d. (ca. 1955).

20 Promotional advertisement for *The Battle of the Bulge*.

21 William Paul in "The Aesthetics of Emergence" contrasts these screen/spectator relationships in terms of movement into and out of the frame and notes that both 3-D and widescreen processes have "the common aim of breaking down our sense of the frame."

22 Comparison of the participation effect produced by widescreen cinema to the theatrical experience constitutes a major thread of the industry discourse surrounding CinemaScope, as James Spellberg points out in "CinemaScope and Ideology," *Velvet Light Trap*, no. 21 (Summer 1985), 30–1.

23 André Bazin, "Theater and Cinema – Part Two," in *What Is Cinema?* vol. 1, trans. Hugh Gray (Berkeley: University of California Press, 1967), 102.

24 Quoted in ibid., 92.

25 Christian Metz argues that the cinema's impression of reality produces a sense of participation, which informs every film, giving us "the feeling that we are witnessing an almost real spectacle." See *Film Language: A Semiotics of the Cinema* (New York: Oxford, 1974), 4. Some sense of participation undoubtedly exists in all cinema, even in pre-widescreen films, but widescreen increased and expanded this sense to a point that it predominated.

26 Spellberg, "CinemaScope and Ideology," 30–1.

27 Ibid., 31.

28 Ironically, although the cinema of the 1950s modeled itself after the experience of the the-
ater, the theater itself had evolved, over the past two centuries, closer and closer toward the cinema. Eighteenth-century theaters, for example, lit the auditorium as well as the stage, establishing a spatial continuum between the two. Nineteenth-century theater began to separate these two spaces by lighting one (the stage) but not the other (the audience). At the same time, late nineteenth-century dramaturgy, which began to create a more realistic world onstage through the use of three-dimensional set design and lighting, transformed theater audiences from knowing participants with the actors in the construction of a dramatic illusion into voyeurs who looked in on a seemingly autonomous world.

29 Charles Einfeld, "CinemaScope and the Public," in Quigley, *New Screen Techniques*, 182.

30 Spellberg, "CinemaScope and Ideology," 30. See also Thomas Pryor, "Fox Films Embark on 3-Dimension Era," *New York Times* (February 2, 1953). Spellberg has examined the industry's discourse on CinemaScope in both advertising and trade magazines in terms of the identification of it with theatrical forms. As he points out, "In its new position in the late 1950s, Hollywood was more like Broadway. Hollywood was less a mass medium and more a specialized form of entertainment" (p. 31).

31 *Life* (March 9, 1953), 35.

32 Darryl Zanuck, "CinemaScope in Production," in Quigley, *New Screen Techniques*, 156.

33 *Newsweek* (September 28, 1953), 96.

34 Memo, Zanuck to Spyros Skouras, January 27, 1953. Zanuck folder, box 116, Sponable Collection, Columbia University Libraries.

35 Todd-AO folder, box 120, Sponable Collection.

36 *Film Daily* (October 10, 1955), 7.

37 After initial demonstrations of CinemaScope in Los Angeles in mid-March 1953, one exhibitor remarked that with the expansiveness of the CinemaScope frame, there was "so much to see that the viewer was not conscious of the limitations of the framework"; *Hollywood Reporter* (April 24, 1953), 6, quoted by James Spellberg, "Technology and the Film Industry: The Adoption of CinemaScope" (Ph.D. diss., University of Iowa, 1980), 210.

41

Big Boom in Outdoor Movies (1956)

Frank J. Taylor

In the up-or-down show business, the hot box-office bonanza nowadays is a Cinderella stepchild of the motion-picture industry known in Hollywood's vernacular as "the ozoners." Until recently, this stepchild was haughtily ignored by movie tycoons; now Cinderella is being welcomed into the cinema fold with open arms. This change of heart is justified; the once-despised orphan now brings home almost one fourth of Hollywood's income, sufficient to be the difference between profit and loss.

As might be suspected, an "ozoner" is one of those weird-looking open-air drive-in movies which stud the landscape outside American and Canadian cities, a phenomenon of the motor age found nowhere else on earth. In an ozoner, the customers bring their own seats, those of the family car. The management obligingly provides a parking spot in front of the lofty screen, plus plenty of fresh air, hot dogs, pizza pies, pop and popcorn, along with jumbo screen stars two or four stories high. Anybody who wearies of the evening's drama can stretch out and go to sleep. About half of the patrons, knowing they are going to sack it before the show is over, come in their pajamas.

"Stand by the exit gate and peek into the cars as they leave a drive-in movie," suggested stocky, exuberant Robert L. Lippert, dean of open-air cinema enterprisers, whose

chain of twenty-three ozoners stretches from Southern Oregon to the California–Mexico border. "You'll get an eye-opener," continued Lippert. "In nine out of ten cars you'll see young children asleep on the back seat and on the floor. That's why the ozoners are going over big. The drive-in movie is the answer to the sitter problem, and to the downtown parking problem. It's the answer to the young family's night out. It's the neighborhood theater of the future."

The enthusiasm flashing from Bob Lippert's black eyes is understandable. He is one of the fortunate pioneers who bet on ozone cinema when the well-heeled operators of "the hardtops," as Hollywood terms the conventional four-walls-and-a-roof movie houses, were laughing off the early and primitive drive-ins as a passing fad.

"Movie people thought I was absolutely crazy when I went around talking the butcher, the baker, and anybody who'd listen into putting a few dollars in those early drive-ins," recalled Lippert, who did just that to raise capital for his first ozoner in Sacramento, opened a dozen years back. Its lofty flapping canvas screen made the movie lovers look pretty grotesque when the wind blew.

But by what Lippert calls "the trial and error system," he solved the screen problem, and other problems as well, and moved up

Excerpted from Frank J. Taylor, "Big Boom in Outdoor Movies." *Saturday Evening Post 229* (September 15, 1956), 31, 100–2. Reprinted with permission of the *Saturday Evening Post*.

and down California's Central Valley, persuading other businessmen to risk dollars in additional open-air cinemas – four in Fresno, two in Modesto, until the chain of twenty-three extended from El Centro, near the Mexican border, to Medford, in Southern Oregon. Those who bet with Lippert on his ozoners shared the jack pot along with him.

By 1956, Box Office, the trade magazine that styles itself "the pulse of the motion-picture industry," reported that there were more than 5000 of the drive-in movies in the United States and Canada. Last year, when only a dozen or so new conventional theaters were opened in the entire country, 389 new drive-ins were launched at a cost of $79,880,000 according to the Box Office survey. The pulse of the drive-ins is beating young and strong; that of many of the 13,000 older, conventional theaters is flickering. As the older picture houses are abandoned, few are being replaced, because it costs $500 per seat to replace them, and only half that much to provide space for the bring-your-own-seats of the drive-in movie patrons, who, incidentally, spend as much for food and soft drinks at the concession stand as they do for entrance tickets. As a magnet for collecting nickels, dimes, quarters, and even dollars, the ozoner ranks with Coney Island.

The boom in drive-ins is a nationwide phenomenon. Weather has little influence on it. Illinois, for example, has 126 drive-ins, about average for a populous state. Pennsylvania has 226, North Carolina 274, more than California with 174. Texas boasts 472, many of them mushrooming out of the open prairie, midway between three or four cities, where each is "the neighborhood movie for four hundred square miles." Canada has 221 drive-in movies, a number of them all-year-'round operations, despite the cold winters. Scores of open-air movies in the northern states stay open through the winter. In some the owners provide small electric heaters for patrons' cars; other operators give each car owner a gallon of gas to keep the motor idling and run the car heater.

A surprise angle to the mushroom growth of the drive-ins is that nearly all of them were launched by comparative amateurs in the motion-picture entertainment field. While professional showmen kept on building hard-tops, landowners, merchants, real estaters, barbers, even farmers, with shoestrings for backers, converted cow pastures into open-air cinemas. [...]

A lot of these amateur amusement entrepreneurs, who did not know what was in the book and what wasn't, resorted to gimmicks to lure patrons that are rated as downright unethical by veteran motion-picture exhibitors. Several Texas drive-ins, for example, operate laundries as a side line. The housewife, who might otherwise be spending the evening at home with the washing machine, drops her washing at the gate as the family enters the drive-in, and picks it up freshly laundered as she leaves – for a small consideration, of course. Some drive-ins offer warmed milk for babies, and fresh diapers, if their infant patrons forget to bring along a spare pair of pants. Others maintain nurseries and playgrounds for small fry, driving ranges for bored dads, open-air dance floors for teenagers. Some offer "spook" programs, four shows lasting from midnight to dawn!

"The hottest firecracker in the drive-in-theater business," to quote an admiring film distributor, is Stanford Kohlberg, a short, round, swarthy character with intense blue eyes, who operates the Starlite Drive-In Theater on Highway U.S. 20, southwest of Chicago, which is a battleground of the ozoners. Kohlberg, who hails from an old Omaha vaudeville family, has tried so many come-ons to lure customers that he is rated as unfair competition by his more conservative rivals.

To kick off the 1956 summer season, for instance, Kohlberg lined up $20,000 worth of live talent – bands, crooners, dancers and acrobats – for the last weekend in May. Dramatizing the weather gamble, which is the drive-in operator's nightmare, the heavens cut loose with the most torrential downpour Chicago had seen in years. But Kohlberg's troupers went on with the show, the crooners doing their best in the deluge that made them sound as though they were singing under water. And, pointing up the devotion of drive-in fans for their favorite amusement, more than 1,000 customers turned out, in the face of storm warnings, to watch the show through moaning windshield wipers.

[. . .] Admission for adults is $1.25; youngsters under twelve, as many as can be packed in a car, are free, and each gets a door prize. The $1.25 pays for the movie, for dancing under the stars to music from name bands. It includes free milk for babies and free diapers if young mothers forget them. Kohlberg has a Kiddieland for youngsters too small to be interested in cinema drama. He has a miniature golf course and driving range for anyone in the family not interested in the picture. Three concession buildings purvey soft or hot drinks, pizza pies, hot dogs, hamburgers at popular prices. For one dollar Kohlberg sells his patrons a chicken dinner. One of his more brilliant ideas is the "Starlite Happiness Book," good for five or ten or fifteen dollars' worth of entertainment and food, sold on credit to any holder of a department-store or oil-company credit card. Kohlberg bills his charge accounts at the end of thirty days.

"Parents know their youngsters won't wind up in a beer hall," says Kohlberg. "With a Happiness Book a youth brings his girl to the Starlite, where we don't sell any alcoholic drinks. We even have attendants in the rest rooms to see that nobody spikes the soft drinks. The drive-in is the answer to the problem of wholesome amusement for teenagers. I know, because I have seven girls and two boys, ranging from college age to three months."

This is a far cry from the early-day drive-ins, which were labeled "passion pits" by their hardtop competitors, because sin and cinema were thought to be inseparable within the confines of darkened automobiles. In the province of Quebec, Canada, drive-ins are still taboo, largely because the Catholic Church has not yet lifted an early ban on them. But elsewhere in Canada and all over the United States, the passion-pit problem seems to have resolved itself. The bulk of the patrons are young couples with children, to whom the drive-in is an opportunity to spend an evening out without investing in either a sitter or a parking space. The roughs, who apparently don't approve of the company of young parents with kids sleeping in the back seat, have gone elsewhere. To discourage the rowdy element and the liquor drinkers, the larger ozoners have special officers, with flashlights, patrolling the ramps.

In the Starlite Drive-In, Kohlberg can accommodate more patrons than Chicago's largest downtown theater. Several of his competitors whose drive-ins ring Chicago can do the same. The Essaness chain, which operates eleven hardtops as well as four ozoners, has about the same capacity in its largest drive-in, the Harlem Avenue Outdoor. Another, the new Bel-Air, which turned an unsightly old city dump on Cicero Avenue into a plush drive-in, has parking space for 2500 cars plus 1000 seats for customers who park outside and walk in. The M. & R. chain, which built the Bel-Air, also runs the Double Drive-In, with two movies showing at the same time on opposite sides of the huge metal screen. Ralph Smitha, manager of Essaness, once tried a four-screen drive-in, which wasn't a success. Smitha still considers the four-screener a great idea, even if the moviegoers didn't go for it.

"The drive-in attracts brand-new movie patrons," says Smitha. "Young families with children, young people with aged parents, people with dogs they won't leave at home, teen-agers, and college kids. You have to be where the customers can drive to your theater easily."

Smitha and most drive-in operators don't like to be close to shopping centers or race tracks on account of traffic congestion. They try to locate on a major highway into a city, because on hot summer nights many apartment-house dwellers like to drive out to the country for fresh air, just as young mothers yearn to escape the house for an evening.

"People like to go out without dressing up," says Smitha. "They can go to a drive-in in any kind of clothes."

The drive-in operators prefer not to be too near to roadside taverns or "clubs" that attract rowdies. Most drive-ins are now strictly chaperoned. Some work closely with churches and schools, offering their facilities free for Easter sunrise services and for outdoor civic gatherings.

Once he has his acreage, the drive-in proprietor, often a syndicate of local investors, lays it out, clamshell shape, with a screen and office where the clamshells would hook together. The ramps are graded in curves facing the screen, under which the office is usually located. It takes miles of underground wiring to connect the in-car speakers, located on posts between cars. The posts also house the outlets into which are plugged the small electric heaters which plushier drive-ins offer as an inducement on cold evenings. In these drive-ins, every car, as it passes the ticket gate, is issued a car heater or, if the occupants don't want heat, a brass check; as they leave, the patrons turn in either a heater or the brass check.

In the center of the clamshell is the low concession building, which also houses the projectors and the toilet facilities. The combination cafeteria-soda fountain-candy counter is an all-important part of the drive-in, because the sale of food, hot and cold drinks, and candy accounts for a big bite of the drive-in's take. Many drive-in operators figure they can offer to run the movie on a bare break-even basis and make their profit from food, candy and drink sales. Some early drive-ins employed car hops to peddle food and drink. Now they run teasers on the screen, urging the patrons to come and get it, cafeteria style. They sell more over the counter, and sell fast. [...]

The drive-in boom is definitely a post-war phenomenon. In the past decade the number of drive-ins has leaped from 500 to almost 5000. During that time, the price tag on a 1000-car ozoner increased, depending on the cost of fifteen to fifty acres of pasture on a major highway near a center of population, from $50,000 to $500,000. The drive-in operators, most of them enterprisers easing their way into a fantastic new business, have accumulated a lot of lore on the habits of their patrons.

Instead of improvising, as the drive-in pioneers had to do, operators now can order their drive-in complete, except for land and ramps, from the Radio Corporation of America, which has come by a major stake in the business more or less by accident. RCA makes the bulk of the projectors, speakers, and even screens for the new open-air theaters. Another source is National Theater Supply. RCA even offers a drive-in package deal, including financing, to good prospects who have fifteen or more acres on a highway near a population center.

This makes a nice chunk of business. An average modern 1000-car drive-in is a $250,000 investment, including some $65,000 to $70,000 worth of electrical equipment, and a $25,000 metal screen that a 50-mile wind can't topple. It includes also a $45,000 refreshment building, and $25,000 worth of cafeteria equipment, all-important because up to 40 per cent of a successful drive-in's income is from the sale of food and soft drinks. A sizable drive-in has an annual gross income of $750,000. [...]

While the tall-talking Texans can boast that they have the most drive-ins, the Californians and the Floridians have been able to claim the poshest ozoners, at least until recently. In Southern California, where dependable weather makes drive-in cinemas an all-year-around entertainment business, the operators have prided themselves on their landscaping and architectural designing. At best, drive-ins are anything but beautiful in the daytime, although at night the soft lights, the color on the screen, the stars above, and the neon entrances give them a certain eerie glamour. During the past two or three years, eastern operators, particularly in New Jersey and New York and other northern states, have invested sizable sums of money on landscaping, on the theory that it is in the daytime that Mrs. Housewife decides whether or not she would like to go to the movies, and which one she would like to see that night.

In recent years, many of the larger drive-ins have merged into chains. Scores of independent owners have turned their drive-ins over to chains to operate. The giant among the chains is Pacific-Drive-In Theaters, which has 38 major outdoor cinemas in and around Los Angeles, which is the drive-in hotbed of the country. Pacific-Drive-In is unique in another respect: it was bought by four veteran Hollywood movie tycoons who sensed the phenomenal potential of the outdoor cinema in time to capture the lion's share of the good sites for super drive-ins in the area. This has given Pacific an advantage enjoyed by drive-ins of no other area. Because of its mass coverage, Pacific can outbid the hardtops for first runs of big pictures, and frequently does so. Often half a dozen of Pacific's drive-ins will kick off a première simultaneously with two or three of the downtown Los Angeles and Hollywood movie palaces.

Whether or not this is worth while, except to prove that drive-ins are no longer the orphans of the movie industry, is a moot question. First-run pictures are rented by the exchanges on a bid basis which may give the distributor up to 70 per cent of the gate take, plus a flat minimum guarantee, leaving the drive-in operator less than a third. If he waits for a second run, the operator may keep up to two-thirds of the gate, the distributor one-third. Outside Southern California, drive-in operators have taken the attitude that they don't need first-run pictures to fill their ramps; second-runs will do just as well, because families are coming out for an evening anyway, so why not wait for a better break on the take?

In the East and Midwest, the drive-in chains have spread risks, weatherwise especially, by scattering their operations over large areas. The Loew chain operates twenty-six drive-ins extending from Connecticut to Florida. Smith Management Company of Boston has drive-ins throughout New England and the Middle Atlantic states and the Midwest, including the 2600-car Timonium, outside Baltimore. The whopper of all drive-ins, the 3000-car Troy, near Detroit, is in the Affiliated Theaters group. This giant is regarded as about as large as ozoners can be built, partly because of traffic problems, partly because of the distance from the screen to the back ramp. But the trend generally is toward larger drive-ins. There are now seventy in the country with a capacity of 1000 cars or more, including several that can accommodate more than 2000 cars. The latter have a greater seating capacity than Radio City Music Hall, the country's largest four-wall motion-picture palace.

Ever since the drive-ins began to flourish, Hollywood's most agile minds have been trying to figure out what type of cinema appeals most to outdoor movie fans. The answer seems to be action pictures in color. Color is all-important, because color pictures can be seen distinctly on the screen half an hour earlier than black and white. "Critic pictures don't pull in drive-in customers," one operator explained. "Drive-in movie fans like westerns, or any picture with action that fits into the holiday mood." [...]

The motion-picture industry now accepts the drive-in as "a phase of American life based on the decentralization of cities, along with supermarkets, shopping centers, and Levittowns," as one studio executive, David Lipton, of Universal-International Pictures, puts it. "The shift in population caused a shift in theaters. One modern drive-in takes the place of four little old-style neighborhood theaters. It is a phenomenon of the motor age, here to stay, so we might as well like it."

42

Free Lances (1929)

Alexander Bakshy

Standardized mass production on a world scale has made Hollywood the dominating force in the world of cinema. Thanks to Hollywood the making of motion pictures has become an industry, and though we may not rejoice in this fact as much as some of our friends in Russia seem to, we must admit that it is in accord with all modern developments; if we have machine-made and standardized homes, clothes, food, newspapers, and radios, why not also movies? Moreover, Hollywood satisfies a certain social need by providing its entertainment in quantities and qualities which are demanded by the countless numbers of its consumers, and which could not be supplied except by an organized industry.

On the other hand, of course, there are the obvious drawbacks of industrial standardization: banned is artistic and intellectual culture; banned, independence of outlook and originality of treatment. The resultant product is inevitably bilge, no matter how glorified or how skilfully decked out in borrowed plumes of a vulgarized and usually outlived artistic fashion.

Thus, among people who resent the effects of Hollywood, there has grown up a demand for motion pictures of a superior artistic and intellectual appeal. In America the first attempt to satisfy this demand came with a series of Sunday showings organized by the Film Arts Guild in 1925. This was followed by the establishment of permanent picture houses in New York such as the Fifth Avenue, the Fifty-fifth Street, the St. George's in Brooklyn, the Little Carnegie, and the latest of them all, the Film Guild Cinema, besides a number of other similar little picture houses in other parts of the country. The movement is undoubtedly showing signs of rapid progress. But though numerical growth is an important factor in the situation, the success of the movement will largely depend on the artistic policy pursued by its sponsors. In this respect, it must be admitted, not everything is as well as it should be. The little cinema houses certainly deserve every credit for introducing to this country a number of foreign pictures of outstanding merit. They popularized "The Cabinet of Dr. Caligari," "Ballet Mécanique," "Potemkin"; and, more recently, "The Symphony of Berlin," "Thérèse Raquin," "Ivan the Terrible," "The End of St. Petersburg," and "Ten Days That Shook the World." But side by side with these truly remarkable achievements of cinematic art the little theaters have also tried to foist on the public as genuine masterpieces works puerile and utterly inept.

There is so much that can be done by these experimental theaters in the way of real artistic leadership that one is apt to grow impatient with the lack of vision displayed by the majority of them. An agreeable exception is the Film Guild Cinema, whose director, Symon Gould, showed commendable daring

Excerpted from Alexander Bakshy, "Free Lances." *Nation* 128 (March 13, 1929), 324–5.

in selecting Frederick Kiesler for his architect. At present it is still too early to pass an opinion on the most original part of Mr. Kiesler's design – his use of side-walls for additional projection – for the installation of this feature has not yet been completed. But the very attempt to build "a 100 percent cinema house," whether successfully realized or not, is of tremendous importance. From now on no picture house making any claim to distinction will be able to content itself with copying the popular, essentially stagy, designs of today. It will have to tackle the aesthetic problem of the screen as an architectural feature – one of the most important in the art of motion picture – and for raising this problem, as well as for many other interesting innovations, Mr. Kiesler and Mr. Gould deserve the gratitude of all believers in cinematic progress. [...]

Cover for Surrealist and Fantastic Film Festival at 5th Avenue Playhouse (1941)
The programs (1941–2)

1 *The Blood of a Poet* (Cocteau)
   Lot in Sodom (Watson and Webber)
   Object Lesson (Young)
   Carmen (featuring Chaplin)
2 *Adventures of Prince Achmed* (Reiniger)
   The Blue Light (Balacz)
3 *The Robber Symphony* (Feher)
   Fall of the House of Usher (Watson and Webber)
   Joy of Living (Hoppin and Gross)
   Emak Bakia (Man Ray)
   Modern Inventions (Disney)
4 *The Living Dead* (Oswald)
   Vampire (Dreyer)

43

Sure-Seaters Discover an Audience (1952)

Stanley Frank

In the past two years several hundred theater owners, who are not in the entertainment business for their own amusement, seem to have gone to a good deal of trouble to alienate their affection for money. They have built new movie houses, or renovated old ones extensively, blandly ignoring gloomy predictions that the industry is withering on the vine. Even more rashly, they have introduced a policy of showing only "good," highbrow films, flouting H.L. Mencken's dour observation that "no one ever went broke underestimating the taste of the American public."

These theaters are known in the trade as "art" houses or "sure-seaters," and represent the most encouraging trend in the movies since television aerials began to cast menacing shadows over box offices. A sure-seater is a small theater – 300 to 750 capacity – that specializes in showing mature, sophisticated foreign and domestic pictures. The definition has undergone a radical change of interpretation lately. Hollywood wits once said the sure-seater was aptly named because a patron always was sure to get a seat. The gag has fallen flat because, with the proper attraction, every seat in a sure-seater is pretty sure to be filled.

There are 470 sure-seaters in the United States today, about twice as many as there were two years ago when exhibitors began to blame television, the recession and the sticky international situation for the sharp slump in attendance. In addition, there are 1,500 other theaters that are booking a steadily increasing ratio of art pictures in preference to run-of-the-mill Hollywood products. These outlets account for a small percentage – no more than one twentieth – of the total business done by the country's 19,000 movie houses, but they are exerting an influence on traditional Hollywood attitudes and distribution methods out of all proportion to their immediate impact on the box office.

Pictures treating sensitive themes and social problems realistically always were regarded by Hollywood as well intentioned, but, none the less foolish, invitations to deficits. Companies that tried to raise the cultural level of the cinema invariably were swamped with red ink in the backwash of public indifference. The boom sure-seaters are enjoying, however, is leading some executives in the industry to believe that serious pictures can be:

1. A source of important income if they are properly introduced and built up in prestige by first-run releases in sure-seaters;
2. Made on low budgets in this country, although production costs are two to five times greater than they are in England, France and Italy, heretofore the chief suppliers of art pictures;

Excerpted from Stanley Frank, "Sure-Seaters Discover an Audience." *Nation's Business* 40 (January 1952), 34–6, 69.

3. Instrumental in recapturing the "lost audience."

The lost audience is to Hollywood what the morality of the younger generation is to educators and the state of the union is to deep thinkers. It is a handy springboard for viewing with alarm. In his book, "The Great Audience," Gilbert Seldes made a statement to the effect that hardly anyone past 40 ever goes to the movies. This sweeping generalization is: (a) manifestly exaggerated, as a quick look at the audience in a sure-seater will demonstrate; (b) hardly a startling revelation.

The movies, like all mass entertainments – sports, radio, television, popular music, dancing – largely are supported by young folks.

As we grow older, most of us become more discriminating – and smarter. We seek relaxation in ease rather than excitement. [...]

It can be argued that if the public wanted "good" pictures it could have had them long ago by the simple expedient of supporting such films at the box office. Critics who took a dim view of the mass American audience's intelligence have been forced to revise that estimate as a result of some startling developments in the past two years.

Sir Laurence Olivier's British-made "Hamlet," a highbrow offering if ever there was one, played in 30 RKO theaters in New York in February, 1950, on a Monday and Tuesday, the worst days of the week. It grossed $250,000, an all-time high on the circuit for those two days. "Red Shoes," a pure fantasy expressed in ballet, has grossed $5,000,000 with more than half its potential outlets still to go.

Three pictures with Italian dialogue and English subtitles – "The Bicycle Thief," "Open City" and "Bitter Rice" – were released in 8,000 theaters and showed profits. "Devil and the Flesh," a French film, cleared $260,000 during a 36-week run in one sure-seater, the Paris in New York. The Sutton Theater, also in New York, is easily the most successful movie house in America in relation to seats – 550 – and profits. Its art

pictures, usually British, run longer than six months on the average. One of the big money-makers last summer was a remake of that venerable costume piece, "Cyrano de Bergerac."

Those pictures were made in four countries and three languages. (Four languages, if you include theatrical British, which sometimes requires subtitles for comprehension by American audiences.) The pictures ranged in appeal from a soaring classic ("Hamlet") to a stark incident in the life of a laborer ("The Bicycle Thief"). Only two of the films boasted a star whose name on the marquee meant anything in this country. The pictures had only one thing in common. All were first presented in sure-seaters.

Several of the pictures unquestionably could have been booked into the 6,000-seat Radio City Music Hall in New York, the No. 1 showcase of the industry. A few years ago distributors were cutting their own, and competitors', throats to get into the Music Hall. Today, they are by-passing it and other palaces and releasing their products in theaters that have one tenth the capacity. Why? It's a better financial deal for the long haul.

Launching a feature picture in a downtown palace in any city is an expensive proposition. Advertising, publicity and exploitation costs are at least $7,000. That figure can go as high as $40,000 for a Broadway opening if the distributor wants to impress exhibitors throughout the country. If the theater is part of a chain, as most first-run houses are, its own and the home office's overhead add another $7,000 a week before the doors are opened. The picture runs one week, two at the most, and then the expensive, laborious process starts all over again.

The economics of a sure-seater are much simpler. Elaborate advertising and promotion campaigns are unnecessary because the theater has a steady clientele and can't handle big crowds anyway. A sure-seater is splurging if it spends $4,000 on a new picture. The gimmick, however, is that this cost drops to a few hundred dollars a week for modest newspaper ads after the picture has been introduced. The independent sure-seater exhibitor can afford to give the distributor a larger share of the gross receipts than a chain operator because his rent and overhead are low and promotion-wise he is riding on velvet after the first week.

Extended runs are the keys to a sure-seater's success. The longer a picture plays, the less expensive it is to keep it before the public. By reducing costs to the bone, it is possible to make more money with a picture that starts off grossing $6,000 a week and gradually goes down to $2,000 weekly in a sure-seater than it is with a picture that takes in $20,000 in a big house in one week, then goes off the boards.

"That's only part of the story," says Max Youngstein, national director of advertising and publicity for United Artists. "The sure-seater gives word-of-mouth publicity, which really sells movies, a chance to catch up with the merits of a picture.

"The average movie opens on a Thursday to catch favorable reviews and comment for the big week-end trade. Business invariably falls off on Monday and continues slow the rest of the week, so the audience is hypoed with a new attraction the next Thursday. The picture goes into the neighborhood circuits with only three good days of build-up behind it and plays there another four, five days. Then it goes into the cheap 'grind' houses and in six months it's dead.

"Compare that to the steady prestige a picture builds in a sure-seater. The capacity is so small that the audience is spread over a period of two or three weeks. In big metropolitan centers it may play for several months. The Sutton Theater has shown pictures for as long as nine months. All right. People keep on talking about the picture and small ads continue to appear in the papers, stimulating interest among the mass audience for release on the circuits, where the juicy profits are made.

"Sure-seaters never have been exploited properly because the major studios still stick to distribution methods that have ruined more than one fine picture. MGM's 'Intruder in the Dust' is cited as a classic example of a great picture that flopped. Sure it did, because it opened in a Broadway house that featured Westerns, confusing the theater's regular clientele. Had it gone into a sure-seater and acquired the word-of-mouth praise it deserved, it wouldn't be remembered as an artistic triumph and a commercial failure.

"Sure-seaters are not the answer to all the movies' headaches. All I claim is that they can keep the movie-going habit alive among mature people and, at the same time, pipe down untrue cultural criticism that hurts the industry's public relations. The essential job of a producer, one that should occupy 95 per cent of his attention, is to give people what they want in the best possible taste. The remaining five per cent of his effort should be devoted to raising artistic standards. The sure-seater encourages such attempts by reducing the element of financial risk.

"Many art pictures have failed because they were dull. They didn't have to be. 'Hamlet' and 'Henry the Fifth' were straight Shakespeare, but they were as exciting as a cops-and-robbers chase."

Time was when sure-seaters depended exclusively on foreign studios for their attractions, giving rise to the myth that Hollywood was far inferior to the European masters. The truth is that only one or two percent of all pictures made abroad ever see the light of day in this country. The rest can't be shown here for fear the customers will tear up the seats. It was not by design that sure-seaters formerly showed "The Cabinet of Dr. Caligari" three times a year or brought back repeatedly "by popular demand" such gems as "Pygmalion" and "Mayerling." There were not enough new art pictures available to supply the demand.

Foreign production costs were so low that a few small European companies could afford to make an occasional picture with limited appeal. American studios, saddled with high overheads, had to beam their products to the mass audience. That idea was thrown out of the window by Stanley Kramer, the latest boy wonder of the industry who demonstrated with "Champion" and "Home of the Brave," that fine films could be made on low budgets in Hollywood.

Each picture was produced for $400,000, an unheard of figure in this day, and cleared a combined profit of $1,000,000. Kramer didn't hit the jackpot in sure-seaters, of course. There is a pretty rigid formula that governs movie profits. A picture must do 1.9 times the cost of production and negatives distributed to exhibitors before it breaks even. Kramer, therefore, had to gross $760,000 on each picture before he was off the hook and that kind of money can be made only on the big circuits. The attention the pictures stirred up in the sure-seaters paved the way for a general release which otherwise might not have been given Kramer.

Kramer didn't use high-salaried stars, fancy sets or color, which can add $600,000 to the over-all cost of a picture. He merely followed an old maxim of the theater – the play's the thing. Kramer's themes were engrossing, handled realistically and people came a-running.

The sure-seater has a subtle snob appeal that helps at the box office. You go into a theater that has a few tasteful paintings in the lobby and a maid serves you a demitasse of coffee. You've just paid top admission prices, but the coffee creates a pleasant aura. Then you're shown to a comfortable seat in a well mannered audience.

The show lasts two hours; there is no Class C horror or murder mishmash to pad out a double-feature program. You see a picture that assumes you have average intelligence and it's such a refreshing switch that you are flattered to be among such perceptive folks who are sharing the experience.

The brisk sure-seater business suggests that the market for truly worth-while movies is expanding steadily. Maybe, to paraphrase Mencken, no one will go broke crediting the American public with good taste.

44

Some Considerations on the Rise of the Art-Film Theater (1956)

John E. Twomey

Roger Manvell, in his new book *The Film and the Public*, gives a penetrating analysis of the important question of film art *vs.* film commercial. Judging the film in relation to the other media of mass communication, Manvell notes a situation peculiar to the cinema which he feels has inhibited its artistic growth. He writes:

> There is still, after fifty years, almost no specialization in the presentation of cinema entertainment, at least as far as the English-speaking film is concerned. If a picture is to be financially successful, whether it be comedy, satire, melodrama, or tragedy, Western or musical, slapstick, or fantasy, it must pass through the same routine of exhibition. This is very different from the conditions which affect the production of printed publications, broadcasting (in Britain), and even the "live" theatre; in all of these different tastes are deliberately fostered and specialization in kinds and grades of entertainment and information is the very essence of the policy of production. The only specialized form of provision in the cinema occurs in the newsreel theatres and particularly in the few cinemas which screen foreign-language films, and in privately organized film societies.[1]

Evidence generally bears out Manvell's views, but the postwar increase in art theaters ("specialized cinemas" in Britain), film societies, and the nontheatrical distribution of film has encouraged those who feel a need for more "artistic" motion pictures. Many art-film patrons see a renaissance in American movie tastes in the initial successes of many newly established art-film theaters and in the influence of art films on Hollywood picture standards.[2]

An important aspect of the growth of the art film has been its increasing appearance on American screens at the same time that television has been creating Hollywood's greatest economic crisis. From 1948 through 1954, the regular movie-house attendance declined some forty million.[3] During this period, theater closures were hitting an all-time high; and exhibitors, in order to stay solvent, came to rely on the innovations of 3-D, drive-in theaters, popcorn concessions, and movies made by the various wide-screen techniques. Some exhibitors began seeking out films of quality to show in small intimate theaters under the title of "adult entertainment" or "art."

Today, there are 226 motion-picture theaters devoting their entire screening time to films from other countries, reissues of old-time Hollywood "classics," documentaries, and independently made films on off-beat themes.[4] This figure does not include those theaters located in foreign-language neighborhoods which show foreign films unsubtitled.[5] Another 400 theaters are run on a part-time art-film basis. Art-film theaters are found primarily in large metropolitan areas and in college and university communities. These theaters represent only an infinitesimal part of the 15,029 permanent four-walled motion-picture theaters in the United States, and are found in only seventy communities. Nevertheless, they represent a distinct change in motion-picture appetites in America.

It is difficult to explain the significance of the emergence of the art-film theaters, their audiences, and what meaning these theaters have. This difficulty stems primarily from the dual nature of the motion picture. Created as a commercial product, the film is an economic unit governed by the practices of our capitalistic economy. On the other hand, and seemingly in conflict with its economic nature, a motion picture is the creation of artists. A third element, public taste, must also be considered in any analysis of the popularity of a film or film type. Roger Manvell relates these three factors when he states:

> Every picture is a gamble in public taste, and investment in an artist's ideas is the risk which the company always has to take. Even the formula picture is a risk, because the mere mixture of popular themes and actors may not finally combine into a film which makes the money flow back. Every film is a unique event, a unique voyage into the difficult, shifty seas of popular taste.[6]

Of the many factors that have contributed to the building of American audiences interested in art films, the establishment of film libraries and the study of film appreciation in colleges and universities have been important. Chief among film libraries is the Museum of Modern Art, which was begun in 1935, and now contains prints of most of the outstanding foreign motion pictures, American classics, and films of historic value. Maintaining an extensive lending service, the Museum has been a prime mover behind the serious study of the film in American universities.

The widespread wartime use of documentary film – a type of motion picture greatly neglected in the United States because of its presumably small commercial value – helped create audience interest in new film themes and techniques. Of the many 16-mm. movie societies to emerge, the most successful has been "Cinema 16," an educational, nonprofit organization which was incorporated in New York City in 1947. The reason for its organization and subsequent success – it grew from a membership of less than 100 to over 6,000 – must be sought in relation to the type of film it has presented. In the words of its founder,

> Cinema 16 offers films that comment on the state of man, his world and his crises, either by means of realistic documentation or through experimental techniques. It "glorifies" nonfiction....It hails a film that is a work of art, but will not hesitate to present a film that is important only because of its subject matter. Its avant-garde films comment on the tensions and psychological insecurity of modern existence or are significant expressions of modern art. Its social documentaries stimulate rather than stifle discussion and controversy.[7]

Elimination of the former monopolistic trade practices of large film producers and distributors also played an important role in preparing the way for the postwar successes of the art film. In the 1940s, a series of federal court decisions stopped such trade practices as blind-buying and block-booking which had long maintained a strangle hold on motion-picture exhibitors throughout the United States. Greater freedom for exhibitors in the selection of films was one result of these court decrees. Some exhibitors used this opportunity to rent foreign or independently made motion pictures, especially when Hollywood film production dropped drastically following the court rulings.

Essentially, postwar films from abroad stimulated the growing interest in motion pictures which did not follow the usual Hollywood formulae. Although the screening of foreign productions in the United States was not a new development, certain events in the postwar period promoted greater acceptance of these films as well as a new popularity among American moviegoers.[8] [...]

Two events are largely responsible for the foreign film's quick gain of a faithful and expanding audience in the United States: J. Arthur Rank's ability to have his prestige pictures distributed here and the screening of Italy's *Open City* in New York and later throughout the country. This one Italian picture gained such widespread publicity and mass audiences that its influence on the subsequent popular reception of postwar films from abroad cannot be underestimated.

Roberto Rosselini produced and directed *Open City* in Rome in 1945. He spent less than $18,000 on the picture, used no professional actors or formal working script, and filmed the movie on outdated negative film. But the finished product earned a million dollars in the United States, initiated a Neo-Realistic Italian film era, and created an avid audience for foreign films.

There is no doubt that *Open City* has been an overwhelming success. Similarly, a popular demand did arise, and has continued, for such succeeding Italian films as *Paisan*, *Shoe-Shine*, *Angelina*, and *The Bicycle Thief*. But there is doubt about the reasons for both. Some believe the answer has to do with the growth of American audiences with more mature and sophisticated film interests. Other observers point out that these films have been advertised and exploited as "exotic" motion pictures and that herein lies the clue to their popularity. Arthur Mayer, the man who handled the American distribution and exhibition of *Open City* states frankly:

"Open City" was generally advertised with a misquotation from *Life* adjusted to read: "Sexier than Hollywood ever dared to be," together with a still of two young ladies deeply engrossed in a rapt embrace, and another of a man being flogged, designed to tap the sadist trade. The most publicized scene in "Paisan" showed a young lady disrobing herself with an attentive male visitor reclining by her side on what was obviously not a nuptial couch. "The Bicycle Thief" was completely devoid of any erotic embellishments, but the exhibitors sought to atone for this deficiency with a highly imaginative sketch of a young lady riding a bicycle.[9]

Mayer's disclosures offer important considerations but are by no means a final judgment on the reasons behind the postwar success of foreign films. His comments do, however, further complicate the search for the cultural meaning of the emergence of the art film in the United States.

We know that the potential for the popular reception of quality films has existed for some time. Whether or not the limits of this potential have been reached in the existing art-film audiences remains to be seen. We know too that a series of interrelated social and economic events have provided the means of presenting to discriminating audiences films of artistic quality.

Reiterating the essential facts of the economic aspects of the art film, Arthur Mayer admonishes those of us who praise the newfound popularity of art films solely in the light of artistic taste. He writes:

Those of us who ... realize the necessity for such outposts of culture would be of greater service to our cause if we talked less glowingly about the progress of the art houses and sought more zealously to understand the nature of their current status.

Their problems are many. The two primary difficulties, however, consist of a scarcity of pictures and of patrons ... And until we have art theaters in the Fargos as well as in New York and Pittsburgh the movement will never be built on a solid national foundation.

. . . .

Neither of the ancient bogeys – Hollywood moguls or inflexible exhibitors – stand in the way. All that is necessary is for the intellectuals to stop paying lip service to the better cinema and to start paying admission. When they do so the exciting thing about American movies will be, not how much wider they are, but how much better.[10]

At least, Mayer and many others in the motion-picture business have acknowledged that the art theater is a commercially as well as artistically established institution. No longer is the art film a delicacy for the palates of a few connoisseurs. Mayer's views serve as a reminder that, as the art film emerges from the small screening rooms of a few specialized film societies and art-film theaters and reaches for a mass audience, a greater understanding of both its peculiar appeal and its potential market becomes essential.

Notes

1   (Harmondsworth, England: Penguin Books Ltd., 1955), 187–188.
2   Although the old formulas still prevail in Hollywood, there has been a marked increase in experimentation, the use of new themes, the use of foreign actors, locations and story content, and, most important, a tendency toward realism which can be said to be in some degree influenced by the success of art films in the United States.
3   *The Film Daily Year Book* (New York: The Film Daily, 1955), 141.
4   Ibid., 143.
5   The great majority of these films are never seen in art-film theaters. They are principally shown without subtitles in foreign-language neighborhoods. Very few of the 43 films imported from Mexico last year were shown outside of the Southwest or the Spanish-speaking neighborhoods in large urban centers.
6   Manvell, *op. cit.*, 189.
7   Amos Vogel, "Cinema 16," *Hollywood Quarterly*, IV (Summer, 1950), 420.
8   The importation of films from abroad began as a successful commercial venture in the early twenties. Joseph Burstyn and Arthur Mayer of New York and Abraham Teitel of Chicago were pioneers in this field. Abe Teitel was one of the first to make personal trips to Germany and Russia in the early twenties to bring home to special audiences the films of quality being produced at that time. Among the few art theaters established before the postwar boom was Teitel's World Playhouse, which opened at the time of the Chicago World's Fair in 1933.
9   *Merely Colossal* (New York: Simon and Schuster, 1953), 233.
10 "Hollywood Verdict: Gilt But Not Guilty," *Saturday Review* (Oct. 31, 1953), 44–47.

Film schedules for New York City repertory cinemas, Wednesday, June 24 to Tuesday, June 30, 1981

St. Mark's

Wednesday–Thursday	*La Cage aux Folles II* (France 1981)
	The Stunt Man (USA 1980)
Friday–Tuesday	*Tess* (Great Britain 1980)
Friday–Saturday midnight	*Rockers* (Jamaica 1978)

Theatre 80

Wednesday	*The Blood of a Poet* (France 1930)
	L'affaire est dans le sac (France 1932)
	Zero for Conduct (France 1933)
Thursday	*Charlie Chan on Broadway* (USA 1937)
	Charlie Chan at Monte Carlo (USA 1937)
Friday	*Rebecca* (USA 1940)
	Spiral Staircase (USA 1946)
Saturday–Sunday	*A Night at the Opera* (USA 1935)
	A Day at the Races (USA 1937)
Monday	*Night Nurse* (USA 1931)
	The Purchase Price (USA 1932)

Bleeker Street

Wednesday	*McCabe and Mrs. Miller* (USA 1971)
	Thieves Like Us (USA 1974)
Thursday	*Masculin Féminin* (France 1966)
	Band of Outsiders (France 1964)
Friday	*Wise Blood* (USA 1979)
	Blow-Up (Great Britain 1966)
	Ladies and Gentlemen, The Rolling Stones (USA 1973)
Saturday	*Children of Paradise* (France 1944)
Sunday	*Quadrophenia* (Great Britain 1979)
Monday	*Sworn Brothers* (Japan 1969)
	Life and Opinion of Zatoichi (Japan 1962)

Cinema Village

Wednesday–Thursday	*1900* (Italy 1976)
Friday–Saturday	*Taxi Driver* (USA 1976)
	New York, New York (USA 1977)
Sunday–Tuesday	*Incredible Shrinking Woman* (USA 1981)
	Incredible Shrinking Man (USA 1957)

Eighth Street

Wednesday–Tuesday	*House of Wax* (in 3-D) (USA 1953)
Wednesday midnight	*Fritz the Cat* (USA 1972)
Thursday midnight	*The Harder They Come* (Jamaica 1972)
Friday–Saturday midnight	*Rocky Horror Picture Show* (Great Britain 1976)
Sunday midnight	*A Clockwork Orange* (Great Britain 1971)
Monday midnight	*Female Trouble* (USA 1974)

Harold Clurman Theatre: Series of Rock 'n' Roll Movies

Wednesday–Thursday	*American Hot Wax* (USA 1978)
	Roadie (USA 1980)
Friday–Saturday	*The Kids are Alright* (Great Britain 1979)

Sunday	*Tommy* (USA 1975)
Monday–Tuesday	*The Grateful Dead* (USA 1977)
	Wild in the Streets (USA 1968)
	Rock 'n' Roll High School (USA 1979)

Regency Murder Mystery Series

Wednesday	*Get Carter* (Great Britain 1971)
	Dirty Harry (USA 1971)
Thursday–Saturday	*Private Life of Sherlock Holmes* (USA 1970)
	Murder on the Orient Express (USA 1974)
Sunday–Tuesday	*Out of the Past* (USA 1947)
	They Won't Believe Me (USA 1947)

Thalia

Wednesday	*Singin' in the Rain* (USA 1952)
	The Band Wagon (USA 1953)
Thursday	*Baby Face* (USA 1933)
	Juke Girl (USA 1942)
Friday–Saturday	*High Heels* (France 1972)
	Dandy, the All-American Girl (USA 1977)
Sunday	*Magic Flute* (Sweden 1973)
	Beethoven (France 1936)
Monday	*Apocalypse Now* (USA 1979)
Tuesday	*Exterminating Angel* (Mexico 1962)
	Nazarin (Mexico 1958)

Carnegie Hall Cinema

Wednesday–Thursday	*Days of Heaven* (USA 1978)
	Pretty Baby (USA 1978)
Friday–Sunday	*Numéro Deux* (France 1975)
Monday–Tuesday	*Dr. Strangelove* (USA 1964)
	Casino Royale (USA 1967)

Mini Cinema

Wednesday	*Cat on a Hot Tin Roof* (USA 1958)
	Conspirator (USA 1949)
Tuesday–Saturday	*How to Marry a Millionaire* (USA 1953)
	Gentlemen Prefer Blondes (USA 1953)
Sunday–Tuesday	*The Lady Vanishes* (Great Britain 1938)
	The 39 Steps (Great Britain 1938)

Hollywood Twin I

Wednesday–Saturday	*The Young Lions* (USA 1958)
	The Men (USA 1950)
Sunday–Tuesday	*Old Acquaintance* (USA 1943)
	Harriet Craig (USA 1950)

Hollywood Twin II

Wednesday–Saturday	*A Boy and His Dog* (USA 1975)
	Dark Star (USA 1974)
Sunday–Tuesday	*A Face in the Crowd* (USA 1957)
	On the Waterfront (USA 1954)

45

Domestic Theatrical and Semi-Theatrical Distribution and Exhibition of American Independent Feature Films: A Survey in 1983

Betsy McLane

In the past five years, American independent features have been widely heralded as our cinema's best hope for personal artistic expression. From John Sayles' well-publicized odyssey through *The Return of the Secaucus Seven*, Hollywood hackdom, and *Baby It's You*, to the feature documentary travails of Connie Field with *The Life and Times of Rosie the Riveter*, from Barbara Kopple's *Harlan County U.S.A.* to John Lowenthal's *The Trials of Alger Hiss*, new "serious" independents seem to surface monthly. Along with the rising number of people turning their talents to making "small," "personal," or "regional" films, there is a select, but growing, audience for movies made outside the Hollywood tradition. Still miniscule compared to the audience for an *E.T.* or *Tootsie*, this theatrical and semitheatrical market is increasingly important, and its importance is being recognized. There is still by no means a smooth or well-marked road for American independent production. Perhaps the way of independent creation should by definition be rocky. Likewise, there is no one reliable method for independent films to reach their potential audience. Distribution and exhibition methods have yet to fully define and develop the audience for independent product, but

prospects are more promising than ever before. [...]

Features like Dennis Hopper's *Out of the Blue*, Susan Seidelman's *Smithereens*, or even Paul Bartel's *Eating Raoul* may never make it to Paducah, Kentucky, or Poland Spring, Maine, despite the fact that they have played to admiring audiences at festivals around the world and at theaters in New York and Los Angeles. Exhibition of American independent films has historically been centered only in the major cities, specifically in New York, with perhaps a nod in the direction of Boston, Chicago, Los Angeles. Only the culturally advantaged city dweller could be counted on to support non-Hollywood movies. This situation is changing somewhat as the specialized segment of the moviegoing public that patronizes a diversified lineup of films makes its presence known. Of the 5,000 theaters not affiliated with a major chain, around 400 play specialized and art films. The greatest number of these are still in the major urban areas, but they now exist in urban America from Florida to Colorado. Places as diverse at Montpelier, Vermont, and Eugene, Oregon, manage to support fulltime repertory and/or art houses.

Excerpted from Betsy McLane, "Domestic Theatrical and Semi-Theatrical Distribution and Exhibition of American Independent Feature Films: A Survey in 1983." *Journal of the University Film and Video Association* 35, no. 2 (Spring 1983), 17–24.

New York is still the key city, and although it's more difficult and more expensive to open a film there than anywhere else in the United States (because of high advertising costs, exorbitant theater overhead, inaccessibility of critics), it still offers the greatest variety of venues. With a tradition of showing modern independents that can be traced back to the fact that European art house films arrived on the East Coast and often never made it West of the Hudson River, New York remains the most eclectic and adventurous movie-watching city in America. Along with the multitude of regular commercial theaters which sometimes program independents, there are revival houses like the Thalia, the Regency, the Bleeker Street, and the Hollywood Twin. More important to the life of independent films are the showcases like Dan Talbot's New Yorker (aligned with his New Yorker Films), Joseph Papp's Public Theatre, and especially the Film Forum. The Film Forum, under the direction of Karen Cooper, is one of the most avant garde feature theaters in the country. It practices an aggressive policy of showing the best of new foreign and American cinema.

The Film Forum is unique in that it programs new films almost exclusively. Other theaters around the country that regularly run American independents usually also rely heavily on foreign classics, Hollywood revivals, midnight cult movies, and standard Hollywood releases to draw audiences. Multiple theater operations like the Nickelodeon chain in New England, Laemmle Theatres in Los Angeles, the Biograph in Washington, DC, and Landmark Theatres, located primarily in the West, provide the most substantial commercial markets for American independents. Along with their visibility among moviegoers, they maintain standing relationships with the key distributors of independents. Single theater operations, which also tend to offer a mix of non-mainstream films, are sometimes even more adventurous in programming than the chains. Theaters such as The Walnut Street in Philadelphia, and Long Island's Community Cinema are generally programmed at the discretion of one or two devoted and knowledgable film fanatics. They tend to reflect a more personal sensibility along with responsibility to the cultural needs of the community and an eye to box-office receipts. Of course, they offer smaller returns to distributors and producers, since in most cases they book pictures for one or two nights rather than for week-long runs. They also lack the promotional power of the chains, although in individual markets they may have dedicated followings.

Building such a following is key to the growth of a larger market for American independents. Outside the major cities, specialty cinemas have survived chiefly in college town enclaves where adventurousome audiences are built-in fixtures. For almost any audience, independent features require individual promotional handling. There is no ready-made Hollywood star hook or special effects to attract people. The films need to be sold on specialized bases to targeted regional audiences. So along with standard media advertising, both chains and single theater operations often rely on printed schedules to publicize their offerings. In many ways these handbills, available at the theaters, and often at their locations or through the mail to regular patrons, are more important and cost effective than advertising in newspaper, radio and television. A month-long listing of screenings helps to build interest and that all-important word of mouth. As people decide to plan their moviegoing activity days in advance, the pattern of theater attendance shifts dramatically from spur of the moment or Saturday night date filmgoing. This pre-planning in part reflects the growth of a more sophisticated film public.

Grouping a series of pictures on one page tends to transfer aesthetic credibility and audience interest from one to another. This technique of cluster promotion has not been lost on UA Classics, which now advertises a batch of currently released films in a single newspaper or magazine block, no matter where they may be showing. The older art house distributors have used this approach for years in film periodicals, depending on the name of Janus or New Yorker to sell a selection of films. Creating a strong corporate image for both distributor and exhibitor through such localized advertising makes a great deal of sense when trying to reach a specialized audience. It has proven to work well for such diverse houses as the Newart in Los Angeles, which serves a diversified media-land clientele of millions, to the Savoy in Montpelier, the tiny isolated capital of Vermont. It is a technique that could well be exploited further by distributors.

Regular direct mail publicity is one of the most effective audience targeting techniques for another branch of exhibitors of American independent, museum and gallery type screens. The majority of these are devoted principally to independents, who are less in the mainstream of narrative film than the feature makers discussed so far. Focusing on experimental film and video, short and feature documentaries, films about art, as well as some fictional features, places like the Anthology Film Archive, The Whitney Museum, and The Kitchen in New York; The Walker Art Center in Minneapolis/St. Paul; the Hirschhorn Museum In Washington, DC; and the Pacific Film Archive in Berkeley program audacious mixtures of traditional and vanguard media. Most of these organizations are non-profit and are concerned with properly showcasing the work of "artists." Audiences expect something out of the ordinary when they patronize these theaters. Film makers gain a great deal of prestige from such screenings, and they serve to generate publicity that reaches an art-conscious audience. Distributors expect nominal returns, and when they go to the

trouble of cultivating these bookings, they do so to provide recognition for the film maker and goodwill for the company. Museum showings have long-term benefits in establishing an audience for independents, rather than any short-term profit for the distributor.

Independent features are also occasionally booked into mass audience first-run and neighborhood movie houses, particularly in multi-screen situations. Except in rare cases like the sixteen-screen Cineplex in Los Angeles and Toronto that regularly schedule foreign and independent features, a small film is lost in the undifferentiated flow of mass studio product. Mass-market exhibitors are often simply filling holes in their calendars, and are reluctant to allot the extra promotional support that an American independent demands. A more logical venue for independent films would seem to be college dates that could exploit their topical, and often youth-oriented aspects. Certainly student organizations like Cornell Cinema in Ithaca, Cinema Texas in Austin, and countless other film societies from Yale to The University of Arizona account for scores of individual and repertory foreign film bookings. Colleges tend to choose well-known, but seldom seen older foreign films, hot newer foreign directors, Hollywood revival series in genre or movie-star modes, cult movies and money-making newer Hollywood releases. College film bookers are geared toward the major nontheatrical feature distributors like Swank, Films Incorporated, Corinth, and MGM/UA 16, which are set up to serve the 16 mm educational markets. Independent American features do play the college circuit, but mainly when they can be financed by a savvy programmer, who also includes James Bond and Clint Eastwood in the lineup. [. . .]

46

The Harlem Theater: Black Film Exhibition in Austin, Texas: 1920–1973

Dan Streible

When we think of the history of the traditional, American, moviegoing experience, a number of images come to mind: the mighty Wurlitzer organ accompanying a movie palace's silent-era feature, the iconic searchlights proclaiming a Golden Age Hollywood premiere, teenagers cruising at the local drive-in, an audience of otherwise sensibly attired adults wearing cardboard 3-D glasses, and more recently, young adults carrying five-dollar bills to the cineplex at the end of the mall in order to see the latest sequel. But while these iconic, even stereotypical, images suggest something of the truth behind the American movie theater's history, they also omit much of the social reality that has co-existed along with these instances of the mainstream filmgoing experience. While Hollywood features and first-run urban theaters may have greater single importance than any other mode of exhibition, a number of other important alternatives have fleshed out audiences' encounters with film.

One such alternative, with a fascinating yet understudied history all its own, was the Black movie house circuit that existed in the United States from (at least) 1907 until the 1970s.[1] With the project in mind of examining the cultural, social, and economic history of Black film theaters, I will discuss in this essay the development of Black film theaters in Austin, Texas, focusing especially on that city's longest standing and most prominent "show," the Harlem Theater.

Although movies came to the Texas capital before the turn of the century, and all-movie theaters began to proliferate there during America's post-1905 nickelodeon boom, the first recorded "colored" film theater – the Dixie-Dale – opened in Austin in 1920 under the management of Joseph Trammell. I found no other details about Trammell or the Dixie-Dale, but it is recorded that after two years the theater was renamed the Lincoln and managed by A.C. Lawson until it closed in 1928 or 1929. Austin also supported a second Black movie house in the 1920s. The Lyric, which opened in 1922, just one block east of the downtown Lincoln, was owned and operated by Dr. Everett H. Givens, a practicing dentist (with an office next door) who would become Austin's most prominent Black civic leader from the 1930s until his death in 1962. For reasons unclear at this point, Dr. Givens' Lyric, which changed its name to the Dunbar when A.C. Lawson took over its management in 1929, survived the Lincoln by a few years, closing in 1931. Whether the first Black film theaters in Austin closed due to the Depression, the cost of

Dan Streible, "The Harlem Theater: Black Film Exhibition in Austin, Texas: 1920–1973" originally appeared in Manthia Diawara (ed.), *Black American Cinema* (New York: Routledge, 1993), 221–36.

converting to sound, or some other reason, is impossible to judge given the paucity of data available about these enterprises.

However, placing the existence of the Lincoln and the Lyric in the contexts of both African American life in Austin and the concurrent national Black film theater scene enhances a historical understanding of these two houses both as businesses and as entertainment venues. From a national perspective, we know that the motion picture theater, with its roots in the Jim Crow era, had always been subject to racial segregation. Sometimes Black patrons were restricted to balconies or other special sections of the theater, but Black-only theaters were common in the United States from at least 1910, a year when a Black newspaper in Washington wrote matter-of-factly that "there are separate motion picture theaters among the whites and blacks in this country."[2] Although at the turn of the century "there was hardly a theater for colored people in the entire United States,"[3] by 1925, there were at least 425 Black theaters (of all types), virtually all of which offered films "in whole or part." Of these, nearly half were, like the Lyric and possibly the Lincoln, Black-owned.[4]

But ownership of Black movie houses, in contrast to the first-run, White theaters of the day, was not done by regional or national chains, nor by affiliated circuits; because houses operated independently, the dynamics of local conditions affected theaters like the Lincoln as much as national structures did. Historically, social and economic conditions changed greatly for Austin's Black community when its first Black movie houses appeared. During and after Reconstruction, Black neighborhoods had existed in several locations around Austin: Clarksville in west Austin, Kincheonville to the south, Gregoryville in East Austin, Masontown in the southeast, Horse's Pasture and Wheatville to the north, and so on.[5] Compared to other towns of the time, particularly in the South, race relations were fairly calm, albeit within the practice of institutionalized racism. The town boasted "three colleges and institutions for colored people,"[6] maintained some neighborhoods (such as Masontown) that were racially integrated among Blacks, Whites, Hispanics, and Asians, and in general obtained a reputation as a town without the major problems of racial violence that plagued most American communities. But during the 'teens segregation patterns began to develop.[7] In 1919 a White representative of the young NAACP was beaten by a White mob in the middle of downtown, and in the 1920s "the city of Austin created a 'Negro district' in East Austin ... induc[ing] blacks to move there" by implementing tough zoning laws elsewhere.[8] So it was that the majority of Austin's African American population (which has consistently remained at just below 20 percent of Austin's total) became concentrated in an area east of downtown and between 12th Street to the north and 7th Street to the south.

Not surprisingly, then, both of Austin's silent-era Black theaters were built on East 6th Street, near the racial dividing line of East Avenue, within the only downtown shopping and dining district that served Black patrons,[9] yet away from the White theater district on the city's main thoroughfare of Congress Avenue. I could uncover little information, however, that would indicate the nature or reception of these early movie houses. Longtime Austin resident L.C. Jones recalled visiting the Lincoln as a child, where he remembers a piano player accompanying the motion picture entertainment. Lonnie Bell, who wrote for the Black press in Austin for 50 years, indicates that in the 1920s both the Lyric and the "Lawson Lincoln Theatre" were among the very few venues for Black entertainment in the city and so "did well before the Great Depression in '29."[10] Other information about Everett Givens also indicates that he made the Lyric/Dunbar into a focal point for the Black community, viewing the theater as a civic improvement project as much as a business investment.[11] That these two movie houses were well received and supported by the Black community can also be inferred from the fact that a 1940 account of Austin history prepared by students at Til-lotson College (a Black institution) referred to the era of 1905 to 1929 as a time when "privately owned amusement centers were developed" by Blacks – even though no other Black amusements of record were insti-tuted during this period.[12]

As I mentioned earlier, the cause for these theaters' demise cannot be established abso-lutely, but several factors undoubtedly offer reasonable explanations. Bell's assertion that it was the economic devastation of the Depression that closed the Lincoln and Dun-bar makes logical economic sense. Black theater owners, like even the big-time oper-ators, would have been hit hard as the US economy collapsed. Moreover, inasmuch as movie tickets are purchased with "disposa-ble" income, Black patrons would have been especially likely to curtail their moviegoing since even before the Depression Blacks in Austin earned only one-half the wage of White workers.[13] More specifically, both houses in Austin would have found it even more difficult to cope with the hard times if they attempted to make the costly transition to sound technology in the late twenties or early thirties. The Dallas Film Board of Trade's statistics on Texas theaters indicate that many theaters, especially independently operated ones, closed in the early thirties, having no sound. (In Austin, two of the five White houses, the Crescent and Star, also went out of business in 1929 to 1931.) Furthermore, one-third of Texas' 30 "colored theaters" were listed as "closed, no sound" by the mid-1930s.[14] Other factors may have led to the closure of the Lincoln and Dunbar, but, given the theaters' dependence on the patron-age of a small, economically marginalized population, in the midst of a severe depression their failure is not surprising.

But the history of Black film theaters in Austin did not end with the closing of the Dunbar in 1931. In that same year, real estate was purchased and construction begun on a new movie house that would serve as the hub of Black filmgoing in Austin for the next 40 years. The Harlem Theater,

which opened on October 5, 1935,[15] distin-guished itself from the earlier theaters – and all subsequent ones – by being located in the heart of East Austin, at 1800 E. 12th Street, where it could better attract Black movie-goers.

However, before discussing the reasons for the Harlem's longevity, I point out that although it was Austin's only exclusively Black theater, it was not without its competi-tor for Black audiences. All accounts of Aus-tin in the 1930s and forties agree that the Ritz Theater was the only other house that admitted Black patrons on a regular basis, though customers there were limited to bal-cony seating and made to use a separate entrance. The Ritz, located on the same block of East 6th Street where the Lincoln operated, opened in 1930 under White man-agement, showing a variety of second-run Hollywood films. Manager J.J. Hegman (and his son after him) maintained the segregated seating policy until the Ritz's closing in the early 1960s. More prominent Austin houses, such as those first-run members of the pres-tigious Interstate Theater circuit (the Para-mount, Texas, State, and Queen), advertised "colored midnight shows" from time to time as part of the chain's overall marketing scheme.[16] Thus, while there was some com-petition for the Black filmgoing audience, seg-regated, White-managed theaters did not attempt to offer African Americans the film-going experience and environment of an all-Black house like the Harlem; however, the Ritz balcony and special events at other White movie establishments did continue to cultivate and maintain Black filmgoing in the Depression, when no Black Austin theaters were open.

When the Harlem opened in the midst of America's Depression in late 1935, the the-ater soon established itself as one of Austin's most visible and stable Black-owned busi-nesses. In film industry terms, the Harlem's success was small. With only 14,000 African American residents in 1936, Austin's marketplace for Black films was extremely limited, and the theater never expanded nor led to a chain of others. But, through a combination of strategic location, product differentiation, managerial conservatism, and diversification, the Harlem Theater was able to become a profitable local business in the midst of an industry whose structure tended to favor national giants.

Like the Lyric before it, the Harlem was established by a middle-class, Black Austin native who had been educated at Tillotson College and operated successfully in other local business before embarking on a risky career in the amusement industry. But George F. Jones, who was already in his forties when he opened the Harlem,[17] had also had some experience in programming films for Black audiences. His older brother Evie had purchased an Edison projector in the 'teens and traveled to tent shows in the South and Black churches in Philadelphia showing "church movies" (that is, filmed passion plays) to all-Black audiences.[18] After college, five years as a postal clerk, and ten years as a bookkeeper, George F. Jones himself had worked as the head of Prairie View, Texas' Auditorium (a film theater) while employed as a clerk at Prairie View State College (1925–35).[19] With his wife, Sadie, a Prairie View graduate and educator, Jones was active in the Austin real estate market[20] and their "co-partnership" became known for "accumulating valuable real estate holdings."[21] For the last two decades of his life Jones devoted most of his efforts to managing the Harlem, setting up residence next door to the corner theater upon his return to Austin from Prairie View. While his establishment may not have been unique for its time (there were more than three or four hundred Black theaters in the country), the Harlem was remarkable for being only one of seven US theaters owned and operated by Blacks.[22]

As an experienced theater manager, real estate buyer, and member of Austin's African American community, George Jones no doubt realized the importance of the theater's strategic location in determining its success at attracting moviegoers. East 12th Street was essentially the Main Street of East Austin.[23] The area around the Harlem represented a microcosm of African American life: it was both a quiet neighborhood of residences, churches, grocers, drug stores, beauty shops, and cafés, and a place to be "going up on the cuts" – a street where the action and entertainment were, in the form of taverns, beer joints, and (a block away) the Cotton Club and Paradise Inn for music and dancing.[24] The Harlem was also part of "The End," that area around 12th and Chicon Streets (one block away) where Austin's streetcars, until their cessation in 1940, stopped and turned back toward downtown.[25] In essence, those factors which determined that White theaters were centrally located along Congress Avenue – transportation proximity, pedestrian traffic, shopping convenience, high visibility – similarly made East 12th the choice location for a successful Black movie house.

In terms of architecture and facilities, the Harlem was much like smaller, second-run houses found in towns across the country. The green, two-story, art deco exterior featured a neon marquee topped by the letters of the theater's name in lights. A small walk-up ticket window was flanked on either side by double doors and permanent lobby card and one-sheet poster displays. Inside, a small carpeted lobby led to the air-cooled auditorium, where chairs were divided into three sections by two aisles. Restrooms were on either side of the smallish movie screen, with a stage in front and dressing rooms hidden behind. Double wide "necking seats" were conspicuous at the ends of every other row on the center aisle. Upstairs there was no balcony, but small screening rooms were situated on both sides of the main projection booth, where two 35 mm projectors were installed. The manager's office was maintained just off the right-hand side of the lobby.

The seating capacity of the Harlem is a matter of some confusion. Various printed sources put the number of seats variously at 685, 500, 480, and even as low as 250. Obviously the number probably changed slightly over time. George Jones made some renovations in the 1940s, and in the fifties a wider screen was installed. But judging from employees' oral accounts and photographic evidence, the higher numbers seem more accurate. Those numbers also indicate that the Harlem was of average house size, both for Black theaters and for second-run theaters in general.

But while the Harlem building may have been unexceptional, its programming in the 1930s and forties often set it apart from the other theaters in Austin. The basic format that Jones followed often mimicked the usual bill of movie fare found elsewhere: Saturday matinees, midnight shows, Fox Movietone newsreels, action serials, double features of Republic "B" Westerns and Hollywood "A" films, with occasional cartoons, and so on. In this respect, Black audiences got and enjoyed the same films and film stars as White audiences across the country. The Harlem programming during this period was difficult to identify in specific detail, but some of the features advertised included *Tropic Holiday* (1938, Dorothy Lamour), *Charlie Chan's Murder Cruise* (1940), *Too Hot to Handle* (1938, Clark Gable), and later, *Within These Walls* (1945, Thomas Mitchell), *Firebrands of Arizona* (1944, Republic), *A Tree Grows in Brooklyn* (1945, Elia Kazan), and *Sealed Verdict* (1948, Ray Milland). But, as George F. Jones' nephew and Harlem employee, L.C. Jones, reported, Black theaters were usually considered last-run possibilities for the major Hollywood studios' product. Big star vehicles usually took a year or more to reach the Harlem, and prestige pictures sometimes never made it. The Harlem playbill for August 23–7, 1940 confirms this account: a recent Charlie Chan release was playing the same weekend as *Tropic Holiday* and *Too Hot to Handle*, both of which had been released two years earlier.[26]

But the Harlem distinguished itself in a more important way by offering the only Austin outlet for the all-Black productions made outside of the Hollywood studios. Again specific programming instances were difficult to identify, since newspapers did not list the Harlem's showtimes, but several sources confirm that the theater attempted to run Black productions when they were available. Horace Marion, a 30-year employee, recalled that during Jones' tenure the Harlem featured a number of all-Black movies, especially Westerns starring Herb Jeffrey and some Black gangster pictures. In addition, Jay Knowles, an Austin film collector, owns a number of posters which had originally hung in the Harlem; they advertise such films as *Killer Diller* (1948, starring Butterfly McQueen and Nat King Cole), *She's Too Mean for Me* and *Up Jumps the Devil* (starring Black comic actor Mantan Moreland.)[27] It should be added, however, that although there was a major distributorship for Black films in Dallas (Sack Amusement Enterprises), the Hollywood distributors and White exhibitors conspired to keep Black productions marginalized. First, it was stipulated that Black productions would only be circulated in theaters having 75 percent or more Black patronage. Secondly, they "attempted to set low rental rates for colored cast plays," making the business of all-Black productions hardly profitable.[28] Thus, it remains uncertain whether the Harlem showed mostly regular movie fare because the Hollywood oligopoly offered little else, or because the management and audience actually preferred Roy Rogers to Herb Jeffrey.

As with White movie houses of the era, the Harlem of the 1930s and forties also supplemented its film programming with live entertainment and other attractions. Musicians, touring circuit shows of Black dance/variety groups, or individual performers such as the local favorite "Cherokee Bill" (a trickshooter and stunt artist) would appear on weekends and late-night bills. And Tuesday nights featured drawings for prizes donated by local merchants ("bicycles, watches, and groceries").[29]

Similarly, just as all-Black entertainments (both live and filmed) constituted a product Austinites could never or seldom find at the Ritz, the Black staff at the Harlem provided filmgoers with an environment that was surely more appealing to most than the segregated trappings of the downtown movie houses. While the Interstate theaters employed Black porters and maids (and *all* of their porters and maids were Black), the ticket girls, ushers, managers, and concessionaires were White.[30] However, all positions at the Harlem were filled by Black employees – with the single exception of the projectionists. Jones hired only union projectionists, and the local IATSE/MPMO was not integrated until the 1960s.[31]

But for a small neighborhood theater like the Harlem, any sort of product differentiation – whether it was with films, live acts, or "ambience" – would have failed to produce enough box office for the theater's survival. As with any theater, the bulk of the profit came not from 15- and 25-cent admissions, but from concessions. On this count, the Harlem again distinguished itself as unique among Austin theaters. In addition to the usual popcorn, candy, and soft drink sales, the Harlem operated a confectionery. L.C. Jones recalled that he was hired by his uncle George to run the Harlem Confectionery (it was sometimes listed as a separate business in the city directory) at the theater. This concession stand served moviegoers at a counter inside the lobby and also sold to walk-up customers on the street through a screened window that opened onto the Salina Street side of the building. The confectionery sold not only popcorn, candy, and drinks, but also ice cream, pickles, and chili burgers. On the opposite side of the theater, in the lot between the Jones residence and the Harlem, an outdoor "watermelon garden" featured umbrella-protected picnic tables where film and food customers could sit. By diversifying his movie house with such supplementary services, Jones created a popular neighborhood establishment with broad appeal, much as the drive-in operators of the 1950s or the picture palace entrepreneurs of the 1920s did.

Within the structures of a segregated society and economy, the Harlem capitalized on the possibilities of a movie house supported only by Black patrons, but its growth was necessarily limited by market size. Rather than attempt to expand into other theater holdings, Mr. and Mrs. Jones used such profits as they made to invest in real estate and maintained the Harlem in its original form until Mr. Jones' death in 1951.

But a transition to White ownership of the Harlem had already begun a few years before. According to several interviewees, Texas film businessmen named Frank Lucchese and Jack Adams had purchased a half interest (possibly the silent partner Mr. Fry's share) in the Harlem during the late 1940s. When George F. Jones died, his widow sold the remaining share of the business to Lucchese as well. Then, in 1952, Frank Lucchese turned the Harlem over to his brother Sam, who managed the theater under the same policies as Jones until 1960.

The background to the Luccheses' involvement with the Black theater business is of some interest here, as it serves to illustrate the long and intricate tradition that ethnic film theaters possess.[32] The Lucchese family's interest in film theaters dates back to the first Sam Lucchese (1867–1929), an Italian immigrant and Texas bootmaker who bought a small San Antonio film theater which expanded into a chain of local houses (including the Nacional and Zaragosa) playing only Mexican/Spanish-language films. Son Frank managed the lucrative theaters until selling out in the 1930s. Then, in 1945, two Dallas film distributors, Jack Adams and Bob Warner, banded with Sam Lucchese, Jr., to form the Triad Amusement Company, which purchased two of Dallas' Black theaters, the Century and the State. For various reasons, a deal was struck in which Frank Lucchese left Austin in order to take over the Dallas Theaters, while his brother Sam moved from Dallas in order to take over management of the Harlem *and* of the Cactus Theater.[33] The latter, opened in 1939, was a White theater on East 6th which had been doing poor business but was somehow forced into the deal that enabled the Luccheses to acquire the Harlem.

With the arrival of Sam Lucchese, then, the Austin Black film theater entered into a new phase of its history: several changes were eventually made at the Harlem, and a new Black theater, the Carver, was opened where the Cactus had been. At both theaters, Lucchese continued to hire only Black employees (with the exception of himself and his son). Programming policies at the two theaters were basically identical, but strategies were put in place that differed slightly from those practiced by George Jones.

Second-run Hollywood movies still made up most of the programming, but Lucchese, either because of his distributor connections or his race, was able to secure more desirable film product and do it more quickly than Jones had been able to do. Six-month clearances were still common for the Harlem, but the theater was able to book prestige films like *The Ten Commandments* and the reissued *Gone With the Wind*. Very few all-Black productions were booked, but whenever Hollywood vehicles for Black stars of the 1950s (Dorothy Dandridge, Sidney Poitier, Harry Belafonte, and so on) became available they met with success at both shows, particularly at the Harlem.

A more significant policy shift, however, was Lucchese's successful attempt to program Hollywood genres which were, according to the "conventional wisdom," supposed to be most appealing to ethnic audiences: horror films and action films. Action/adventure films, Westerns, and gangster pictures usually did well at any time, Sam Lucchese III recalled from his days working for his father at the Harlem. Revivals of *Dracula*, *Bride of Frankenstein*, and the like made for successful midnight shows, which by the 1950s attracted mostly teenage audiences. As the Harlem's teen audience increased, rock and roll movies, from *Blackboard Jungle* (1955) on, also proved more popular than the usual run of films.

Live shows featuring touring Black variety groups continued to be popular, but were hired with less frequency as the decade wore on. A particularly popular act was a group known as the Brown Skin Models, who appeared several times at the Harlem for midnight weekend performances. But as professional touring groups began to dwindle on the film circuit, they were replaced at the Harlem by talent shows. Local performers would compete, on a weekly or monthly basis, for prizes given by area businesses.

In addition to continuing the Harlem's tradition of a film theater for the African American community, Lucchese also attempted to keep a sagging box office up by competing more vigorously for the audience's ticket money. Like George F. Jones, he almost never took out advertising space in either the White or Black newspapers, but he did expand the Harlem's advertising practices. Flyers hyping the coming week's films were printed weekly and left in stacks at grocery stores, druggists, liquor stores, and restaurants around East Austin. Secondly, permanent one-sheet displays were installed in 15 to 20 locations throughout the East End, and posters advertising the Harlem movies were changed twice each week. Finally, the Lucchese management attempted to offer Harlem patrons more appealing movie technology. Bids for 3-D installation were taken, but decided against. However, sometime around 1956 to 1957, Cinemascope equipment was purchased and a new, wider screen was built.

Although the success of the Harlem was limited in this era of falling movie attendance, the Carver – which Lucchese had never wanted to operate anyway – had an even slimmer profit margin. The theater was much smaller (only 250 seats) and suffered from the competition offered by the Ritz and later the Yank, which programmed similar second-run films and some Spanish-language films. Although Lucchese tried to promote the Carver's opening by inviting Black civic leaders to the premiere, even that evening's crowd failed to fill the theater.[34] The theater's downtown location was no longer a desirable characteristic, as Austinites moved further and further away from the small area between the state Capitol building and the Colorado River. Ticket sales at the Carver in the late 1950s were sometimes as little as ten dollars a day. The second Black film theater remained a liability for the Lucchese operation. Within a year of Sam Lucchese's death in December 1960,[35] the Carver Theater closed. During the next ten years it re-opened under four different names: The Carlos (1964–5), The Capri (operated by Paul Mathieson, 1965–73), The Vagabond (1974) and The Sun (1975). Billed as an "art theater," the dollar-house fluctuated between programming X-rated skin flicks and revival/repertory films. Although its features occasionally had a Black or ethnic orientation (a documentary series about Black musicians, a horror triple feature),[36] the East 6th Street theater always played to integrated audiences after 1961.

The Harlem, however, remained a Black film theater throughout the 1960s. While the new management never had to turn away White customers (as Sam Lucchese had done on a number of occasions earlier in his tenure), the business attempted to continue to program for Black audiences. Little is known about how the Harlem was run by its second White owner, Vernon L. Smith, from 1962 on. Sam Lucchese's son recalled that Smith was from Dallas, and probably had a background with a distribution firm there. Josephine Ramey, who sold tickets at the Harlem for Smith, recalled only that as a film programmer he "didn't have the pull" of the previous owners, and business fell off considerably before Smith sold the Harlem (to Andy Majek) some time around 1970.

But the real reason that the Harlem went into decline in the 1960s was not so much related to management styles or to the quality of films, as it was to the changing social conditions in Austin and the nation. Up through even the late 1950s the White Interstate theaters had a written policy which instructed employees to inform customers that "this theater does not cater to Negro patronage at this time."[37] In December 1960, when University of Texas' Students for Direct Action began to demand desegregation by marching in front of the Texas and Varsity theaters,[38] Interstate attempted to discredit the protestors.[39] But the incident-plagued trend toward public integration persisted throughout the decade. As African Americans generally became accustomed to using what had been White-only facilities – such as movie theaters – the ability of the Harlem to compete for the Black audience lessened. With the potential for African American citizens to attend any theater or drive-in in town, the need for an exclusive Black theater became more and more irrelevant to many residents of East Austin.

Nevertheless, in July 1973, the Harlem, after having been closed for six months, re-opened under the interracial management team of John Hutkin (a local sound engineer), Dennis Baum (an investment counselor), and Willie Winn (who had held various jobs in East Austin). The renovated theater, it was announced, would institute a new, "Black-oriented screen policy," "designed to serve its community."[40] For the remainder of the year, the Harlem showed three features a week, with matinees and midnight shows on weekends. The specifics of its programming can be traced accurately, since for the first time in its 40-year history the theater began to advertise in the local newspaper. In 1973 the Harlem played most of the wave of "blaxploitation" films that were being shown at the other Austin theaters as well – *Superfly TNT*, *Hit Man*, *Trick Baby*, *Blacula*, *Black Caesar*, *Death Master*, and *Trouble Man*. The new owners showed an occasional non-Black film with the traditional action/horror appeal (*Soylent Green*, *For a Few Bullets More*), but preferred Black music films (*Wattstax*) and Hollywood movies by African American directors and/or with Black subjects (*The Great White Hope*, *Across 110th Street*, *Buck and the Preacher*). It is difficult to assess how well the theater was doing financially during this brief period, or in what way its clientele had changed, but such concerns became irrelevant on December 30, 1973, when the Harlem Theater burned to the ground.[41]

But had fire not destroyed the East Austin institution, it is doubtful that the Harlem could have survived much longer as a Black movie theater. Although the East 12th Street neighborhood remains predominantly African American, the establishment of a Black theater remains predicated on the assumption that there is a need in the community for services denied in White businesses.[42] The Harlem, like other East Austin businesses of its day, was a creation of segregation; one needed a Black movie house because African Americans were excluded from all other movie houses. It was created in an era when, under the advice of conservative leaders like Booker T. Washington and Dr. Everett H. Givens, African Americans were encouraged to make the most of their separate lot rather than insist on integration. "There are better five-cent theaters conducted by colored Americans than any controlled by the Whites, and why do you insist on going where you are not wanted?" the "Negro press" of 1910 told movie patrons.[43] With a philosophy of an integrated economy replacing one of a separate African American economy, by the 1960s the days of the exclusively Black film theater were numbered.

Notes

1 In researching this paper the earliest reference I found to a particular Black movie house was 1910, but Greg Waller has presented evidence of a Black-run nickelodeon that opened in 1907. "Black Moviegoing and Film Exhibition in Lexington, Kentucky, 1906–1927." Paper presented at the Society for Cinema Studies Conference, Washington, DC, May 27, 1990.
2 *Washington Bee*, July 9, 1910, 4.
3 *Negro Yearbook*, 1912, 24.
4 *Negro Yearbook*, 1931–2, 379.
5 "The Early Days in East Austin," *Austin American-Statesman*, March 2, 1986, D41.
6 *Austin City Directory*, 1903–4, 4. The schools were Tillotson College, Samuel Huston College, and the Texas Colored Deaf, Dumb, and Blind Institute in northwest Austin.
7 Martha Doty Freeman, *East Austin: An Architectural Survey*. MS, 1980.
8 "The Early Days in East Austin," D41.
9 Longtime member of Austin's Black press, Lonnie Bell, wrote that East 6th Street was "the only place blacks" could eat, drink, shop for clothes, etc. See "A Look at Austin Black History from World War I to 1983," *East Austin Times*, February 11, 1983, 6. L.C. Jones, who came to Austin in the 1920s and later worked on East 6th in the clothing business, confirmed this in our interview.
10 Bell, 6.
11 Jeanette H. Flachmeier, "Pioneer Austin Notables," vol. II, 1980, 32. Givens reportedly arranged for children who did not have ticket money to earn passes by doing work.
12 J. Mason Brewer, (ed.), *An Historical Outline of the Negro in Travis County* (1940), 34.
13 Ibid.
14 *1936 Texas Theater Guide*.
15 Le Verne Green, "Flames Engulf an Era, Black Celluloid Heroes," *Austin American Statesman* (January 20, 1974), II, 9.
16 *1942 Yearbook: A Round-Up of Showmanship Ideas for Every Month of the Year*. Interstate Theaters. Hoblitzelle Collections, HRC, University of Texas at Austin.
17 The Harlem property was also invested in by a silent partner, a Mr. and Mrs. Fry, according to both L.C. Jones and Travis County courthouse deeds for 1931.
18 As reported by L.C. Jones and his sister Evelyn Hamilton.
19 J. Mason Brewer, *A pictorial and historical souvenir of Negro life in Austin, Texas, 1950–51*, 7. The notes also seem to indicate that George Jones had also done some type of film programming while working at the "DB&O," Austin's school for deaf and blind orphans.
20 Ibid. Travis County courthouse records also confirm this.
21 Ibid.
22 *Negro Handbook 1942*, 37. The other Black movie houses were in Paris, Texas; Washington, DC; Arkansas, Virginia, and Ohio (two).
23 "The Early Days in East Austin," D42.
24 Ibid. Also, confirmed by the L.C. Jones interview, November 30, 1988.
25 Dr. Everett Givens' dental practice had also moved to this area (1203 Chicon), further indicating the location's importance to the Black community.

26 *The Austin Informer*, August 24, 1940, 5.
27 The latter two films were released by Ted Toddy, a White Atlanta producer who "made black pictures with black casts" in the forties and also distributed the films of Black producer Oscar Micheaux. From an interview of David F. Friedman by David Chute, "Wages of Sin," *Film Comment* (August 1986), 38.
28 *Negro Handbook 1943*, 261–2.
29 Green, 1974 (cited above).
30 From employee records in the Hoblitzelle Theater Arts Collection, Harry Ransom Humanities Research Center, University of Texas at Austin.
31 This, according to Jim Malloy, former head of Austin's projectionists' union, who worked at the Harlem occasionally. This was not the case nationwide, however. In 1930 100 of the union's 2,600 motion picture operators were Black, though they were limited to work in the "colored belt" and could not vote in or attend regular union meetings. For a short time the 12 operators in Harlem had split off from IATSE and formed their own union, United Association of Colored Motion Picture Operators. See *Negro Membership in American Labor Unions*, Department of Research and Investigations/National Urban League, 1930, 96–7.
32 This material taken from interviews with Sam Lucchese, November 28, 1988, and from biographical files in the Barker Texas History Center, University of Texas at Austin.
33 This Cactus was owned by Austin's veteran theater entrepreneur, Richard S. "Skinny" Pryor, whose son "Cactus" not only worked at his namesake theater, but later went on to fame as an entertainer in radio, television, newspapers, and films.
34 Josephine Ramey, who worked at the Harlem as ticket salesperson for many years, worked at the Carver on its opening night. Interviewed December 1, 1988.
35 Lucchese was killed by a 17-year-old employee while leaving the Harlem late one night. "Trio Charged in Gun Death," *Austin American-Statesman*, December 7, 1960, 15; "Lucchese, 52, owner of Harlem and Carver shot in head," *Austin American-Statesman*, December 14, 1960.
36 C.A. Richardson, "Capri Theater Aids Hopper Movie," n.d. Clipping in Austin History Center file, AF-M8300 (21).
37 Interoffice communications from Interstate General Office, Dallas, to all city managers, June 10, 1954 and June 7, 1956. In the Hoblitzelle Theater Arts Collection.
38 "Racial Fuss Closes Door to Theatre," *Austin American-Statesman*, December 10, 1960. "Integration Group Mills at Theatres," December 11, 1960.
39 Jim Malloy maintained that the local Interstate manager commissioned him to install a hidden camera (!) in front of the Varsity so that protesters could be recorded on film by the ticket seller. Malloy built in the hidden camera and set up a screening of the final product for several Interstate managers who met at the Austin Hotel. He was not privy to their secret meeting, but he assumed that they were looking for political undesirables among the group, in order to smear their cause.
40 "Harlem Theater Re-Opens," *Austin American-Statesman*, July 16, 1973, 59.
41 Green, 1974. Today the property where the Harlem was built remains an empty lot. However, the memory and legacy of the theater's role in the East Austin community were paid tribute in 1989 when students from Austin Community College painted a colorful mural replica of the Harlem. On the facade of the closed Elks Lodge building, just a few blocks from where the theater originally stood, a life-sized representation of the deco building is now on public display (complete with three-dimensional marquee reproducing the Harlem's cutout letters).
42 See Robert H. Kinzer and Edward Sagarin, *The Negro in American Business: The Conflict Between Separation and Integration* (New York: Greenberg, 1950).
43 *Washington Bee*, June 4, 1910, 1.

Archives consulted

Austin Texas History Center, Austin Public Library, Austin, Texas.
Barker Texas History Center, University of Texas at Austin.
Hoblitzelle Collection, Theater Arts Collection, Harry Ransom Humanities Research Center, University of Texas at Austin.
Travis County Courthouse, Deeds and Records, Austin, Texas.

Interviews

Hamilton, Evelyn. Santa Monica, California (via telephone). November 30, 1988.

Jones, L.C. Former employee of the Harlem and Carver Theaters: nephew of the Harlem's original builder/owner. Austin, Texas. November 30, 1988.

Jones, Alice. Former employee of the Harlem and Carver Theaters. Austin, Texas. November 30, 1988.

Knowles, Jay. Private collector; Harlem patron. Austin, Texas. October 27, 1988.

Lucchese, Sam. Former employee of Harlem and Carver Theaters; son of the second owner of the Harlem. Austin, Texas. November 28, 1988.

Malloy, Jim. Motion Picture Operator. IATSE. Austin, Texas. December 1 and 2, 1988.

Ramey, Josephine. Ticket salesperson at the Harlem. Austin, Texas. December 1, 1988.

Other sources consulted

1936 Texas Theater Almanac. Dallas: Dallas Film Board of Trade, 1936.

1938 Texas Theater Guide, 14th edition. Dallas: Dallas Film Board of Trade, 1939.

1942 Yearbook: A Round-Up of Showmanship Ideas for Every Month of the Year. Dallas: Interstate Theatres, 1942.

1955 Texas Theater Guide.

1956–57 Texas Theater Guide.

1960 Texas Theater Guide.

Abajian, James de T. *Blacks in Selected Newspapers, Censuses, and Other Sources*.

The Afro-American Texans. University of Texas at San Antonio, Institute of Texan Cultures, 1975.

Austin American-Statesman.

Austin City Directory.

Austin History Center, clippings file.

Barker Texas History Center. Biography files: J.J. Hegman, Sam Lucchese, Dr. Everett H. Givens.

Bell, Lonnie. "A Look at Austin Black History from World War I to 1983." *East Austin Times* (February 11, 1983), 6.

Bell, William K. *A Business Primer for Negroes*. New York, 1948.

Bogle, Donald. *Blacks in American Films and Television: An Encyclopedia*. New York: Garland, 1988.

——. *Toms, Coons, Mulattoes, Mammies and Bucks*. New York: Von Nostrand Reinhold, 1972.

Brewer, J. Mason. *An Historical Outline of the Negro in Travis County*. Austin: Sam Huston College, 1940.

——. *A Pictorial and Historical Souvenir of Negro Life in Austin, Texas: 1950–51. Capital City Argus*.

Chute, David. "Wages of Sin," *Film Comment* (August 1986), 32–48.

Cripps, Thomas. *Black Film as Genre*. Bloomington: Indiana University Press, 1978.

——. *Slow Fade to Black: The Negro in American Film*. Oxford: Oxford University Press, 1977.

The Crisis: A Record of the Darker Races. NAACP journal, 1910–

East Austin Times.

Fachmeier, Jeanette Hastedt. *Pioneer Austin Notables*, vol. 2. Austin, 1980, 29–33.

Freeman, Martha Doty. *East Austin: An Architectural Survey*. Unpublished MS. 1980.

Fuller, M.A.B. (comp.). *Historical Booklet of Religious, Business and Professional Men and Women*. 1948. Austin Texas History Center, A 920 Fu.

Guzman, Jessie Parkhurst, (ed.). *Negro Yearbook 1952*. New York: William H. Wise & Co., 1952.

Hall, Bruce H. "The Negro and His Pleasures." *Opportunity* (May 1937), 138, 156.

The Illustrated News (Austin).

Kinzer, Robert H. and Edward Sagarin. *The Negro in American Business: The Conflict between Separation and Integration*. New York: Greenberg, 1950.

Klotman, Phyllis Rauch. *Frame by Frame – A Black Filmography*. Bloomington: Indiana University Press, 1979.

Murray, Flo (ed.). *The Negro Handbook*. New York: Wendell Malliet & Co., 1942–9.

Murray, James. *To Find an Image: Black Films from Uncle Tom to Superfly*. Indianapolis: Bobbs-Merrill, 1973.

Negro Digest.

Negro Membership in American Labor Unions. Department of Research and Investigations, National Urban League. New York: Negro US Press, 1930.

Operation Impact: Working Papers on East 11th & 12th Street Area. MS February 16, 1988.

Simons, Ada (ed.). *Delta Sigma Phi Present the Black Heritage Exhibit: A Pictorial History of Austin, Travis County, Texas' Black Community, 1839–1920*. n.d.

The Voice (Austin).

Work, Monroe N. (ed.). *Negro Year Book 1912–1938*. Tuskegee: Negro Yearbook Publishing Co.

47

The Exhibitors (1972)

Stanley H. Durwood

"...It is not a policy of our corporation to use commercial advertising for income on our screen. We are selling the public one item – a particular motion picture – and to use the screen for other purposes detracts from this item...."

Durwood Theatres, now known as American Multi-Cinema, was founded in 1920 by Edward D. Durwood. In 1947 the company operated one theatre in Kansas City and 11 others in cities in the Missouri–Kansas area. In 1963 we opened the Parkway Theatres in the Ward Parkway Shopping Center in Kansas City. They were the first twin theatres in the world with a common lobby, box-office, projection booth and concession stand. In 1966, the company opened the world's first four-theatre complex, the Metro Plaza Theatres in Kansas City. In 1969, the first six-theatre complex, the Six West Theatres in Omaha, were opened. Currently, the company operates over 120 theatre screens in nine states and plans to open at least 40 additional screens.

Since American Multi-Cinema has planned its expansion program on the basis of constructing twin-, four- and six-theatre complexes throughout the country, we have established our own marketing department, which analyzes the market potential of cities throughout the United States. Our initial concern is the potential number of movie-goers within a geographic area.

We consider all cities that have a population in excess of about 100,000 as potential locations for a multi-theatre operation. Next, we evaluate the growth potential of each city and the particular future growth areas within a city. We also attempt to evaluate the population centers by various economic and demographic considerations, including average age, income, education, and occupation of residents. We prefer to locate theatres in growing middle-class areas, inhabited by college-educated families and potentially college-educated young people. These groups are the backbone of the existing motion picture audience, and our future audience.

Once we have evaluated the market potential of a particular city, we proceed to find the locations of all the existing theatres and determine how many additional theatres can be economically supported, in order to set our specific plans for development within a

Excerpted from Stanley H. Durwood, "The Exhibitors." In William A. Bluem and Jason E. Squire (eds.), *The Movie Business: American Film Industry Practice* (New York: Hastings House, 1972), 220–3. Reprinted with permission from Hastings House.

particular city. As examples, we may determine that in a city the size of Dallas, we would like to erect between five and eight multi-cinema locations; in a city like Denver, three; or in a city like Philadelphia, 14 multi-theatre locations.

After our plans are set, the workload shifts to our real estate department. We locate all our theatres within shopping centers, in prime retail space. Since we are constructing only multi-theatres in units of two, four or six, containing between 200 and 400 seats in each theatre, the design of our theatres is fairly standard. We do not create a new form for each shopping center; but we construct our theatres to fit the pattern of the shopping center's motif.

The cost of operating theatre chains can be broken down into four basic areas: (1) rental cost of the motion picture, (2) advertising cost for the motion picture, (3) direct cost of operating the theatre itself, and (4) overhead cost of the entire theatre chain's executive management.

Each picture released by a particular distributor is licensed to us in each of our theatres on an individual basis. In some areas, we license pictures on a competitive basis (i.e., we compete through bidding with other theatres operated by other exhibitors) while in other areas, we license our pictures through negotiation, on a non-competitive basis.

Almost all of our pictures are licensed from distributors on the basis of a percentage of gross receipts. This might be a straight percentage, such as 50% of the income derived from the exhibition of a picture over a certain number of weeks. Another form of percentage license provides that we keep the first amount of dollars to cover our operating overhead, and the distributor receives 90% of the gross receipts in excess thereof, while we retain the remaining 10%. This is a *90/10 over-the-house expense* deal. Often, these deals are combined so that the distributor would receive whichever is higher between a 90/10 over-the-house expense deal, and a direct percentage of the gross receipts. At times, pictures are licensed on a flat rental basis,

but such deals generally take place on second-feature pictures, and to theatres of minimal grossing potential.

The basic operating cost of a theatre itself includes such elements as salaries to employees, rent to the shopping center, amortization of the cost of the furnishings and fixtures of the theatre, including cost of seats, projection equipment, screen, concession equipment, maintenance costs, cost of concession items, supplies, tickets, and incidental costs. In operating a circuit, we also have management overhead costs, which include the salaries of the film buyers, theatre operation executives, the accounting and financial departments, legal fees, and auditors.

For first-run motion pictures, advertising is generally shared on a cooperative basis between distributor and exhibitor, in accordance with the percentage of film rental earned on a motion picture. If the deal is a 90/10 over-house expense, the distributor will pay 90% of the advertising.

On the first sub-run break of motion pictures in major cities, the advertising is divided on a different basis. The picture is licensed to a certain number of theatres in one area – as determined by the distributor – and each theatre is asked to contribute a set proportion of dollars (i.e., $50, $100, $150) over the theatre's normal advertising budget for the sub-run campaign. The distributor, in turn, will contribute a certain proportion to the amount financed by the theatres. Although advertising costs vary with pictures, we estimate that an average of 6% to 8% of the theatres' box-office grosses are expended in advertising dollars. It is not a policy of our corporation to use commercial advertising for income in any of our theatres. We are selling the public one item – a particular motion picture – and to use the screen for other purposes detracts from this item.

The general policy of our corporation is not to use double-bills in indoor theatres. They are used only to bring back two successful pictures as one show. It is our opinion that people most often want to see just one particular picture, and do not care for a second feature. The drive-in public, on the other hand, has come to expect a bargain of two or more pictures for their evening's entertainment. The combination of *A Man Called Horse* and *Cheyenne Social Club* or two of the James Bond pictures, are pair-ups that achieved great success. With respect to shorts and cartoons, these are used only as fill-ins for time schedules. Often, when a picture runs an hour and a half, the time schedule may be on a two-hour basis, so a 10- or 15-minute short or cartoon is used to fill out the program.

Our theatres must be booked differently, of course. In Lansing, Michigan, we cater to a large number of students from Michigan State University, and their movie-going fare differs greatly from theatres located in upper-income, conservative, middle-class areas. Our theatre in St. Petersburg, Florida, attracts audiences of older people who are not interested in the provocative problems of the day and for whom a film like *Getting Straight* has no appeal. We must cater to their tastes by showing musicals like *Funny Girl* and *Hello, Dolly! Easy Rider*, which had such great success throughout the country, should not be exhibited in our theatres in St. Petersburg. On the other hand, I would not recommend playing *Hello, Dolly!* on a third or fourth run in Lansing, Michigan. I could, however, bring *Easy Rider* back to Lansing. I suspect there will always be an audience for that picture in that town.

We are the originators of the multiple-theatre complex, and are continuing to build theatres on that basis. In essence, variety is the key to the multiple-theatre operation. Adults may attend a picture with adult appeal, while their children are in the adjacent theatre attending a film specifically designed for children. Certainly, some pictures are held over, but if you are operating four or six theatres in a complex, at least one or two new pictures are added to the films each week.

Economically, the multiple-theatre operation benefits the distributor. A theatre operator who has one large theatre within an area has a higher overhead than a theatre operated as part of a multiple-theatre complex. With this high overhead, the exhibitor cannot hold a picture for a long period of time. Once the picture falls below a certain gross, the exhibitor must put in a new picture. In a multiple-theatre operation, the house expense of a particular screen is much less, so the picture can be held in that theatre at a lower gross. This gives the distributor the benefit of having his picture before the public for a longer period of time. A short run, in my opinion, deprives the distributor of income to which he is entitled.

We are convinced that the multi-theatre concept is economically right for our form of operation and the motion picture distributor, and that it will play a large part in the future of the motion picture industry.

48

The K-Mart Audience at the Mall Movies

William Paul

During the late 1970s, a crisis sensibility began to overtake Hollywood. In 1977, there was a mild panic in response to a sudden 7.5 percent decline in movie theater attendance in 1976 after a two-year surge in 1974–5. After a decade of almost continuous growth and record revenues, the years 1990–1 saw ticket sales decline sharply, in fact to their lowest level since 1976.[1] A similarly bleak sense of crisis lowered over Hollywood, one that has continued even after box office began to pick up again in the following year.[2] Never before in the history of Hollywood has an individual film been able to make as much money as it can today. But the demand for sure-fire blockbusters and commensurately escalating budgets has also meant that never before had any individual film been able to lose so much money. As a consequence, it's very easy to go from a buoyant boom to a gloomy bust in a very short time.

Crises come very easily to Hollywood since movie production is probably the world's largest crap shoot, or, as a *Variety* writer surveying 1993 box office put it, "What keeps the movie business so interesting and media pundits so busy is that the search for a sure thing has a success rate right up there with playing slot machines in Vegas."[3] Every new film is like a roll of the dice or a spin of the slot machine with every player trying to calculate odds that might well be incalculable. The extraordinary success of Arnold Schwarzenegger movies was enough to make Columbia willing to gamble $80 million on *The Last Action Hero*, but it turned out to be a bad bet, with a $28 million loss.[4] Still, 20th Century-Fox saw sufficiently good odds in previous Schwarzenegger successes to place a $100 million-plus bet on *True Lies*, even though Schwarzenegger is completely miscast in that film. The stakes are enormous, far beyond what anyone might have imagined during the crisis of the late 1970s. Furthermore, the intervening 17 years saw radical changes in distribution, marketing and exhibition that make the crisis of the early 1990s different. In fact, the current situation arises from changes brought about by a response to the crisis of the 1970s, which was really a crisis of confidence in Hollywood's sense of its audience.[5]

In the late 1970s, an apparent fickleness of audience taste coupled with an increasing selectivity in moviegoing raised new questions for Hollywood's executives: who were these viewers and why did they go to the movies? Not only did Hollywood wonder why they went to a movie, but why they went to *any* movie? In the mid-1970s Ned Tanen, executive vice president of Universal, could declare, "The truth is, although nobody likes to bring it up, we can't find twenty-five films a year worth making."[6]

William Paul, "The K-Mart Audience at the Mall Movies." *Film History* 6 (1994), 487–501. Reprinted with permission from John Libbey & Company, Limited.

What this executive actually meant was they could no longer find 25 films a year that would appeal to an audience they felt increasingly remote from them and unpredictable. The crisis of 1991 also has to do with uncertainty about what motivates an audience, but it is of a different order in large part because it reflects changes in the way Hollywood addressed its audience over the last couple of decades.

Exploitation Psychology

Changes in exhibition practices that were a response to the previous sense of crisis have led to a consequent transformation of the *kinds* of movies that get produced. In effect, exhibition has become the tail that wags the dog as it inescapably makes demands for product that can most appropriately fit new modes of exhibition. There is a kind of reciprocal influence that exists between film-producing companies and their audience that is determined by the way the companies address their audience: new exhibition practices which occur in response to changing demographics (shifts in geographic and age distribution of the audience) and market pressures, in turn, help transform audience expectations of the moviegoing experience. The period I am concerned with here presented one of the clearest examples of this process in American film history, largely because it saw the most radical break with past exhibition practices: favorable audience reaction to a number of films whose subject matter would once have marked them as exploitation product led to an exploitation releasing strategy that eventually became applied to all films. The films in turn became marked as exploitation product by virtue of the releasing strategy.[7] The responses of the audience may help determine marketing strategies, but the marketing strategies effectively reconstitute the audience. The manner in which the films are presented to the audience effectively tells us something about who Hollywood thinks its audience is.

While there had been a general decline in movie theater attendance from the mid-1960s through the early-1970s, with 1973 representing the worst year since the leveling off of the post-Second World War decline in the late 1950s, individual films were reaping theatrical revenues on an unheard-of scale, generally surpassing the grosses of even the biggest blockbusters from the 1950s. And the success of these individual films led to lopsided box-office returns. There was a striking example of films released in 1975 that had earned more than $2 million, which was then considered the minimum necessary to break even: out of 79 films that reached the magic $2 million figure, a mere 15 accounted for 57 percent of combined domestic rentals, monies returned to the producing companies from the US–Canada market.

Moving away from the golden age of theatrical exhibition when the margin of economic difference between success and failure was of a much smaller scale, this new development proved to have such lasting effect that an astute movie business observer writing in *Variety* in 1986 could state flat-out:

> In the film business, an unchanging parameter is that the top 10 per cent of films account for 40–50 per cent of the business of *all* films in concurrent release. If there are 200 films released in a year, 20 of them will generate nearly one-half the b.o. of all 200.[8]

This was a statement, however, that could only apply to post-television Hollywood, when the regular moviegoing audience had disappeared. Every film had to succeed in the marketplace entirely on its own, but in a crowded marketplace how could it attract the attention that was a necessary prelude to success? It was in this period that it became a commonplace in Hollywood to think that every film had to be an event to succeed in this marketplace. So, even though individual films in the seventies could make enormous amounts of money, production dropped sharply as each producing company tried to concentrate its production on the event films, the films that would land in the top 10 percent to generate half the company's income.

Within a decade, the cries of product shortage common throughout the seventies were succeeded by new concerns about product glut![9] This shift came about through the development of the aftermarket, the videotape as a major form of distribution and the continuing growth of pay-cable television. The majority of films might still have trouble making their cost back from theatrical distribution, but video in its various forms buoyed confidence by promises of profit margins in the post-theatrical market. Since the number of people buying tickets remained remarkably steady throughout this period, video did not so much cut into active moviegoing as expand the market for feature films.[10] And since theatrical exposure is often a key factor in the success of a film on video, theatrical exhibition was actually given a new *raison d'être* in this period: a necessary spring board for the lucrative tape market.

Saturating the Market

For all the changes that videotape would help introduce, the mid-1970s product shortage and its concomitant sense that every film had to be an event did itself have a lasting impact on film exhibition in one striking way. In June of 1975, Universal simultaneously opened *Jaws* in about 500 theaters at once, promoting the film with a massive television ad campaign. The very way in which the film was exhibited helped make it an event, something of a necessary strategy for Universal because it was the only film the company released for the next three months. Mass releasing was a mode of exhibition distributing companies had been experimenting with ever since it proved successful with the low-budget *Trial of Billy Jack* in 1971, but *Jaws* was the first time since *Duel in the Sun* that the strategy had been applied to a bigbudget, glossy production, and it seemed to work.

Significantly, the *Duel in the Sun* release was unusual in 1946, one which producer David O. Selznick described as a revolutionary "multiple-booking plan" involving "enormously and unprecedentedly heavy newspaper and radio advertising by territories." Selznick, realizing he had not come up with another "*Gone With the Wind*," used the mass release as a way of capitalizing on advance audience interest and countering potential bad word of mouth. Nevertheless, he eventually came to regret it, writing in a memo that "the advertising and ballyhoo on *Duel* was damaging and was a complete contradiction of our former 'Tiffany' standards ...even if I am wrong in exaggerating the extent of the loss to my position, there is the matter of my family to think of..."[11] But if the release strategy contradicted the kind of movie Selznick thought he had produced, *Jaws* truly was material that in the past would have been considered exploitation; what made it different was the big budget, the major stars, and a change in the cultural environment that made no one connected with the film worried about sullying their families. The film might have had the trappings of A films in the past, but its exploitation release was appropriate to its content and genre.[12]

Nowadays when *The Lion King* can premiere in 2,552 theaters simultaneously, 500 theaters would count as a limited opening, but *Jaws* at least helped establish the future method for distributing films, one that would become set in stone by the middle of the next decade: extensive advertising on prime-time national television to generate name-recognition followed by opening of the film in as many markets as possible to take advantage of all the national advertising.[13] Once advertised this way, the film should be easily available to its audience, as easily as any other mass-produced item. To say this method became set in stone is to be quite literal in that it effectively became institutionalized by the ascendancy of a new institution: the multiplex. There are, of course, a number of reasons for the multiplex, but the one of most interest to me here is the way it provided the perfect set-up for the new releasing strategy since it could make readily available all mass-advertised films to their mass audience in the most convenient form. Viewers wouldn't have to search for the film they saw adver-tised on television. All they'd have to do is show up at the local multiplex.

This exhibition strategy turned out to be, for the most part, a radical reversal of past releasing patterns, and with this reversal, the movie distributors effectively changed the way they had addressed their audience in the past. Up through the 1970s, distribution was based on principles of exclusivity. Vir-tually every major release was tiered through a series of runs, with each tier effectively inscribing a somewhat different audience. The movie might be the same, albeit a bit older, but seeing it in your small neighbor-hood movie theater in second-run made of it a different experience from seeing it in one of the big downtown movie palaces. If execu-tives in the mid-1970s began to worry about how to position each movie as an event, they could turn to an earlier model when the first-run theaters of the post-war era attempted to transform exhibition into an event.

The culmination of this booking strategy came in the 1950s and 1960s when the most lavishly produced films of the year would open solely in the biggest cities in the coun-try, on a reserved-seat basis and with only two shows a day, imitating the classy pattern set by live theater. Exclusivity had its own marketing value by effectively lending an aura to each film: the small number of first-run theaters – they accounted for only a quarter of the total theaters in the United States – gave anything that was seen in those theaters a distinctive stature. And when they were shown in even fewer the-aters with advanced ticket purchases required, they were immediately made even more special.

The value of giving special value by exhib-ition practices was thrown into question by the disastrous 1969–70 seasons that even-tually saw the ledger books of all the major

film companies turn red. *The Sound of Music*, released in 1965 on a reserved-seat, limited-run basis, ended up with over $70 million in rentals, an extraordinary figure for the period, far outdistancing every other film of the decade and effectively setting a goal for every studio to try to reach. Unheard-of losses turned out to be the eventual destination, however, as every studio found its monies tied up in a small number of megabudget musicals that failed to duplicate *The Sound of Music's* success. The immediate response of the major studios was to limit costs and prod-uct. Exclusivity had seemingly lost its value in marketing films.

At the same time that the studios were moving toward disaster with the megabudget musicals, theater chains were trying to shore up their economic base through the discovery of the suburban market. Even with the growth of the suburbs after the Second World War and the intensified suburban flight of the 1960s, big downtown movie theaters continued to exist as important venues for first-run. But they lost some of their dominance with the building of new suburban theaters. Located near new shop-ping malls or in isolated spots along inter-urban highways, these theaters followed the model set by downtown theaters since it was appropriate to the tiered releasing policies of the major studios: they were generally free-standing structures with large auditoriums of 500–1,500 seats, and most often with single screens.

Multiplexing

The first twin theater was built in 1964, but single screens dominated in this period of building; the aim was to duplicate in scaled-down fashion the experience of the down-town theater. Exclusivity was still the aim, but now it was an exclusivity that the down-town had to share, often against its will, with the suburb.[14] Within two decades, how-ever, the exclusive downtown theater would virtually disappear from most mid-sized cities and become an endangered species in large cities. The suburban theater became so dominant that currently a trip to the suburbs is necessary in some urban areas in order to see first-run product.[15]

If the development of a network of first-run suburban theaters made the mass booking of films like *Jaws* feasible, this kind of booking strategy effectively helped change the course of theater building. The second wave of theater growth, beginning in the late 1970s, moved in a different direction. In 1978, only 10 percent of indoor theaters were multiplexed, with twin theaters accounting for 80 percent of those.[16] Freestanding theaters built in the 1960s were cut down the middle to create, however awkwardly, twinned theaters, and downtown movie palaces, if they continued to survive, did so by turning their balconies into separate theaters or abandoning movies altogether to become performing arts centers. This tentative move toward multiple screens escalated during the 1980s when one of the greatest explosions of new theater building in the history of motion pictures took place.[17] Multiplexes, some so large they became malls unto themselves, began to ring cities throughout the US in rapidly increasing numbers.[18] In 1979, there were 16,901 "screens" in the United States; by 1990, the number had grown to 23,689, as *Variety* triumphantly noted, "the highest count in the nation's history," even though "screen" in the past always referred to a single theater.[19] Multiplexes had become such a dominant form of exhibition that the Motion Picture Association of America now just lists screens rather than theaters. It's as if the actual number of theaters in the country had become the irrelevant statistic. The screen is the defining factor.

The very structure of these theaters created a new kind of moviegoing experience for film patrons. No longer offering just one film, these theaters, more in the mode of a television set than older film theaters, offered up at least six to ten different films and, in more extravagant outbursts, as many as 20. Film began to be merchandised like wares in a variety store, with everything to please a range of interests and tastes, in theory at least, available under one roof. Much as Kresge's, once an also-ran to Woolworth's, transformed itself into one of the country's preeminent retailers as "K-Mart" by abandoning downtown locations for more expansive suburban plants, the multiplex cinemas became the dominant force in film exhibition by following a similar retailing strategy.

But there was also one clear advantage the multiplexes had over K-Mart: since most of these theaters are first-run, they inescapably defined themselves as quality theaters. In the past, the quality of a theater might be defined by its elaborate architecture which designated it as the appropriate venue for the biggest and best films of the year. The building lent its aura to the product. Now the process is reversed and the quality product lends its aura to the undistinguished settings. Second-run became the province of home video, some of it sold by K-Mart in fact, while subsequent runs were handled by the various stages of television distribution: pay-per-view, pay-cable networks, network television and syndication. But the very different venue at which first-run also arrived in this period has effectively changed our notions of what constitutes a first-run movie.

Marketing Fallout

The marketing strategy of mass distribution has clearly made the multiplex a particularly viable exhibition form for the distribution companies. With the average film now costing $29.9 million to produce with an additional $14 million for prints and advertising, the multiplex offers a couple of key advantages. The heavy investment in television advertising, often, now, at the expense of local newspaper ads, requires that the film be non-exclusive, as readily available for immediate consumption as any other nationally advertised product. Further, the very high costs of producing and releasing films demand a quick return on investments to avoid ever-mounting interest payments on loans used for production and distribution.

The economic pressure is supported by industry wisdom that a strong first week is essential for the success of a film. Oddly, this is more a matter of faith than fact. It's actually impossible to prove that a film could not build slowly, as if often did in the past, but the current system actively discourages that. If the release of each film becomes something of a national event by virtue of the media blitz, every first week that does slow business must necessarily seem like a failed event: the film fizzles before it's given the chance to fizz.[20] In a sense, the audience is no longer allowed to discover films on its own, and the only real "sleepers" are films that do better business than advance marketing research had anticipated.

Any film which does not manage to survive the first-week blitz, is liable to disappear from theatrical life very quickly. This is actually a reverse of what was expected as multiplexes began to dominate exhibition. Initially, there was some sense that the great number of screens would enable "underperforming" films to hang on and build up an audience. This might in fact work during a period of product shortage, but now there are always other films waiting to take their place. And even films with $40–$50 million dollar budgets like *I'll Do Anything* and *Wyatt Earp*, to take two recent examples, can find themselves out of distribution within a month of release.

National advertising may help impulse buying to the extent that a title may come to mind when the patron reaches the box office. The theater chains seem aware of this to the extent that many of them now print brochures that contain guides to current releases to help guide the patron through the plethora of choices that the average multiplex offers. But there is impulse buying of another sort that is crucial to theaters, and that centers around the concession stand. The multiplex theater is a boon to the concession stand because it promotes more foot traffic by it than a single-screen theater does.[21] And the concession stand is a major source of profit for theaters, with "the proportion of profit in refreshment revenue…considerably greater" than that of the box office.[22] In 1989, for example, tickets cost patrons $5.03 billion, while concessions hit them for $1.35 billion. Furthermore, because the distributor may take away a good deal of the ticket receipts for the film rental, "At some theaters, [the concessions] account for 90 per cent of the profits."[23] In most multiplexes, the candy counter is central to the building's architecture: it is generally the first thing you see upon entering, and something you generally move by in leaving.

Every theater is a piece of real estate, and the escalation of land values in the 1980s helped put the final nail in the coffin of downtown movie palaces. As downtowns across the country became primarily business centers valued for their potential as office space, the large spaces given over to theaters became increasingly cost ineffective. The per-square-foot value of office space was simply a better investment. If theaters offered the lowest return per square foot in the center of a city, they could nonetheless have a real value for indoor malls since they could bring people into them and help promote foot traffic.[24] As a result malls generally give theaters preferential treatment in their leases, and they place the theaters in such a way that their exact location remains somewhat mysterious.[25] Where the anchor stores are always clearly visible from the exterior, the only external sign of a multiplex is generally a marquee placed near the entrance to the mall. The theater itself is often off in an obscure corner, usually unmarked on the outside, and often requiring an extensive trip through the mall to find.

The K-Mart Look

The other way out of the real estate bind of downtown theaters is the theater *as* mall. Although population and other shopping centers might eventually grow up around them, these theater malls are built at remote locations that have easy access to highways. They are often found on the sites of the former drive-ins that went up in the post-war period to accommodate both the move to the suburbs and the baby boom. Two of the largest theater chains now operating, General Cinema and National Amusements, in fact began as chains of drive-in theaters, and many of their multiplexes stand on the grounds of former drive-ins. Further, these theater malls play up "the movies" rather than any individual movie. Externally, they tend to be generally nondescript, with large marquees simply listing film titles next to auditorium numbers. If there is anything special about the product, no moviegoer would know that until getting inside the lobby where one poster might dominate another, but not often. It's in the theater mall's interest to sell all films equally, although it must also realize that some films can act as come-on draws for others. This is the reason they hand out the guides at the box office.

Finally, the theater malls offer the big theater chains the cost-effectiveness of uniformity. They are made up of a common and infinitely repeatable architectural design, somewhat modular in approach so that the number of screens actually contained within the multiplex won't change the overall look of the theater. These chains create theater malls with as familiar a look as K-Mart or McDonald's or other retail outlets with a national base.[26] The uniformity in effect helps give the theater a kind of brand-name recognition designed to assure an audience by its very familiarity.

So, what does this form of exhibition have to do with the kind of audience that goes to these theaters? For one thing, the theaters certainly posit an audience familiar and comfortable with mass retailing strategies. And in fact the publicizing of movies has changed as radically as the exhibition strategy over the past couple of decades. Where publicists working in Hollywood studios once generally rose up through the ranks of the studio hierarchy, more and more frequently Hollywood

has begun to draw on outsiders, on people with extensive backgrounds in advertising and with little experience in the movie industry.[27] One of the key aspects of this shift in the nature of both movies and the moviegoing experience is the way the film industry addresses its audience through commercials. There is now a concern to treat each individual movie as a brand and try to build up a kind of brand-name recognition for it before it opens. In effect, the various auditoriums in a multiplex function like a chain store's showroom displays of competing products: the strategy of exhibitors is to try to get potential patrons to recognize and purchase their brand.

There is, of course, one problem with this supermarket analogy, as there is with all the industrial and retailing analogies that have been applied to the "dream factory" in the past. The movies represent a peculiar "industry" since each product which that industry turns out is unique and has a very limited "shelf life." This life has been extended by the growth of the aftermarkets, but compared to other kinds of products, movies achieve a "brand name recognition" that is decidedly short term. In a "secret" staff memo that was almost immediately leaked to *Variety*, Disney Studios head Jeffrey Katzenberg put it this way:

> Thanks to the dictates of the blockbuster mentality, the shelf life of many movies has come to be somewhat shorter than [that of] a supermarket tomato.[28]

Katzenberg is clearly correct, but his language is also quite revealing. If you do think of your "product" in terms of shelf life, then the logical next step is to think of it in terms of modern marketing techniques.[29] Katzenberg can see something wrong with this system, but he can't really step outside of its way of thinking.

In the classical studio period, the companies themselves as well as the stars they held under contract might have functioned like brand names to assure audiences of a certain quality in their pictures, but there was little sense at that time that an individual film might have become a brand name that could fuel a wide variety of ancillary markets. Today's ancillary markets and cross-promotion tie-ins help lead to the treatment of the individual film as a brand name: if a studio can get McDonald's to spend $40 million to help promote *Dick Tracy* by setting up a "Dick Tracy Crimestoppers Game" as a promotion for itself, then it has to treat *Dick Tracy* the film, as opposed to the game, the lunch box, the contest, or the tee shirt, as the flagship object that establishes the brand.[30] One "old-time" Hollywood executive quoted by *Variety* objects to the new approach for the simple reason that the product is different: "When you have people talking about brand identification and product launches, you forget what you're selling... These guys think they're selling toothpaste. It's just a movie! You sell it like a movie."[31] The executive has a point, but his response also begs the question: how, exactly, do you sell something like a movie? Is the product itself ever the sole determining factor?

Mass advertising was initially a response to an exhibition strategy, not to the product itself. That strategy has now become so entrenched that it must effectively drive marketing. In the past, the slow release of a film through a system of tiers depended primarily on local advertising and, the most intangible of all Hollywood marketing strategies, word-of-mouth. Now, in effect, the word-of-mouth must exist before any moviegoer has actually seen the film, a peculiar situation to be sure. If a movie opens wide, as most major studio movies do now and the very exhibition system demands that they do, there must already be widespread interest in it.[32] Hence, the rise of mass-media advertising. But if the advertising was a response to exhibition, it inevitably had both to impact on the way we understand the product and ultimately affect the nature of the product as well.[33] Something that is exclusive and hard to see will necessarily seem different to us than something readily available for mass consumption. The object must eventually be able to fit the selling strategy.

In the early days of multiplexing, there was some thought that the multiple theaters would make for the availability of more diverse product.[34] A stronger, more popular film in a larger auditorium would help a specialty film in the smaller hall either because of overflow from the more popular film or because of the kind of impulse buying the multiplex, like any other mass retailer, tries to encourage. As it has turned out, the reverse seems to be more the case: specialty items tend not to make it to mall theaters.[35] K-Mart might offer everything under one roof, but there are definite limits to what it might sell. There are, of course, no mink coats or sterling silver, but even in other areas there are definite limitations dictated by the kind of marketing strategy behind mass-driven chain stores. In the book section, for example, you are most likely to find Danielle Steele, Stephen King, John Grisham, and their epigones. There are items that simply do not sell well within the mall-theater system. Most strikingly, foreign-language film distribution has greatly declined since the advent of the multiplex. There are a number of reasons for this, but the lack of specialty theaters remains a major one. A foreign-language film really needs an art house to promote it; its location makes it something special. In the context of a multiplex, it becomes merely another product, and one for which the mass audience holds little interest. In the early 1960s, Federico Fellini's *La Dolce Vita* could move through first-run art house showings to a wider distribution that would eventually enable it to take in ca. $70 million in current dollars. It's impossible to imagine anything like that happening in the current market.

But if the decline in foreign-language film distribution defines what can't survive in a multiplex market, what films are especially well positioned to thrive in it? Most older films were released in tiered fashion. Most, but not all. In 1953 Warner Bros. premiered *The Beast From 20,000 Fathoms* in 1,422 theaters and, a year later, *Them* in 2,000. In both cases, the word "theaters" means something a good deal larger than what we would now think of.[36] These bookings were high enough to rate brief items in *Variety*, but they were not entirely unheard of. Rather, they represented a very particular type of exhibition policy of the period, one strictly reserved for exploitation movies. Exploitation films, as their name indicates, were made for quick turnover. They were low-budget works that would draw on highly marketable features, like sex, violence, technical gimmicks, or timeliness, to ensure a quick turnover and tidy profit. They were targeted at a large number of initial patrons titillated by the exploitable elements. Exceptional films might emerge from the exploitation market every now and then, but for the most part they could not expect to increase box office through word-of-mouth. In these movies, the come-on was what sold them.

In the 1950s, exploitation was firmly entrenched in the realm of B-genres like horror and science fiction, which account for the two titles cited above, *policiers*, and lurid crime melodramas. By the 1980s, an exploitation marketing strategy had been set in place to exhibit films, but the films themselves were different at least in terms of budget. Exhibition became dominated by megabudget exploitation films. Film types once considered almost exclusively B-movie fare became the most touted genres of the year: horror, science fiction, cop movies, films based on comic strips and cartoons, films based on old TV/radio shows. The most explicit recognition of this trend came with *Raiders of the Lost Ark* in 1981. The film openly acknowledged its roots in B-film production, but did so with an A-film budget, lavishing millions of dollars on set design and special effects.

The reasons for this shift are complex since it is grounded in a striking change in audience taste. Taste itself is a consequence of too many factors, social and personal, to warrant explanations of simple economic determinism. Nevertheless, as marketing and exhibition have affected audience experience of a movie, they have clearly played an important role in the transformation of what an audience *wants* from a movie. The marketing system required by mass exhibition calls for a product which has highly exploitable elements, one that can effectively establish its flavor and its excitement within the constrictions of an extremely brief television commercial. It's not very easy to make an intimate drama look exciting in the context of a 30-sec spot, so questions of how to market the "product" necessarily come into play before the "product" is put into production. If it won't play well as a TV spot, there's a good chance it won't get produced. Furthermore, the wide opening demands an audience at the very beginning that will have a precise set of expectations which the movie will pay off one by one. The whole system of marketing and exhibition simply favors exploitation fare.

Exploitation and the Aftermarket

To say that Hollywood production decisions are driven by the marketplace is hardly news. What is new in the 1990s are the ways in which the marketplace has reconfigured itself through a massive expansion. One reason offered by the product shortage of the mid-1970s was the "somewhat inelastic overall market potential".[37] Within a decade, however, the market became a good deal more elastic than anyone in the 1970s might have anticipated. As I noted earlier, the product shortage that became an unexpected product glut in such a short period of time owes everything to the rise of home video. Since income from sales and rentals of videotape now surpass those of first-run theatrical exhibition, home video by a change of venue has effectively made second-run economically primary, an impossible feat for theatrical second-run. Home video certainly changes the way an audience experiences a movie, but it remains difficult to determine if home video affects the kind of movies that get made.[38]

It is clear, however, that other aspects of the aftermarket are helping to determine what gets produced.[39] Can a movie be turned into a theme park attraction that a producing studio owns? What are its chances for being reconfigured as a video game? The latter is a question made important by its market: as *Variety* noted, "videogames, mostly produced by companies outside the Hollywood loop, now earn more than movies domestically . . . Domestically, videogames generated between $5–7 billion dollars in 1993, while total US box office for features was closer to $5 billion."[40] With the aftermarket surpassing the "primary" market, demand grows for the former to impact on the latter. Dan Gordon, screenwriter on *Surf Ninja*, partially financed by the videogame company Sega, stated bluntly, "I try and write action sequences that will serve the movie and provide the spring-board for the videogame."[41] If a movie has sufficient "gameability," a premise that can produce a challenging videogame, then even a flop might achieve success as an arcade game.[42] With movie companies ever increasing their corporate involvement in a multimedia universe, it is perhaps inevitable that the ability to translate a film project into another medium will be a key factor to green-lighting its production.[43] The videogame machines that line the lobby walls of the multiplex theaters best signal the synergy between movies and videogames, the fact that both seem to offer comparable experiences to some of their patrons.[44]

In this new expanded media universe, what is the future of the theatrical feature film? Hollywood has effectively changed the way it addresses its audience over the last two decades, and that change has become institutionalized by the building boom in multiplex theaters. If audiences tire of the exploitation fare encouraged by the exploitation market, can Hollywood once again change its manner of address? Certainly, a number of executives like Katzenberg have attacked the "event" mentality that they feel led to the earlier crisis of 1970 and has now returned with a vengeance. But to acknowledge this is also to ignore how different the marketing of films is now. Other executives simply worry what the next event will be, and that might well be a more realistic approach to the current situation. The decline of science fiction, horror, and actioners, in that order, has left them uncertain what the audience actually wants. The success of *Pretty Woman* and *Ghost* back in 1990 and more recently *Sleepless in Seattle* in 1993 suggested that there might be value in films aimed more directly at women, who tend to be left out of the exploitation market, but, according to *Variety*, "Studios are also hesitant to bank on female audiences to turn a profit. 'Most moviegoers are men,' says 20th Century-Fox production exec Melissa Bachrach."[45] If a Hollywood executive says this, there are no doubt demographic studies to prove it, but the observation contradicts the consensus of old Hollywood that most audiences were women. If men dominate now, it might well be a consequence of the exploitation market which has always been aimed primarily at them.

Can this change? Years ago, the future of the movies seemed to lie in the then newborn video-cassette market. But that industry has turned out to be as market driven as theatrical movies. Still, the oft-predicted demise of Hollywood and the theatrical film has yet to occur. Perhaps there is simply a need to change marketing strategies every couple of decades. The top tier of exclusive, theatrical-style exhibition that was added to release schedules via reserved-seat showings in the 1950s was one such change, but it was easy to establish within existing structures of exhibition. How much the multiplex phenomenon dictates exhibition strategies remains to be seen. The only certainty is that the need for change will lead to change. Change might be as minimal as the move to reserved seats in the 1950s, extending the tiering system to its farthest reaches, or it might be as radical as the dramatic revamping of production, distribution, and exhibition that has taken place over the last 15 years. Whatever happens, it's likely that Hollywood will be speaking to us in a different way over the next decade, and what we expect when we go out to a movie then will be different from what we expect today.

Addendum

As this issue was going to press [1994], *Variety* ran a lead story headlined "Here Come the Megaplexes: Exhibs Usher in 24-Screen Destinations." The story reports a new wave in theater building that confirms the trends in exhibition outlined in the preceding article: super multiplexes – or "megaplexes" in *Variety*speak. Every possible thing is contained under one roof, with free-standing theaters independent of malls that can operate as destinations in themselves by being "coupled with entertainment centers encompassing everything from minature golf and virtual reality games to 'food courts' and toddler compounds."[46] This new trend runs counter to industry fears of overbuilding, but the *Variety* writer speculates that the new theaters – a logical extension of the "theater malls" described in the current article – might render the original mall theater obsolete and ultimately replace rather than add to them.

Notes

1 According to the Motion Picture Association of America, attendance declined by 5.9 percent in 1990, then by another 4.0 percent in 1991. The rebound in 1992 and 1993 still did not bring attendance levels back to the 1989 record.

2 A recent *Variety* article on the weak first quarter of 1994 suggests that anxiety levels continue. Following a subtitle, "Glorious Summer Start Can't Erase Spring of Discontent," the article begins, "It's difficult to recall a time when relations between exhibitors and distributors have been more brittle." Leonard Klady, "Exhibs' Hard Feelings Linger," *Variety*, June 6–12, 1994.

3 John Brodie, "Franchise Frenzy in H'wood," *Variety*, January 3–9 1994, 1, 66.

4 John Evan Frook, "Sony Calculates Comeback: 'Hero's' Flameout Was Not Rocket Science," *Variety*, May 2–8, 1994, 1, 103.

5 For a more detailed discussion of this earlier "crisis," see William Paul, "Hollywood Hara-kiri: Notes on the Decline of an Industry and Art," *Film Comment* 13, no. 2 (March–April 1977), 40–3, 56–62.

6 Robert Lindsey, "Hollywood Scenario: Boom and Bust," *New York Times*, September 26, 1975, 28.

7 I have written more extensively about the rise of the gross-out and the high-budget exploitation film in *Laughing Screaming: Modern Hollywood Horror and Comedy* (New York: Columbia University Press, 1994).

8 A.D. Murphy, "Ancillaries No Alibi for B.O. Blahs," *Variety*, July 16, 1986, 26. Murphy also claimed this was not a distinctive feature of the film business: "All broad-based art forms are driven and sustained by a handful of successes. There are lots of books, records, films and TV shows offered each day to the public; only a few make it big." Still, it should be noted that the difference in revenue between a successful film and a weak film grew immeasurably larger in the post-studio period.

9 Lawrence Cohn's analysis of the increase in production makes clear that home video was the driving force: "While a very low budget project can successfully bypass theatrical and earn back its cost in strictly ancillary markets (such as the made expressly for homevideo exercise programs), most features require theatrical exposure to justify their existence and get the ball rolling. As a result, many of the new indie distribs are merely walking their pictures through the theatrical release, at minimum cost, en route to the more lucrative ancillaries." Cohn, "Overproduction Hurts Distribs," *Variety*, February 25, 1987, 1, 86.

10 As A.D. Murphy noted in analyzing a box-office recession of the mid-1980s, "For a quarter of a century, the number of tickets sold annually by US theaters has ranged up and down around 1.03 billion...By 1962, the impact of television (and an enlarged leisure-time spectrum) on film attendance had exhausted itself...Instead of looking at new video gadgets as a threat, it should be kept in mind that the combination of old and new

exhibition markets results in more people, watching more films, more often, than at any other time since the invention of film and camera nearly 100 years ago." Murphy (1986), 3, 26.

11 Selznick, *Memo from David O. Selznick* (New York: The Viking Press, 1972), 356–9.

12 The obvious precedent for the release of *Jaws* was another high-budget horror film from two years earlier, *The Exorcist* (1973). See my discussion of the release of *The Exorcist* in *Laughing Screaming* (287–90) for how audience response led Warner Bros. toward more of a mass booking release than they originally intended.

13 Advertising costs offer the clearest evidence of this shift in marketing. According to a Motion Picture Association of America chart, average advertising costs between 1980 and 1993 nearly quadrupled, from $3.5 million to $12.1 million. In 1991, a studio executive complained to *Variety*, "Movie marketing has become totally media driven, neglecting the exploitation of publicity, promotion and word-of-mouth." Anne Thompson, "Studios Shifting to Mad Ave's Savvy Sell," *Variety*, April 1, 1991, 87.

14 Difficulties experienced by the exclusive first-run theaters of Chicago in the Near North Side and the Loop by the mid-1970s are exemplary of this shift: "Whereas outlyers here once had to fight to get major bookings on a first run basis, that situation has been reversed, with near north exhibitors and an occasional Loop house now seeking track product and suppliers looking for additional track houses." Lloyd Sachs, "Near North Side Vis-A-Vis Loop and Suburbs; Chicago Altering," *Variety*, March 31, 1976, 19. See also Lloyd Sachs, "Loop Comes To Day-Date Policy; Downtown Grief," which makes clear that marketing strategies were affecting the booking policies of downtown theaters: "Distribs have backed away from exclusive runs in the Loop, he [Plitt theater booker Jerry Winsberg] said, because 'There just aren't enough pictures that lend themselves to spending money in the Loop and then in outlying houses, in terms of advertising.'" *Variety*, June 2, 1976, 7.

15 "What we have found today is that many, many of the prime theaters in the country are in shopping malls," says marketing consultant Martin Levy, "and that's a major revolution in distribution in the last five or ten years. There are many cities in which a first-run, quality film will only open in four or five theaters, and they will all be out in [suburban] communities, and generally they will be in shopping centers." This quotation is from a 1983 article; since this point, most of the downtown movie palaces have disappeared as venues for first-run exhibition. William Severini Kowinski, "The Malling of the Movies," *American Film* (September 1983), 55.

16 Gary R. Edgerton, *American Film Exhibition and an Analysis of the Motion Picture Industry's Market Structure 1963–1980* (New York: Garland Publishing, 1983), chart on p. 139.

17 A *Variety* article published in 1984 noted that "Totals (of screens) had gradually risen from 1964 to 1984," with 1984 seeing the "highest number of screens since 1948." Furthermore, "Scores of additional screens" that had recently been added to the nation's total were "almost entirely in new multiplexes . . ." Will Tusher, "US Exhibs Showing New Growth," *Variety*, November 28, 1984.

18 Because it did not have the same kind of suburban flight as most other American cities, New York City remains the largest urban film market in the country, but the fate of the oldest Broadway theaters reflects changes taking place elsewhere. In the 1970s, these old palaces turned themselves into twin theaters by adding a screen to the balcony. By the 1990s, a theater of only two screens was no longer a viable use of real estate: the Criterion, which had not only twinned its auditorium but added four small theaters to its basement, became the only one of the original Broadway film palaces that was not torn down. In fact, the Loew's chain tore down its three remaining large-scale movie theaters in Manhattan to replace them with newly built multiplexes.

19 Will Tusher, "Nation's Screen Tally Reached a New High in '90," *Variety*, January 28, 1991, 3.

20 "The hundreds of new theaters that can present anywhere from 6 to 18 movies at a time provide opportunity for the increasingly important independent filmmakers and small distribution companies. But the peril in such numbers is that failure can be quicker and have more impact . . . 'Since there is so

much film for exhibitors to choose from, you have to open strong or exhibitors will pull your movie,' said the president of distribution and marketing at 20th Century-Fox, Tom Sherak. 'A year ago a movie used to have a minimum shelf life of two weeks. Now it's only one week, and then the movie is double-billed. In and out.' " Aljean Harmetz, "New Movies Battle for Theaters," *New York Times*, October 14, 1987, C23.

21 A measure of the concession stand's importance is the quick reaction of theater chains to reject claims about theater popcorn made by the Center for Science in the Public Interest. See Paul F. Young, "Popcorn Peril Puts Theater Owners on the Hot-Oil Seat," *Variety*, May 2–8, 1994, 13, 20.

22 Thomas Guback, "The Evolution of the Motion Picture Theater Business in the 1980s," *Journal of Communication* (Spring 1987), 63–4. Guback reprints a chart from the US Department of Commerce that shows concession revenue as a percentage of admission revenue rose from 14.62 percent in 1967 to 23.26 percent in 1982.

23 Charles Fleming, "Snackbar Slowdown Bitter Pill for Exhibs," *Variety*, January 21, 1991, 3. An article on shopping-center theaters in a real estate journal from the same year notes, "in a theater it often is not the movie, but the ancillary concessions that generate the most revenues available to the theater operator." Earl L. Segal, Edward M. Rogers, "Negotiating the Shopping Center Movie Theater Lease," *Real Estate Review* (Summer 1991), 84.

24 Guback points out that the building boom of the 1980s, "is closely tied to the growth of shopping malls and does not necessarily represent a significant capital investment on the part of exhibitors themselves." Some of this building boom, then, was spurred on by the desires of the shopping mall developers, who put up much of the cost of theater building. Guback, 71.

25 Guback notes, "In cases where the exhibitor advances some construction money to the developer, the rent for the premises is reduced accordingly." Guback, 69. Segal and Rogers detail the special arrangements shopping centers make in their rental agreements with theatres, 82–7.

26 In writing this, I do not intend to update Douglas Gomery's assertion that the movie theater chains forming in the mid-1910s followed the pattern set by chain stores such as Sears–Roebuck, Woolworth's, and A&P because I think this analogy needs some qualification. While the theater chains might have followed some of the marketing and accounting strategies of the chain stores, they also aimed to position themselves as high class, which made them something quite different. Gomery himself seems to recognize this in his discussion of Balaban & Katz as the chain that set the mode for nationwide chains: "Balaban & Katz proved that the movie entertainment business was not one of simple *mass* market appeal." Furthermore, while the retail chains Gomery cites managed to establish themselves by offering low prices, "Prices [in Balaban & Katz theaters] were higher than the usual five and ten cents and sometimes reached a dollar for the best seats on the best night of the week for the top attractions." While similar designs for these movie palaces might be used in different cities, the theater chains for the most part did not aim for the kind of uniformity that is typical in multiplex building since that itself would have denied their aspirations to quality. Where the movie palaces might have imitated the Paris Opera, there was no confusing the interiors of Woolworth's stores, all uniform, with the very distinctive downtown Chicago Marshall Field, itself an imitation of a Paris department store. Gomery, *Shared Pleasures: A History of Movie Presentation in the United States* (Madison: University of Wisconsin Press, 1992), 35, 36, 55.

27 "For the first time, top-level advertising decisions are being made, not by old movie hands, but by marketing professionals, recruited from agencies or other industries... While marketing chiefs traditionally rose through studio publicity and ad departments, four major studios now have looked outside in filling their top posts and a fifth is expected to be announced shortly." Thompson (April 1, 1991), 1.

28 "The Teachings of Chairman Jeff," *Variety*, February 4, 1991, 24.

29 One of the oddest examples of this is the use of the word "franchise" as in "franchise picture" to denote a film that holds out the possibility for endless sequels if the original

has sufficient drawing power. See Brodie (January 3–9, 1994), 1, 66.

30 Thompson (April 1, 1991), 87.

31 Ibid.

32 Some films that will admittedly have a more limited appeal, like *Barton Fink* and *The Commitments*, may be "platformed," which means opening at a limited number of theaters and moving out from there, something in the manner of the tiering system, but the timing of these platforms is often fairly short, and the aim is still to move the film into a kind of mass-market system. Of course, if these films fail in limited release, they never make it to the mass market.

33 See Cameron Stauth, "The Cineplex Complex," *American Film* (December 1990), 16.

34 Even as late as 1986 Jean Picker Firstenberg could write, hopefully, "The multiplexes greatly increased the number of small venues that could support – without filing a Chapter Eleven – experimental films, artistic films, foreign and independent films." Firstenberg, "A Renaissance in Film Exhibition," *American Film* (November 1986), 73.

35 Guback has written, "Clearly, the proliferation of screens has not necessarily meant a great choice of films for consumers but merely more locations at which to view a smaller number of films. Moreover, release strategies in recent years have turned virtually all theaters into first-run houses in many communities. The second run, therefore, begins with home video and pay TV." Guback, 76.

36 "Plan Fast Playoff For WB 'Beast,' " *Variety*, June 17, 1953, 3, and "2,000 Playdates for WB's 'Them' Within a Month!" *Variety*, June 2, 1954, 5.

37 A.D. Murphy, "Pinch Picture Playoff Patterns," *Variety*, March 17, 1976.

38 Certainly sale of home-video rights has been a factor in facilitating niche marketing, production of films aimed at limited audiences. This might also mean, simply, that independent cinema has greater visibility than ever before in the past.

39 It is a fair measure of how much the market has changed that A.D. Murphy, one of the most astute observers of Hollywood economics, could write in 1978: "A major diversified film production-distribution company – active in music, recreation parks, telefilming, whatever – cannot be expected to lose money on theatrical filmmaking...and make it up on the diversifications. Nor can the secondary markets for features – TV, pay-TV, etc. – be required to create the overall pix profit..." Murphy, "Hits Alone Nourish Biz; More Non-Hits Too Risky," *Variety*, June 14, 1978, 3.

40 John Brodie, Marx, "Two Can Play This Game," *Variety*, December 27, 1993, 1, 74.

41 Ibid., 74.

42 "Gameability Can Elude Even a Blockbuster Pic," *Variety*, December 27, 1993, 74.

43 Over a decade ago, William Severini Kowinski wrote of the mall movie theaters: "The marriage between Americans and the mall is changing not only how movies are promoted and exhibited but perhaps even which movies get made. More films these days are being shown in theaters that are located in shopping centers; not only are the movies themselves available in malls, but so are the books, records, games, toys, mugs, kites, clothes, and dolls that make-up the tie-in merchandise for a growing number of films..." In the intervening period, the potential for tie-ins as a factor in determining production has remained high, so it is likely that the video-game will be an equally potent force in production decisions. Kowinski, 55.

44 These machines also point to the radical difference between the multiplex of today and the movie palace of the past in the deliberate downscale atmosphere. Much as the video-games seem fitting in the multiplex, it would be impossible to imagine the grand lobbies of the old palaces full of pinball machines.

45 Anne Thompson, "Studios Stick to their Guns over Sex Appeal of Pics," *Variety*, January 7, 1991, 109.

46 Paul Noglows, *Variety*, August 22–8, 1994, 1.

49

Modern Times (1993)

Barbara Stones

Throughout exhibition history, doomsayers have regularly predicted the demise of movie theatres. The dire forecasts began with the advent of radio, grew more pronounced when television arrived, and reached a negative crescendo of gloom when the triple threat of videocassettes, cable and satellite services reached full maturity during the 1980s.

To be sure, a full-blown revolution in home entertainment was underway. VCRs, costing some $1,200 when they were first introduced in the seventies, soon plummeted in price to less than $300. By the mid-1980s two-thirds of America's households owned a VCR, and the market was still growing. A proliferation of video stores emerged to flaunt thousands of movie titles for sale or rent on cassette. And then there was cable. By the late 1980s every cable system in the country had at least one movie channel, with more than 90 percent of the systems offering two or more. The pay-per-view concept also gained in popularity. Rather than paying a fee for a month's worth of premium movie channel programming, cable subscribers could instead pay a separate, usually smaller fee for each special event or movie watched, much as they did at a movie theatre's box office. Laser discs debuted in the early 1980s as competition to the videocassette. Laser discs played back a superior video image and theoretically would never wear out, but disc players were generally much more expensive th[a]n VCRs, plus they lacked the VCR's ability to record.

Far from folding under the onslaught of these home entertainment systems, exhibition entered a stage of dramatic growth that climaxed with a record 23,000 movie screens in place by the end of the 1980s. The expanded ancillary market for films generated a gold mine of new profits that studios promptly pumped back into increased production. After battling a drought of pictures for years, exhibition was enjoying a deluge.

Despite the competition from VCRs and cable, the moviegoing audience remained stable during the '80s with more than one billion tickets sold in the U.S. each year. What became abundantly clear was that all the new media depended on movie marketing and box office success to attract home audiences. Movie theatres retained the enviable position of launching a film in its first release. Despite a shortening of the "release window" – an industry term for that period of time between the end of a film's first run and the start of its subsequent release to ancillary markets – going to a movie theatre was still the only way to see the latest pictures with top stars. And of course, it was the only way *ever* to see a movie in the richness of detail and sound that the filmmaker originally intended, all while enjoying a shared

Excerpted from Barbara Stones, *America Goes to the Movies* (North Hollywood, California: National Association of Theatre Owners, 1993), 231–49. Reprinted courtesy of the National Association of Theatre Owners.

emotional experience in a darkened auditorium full of people.

Mindful of the increasing sophistication of big screen televisions and home stereo systems, exhibition embarked on an aggressive campaign to upgrade screen presentation and all aspects of the moviegoing experience. Theatre complexes expanded into larger, more stylish showhouses. The 1980s saw a trend away from twin, triple and four-screen theatres to new and remodelled complexes featuring six, ten or more auditoriums. The multiple screen theatre had outgrown the shopping mall and increasingly emerged as a free-standing complex. "There are a number of reasons why theatres wanted to be free standing now," explained veteran Midwestern exhibitor Herb Brown. "First of all if you are in a mall generally you have certain constraints. The mall might want to close at 10 and then they start designating certain exits that will be available to your people when they get out at 11 or 12 or one in the morning. If you are doing business and you have a line or a big crowd, you don't want to be concerned about these people lining up in front of the mall stores."

Modern multiplexes saw plain-faced functional designs give way to those with more imagination, color and neon. Lobbies expanded to embrace huge, brightly-lit concession counters with an expanded array of snack choices. Seats became wider and more comfortable. "Probably the biggest improvement we've made in seating was the cupholder arm rest," remarked veteran circuit executive Vincent Guzzo. "They didn't work at first. We couldn't figure out how to hold them on there. They were too wide and the seat bucket wouldn't come up or wouldn't go down. People would bang into them with their knees. We made them out of wood for a long time. They were expensive. We couldn't figure out a way to make all of the drink sizes fit. It was about a two year cycle before we got one that really worked."

Cleanliness and regular maintenance were re-emphasized; courteous staff service became a top priority. Showtimes were staggered with military-like precision to eliminate lines and maintain a smooth traffic flow at all times. The advent of computerized ticketing and credit card advance sales put a crowning touch of convenience on the whole moviegoing experience. "You stand in line and you see someone just scanning the board and you realize what's going on," said veteran Florida-based exhibitor Arthur Hertz of the multiplex experience. "It's like going to a smorgasbord and they'll see what appeals to them at the moment. There is a psychology to having a lot of small auditoriums playing a lot of pictures. If you are sold out of one, there are still choices for people to come in and see something else. They're not usually going to walk away and say 'the hell with it, I'm going home.' They'll see something else."

The centerpiece of a successful multiplex is its focus on economies of scale. Multiple auditoriums that share a common parking lot, box office, lobby, restrooms and concession area reduce overhead expenses and generate more profit per square foot. Behind the scenes, theatre circuits pursued the economies of centralized purchasing and utilized computers to track inventory and prevent spoilage.

The 1980s witnessed the birth of the mega-multiplexes, wondrous theatre complexes that put a new premium on style, service, comfort and screen presentation. In 1982, Canada's Cineplex theatre circuit, which had startled the industry three years earlier with the opening of the world's first 18-plex in Toronto, gained a foothold in the U.S. market when it opened the $3 million, 14-screen Beverly Center Cineplex inside a sprawling new upscale Los Angeles shopping mall. The sleek new complex was kept spotlessly clean, and included Perrier and Cadbury's chocolates among its concession choices. The complex would typically put a popular, well-advertised film on as many as three or four screens at a time, and cut back the number of screens as interest in the film declined.

Fueled by its North American successes, the company bought out a major Canadian chain to emerge as Cineplex Odeon. The company continued its expansion into the American market. In 1985 after buying out the Plitt circuit, Cineplex Odeon became, overnight, the fourth-largest theatre chain in the United States. Soon after it joined with MCA, parent company of Universal Studios, to build and jointly operate what was then the world's largest cinema complex. The 18-screen mega-multiplex, located adjacent to Universal Studios in Los Angeles, which could accommodate up to 6,000 patrons, opened in 1987. Some 38,000 patrons showed up for its July, 1987 opening weekend and the venue remains one of the most successful theatre complexes in the U.S.

But by the early 1990s, if you wanted to see the biggest theatre in the Western Hemisphere – 6,000 seats, spread over 20 screens, spread over 125,000 square feet of property – you had to first journey into America's heartland to an area not far from Motor City, U.S.A. There stood the Studio 28, a 20-plex owned by Jack Loeks in Grand Rapids, Michigan. In the early 1990s prominent theatre circuits announced plans for even *bigger* mega-multiplex theatres. Mammoth 24-screen theatre complexes were set for construction.

In sharp contrast to the rise of super-colossal theatres came the 1980s phenomenon of the discount "dollar" house, a theatre that presented sub-run features at a fraction of their first-run prices. The traditional audience for the dollar house is the audience on a low or fixed income: the elderly, the poor or the student. "There are many people in the country that can't afford more than a dollar for a movie ticket," explained Texas-based exhibition executive Randy Hester. His circuit operated dozens of dollar houses in the 1990s.

"We've always felt that there's a place for sub-run," said Virginia-based circuit owner Sam Bendheim III. "It is a different audience and this is our feeling: It does not take away from the first-runs because those people are not going to go anyway. We have found that we are bringing in people who haven't been to the movies in years because of the cost, because they have large families and they can't afford the whole experience, or because they're on fixed incomes. But they would rather see a movie in a theatre than rent a video."

Exhibition's business climate during the 1980s was marked by an intense phase of consolidation that saw a handful of companies grow to dominate the industry. "The consolidation took place for several reasons," explained exhibition veteran Joel Resnick, "One, the inherent fear of how we are going to do business in an atmosphere that wouldn't let us split. And two, theatre owners got offered deals they never dreamt they could get offered. Why not sell when you could get more money than you could ever make?" Regional circuits that had weathered decades of exhibition's struggles faced the choice of a lucrative buy-out offer or the difficult prospect of competing against the financial clout of a major national chain. Scores of these smaller circuits sold out, their theatres submerged into new corporate identities.

Beginning in 1986, the parent companies of major Hollywood studios began to enter exhibition by purchasing interests in national theatre circuits. But unlike the vertically-integrated studio-owned theatres of the 1930s and 1940s, theater chains owned or partially owned by studio parent companies are typically run by independent management teams and boards of directors.

As a result of the fierce competition for market share, some areas of the country were overbuilt with too many screens, turning once profitable venues into poor performers for the competing circuits. Saddled with debt from what one veteran exhibitor called the "feeding frenzy" to acquire theatres at prices many times their market worth, some of the major circuits faced a period of retrenchment at the end of the decade and began to raise cash by selling off some of their theatres, usually venues in smaller markets. As a result, some regional circuits that resisted the tide of consolidation would come to increase their screen totals and grow to greater prominence. [...]

[...] [P]undits have been predicting the demise of the motion picture theatre virtually since the medium's inception. First the introduction of wireless radio was to have signaled the movies' death-knell; then the arrival of television; then home video and cable; and most recently pay-per-view. With family entertainment conveniently located in the living room of every American's home in the '90s, again the question is posed: "Who needs to drive out to a theatre to watch a movie?"

Well, actor Harrison Ford, for one. "Going to the movies is one of the last things we do together as a people, one of our last community rituals," Ford told *Vanity Fair* in a 1993 interview. "We enter a darkened room as a group of strangers and we all watch the same images up on the screen and we generally share the same reactions – the same emotions – to these images. If we are lucky, if the movie is good, we watch something that reminds us of our commonality and our humanity. That makes it very different from sitting at home watching a VCR by yourself or with one other person."

And, of course, Ford has perfectly distilled the enduring appeal of moviegoing. Almost everyone seems to agree that new technologies and the "freshness" of newly-released first-run films keep the moviegoing experience exciting, but it is the *sharing* of the out-of-home experience with others that makes it unique and irreplaceable.

Or, as Sony Pictures Entertainment chairman Peter Guber once explained, "We can expand our business to the farthest points of the earth, repeat movies in a dozen new formats and technologies, blaze new pathways into home entertainment, but there is no substitute for the shared emotion of going to the movies – the 20th century version of the tribal campfire."

The tribal campfire burns on.

50

From Exhibition to Reception: Reflections on the Audience in Film History

Robert C. Allen

As recently as 1975, when I taught my first film history class, film history still was almost universally taken to mean the history of films. Not all films, of course, just those films a teacher could nominate with a straight face as "art" in defending his or her course to a colleague in art history or literature. Ironically, the first film "theory" that French, then British, and finally American scholars took up in opposition to this cinematic New Criticism – the "auteur theory" – merely bolstered the historiographic notion that film history was to be studied as a succession of texts. The corpus of film history – especially American film history – was certainly modified as a result of auteurism, but the idea that film history rested upon the interpretation of a body of texts remained unchallenged. Any hopes of dethroning the text in film studies and textual interpretation in film history were dashed in the mid-1970s as auteurism was succeeded by structuralism, semiotics, and Lacthusserianism. Film history was to take a very back seat indeed during the reign of high theory, which is not surprising given its resolutely ahistorical and thoroughly conventionalist underpinnings. All the cool graduate students were analyzing texts. Anyone interested in questions of history was clearly not with the program; and

anyone interested in non-cinetextual historical questions – economic structures, the relationship between cinema and other forms of popular entertainment, technology, the organization of labor, or what might have gone on the billions of times the texts of film history were "read" by viewers – was also a damned empiricist!

And yet as I prepared that first set of film history lectures, issues of context not textual interpretation troubled and fascinated me most – a fascination, I must admit, that owed more to intellectual perversity than prescience. Specifically, I was struck by how little the audience or even exhibition featured in the received film history we all learned in film courses or read about in survey accounts. Except for the legendary viewers who dove under their seats at the sight of Lumière's train coming into the station; the countless immigrants to the US who, we are told, learned American values in the sawdust-floored nickelodeons of the lower East Side; and those who, to a person it would seem, applauded Al Jolson's "You ain't seen nothin' yet" in 1927;[1] film history had been written as if films had no audiences or were seen by everyone and in the same way, or as if however they were viewed and by whomever, the history of "films" was distinct from and

Robert C. Allen, "From Exhibition to Reception: Reflections on the Audience in Film History" originally appeared in *Screen* 31, no. 4 (Winter 1990), 347–56.

privileged over the history of their being taken up by the billions of people who have watched them since 1894.

Furthermore, a good deal of what had been written about film audiences was supported (if at all) by the flimsiest of evidence and yet was couched in terms of unqualified generalization. In one of my early lectures I got to the point in American film history when films had been successfully introduced as vaudeville acts (ca. 1896). But quickly thereafter (ca. 1897), as I had read in all the standard histories, audiences became so disenchanted with the movies that theater managers began to use them as "chasers" – acts so unpopular that they drove the audience from the theater. The words stuck in my throat. I couldn't "profess" this moment of film history. As a result, I was driven back to more contemporaneous sources and to a wider consideration of the contexts within which early films were received. I'll not belabor the "chaser" issue further here, except to say that nearly 15 years later I'm far from convinced that films universally sank into a trough of audience disdain during this period or that vaudeville managers routinely used movies they knew their audiences did not want to see to clear the house.[2]

Over the past 15 years, a number of scholars in the US and elsewhere at least have added exhibition to the agenda of film history, demonstrating, among other things, how important exhibition was as an historical determinant in the development of the film industry in the US. In the process, they have also suggested something of our appalling ignorance of the most basic facts of exhibition history: differences in exhibition practices among cities and towns, the likely audiences for the tens of thousands of exhibition venues across the US and over time, and the complexities of the relationship between moviegoing and other social practices. Today I would hope that no film scholar would write a serious film history with the near total elision of the audience that characterized such works 15 years ago, and I would similarly hope (although I know in fact they are) that

film history classes would not be taught without some minimal attention being given to the conditions under which viewers actually saw films.

In 1983 Philip Corrigan declared the history of film audiences to be "still almost completely undeveloped, even unconsidered." He argued that the problem of the audience in film history could usefully be recast within the rubric of cultural studies.[3] What I would like to propose here is taking Corrigan's reconsideration of the audience in film history a step further: namely the enlarging of the notion of exhibition and the audience to encompass a more general historical concern with reception – a move implied in the work of a growing number of film scholars. I am using the term reception here to mean the most inclusive category of issues surrounding the confrontation between the semiotic and the social. Reception thus conceived would have at least four overlapping but theoretically and methodologically distinct components.

1 Exhibition

Exhibition here designates the institutional and economic dimensions of reception – that is, the nature of the institutional apparatus under whose auspices and for whose benefit films are shown; the relationship between exhibition as that term has been used within the industry and other segments of the film business; and the location and physical nature of the sites of exhibition.

Although no study has systematically charted the nature and historical development of exhibition in the US, a number of individual studies have suggested something of the previously unacknowledged variety of exhibition practices, particularly during the first two decades of the commercial exploitation of the movies. The first thing these studies are discovering is that New York City – the place from which many of our generalizations about moviegoing across the country are taken – is probably *sui generis* with respect to exhibition. As soon as we look at cities in other parts of the country, smaller cities without large immigrant populations, and small towns and villages, a very different exhibition picture emerges.

For example, concentration on early moviegoing as an urban phenomenon has obscured the fact that during the first decade of the movies' commercial growth, 71 percent of the population of the United States lived in rural areas or small towns. The first audiences for the movies in these areas were not to be found in vaudeville theaters (the towns were too small to support them) or storefront movie theaters (which, if they came at all, came later), but in tents, amusement parks, the local opera house, YMCA hall, public library basement – wherever an itinerant showman could set up his (/her? – were there any female itinerant exhibitors?) projector. Edward Lowry has suggested that one consequence of small communities' reliance upon itinerant showmen was that their audiences attached much more importance to the exhibitor – who, after all, was the present, human agent of their filmgoing pleasure – than to the producers of the films he showed.

For years, traveling exhibitors provided the only opportunities for moviegoing to millions of Americans. The dispatching of Lumière "operators" around the world in 1896 has left the impression that exposure to motion pictures, at least in the West, was universal and simultaneous. However, the more we learn about US exhibition patterns, the more aware we become of just how long it took the movies to reach some parts of the country. Although we know that films were shown in some remote locations (Klondike mining camps in 1898 for example), one itinerant showman claimed to have given the first movie exhibition in Arizona during the 1911–12 season. Furthermore, although many traveling exhibitors ceased operation with the spread of permanent exhibition in the 1910s, there were still itinerant showmen on the road as late as 1947. One showman, who worked the small towns of North

and South Carolina, Virginia, and Georgia, recalled that one of his best customers was a woman who had never seen the movies until he set up his tent in her village for the first time in the mid-1930s.[4]

For some time now my graduate students and I have been charting exhibition patterns in cities and towns throughout North Carolina between 1896 and 1915. Without exception, the exhibition situation contrasts sharply with that in New York. Permanent exhibition for example was not established even in the largest North Carolina city until 1906. The first permanent theaters were not located in working-class ghettos but invariably in the center of the downtown business district. Most of these theaters attempted to attract a middle-class clientele from the outset. In some cases itinerant showmen were the first to bring movies to the community, but more often than not in the case of large towns, the first sustained exhibition programs took place in amusement parks, which were constructed at the end of street car lines to encourage ridership. My favorite example is the mountain community of Asheville, NC where, in the summer of 1902, movies were projected on a screen erected on an island in the middle of a lake. Many Ashevillians saw their first movie from the stern of a canoe.[5]

The history of non-commercial exhibition has hardly even been considered and has certainly not been written about, despite the fact that film projectors have been marketed for home use since the 1890s, and in 1948 – well before the popularity of Super-8 and half-inch video – more than one million American households owned movie cameras.[6] We have also yet to explore the history of the use of movies in schools – another important non-commercial site of filmic reception.

2 Audience

Obviously, at the most basic level this term designates the "who" of reception. The direct study of contemporary audiences is already fraught with enormous theoretical and methodological problems, which are, of course, multiplied greatly when questions of audience are cast in the past tense. Although some contemporaneous and "independently" collected data on American movie audiences is available to scholars (the Gallup Poll surveys of audience movie preferences in the 1940s, for example), we know much less in gross demographic terms about the audiences for movies than we do about the historical audiences for broadcasting. In large measure this is because, as Motion Picture Association of America President Eric Johnson noted in 1946, the Hollywood film industry knew less about itself than any other American industry. As an industry executive characterized market research in Hollywood a few years later, "We stand in the dark and throw a rock and [if] we hear a crash, [we assume] we've hit the greenhouse."[7] But leaving the practicalities of historical audience research aside for a moment, the study of historical audiences for the movies should include, for starters, an attempt to determine the size and constitution of the audiences for various films; and the relationship of moviegoing patterns to race, gender, class, ethnicity, and other variables.

To give another American example from the early period: although immigrants in New York City did go to nickelodeons between 1906 and 1912, not all immigrant groups were equally attracted to the movies. Jewish immigrants frequently went to the movie theaters that sprang up on the Lower East Side after 1905, but relatively fewer Italian immigrants, who lived in large numbers in an adjacent neighborhood, went. Why? The best answer I can come up with is that Jews came to the US to stay and they came as families. Eighty-five percent of Italian migration to the US between 1885 and 1915 was single men between the ages of 18 and 35 who came to New York to dig the subways or build the Brooklyn Bridge. Then the vast majority returned home to Italy. For many in this group the movies were an irrelevant extravagance.

We have just begun to uncover the history of black exhibition in the US. In the South blacks were barred from "white" theaters until the 1960s or were forced to sit in restricted areas of the auditorium. By 1915 however, the black ghettoes of a number of southern cities featured black theaters which served as important cultural centers for the community and provided an outlet for black films.[8]

Within the category of audience, I'm also talking about the social meanings attached to moviegoing, in the same way that Janice Radway talks about the social meanings of reading romantic novels.[9] Obviously, the social meaning ascribed to the viewing of a European art film at Lincoln Center or the NFT is different from being part of the audience for *Debbie Does Dallas* a few blocks away on Times Square or in Soho.

As Ien Ang's *Desperately Seeking the Audience* (Routledge, forthcoming) makes abundantly clear with respect to the television audience, "audience" is as much a discursive as a social phenomenon. Individuals are not only solicited but constructed as audience members through industry attempts at marketing research, advertising, promotions, the decor of movie theaters, etc. The discourse constructs some audience groups more precisely and differently than others. Diane Waldman, for example, has argued that women filmgoers have been "pursued" through advertising, publicity stunts, and other promotional devices "to a degree disproportionate with their actual representation in the filmgoing audience." Other groups – blacks and other identifiably non-WASP ethnic groups, for example – have for the most part been omitted from Hollywood's construction of "the audience" for the movies. Mary Beth Haralovich's extensive work on Hollywood advertising has examined both the industry's self-representational strategies as well as those for interpellating viewers.[10] We need to ask whom the industry and their agents have thought they were talking about when they talked about "the audience." What presumptions lie behind not only advertising and promotion, but also studio pronouncements and internal discourse regarding "popularity," "box office," and films that "work" with particular audiences?

3 Performance

By this I mean the immediate social, sensory, performative context of reception. We tend to talk of films being "screened" as if the only thing going on in a movie theater were light being bounced off a reflective surface. Obviously, at a number of levels there is much more going on during a film-viewing situation than that. Again, we have only begun to chart the enormous variety of cinema performance and changes over time. A look at what I'm calling performance serves to remind us that film has been merely one component of reception. Given the rather phenomenologically impoverished nature of commercial film viewing in the US and the UK these days, it is easy to overlook the fact that in the 1920s in America, for example, many viewers were not particularly interested in what feature film was playing. They were attracted to the theater by the theater itself, with its sometimes bizarre architectural and design allusions to exotic cultures, its capacious public spaces, its air conditioning in the summer, and its auditorium, which may have been decorated to resemble the exterior of a Moorish palace at night – complete with heavenly dome and twinkling stars. Regardless of what feature the theater chain had secured from the distributor that week, there was sure to be a newsreel, a comedy short, a program of music by pit orchestra or on the mighty Wurlitzer, and, in many theaters, elaborate stage shows. Trade papers from the 1920s (*Moving Picture World* in particular) provided smaller exhibitors with suggestions for lobby displays, promotional tie-ins, publicity stunts, as well as stage shows to complement particular films or genres of films.

In a fascinating paper, Mary Carbine has pointed out the role of black movie theaters on the South side of Chicago as providing a venue for jazz and blues.[11] Louis Armstrong, Fats Waller, Erskine Tate, Earl Hines, and other legendary black musicians provided musical accompaniment for mainstream Hollywood films. Ads in black newspapers featured the pit orchestra much more prominently than the film. At times, the jazz bands provided not so much accompaniment to the film as counterpoint. A critic complained that "Race orchestras discolor the atmosphere that should prevail in the picture house by not characterizing the photoplay. [...] During a death scene flashed on the screen, you are likely to hear the orchestra jazzing away on 'Clap Hands, Here Comes Charlie.'"

4 Activation

I'm borrowing this term from reception theory in literature to denote how particular audience groups make or do not make sense, relevance, and pleasure out of particular moments of reception. Again, this is obviously difficult to determine with regard to contemporary reception and even more so with regard to reception in the past – as Janet Staiger has pointed out.[12]

It is important to note that I'm not talking here of individual activations of filmic texts. In the first place, except for critical discourse we have little evidence of this, and even if we did they would have little relevance except where they represented a more generalizable appropriation of the text. Rather we are trying to locate what realists would call the "generative mechanisms" that operate variably and with uneven force in producing the myriad readings of individual texts among viewers and over time.[13] Thus, charting the location of theaters in cities, hamlets, and villages, or unearthing box-office records for a particular film, or reconstructing the critical discourse surrounding a given filmic text has a relevance for the history of filmic reception not in itself but only in relation to what these data might suggest about the underlying structures of reception, their interaction, variability, modification over time or resistance to change. I would argue that without the realist notion of generative mechanisms or underlying structures, the historical study of filmic reception becomes either an empiricist fool's errand (in which the scholar is guided by a misplaced faith that by collecting all the available data, he/she can arrive at the truth of the history of film viewing) or merely a game.

It is here that work on film viewing (both historical and contemporary) touches upon and may benefit from reader-oriented theoretical and critical work being undertaken in literature, cultural studies, and media studies. Clearly, for example, what viewers have "made" of films has involved the mobilization of a number of sets of abilities and competences, ranging from the perceptual to the cognitive, and from the affective to the cultural. Some levels, obviously, would seem to yield to historical investigation more easily than others. Although it is difficult and the knowledge yielded enormously speculative, we can attempt to contextualize historical activations of filmic texts by taking a stab (and that's all it is) at the cultural repertoires audiences might have brought with them to the theater. Or, to use Bennett and Woollacott's terminology, we might attempt to examine a given film's *inter-textuality*: "the social organisation of the relations between texts within specific conditions of reading."[14]

To give but one example of a vexing historical problem requiring both textual and inter-textual analysis, let me raise the small matter of the relationship between patterns of style and narration in early cinema and how audiences made sense and pleasure out of their engagements with these texts. Any number of early narrative films (1900–5) cannot be "read" smoothly by contemporary viewers according to the conventions of classical narrative. They contain repeated action, "unexplained" ellipses, or other features that to us mark them as primitive or their surviving prints as possible victims of some sort of mutilation. Are there inter-titles missing from existing prints? Were screenings of these films accompanied by an interlocutor, who provided the missing narrational links? Were audiences in 1900 similarly perplexed by these story-telling strategies? A closer look at the inter-textual contexts of the reception of these films is helping to account for their textual structures. In his analysis of *Life of an American Fireman*, Charles Musser suggests that its repeated narrative action draws upon what would have been well-known and understood conventions of magic lantern shows.[15] Patrick Loughney, an archivist at the Library of Congress, has discovered that many early filmic narratives reference popular stage productions mounted just before or at the same time as the film's release. Thus some of the "missing" narrative information in some early narratives might have been supplied by the audience, in the form of their knowledge of the theatrical text which was being referenced by the film.

Let me end by at least mentioning two additional reasons the historical study of reception might be of more than antiquarian interest. The first is pedagogic. In my film history classes I sometimes have students conduct a study of exhibition in their hometowns. They use old newspapers, city directories, fire insurance maps, municipal ordinances, interviews with their grandparents, and surviving architecture to uncover something about their community that they didn't know. This kind of assignment can have several effects. First, it helps to break down what students all too frequently perceive as the barrier that exists between producers of knowledge (someone else) and themselves. A student can be wonderfully empowered by becoming the world's leading expert on the history of film exhibition in Shelby, NC. Second, students learn something about the way history gets conducted and written: the process of question-framing, collection of evidence, the exercise of historical judgment, etc. Third, they frequently learn what has been written *out* of the history of their community and region. Invariably, black audiences and theaters have left the faintest historical traces, and yet when students talk with people who attended these theaters in the 1920s and 1930s, they find how important these theaters were to the cultural life of the black community. And fourth, I can honestly tell my students that the work they are doing is not a mere exercise – each study helps us better to understand the complexities and variety of filmic reception.

Although I have concentrated in this article on the history of filmic reception in the United States – where my own work has been located – the historical study of reception may help to open up film history for parts of the world we have too often seen as having no film history. When Roy Armes was writing *Third World Filmmaking and the West*, he told me he was struck by the fact that for the most part film history of the third world has meant film production history. It is as if, he said, film history erupts in Bolivia or Chile or Senegal only when there is a notable (usually notable in terms of Western notions of aesthetic worth) director or film movement in evidence in that country. The rest of the time, these countries are written about as if film is not a part of their cultures. But, of course, in many cases indigenous film movements are historical anomalies in the course of a larger history of filmic reception, as millions and millions of people continue to watch films – films made on the other side of the world for very different audiences. One of the challenges for film history is to write back in this enormous and enormously important history.

In short, what I'm calling for is the study of the historical conditions of filmic reception, a study which may lead us to a better understanding of the mechanisms of reception – how these mechanisms are formed, sustained, change, and vary. In effect, we need to ask: what generalizable forces help to account for the unstudiable and, for any individual investigator, incomprehensibly numerous and diverse instances of reception that have occurred since 1895 and continue as you read this?

Notes

1 Indeed, in their rush to celebrate sound technology, historians of American cinema have ignored the fact that there was serious audience resistance to the introduction of the talkies in the late 1920s in some parts of the US. As late as January 1929, for example, a survey of moviegoers in Syracuse, New York, found that only 50 percent preferred talkies to silents, and only 7 percent favored elimination of silent films. See Henry Jenkins III, "Shall We Make It for New York or for Distribution: Eddie Cantor, *Whoopie*, and Regional Resistance to the Talkies," *Cinema Journal* 29, (Spring 1988), 32–52.

2 I laid out my arguments against the "chaser theory" in "Contra the Chaser Theory," *Wide Angle* 3 (1979), 4–11. See also my exchange with Charles Musser on the subject in *Studies in Visual Communication* 10 (1984), 24–52.

3 Philip Corrigan, "Film Entertainment as Ideology and Pleasure: A Preliminary Approach to a History of Audiences," in James Curran and Vincent Porter (eds.), *British Cinema History* (London: British Film Institute, 1983), 24–35.

4 On itinerant film exhibition in the US see: Edward Lowry, "Edwin J. Hadley: Traveling Film Exhibitor," *Journal of the University Film Association* 28 (1976), 5–12; Burnes St. Patrick Hollyman, "The First Picture Shows: Austin, Texas (1894–1913)," *Journal of the University Film Association* 29 (1977), 9–22; David O. Thomas, "From Page to Screen in Smalltown America: Early Motion Picture Exhibition in Winona, Minnesota," *Journal of the University Film Association* 33 (1981), 3–14; Calvin Pryluck, "The Itinerant Movie Show and the Development of the Film Industry," *Journal of the University Film Association* 35 (1983), 11–22; Mark E. Swartz, "Motion Pictures on the Move," *Journal of American Culture* 9 (1986), 1–8.

5 I discuss early exhibition in Durham, North Carolina, in *Film History: Theory and Practice* (New York: Alfred A. Knopf, 1985), 202–7. On the role of amusement parks in early exhibition, see Lauren Rabinowitz, "Temptations of Pleasure: Cinema, Sexuality, and the Turn-of-the-Century Amusement Park," *Camera Obscura*, forthcoming; Greg Waller, "Situating

Motion Pictures in the Pre-Nickelodeon Period: Lexington, Kentucky 1897–1906," [*Velvet Light Trap* 25 (1990), 12–28]; and Charlotte Herzog, "The Archaeology of Cinema Architecture: The Origins of the Movie Theater," *Quarterly Review of Film Studies* 9 (1984), 11–32.

6   Some interesting work *is* being done on "amateur" filmmaking practices, particularly that by Patricia R. Zimmerman. See, for example, "Hollywood, Home Movies, and Common Sense: Amateur Film as Aesthetic Dissemination and Social Control, 1950–62," *Cinema Journal* 27 (1988), 23–44; and "Trading Down: Amateur Film Technology in Fifties America," *Screen* 29, no. 2 (1988), 40–51.

7   Bruce Austin, *The Film Audience: An International Bibliography of Research* (Metuchen, NJ: Scarecrow Press, 1983), xx, xxii.

8   On immigrant audiences for early movies see my "Motion Picture Exhibition in Manhattan: Beyond the Nickelodeon," *Cinema Journal* 18 (1979), 2–15, and Judith Mayne, "Immigrants and Spectators," *Wide Angle* 5, 32–41. As Pryluck (p. 17) has pointed out, in 1900 immigrants constituted only 7.7 percent of the rural population of the US, which itself represented 71 percent of the total population.

9   Janice Radway, *Reading the Romance: Women, Patriarchy, and Popular Literature* (Chapel Hill: University of North Carolina Press, 1985).

10   Diane Waldman, "From Midnight Shows to Marriage Vows: Women, Exploitation, and Exhibition," *Wide Angle* 6, 40–9; Mary Beth Haralovich, "Mandates of Good Taste: The Self-Regulation of Film Advertising in the Theatres," *Wide Angle* 6, 50–7; "Film History and Social History: Reproducing Social Relationships," *Wide Angle* 8, 4–14, and "Advertising Heterosexuality," *Screen* 23, no. 2 (1982), 50–60.

11   Mary Carbine, "The Finest Outside the Loop: Motion Picture Exhibition in Chicago's Black Metropolis," *Camera Obscura*, forthcoming.

12   Janet Staiger, "The Handmaiden of Villainy: Methods and Problems in Studying the Historical Reception of a Film," *Wide Angle* 8, 19–27.

13   On the relationship between realism (as a position within the philosophy of science) and film study, see Terry Lovell, *Pictures of Reality* (London: BFI, 1980).

14   Tony Bennett and Janet Woollacott, *Bond and Beyond: the Political Career of a Popular Hero* (London: Macmillan, 1987), 45. Michael Budd provides a useful model for analyzing the critical discourse produced in response to a given film. See "*The Cabinet of Dr. Caligari*: Conditions of Reception," *Cine Tracts* 12 (1981), 41–9.

15   Charles Musser, "The Early Cinema of Edwin S. Porter," *Cinema Journal* 19 (1979), 1–35.

★ ★ ★ ★ ★ ★ ★ ★ ★ ★ ★ ★ ★

PART V

Research and Resources

★ ★ ★ ★ ★ ★ ★ ★ ★ ★ ★ ★ ★

A Guide to Research and Resources

While this guide to research and resources in the history of film exhibition and moviegoing covers a considerable amount of ground, I have been selective, particularly in terms of listing material that originally appeared in the motion picture industry trade press, general interest magazines, and specialized business and architectural periodicals. The emphasis is clearly on the United States, though I have included a sampling of the research done on exhibition in other nations, which I will refer to when appropriate.

The bibliography covering the literature of film exhibition compiled by Dan Streible for the *Velvet Light Trap* (1990) is an indispensable reference, as are two major works that offer annotated listings: *The Film Index* (pre-1930s) and *The New Film Index* (1930–70). Aspects of this field are also covered in other bibliographic sources, virtually all of which are now available online: *Avery Index to Architectural Periodicals*, *Reader's Guide to Periodical Literature*, *Music Index*, and *America: History and Life*, the last of which includes all manner of local history studies (see, for instance, Boyer 1988; Schneider 1988; Sorenson 1990). In fact, given the sorts of questions raised by the history of film exhibition and moviegoing, it is also worth consulting bibliographies across a range of other disciplines, including business, economics, theater, law, and art.

As several of the recent essays reprinted in this book suggest, the trade press is an essential source of information about exhibition practices, offering not only feature articles, new items, and statistical data, but also editorials, advice columns, advertisements, and illustrations. See, in particular, *Moving Picture World* (1910–30), which merged into *Exhibitor's Herald World* (1929–30), and then became *Motion Picture Herald* (1931–72), featuring a special monthly supplement entitled "Better Theatres." See also:

- *Billboard* (1910–)
- *Boxoffice* (1932–63)
- *Film Daily Year Book of Motion Pictures* (1920–)
- *International Motion Picture Almanac* (1933–)
- *Motion Picture News* (1910–30)
- *Motion Picture Exhibitor* (1918–)
- *Motography* (1911–18)
- *Nickelodeon* (1909–11)
- *Theatre Catalog* (1940–57)
- *Variety* (1905–)

Among the special journal issues devoted to movie theaters, exhibition, and moviegoing are:

- *Brickbuilder* 23 (February 1914) on movie theaters and terra cotta architecture
- *Architectural Forum* 42 (June 1925) on the design of contemporary theaters
- *Architectural Record* 104 (November 1948) on new theater architecture

311

- *Velvet Light Trap* 25 (1990) on exhibition/ conditions of reception
- *Film History* 6 (1994) on the history of film exhibition
- *Iris* 17 (1994) on movie spectators and audiences

The major specialized archival collections include:

- **Theatre Historical Society of America**
  Elmhurst, Illinois
  www.historictheatres.org
- **National Association of Theater Owners Collection**
  Harold B. Lee Library, Brigham Young University
  www.lib.byu.edu/byline/index.html
- **Hoblitzelle and Interstate Theater Collection**
  Harry Ransom Humanities Research Center, University of Texas at Austin
  www.lib.utexas.edu/hrc/home.html
- **B'hend and Kauffman Collection**
  Academy of Motion Picture Arts and Sciences Library
  Beverly Hills, CA
  www.oscars.org/cmps/mhl/index2.html

In addition, local, city, county, and state archives and historical societies are all well worth consulting, as are public libraries, university and college holdings, and privately held collections.

The best single-volume history of what he calls "movie presentation in the United States" is Gomery's *Shared Pleasures* (1992), which includes important material on technological innovations, "alternative" screening sites, and the role of commercial television, video, and cable television as outlets for film exhibition. Stones' *America Goes to the Movies* (1993) makes extensive use of photographs and effectively draws on interviews with veteran exhibitors. Other well-illustrated works that focus primarily on

movie theaters are Naylor (1987), Margolies and Gwathmey (1991), Valentine (1994), and Headley (1999).

Bluem and Squire's *The Movie Business* (1972), Kindem's *The American Movie Industry* (1982), and Balio's *The American Film Industry* (1985) and *Hollywood in the Age of Television* (1990) are very useful anthologies that feature sections on exhibition, as do histories of the economics of the motion picture industry by Seabury (1926), Huettig (1944), and Wasko (1994). Allen and Gomery put film exhibition and the practice of writing local history at the center of their textbook, *Film History: Theory and Practice* (1985). Of the many general histories of American cinema, all the volumes currently available in Scribner's History of American Cinema series are well worth consulting. The volumes by Musser (1990), Bowser (1990), and Koszarski (1990) on the silent era are particularly thorough in detailing exhibition practices. For an influential contemporary view of this era, read – with a good sense of skepticism – Ramsaye's *A Million and One Nights* (1926). Among the many other works that survey the entire silent period, several stand out: Pratt makes effective use of trade press accounts in *Spellbound in Darkness* (1973); Ross comprehensively examines working-class moviegoing throughout the silent era in *Working-Class Hollywood* (1998), following up and revising May's 1980 study of the relation between the movies and the emergence of a mass culture; Nasaw (1993) situates movies within the larger context of early twentieth-century show business. In *Main Street Amusements* (Waller 1995) I look at all aspects of film exhibition and moviegoing from 1896 to 1930 in one small community. Stokes and Maltby gather a broad selection of current research on moviegoing through the 1930s in their 1999 anthology, *American Movie Audiences*.

Historians interested in film exhibition and moviegoing practices have been particularly drawn to the first 20 years of the silent era, which saw the development and consolidation of the American film industry, the growing prominence of a particular form of narrative film (which would later be a hallmark of the classic Hollywood cinema), and the increasingly significant role of picture shows and the movies in the daily life of people across the United States. There was, as Musser (1990) demonstrates, a flurry of entrepreneurial endeavors during the "novelty year" of 1896–7 when audiences first viewed projected moving pictures. Much of the most influential research in the cultural history of American cinema has focused on the situation through the early 'teens in New York City, specifically, the number and location of screening sites in Manhattan, the role of moving pictures in other entertainment venues (like vaudeville theaters), and the audience for film among the city's middle classes and immigrant populations, across lines of gender, age, and race. This research – still very much in process – has been essential for the major revisioning of film history since the early 1980s. See, in particular, the work of Robert C. Allen, including the 1980 book based on his Ph.D. dissertation, *Vaudeville and Film 1895–1915: A Study in Media Interaction*, and a series of influential articles (1979a, 1979b, 1979c, 1985), and Charles Musser, in comprehensive studies like *Before the Nickelodeon: Edwin S. Porter and the Edison Manufacturing Company* (1991) and *The Emergence of Cinema: The American Screen to 1907* (1990). Musser also produced a documentary film based on this research, entitled *Before the Nickelodeon* (1982). Current debate over early theaters and audiences in Manhattan can be traced through the pages of *Cinema Journal* (see Singer 1995; Allen 1996; Higashi 1996; Singer 1996). In *The Red Rooster Scare: Making Cinema American, 1900–1910* (1999), Abel helps expand the terms of this debate by moving outside Manhattan and linking the exhibition of imported films to the increasing "Americanization" of the US film industry.

Other recent research has tended to focus on specific localities and audiences during the nickelodeon era and into the 'teens. Together, this work offers a complex and revealing portrait of America encountering the twentieth century via this new form of popular entertainment. Again, New York City has attracted the most attention (see Weiss 1993), with studies of film exhibition in Harlem (Griffiths and Latham 1999), and of the city's working-class female (Peiss 1986), Italian immigrant (Bertellini 1999a, 1999b), and Jewish immigrant audiences (Thissen 1999). Stamp (2000) effectively continues this work into the 'teens, focusing on female moviegoing. Scholars have also looked to other industrialized areas with large ethnic and first-generation immigrant populations (Mayne 1982; Ewen 1985). Rosenzweig's examination in *Eight Hours for What We Will: Workers and Leisure in an Industrial City, 1870–1920* (1983) of the movies and other leisure activities in Worcester, Massachusetts, remains a model of working-class history. Rabinovitz foregrounds issues of gender and situates moving picture theaters in the context of amusement parks and other commercial venues in *For the Love of Pleasure: Women, Movies, and Culture in Turn-of-the-Century Chicago* (1998). Lindstrom (1998) traces the urban geography informing the nickelodeon era in Chicago (see also Grieveson 1999, and, for a later period, Cohen 1990), a city also examined by Luckett (1995) and Carbine (1990), who looks at African American moviegoing practices. For some sense of moving picture shows and audiences during the silent era outside the United States, see Veronneau (1994) and Lacasse (1999) on Quebec, Fullerton (1993) on Sweden, Hughes (1996) on South India, and Chenan (1996) on Great Britain.

Other case studies of the nickelodeon period and after – concerned with the location, operation, and patronage of early theaters – take up a range of quite distinct localities, including: New Orleans (Brear 1951), Rochester, New York (Pratt 1959), Austin, Texas (Hollyman 1977), Boston (Merritt 1985), Milwaukee (Kmet 1979, DeBauche 1999), Winona, Minnesota (Thomas 1981a, 1981b), Los Angeles (Ogihara 1990), Philadelphia (Woal 1994), Atlanta (Gue 1999), Baltimore (Headley 1974, 1981), Denver (Warren 1960), Knoxville, Tennessee (Thomas 1990, 1993), Lexington, Kentucky (Waller 1995), and Washington, DC (Headley 1999).

For contemporary magazine accounts of the nickelodeon phenomenon, see Currie (1907), Patterson (1907), Pierce (1908), and Vorse (1911). The emerging trade press during this period not only frequently reports on but also attempts to monitor and direct the business of film exhibition. See, among countless examples from *Moving Picture World*, Bush (1914), and the several selections from the trades that Pratt reprints in *Spellbound in Darkness*. The 'teens also saw a number of public recreation surveys undertaken with progressive zeal, like Davis' *The Exploitation of Pleasure: A Study of Commercial Recreation in New York City* (1911) and Foster's 1914 study of theaters in Portland, Oregon. With respect to the movies, the most comprehensive of these surveys is Phelan's *Motion Pictures as a Phase of Commercialized Amusement in Toledo, Ohio* (1919; abridged in Holliday 1919). Hansen's *Babel and Babylon: Spectatorship in American Silent Film* (1991) offers a particularly effective theorization of moviegoing practices in the silent era. Focusing on issues of class, ethnicity, and gender, Hansen considers whether the nickelodeon constituted a significant public sphere. For other approaches to early moviegoing, see Uricchio and Pearson (1993, 1994), who take up the discursive construction of the nickelodeon audience, and Crafton (1990).

Before and well after the rise of the nickelodeon, moving pictures were screened at a variety of different sites (see Waller 1990), frequently by traveling exhibitors, the most successful of whom was Lyman H. Howe. Howe's career is fully analyzed by Musser in *High-Class Moving Pictures: Lyman H. Howe and the Forgotten Era of Traveling Exhibition, 1880–1920* (1991). Carol Nelson, Musser's collaborator on this volume, also directed the award-winning documentary, *Lyman H. Howe's High-Class Moving Pictures* (1983). Other small and large-scale itinerant exhibitors are discussed by Lowery (1976), Pryluck (1983), Swartz (1987a), and Fuller (1996, 1999). There is little information on the major sites and circuits worked by these traveling exhibitors, but see Waller (1999a) for the role of moving pictures at chautauqua assemblies, and Rosini, whose 1998 dissertation looks at Protestant churches as exhibition sites throughout the silent era. Waldman (1986) examines a quite different sort of non-theatrical site, the YMCAs in company-owned mining towns during the 1920s.

A number of the sources already cited (particularly Musser 1990) consider the ways that moving pictures and live performances were combined for programs in the early silent era. Understandably, the role of live music/sound in the exhibition of silent film has proven to be a topic not only of abiding nostalgia but also of detailed scholarly research. See, for instance, Anderson (1987, 1988) and Marks (1996). Berg (1976) notes that as early as 1910 the *Moving Picture World* offered regular columns of advice for musicians working in theaters that screened films. This trade journal also devoted much attention to lecturers who presented spoken accompaniment in certain venues (see, for example, Bush 1912), and it lobbied strongly to reform what editor Louis Harrison Reeves criticized as "jackass music" (Reeves 1911).

See Anderson (1997) for a discussion of this campaign. (On the role of lecturers – *benshi* – in Japanese film exhibition, see, for example, Dym 1998.) A similar column began in *Motion Picture News*, in 1912 and later in music industry trade journals like *Metronome* (beginning in 1916) and *Melody Magazine* (beginning in 1922). In a major 1996 article, Altman challenges certain assumptions that have informed earlier discussion of silent film music, notably the truism that moving pictures in the pre-1915 period were always shown with some sort of live sound accompaniment.

Several handbooks were available for silent film accompanists, including Lang and West's *Musical Accompaniment of Moving Pictures* (1920) and Rapee's *Motion Picture Moods for Pianists and Organists* (1924) – both volumes were reprinted in 1970 by Arno Press as part of its invaluable series, "The Literature of Cinema." Landon (1983) and Bowers (1986) discuss theater organs during this period. Aldridge (1973, 1982), Marsh (1984), and Koszarski (1990) consider various types of stage shows during the later silent era, as do most commentators who discuss the operation of the picture palace. Kraft shifts the focus onto the musicians themselves, particularly during the transition to sound, in *Stage to Studio: Musicians and the Sound Revolution, 1890–1950* (1996); see also Fones-Wolf (1994).

The role of live music in movie presentation also figures prominently in virtually all of the early handbooks designed to provide practical advice for the picture show owner or theater manager. These guides also cover a range of other topics: theater design, economics, promotional activity, staffing, programming, projection, and public relations. See, especially, Jenkins and DePue, *Handbook for Motion Picture and Stereopticon Operators* (1908); Hodges, *Opening and Operating a Motion Picture Theater: How It Is Successfully Done* (1912); Richardson, *Motion Picture Handbook: A Guide for Managers and Operators of Motion Picture Theaters* (1912); and Hulfish, *Motion-Picture Work: A General Treatise on Picture Taking, Picture Making, Photo-Plays, and Theater Management and Operation* (1915). From the later silent period, see Balaban and Katz, *The Fundamental Principles of Balaban and Katz Theatre Management* (1926); Barry and Sargent, *Building Theatre Patronage: Management and Merchandising* (1927); and Franklin, *Motion Picture Theater Management* (1928). For other discussions of the role of movie theater ushers, see Deutsch (1980) and Rosenberg (1995). Hark (1994) analyzes the role of gender across several of these manuals.

Much of the material already cited includes information about the design, architecture, construction, and outfitting of the moving picture theater, which by the mid-'teens had become a fixture of the American commercial landscape. The one-volume histories by Stones and Valentine pay particular attention to these topics, as do a great number of specialized articles in architectural journals. See the bibliographies by Stoddard (1978) and Dyal (1981) and, for example, the special number of the *Brickbuilder* (February 1914) devoted to moving picture theaters, as well as Kinsila's *Modern Theater Construction* (1917) and Whittemore's 1917 articles. In a series of well-researched studies, Herzog (1977, 1980, 1981, 1984) explores the origins and the transformation of the film theater up to and including grand-scale picture palaces.

There is no question but that the massive, metropolitan-area, visually spectacular first-run theaters built from the mid-'teens through the early 1930s have filled a major place in the history of film exhibition in America – as palaces or cathedrals, as influential screening sites, and as cultural icons. The literature on picture palaces and smaller venues from this era is vast, including a host of case studies of individual theaters published in *Marquee*, the journal of the Theatre

Historical Society, a valuable resource, well-indexed and available on microfilm. (See also, for example, Triponi 1990.) Standard accounts of the picture palace are Hall's *The Best Remaining Seats* (1961) and Naylor's *American Picture Palaces: The Architecture of Fantasy* (1981). These should be supplemented by surveys by Sharp (1969), Pildas and Smith (1980), and Naylor (1987), and by contemporary accounts of theaters during the 1920s in general interest magazines (see Lewis 1929 and Reinhart 1929), in specialized journals devoted to the motion picture (see Clarke 1926 and Stern 1927), and in pieces written by and for professional architects, such as the special issue of *Architectural Forum* (June 1925). Among more recent historians, Gomery (1978, 1979b, 1990c) analyzes the economics of the picture palace in terms of chain-store practices, and May (1980) argues that these grand theaters were crucial in the development of American mass culture. Ross' discussion of picture palaces in *Working-Class Hollywood* is a particularly useful summary of current research. For a sense of the situation outside the United States, see Thorne (1976) on picture palaces in Australia, Atwell (1980) on British cinemas, and Shand (1930) on modernist theater design in Europe.

Valuable sources for the industry's sense of its own exhibition practices and the audiences it was attracting during the late silent period are two volumes of public (or public relations) statements: *The Story of the Films* (1927) and *The Community and the Motion Picture: Report of the National Conference on Motion Pictures* (1929). Seabury's *The Public and the Motion Picture Industry* (1926), on the other hand, is a highly critical view that foregrounds serious problems with exhibition, including block-booking, vertical monopolization, and the dominance of first-run theaters. Gomery has explored these issues in a series of influential articles (1979b, 1982a, 1985c), which culminated in the section on

the "business history" of movie presentation in *Shared Pleasures*. Waller (1995) and Fuller (1996) look at exhibition practices outside the metropolis in the 1920s, as does Potamianos in a 1998 dissertation that examines Sacramento and Placerville, California, up through 1936. "Colored" theaters and segregated seating policies affecting African American audiences were a basic aspect of moviegoing in America from the nickelodeon period onward. Research has focused on the silent era; see Waller (1992, 1995) and Carbine's excellent study of theaters, musical performance, and audiences in Chicago (1990). For a sense of Jim Crow practices in later periods, see, for example, Turner and Kennedy (1947), McKay (1954), Feagans (1965), and Streible (1993).

There is a wealth of material on Hollywood's conversion to sound films in the late 1920s, some of which (such as Gomery 1985d and Crafton 1997) pays more than passing attention to the effects on film exhibition. The "Better Theatres" monthly supplement to *Exhibitor's Herald World* (which in 1931 became *Motion Picture Herald*) regularly gave exhibitors advice on problems with sound equipment, as well as many other aspects of theater operation, from projection to promotion. This trade journal (and, later, the *Theatre Catalog*) is an essential source of information about the period. Ricketson's *The Management of Motion Picture Theatres* (1938) provides another valuable perspective, particularly when read in the context of the earlier manuals I have cited.

Hollywood's transition to sound movies meant the end of live musical accompaniment and, therefore, a more standardized program across the United States. Recent research does suggest, however, that there was still significant local variation in the function of the movie theater, the behavior of movie audiences, and the make-up of the film program at least well into the 1930s. Doherty (1999), for example, draws on trade magazines in his reconsideration of the behavior of early sound film audiences. Klenotic's case study of Springfield, Massachusetts, between 1926 and 1932 points out the continuing significance of class and ethnicity in moviegoing and exhibition practices (1998; see also his 1996 dissertation). My own work on small-town Kentucky theaters (1999b) emphasizes the role of race, region, and locality. See also my documentary, *At the Picture Show* (1993), which looks at the role of the movie theater in one small rural town from the 1920s into the 1940s. Other recent case studies dealing with exhibition during the Depression include Bjork (1989) on Seattle and dissertations by Testa (1992) on Providence, Rhode Island, and Wilson (1999) on Wichita Falls, Texas, and the Interstate Theatre Circuit. Two lengthy feature articles in the *Saturday Evening Post* offer a quite different sort of case study, viewing the industry from the vantage point of a single exhibitor (Sprague 1937; Roney 1939).

Popular journalism is also a good source for contemporary reactions to certain exhibition practices associated with the Great Depression – particularly double features, premium giveaways, and other promotional strategies. *Business Week*, for example, regularly covered film exhibition, as in a 1934 article, "Premium Thriller." For contemporary views of bank nights see Kresensky (1935) and Parkhill (1937); for the practice of booking double features, see articles in the *Harvard Business Review* by Beach (1932) and Chambers (1938). The movie premiere, a quite different and yet also highly visible form of film exhibition that also flourished in this era, is described by Costello (1941) and effectively analyzed by Karnes (1986) and Bernstein (1999).

For information about run-zone-clearance policies, which dictated when and where films could be shown, and other aspects of the larger system of film exhibition in the United States during the heyday of the five

major studios' oligopoly in the 1930s and 1940s, see Huettig (1944), and also Cassady (1933), Whitman (1938), and Balio (1985). The long-standing practice of block-booking – strongly contested by independent exhibitors and many civic groups – received a great deal of contemporary attention; see Seabury (1926) and Wilbur (1938). For later assessments of this practice, see Mayer (1958) and Kenney (1979). Legal scholars, in particular, have focused on the government's anti-trust case against the vertically integrated major studios, companies that dominated the exhibition market through their ownership of first-run theaters in major metropolitan areas and through their distribution policies. Among other assessments, see Armstrong (1947, 1952), McDonough and Winslo (1949), Borneman (1951), Whitney (1955), Cassady (1958, 1959), and Jacobs (1983). The government's protracted effort culminated in the Supreme Court's 1948 decision in the Paramount case, which required the studios to divest themselves of their theater holdings and no longer rely on block-booking and certain other practices that restrained trade. The actual opinions in the Paramount case are available in "Cases Adjudicated in the Supreme Court at October Term, 1947," in *United States Reports* Volume 334 (Washington: Government Printing Office, 1948), 100–81. Conant's *Antitrust in the Motion Picture Industry* (1960) – supplemented by his 1981 reconsideration of the Paramount case – is still the standard work in this area. It contains a full listing of other relevant court cases.

By one estimate almost 20 percent of the 20,000 movie theaters in operation in 1930 had closed by 1932 (Balio, 1993), the same year that saw the less-than-stunning debut of the RKO Roxy Theatre at Radio City Music Hall, marking for all purposes the end of picture palace construction in the United States. Architectural discourse on the movie theater in the 1930s and the 1940s shifted to a concern with smaller, more streamlined and "modern" venues. See, for example, Adams (1930), Graf (1938), and the June 1932 issue of *Architectural Record*. As Gomery (1992) notes, specialized newsreel theaters were one new exhibition site that did prosper in this period. See Peet (1931) for a contemporary view and Grenz (1982) for an in-house history of Trans-Lux, which operated the major chain of newsreel theaters.

Valentine (1994) makes a convincing case that S. Charles Lee, who designed more than 300 theaters between 1926 and 1950, was the most influential architect of this period. For his own commentary on the influence of "West Coast Designers," see Lee (1948). Paul (1996) and May (1987, 1993, 2000) point to the significance of another prolific, well-known architect, Ben Schlanger. In a score of articles published between 1931 and 1951, Schlanger argued for the virtues of small, efficient theaters with unadorned auditoria and large screens, tailored for the particular film-viewing experience encouraged by Hollywood feature films. His influence is apparent in many of the designs, new projects, and remodeled theaters that are pictured in *Architectural Forum* and *Architectural Record* during the 1940s. Schlanger is a central figure in Paul's essay on the historical changes in both the technology and the architecture of the movie screen. May sees Schlanger's work in the context of a larger movement in design that was tied directly to the ascendancy of "America's first *national* mass audience" and to the creation of a new "national vision" – what came to be known as the "American way."

Schlanger's ideas also figure prominently in Stote's *The Motion Picture Theater: Planning, Upkeep* (1948), an anthology published by the Society of Motion Picture Engineers. This book provides an important perspective on the business of film exhibition at a point when box-office revenues had begun to drop precipitously. For a sampling of other views of this period, see, for instance, the optimistic statement by theater chain magnate Charles P. Skouras (1947) and three lengthy feature articles: a profile of a theater manager in the *Saturday Evening Post* (Thruelsen 1947) and two pessimistic pieces in *Fortune* (August 1948 and April 1949).

The so-called "Suburban Movie House" pictured in *Architectural Record* (October 1951) offers one vision of the new movie theater, but the only substantive growth in the industry was in drive-in theaters, which proliferated even as hardtops closed down. There is a wealth of material in the popular press on the drive-in phenomenon, including articles in *Life* (September 24, 1951) and *Business Week* (May 9, 1953); see also Durant (1950), Cullman (1950), Luther (1951), and Hines (1952); later studies include Horton (1976), Giles (1983), and Austin (1985), as well as full-length histories by Reddick (1986) and Segrave (1992). Linking the drive-in with the practices of the early silent era, Cohen (1994) offers the most intriguing recent interpretation of this bit of Americana. Goldsmith (1999) looks at the drive-in phenomenon in Australia.

Like the drive-in, the various widescreen processes marketed in the 1950s garnered much contemporary press, some of which deals with the actual exhibition of widescreen (and also 3-D) films. See, for example, *Fortune*'s account of Cinerama (1953), Tyler on 3-D movies (1953, 1954), and Macgowan on the entire widescreen phenomenon (1956, 1957). There has since been considerable research in this area, including dissertations by Spellerberg (1980), Erffmeyer (1985), and Hincha (1989), as well as books by Wysotsky (1971), Carr and Hayes (1988), and Hayes (1989). The standard work is now Belton's *Widescreen Cinema* (1992), which draws on his earlier articles (1985, 1987, 1988).

Though Hollywood's experiments with widescreen processes date from the early 1930s, around the same time that the first drive-in opened in Camden, New Jersey, it was in the 1950s that drive-ins and wide-screen movies became central to the industry and part of the larger public discourse about theaters and moviegoing. The situation is roughly comparable with art cinemas, though these never figured as prominently in the culture and in the industry as did drive-ins. Wilinsky's 1997 dissertation examines the emergence of art film theaters during the post-Second World War years in the United States. For this period, also see Frank (1952), Twomey (1956), Adler (1959), and *Business Week*'s article on the phenomenon (March 22, 1958). Later, when art cinemas had in most cases adopted a repertory format, Austin (1984) analyzed the art theater audience. Phelps (1983) surveys the art-house situation in England, while Neale (1980) and O'Pray (1980) consider more radical attempts in Britain at a truly "oppositional" form of exhibition. Josephson (1926), Mindlin (1928), Bakshy (1929), and Blake (1933) provide accounts of the "little cinema movement," an important early manifestation of the art cinema. For more on the exhibition of European art films in the United States, see Mayer (1964), Ogan (1990), and Guzman (1993). Film societies in cities and college communities were crucial in opening up the possibilities of US film exhibition from the 1950s into the 1970s. Material on Cinema 16, the influential New York City film society, includes the statement of its founder, Amos Vogel (1949), and also Schreiber (1952) and Dobi (1984). There has been less research on the significance of the American film festival as a particular exhibition site and occasion, but see Petrie's dissertation on the Sundance Institute (1987).

Paletz and Noonan's lengthy interviews in *Film Quarterly* (1965) with three quite different exhibitors (who operate drive-ins, art cinemas, and porn houses) provide a good introduction to changes in the industry in the 1960s. Edgerton's *American Film Exhib-* *ition and an Analysis of the Motion Picture Industry's Market Structure, 1963–1980* (1981) and Wyatt's 1998 essay offer an overview of these changes, which included, most notably, the introduction of the multiplex theater (see Willson 1974; Edgerton 1982; Paul 1994) and, particularly in the 1970s, the success of four-wall exhibition strategies (see Beaupre 1978; Wasser 1995). In 1969, the Society of Motion Picture and Television Engineers published a manual edited by Kloepfel covering motion picture projection and presentation. For views from the 1970s, see Bluem and Squire (1972), *Architectural Record*'s portfolio of theaters (1972), and a series of pieces by Mayer (1973, 1974, 1976, 1977). The midnight movie as a particular exhibition strategy that thrived from the late 1960s into the early 1980s is taken up by Austin (1981), Strout (1981), Samuels (1983), Hoberman and Rosenbaum (1983), and Waller (1991). Drawing extensively from sources like *Variety* and the *Wall Street Journal*, Gomery's case studies of the Cineplex Odeon chain (1990a, 1990b, 1990d) highlight one direction in film exhibition during the 1980s, a period also considered by Guback (1987) and Donahue (1987). Wasko (1994) looks at subsequent developments in the industry, focusing on the acquisition of theaters by major distributors and thus the increasing consolidation of first-run film exhibition in America.

Like many other contemporary commentators, Wasko also underscores the role of television and video as important exhibition "windows" for Hollywood product. Of course, the connections between American television and Hollywood, and, more specifically, the role of television as a site for film exhibition, go back to the late 1940s. Balio's anthology, *Hollywood in the Age of Television* (1990), is an important resource, and Gomery treats this topic at length in *Shared Pleasures* and in several articles (1984a, 1985a). See also dissertations by Schnapper (1975), White

(1990), and Brett (1995) and articles by Taylor (1972), McGilligan (1980), and Belton (1987). Two early statements on the relations between television and film exhibition are Goldwyn (1949) and Luther (1950), written at a time when it still looked as if movie theaters would become the prime site for presenting big-screen television. On the history of what was then called "theatre television," see Little (1948), Goldsmith (1948), Hodgson (1949), Kreuzer (1949), McCoy and Warner (1949), Schlanger and Hoffberg (1951a), and Gomery (1985b, 1989b).

Among the reams of material written about Hollywood in the age of video, there are a good many titles that consider the implications of and practices associated with home video (or, later, laserdisc and DVD) as a type of film exhibition or a substitute for film exhibition. See, for example, Agostino, Terry, and Johnson (1979), Waterman (1985), Levy (1989), Johnson (1989), Moret (1991), and De Silva (1994). Of particular interest are the following essays, which highlight certain key issues concerning contemporary film-on-video viewing practices: Andrew's comparison of the experience of watching films in a public versus a private setting (1988); Austin's study of home video as a sort of "second-run theater" in the exhibition cycle (1990); Hansen's speculations about the parallels between the contemporary film-viewing and early cinema practices (1993); and Klinger's analysis of the discourse concerning home theater systems (1998).

Canned food drive and *Tom Sawyer* promotion (ca. 1932)

Research Projects in the History of Moviegoing and Film Exhibition

As the readings collected in this book demonstrate, the cultural history of film can always be explored from a local as well as a national perspective, from the bottom up as well as the top down. Like the readings, the Guide to Research and Resources offers a range of topics and models for exploring the history of film exhibition and moviegoing. Here are a few of the possibilities, which are readily adaptable to a range of localities within and outside the United States:

1 Examine the public discourse concerning some aspect of film exhibition and moviegoing. This project might focus on representations of the movie audience (as childlike, for example, or working class), of a particular exhibition site (the drive-in, the multiplex, the art cinema), of a unique occasion (the Saturday matinee, the midnight movie), or of a specific historical period. The project should draw on a range of sources, from general-interest magazines to more specialized journals, as well as any relevant cartoons, photographs, film footage, advertisements, and other pieces of visual evidence.

2 Analyze the film exhibition business since 1990, using sources like the trade press, major newspapers, business periodicals, and interviews with representatives of theater chains and independent venues. What do you identify as the major trends in this period? What principles and policies govern this business? Is the theatrical exhibition of moving pictures today significantly different than it was in 1980 or 1990?

3 Compile a thorough case study of the most prominent multiplex in your immediate vicinity, considering its design, ownership, operation, and booking policies over at least the past year. Observe this screening site; interview patrons and employees. What audience(s) does it draw? What sort of moviegoing experience does it offer?

4 Profile the current state of film-exhibition practices and occasions, using one locality for the case study. What sort of variety do you see in the array of movie theaters and non-theatrical venues? This study might be expanded to include video-rental outlets and cable television stations, or it might involve a comparative look at one or more earlier periods, say 1920 and 1955.

5 Focus on film-programming practices during a particular historical period: what's on the bill? How is the program arranged? Is there any use of live performance or advertising? How do these practices change over a period of months, years, or decades in a particular locality? Is there any variation from place to place at a given time?

6 Document the local history of film exhibition by focusing on one object of investi-

gation. For example: (a) the history of a specific theater or of the moviegoing activities in a given neighborhood; (b) the local situation during a discreet period, for example, the nickelodeon era or the Second World War years; (c) the controversy surrounding desegregation or community-based censorship initiatives; (d) the local experience of what has come to be taken as a significant moment in film history, such as the first exhibition of moving pictures, the premiere of *The Birth of a Nation*, the conversion to sound, or the introduction of widescreen films in the 1950s.

7 Conduct an oral history interview (or a set of related interviews) with, for example, people who owned theaters or worked as managers, projectionists, musicians, ushers, ticket-takers, and so on; or interview people in the community who might be able to speak to the larger role of movie theaters in the public sphere (city officials, clergy, censors, owners of competing forms of commercial entertainment); or interview moviegoers, both die-hard fans and casual moviegoers. Depending on the people you are able to interview, this project can be focused on an individual theater, neighborhood, time-period, or issue, or on a particular type of film exhibition or a certain kind of moviegoing experience.

Valerie Raleigh Yow's *Recording Oral History* (Thousand Oaks, California: Sage Publications, 1994) offers some basic guidelines for conducting oral history interviews:

(a) Prepare a preliminary list of topics and potential questions.

(b) Informally discuss the topics with the prospective interviewee.

(c) Prepare an interview guide with specific, clear, non-condescending questions that you will ask. Formulate both broad and narrowly focused questions. Test your recording equipment.

(d) Begin by asking about biographical information (personal background, family, school, work). Always listen carefully to the interviewee. Follow the guide you have prepared but leave room for follow-up questions and for pursuing topics that may emerge during the interview.

(e) Ask interviewees to suggest other people who might be able and willing to be interviewed for the project.

(f) Carefully label and safeguard interview tapes.

Interviews can be a major source of information, but as Robert C. Allen and Douglas Gomery explain in *Film History: Theory and Practice* (207–11), there are several other resources that are quite useful when working on what they call "local film histories." They mention, in particular: city directories and business directories (for identifying theater locations, adjacent businesses, owners, and managers); fire insurance maps (to help determine the size and design features of theaters); public records (for possible information about licenses, building permits, property taxes, ordinances, and codes relating to moving picture theaters and other places of commercial amusement); and any available histories of the locality (which often must be read with more than a little skepticism). As Allen and Gomery note, local newspapers – likely to be found only on microfilm – are an invaluable source of information, not only through advertisements and amusement pages, but also through news stories, editorials, and cartoons. So, too, are any photographs that show the architecture, audiences, promotion, or location of local movie houses. Look for photographs, paper ephemera (like posters, handbills, postcards, programs), and related information at public libraries, university collections, and other archives, including city, county, and state historical archives.

Bibliography

Abel, Richard 1999: *The Red Rooster Scare: Making Cinema American, 1900–1910*. Berkeley: University of California Press.

Adams, Arthur Frederick 1930: Expressing the Modern Spirit of Design in the Small Theater. *Exhibitor's Herald World* 99 (April 12, 1930), 11, 30–1.

Adler, Kenneth P. 1959: Art Films and Eggheads. *Studies in Public Communication* 2, 7–15.

Agostino, Donald E., Herbert A. Terry, and Rolland C. Johnson 1979: *Home Video: A Report on the Status, Projected Development and Consumer Use of Videocassette Recorders and Videodisc Players in the United States*. FCC Network Inquiry Special Staff.

Aherne, Eugene 1913: *What and How to Play for Pictures*. Twin Falls, Idaho: Newsprint.

Aldridge, Harry Belden 1973: Live Musical and Theatrical Presentations in Detroit Moving Picture Theatres: 1896–1930. Unpublished Ph.D. dissertation, University of Michigan.

Aldridge, Henry B. 1982: The Role of the Stage Show in Film Exhibition: The Case of Detroit's Capitol Theatre. *Journal of Popular Film and Television* 10, no. 2, 66–71.

Allen, Robert C. 1979a: Motion Picture Exhibition in Manhattan, 1906–1912: Beyond the Nickelodeon. *Cinema Journal* 18, no. 2, 2–15.

Allen, Robert C. 1979b: Vitascope/Cinématographe: Initial Patterns of American Film Industrial Practice. *Journal of the University Film Association* 31, no. 2, 13–18.

Allen, Robert C. 1979c: Contra the "Chaser Theory." *Wide Angle* 3, no. 1, 4–11.

Allen, Robert C. 1980: *Vaudeville and Film 1895–1915: A Study in Media Interaction*. New York: Arno Press.

Allen, Robert C. 1985: The Movies in Vaudeville: Historical Context of the Movies as Popular Entertainment. In *The American Film Industry*, ed. Tino Balio, rev. ed. Madison: University of Wisconsin Press, 57–82.

Allen, Robert C. 1990: From Exhibition to Reception: Reflections on the Audience in Film History. *Screen* 31, 347–56.

Allen, Robert C. 1996: Manhattan Myopia; Oh! Iowa! *Cinema Journal* 35, no. 3, 75–103.

Allen, Robert C., and Douglas Gomery 1985: *Film History: Theory and Practice*. New York: Alfred A. Knopf.

Altman, Rick 1996: The Silence of the Silents. *Musical Quarterly* 80, 649–719.

American Architect 1920: The Artificial Illumination of Motion Picture Theatres, 1920. *American Architect* 118, 645–7, 678–81.

American Architect 1927: Modern Tendencies in Theatre Design. *American Architect* 12, 681–90.

Anderson, Gillian B. 1987: The Presentation of Silent Film or, Music as Anaesthesia. *Journal of Musicology* 5, 257–92.

Anderson, Gillian 1988: *Music for Silent Films: 1894–1929*. Washington: Library of Congress.

Anderson, Tim 1997: Reforming "Jackass Music": The Problematic Aesthetics of Early American Film Music Accompaniment. *Cinema Journal* 37, no. 1, 3–22.

Andrew, Dudley 1988: Film and Society: Public Rituals and Private Space. *East West Film Journal* 1, no. 1, 7–22.

Architect and Engineer 1915: Development of the Moving-Picture Theatre. *Architect and Engineer* 40 (February 1915), 51–60.

Architect's Journal 1935: The Cinema, a Symposium. *Architect's Journal* 82, 657–718.

Architects' and Builders Magazine 1910: The Moving Picture Theatres. *Architects' and Builders Magazine* 12, 319–22.

Architectural Forum 1922: Two San Francisco Motion Picture Theaters. *Architectural Forum* 37, 183–8.

Architectural Forum 1925a: The Work of Thomas W. Lamb, Architect. *Architectural Forum* 42, 377–80.

Architectural Forum 1925b: The Planning of the Motion Picture Theater. *Architectural Forum* 42, 385–8.

Architectural Forum 1942: Today Theater, Chicago, Illinois. *Architectural Forum* 76 (February 1942), 123–6.

Architectural Forum 1943: Moving Picture Theater. *Architectural Forum* 78 (May 1943), 113–15.

Architectural Forum 1944a: Theater: A California Movie House. *Architectural Forum* 81 (August 1944), 109–12.

Architectural Forum 1944b: Postwar Project for a Motion Picture Theater. *Architectural Forum* 81 (October 1944), 130–1.

Architectural Forum 1948: Small Theater Provides High Technical Standards for Rural Moviegoers. *Architectural Forum* 89 (October 1948), 95.

Architectural Forum 1949: Colorful Movie Theater. *Architectural Forum* 91 (November 1949), 95–7.

Architectural Record 1932: Portfolio of Theaters. *Architectural Record* 71, 421–8.

Architectural Record 1934a: A News Reel Movie in a Railroad Station. *Architectural Record* 75, 234.

Architectural Record 1934b: Drive-in Theater, Camden, New Jersey. *Architectural Record* 75, 235.

Architectural Record 1944a: The Theatre for Motion Pictures. *Architectural Record* 95 (June 1944), 83–94.

Architectural Record 1944b: Good Sight-Lines in a 900 Seat Theater. *Architectural Record* 95 (June 1944), 100–1.

Architectural Record 1948: Theaters. *Architectural Record* 104 (November 1948), 120–44.

Architectural Record 1949: Where Parking Is No Problem. *Architectural Record* 105 (January 1949), 84–7.

Architectural Record 1951: Suburban Movie House. *Architectural Record* 110 (October 1951), 163–5.

Architectural Record 1972: Theatres. *Architectural Record* 152, no. 4, 115–18.

Architecture and Building 1911: The Moving Picture Theatre. *Architecture and Building* 43, 319–22.

Armagnac, Alden P. 1950: Supermovies Put You in the Show. *Popular Science* 157 (August 1950), 74–8.

Armstrong, W.P. 1947: The Sherman Act and the Movies. *Temple Law Quarterly* 20, 442–71.

Armstrong, W.P., Jr. 1952: Sherman Act and the Movies: A Supplement. *Temple Law Quarterly* 26, 1–21.

Arnold, Robert Franklin 1994: The Architecture of Reception: Perspective and Ideological Functions in Visual Representation. Unpublished Ph.D. dissertation, University of Iowa.

Atwell, David 1980: *Cathedrals of the Movies: A History of British Cinemas and Their Audiences*. London: Architectural Press.

Austin, Bruce A. 1981: Portrait of a Cult Film Audience. *Journal of Communication* 31, no. 2, 43–54.

Austin, Bruce A. 1983: *The Film Audience: An International Bibliography of Research.* Metuchen, New Jersey: Scarecrow Press.

Austin, Bruce A. 1984: Portrait of an Art Film Audience. *Journal of Communication* 34, no. 1, 74–87.

Austin, Bruce A. 1985: The Development and Decline of the Drive-In Movie Theater. In *Current Research in Film: Audiences, Economics, and Law* 1. Norwood, New Jersey: Ablex, 59–91.

Austin, Bruce A. 1986: Cinema Screen Advertising: An Old Technology with New Promise for Consumer Marketing. *Journal of Consumer Marketing* 3, no. 4, 45–56.

Austin, Bruce A. 1989: *Immediate Seating: A Look at Movie Audiences.* Belmont, California: Wadsworth.

Austin, Bruce A. 1990: Home Video: The Second-Run "Theater" of the 1990s. In *Hollywood in the Age of Television*, ed. Tino Balio. Boston: Unwin Hyman, 319–49.

Bachman, Gregg Paul 1995: The Last of the Silent Generation: Oral Histories of Silent Movie Patrons. Unpublished Ph.D. dissertation, Union Institute.

Bachman, Gregg 1997: Still in the Dark – Silent Film Audiences. *Film History* 9, 23–48.

Bailie, Douglas 1996: Cinemas in the City: Edmonton from the Nickelodeon to the Multiplex. *Prairie Forum* 21, 239–62.

Bakshy, Alexander 1929: Free Lances. *Nation* 128, 324–5.

Balaban, Barney, and Sam Katz, 1926: *The Fundamental Principles of Balaban and Katz Theatre Management.* Chicago: Balaban and Katz.

Balaban, Carrie 1941: *Continuous Performance.* New York: A.J. Balaban Foundation.

Balio, Tino, ed. 1985: *The American Film Industry*, rev. ed. Madison: University of Wisconsin Press.

Balio, Tino, ed. 1990: *Hollywood in the Age of Television.* Boston: Unwin Hyman.

Balio, Tino 1993: *Grand Design: Hollywood as a Modern Business Enterprise, 1930–1939.* New York: Charles Scribner's Sons.

Barber, X. Theodore 1993: Evenings of Wonders: A History of the Magic Lantern Show in America. Unpublished Ph.D. dissertation, New York University.

Barrons 1978: Movie Theaters, Soft Drinks Prove Profitable Combo for General Cinema. *Barrons*, July 10, 1978, 32–3.

Barry, John F., and Epes W. Sargent 1927: *Building Theatre Patronage: Management and Merchandising.* New York: Chalmers Publishing Company.

Basque, Christine 1995: The Paradoxes of Paradise: Elements of Conflict in Chicago's Balaban and Katz Movie Palaces. *Marquee* 27, no. 2, 4–11.

Beach, Edward R. 1932: Double Features in Motion Picture Exhibition. *Harvard Business Review* 10, 505–15.

Beardsley, Charles 1983: *Hollywood's Master Showman: The Legendary Sid Grauman.* New York: Cornwell.

Beaupre, Lee 1978: Industry. *Film Comment* 14, no. 5, 68–72, 77.

Belton, John 1985: CinemaScope: The Economics of Technology. *Velvet Light Trap* 21, 35–43.

Belton, John 1987: The Pan & Scan Scandals. *Perfect Vision* 1, no. 1, 41–9.

Belton, John 1988: Cinerama: A New Era in the Cinema. *Perfect Vision* 1, no. 4, 78–90.

Belton, John 1992: *Widescreen Cinema.* Cambridge, Massachusetts: Harvard University Press.

Berg, Charles M. 1975: The Human Voice and the Silent Camera. *Journal of Popular Film* 10, 165–77.

Berg, Charles M. 1976: *An Investigation of the Motives for and the Realization of Music to Accompany the American Silent Film, 1897–1927.* New York: Arno Press.

Bernstein, Matthew 1995: A Tale of Three Cities: The Banning of *Scarlet Street. Cinema Journal* 35, no. 1, 27–52.

Bernstein, Matthew 1999: Selznik's March: The Atlanta Premiere of *Gone with the Wind. Atlanta History* 43, no. 2, 7–33.

Bertellini, Giorgio 1999a: Shipwrecked Spectators: Italy's Immigrants at the Movies in New York, 1906–1916. *Velvet Light Trap* 44, 39–53.

Bertellini, Giorgio 1999b: Italian Imageries, Historical Feature Films, and the Fabrication of Italy's Spectators in Early 1900s New York. In *American Movie Audiences: From the Turn of the Century to the Early Sound Era*, eds. Melvyn Stokes and Richard Maltby. London: British Film Institute, 29–45.

Beynon, George W. 1921: *Musical Presentation of Motion Pictures*. New York: Schirmer.

Bjork, Ulf Jonas, 1989: Double Features and "B" Movies: Exhibition Patterns in Seattle, 1938. *Journal of Film and Video* 41, no. 3, 34–49.

Blackall, C.H. 1914: New York Moving Picture Theater Law. *Brickbuilder* 23, 46–50.

Blake, Francis 1933: Something New in the Motion Picture Theatre. *Close Up* 10, 154–7.

Blanchard, S. 1983: Cinema-Going, Going, Gone! *Screen* 24, nos. 4–5, 108–13.

Bluem, A. William, and Jason E. Squire 1972: *The Movie Business: American Film Industry Practice*. New York: Hastings House.

Boblitz, K. Sherwood 1920: Where "Movie Playing" Needs Reform. *Musician* 25 (June 1920), 8, 29.

Boller, Robert 1930: Designing the Theatre Exterior. *Exhibitor's Herald-World* 99 (April 12, 1930), 23–6; (May 10, 1930), 21–3, 63.

Bordwell, David, Janet Staiger, and Kristin Thompson 1985: *The Classical Hollywood Cinema: Film Style & Mode of Production to 1960*. New York: Columbia University Press.

Borneman, Ernest 1951: United States vs. Hollywood: The Case History of an Anti-trust Suit. *Sight and Sound* 19, 418–20, 424, 448–50.

Bowers, Q. David 1986: *Nickelodeon Theatres and Their Music*. Vestal, New York: Vestal Press.

Bowser, Eileen 1990: *The Transformation of Cinema, 1907–1915*. New York: Scribner's.

Boyer, Diane 1988: Glitter Amidst Adobe: Tucson's Fox Theatre. *Journal of Arizona History* 29, 303–22.

Breard, Sylvester Quinn 1951: A History of Motion Pictures in New Orleans, 1896–1908. Unpublished M.A. thesis, Louisiana State University.

Brennan, William B., Jr. 1972: The Development of Special Forms of Film at World Expositions (1900–1970). Unpublished Ph.D. dissertation, Northwestern University.

Brett, Roger 1976: *Temples of Illusion*. Providence, Rhode Island: Brett Theatrical.

Brett, Steven Joseph 1995: The Shrinking Screen: The Increasing Intersection of Hollywood Film and Television Programming. Unpublished Ph.D. dissertation, Northwestern University.

Brickbuilder 1914: Moving Picture Theaters. *Brickbuilder* 23, 51–8.

Bullock, E.C.A. 1925: Theater Entrances and Lobbies. *Architectural Forum* 42, 369–72.

Bush, W. Stephen 1908: Hints to Exhibitors. *Moving Picture World* 3, 317.

Bush, W. Stephen 1912: The Picture and the Voice. *Moving Picture World* 14, 429.

Bush, W. Stephen 1914: New Theatres – New Exhibitors. *Moving Picture World* 22, 1049.

Business Week 1934: Premium Thriller. *Business Week* (December 8, 1934), 24.

Business Week 1938: Double-Movie Scrap. *Business Week* (March 5, 1938), 45–6.

Business Week 1953: Drive-In Theaters: Happy but Griping. *Business Week* (May 9, 1953), 129–30.

Business Week 1958: Film Chain Finds Cure for Box-Office Blues. *Business Week* 39 (March 22, 1958), 72–6.

Campbell, James R. 1922: *Motion Picture Projection*, 3rd ed. New York: Technical Book Company.

Carbine, Mary 1990: "The Finest Outside the Loop": Motion Picture Exhibition in Chicago's Black Metropolis, 1905–1928. *Camera Obscura* 23, 9–41.

Carr, Robert E., and R.M. Hayes 1988: *Wide Screen Movies: A History and Filmography of Wide Gauge Filmmaking.* Jefferson, North Carolina: McFarland.

Cassady, Ralph, Jr. 1933: Some Economic Aspects of Motion Picture Production and Marketing. *Journal of Business of the University of Chicago* 6, 113–31.

Cassady, Ralph, Jr. 1958: Impact of the Paramount Decision on Motion Picture Distribution and Price Making. *Southern California Law Review* 23, 325–90.

Cassady, Ralph, Jr. 1959: Monopoly in Motion Picture Production and Distribution: 1908–1915, *Southern California Law Review* 32, 325–90.

Chambers, R. 1938: Double Features as a Sales Problem. *Harvard Business Review* 26, 226–36.

Chambers, Robert 1950: Problems in Motion Picture Theatre Management. Unpublished Ph.D. dissertation, Harvard University.

Chenan, Michael 1996: *The Dream that Kicks: The Prehistory and Early Years of Cinema in Britain.* London: Routledge.

Christian Century 1933: Movie Exhibitors Ask Church Cooperation. *Christian Century* 50, 140.

Christman, Roy 1988: Movie Theaters in the Maintenance of Rural Communities in Kansas. *Great Plains Research* 8, 299–313.

Clarke, Eric T. 1926: An Exhibitor's Problems in 1925. *Transactions of the Society of Motion Picture Engineers* (January 1926), 46–57.

Cocks, Orrin G. 1920: The Motion Picture and the Upbuilding of Community Life. *Proceedings of the National Conference of Social Work* 47, 311–13.

Cohen, Lizabeth 1990: *Making a New Deal: Industrial Workers in Chicago, 1919–1939.* Cambridge: Cambridge University Press.

Cohen, Mary Morley 1994: Forgotten Audiences in the Passion Pits: Drive-In Theatres and Changing Spectator Practices in Post-War America. *Film History* 6, 470–86.

Collier, John 1908: Cheap Amusements. *Charities and the Commons* 20 (April 1908), 73–6.

Columbia Law Review 1936: The Motion Picture Industry and the Anti-Trust Laws. *Columbia Law Review* 36, 635–52.

The Community and the Motion Picture: Report of the National Conference on Motion Pictures Held at the Hotel Montclair, New York City, September 24–27, 1929 1929: N.p. Motion Picture Producers and Distributors of America.

Conant, Michael 1960: *Antitrust in the Motion Picture Industry.* Berkeley: University of California Press.

Conant, Michael 1981: "The Paramount Decrees Reconsidered." *Law and Contemporary Problems* 44, no. 4, 79–107.

Connelly, Eugene LeMoyne 1940: The First Motion Picture Theater. *Western Pennsylvania Historical Magazine* 23, no. 1, 1–12.

Connor, Edward 1966: 3-D on the Screen. *Films in Review* 17, no. 3, 159–74.

Coombs, Jan 1994: Big Ambitions in a Small Town: The Story of J.P. Adler and the Movies. *Wisconsin Magazine of History* 78, no. 2, 82–109.

Costello, Michael 1941: They Pronounce It Pre-Meer. *Commonweal* 33, 294–6.

Crafton, Donald 1990: Audienceship in Early Cinema. *Iris* 11, 1–12.

Crafton, Donald 1997: *The Talkies: American Cinema's Transition to Sound, 1926–1931.* New York: Scribner's.

Crane, C. Howard 1925: Observations on Motion Picture Theaters. *Architectural Forum* 42, 381–4.

Craw, George Rockhill 1911: Swelling the Box Office Receipts. *Moving Picture World* 8, 1059–60.

Cromie, Robert 1938: Thoughts on the Cinema. *Architect's World* 1, 252–4.

Cullman, Marguerite W. 1950: Double Feature – Movies and Moonlight. *New York Times Magazine* (October 1, 1950), 22, 68–9, 72.

Currie, Barton W. 1907: The Nickel Madness. *Harper's Weekly* 51, 1246–7.

Cutter, Walter A. 1948: Psychology of the Theater. In *The Motion Picture Theater: Planning, Upkeep* ed. Helen M. Stote. New York: Society of Motion Picture Engineers, 14–21.

Daly, David Anthony 1978: A Comparison of Exhibition and Distribution Patterns in Three Recent Feature Motion Pictures. Unpublished Ph.D. dissertation, Southern Illinois University at Carbondale.

Davis, Michael 1911: *The Exploitation of Pleasure: A Study of Commercial Recreation in New York City.* New York: Russell Sage Foundation.

DeBauche, Leslie Midkiff 1999: Reminiscences of the Past, Conditions of the Present: At the Movies in Milwaukee in 1918. In *American Movie Audiences: From the Turn of the Century to the Early Sound Era*, eds. Melvyn Stokes and Richard Maltby. London: British Film Institute, 129–39.

DeCordova, Richard 1990: Ethnography and Exhibition: The Child Audience, the Hays Office, and Saturday Matinees. *Camera Obscura* 23, 91–107.

Dekom, Peter, Michael I. Adler, David Ginsburg, and Michael H. Lauerm, eds. 1980: *The Fifth Annual UCLA Entertainment Symposium: The Selling of Motion Pictures in the '80s: New Producer/Distributor/Exhibitor Relationships.* Los Angeles: Regents of the University of California.

Dench, Ernest A. 1916: Exhibiting Motion Pictures in a Mining Town. *Coal Age* 9, 764–5.

De Silva, Indrawansa 1994: Understanding Motion Picture Audiences in the Age of Home Video: A Synthesis of Communication and Economic Approaches. Unpublished Ph.D. dissertation, Michigan State University.

Denvir, Bernard 1983: Things Ain't What They Used To Be. *Films and Filming* 343, 25–7.

Deutsch, James L. 1980: The Rise and Fall of the House of Ushers: Teenage Ticket Takers in the Twenties Theaters. *Journal of Popular Culture* 13, 602–8.

Dickey, Sara Ann 1988: Going to the Pictures in Madurai: Social, Psychological, and Political Aspects of Cinema in Urban Working Class South India. Unpublished Ph.D. dissertation, University of California, San Diego.

Dobi, Stephen J. 1984: Cinema 16: America's Largest Film Society. Unpublished Ph.D. dissertation, New York University.

Doherty, Tom 1999: This Is Where We Came In: The Audible Screen and the Voluble Audience of Early Sound Cinema. In *American Movie Audiences: From the Turn of the Century to the Early Sound Era*, eds. Melvyn Stokes and Richard Maltby. London: British Film Institute, 143–63.

Donahue, Suzanne Mary 1987: *American Film Distribution: The Changing Marketplace.* Ann Arbor, Michigan: UMI Research Press.

Downs, Anthony 1953: Drive-Ins Have Arrived. *Journal of Property Management* 18, 149–53.

Durant, John 1950: The Movies Take to the Pastures. *Saturday Evening Post* 223 (October 14, 1950), 24–5, 85, 89–90.

Dutton, William S. 1931: Getting on in the World: New Jobs in the Theater. *Saturday Evening Post* 203 (May 23, 1931), 49, 62.

Dyal, Donald H. 1981: *Movie Theatre Architecture: A Bibliography*. Monticello, Illinois: Vance Bibliographies.

Dym, Jeffrey Albert 1998: Benshi, Poets of the Dark: Japanese Silent Film Narrators and Their Forgotten Narrative Art of Setsumei, 1896–1939. Unpublished Ph.D. dissertation, University of Hawaii.

Eberson, John 1925: A Description of the Capitol Theater, Chicago. *Architectural Forum* 42, 373–6.

Eckert, Charles 1978: The Carole Lombard in Macy's Window. *Quarterly Review of Film Studies* 3, no. 1, 1–21.

Edelhertz, Bernard 1927: The Soul of a Master Showman. *American Hebrew* 120, 641–2, 671.

Edgerton, Gary R. 1981: *American Film Exhibition and an Analysis of the Motion Picture Industry's Market Structure, 1963–1980*. New York: Garland Press.

Edgerton, Gary 1982: The Multiplex: The Modern American Motion Picture Theatre as Message. *Journal of Popular Film* 9, 158–65.

Edwards, Gregory J. 1985: *The International Film Poster: The Role of the Poster in Cinema Art, Advertising, and History*. Salem, New Hampshire: Salem House.

Embury, Aymar 1914: Architectural Treatment of the Moving Picture Theatre. *Brickbuilder* 23, 37–9.

Erffmeyer, Thomas Edward 1985: The History of Cinerama: A Study of Technological Innovation and Industrial Management. Unpublished Ph.D. dissertation, Northwestern University.

Ewen, Elizabeth 1985: *Immigrant Women in the Land of Dollars: Life and Culture on the Lower East Side, 1890–1925*. New York: Monthly Review Press.

Faber, Ronald J., Thomas C. O'Guinn, and Andrew P. Hardy 1988: Art Films in the Suburbs: A Comparison of Popular and Art Film Audiences. In *Current Research in Film: Audiences, Economics, and Law* 4. Norwood, New Jersey: Ablex, 45–53.

Feagans, Janet 1965: Atlanta Theatre Segregation: A Case of Prolonged Avoidance. *Journal of Human Relations* 13, 208–18.

Ferguson, Stanley 1942: Gone with the Sound Track. *New Republic* 106, 426–7.

Fernett, Gene 1982: Itinerant Roadshowmen and the "Free Movie" Craze. *Classic Images* 88, 12–13.

Field, Audrey 1974: *Picture Palace: A Social History of the Cinema*. London: Gentry Books.

Fielding, Raymond 1970: Hale's Tours: Ultrarealism in the Pre-1910 Motion Picture. *Cinema Journal* 10, no. 1, 34–47.

Fisher, Boyd 1912: The Regulation of Motion Picture Theaters. *American City* 7, 520–1.

Fones-Wolf, Elizabeth 1994: Sound Comes to the Movies: The Philadelphia Musicians' Struggle against Recorded Music. *Pennsylvania Magazine of History and Biography* 118, nos. 1–2, 3–31.

Foreman, Henry James 1934: *Our Movie Made Children*. New York: Macmillan.

Fortune 1948: What's Playing at the Grove? *Fortune* 38 (August 1948), 94–9, 134, 136–8.

Fortune 1949: Movies: End of an Era? *Fortune* 39 (April 1949), 99–102, 135–50.

Fortune 1953: Cinerama: The Broad Picture. *Fortune* 47 (January 1947), 122–3, 144–50.

Fosdick, Raymond B. 1911: *Report on the Conditions of Motion Picture Shows in New York*. New York: Office of the Commissioner of Accounts.

Foster, William Trufant 1914: *Vaudeville and Motion Picture Shows: A Study of Theaters in Portland, Oregon*. Portland: Reed College.

Francisco, Charles 1979: *The Radio City Music Hall: An Affectionate History of the World's Greatest Theatre*. New York: E.P. Dutton.

Frank, Stanley 1952: Sure-Seaters Discover an Audience. *Nation's Business* 40, 34–6, 69.

Franklin, Harold B. 1928: *Motion Picture Theater Management*. Garden City, New York: Doubleday, Doran and Company.

Franzheim, Kenneth 1925: Present Tendencies in the Design of Theater Facades. *Architectural Forum* 42, 365–8.

Fried, Frederick 1984: The Not-So Silent Films and Some Sound Effects. *Musical Box Society International* 30, 176–83.

Fuller, Kathryn Helgesen 1993: Shadowland: American Audiences and the Moviegoing Experience in the Silent Era. Unpublished Ph.D. dissertation, Johns Hopkins University.

Fuller, Kathryn H. 1996: *At the Picture Show: Small-Town Audiences and the Creation of Movie Fan Culture*. Washington: Smithsonian Institution Press.

Fuller, Kathryn Helgesen 1999: Viewing the Viewers: Representations of the Audience in Early Cinema Advertising. In *American Movie Audiences: From the Turn of the Century to the Early Sound Era*, eds. Melvyn Stokes and Richard Maltby. London: British Film Institute, 112–28.

Fullerton, John 1993: Intimate Theatres and Imaginary Scenes: Film Exhibition in Sweden before 1920. *Film History* 5 (1993), 457–77.

Gaines, Jane 1990: From Elephants to Lux Soap: The Programming and "Flow" of Early Motion Picture Exploitation. *Velvet Light Trap* 25, 29–43.

Geary, Helen Brophy 1983: After the Last Picture Show. *Chronicles of Oklahoma* 61, no. 1, 4–27.

Giles, Dennis 1983: The Outdoor Economy: A Study of the Contemporary Drive-In. *Journal of the University Film and Video Association* 35, no. 2, 66–76.

Glase, Paul E. 1948: The Motion Picture Theatre in Reading: Silent Drama Days – 1905–1926. *Historical Review of Berks County* (January 1948), 35–44.

Glazer, Irving R. 1986: *Philadelphia Theatres, A-Z*. New York: Greenwood Press.

Goldsmith, Alfred N. 1948: Theater Television – A General Analysis. In *The Motion Picture Theater: Planning, Upkeep*, ed. Helen M. Stote. New York: Society of Motion Picture Engineers, 318–44.

Goldsmith, Ben 1999: "The Comfort Lies in All the Things You Can Do": The Australian Drive-In-Cinema of Distraction. *Journal of Popular Culture* 33, no. 1, 153–64.

Goldwyn, Samuel 1949: Hollywood in the Television Age. *Hollywood Quarterly* 4, 145–51.

Gomery, Douglas 1978: The Picture Palace: Economic Sense or Hollywood Nonsense. *Quarterly Review of Film Studies* 3, no. 1, 23–36.

Gomery, Douglas 1979a: Saxe Amusement Enterprises: The Movies Come to Milwaukee. *Milwaukee History* 2, no. 1, 18–28.

Gomery, Douglas 1979b: The Growth of Movie Monopolies: The Case of Balaban & Katz. *Wide Angle* 3, no. 1, 44–63.

Gomery, Douglas 1981a: The Warner Theatre: Architectural Splendor in Milwaukee. *Marquee* 12, nos. 1–2, 27–31.

Gomery, Douglas 1981b: The Economics of U.S. Film Exhibition Policy and Practice. *Cine-Tracts* 12, 36–40.

Gomery, Douglas 1982a: Movie Audiences, Urban Geography, and the History of the American Film. *Velvet Light Trap* 19, 23–9.

Gomery, Douglas 1982b: Splendor in Paradise: The Paramount in Palm Beach. *Marquee* 14, no. 4, 3–6.

Gomery, Douglas 1983: Movie-Going during Hollywood's Golden Age. *North Dakota Quarterly* 51, no. 3, 36–43.

Gomery, Douglas 1984a: Failed Opportunities: The Integration of the U.S. Motion Picture and Television Industries. *Quarterly Review of Film Studies* 10, no. 2, 219–28.

Gomery, Douglas 1984b: The Skouras Brothers: Bringing Movies to St. Louis and Beyond. *Marquee* 16, no. 1, 18–21.

Gomery, Douglas 1985a: The Coming of Television and the "Lost" Motion Picture Audience. *Journal of Film and Video* 37, no. 3, 5–11.

Gomery, Douglas 1985b: Theatre Television: The Missing Link of Technological Change in the U.S. Motion Picture Industry. *Velvet Light Trap* 21, 54–61.

Gomery, Douglas 1985c: U.S. Film Exhibition: The Formation of a Big Business. In *The American Film Industry*, ed. Tino Balio, rev. ed. Madison: University of Wisconsin Press, 218–28.

Gomery, Douglas 1985d: The Coming of Sound: Technological Change in the American Film Industry. In *The American Film Industry*, ed. Tino Balio, rev. ed. Madison: University of Wisconsin Press, 229–51.

Gomery, Douglas 1986a: Hollywood's Business. *Wilson Quarterly* 10, no. 3, 43–57.

Gomery, Douglas 1986b: The Popularity of Filmgoing in the United States, 1930–1950. In *High Theory/Low Culture: Analyzing Popular Television and Film*, ed. Colin McCabe. New York: St. Martin's Press, 71–9.

Gomery, Douglas 1989a: The Story of the Augusta Theatre. *Marquee* 21, no. 2, 3–8.

Gomery, Douglas 1989b: Theatre Television: A History. *SMPTE Journal* 98, no. 2, 120–3.

Gomery, Douglas 1990a: If You've Seen One, You've Seen the Mall. In *Seeing Through Movies*, ed. M.C. Miller. New York: Pantheon, 49–80.

Gomery, Douglas 1990b: Thinking about Motion Picture Exhibition. *Velvet Light Trap* 25, 3–11.

Gomery, Douglas 1990c: The Movie Palace Comes to America's Cities. In *For Fun and Profit: The Transformation of Leisure into Consumption*, ed. Richard Butsch. Philadelphia: Temple University Press, 136–51.

Gomery, Douglas 1990d: Building a Movie Theater Giant: The Rise of Cineplex Odeon. In *Hollywood in the Age of Television*, ed. Tino Balio. Boston: Unwin Hyman, 377–91.

Gomery, Douglas 1992: *Shared Pleasures: A History of Movie Presentation in the United States*. Madison, Wisconsin: University of Wisconsin Press.

Graf, Don 1938: The Design of the Cinema. *Pencil Points* 19, 337–40, 399–406, 443–8.

Grenz, Christine 1982: *Trans-Lux: Biography of a Corporation*. Norwalk, Connecticut: Trans-Lux Corporation.

Grieveson, Lee 1999: Why the Audience Mattered in Chicago in 1907. In *American Movie Audiences: From the Turn of the Century to the Early Sound Era*, eds. Melvyn Stokes and Richard Maltby. London: British Film Institute, 79–91.

Griffiths, Alison, and James Latham 1999: Film and Ethnic Identity in Harlem, 1896–1915. In *American Movie Audiences: From the Turn of the Century to the Early Sound Era*, eds. Melvyn Stokes and Richard Maltby. London: British Film Institute, 46–63.

Guback, Thomas 1987: The Evolution of the Motion Picture Theater Business in the 1980s. *Journal of Communication* 37, no. 2, 60–77.

Gue, Randy 1999: Nickel Madness: Atlanta's Storefront Movie Theaters, 1906–1911. *Atlanta History* 43, no. 2, 34–44.

Gunning, Tom 1994: An Aesthetic of Astonishment: Early Film and the (In)credulous Spectator. In *Viewing Positions: Ways of Seeing Film*, ed. Linda Williams. New Brunswick, New Jersey: Rutgers University Press, 114–33.

Guzman, Anthony Henry 1993: The Exhibition and Reception of European Films in the United States during the 1920s. Unpublished Ph.D. dissertation, University of California at Los Angeles.

Hall, Ben M. 1961: *The Best Remaining Seats*. New York: Bramwell House.

Hampton, Benjamin B. 1931: *A History of the Movies*. New York: Covici Friede.

Handel, Leo A. 1950: *Hollywood Looks at Its Audience: A Report of Film Audience Research*. Urbana: University of Illinois Press.

Hansen, Miriam 1983: Early Silent Cinema: Whose Public Sphere? *New German Critique* 29, 147–84.

Hansen, Miriam 1988: Reinventing the Nickelodeon: Notes on Kluge and Early Cinema. *October* 46, 179–98.

Hansen, Miriam 1991: *Babel and Babylon: Spectatorship in American Silent Film*. Cambridge, Massachusetts: Harvard University Press.

Hansen, Miriam 1993: Early Cinema, Late Cinema: Permutations of the Public Sphere. *Screen* 34, 197–210.

Haralovich, Mary Beth 1984: Motion Picture Advertising: Industrial and Social Forces and Effects, 1930–1948. Unpublished Ph.D. dissertation, University of Wisconsin, Madison.

Haralovich, Mary Beth 1985: Film Advertising, the Film Industry, and the Pin-Up: The Industry's Accommodations to Social Forces in the 1940s. In *Current Research in Film: Audiences, Economics, and the Law* 1, ed. Bruce A. Austin. Norwood, New Jersey: Ablex Publishing Company, 127–64.

Hark, Ina Rae 1994: The "Theater Man" and "The Girl in the Box Office." *Film History* 6, 178–87.

Harrison, P.S. 1935: Give the Movie Exhibitor a Chance! *Christian Century* 52, 819–21.

Haver, Ronald 1981: The Perils of Movie-going. *American Film* 6, no. 7, 46–8.

Havig, Alan 1982: The Commercial Amusement Audience in Early 20th-Century American Cities. *Journal of American Culture* 5, 1–19.

Hawkins, Richard C. 1953: Perspective on 3-D. *Quarterly Review of Film, Radio and Television* 7, 281–4.

Hayes, R.M. 1989: *3-D Movies: A History and Filmography of Stereoscopic Cinema*. Jefferson, North Carolina: McFarland.

Heacock, Ralph H. 1955: Wide Screens in Drive-In Theatres. *Journal of the SMPTE* 64, no. 2, 86–7.

Headley, Robert Kirk, Jr. 1974: *Exit: A History of the Movies in Baltimore*. Baltimore: Privately published.

Headley, Robert K., Jr. 1981: Nickelodeon Finances and Operations, 1909–1911: The Horn Theatre, Baltimore, Maryland. *Marquee* 13, no. 1, 21–2.

Headley, Robert K., Jr. 1999: *Motion Picture Exhibition in Washington, D.C.: An Illustrated History of Parlors, Palaces and Multiplexes in the Metropolitan Area, 1894–1997*. Jefferson, North Carolina: McFarland.

Herzog, Charlotte 1977: Movie Palaces and Exhibition. *Film Reader 2*, 185–97.

Herzog, Charlotte 1980: The Motion Picture Theatre and Film Exhibition – 1896–1932. Unpublished Ph.D. dissertation, Northwestern University.

Herzog, Charlotte 1981: The Movie Palace and the Theatrical Sources of Its Architecture. *Cinema Journal* 20, 15–37.

Herzog, Charlotte 1984: The Archaeology of Cinema Architecture: The Origins of the Movie Theater. *Quarterly Review of Film Studies* 9, 11–32.

Higashi, Sumiko 1996: Dialogue: Manhattan's Nickelodeons. *Cinema Journal* 35, no. 3, 72–4.

Hincha, Richard 1985: Selling CinemaScope: 1953–1956. *Velvet Light Trap* 21, 44–53.

Hincha, Richard Emil 1989: Twentieth-Century Fox's Cinemascope: An Industrial Organization of Its Development, Marketing, and Adoption. Unpublished Ph.D. dissertation, University of Wisconsin, Madison.

Hines, Al 1952: The Drive-Ins. *Holiday* 12 (July 1952), 6–10.

Hoberman, J., and Jonathan Rosenbaum 1983: *Midnight Movies*. New York: Harper and Row.

Hodges, James Floyd 1912: *Opening and Operating a Motion Picture Theater: How It Is Successfully Done*. New York: Scenario Publishing Company.

Hodgson, Richard 1949: Theatre Television System. *Journal of the Society of Motion Picture Engineers* 52, 540–8.

Hoffman, H.F. 1911: The Murder of *Othello*. *Moving Picture World* 9, 110.

Holliday, Carl 1919: The Movies in an Average City. *American City* 21, 59–69.

Hollyman, Burnes St. Patrick 1977: The First Picture Shows: Austin, Texas, 1894–1913. *Journal of the University Film Association* 29, no. 3, 3–8.

Horton, Andrew 1976: Turning On and Tuning Out at the Drive-In: An American Phenomenon Survives and Thrives. *Journal of Popular Film* 5, 233–44.

Howe, Frederic C. 1914: What to Do with the Motion-Picture Show? Shall It Be Censored? *Outlook* 100, 412.

Hubbard, P.J. 1985: Synchronized Sound and Movie-House Musicians, 1926–29. *American Music* 3, 429–41.

Huettig, Mae D. 1944: *Economic Control of the Motion Picture Industry*. Philadelphia: University of Pennsylvania Press.

Hughes, Stephan Putnam 1996: Is There Anyone Out There? Exhibition and the Formation of Silent Film Audiences in South India. Unpublished Ph.D. dissertation, University of Chicago.

Hulfish, David 1915: *Motion-Picture Work: A General Treatise on Picture Taking, Picture Making, Photo-Plays, and Theater Management and Operation*. Chicago: American Technical Society. Rpt. New York: Arno Press, 1970.

Illinois Law Review 1938: Restraints on Motion Picture Exhibition and the Anti-Trust Laws. *Illinois Law Review* 33, 424–46.

Illinois Law Review 1947: Price-Fixing in the Motion Picture Industry. *Illinois Law Review* 42, 630–46.

Jacobs, Lea 1983: The Paramount Case and the Role of the Distributor. *Journal of the University Film and Video Association* 35, no. 1, 44–9.

Jacobs, Lewis 1939: *The Rise of the American Film: A Critical History*. New York: Harcourt, Brace.

Jenkins, C. Francis, and Oscar D. DePue 1908: *Handbook for Motion Picture and Stereopticon Operators*. Washington, DC: Knega.

Johnson, Keith F. 1981: Cinema Advertising. *Journal of Advertising* 10, no. 4, 11–19.

Johnson, Keith F. 1989: An Investigation of the VCR Viewing Environment. Unpublished Ph.D. dissertation, University of Georgia.

Josephson, Matthew 1926: The Rise of the Little Cinema. *Motion Picture Classic* 24, no. 1, 34–5, 69, 82. In *Spellbound in Darkness*, ed. George Pratt, rev. ed. Greenwich, New York: New York Graphic Society, 1973, 483–8.

Jowett, Garth S. 1976: *Film: The Democratic Art*. Boston: Little, Brown.

Jowett, Garth S. 1982: The First Motion Picture Audiences. In *Movies as Artifacts: Cultural Criticisms of Popular Film*, ed. Michael Marsden, et al. Chicago: Nelson-Hall, 14–25.

Kalmus, Herbert 1953: Technicolor and New Screen Techniques. In *New Screen Techniques*, ed. Martin Quigley, Jr. New York: Quigley Publishing, 78–81.

Karnes, David 1986: The Glamorous Crowd: Hollywood Movie Premieres Between the Wars. *American Quarterly* 38, 553–72.

Katz, Samuel 1927: Theatre Management. In *The Story of the Films*, ed. Joseph P. Kennedy. Chicago: A.W. Shaw, 263–84.

Kauffman, Stanley 1965: Are We Doomed to Festivals? *New Republic* 153 (October 2, 1965), 30–2.

Kautzenbach, George 1972: Columbia University and the Rivoli Theater. *Journal of Popular Culture* 6, 301–22.

Kennedy, Joseph P., ed. 1927: *The Story of the Films*. Chicago: A.W. Shaw.

Kenney, Roy Wallace 1979: The Economics of Block-Booking. Unpublished Ph.D. dissertation, University of California at Los Angeles.

Kerbel, Michael 1977a: Edited for Television. *Film Comment* 13, no. 3, 28–30.

Kerbel, Michael 1977b: Edited for Television II. *Film Comment* 13, no. 4, 38–40.

Kerr, Eleanor 1940: *The First Quarter Century of the Motion Picture Theatre*. New York: Potter.

Kindem, Gorham, ed. 1982: *The American Movie Industry: The Business of Motion Pictures*. Carbondale: Southern Illinois University Press.

Kinsila, Edward Bernard 1917: *Modern Theater Construction*. New York: Moving Picture World.

Kirby, Lynne 1997: *Parallel Tracks: The Railroad in Silent Cinema*. Durham, North Carolina: Duke University Press.

Klaber, John J. 1915: Planning the Moving Picture Theatre. *Architectural Record* 38, 540–54.

Klenotic, Jeffrey F. 1996: A Cultural Studies Approach to the Social History of Film: A Case Study of Moviegoing in Springfield, Massachusetts, 1926–1932. Unpublished Ph.D. dissertation, University of Massachusetts, Amherst.

Klenotic, Jeffrey F. 1998: Class Markers in the Mass Movie Audience: A Case Study in the Cultural Geography of Moviegoing, 1926–1932. *Communication Review* 2, 461–95.

Klinger, Barbara 1997: Film History Terminable and Interminable: Recovering the Past in Reception Studies. *Screen* 38, 107–28.

Klinger, Barbara 1998: The New Media Aristocrats: Home Theater and the Domestic Film Experience. *Velvet Light Trap* 42, 4–19.

Kloepfel, Don V., ed. 1969: *Motion-Picture Projection and Theater Presentation Manual*. New York: Society of Motion Picture and Television Engineers.

Kmet, Jeffrey 1979: Milwaukee's Nickelodeon Era: 1906–1915. *Milwaukee History* 2, no. 1, 2–7.

Knudsen, Vern O., and Cyril M. Harris 1948: Acoustical Design of the Theater. *Architectural Record* 104 (November 1948), 139–44.

Kobal, John, and V.A. Wilson 1983: *Foyer Pleasure: The Golden Age of Cinema Lobby Cards*. New York: Delilah.

Koszarski, Richard 1990: *An Evening's Entertainment: The Age of the Silent Feature Picture, 1915–1928*. New York: Scribner's.

Kraft, James P. 1993: Work and Technological Change: Musicians and the Film Industry, 1926–1940. *Business and Economic History* 22, 256–61.

Kraft, James P. 1994: The "Pit" Musicians: Mechanization in the Movie Theaters, 1926–1934. *Labor History* 35, no. 1, 66–89.

Kraft, James P. 1996: *Stage to Studio: Musicians and the Sound Revolution, 1890–1950*. Baltimore: Johns Hopkins University Press.

Kresensky, R. 1935: Bank Night. *Christian Century* 52, 1034–5.

Kreuzer, Barton 1949: Progress Report – Theatre Television. *Journal of the Society of Motion Picture Engineers* 53, no. 2, 128–36.

Krows, Arthur Edwin 1935: The Exhibitor Says "No." *Outlook* (May 1935), 30–6.

Kusell, H.O. 1936: Bank Night. *New Republic* 86, 363–5.

Lacasse, Germain 1999: American Film in Quebec Theater. *Cinema Journal* 38, no. 2, 98–110.

Lafferty, William 1990: Feature Films on Prime-Time Television. In *Hollywood in the Age of Television*, ed. Tino Balio. Boston: Unwin Hyman, 235–56.

Lang, Edith, and George West 1920: *Musical Accompaniment of Moving Pictures*. Boston:

Boston Music Company. Rpt. New York: Arno Press, 1970.

Landon, John W. 1974: *Jesse Crawford*. Vestal, New York: Vestal Press.

Landon, John W. 1983: *Behold the Mighty Wurlitzer: The History of the Theatre Pipe Organ*. Westport, Connecticut: Greenwood Press.

Laycock, George 1952: Free Shows Pay Off in Kentucky. *Nation's Business* 40 (November 1952), 84–5.

Lee, S. Charles 1948: Influence of West Coast Designers on the Modern Theater. In *The Motion Picture Theater: Planning, Upkeep*, ed. Helen M. Stote. New York: Society of Motion Picture Engineers, 32–9.

Lescarboura, Austin C. 1919: *Behind the Motion Picture Screen*. New York: Scientific American.

Levy, Mark, ed. 1989: *The VCR Age: Home Video and Mass Communications*. Newbury Park, California: Sage.

Lewis, Howard Thompson 1930: *Harvard Business Reports. Volume 8: Cases on the Motion Picture Industry*. New York: McGraw-Hill.

Lewis, Lloyd 1929: The De Luxe Picture Palace. *New Republic* 58 (March 27, 1929), 175–6.

Life 1951: Drive-In Film Business Burns up the Prairies. *Life* 31 (September 24, 1951), 104–6.

Lincoln, Freeman 1955: The Comeback of the Movies. *Fortune* 51 (February 1955), 127–31, 155–8.

Lindstrom, Julie Ann 1998: "Getting a Hold in the Life of the City": Chicago Nickelodeons, 1905–1914. Unpublished Ph.D. dissertation, Northwestern University.

Little, Ralph V. 1948: Developments in Larger-Screen Television. *Journal of the Society of Motion Picture Engineers* 51, no. 1, 37–46.

Locher, Harriet Hawley 1926: Making the Neighborhood Motion Picture Theater a Community Institution. *Educational Screen* (April 1926), 203–5, 397–401.

Logan, H.L. 1948: Lighting Movie Theater Interiors. *Architectural Record* 104 (November 1948), 145–7.

Lowery, Edward 1976: Edwin J. Hadley: Traveling Film Exhibitor. *Journal of the University Film Association* 28, no. 3, 5–12.

Luckett, Moya 1995: Cities and Spectators: A Historical Analysis of Film Audiences in Chicago, 1910–1915. Unpublished Ph.D. dissertation, University of Wisconsin, Madison.

Luther, Rodney 1950: Television and the Future of Motion Picture Exhibition. *Hollywood Quarterly* 5, 164–77.

Luther, Rodney 1951: Drive-In Theatres: Rags to Riches in Five Years. *Hollywood Quarterly* 5, 401–11.

Lynch, W.F. 1961: Let's Have Film Festivals. *America* 104, 753–6.

McCarthy, Kathleen D. 1976: Nickel Vice and Virtue: Movie Censorship in Chicago, 1907–1915. *Journal of Popular Film* 5, 37–55.

McCoy, John E., and Harry P. Warner 1949: Theatre Television Today – Part I. *Hollywood Quarterly* 4, no. 2, 160–77.

McDonough, John R., Jr., and Robert T. Winslo 1949: The Motion Picture Industry: United States v. Oligopoly. *Stanford Law Review* 1, 385–427.

McGilligan, Patrick 1980: Movies are Better than Ever – On Television. *American Film* 5, no. 4, 52–3.

Macgowan, Kenneth 1956: The Screen's "New Look" – Wider and Deeper. *Quarterly Review of Film, Radio and Television* 11, 109–30.

Macgowan, Kenneth 1957: The Wide Screen of Yesterday and Tomorrow. *Quarterly Review of Film, Radio and Television* 11, 217–41.

McKay, Robert B. 1954: Segregation and Public Recreation. *Virginia Law Review* 40, 697–731.

Mclane, Betsy 1983: Domestic Theatrical and Semi-Theatrical Distribution and Exhibition of American Independent Feature Films: A Survey in 1983. *Journal of the University Film and Video Association* 35, no. 2, 17–24.

Margolies, John, and Emily Gwathmey 1991: *Ticket to Paradise: American Movie Theaters and How We Had Fun.* Boston: Little, Brown.

Marks, Martin M. 1996: *Music and the Silent Film: Contexts and Case Studies, 1895–1924.* New York: Oxford University Press.

Marsh, John L. 1984: Vaudefilm: Its Contribution to a Moviegoing America. *Journal of American Culture* 7, no. 3, 77–84.

May, Lary 1980: *Screening Out the Past: The Birth of Mass Culture and the Motion Picture Industry.* New York: Oxford University Press.

May, Lary 1987: Making the American Way: Moderne Theatres, Audiences, and the Film Industry 1929–1945. In *Prospects, An Annual of American Cultural Studies*, ed. Jack Salzman. New York: Cambridge University Press, 89–124.

May, Lary 1993: Designing Multi-Cultural America: Modern Movie Theaters and the Politics of Public Space 1920–1945. In *Movies and Politics: The Dynamic Relationship*, ed. James Combs. New York, Garland, 183–235.

May, Lary 2000: *The Big Tomorrow: Hollywood and the Politics of the American Way.* Chicago: University of Chicago Press.

Mayer, Arthur 1947: An Exhibitor Begs for "B"s. *Hollywood Quarterly* 3, 172–7.

Mayer, Arthur 1953: *Merely Colossal.* New York: Simon and Schuster.

Mayer, Arthur 1958: Hollywood's Favorite Fable. *Film Quarterly* 12, no. 2, 13–20.

Mayer, Michael 1964: *Foreign Films on American Screens.* New York: Arco.

Mayer, Michael 1973: *The Film Industries: Practical Business/Legal Problems in Production, Distribution, Exhibition.* New York: Hastings House.

Mayer, Michael 1974: Film as Business: New Trends in Exhibition. *Take One* 4, no. 5, 48+.

Mayer, Michael 1976: Film as Business: New Trends in Exhibition Deals. *Take One* 5, no. 4, 31–2.

Mayer, Michael 1977: Film as Business: The Exhibition License. *Take One* 5, no. 6, 29–30.

Mayne, Judith 1982: Immigrants and Spectators. *Wide Angle* 5, no. 2, 32–41.

Meloy, Arthur S. 1916: *Theatres and Motion Picture Houses.* New York: Architects' Supply and Publishing Company.

Merritt, Russell 1985: Nickelodeon Theaters, 1905–1914: Building an Audience for the Movies. In *The American Film Industry*, ed. Tino Balio, rev ed. Madison: University of Wisconsin Press, 83–102.

Miller, Mark Stuart 1994: Promoting Movies in the Late 1930s: Pressbooks at Warner Bros. Unpublished Ph.D. dissertation, University of Texas at Austin.

Milnar, Emil M. 1922: Motion Picture Theatre Data. *Pencil Points* (June 1922), 29–30; (July 1922), 10–13+; (September 1922), 13–15+; (October 1922), 32–4+; (November 1922), 27–9+.

Mindlin, Michael 1928: The Little Cinema Movement. *Theatre* (July 1928), 18, 62.

Moret, Daniel Loren 1991: The New Nickelodeons: A Political Economy of the Home Video Industry with Particular Emphasis on Video Software Retailers. Unpublished M. S. thesis, University of Oregon.

Morrison, Craig 1974: From Nickelodeon to Picture Palace and Back. *Design Quarterly* 93, 6–9.

Morrison, A. Craig, and Lucy Pope Wheeler 1978: *Nickelodeon to Movie Palace: Ten Twentieth Century Theaters 1910–1931.* Washington, DC: Historic American Buildings Survey, US Department of the Interior.

Moving Picture World 1910a: The Awakening of the Exhibitor. *Moving Picture World* 6, 47–8.

Moving Picture World 1910b: Mrs. Clement and Her Work. *Moving Picture World* 7, 859–60.

Musser, Charles 1981: The Eden Musee: Exhibitor as Creator. *Film and History* 11, no. 4, 73–83.

Musser, Charles 1984a: The "Chaser" Theory: Another Look at the "Chaser Theory." *Studies in Visual Communication* 10, no. 4, 24–44.

Musser, Charles 1984b: The Nickelodeon Era Begins: Establishing the Framework for Hollywood's Mode of Representation. *Framework* 22/23, 4–11.

Musser, Charles 1990: *The Emergence of Cinema: The American Screen to 1907*. New York: Scribner's.

Musser, Charles, with Carol Nelson 1991a: *High-Class Moving Pictures: Lyman H. Howe and the Forgotten Era of Traveling Exhibition, 1880–1920*. Princeton, New Jersey: Princeton University Press.

Musser, Charles 1991b: *Before the Nickelodeon: Edwin S. Porter and the Edison Manufacturing Company*. Berkeley: University of California Press.

Musser, Charles 1995: Reading Local Histories of Early Film Exhibition: Sylvester Quinn Breard's "A History of the Motion Pictures in New Orleans." *Historical Journal of Film, Radio and Television* 15, 581–9.

Musser, Charles 1999a: Nationalism and the Beginnings of Cinema: The Lumière Cinématographe in the United States, 1896–1897. *Historical Journal of Film, Radio and Television* 19, no. 2, 149–76.

Musser, Charles 1999b: Reading Local Histories of Early Film Exhibition, Part II: Roger William Warren's "History of Motion Picture Exhibition in Denver, 1896–1911." *Historical Journal of Film, Radio and Television* 19, 247–55.

Nasaw, David 1993: *Going Out: The Rise and Fall of Public Amusements*. New York: Basic Books.

Naylor, David 1981: *American Picture Palaces: The Architecture of Fantasy*. New York: Van Nostrand Reinhold.

Naylor, David 1987: *Great American Movie Theaters*. Washington, DC: Preservation Press.

Neale, Steve 1980: Oppositional Exhibition: Notes and Problems. *Screen* 21, no. 3, 45–56.

New Yorker 1951: In Sync. *New Yorker* 27 (May 5, 1951), 23–5.

Ogan, Christine 1990: The Audience for Foreign Films in the United States. *Journal of Communication* 40, no. 4, 58–77.

Ogihara, Junko 1990: The Exhibition of Films for Japanese-Americans in Los Angeles in the Silent Film Era. *Film History* 4, 81–7.

O'Leary, Brian 1996: Local Government Regulation of the Movies: The Dallas System, 1966–93. *Journal of Film and Video* 48, no. 3, 46–57.

O'Pray, Michael 1980: Authorship and Independent Film Exhibition. *Screen* 21, no. 2, 73–8.

Paletz, David, and Michael Noonan 1965: The Exhibitors. *Film Quarterly* 19, no. 2, 14–40.

Parkes, Graham 1987: Reflections on Projections: Changing Conditions in Watching Film. *Journal of Aesthetic Education* 21, 77–82.

Parkhill, Forbes 1937: Bank Night Tonight. *Saturday Evening Post* 210 (December 4, 1937), 20–2, 82.

Patterson, Joseph Medill 1907: The Nickelodeons: The Poor Man's Elementary Course in the Drama. *Saturday Evening Post* 180 (November 23, 1907), 10–11, 38.

Paul, William 1994: The K-Mart Audience at the Mall Movies. *Film History* 6, 487–501.

Paul, William 1996: Screening Space: Architecture, Technology, and the Motion Picture Screen. In *The Movies: Texts, Receptions, Exposures*, eds. Laurence Goldstein and Ira Konigsberg. Ann Arbor: University of Michigan Press, 244–73.

Pawley, Fredric Arden 1932: Design of Motion Picture Theaters. *Architectural Record* 71, 429–38.

Pearson, Roberta E., and William Uricchio 1999: "The Formative and Impressionable Stage": Discursive Constructions of the Nickelodeon Child Audience. In *American Movie Audiences: From the Turn of the Century to the Early Sound Era*, eds. Melvyn Stokes and Richard Maltby. London: British Film Institute, 64–75.

Peet, Creighton 1931: The New Movies: Trans-Lux. *Outlook and Independent* (March 25, 1931), 442.

Peiss, Kathy 1986: *Cheap Amusements: Working Women and Leisure in Turn-of-the-Century New York*. Philadelphia: Temple University Press.

Penley, Constance, ed. 1988: *Feminism and Film Theory*. New York: Routledge.

Pereira, P.R. 1914: The Development of the Moving Picture Theater. *American Architect* 106, 177–82.

Peterson, S. 1982: A Movie House Is an Enlarged Camera Obscura for the Sale of Popcorn, a Darkroom for Star-Gazing Right Side Up. *Film Culture* 70–1, 2–12.

Petrie, David Terry 1987: The Sundance Institute: The First Four Years. Unpublished Ph.D. dissertation, Brigham Young University.

Phelan, J.J. 1919: *Motion Pictures as a Phase of Commercialized Amusement in Toledo, Ohio*. Social Survey Series III (August 1919). Toledo: Little Book Press.

Phelps, Guy 1983: Art-House. *Sight and Sound* 53, no. 1, 12–14.

Pierce, Lucy France 1908: The Nickelodeon. *World Today* (October 1908), 1052.

Pildas, Ave, and Lucinda Smith 1980: *Movie Palaces: Survivors of an Elegant Era*. New York: Clarkson N. Potter.

Popper, H.R. 1947: Palace Builder. *Theatre Arts* 31, 55–6.

Potamianos, George Peter 1998: Hollywood in the Hinterlands: Mass Culture in Two California Communities, 1896–1936. Unpublished Ph.D. dissertation, University of Southern California.

Pratt, George C. 1959: No Magic, No Mystery, No Sleight of Hand: The First Ten Years of Motion Pictures in Rochester. *Image* 8, no. 4 (December), 159–211.

Pratt, George C. 1973: *Spellbound in Darkness*, rev. ed. Greenwich, New York: New York Graphic Society.

Preddy, Jane 1988: *Temples of Illusion: The Atmospheric Theatres of John Eberson*. New York: Betha and Karl Leubsdorf Art Gallery, Hunter College.

Preddy, Jane 1990: Glamour, Glitz and Sparkle: The Deco Theatres of John Eberson. In *1989 Annual of the Theatre Historical Society*. Chicago: Theatre Historical Society, 1–39.

Pribram, E. Deidre, ed. 1988: *Female Spectators: Looking at Film and Television*. London: Verso.

Pryluck, Calvin 1983: The Itinerant Movie Show and the Development of the Film Industry. *Journal of the University Film and Video Association* 25, no. 4, 11–22.

Rabinovitz, Lauren 1998: *For the Love of Pleasure: Women, Movies, and Culture in Turn-of-the-Century Chicago*. New Brunswick, New Jersey: Rutgers University Press.

Ramsaye, Terry 1926: *A Million and One Nights: A History of the Motion Picture Through 1925*. Rpt. New York: Simon and Schuster, 1986.

Rapee, Erno 1924: *Motion Picture Moods for Pianists and Organists*. New York: G. Schirmer. Rpt. New York: Arno Press, 1970.

Rapee, Erno 1925: *Encyclopedia of Music for Pictures*. New York: Belwin. Rpt. New York: Arno Press, 1970.

Rapp, George L. 1930: History of Cinema Theater Architecture. In *Living Architecture*, ed. Arthur Woltersdorf. Chicago: A. Kroch, 55–64.

Reddick, David Bruce 1986: Movies Under the Stars: A History of the Drive-In Theatre

Industry, 1933–1983. Unpublished Ph.D. dissertation, Michigan State University.

Reeves, Louis Harrison 1911: Jackass Music. *Moving Picture World* 21, 124–5.

Reinhart, Charles G. 1929: Halls of Illusion. *Saturday Evening Post* 201 (May 11, 1929), 16–17, 166–8.

Richard, Frank Herbert 1910: Posteritis. *Moving Picture World* 6, 987.

Richardson, Frank Herbert 1912: *Motion Picture Handbook: A Guide for Managers and Operators of Motion Picture Theaters*. New York: Moving Picture World.

Ricketson, Frank H., Jr. 1938: *The Management of Motion Picture Theatres*. New York: McGraw-Hill.

Ripley, John W. 1971: Song-Slides: Helper to Unify U.S. Communities and Sell Sheet Music. *Films in Review* (March 1971), 147–52.

Risenfield, Hugo 1926: Music and Motion Pictures. *Annals of the American Academy of Political and Social Science* 128, 58–62.

Robinson, David 1996: *From Peep Show to Palace: The Birth of American Film*. New York: Columbia University Press.

Roney, Carlie Beach 1939: Show Lady. *Saturday Evening Post* 211 (February 18, 1939), 23, 36, 38–40.

Rosenberg, Ben 1995: An Usher's Life – Part I. *Marquee* 27, no. 2, 18–26.

Rosenzweig, Roy 1983: *Eight Hours for What We Will: Workers and Leisure in an Industrial City, 1870–1920*. New York: Cambridge University Press.

Rosini, Vincent Thomas 1998: Sanctuary Cinema: The Rise and Fall of Protestant Churches as Film Exhibition Sites, 1910–1930. Unpublished Ph.D. dissertation, Regent University.

Ross, Stephen J. 1998: *Working-Class Hollywood: Silent Film and the Shaping of Class in America*. Princeton, New Jersey: Princeton University Press.

Ross, Stephen J. 1999: The Revolt of the Audience: Reconsidering Audiences and Reception during the Silent Era. In *American Movie Audiences: From the Turn of the Century to the Early Sound Era*, eds. Melvyn Stokes and Richard Maltby. London: British Film Institute, 92–111.

Rosse, Herman 1928: Suggestions for Modern Movie Palaces. *Theatre Arts Monthly* 12, 853–6.

Rothafel, Samuel L. 1910: Dignity of the Exhibitor's Profession. *Moving Picture World* 6, 289.

Rothafel, Samuel L. 1921: Making the Program. *Mentor* 9 (July 1, 1921), 33.

Rothafel, Samuel L. 1925: What the Public Wants in the Picture Theater. *Architectural Forum* 42, 361–4.

Rotzoll, Kim 1987: The Captive Audience: The Troubled Odyssey of Cinema Advertising. In *Current Research in Film: Audiences, Economics, and Law* 3, ed. Bruce A. Austin. Norwood, NJ: Ablex, 72–87.

Samuels, Stuart 1983: *Midnight Movies*. New York: Collier.

Sargent, Epes Winthrop 1915: *Picture Theater Advertising*. New York: Chalmers Publishing Company.

Schaefer, Eric 1999: *"Bold! Daring! Shocking! True!" A History of Exploitation Film, 1919–1959*. Durham, North Carolina: Duke University Press.

Schatz, Thomas 1997: *Boom and Bust: American Cinema in the 1940s*. New York: Scribner's.

Schlanger, Ben 1931: Reversing the Form and Inclination of the Motion Picture Theater Floor Improving Vision. *Society of Motion Picture Engineers Journal* 17, 161–71.

Schlanger, Ben 1932: New Theaters for the Cinema. *Architectural Forum* 57, 253–60.

Schlanger, Ben 1937: Motion Picture Theaters. *Architectural Record* 81 (February 1937), 17–24.

Schlanger, Ben 1938: Cinemas. *Architectural Record* 84 (July 1938), 113–15.

Schlanger, Ben 1944a: The Theater for Motion Pictures: The Theater Plan. *Architectural Record* 95 (June 1944), 85–90.

Schlanger, Ben 1944b: Postwar Project for a Motion Picture Theater. *Architectural Forum* 81 (October 1944), 130–1.

Schlanger, Ben 1948: Advancement of Motion Picture Theater Design. In *The Motion Picture Theater: Planning, Upkeep*, ed. Helen M. Stote. New York: Society of Motion Picture Engineers, 3–13.

Schlanger, Ben, and William A. Hoffberg 1951a: Effects of Television on the Motion Picture Theater. *Society of Motion Picture and Television Engineers Journal* 56, 39–43.

Schlanger, Ben, and William A. Hoffberg 1951b: New Approaches Developed by Relating Film Production Techniques to Theater Exhibition. *Society of Motion Picture and Television Engineers Journal* 57, 231–7.

Schnapper, Amy 1975: The Distribution of Theatrical Feature Films to Television. Unpublished Ph.D. thesis, University of Wisconsin, Madison.

Schneider, Donald 1988: The Controversy over Sunday Movies in Hastings, 1913–1929. *Nebraska History* 69, no. 1, 60–72.

Schreiber, Flora Rheta 1952: New York – A Cinema Capital. *Quarterly Review of Film, Radio and Television* 7, 264–73.

Scientific American, 1927: The "Movie" Theater Up-to-Date. *Scientific American* 137, 516–17.

Scott, Irvin L. 1931: A Motion Picture Theater for a Suburban Town. *Architectural Record* 70, 111–15.

Seabury, William Marston 1926: *The Public and the Motion Picture Industry*. New York: Macmillan.

Segrave, Kerry 1992: *Drive-In Theaters: A History from Their Inception in 1933*. Jefferson, North Carolina: McFarland.

Seldes, Gilbert 1937: *The Movies Come from America*. New York: Scribner's.

Severns, Patricia 1987: The History of the Princess Theatre, 1916–1926. Unpublished M.A. thesis, Northeast Missouri State University.

Sexton, Randolph Williams, and Benjamin Franklin Betts 1927: *American Theatres Today*. New York: Architectural Book Publishing.

Shand, Philip Morton 1930: *Modern Picture-Houses and Theaters*. Philadelphia: J.P. Lippincott.

Sharp, Dennis 1969: *The Picture Palace and Other Buildings for the Movies*. New York: Praeger.

Shaw, H.F. 1937: Do You Hold Hands at the Movies? A Theater Manager's Bank Night and Other Headaches. *American Magazine* (August 1937), 38–9.

Sherman, Stratford P. 1986: Movie Theaters Head Back to the Future. *Fortune* (January 1986), 90–4.

Singer, Ben 1995: Manhattan Nickelodeons: New Data on Audiences and Exhibitors. *Cinema Journal* 34, no. 3, 5–35.

Singer, Ben 1996: New York, Just Like I Pictured It . . . *Cinema Journal* 35, no. 3, 104–26.

Sklar, Robert 1975: *Movie-Made America: A Cultural History of American Movies*. New York: Random House.

Skouras, Charles P. 1947: The Exhibitor. *Annals of the American Academy of Political and Social Science* 254, 26–30.

Sloman, Tony 1983: West End Nightmare. *Films and Filming* 348, 13–15.

Smith, Joe E. 1979: Early Movies and Their Impact on Columbia. *Missouri Historical Review* (October 1979), 72–85.

Smoodin, Eric 1995: "Compulsory" Viewing for Every Citizen: Mr. Smith and the Rhetoric of Reception. *Cinema Journal* 35, no. 2, 3–23.

Snyder, Robert W. 1989: *The Voice of the City: Vaudeville and Popular Culture in New York*. New York: Oxford University Press.

Sorenson, John 1990: *Our Show Houses: The History of Movie Theaters in Grand Island, Nebraska.* Grand Island, Nebraska: Hall County Historical Society Press.

Spellerberg, James Edward 1980: Technology and the Film Industry: The Adoption of Cinemascope. Unpublished Ph.D. dissertation, University of Iowa.

Sprague, Jesse Rainsford 1937: Small-Town Movie Theater. *Saturday Evening Post* 210 (August 14, 1937), 23, 62–4.

Squires, Jason, ed. 1983: *The Movie Business Book.* New York: Simon and Schuster.

Stabinger, Karen 1982: The Shape of Theaters to Come. *American Film* 7, no. 10, 34–8.

Staiger, Janet 1986: The Handmaiden of Villainy: Methods and Problems in Studying the Historical Reception of a Film. *Wide Angle* 8, no. 1, 19–28.

Staiger, Janet 1990: Announcing Wares, Winning Patrons, Voicing Ideals: Thinking about the History and Theory of Film Advertising. *Cinema Journal 29*, no. 3, 3–31.

Staiger, Janet 1992: *Interpreting Films: Studies in the Historical Reception of American Cinema.* Princeton, New Jersey: Princeton University Press.

Stamp, Shelley 2000: *Movie-Struck Girls: Women and Motion Picture Culture after the Nickelodeon.* Princeton, New Jersey: Princeton University Press.

Stepanian, Laurie Anne, 1988: Harry Davis, Theatrical Entrepreneur, Pittsburgh, Pennsylvania, 1893–1927. Unpublished Ph.D. dissertation, University of Missouri-Columbia.

Stern, Seymour 1927: An Aesthetic of the Cinema House. *National Board of Review Magazine* (May 1927), 7–10, 19.

Stoddard, Richard 1978: *Theater and Cinema Architecture: A Guide to Information Sources.* Detroit: Gale.

Stokes, Melvyn, and Richard Maltby, eds. 1999: *American Movie Audiences: From the Turn of the Century to the Early Sound Era.* London: British Film Institute.

Stones, Barbara 1993: *America Goes to the Movies: 100 Years of Motion Picture Exhibition.* North Hollywood, California: National Association of Theatre Owners.

Stote, Helen M., ed. 1948: *The Motion Picture Theater: Planning, Upkeep.* New York: Society of Motion Picture Engineers.

Straw, Will 2000: Proliferating Screens. *Screen* 41, 115–19.

Streible, Dan 1990: The Literature of Film Exhibition: A Bibliography on Motion Exhibition and Related Topics. *Velvet Light Trap* 25, 80–119.

Streible, Dan 1993: The Harlem Theater: Black Film Exhibition in Austin, Texas: 1920–1973. In *Black American Cinema*, ed. Manthia Diawara. New York: Routledge, 221–36.

Strout, Andrea 1981: In the Midnight Hour. *American Film* 6, no. 4, 34–7, 72–3.

Swami, Sanjeev 1998: Dynamic Marketing Decisions in the Presence of Perishable Demand. Unpublished Ph.D. dissertation, University of British Columbia.

Swartz, Mark E. 1987a: Moving Pictures on the Move. *Journal of American Culture 9*, no. 3, 1–7.

Swartz, Mark E. 1987b: An Overview of Cinema on the Fairgrounds. *Journal of Popular Film and Television* 15, no. 3, 102–8.

Taylor, Frank J. 1956: Big Boom in Outdoor Movies. *Saturday Evening Post 229* (September 15, 1956), 31, 100–2.

Taylor, Ryland A. 1972: The Repeat Audience for Movies on TV. *Journal of Broadcasting* 17, no. 1, 95–100.

Testa, Richard Louis, Jr. 1992: Movie Exhibition Practices and Procedures during the Hollywood Studio Era in Providence, Rhode Island. Unpublished Ph.D. dissertation, University of Maryland.

Theatre Television Committee 1949: Theatre Television. *Journal of the Society of Motion Picture Engineers 52*, no. 3, 243–67.

Thissen, Judith 1999: Jewish Immigrant Audiences in New York City, 1905–14. In *American Movie Audiences: From the Turn of the Century to the Early Sound Era*, eds. Melvyn Stokes and Richard Maltby. London: British Film Institute, 15–28.

Thomas, David O. 1981a: From Page to Screen in Small Town America: Early Motion Picture Exhibition in Winona, Minnesota. *Journal of the University Film Association* 33, no. 3, 3–13.

Thomas, David O. 1981b: Winona Nickelodeon Theatres 1907–1913: The Battle for Local Control. *Marquee* 13, no. 1, 12–16.

Thomas, John Kyle 1990: Of Paramount Importance: American Film and Cultural Home-Rule in Knoxville, 1872–1948. Unpublished Ph.D. dissertation, University of Tennessee.

Thomas, John Kyle 1993: The Cultural Reconstruction of an Appalachian City: Knoxville, Tennessee and the Coming of the Movies. *Journal of East Tennessee History* 65, 34–52.

Thompson, Toby 1983: The Twilight of the Drive-In, *American Film* 8, no. 9, 44–9.

Thorne, Ross 1976: *Picture Palace Architecture in Australia*. South Melbourne: Sun Books.

Thorp, Margaret 1939: *America at the Movies*. New Haven: Yale University Press.

Thruelsen, Richard 1947: Men at Work: Movie-House Manager. *Saturday Evening Post* 220 (November 15, 1947), 36–7, 84, 88–92, 95.

Toler, J.H. 1945: Air Conditioning Wanted for New and Remodeled Theatres. *Domestic Engineering* 165, 113–14.

Triponi, Marianne 1990: The Ironwood Theatre in Context: Movie Palace as Symbol. *Journal of American Culture* 13, no. 4, 1–8.

True, Lyle C. 1924: *How and What to Play for Moving Pictures*. San Francisco: Music Supplement.

Turner, Max W., and Frank R. Kennedy 1947: Exclusion, Ejection, and Segregation of Theatre Patrons. *Iowa Law Review* 32, no. 4, 631–54.

Twomey, John E. 1956: Some Considerations on the Rise of the Art-Film Theater. *Quarterly Review of Film, Radio and Television* 10, 239–47.

Tyler, Parker 1953: Era of the Three-D's. *New Republic* (May 18, 1953), 22–3.

Tyler, Parker 1954: Movie Note. *Kenyon Review* 16, 468–72.

University of Chicago Law Review 1946: The Sherman Act and the Motion Picture Industry. *University of Chicago Law Review* 13, 346–61.

University of Pennsylvania Law Review 1947: Judicial Regulation of the Motion-Picture Industry. *University of Pennsylvania Law Review* 95, 662–75.

Uricchio, William, and Roberta E. Pearson 1993: *Reframing Culture: The Case of the Vitagraph Quality Films*. Princeton, New Jersey: Princeton University Press.

Uricchio, William, and Roberta E. Pearson 1994: Constructing the Mass Audience: Competing Discourses of Morality and Rationalization in the Nickelodeon Period. *Iris* 17, 43–54.

Valentine, Maggie 1994: *The Show Starts on the Sidewalk: An Architectural History of the Movie Theatre*. New Haven: Yale University Press.

Veronneau, Pierre 1994: The Creation of a Film Culture by Travelling Exhibitors in Rural Quebec Prior to World War I. *Film History* 6, 250–61.

Vincent, Richard Charles 1983: The Cinema and the City: An Analysis of Motion Picture Theater Location in Selected United States Urban Areas. Unpublished Ph.D. dissertation, University of Massachusetts.

Vogel, Amos 1949: Film Do's and Don'ts. *Saturday Review* 32 (August 20, 1949), 32–4.

Vorse, Mary Heaton 1911: Some Picture Show Audiences. *Outlook* 98 (June 24, 1911), 441–7.

Waldman, Diane 1984: From Midnight Shows to Marriage Vows: Women, Exploitation and Exhibition. *Wide Angle 6*, no. 2, 40–8.

Waldman, Diane 1986: Rockefeller, the YMCA and the Company Movie Theater. *Wide Angle 8*, no. 1, 41–51.

Waller, Gregory A. 1989: Introducing the "Marvellous Invention" to the Provinces: Film Exhibition in Lexington, Kentucky, 1896–1897. *Film History* 3, 223–34.

Waller, Gregory A. 1990: Situating Motion Pictures in the Prenickelodeon Period: Lexington, Kentucky, 1897–1906. *Velvet Light Trap* 25, 12–28.

Waller, Gregory A. 1991: Midnight Movies: 1980–1985: A Market Study. In *The Cult Film Experience: Beyond All Reason*, ed. J.P. Telotte. Austin: University of Texas Press, 167–86.

Waller, Gregory A. 1992: Another Audience: Black Moviegoing, 1907–1916. *Cinema Journal* 31, no. 2, 3–24.

Waller, Gregory A. 1993: Black Nickelodeon. *Black Film Review* 7, no. 4, 28–31.

Waller, Gregory A. 1995: *Main Street Amusements: Movies and Commercial Entertainment in a Southern City, 1896–1930*. Washington, DC: Smithsonian Institution Press.

Waller, Gregory A. 1999a: Motion Pictures and Other Entertainment at Chautauqua. In *Cinema at the Turn of the Century*, eds. Roberta Pearson, Claire Dupre la Tour, and Andre Gaudreault. Quebec: Editions Nota Bene, 81–9.

Waller, Gregory A. 1999b: Hillbilly Music and Will Rogers: Small-Town Picture Shows in the 1930s. In *American Movie Audiences: From the Turn of the Century to the Early Sound Era*, eds. Melvyn Stokes and Richard Maltby. London: British Film Institute, 164–79.

Waltz, Gwendolyn S. 1991: Projection and Performance: Early Multi-Media in the American Theatre. Unpublished Ph.D. dissertation, Tufts University.

Warner, Harry M. 1927: Future Developments. In *The Story of the Films*, ed. Joseph P. Kennedy. Chicago: A.W. Shaw, 330–5.

Warren, Roger William 1960: History of Motion Picture Exhibition in Denver, 1896–1911. Unpublished M.A. thesis, University of Denver.

Wasko, Janet 1994: *Hollywood in the Information Age: Beyond the Silver Screen*. Austin: University of Texas Press.

Wasser, Frederick 1995: Four Walling Exhibition: Regional Resistance to the Hollywood Film Industry. *Cinema Journal* 34, no. 2, 51–65.

Waterman, David 1985: Prerecorded Home Video and the Distribution of Theatrical Feature Films. In *Video Media Competition: Regulation, Economics, and Technology*, ed. Eli M. Noam. New York: Columbia University Press, 221–43.

Weiss, Ken 1993: The Role of the Immigrant Audience in the Development of Motion Pictures. Unpublished Ph.D. dissertation, City University of New York.

White, Timothy 1990: Hollywood's Attempt to Appropriate Television: The Case of Paramount Pictures. Unpublished Ph.D. dissertation, University of Wisconsin, Madison.

Whitman, William F. 1938: Anti-Trust Cases Affecting the Distribution of Motion Pictures. *Fordham Law Review* 7, 189–202.

Whitney, Simon 1955: Vertical Disintegration in the Motion Picture Industry. *American Economic Review* 45, 491–8.

Whittemore, Charles A. 1914: The Moving Picture Theatre. *Brickbuilder* 23, 41–5.

Whittemore, Charles A. 1917a: The Motion Picture Theater. *Architectural Forum* 26, 179–86.

Whittemore, Charles A. 1917b: The Moving Picture Theatre. *Architectural Forum* 27, 13–18, 39–43, 67–72.

Widen, Larry, and Judi Anderson 1986: *Milwaukee Movie Palaces*. Milwaukee: Milwaukee Historical Society.

Wilbur, Ray Lyman 1938: Who Should Select America's Movies? *National Parent–Teacher* 32, 23, 29.

Wilcox, Roy, and H.J. Schlafly 1949: Demonstration of Larger Screen Television in Philadelphia. *Journal of the Society of Motion Picture Engineers* 52, no. 5, 549–60.

Wilinsky, Barbara Jean 1997: Selling Exclusivity: The Emergence of Art Film Theatres in Post World War II United States Culture. Unpublished Ph.D. dissertation, Northwestern University.

Williams, Linda, ed. 1994: *Viewing Positions: Ways of Seeing Film*. New Brunswick: Rutgers University Press.

Willson, Robert F., Jr. 1974: *The Exorcist* and Multicinema Aesthetics. *Journal of Popular Film* 3, 183–7.

Wilson, Ronald W. 1999: Northwest Texas Movie Shows: The Interstate Theatre Circuit and Motion Picture Exhibition in Wichita Falls, Texas, 1935–1955. Unpublished Ph.D. dissertation, University of Kansas.

Wilson, J. Victor 1914: Strand Theater, New York. *American Architect* 106, 183–4.

Woal, Linda 1994: When a Dime Could Buy a Dream: Siegmund Lubin and the Birth of Motion Picture Exhibition. *Film History* 6, 152–65.

Wyatt, Justin 1998: From Roadshowing to Saturation Release: Majors, Independents, and Marketing/Distribution Innovations. In *The New American Cinema*, ed. Jon Lewis. Durham, North Carolina: Duke University Press, 64–86.

Wysotsky, Michael Z. 1971: *Wide Screen Cinema and Stereophonic Sound*. New York: Hastings House.

Index

Across 110th Street, 275
advertising and promotion, 5, 60–1, 100, 114,
    266–7, 280, 293 n. 13, 294 n. 27, 315;
    inside theater, 60–1, 66–7; national
    advertising campaigns, 85, 86, 94–5, 97,
    124–5, 131, 132–4, 240–4, 284–6, 287,
    289–90; on radio, 132; posters, 60–1, 63,
    68–9, 131, 177, 261, 274; promotional
    strategies, 131–2, 137, 156, 176, 190–1,
    192–5, 200–2, 248–9, 272; trailers, 132; *see
    also* bank night
Affiliated Committees for Better Films, 164
airdomes, 12, 59, 73
Albuquerque, 206
Allen, Robert, 91
Allen, Weldon, 203–10
Althusser, Louis, 239
American City, 12
American Federation of Musicians (AFM), 130
American Mutoscope Company, 23
amusement parks, 20, 29, 37, 241, 242, 302,
    313
Andrew, Dudley, 7
Angelina, 261
Anna and the King of Siam (1946), 207
architecture, 5, 12, 311, 315, 317–18;
    "atmospheric" style, 95–6, 106–8;
    "colloquial" style, 81–2; Harlem Theater,
    271; interior design, 105, 106–8, 110–11,
    229, 297; "modern functional" style, 221–3,
    224, 225–7, 229–31, 318; multiplex, 280;
    terra cotta, 81–2
Are You With It?, 203
Armat, Thomas, 13, 14, 19, 21, 22, 23
art cinemas, 3, 235–6, 252–3, 254, 255–8,
    259–62, 265–7, 289, 319
Ash, Paul, 127

Aspley, Bruce, 178
"At the Picture Show" (song), 92
audiences, 5, 80, 87, 110, 302–6; African
    American, 5, 176, 236, 268–76, 304, 313,
    316; children and youth, 31, 34, 36, 43 n.
    17, 47, 51, 52, 60, 64, 78, 86, 92, 96–7,
    111–12, 138–9, 151–2, 153–4, 156–7,
    159–68, 200, 249; drive-in, 249–50;
    immigrant, 5, 11–12, 30–5, 50–3, 155, 300,
    303, 307 n. 8, 313; middle-class, 11, 38–41,
    89–94, 302, 313; women, 31–2, 51–2, 64,
    66–7, 190, 291, 303, 313; working-class, 5,
    11, 27–41, 312
Autry, Gene, 180, 184

Baby It's You (1982), 265
Baker, Charles, 33
Balaban, Barney, 126–8, 133
Ballet Mécanique, 252
Balsley, Charles H., 21
Band Drill, 16, 17
bank night, 173, 190–1, 193, 208, 317
Bartel, Paul, 265
Battle of the Bulge, The (1965), 241
Baudry, Jean-Claude, 238
Bazin, André, 238
Beast from 20,000 fathoms, The (1953), 289
Berlin, Irving, 92
Best Years of Our Lives, The (1946), 207
Bial, Albert, 13, 14, 15, 22, 23
Big Sleep, The (1946), 207
biograph, 23, 24
Birth of a Nation, The (1915), 4, 40
Bitter Rice (1948), 256
Black Caesar (1973), 275
Black Fury (1935), 179
Black Narcissus (1946), 203, 204

Blackboard Jungle (1955), 274
Blacula (1972), 275
Blair Camera Company, 22
blaxploitation films, 275
Blue Sky Boys, 182
Body and Soul (1981), 204
Boomerang (1976), 207
Bordwell, David, 4
Bowers, Q. David, 6
Bowser, Eileen, 4
Brickbuilder, 12
Bride of Frankenstein, The (1935), 179, 274
Buck and the Preacher (1971), 275
Bufwack, Mary A., 182
burlesque, 28, 29, 33, 46, 151
Bush, W. Stephen, 89
Butler, Elizabeth, 32

Cabinet of Dr. Caligari, The (1919), 252, 257
Callahan Brothers, 182
Capitol Theatre (Chicago), 106–8
Carbine, Mary, 304
Carnegie Hall, 207
Casbah, 203
censorship, 7 n. 5, 28, 36–8, 45 n. 41, 50, 78,
    123, 151–2, 163, 201
Chandler, Edward, 31
Charlie Chan's Murder Cruise (1940), 272
Cherokee Bill, 272
Children's Motion Picture League, 163
CinemaScope, 238, 241–4
"Cinematograph Man, The" (song), 92
Cinerama, 238, 241, 244
Cinerama Holiday, 241
Cloak and Dagger (1946), 207
Cocteau, Jean, 242
Collier, John, 11
concessions, 1, 61–2, 66, 204–5, 209, 248,
    249, 250, 259, 273, 287, 294 n. 21
Coon Creek Girls, 182, 183
Cotton States Exhibition, Atlanta, 14
Curly Top (1935), 179
Cyrano de Bergerac, 256

Darrow, Clarence, 130
Daughters of the American Revolution, 163
Davis, L.O., 179
Davis, Michael, 91–2
Death Master, 275
DeMille, Cecil B., 96
Devil is a Woman, The (1935), 179

Dickson, W.K.L., 13
dime museums, 29, 33
double features, 2, 3, 6, 117, 189, 191, 204,
    208, 214, 216, 280, 317
Double Life, A (1947), 203
Dracula (1931), 274
drive-ins, 1, 2, 3, 235, 237, 247–51, 259, 268,
    273, 275, 281, 288, 318
Duel in the Sun (1946), 284
Duel, The, 206
Duke of Paducah, 182
Durwood Theatres, *see* Multi-Cinema
Durwood, Edward A., 279

Early, James, 31
Eastman Company, 22
Eating Raoul (1982), 265
Edison Manufacturing Company, 21, 22, 24
Edison, Thomas A., 13, 14, 22
eidoloscope, 13, 18
End of St Petersburg, The (1927), 252
exhibition: block-booking, 173–4, 207–8,
    211–12, 214–17, 260, 316, 317; booking
    films, 178, 199–200, 203–10, 251, 257,
    280; chain-store practices, 5, 85–6, 124–30,
    288–9, 294 n. 26, 316; independent
    theaters, 173, 189–91, 197–202, 203–10,
    211–12, 215–18, 233, 236, 266, 268–76;
    listening to and attracting the audience, 59,
    71, 110–15, 122–3, 206–7; run, zone,
    clearance system, 189, 199, 203, 207–8,
    217–18, 285, 317; saturation booking, 236,
    284–6; start-up and operating expenses,
    54–9, 197–200, 204–6, 222, 250–1, 280;
    state rights, 22–5; theater chains, 1–2, 40,
    124–34, 176, 189–91, 217, 233, 236,
    247–9, 251, 256, 266, 269, 270, 273,
    279–81, 285, 287, 297–8; traveling
    exhibition, 6, 271, 302, 306 n. 4, 314; *see
    also* concessions

Fairbanks, Douglas, 91
Famous Players, 96, 104, 124
Fedeli, Fred, 30–1, 37
Federation of Women's Clubs, 163
Feretti, Aduino, 28
Field, Connie, 265
Film Arts Guild, 252
Film Guild Cinema, 252–3
Firebrands of Arizona (1944), 272
Fitzgerald, Cissy, 20

For a Few Bullets More, 275
Ford, Charles E., 20
Ford, Harrison, 299
Foucault, Michel, 167
Fox Company, 96, 211
Fox, Curly, 180
Franklin, Harold B., 175

Gallant Bess, 207
Gammon, Frank, 13, 14, 15, 17, 21, 22–3
Georgia Wildcats, 180, 184
Ghost (1990), 291
Girl and Her Trust, The (1912), 12
Girls of the Golden West, 182
Givens, Dr. Everett H., 268
Golden West Cowboys, 184
Gomery, Douglas, 91
Gone With the Wind, 274, 284
Gordon, Dan, 291
Gordon, Nathan and Isaac, 28
Graf, Max, 28
Grauman, Sid, 127
Great Mr. Handel, The, 206
Great White Hope, The, 275
Green, William, 130
Griffith, D.W., 7, 90

Hall, G. Stanley, 27
Hamlet (1948), 256, 257
Hammerstein, Oscar, 90
Hartt, Rollin Lynde, 35
Hays Office, 163, 165–7
Hays, Will, 165, 166
Heath, Steven, 238–40
Hegman, J.J., 270
Heise, William, 13
Henry V (1944), 206, 257
Hit Man (1972), 275
Holland, Andrew, 21
Hopkins, Eurio, 21
Hopkins, J.D., 18
Hopper, Dennis, 265
Hotaling, Arthur, 20
Hottentot, The, 165
How to Marry a Millionaire (1953), 242
Howe, Frederic, 31
Hoyt, Professor G., 30, 35, 38
Humoresque (1946), 207

I Remember Mama (1948), 208
If Winter Comes, 206

I'll Do Anything, 287
Imitation of Life (1934), 179
In Old Kentucky (1935), 179
Irwin, May, 20
It Happened One Night (1934), 179
Ivan the Terrible (1944/46), 252

Jacobs, Lewis, 6–7
Jaws (1975), 284
Jeffrey, Herb, 272
Jenkins, C. Francis, 13, 14, 19
Jesse James (1939), 179
Jones, George F., 271–3
Jowett, Garth, 167
Judge Priest (1935), 179

Katz, Sam, 124, 126–34
Katzenberg, Jeffrey, 288
Keene, Tom, 184
Keith, B.F., 18
Kett, Joseph, 162
Kid from Brooklyn, The, 207
Kiefaber, Peter, 20
Killer Diller (1948), 272
Kincaid, Bradley, 183
kinetoscope, 13–14, 15
Kohlberg, Stanford, 248–9
Kopple, Barbara, 265
Koster & Bial, 13, 14, 15, 22, 23
Koszarski, Richard, 4
Kramer, Stanley, 258
Kuhn, Edmund, 15

Lair, John, 182
Lasky Corporation, 96, 104
Last Action Hero, The (1993), 282
Late George Appleby, The, 207
Lawson, A.C., 268
Ledford, Lily Mae, 183
Leigh sisters, 16
Lexington, Kentucky, 1–2
Life and Times of Rosie the Riveter, The (1980), 265
Life Begins at 40 (1935), 179
Lindsay, Vachel, 27
Lion King, The (1994), 284
Lippert, Robert J., 247
Little Christopher Columbus, 16
Little Clifford, 182
Loew's, 96
Lowenthal, John, 265
Lucchese, Frank (Sr. and Jr.), 273

Lucchese, Sam (Sr. and Jr.), 273–5
Lumière cinématographe, 23, 24
Lynd, Robert and Helen, 96–7, 162

McGaddy, Michael, 28
McLoughlin, Edmund, 22
McMichen, Clayton, 183–4
Macomber Affair, The, 207
Macon, Uncle Dave, 180
Majek, Andy, 275
Malone, Bill C , 180
Manvell, Roger, 259
Marie Gallante (1934), 180
matinee screenings, 3, 64, 86, 163–7, 179, 200
May, Lary, 40, 41
Mayer, Arthur, 261–2
Mayerling (1935), 257
Mayon, John, 17
Mellen, James H., 37
melodrama (stage), 29, 33, 34, 46, 47, 50
Mencken, H.L., 255
MGM, 96, 208–9
Miller, Fiddlin' Slim, 182
Miller, W.R., 17, 21, 22
Miracle of the Bells, The (1948), 208
Miracle on 34th Street (1994), 207
Mitchell, Alice Miller, 159
Mitry, Jean, 238
Monroe, Bill and Charlie, 182
Monroe Doctrine, The, 16, 17
Motion Picture Association of America, 286
Motion Picture Producers' and Distributors' Association (MPPDA), 163, 165–6
Moving Picture World, 12
Multi-Cinema, 279–81
multi-screen theaters, 1–2, 3, 4, 5, 6, 174, 236, 267, 268, 279–81, 284–92, 293 n. 15, 293 n. 18, 295 n. 43, 297–8, 319
Murphy, Edward, 21
Musser, Charles, 3, 4
My Darling Clementine (1946), 207

Naked City, The (1948), 203
National Board of Review, Committee on Films for Young People, 164
National Committee for Better Films, 164, 167
nickelodeons, 2, 3, 11–12, 27–35, 41 n. 5, 46–8, 91–4, 174, 239, 268, 300, 313–14

non-theatrical exhibition, 6, 91, 166, 236, 259, 260, 267, 302, 314
Northwest Mounted Police Company, 180

Oermann, Robert K., 182
Oklahoma! (1955), 243
Open City (1945), 256, 261
Out of the Blue (1980), 265
Outlaw, The (1943), 206

Paine, R.S., 21
Paisan, 261
Paramount Case, 174, 204–5, 260, 317
Paramount Pictures Corporation, 40, 94–5, 96, 97, 104, 124, 129
Paul, Robert, 16
Paul, William, 3
People's Institute, 46
Pickford, Mary, 91
picture palaces, 1, 2, 6, 39–40, 85, 89–90, 95–7, 104–5, 106–8, 109, 126–8, 176, 184, 235, 239, 244, 256, 268, 273, 286, 304, 315–16
Porter, Edwin S., 21
Pretty Woman (1990), 291
Private Affairs of Bel Ami, The, 207
Proctor, F.F., 24
programming, 2–3, 5, 54–60, 70–1, 101, 111, 116–18, 179, 258, 281; amateur shows, 33, 35, 60, 180, 274; Harlem Theater, 272, 274–5; illustrated songs, 2, 3, 28, 34, 46, 55, 56, 57, 59, 65, 71–2; lectures, 60, 65, 314; live performance in the sound era, 173, 180–5, 248–9, 272, 274; local films, 179; music in the silent era, 15, 64–5, 86, 101, 138–9, 140–3, 144–6, 269, 304, 314–15; of Vitascope films, 16–21; orchestra, 2, 57, 71, 89, 101–2, 117, 142–3, 144–5; organs, 89, 115, 117, 130, 142, 145–6; printed programs, 67, 99, 103, 254; stage shows, 2, 89, 116–17, 127–8, 133, 304, 315; *see also* double features; matinee screenings; repertory theaters
projection, 73–4, 75–6
Publix theaters, 124, 204; advertising/promotion, 130–4; building, 125–6; coming of sound, 129–30; effect of Great Depression on, 134; formation of empire, 127–9; use of chain-store methods, 125–7
Pursued (1947), 207
Pygmalion (1938), 257

radio, 4, 125, 130, 132, 173, 180–5, 242, 256, 290, 296, 299

Raff, Norman, 13, 14, 15, 17, 21, 22–3

Rage in Heaven (1941), 207

Raiders of the Lost Ark (1981), 290

Ramrod (1947), 206

Raymond, John W., 28

Renfro Valley Barn Dance, 182–3

repertory theaters, 1, 2, 236, 263–4, 265–7, 275, 319

Return of the Secaucus Seven, The (1979), 265

Rice, John C., 20

Richardson, C.O., 22

Richardson, F.H., 91

Rieser, Allen F., 17, 22

Ritter, Tex, 180, 184

Rogers, Roy, 272

Rogers, Will, 179

Roosevelt Story, The, 207

Rothafel, Samuel "Roxy", 90, 127

Saturday matinee movement, 163–7

Saunders, Paul, 178

Sayles, John, 265

Sea Waves at Dover, 16

Sealed Verdict (1948), 272

Seidelman, Susan, 265

Seldes, Gilbert, 1

Selznick, David O., 284

Shand, P. Morton, 4

Shea, F., 28

She's Too Mean for Me, 272

Shoe-Shine, 261

Sklar, Robert, 32, 167

Slavin, John, 17

Sleepless in Seattle (1993), 291

Smith, Fiddlin' Abner, 180

Smith, Vernon L., 275

Smitha, Ralph, 249

Smithereens (1982), 265

Snow White (1937), 178

Sound of Music, The (1965), 285

Soylent Green (1973), 275

Spellerberg, James, 242

Staiger, Janet, 4

Stones, Barbara, 6

Strange Wives (1934), 180

Superfly (1972), 275

sure-seaters, *see* art cinemas

Swanson, Gloria, 96

Symphony of Berlin, The, 252

Talmadge, Norma, 96

television, 3, 4, 5, 133, 222, 225, 226, 227, 235, 237, 242, 255, 256, 284, 285, 286, 290, 296, 299, 303, 312, 319–20

Temple, Shirley, 179

Temptation, 207

Ten Commandments, The (1956), 274

Ten Days That Shook the World (1927), 252

theaters, 4–5; air-conditioning, 108, 127, 128, 133, 206, 227, 237; attempts to regulate, 11–12, 36–9, 46–8, 50, 77–9, 151–2, 163–8; community role of, 85, 100–1, 111–12, 116–18, 123, 153–4, 176, 178–9, 193, 195, 201, 227, 228–9, 250; entrances, 104–5, 110; exterior design, 54, 61, 63, 68–9, 104–5, 108, 110, 126–7, 224, 227, 271; for African Americans, 3, 268–76, 303, 304, 316; in Worcester, Massachusetts, 27–32; licensing of, 78–9; lighting in, 5, 66, 78, 101–2, 107, 156, 226; lobbies, 105, 110, 227, 258; location, 4, 91, 126, 222, 248, 249–50, 260, 271, 279–80, 285–6; rural and small-town, 6, 58–9, 88–96, 175–85, 191, 197–202, 203–10, 221–3, 230–1, 302, 316, 317; safety of, 47, 77–8, 81, 230; screen size and dimensions, 3, 174, 219–20, 223, 225–6, 238–44, 253; seating, 33–4, 221–3; sound technology and acoustics, 3, 129–30, 147–9, 150, 226–7, 235, 240, 316; staff, 85, 100–1, 118–22, 204, 249, 273, 297, 315; types of theaters, 2, 12, 54–9, 116–18; ushers, 40, 41, 66, 67, 89, 315; widescreen and large-screen processes, 5, 235, 237, 238–44, 259, 274, 318; *see also* airdomes; art cinemas; drive-ins; multi-screen theaters; nickelodeons; picture palaces; projection; repertory theaters

Them (1954), 290

Thérèse Raquin, 252

Thin Man, The (1934), 179

This Is Cinerama, 241

Thompson, Kristin, 4

Three Little Girls in Blue, 207

Todd-AO, 242, 243, 244

Too Hot to Handle (1938), 272

Tracy, Spencer, 180

Trail of the Lonesome Pine, The (1936), 179

Trammell, Joseph, 268

Tree Grows in Brooklyn, A (1945), 272

Trial of Billy Jack (1971), 284

Trials of Alger Hiss, The (1979), 265

Trick Baby, 275
Tropic Holiday (1938), 272
Trouble Man, 275
True Lies (1994), 282
Tulloch, Donald, 38

Umbrella Dance, 16
Uncle Henry and His Original Kentucky
   Mountaineers, 180
United Artists, 208, 209
Unwritten Law, The, 28, 36
Up Jumps the Devil, 272

vaudeville, 2, 6, 12, 18, 20, 22, 24, 28, 34, 39,
   41 n. 4, 46, 47, 50, 55–6, 59, 60, 71–2, 79,
   88, 89, 91, 92, 117, 127, 129, 130, 131,
   145, 151, 180, 301, 313
video, 5, 235, 284, 286, 290, 292 n. 9, 292 n.
   10, 296, 299, 302, 312, 319
video games, 291, 295 n. 44
Virginian, The (1929), 132

Vitascope, 14–25
Vorse, Mary Heaton, 11, 31

Wake Up and Dream, 207
Walker, Gustave, 18
Walton & Slavin, 16
Walton, Charles, 16, 17
Warner Brothers, 96
Wattstax (1973), 275
White, James, 21
Williams, Percy, 20
Williamson, J.W., 175
Wilton, Alf T., 28
Winters, W.W., 93
Within These Walls (1945), 272
Woman's Municipal League, 46
Wyatt Earp (1994), 287

Zamarro, Carmine, 28
Zanuck, Darryl, 243
Zukor, Adolph, 124